The Role of the EU in the Promotion of Human Rights and International Labour Standards in Its External Trade Relations

Samantha Velluti

The Role of the EU in the Promotion of Human Rights and International Labour Standards in Its External Trade Relations

With Contributions from Francesca Martines

Springer

Samantha Velluti
Sussex Law School
School of Law, Politics and Sociology
University of Sussex
Brighton, UK

Contributed by
Francesca Martines
Department of Law
University of Pisa
Pisa, Italy

ISBN 978-3-030-56746-0 ISBN 978-3-030-56748-4 (eBook)
https://doi.org/10.1007/978-3-030-56748-4

This Springer imprint is published by the registered company Springer Nature Switzerland AG
The registered company address is: Gewerbestrasse 11, 6330 Cham, Switzerland

All this world is heavy with the promise of greater things, and a day will come—one day in the unending succession of days—when beings who are now latent in our thoughts and hidden in our loins will stand upon this earth as one stands upon a footstool, and laugh and reach out their hands amidst the stars.

H. G. Wells, 'The Discovery of the Future', Lecture delivered to the Royal Institution of Great Britain, London, United Kingdom, 24 January 1902.

In memoriam E. V. Velluti

Preface

The focus of this book—the European Union (EU) as a good global actor and its promotion of non-trade values beyond its borders, specifically human rights and international labour standards through trade—continues to attract scholarly attention and still sparks heated debates and controversy. EU human rights conditionality, the human rights impact of EU (trade) measures, the viability and desirability of the trade–labour linkage, the *vexata quaestio* of the extraterritoriality of EU law, just to name a few, are all topics which require ongoing investigation. Above and beyond the key constitutional, institutional and substantive reforms of the 2009 Treaty of Lisbon, the global, national and local contexts within which the EU acts are changing dramatically. Within this constantly evolving setting, the *ancien régime* is confronted with new challenges and problems that require a rethinking of existing approaches and measures. Additionally, at the time of writing, the United Kingdom (UK) has left the EU.

Against this backdrop, the book provides new insights into the promotion and protection of human rights and international labour standards in the EU's external trade relations, building on and stimulating further the already well-engaged scientific dialogue on the nexus between the EU, human rights, labour and trade, i.e. EU human rights and social conditionality.

While writing this book I have come across many people with whom I had the privilege and pleasure to discuss many aspects of this book. I am grateful to all for helping me develop, refine and revisit the various ideas, concepts and arguments presented in this book.

A special thanks to Sue Millns and Donald McGillivray, former and current Head of Sussex Law School. Both have been incredibly supportive and encouraging during the writing of this book. I am also particularly indebted to Francesca Martines who accepted to step in at a later stage and for her key and insightful contributions to the completion of the book.

I would also like to extend my thanks to Brigitte Reschke and Boopalan Renu as well as the production team at Springer for their assistance and for their enduring patience in seeing this project slowly but steadily come to fruition.

Brighton, UK
March 2020

Samantha Velluti

Contents

Abbreviations

AA	Association Agreement
AB	Appellate Body
ACP	African, Caribbean and Pacific Group of States
AFL	American Federation of Labor
AFSJ	Area of Freedom, Security and Justice
AGOA	US African Growth and Opportunity Act
ASEAN	Association of Southeast Asian Nations
BIT	Bilateral Investment Treaty
BLA	Bangladesh Labour Act
CAFTA-DR	Dominican Republic—Central America—United States Free Trade Agreement
CARIFORUM	The Caribbean Forum of the African, Caribbean and Pacific Group of States
CARIS	Centre for the Analysis of Regional Integration at Sussex, University of Sussex, UK
CAS	ILO Committee on the Application of Standards
CAT	UN Convention against Torture
CCC	Clean Clothes Campaign
CCP	Common Commercial Policy
CEACR	ILO Committee of Experts on the Application of Conventions and Recommendations
CEDAW	Convention for the Elimination of Discrimination against Women
CERD	Convention on the Elimination of All forms of Racial Discrimination
CESCR	UN Committee on Economic, Social and Cultural Rights
CET	Common External Tariff
CETA	EU-Canada Comprehensive Economic and Trade Agreement
CFSP	Common Foreign and Security Policy
CIO	Congress of Industrial Organizations
CJEU	Court of Justice of the European Union

CLS	Core Labour Standards
CPA	Cotonou Partnership Agreement
CRC	UN Convention on the Rights of the Child
CSCE	Conference on Security and Cooperation in Europe
CtRC	UN Committee on the Rights of the Child
CU	EU Customs Union
DAG	Domestic Advisory Group
DCFTA	Deep and Comprehensive Free Trade Agreements
DCI	Development Cooperation Instrument
DG	Directorate General
DG DEVCO	DG for International Cooperation and Development
DRD	Declaration on the Right to Development
DWA	ILO Decent Work Agenda
EANO	Economic Assessment of the Negotiated Outcome
EBA	Everything But Arms
EC	European Community
ECHR	European Convention for the Protection of Human Rights and Fundamental Freedoms
ECOWAS	Economic Community of West African States
ECSC	European Coal and Steel Community
EDF	European Development Fund
EEAS	European External Action Service
EEC	European Economic Community
EGAF	European Globalization Adjustment Fund
EIDHR	European Instrument for Democracy and Human Rights
EMU	Economic and Monetary Union
ENI	European Neighbourhood Instrument
EO	European Ombudsman
EP	European Parliament
EPA	Economic Partnership Agreement
ESI	European Structural and Investment
ESPCA	EU-Singapore Partnership and Cooperation Agreement
ETS	EU Emissions Trading System
ETUC	European Trade Union Confederation
EU	European Union
EU-CAAA	EU-Central American Association Agreement
EUCFR	European Union Charter of Fundamental Rights of the European Union
EUSFTA	Free Trade Agreement between the EU and Singapore
EVFTA	EU-Vietnam Free Trade Agreement
FCCC	UN Framework Convention on Climate Change
FDI	Foreign Direct Investment
FIDH	International Federation for Human Rights
FPI	Foreign Portfolio Investment
FTA	Free Trade Agreement

GATS	General Agreement on Trade in Services
GATT	General Agreement on Tariffs and Trade
GC	General Court
GDP	Gross Domestic Product
GPA	WTO Agreement on Government Procurement
GSP	Generalized Scheme of Preferences
GSP+	GSP incentive scheme
HEC	École des Hautes Études Commerciales
HRC	UN Human Rights Committee
HRIA	Human Rights Impact Assessment
IA	Impact Assessment
ICC	International Criminal Court
ICCPR	International Covenant on Civil and Political Rights
ICESCR	International Covenant on Economic, Social and Cultural Rights
ICFTU	International Confederation of Free Trade Unions
ICJ	International Court of Justice
IFC	International Finance Corporation
IIA	International Investment Agreement
ILC	International Labour Conference
ILO	International Labour Organization
ILS	International Labour Standards
IMF	International Monetary Fund
INTA	Committee on International Trade of the EU Parliament
IPA	Investment Protection Agreement
IR	International Relations
ISDS	Investment-State Dispute Settlement
ITLOS	International Tribunal for the Law of the Sea
ITM	Informal Technical Meetings
LABPTA	Labour Provisions in Trade Agreements
LDCs	Least Developed Countries
MFN	WTO Most Favoured Nation principle
MPE	Market Power Europe
NAALC	North American Agreement on Labour Cooperation
NAFTA	North American Free Trade Agreement
NGO	Non-governmental Organization
NPE	Normative Power Europe
NYU	New York University
OAS	Organization of American State Charter
OCTs	Overseas Countries and Territories
OECD	Organization for Economic Cooperation and Development
OHCHR	UN High Commissioner for Human Rights
OJ	Official Journal
OSPAR	Convention for the Protection of the Marine Environment of the North-East
PCA	Partnership and Cooperation Agreement

PCIJ	Permanent Court of International Justice
PPM	Process and Production Method
RMG	Ready-made Garment Industry
RTA	Regional Trade Agreement
SALW	Small Arms and Light Weapons
SDG	Sustainable Development Goal
SFPA	Sustainable Fisheries Partnership Agreement
SIA	Sustainable Impact Assessment
TBR	EU Trade Barriers Regulation
TEU	Treaty on European Union
TFEU	Treaty on the Functioning of the European Union
TGWA	EU Trade, Growth and World Affairs Strategy
TL	Treaty of Lisbon
TPC	Trade Policy Committee
TPEA	US Trade Preferences Extension Act
TPP	Trans-Pacific Partnership Agreement
TRIPS	Trade-Related Aspects of Intellectual Property Rights
TTIP	Transatlantic Trade and Investment Partnership between the EU and the USA
UDHR	Universal Declaration of Human Rights
UK	United Kingdom
UN	United Nations
UNCLOS	United Nations Convention on the Law of the Sea
UNCTAD	United Nations Conference on Trade and Development
US	United States of America
USAID	US Agency for International Development
USJFTA	US-Jordan Free Trade Agreement
USTR	United States Trade Representative
VCLT	Vienna Convention on the Law of Treaties
WCL	World Confederation of Labour
WCO	World Customs Organization
WCED	World Commission Development on Environment and Development
WCSDG	World Commission on the Social Dimension of Globalization
WIPO	World Intellectual Property Organization
WMD	Weapons of Mass Destruction
WTO	World Trade Organization

Chapter 1
The Promotion of Human Rights and International Labour Standards After Lisbon: An Introduction

Samantha Velluti

1.1 Background and Context

The book is the culmination of research spanning a period of four years during which the interconnectedness of the economy and the pace of change has increased at majestic levels with rising uncertainty, social concerns and new regulatory challenges for states and international organisations alike. The strong opposition across many European countries against the conclusion of so-called "mega-regional" trade agreements such as the Transatlantic Trade and Investment Partnership Agreement between the European Union (EU) and the United States of America (US), i.e. TTIP,[1] and the withdrawal of the United Kingdom from the EU—commonly known as "Brexit"—[2]represent a vivid manifestation of the kind of problems that the EU currently faces and the challenges that lie ahead, in-between change and continuity.[3]

Just as politics permeates every aspect of our lives, so too do human rights. There is no facet about life that is not framed in human rights terms or that does not have a human rights dimension or connotation. The level of protection and promotion of human rights thus denotes the level of acceptance of power: human rights as legitimating ideals of democracy still retain a powerful theoretical and ideational supremacy. It is for this reason that 'human rights in modern international relations represent both the best and the worst of times.'[4] Amid this climate of uncertainty

---

[1]For detailed information, European Commission, 'TTIP—News Archive', Department for Trade (DG Trade), https://trade.ec.europa.eu/doclib/press/index.cfm?id=1230, accessed on 14 June 2020; for a critique of TTIP, see De Ville and Siles-Brügge (2017); specifically in relation to the implications of TTIP for labour rights and standards, Tyc (2017).

[2]The departure of the UK from the EU is referred to more commonly with the term of "Brexit" from the amalgamation of the words "British" or "Britain" and the word "exit", see further Sect. 3.5.5 in Chap. 3 of this book.

[3]On the complexities of regulating in times of uncertainty in the EU context, see Larik (2013); specifically in relation to trade, Young (2017).

[4]Forsythe (2018), p. 4.

S. Velluti, *The Role of the EU in the Promotion of Human Rights and International Labour Standards in Its External Trade Relations*,
https://doi.org/10.1007/978-3-030-56748-4_1

and difficult times, the long-term vision that emerges for human rights *lato sensu* is open-ended and depends on agency in context.[5] From this perspective, the twenty-first century holds both dangers to, and promise for, human rights[6] insofar as the future of human rights should not be considered as being predetermined by structural or systemic factors but is instead dependent on and determined by public choice, decisions of a given polity's institutions and bodies.

The incorporation of human rights into international law, via the adoption and ratification of treaties, is considered by many one of the most significant achievements of contemporary history. International human rights law is meant to provide individuals with invaluable protections. And yet, it is hard to refute the conclusion that governments world-wide continue to violate human rights with impunity. Why do more than 150 states (out of 193 that are members of the United Nations (UN), including liberal democracies) still engage in torture? Why does child labour continue to exist in so many countries? Why are millions of people still forced against their will to work? Why does slavery continue to plague most modern economies? Violent suppression of peaceful demonstrations and violations of other fundamental civil, political and internationally recognised labour rights also remain widespread across the globe. The traditional champions of human rights, such as Europe, have floundered amid ongoing economic downturns or slow growth. This state of affairs is not new, nor the recognition that individualist and abstract rights-based formulations of justice are intrinsically problematic and cannot fully capture the multi-faceted forms of human rights breaches taking place in this globalising world.[7] It is evident that ratification of treaties is not the answer, but rather their (effective) enforcement.

Linked to this first set of challenges concerning solely human rights, is the even more vexing question about their interaction with trade. Market regulation has become conspicuously contentious. Lamy -former Director-General of the World Trade Organisation (WTO)—once famously said that trade is often depicted as a villain, 'a symbol of mercantilism, capitalism, the tool through which powerful multinational corporations impose their law over human beings, impairing their economic, social and cultural rights.'[8] Similarly, trade experts and proponents of globalisation often dismiss the human rights impact of trade.[9] This "mutual ignorance" continues to permeate the interaction between human rights and trade to this day, and even more so in the case of social trade. Any attempt at establishing a fruitful relationship between non-trade values and trade is mired in tension and reciprocal suspicion.

The book is situated within this overarching "mutual misunderstanding" and looks at the difficult conceptual problem concerning the relationship between human rights and international labour standards, and trade in EU external (trade) relations. Here, the intended aim is to help diminish this mutual ignorance. To this end, it examines the EU's role in strengthening and promoting the human rights and social dimension

[5] Ibid., at p. 7.

[6] Ibid.

[7] For an excellent critique from the perspective of justice, see Kochenov et al. (2017).

[8] Lamy (2010).

[9] Stiglitz (2002), at p. 5.

of globalisation, identifying its limitations and suggesting ways of overcoming them. Linked to this, it critically evaluates the way the EU has been steadily positioning itself as a key international player in the attempt to improve global governance, through increased cooperation with other international organisations. In this context, as the book will go on to show, the EU not only exports its own norms and policies, uploading its internal *acquis* to the international sphere, but it also employs its various instruments—whether unilateral, bilateral, regional or multilateral- to support the adoption and implementation of international law. Cremona sums it up neatly in saying that, 'the EU maintains a complex web of relations founded on and operating within international law, and these relations mediate between EU law and third countries and international organisations.'[10]

For these reasons, the increased role of the EU as a global actor in the promotion of human rights in its external (trade) relations provides a focal point of analysis not only for EU and International Relations (IR) scholars but also for International and human rights lawyers. Within the copious literature on the international role of the EU[11] it is possible to find learned assessments with rather opposite but equally persuasive conclusions about its place in the world.

1.2 Aims and Significance of the Book

1.2.1 Aims

Following the 2009 Treaty of Lisbon (TL)[12] reforms, the EU's Common Commercial Policy (CCP) is explicitly included as one of the six exclusive competences of the Union and the European Parliament has been given a stronger role in relation to the EU's international agreements. Moreover, the TL has introduced two new Titles (Title V TEU, and Part Five, Title 1 TFEU) which aim at ensuring, among others, more consistency in EU external action. Significantly, the respect for the rule of law, protection of human rights, and the strict observance and development of international law (including respect for the principles of the UN Charter)[13] have now been included among the EU external action's overall objectives and mission statement.[14] The changes introduced by the TL confirm, therefore, that the EU intends to have a significant role outside its territory, not only in relation to the external dimension of its internal market, but also in relation to normative objectives of global justice, such as human rights.

---

[10]Cremona (2019), at p. 64.

[11]Chapter 2 of the book offers a detailed literature review of the EU's role as a global actor.

[12]Treaty of Lisbon Amending the Treaty on European Union and the Treaty Establishing the European Community, 13 December 2007, 2007/C 306/01.

[13]United Nations, *Charter of the United Nations*, 24 October 1945, 1 UNTS XVI, available at: https://www.un.org/en/sections/un-charter/un-charter-full-text/, accessed on 20 February 2020.

[14]Articles 3(5) TEU and 21 TEU.

To put it differently, according to its new mandate post Lisbon the EU is 'morally, politically and legally held to pursue equality amongst wealthy and poorer nations, to support their development and ensure "fairness" between them,'[15] in particular by fostering sustainable economic, social and environmental development. The EU is to be guided by the principles, which inspired its own creation and which it seeks to advance in the world. This mission, which could be equated to a kind of Kantian dogma for the Union's external action, is in many respects the external projection of its internal reality: the EU's single market and the European integration process have been progressively constructed through a variety of legal processes that were based on forms of multilateralism and the rule of law, as a means of responding to geo-political and socio-economic challenges faced by European states after the end of World War II.[16]

However, in relation to the CCP, it should be noted that while Article 207(1) TFEU requires the EU to take into consideration also the general objectives set out in Article 21 TEU in conducting its external trade policy, Article 206 TFEU—which outlines the specific trade policy objectives of the CCP—places a strong emphasis on liberalization.[17] In addition, as the European Commission has itself long recognized,[18] human rights and labour requirements, included in the EU's various external trade instruments, are perceived by non-EU countries as protectionist and asymmetrical instruments that seemingly work to the advantage of developed countries. The role the EU has committed itself to in relation to the promotion of human rights, social rights and international labour standards in its international trade agreements, therefore, raises many complex questions in relation to competence, consistency/coherence and effectiveness as well as legitimacy of EU external action, all of which are the focus of analysis of this book.

To sum up, the changes introduced by the TL to the EU's external competence combined with the legally binding status of the 2000 EU Charter of Fundamental Rights (EUCFR)[19] forces European scholars and lawyers to rethink the role of the EU in global governance, the functioning of the EU system (including the new inter-institutional balance) and the way the promotion of human rights is being pursued through trade internationally.

The book is a timely contribution to the fervent debate about the role of the EU as a global trade and human rights actor and follows an already distinguished body of work on EU human rights conditionality,[20] including the trade-labour linkage,[21] as well as the nature of the EU's human rights obligations when it acts beyond its

[15] Van Vooren et al. (2013), p. 2.

[16] Ibid.

[17] Article 206 TFEU provides that the Union shall contribute to the harmonious development of world trade, the progressive abolition of restrictions on international trade and on foreign direct investment, and the lowering of customs and other barriers.

[18] European Commission (2004).

[19] Charter of Fundamental Rights of the European Union [2000] OJ C364/01.

[20] E.g. Fierro (2002), Bartels (2005).

[21] E.g. Addo (2015), Orbie and Tortell (2011).

borders.[22] The book shows that the EU human rights framework post Lisbon can be operationalized within the realm of the EU external relations regime and specifically in EU external trade policy, in spite of concrete legal (and political) limitations. In this context, the book suggests some proposals for reform to strengthen the EU's human rights obligations in its external trade relations and offers some points for further reflection.

The book addresses a further set of related questions and associated aims.

(i) the definition of adequate strategies to reconcile its internal tensions which manifest themselves most visibly in the gap or mismatch between what the EU purports itself to be, namely its carefully construed image and identity of an organization with a clearly identifiable and enforceable common set of European values, principles and human rights and its practices—in both its internal and external spheres of action—which seem to suggest a different reality;
(ii) the development of credible and valuable linkages between trade and human/social rights (for example, defining acceptable conditionalities which are not considered discriminatory or protectionist in nature), thus ensuring a system of international trade which genuinely promotes more equitable global trade and sustainability, is founded on discourses of social responsibility and justice and is no longer limited to the pursuit of free trade and open market economies.

1.2.2 Significance

The book provides new insights into the promotion and protection of human rights and international labour standards in the EU's external trade relations, building on and stimulating further the already well-engaged scientific dialogue on the nexus between the EU, human rights, labour and trade, i.e. EU human rights and social conditionality. In particular, it provides the basis for developing a new analytical lens for better understanding the role of the EU in promoting human rights and international labour standards in global trade and for critically examining the extent to which and how normative considerations have actually influenced the adoption of EU legal instruments and policy decisions. Its findings seek to act as a prelude to considering how change might be effected and, in particular, they aim at helping to identify criteria and assessment standards that make it possible to qualify, substantiate or reject the claim that the EU is a normative and ethical power.

To recap, the significance of the intended book lies chiefly in subjecting the theoretical assumptions of the EU's role as a global actor to further interrogation in order to assess the legal, political and economic rationales underpinning the role of the EU in promoting human rights and international labour standards in its external trade relations and, more broadly, to evaluate the purported role of the EU as a normative and ethical power. The analysis carried out throughout the book uncovers the extent

[22] E.g. Bartels (2015), Velluti and Tzevelekos (2018).

to which the EU shapes and influences the evolving legal processes, principles, values and institutions of global governance in order to effectively promote the protection of human rights.

1.3 Structure, Methods and Methodology of the Book

1.3.1 Research Methodology and Methods

The fuzziness of the EU's nature, which eschews clear-cut categorisations, requires an overarching research approach that is distinctively interdisciplinary, using insights from political science, IR and law. The book is essentially a legal study blended with a contextual approach, which also embraces social, political and economic analyses. The multi-disciplinary perspective combined with a holistic and explorative analytical approach provides a fresh in-depth examination of the role of the EU as a global player in human rights. The various theoretical and analytical approaches which make up the bulk of the book's overall methodology are presented in key individual chapters, where required for analytical purposes.

This study has relied on a series of documents, papers and reports. First, official documentation of the EU Institutions such as Protocols annexed to the EU Treaties, Presidency Conclusions of the European Council, Communications, Green and White Papers of the Commission, Decisions, Directives, Recommendations and Resolutions of the Council of Ministers and European Parliament, working papers and reports, as well as the decisions of the General Court and the Court of Justice of the EU (CJEU). The investigation also extended to the examination of documents of the International Labour Organisation (ILO) such as Global reports, Working Papers and Meeting documents, the World Trade Organisation (WTO) such as WTO agreements, dispute settlement reports and related documents, WTO selected studies, reviews and profiles and other international organisations. With regard to human rights, some of the chapters of the book also provide coverage of the judgments of the European Court of Human Rights (ECtHR), the Human Rights Committee (HRC), the Inter-American Court of Human Rights (IACHR) and the International Court of Justice (ICJ). Lastly, the book relied on an array of materials that can be categorized as soft law, which has contributed to the development of key arguments or recommendations.

1.3.2 Structure of the Book

As Williams aptly puts it: 'half a century after the EU was formed there is still doubt and angst about the nature of its constitution. We are perhaps no nearer a clear understanding of what the EU is for or the values that govern its development and practice than we were in 1957.'[23] To this day, the EU still has an "uncertain soul",[24] which remains a conundrum for all EU scholars. The opening chapter (Chap. 2) thus examines selected IR literature on the EU's active engagement with the international legal order, namely, the role, place and position of the EU within the international legal order and how the EU is also (re-)shaping it. While the analysis carried out is intentionally descriptive it serves an important purpose to the research aims of the book as it helps to unpack the reasons for the uneven and incoherent promotion of human rights (including social rights) and labour standards. In so doing, it helps to fathom the different, even conflicting objectives that said promotion is said to serve. In this context the study also looks at the EU's "deep trade agenda" and how the CCP in many ways represents the move at international level towards so-called "managed globalization". The main argument put forward is to develop and apply a revisited notion of Normative Power Europe (NPE) to the EU and its external action, which departs from a dichotomic approach towards the relationship between values and interests.

Chapter 3 provides a detailed analysis of the legal framework of the CCP in the light of the constitutional, institutional and substantive changes introduced by the TL, which are particularly important for the conclusion of the EU's international trade agreements and its unilateral trade arrangements. The main purpose of this chapter is to shed light on the significance of these changes with particular reference to the complex question of EU competence in the field of the CCP. In so doing, it takes into account other salient reforms at global, European and domestic levels which impact directly on the further development of the CCP. The analysis shows how the TL changes reflect a broader conceptualization of trade and constitute a response to the challenges of the evolving international trading system and globalization. Particular attention is paid to the effects that Brexit will have on the conclusion of the EU's international trade agreements as well as the increased powers of the European Parliament (EP), its democratizing function in the context of the CCP and the growing importance of the role of national parliaments, qua vox populi, in the negotiation and ratification of international trade agreements.

Chapter 4 offers a detailed account of the EU's political conditionality, which is used to promote non-trade values encompassing the EU's human rights conditionality, and to be distinguished from the narrower form of economic conditionality. The analysis covers its origins and the models used for the human rights clause in EU bilateral agreements as well as its underpinning rationales. In this context, the chapter provides a thorough study of positive and negative conditionality and it identifies the problems of establishing effective monitoring mechanisms. Significantly, the analysis considers the lawfulness of EU political conditionality in accordance with both the Union's internal rules and international law. The examination draws on a series of regional and bilateral trade agreements as well as unilateral trade arrangements to illustrate how EU practice includes both positive and negative conditionality. Ultimately, the chapter shows how EU political conditionality is the litmus test for EU external action, straddling between realpolitik and its normative aspirations.

[23] Williams (2010), at p. 1.

[24] Ibid.

Chapter 5 examines in detail the trade-labour linkage and starts by looking at its foundations and history. It then assesses the EU's increased practice of promoting social rights and international labour standards in its external trade relations, unilaterally through the Generalised System of Preferences (GSP; and largely under its incentive scheme, known as the GSP+), and at regional and bilateral levels via international agreements, which encompass reciprocal or non-reciprocal preferential trade links with third countries. In this context, the chapter unpacks and addresses the tensions in and limitations of the discourse and practice of the EU's promotion of social rights in its external trade relations. It concludes by putting forward recommendations to strengthen the effectiveness of the operationalization of EU social conditionality on the basis of the capabilities approach.[25]

Chapter 6 shifts the focus of analysis to the nature of the EU's human rights obligations in its external trade relations after Lisbon, particularly following the EUCFR's legally binding status. It specifically addresses the difficult question of whether the EU's obligations abroad can be categorized as extraterritorial. The chapter thus starts by providing an account of the phenomenon of extraterritorial jurisdiction by reference to the case law of the ECtHR. It then outlines the jurisdictional model embraced in the chapter and explains why it is an apposite lens for the uniqueness of the EU legal system. The analysis also includes key judgments of the EU Courts, where the legality of EU measures has been called into question by reference to fundamental human rights. Two arguments are presented in this chapter: first, an argument in favour of applying a narrow reading of the duty of due diligence to the EU with a concomitant duty to carry out *ex ante* human rights impact assessment of trade agreements together with *ex post* evaluation of the former's compliance with human rights and, second, a revised notion of the principle of implied powers in the field of human rights so as to better equip the EU with the required competence and instruments to act.

Chapter 7, the concluding chapter of the book, draws together the most salient points made throughout the book and presents some tentative recommendations for future research that address the main limitations of EU conditionality in its external trade relations.

References

International Law

United Nations (1945) Charter of the United Nations, 24 October 1945, 1 UNTS XVI, available at: https://www.un.org/en/sections/un-charter/un-charter-full-text/. Accessed on 20 Feb 2020

[25] Sen (1999), Nussbaum (2011); for a detailed account of the capabilities approach in relation to labour law, see Langille (2019).

EU Primary Law

Charter of Fundamental Rights of the European Union (2000) OJ C364/01
Treaty of Lisbon Amending the Treaty on European Union and the Treaty Establishing the European Community, 13 Dec 2007, 2007/C 306/01

EU Official Documents

European Commission, Communication from the Commission to the European Parliament, the Council, the European Economic and Social Committee and the Committee of the regions, 'The Social Dimension of Globalisation—the EU's Contribution on Extending Benefits to All' COM (2004) 383final

Books and Chapters in Books

Addo K (2015) Core labour standards and international trade. Springer, Heidelberg
Bartels L (2005) Human rights conditionality in the EU's international agreements. OUP, Oxford
Cremona M (2019) Extending the reach of EU law. The EU as an international legal actor. In: Cremona M, Scott J (eds) EU law beyond EU borders. The extraterritorial reach of EU Law. OUP, Oxford, pp 64–111
Fierro E (2002) The EU's approach to human rights conditionality in practice. Martinus Nijhoff Publishers, The Hague
Forsythe DP (2018) Human rights in international relations. CUP, Cambridge
Kochenov D, de Búrca G, Williams A (eds) (2017) Europe's justice deficit?. Hart Publishing, Oxford
Langille B (ed) (2019) The capability approach to labour law. OUP, Oxford
Larik J (2013) Entrenching global governance: the EU's constitutional objectives caught between a Sanguine World view and a daunting reality. In: Van Vooren B, Blockmans S, Wouters J (eds) The EU's role in global governance. OUP, Oxford, pp 7–22
Nussbaum M (2011) Creating capabilities. Harvard University Press, Cambridge, MA
Sen A (1999) Development as freedom. OUP, Oxford
Stiglitz J (2002) Globalisation and its discontents. Penguin, London
Orbie J, Tortell L (eds) (2011) The European union and the social dimension of globalisation. Routledge, London
Van Vooren B, Blockmans S, Wouters J (2013) The legal dimension of global governnace: what role for the European Union? An introduction. In: Van Vooren B, Blockmans S, Wouters J (eds) The EU's role in global governance. OUP, Oxford, pp 1–4
Velluti S, Tzevelekos VP (eds) (2018) Special issue: 'Extraterritoriality of EU law and human rights after Lisbon: the case of trade and public procurement. Europe and the World: A Law Review 2(1)
Williams A (2010) The ethos of Europe. Values, law and justice in the EU. CUP, Cambridge

Journal Articles

Bartels L (2015) The EU's human rights obligations in relation to policies with extraterritorial effects. Eur J Int Law 25(4):1071–1091

De Ville F, Siles-Brügge G (2017) Why TTIP is a game-changer and its critics have a point. J Eur Pub Policy 24(10):1491–1505. https://doi.org/10.1080/13501763.2016.1254273

Tyc A (2017) Workers' rights and transatlantic trade relations: the TTIP and beyond. Econ Labour Relat Rev 28(1):113–128

Young AR (2017) European trade policy in interesting times. J Eur Integr 39(7):909–923. https://doi.org/10.1080/07036337.2017.1371705

Other

Lamy P (2010) Towards shared responsibility and greater coherence: human rights, trade and macroeconomic policy. Speech at the Colloquium on Human Rights in the Global Economy, Co-organized by the International Council on Human Rights and Realizing Rights, Geneva, 13 Jan 2010, available at: https://www.wto.org/english/news_e/sppl_e/sppl146_e.htm. Accessed on 20 Feb 2020

European Commission (2020) TTIP—news archive. Department for Trade (DG Trade), available at: https://trade.ec.europa.eu/doclib/press/index.cfm?id=1230. Accessed on 14 June 2020

Chapter 2
The EU as a Global Actor in an "Inter-Polar" World

Samantha Velluti

2.1 Introduction: Theoretical Understandings of the Nature, Powers and Role of the EU in the World

> 'Our world today is more connected, contested and complex. The European Union needs to take a fresh look at this uncertain environment, in which opportunities and challenges coexist. This will help promote the European Union's interests globally, and ensure our security at home and abroad.'
>
> Federica Mogherini,
>
> Former EU High Representative for Foreign Affairs and Security Policy
>
> Brussels, June 2016

The complex dynamics of a constantly evolving world require an ongoing investigation into the EU's (self-)image, the way it projects its identity and it operates globally. This study is particularly pertinent in the twenty-first century that is taking shape, 'accommodating the rising powers and sensitive to the needs of the global south.'[1]

It draws on Grevi's notion of "inter-polar world".[2] The chapter examines selected literature on the EU's active engagement with the international (legal) order, namely, the role, place and position of the EU within the international (legal) order and how the EU is also (re-)shaping it.[3] This chapter, belated as it is in entering the debate on the EU's actorness in international relations (IR) and role in global governance,[4]

---

[1]Howorth (2010), pp. 455–474.

[2]Grevi (2009); in a constantly evolving world multi-polarity on its own no longer captures the complex challenges faced by "poles" or "powers" due to the interconnectedness of many policy areas and the interdependence and need for cooperation that it creates among "poles" or "powers".

[3]Kochenov and Amtenbrink (2013), pp. 1–18; Cremona (2008), pp. 1–9, at p. 9; Larik (2013), pp. 62–86.

[4]The following broad working definition of global governance is employed in the present chapter: 'The complex of formal and informal institutions, mechanisms, relationships and processes between

S. Velluti, *The Role of the EU in the Promotion of Human Rights and International Labour Standards in Its External Trade Relations*,
https://doi.org/10.1007/978-3-030-56748-4_2

has the benefit of some hindsight.[5] The distinctive nature of EU external relations and action has become a "familiar question",[6] a staple for both EU lawyers and IR scholars. The chapter's intended aim is not to coin and add a new theorization of the EU's role as a global actor to the existing literature. The heterogeneity of the EU's composite nation makes it difficult to elaborate any one size fits all grand theory or single ideal-type of the EU that can provide the basis for an effective, coherent, value-based system of global governance. As Cremona posits, 'the EU should be seen not as a static model, but as a dynamic experiment, a process or a laboratory in which new methods of integration, multi-level and multi-centred governance and new constitutionalism are being worked on and bargained, and are evolving.'[7] Moreover, the various roles of the EU are the result of a balance or tension between different interests, agendas and players within the Union, namely the member states, the EU institutions and non-state actors, all constituting a bundle of interests and values. Even though it is possible to envisage a Union identity behind the multi-faceted roles that the EU has it is necessary to have a more considered integration of its different roles to meet the consistency and coherence of external relations required by the Treaties.[8]

While the analysis carried out is intentionally descriptive it serves an important purpose to the research aims of the book as it helps to unpack the reasons for the uneven and incoherent promotion of human rights (including social rights) and labour standards. In so doing, it helps to fathom the different, even conflicting objectives that this promotion is said to serve. Equally, it eschews 'any claim that the EU is in some way more virtuous than other international actors, or that it is motivated mainly by values, principles or norms, rather than by its own interests.'[9] A more realistic account is one that accepts and is built on the two-fold premise that the EU is not to be understood as replacing states, but rather 'as a means to better manage their interdependence' and that we live in a "partially globalized world".[10] In consequence, within governance institutions and international organisations values, principles and norms, namely normative standards, necessarily co-exist with self-interest.[11] The EU is no exception. At the same time, it should be recalled that the EU's Common Commercial Policy (CCP), by relying increasingly on "governance through trade agreements"[12] with non-EU countries, needs to deal with two sets of inter-related questions: on the one hand, "functional necessities of international markets" and,

and among states, markets, citizens and organizations—both intergovernmental and nongovernmental—through which collective interests are articulated, rights and obligations are established, and differences are mediated'; see Thakur and Langenhove (2006), pp. 233–240, at 233.

[5] I have borrowed this expression from Hatzopoulos, see Hatzopoulos (2007), pp. 309–342.

[6] Búrca (2013), pp. 39–58, at p. 39.

[7] Cremona (2004), pp. 553–573, at 554.

[8] Ibid., p. 565.

[9] de Búrca, above no. 6, at p. 39.

[10] Keohane (2001), pp. 1–13.

[11] Ibid.

[12] Bohnenberger and Joerges (2016), pp. 1–38, at 3.

on the other hand, "normative concerns prevailing in the participating polities" in order to create a transnational ordering of markets.[13] As Polanyi explains, economies are socially embedded and reflect the social concerns and political preferences of a polity.[14] Accordingly, the functioning of an economy cannot be fully understood without taking into account the social context in which it is embedded. Hence, the EU and the transnational ordering of markets that derives from its international trade agreements, need to be understood as parts of larger, historically derived, institutional, or social structures. It follows that accepted normative concerns, that is, the belief that they ought to be followed, need to be part of the EU's external trade policy. The institutional and legal framework arising from the EU's trade agreements, therefore, must be able to subsume liberalisation and normative objectives in which the economies of the participating parties are embedded. However, tensions inevitably arise between the functional necessities of the markets and the normative concerns of the parties that participate.

Additionally, as will be shown throughout the book, the EU pursues different and often conflicting goals, objectives and agendas,[15] such as for example a neoliberal agenda versus a human rights agenda, whose contradictions, in turn, are reflected in the adoption of conflicting measures: either promoting or furthering liberalisation or, on the other hand, regulating or demoting it. The existence of these opposing goals can be seen also in relation to the underlying reasons for the EU's increasing interest in becoming a key player on the international plane. To some extent the EU's motivations are hegemonic and protectionist, i.e. it seeks to exert political and economic domination over other non-EU countries because the failure to export the standards developed within its internal market to others outside the EU would put European firms at a competitive disadvantage. Moreover, by acting as a global regulator, the EU can defend its social preferences without compromising the competitiveness of its industries. At the same time, however, the EU's externalization of its regulatory preferences is driven by altruistic purposes reflecting the legal traditions of those member states with strong constitutional safeguards for the protection of human rights. As it pursues conflicting objectives, oscillating between supranationalism and intergovernmentalism, the EU is a complex and contradictory actor whose "transformative power" remains limited.[16] As Meunier and Nicolaïdis put it, the EU is a "conflicted trade power"[17] rather than 'an idealized actor whose preference for norms is seen as a guarantee of its good faith and disinterestedness.'[18]

In this context, the 2009 Treaty of Lisbon (TL)[19] reform constitutes an attempt to address the above complexities by simplifying the structure of the EU and the way it

---

[13]Ibid, p. 9.

[14]Polanyi (1957), pp. 243–270; see also Polanyi (1944).

[15]E.g. Borzel and Hullen (2014), pp. 1033–1049.

[16]On the EU's transformative power, see García (2015), pp. 621–640.

[17]Meunier and Nicolaïdis (2006), 906–925.

[18]Laïdi (2009), pp. 1–20, at p. 18.

[19]Treaty of Lisbon Amending the Treaty on European Union and the Treaty Establishing the European Community, 13 December 2007, 2007/C 306/01.

operates. The most significant change has been the merging of the EU and the European Community (EC) into one legal entity, that is the EU, which now has a single legal personality.[20] The changes made to the EU and its external action's legal and institutional framework aim at guaranteeing more clarity, coherence and democracy. It should be noted that, while important, these changes have not introduced a new legal basis for EU external relations rather they have amended the Treaties already in force, reinforcing the EU's external (commercial) competence.[21] In this regard, the expansion of exclusive competence in the field of trade and investment policies is decisive for the strengthening of the role of the EU as a global actor.[22] In particular, clearer competences and the broadening of the scope of the CCP,[23] are meant to ensure a more modernised trade policy, allowing the EU to become a stronger and more effective global player in the pursuit of its interests. [24] As will be shown, this is yet to be fully achieved.

The TL also injected a normative dimension into the EU's international relations thus advancing values, principles and objectives that are emphatically presented as "European" and seeking their universal application via explicit reference to the respect for international law.[25] Moreover, the objective of consistency has also been included in the CCP with the obligation for the Union to conduct its policy within the broader context of the principles and objectives of the Union's external action.[26] Overall, the TL 'signifies an *evolutionary* but not a *revolutionary* step'[27] in the development of the EU project.

Nevertheless, these changes have reignited debates on certain aspects of EU external relations law and practice, such as its constitutional nature, the competence of the EU to act on the international plane, the legal status and effect of decisions of international organizations in the EU legal order and their communitarization through the jurisprudence of the Court of Justice of the European Union (CJEU)[28] as well as the overall consistency and coherence of EU external action.[29] As pointed

---

[20]Article 47 TEU.

[21]Article 3(1)e TFEU and Articles 206 and 207 TFEU and 218 TFEU (in relation to the increased powers of the European Parliament (EP) in the CCP); for critical commentary, see Dimopoulos (2008), pp. 101–129; Dimopoulos (2010), pp. 153–170; Müller-Graff (2008), pp. 188–291; Hoffmeister (2011), pp. 83–95; Puig and Al-Haddab (2011), pp. 289–301.

[22]Wessel and Takács (2017), pp.103–117, 106.

[23]Woolcock (2008), pp. 1–6, at 2.

[24]Hoffmeister, above no. 20, at p. 95. However, the phenomenon of "mixed agreements", examined in Chapter 3 of the book, constitutes a challenge to exclusivity.

[25]Articles 3(5) and 21(1) TEU.

[26]Articles 207(1) TFEU; 3(5) TEU.

[27]Crowe (2008), pp. 163–208. Emphasis in italics added by the authors.

[28]Lavranos (2004); Kuijper and Bronckers (2005), pp. 1313–1355; Búrca and Scott (2001), pp. 1–30.

[29]European Commission, Communication on *Europe in the World—Some Practical Proposals for Greater Coherence, Effectiveness and Visibility* COM (2006) 278 final; Herlin-Karnell and Konstadinides (2012/13), pp. 139–167; Hillion (2008), pp. 10–36; Portela and Raube (eds) (2008), pp. 1–10, and specifically on the changes made by the TL, see Cremona (2008), pp. 11–36; in relation to the question of consistency in the EU's CCP, see Müller-Graff, above no. 20, at p. 192.

out by many commentators, these issues reopen the question of the EU's political destiny and highlight how this remains a deeply controversial area both technically and in terms of underlying political values.[30]

The chapter is organized as follows. Section 2.2 provides a selected analysis of the IR literature on the role of the EU as a global actor and claims that a new research methodology providing the epistemological tools to understand the complex and inter-twined connections between interests, values, norms and institutions in the EU needs to be developed. Section 2.3 provides a preliminary account of the EU's promotion of non-commercial objectives through trade relations as part of its self-projection as a global (human rights) actor. This section explains how the promotion of non-commercial objectives through trade has gained significant prominence in EU external action following the entry into force of the TL. This first analysis provides the basis for the in-depth examination carried out in Chap. 3. Section 2.4 looks at the EU's so-called "deep trade agenda" in the broader context of global economic governance spanning the period in-between the twentieth and twenty-first century. In this context, the section looks at the interconnections between the internal and the external sphere of EU action, such as for example the single market and the CCP and exemplified most vividly by the EU's adoption of overarching strategies. Section 2.5 is the conclusion to the chapter. It brings together the main arguments on the EU's role as a global actor with some preliminary points for reflection in light of the withdrawal of the United Kingdom (UK) from the EU, namely Brexit. These points are then re-examined and expanded upon in subsequent chapters of the book.

2.2 The Multi-Faceted Conceptions of the European Union and Its Role as a Global Actor

There is an abundance of literature, largely in the field of IR,[31] on the EU as a global actor interrogating in different ways and from different perspectives the distinctive character of the EU's role in global governance. More specifically, the EU's existence and action continue to spark crucial questions about what the EU is and *should be*, what it does and *should do* and what impact it has and *should have*. Scholars have attempted invariably to answer these questions with a range of different conceptions developed and used to define the unique features of the EU's international identity and role as a global player.

The normative power Europe (NPE) concept is undoubtedly one of the most popular and contested terms that has enriched the academic debate on the role of the

[30] Dashwood and Maresceau (2008), pp. 1–10, at p. 2; Cremona (2008), pp. 34–69.

[31] For a legal analysis of the EU's role as a global actor, see Cremona (1998), pp. 67–94; Cremona, above no. 7; Czuczai and Naert (eds) (2017); Búrca (2011), pp. 649–693; Wetzel (ed) (2012); Vooren et al. (eds) (2013).

EU as a global actor. Since Manners's seminal work on the NPE concept,[32] scholarly attention has turned to ethical and ideational aspects of EU external relations and foreign policy.[33] It is used to refer broadly to the EU's promotion of multilateralism and values such as respect for human rights, democracy and international law,[34] through non-coercive means.[35] In many of the Union's constitutional texts the international identity of the EU is constructed as one largely based on normative powers.[36] As Khaliq aptly maintains: 'it is certainly true that much of the Union's rhetoric in this regard is about external relations inspired by an "ethics of responsibility" towards others due to its possession of political and economic power.'[37] In other words, the EU sees itself as a key actor in the pursuit of the "global common good"[38] with principled behaviour in foreign policy, that is, it acts according to a set of dynamic yet identifiable values, principles and images of the world.[39] The Laeken Declaration, which in many ways still sets out the EU's key objectives and direction for the twenty-first century, refers emphatically to Europe's need to 'shoulder its responsibilities in the governance of globalization. [...] In short, a power (the EU)[40] wanting to change the course of world affairs in such a way as to benefit not just the rich countries but also the poorest. A power seeking to set globalization within a moral framework, in other words to anchor it in solidarity and sustainable development.'[41]

Orbie and Khorana[42] have identified four tenets on which the NPE research programme is based and which significantly contribute to EU critical thinking and scholarship:

---

[32] Manners (2002), pp. 235–258; Manners (2006), pp. 167–180; Manners (2008), pp. 45–60; Manners (2011), pp. 226–247; see also Sjursen (2006), pp. 235–251; Whitman (2013), pp. 171–193.

[33] Gerrits (2009), pp. 1–8; Lucarelli (2008), pp. 23–42.

[34] For a list of values of the EU, see Article 2 TEU which provides that: 'The Union is founded on the values of respect for human dignity, freedom, democracy, equality, the rule of law and respect for human rights, including the rights of persons belonging to minorities. These values are common to the member states in a society in which pluralism, non-discrimination, tolerance, justice, solidarity and equality between women and men prevail.'

[35] Manners conceptualises normative power on the basis of five points: ideational, involving principles, actions, and impact, and having consequences for the world politics, see Manners (2009), pp. 9–24, at pp. 11–15.

[36] Manners (2002), p. 235; Manners (2008), p. 46.

[37] Khaliq (2008), p. 10.

[38] Aggestam (2008), p. 6.

[39] Lucarelli (2006), p. 2.

[40] Author's addition.

[41] Laeken Declaration on the future of the European Union (15 December 2001), in Bulletin of the European Union. 2001, No 12. Luxembourg: Office for Official Publications of the European Communities. "Presidency Conclusions of the Laeken European Council (14 and 15 December 2001)", p. 19–23, available at: https://www.cvce.eu/content/publication/2002/9/26/a76801d5-4bf0-4483-9000-e6df94b07a55/publishable_en.pdf. Accessed on 14 June 2020, p. 3.

[42] Orbie and Khorana (2015), pp. 253–264, at 254.

(1) *focus*: bringing ideas back in the study of EU foreign policy instead of the pre-dominant interest in instruments;
(2) *analytical*: discarding realist and state-centric views and thinking about post-modern notions of power;
(3) *epistemological*: favouring eclecticist and interpretavists accounts that challenge positivist science;
(4) *critical*: opening space for debate on what the EU should be (doing) in world politics, allowing normative theorizing as an alternative to problem-solving approaches.

In a rapidly changing political and legal landscape a broader understanding of the NPE research programme can provide the basis for addressing new questions about the EU and its external relations in the context of an "inter-polar" world. As posited by Howorth, 'the lessons of the EU's performance as an international actor to date could well prove to be utterly irrelevant to its future behavior.'[43] NPE has thus come to replace the concept of civilian power Europe (CPE),[44] according to which the EU is seen as a new Kantian *foedus pacificum* in international relations, largely relying on non-military means to secure peace and stability.[45] A related concept to CPE is that of good citizen Europe (GCE) developed by Dunne.[46] This notion refers to the EU's ability to 'export an expression of individual rights and duties from a bounded polity to a global order'.[47] According to Dunne, the EU employs two approaches: a "solidarist" and a "pluralist" one, respectively. The EU is a "solidarist" entity internally on the assumption that its member states share common interests and values. It relies instead on "pluralist" ideas where "solidarist" concepts cannot be applied externally, that is, to a specific foreign cultural or social context. Dunne argues that the EU's ability to recognize a specific context and culture and to decide when to take a particular course of action in its external relations enables it to take appropriate policies.[48]

---

[43] Howorth (2010), pp. 455–474, at 459.

[44] Bull (1982), pp. 149–164; Duchêne (1973), pp. 1–21; Duchêne (1972), pp. 32–47; Orbie (2006), pp. 123–128; Twitchett (ed) (1976), see Bilal and Hoekman (2019); Frunză et al. (eds) (2013).

[45] Twitchett defines civilian power as having three key features: the centrality of economic power for the achievement of political goals; the primacy of diplomatic cooperation for solving international problems; and the use of legally binding supranational institutions to achieve international progress, see Twitchett (1976); see also Hanns Maull's definition of "civilian power" as involving:

• the acceptance of the necessity of cooperation with others in the pursuit of international objectives;

• the concentration on non-military, primarily economic, means to secure national goals, with military power left as a residual instrument serving essentially to safeguard other means of international interaction; and

• a willingness to develop supranational structures to address critical issues of international management.

Maull (1990), pp. 92–93.

[46] Dunne (2008), pp. 13–28.

[47] Ibid.

[48] Ibid.

This rather optimistic view, however, contrasts with the perception that non-EU countries have of the Union. While the EU is seen by its member states largely as an agent of peace, democracy, development and good governance, non-EU countries consider the EU as a powerful actor whose policies aim at heavily influencing international behavior by prescribing specific (legitimate) actions, establishing and imposing certain international norms and restricting the domestic behavior of other sovereign actors.[49] Following this line of thought, the EU is perceived as a *sui generis* empire[50] with a *mission civilisatrice*.[51] As such, the EU embeds a civilizing narrative in its external relations with non-EU countries claiming to be a pivotal agent of modernity and peace in Europe and beyond.[52] Stivachtis mantains that: 'this process is reminiscent of the "civilizing process" associated with the historical expansion of the European society of states and its gradual transformation to the contemporary global international society.'[53]

While the EU presents some of the features and characteristics of an empire and while we cannot remain oblivious to implications of coloniality stemming from some of its member states' historical past,[54] we cannot nevertheless use empire and coloniality as the sole conceptual vehicles to fully understand the EU project. It can certainly not be denied that the EU utilizes its economic power and leverage to legitimize its geopolitical interests and commercial gains[55] or to externalize its economic norms. In this context, Damro has come up with the notion of market power Europe (MPE),[56] which is based on rational choice and new institutionalist theories and essentially rejects the idea that the EU is normatively constituted and predisposed to act normatively. The economic size of the EU internal market, with its legal and institutional framework, as well as the presence of interest groups, make the EU a market power that has the potential to influence the behaviour of others by externalising its market-related policies and regulatory measures.[57] The idea of the EU being essentially a market power is also in line with external perceptions of the EU, which largely seem to converge on the view that it is predominantly an international economic power rather than a normative power.[58] The main limitation

---

[49]Stivachtis (2018), pp. 91–106, at 92; see also Zielonka (2011), pp. 281–301; for an analysis of the perception of non-EU countries and actors, see Bachmann and Müller (eds) (2015); Casier and Bardeleben (eds) (2018); Chaban and Holland (eds) (2011); Chaban and Holland (eds) (2013); Chaban and Holland (eds) (2018); Waele and Kuipers (eds) (2013), which looks at the perception of various international organisations; Eliasson (2010); Lisbonne-de Vergeron (2012); Lucarelli and Fioramonti (eds) (2010); Pardo (2015); Lucarelli (2013), pp. 1–16; Sicurelli (2010).

[50]Zielonka (2006).

[51]Zielonka (2013), 35–55, at 36; see also Del Sarto (2016), pp. 215–232.

[52]Zielonka (2015), pp. 45–58.

[53]Stivachtis (2008), pp. 71–90.

[54]Edward Keene (2013), pp. 939–956.

[55]Langan (2012), pp. 243–270; Siles-Brügge (2014), pp. 49–62, at 50 and 58.

[56]Damro (2014), pp. 682–699.

[57]Ibid.

[58]Larsen (2014), pp. 896–910.

of MPE perhaps is that it considers market norms as 'objective categories that can be separated from ideas, identities and ideologies.'[59]

What is required therefore is 'a more subtle and systematic assessment that goes beyond "norms versus interests" contrasts'[60] and to develop a research methodology that provides the epistemological tools to understand the complex and inter-twined connections between interests, values, norms and institutions in the EU. In the context of its external trade policy, therefore, the questions should not be posed in dichotomic terms, i.e. whether the EU is a large and powerful trade bloc in pursuit of its own interest, or a facilitator of world-wide liberal trade regimes, or again, as a rule-based system itself, whether the EU hinders or helps in the formation of a rule-based approach to international trade. What is important rather is an examination, which is not limited to the content and substance of the norms and regulations that the EU externalizes but extends also to the way that they are promoted as well as the scale and level of impact that they have. Here, Rosamond's distinction between "market liberalism", "liberalism as the pursuit of peace" and "liberalism as cosmopolitan duty"[61] seems fitting as it shows how the fact that the EU is a purveyor of market liberalism does not preclude it from pursuing, at the same time, normative objectives or, to put it differently, to pursue objectives with normative implications. Each mode of liberalism 'identifies core "subjects" to whom policy/intervention is targeted and through whom liberal outcomes are expected to emerge. And each derives from its premises a clear policy logic (i.e. what type of external policies follow from the ideational premises—in particular, what are the expected outcomes of policy?).'[62] Hence, for the mode of market liberalism the dominant idea is economic liberalism which concerns the normative validity of market order. From this perspective, markets are considered as being the most effective instruments for the efficient allocation of resources and for ensuring human wellbeing, with minimum intervention of the state and negative freedoms of market subjects[63] or in Foucauldian parlance "subjects of interest".[64] The dominant idea of the second mode of liberalism is Kantian republicanism according to which a peaceful world order can only be guaranteed if states adopt a democratic or in Kantian terms a "republican" system, thus ensuring less propensity for conflictual relationships among states globally.[65] The third mode of liberalism is universal human rights, the rationale of which rests on the claim that freedom can only be guaranteed by ensuring that all people enjoy a set of basic rights regardless of spatial, temporal or any other form of difference.[66] These rights are to be guaranteed through democratic means, which inevitably creates a tension with

---

[59] Orbie and Khorana, above no. 42, at 255.

[60] Ibid.

[61] Rosamond (2014), pp. 133–148.

[62] Ibid, p. 140.

[63] Ibid.

[64] Foucault (2008), p. 42.

[65] Rosamond, above no. 60, at 142.

[66] Ibid, at 141.

the negative freedom of the subjects of interests.[67] All three modes have ideational and normative contents which intersect and interact in different ways, sometimes complementing each other, sometimes in contrast with each other.[68] A combination of these modes of liberalism helps us to conceptualise the EU as a power *through* trade: not only is the EU an unquestionable economic power, but it is through this power that it can pursue objectives that go beyond commercial interests and gains directly related to trade.[69] At the same time, it is in the context of trade that the conflict between the EU's commercial interests and the promotion of its values, including fundamental rights, is mostly visible.[70] While the EU's ambitions are very high, in practice it has often failed to meet its expectations[71] and it has been criticized for the incoherent way in which it promotes values in trade, particularly (but not only) with countries in South-East Asia.[72]

Arguably, one of the most distinctive contributions of the EU has been the promotion of principles of procedural justice at all governance levels. As Cremona aptly maintains, 'this is not merely because the Union has pioneered the development of such rule-generating processes within its own legal system, and does not even claim that it has successfully done so (the laboratory role), but rather relies on the fact that thc Union may convincingly both exemplify and express the need for such processes.'[73] With the TL the Treaties now provide the constitutional foundation for these rule-generating processes and, in particular, for the EU's promotion of global normative goals in its external relations.[74]

2.3 The European Union's Promotion of Normative Objectives in Its External Trade Policy

The promotion of non-commercial objectives through trade relations has gained significant prominence in EU external action following the entry into force of the TL and constitutes the most distinctive aspect of the EU's normative and cosmopolitan approach to international politics.[75] In particular, in the context of the EU's "deep

[67] Ibid.

[68] Rosamond, above no. 61, at 144.

[69] Meunier and Nicolaidis (2011), pp. 275–298.

[70] Kerremans and Orbie (2009), pp. 629–641; Manners (2009), pp. 785–803; Orbie and Kerremans (2013), pp. 493–500; Velluti (2016), pp. 41–68.

[71] Bossuyt (2009), pp. 703–722; Leeg (2014), pp. 335–356; Young (2007), pp. 789–811; Young and Peterson (2006), pp. 795–814; Conceição-Heldt and Meunier (2014), pp. 961–979.

[72] Wong (2012), pp. 669–682; Orbie and Khorana, above no. 42; Maass (2012), pp. 215–231; Sicurelli (2015), pp. 230–245.

[73] Cremona, above no. 7, at 558.

[74] Larik (2013), pp. 7–22, at p. 11.

[75] Sjursen (2017), pp. 443–462.

trade agenda"[76] the EU is to conduct its CCP in line with the principles, values and objectives of the Union's external action.[77] In this context, Meunier and Abdelal refer to an EU policy of "managed globalization"-a term first coined by Pascal Lamy when Commissioner of the Directorate-General for Trade as a doctrine of *mondialisation maîtrisée*-[78] which aims at balancing the imperatives of free trade with the objective of promoting non-trade values in the same way as the EU's ongoing attempt to accommodate liberalization with social goals within the internal market.[79] In this context, the EU increasingly claims to act and is expected by EU citizens to act in such a way so as to manage the effects of globalization.[80] From this perspective, Europeanisation ensures the effective systematization of the new transnational processes generated by globalization with the adoption of new regulatory tools. In this sense, the furthering of the European integration process represents a countertendency to globalization.[81] At the same time, the EU is a form of globalization in itself leading to both "supranational and sub-national regionalism".[82] Domestic policy areas have become increasingly subject to European policy-making through processes of "re-nationalization or re-regulation of law", that is, processes of readjustment to supranational standards and re-evaluation of national needs.[83] EU political and economic dynamics have reoriented the direction and shape of national decision-making processes, becoming part of the organizational logic of national politics.[84] There is thus a dialectical relationship between globalization and the European integration process, which are to a great extent overlapping but often conflicting forces.[85] This can be seen in the context of the EU's economic projects, exemplified in particular by the single market, economic and monetary union (EMU) and the various economic processes such as the *Lisbon Strategy* first adopted in 2000.[86] In particular, the *Lisbon Strategy* is a pan-European effort to meet the challenges identified above, namely the strengthening and the co-ordination of the new regulatory tools alongside the Community Method and the identification of viable policy solutions

---

The discussion on the pursuit of non-commercial objectives through the EU's CCP after the entry into force of TL is carried on further in Sect. 3 of Chapter 3 of this book.

[76]Detailed analysis of the EU's "deep trade agenda" is provided in Sect. 4 of this Chapter.

[77]Article 207(1) TFEU.

[78]Pascal Lamy introduced it in his hearings to the EP as the ideological cornerstone of his future tenure as European Trade Commissioner, see Lamy (1999); Lamy (2004).

[79]Meunier and Abdelal (2010), pp. 350–367; see also Orbie et al. (2008), pp. 148–165.

[80]For further discussion about managing globalization, see the special issue of the *Journal of European Public Policy*, Meunier and Jacoby (eds) (2010), pp. 299–448; on the public expectation that the EU should fulfill this role, see 302.

[81]Velluti (2010), p. 64.

[82]Pieterse (1995), pp. 45–68.

[83]Sciarra (2000), pp. 269–292, at p. 288.

[84]Ladrech (1994), pp. 69–88.

[85]Velluti, above no. 81, at p. 65.

[86]European Council, Lisbon Presidency Conclusions, 23 and 24 March 2000, available at: https://www.consilium.europa.eu/en/european-council/conclusions/. Accessed on 14 June 2020.

which increase the EU's competitiveness by way of bolstering, at the same time, the economic and social dimension of the EU.

The TL has to some extent constitutionalized a "managed globalization" approach in the EU Treaties by injecting a normative approach into its external relations through Articles 3(5) and 21(1) and (3)(1) TEU. Article 3(5) TEU[87] establishes the EU objectives to 'promote' the EU's values and interests outside the Union and to 'contribute to' the other norms mentioned as well as an obligation to achieve these objectives.[88] Article 21(1) TEU is similar to Article 3(5) TEU, although as opposed to the latter there is reference to the Union as being required to 'be guided by' rather than 'uphold' and 'promote' principles in its 'action on the international scene'.[89] According to Bartels Article 21(3)(1) TEU[90] extends the scope of application of the EU's external human rights obligations and is thus normatively stronger than the other two provisions in that it refers not only to 'the development and implementation of the different areas of the Union's external action' but also—and significantly—to 'the development and implementation … of the external aspects of [the EU's] other policies'.[91] What this means is that it also covers the external aspects of the EU's internal policies. Taken together these provisions require the EU to respect human rights in its external action and also in its internal policies with an external dimension. On the necessary link between the internal and the external dimension of EU action, Alston and Weiler[92] maintain that:

> 'the Union can only achieve the leadership role to which it aspires through the example it sets to its partners and other States. Leading by example should become the *leitmotif* of a new EU human rights policy. […] This analysis thus makes no fundamental distinction

[87] Article 3(5) TEU provides that: 'In its relations with the wider world, the Union shall uphold and promote its values [as defined in Article 2 TEU] and interests and contribute to the protection of its citizens. It shall contribute to peace, security, the sustainable development of the Earth, solidarity and mutual respect among peoples, free and fair trade, eradication of poverty and the protection of human rights, in particular the rights of the child, as well as to the strict observance and the development of international law, including respect for the principles of the United Nations Charter.'

[88] Declaration 41 includes among the objectives of Article 352 TFEU the objectives laid out in Article 3(5) TEU; see also Case C-366/10, *Air Transport Association of America* [2011] ECR I-13755; the CJEU refers to Article 3(5) TEU and states that: 'Under Article 3(5) TEU, the European Union is to contribute to the strict observance and the development of international law. Consequently, when it adopts an act, it is bound to observe international law in its entirety, including customary international law, which is binding upon the institutions of the European Union' (para. 101).

[89] Article 21(1) TEU provides that: 'the Union's action on the international scene shall be guided by the principles which have inspired its own creation, development and enlargement, and which it seeks to advance in the wider world: democracy, the rule of law, the universality and indivisibility of human rights and fundamental freedoms, respect for human dignity, the principles of equality and solidarity, and respect for the principles of the United Nations Charter and international law.'

[90] Article 21(3)(1) TEU provides that: 'the Union shall respect the principles and pursue the objectives set out in paragraphs 1 and 2 in the development and implementation of the different areas of the Union's external action covered by this Title and by Part Five of the Treaty on the Functioning of the European Union, and of the external aspects of its other policies.'

[91] Bartels (2014), pp. 1071–1091, at 1074–1075.

[92] Alston and Weiler (1999), at 5–6.

> between the internal and external dimensions of the Union's human rights policy. To use a metaphor, it is clear that both must be cut from a single cloth.'

The EU's foundation and existence rest on a loose ideal of integrated Europe of prosperity and stability, which helps explain its survival and resilience in the face of ongoing economic and political centrifugal forces.[93]

The importance of the adherence to a constantly evolving set of substantive values in the EU's external relations has thus become part of the EU's *raison d'être*.[94] Similarly, Weiler considers values as part of the Union's constitutional development and a representation of its collective identity.[95] Not only is the EU expected to work for peace and economic prosperity within its borders; it is equally expected to act upon and uphold the same values in the international sphere.[96] As posited by De Búrca[97]:

> 'the EU's capacity to manage globalization and its potential to exercise international leadership on a range of crucial global challenges are important aspects of its *raison d'être* today. The EU's capacity to provide its member states and citizens with collective power and a coordinated problem-solving capability, to offer an alternative socio-economic and geopolitical model to those of other existing and rising powers, and to offer global leadership on some of the most pressing transnational challenges, provides a powerful rationale for the EU's existence today.'

In this context, Articles 3(5) and 21(1) TEU provide the legal foundations for the EU to act on the international arena according to its own set of principles and values. Hence, trade can be leveraged as an instrument for the pursuit of broader non-commercial objectives outside of the EU. Article 21(2) TEU is a significant innovation of TL as it unequivocally streamlines and codifies these objectives as part of the EU's external relations legal framework.

Specifically, in relation to the EU's external trade policy, it can be maintained that the CCP as redesigned by the TL reflects the EU's ambition to become a global actor.[98] According to Dimopoulos, Article 21 TEU provides the legal foundation that legitimizes the inclusion of human rights clauses in the EU's trade agreements.[99] It would seem that the TL has thus addressed the legal gap in the EU Treaties as held by the CJEU in Opinion 2/94. Here, the Court stated that none of the Treaty provisions conferred powers to the EU to adopt fundamental rights rules, including human rights clauses in trade agreements.[100] While the EU's commitment to the promotion of the respect for (fundamental) human rights is one of the EU's unique features[101]

---

[93] Wolf (2012).

[94] Búrca (2014), pp. 21–37; see also Herlin-Karnell (2012), pp. 1225–1246.

[95] Weiler (2002), pp. 563–580.

[96] De Búrca, above no. 94, at p. 35.

[97] Ibid, p. 37.

[98] Bungenberg (2010), pp.123–151.

[99] Dimopoulos, above no. 21, at 164.

[100] Opinion 2/94, *Accession by the Communities to the Convention for the Protection of Human Rights and Fundamental Freedoms* [1996] ECR I-1759.

[101] Witte (2011), pp. 127–147, at pp. 142–143.

the inconsistent way in which the EU is committed to human rights protection both internally and externally is one of the reasons why the EU's legitimacy to act in this area is subject to constant criticism.[102]

Even though the EU might display significant inconsistencies or limitations in the way that it promotes its non-commercial objectives through trade, the changes introduced by the TL nevertheless provide the EU with the potential of being a transformative power *through* trade. Hence, what type of global actor the EU intends to be and which objectives it pursues through trade become relevant in determining the rules of global economic governance.

2.4 The European Union's Deep Trade Agenda and Narratives of Self-Projection

The diversification of international economic relations and regulation and related fragmentation of production processes and supply chains combined with the advances in information technology (IT) and transportation—which are frequently referred to in the context of globalization-explain why, in the course of the twentieth century, the international trading system has undergone significant changes with the full or partial demise of the "old" and the rise of "new" sites of power. These changes have transformed the very nature of inter and intra-firm relationships, which are then reflected in the changing patterns of trade, investment, and production.[103] Most importantly, they underline the growing need for "deeper integration" and explain the 'increased focus on the harmonization and dissemination of pro-competitive regulatory frameworks in order to facilitate market access and the operation of firms doing business abroad.'[104] The aim is to go beyond non-discrimination requirements by way of improving both 'market contestability and rules of operation for multinational firms'.[105] The notion of "deep integration"[106] is thus central to understanding the transformations, which are taking place in the context of an increasingly globalized

[102] Ibid; see also Egan and Pech (2015); Velluti, above no. 70.

[103] Gasiorek and Holmes (2010), pp. 139–156.

[104] Araujo (2016), p. 2; see also Hoekman and Kostecki (2001), pp. 413–458, at pp. 414–415.

[105] Melo Araujo, above no. 104, at p. 15.

[106] "Deep integration" is a term developed by Lawrence and can be defined as the convergence of "behind-the-border" or domestic policies and rules such as competition, public procurement, intellectual property (IP), investment, health and safety standards and financial regulation, see Lawrence (1996), p. XVIII. More specifically, "deep integration" can be examined from the perspective of *process* and/or *outcome* of the process. In the former case, "deep integration", be it public or market driven, refers to the removal of barriers to trade that are domestic or "behind the border" such as domestic rules and regulations that may affect both home and foreign firms and also foreign access to trade; in the latter case, the degree and nature of firm level interaction within and across borders both with other firms and with their own subsidiaries. More broadly, "deep integration" can be defined as the explicit actions by governments to reduce the market segmenting effect of domestic regulatory policies through coordination and cooperation. Hence, deep market integration requires deep institutional and policy integration; see Hoekman and Konan (1999).

world economy at market, institutional and policy levels. The EU has been one of the strongest advocates for including so-called "deep disciplines" in the context of the WTO, both during the 1986 Uruguay Round and the Doha Round negotiations, which were launched in 2001. Given the unlikely prospect of success of the comprehensive reforms envisaged in the Doha Round, the EU's "deep trade agenda"—namely the push for further trade liberalization focusing on the removal of domestic non-tariff regulatory measures and, at the same time, the attempt to introduce regulatory disciplines within the sphere of international trade law—has shifted towards bilateralism and regionalism.[107]

The launch of the 2006 *Global Europe Strategy*[108] signalled this change in the EU's external trade policy with the conclusion of the so-called "new generation of free trade agreements" (FTAs) and deep and comprehensive FTAs (DCFTAs). In particular, the EU abandoned its previous policy of focusing largely on multilateral trade liberalization and increasingly moved towards the conclusion of bilateral and regional trade agreements. Linked to this, since the adoption of the afore-mentioned strategy the content of the EU's trade agreements has become more commercially driven rather than focusing mainly on political and security objectives, with their intended aim being chiefly the increase of market access in emerging economies such as Southeast and East Asia.[109] The EU's "deep trade agenda", as formulated and implemented since the *Global Europe Strategy*, also raises important questions in relation to the EU's narratives of self-projection and its actorness on the international plane, particularly since the TL. Some commentators are quite skeptical about the EU's commitments to non-commercial values and principles given that the *Global Europe Strategy* was conceived with the idea of providing an external dimension to the EU's revised *Lisbon Strategy on Growth and Jobs*, the focus of which was largely on the EU's global competitiveness[110] by way of promoting further liberalization of the internal market combined with the integration of new policy areas such as competition, research and development, the environment and education, to achieve this ambitious and overarching goal.[111] Melo Araujo posits that: 'as the EU's trade policy becomes ever more commercially driven and, arguably, less imbued with

[107]Melo Araujo, above no. 104, at p. 2.

[108]European External Action Service (EEAS), *A Global Strategy for the European Union's Foreign and Security Policy—Shared Vision, Common Action: A Stronger Europe*, June 2016, available at: https://eeas.europa.eu/sites/eeas/files/eugs_review_web_0.pdf. Accessed on 20 October 2019.

[109]Woolcock (2007).

[110]The Lisbon Strategy's aim was to make the EU 'the most competitive and dynamic knowledge-based economy in the world capable of sustainable economic growth with more and better jobs and greater social cohesion', by 2010, see Presidency Conclusions of the European Council in Lisbon, 23 and 24 March 2000, available at: consilium.europa.eu/uedocs/cms_data/docs/pressdata/en/ec/00100-r1.en0.htm. Accessed on 14 June 2020.

[111]European Commission, Communication (2005), p. 24; for critical analysis, see Velluti, above no. 80, pp. 164–168.

narratives concerning non-trade values, it may be questioned whether such representations of the EU's approach to external relations are entirely reflective of reality.'[112] Nevertheless, the EU's self-perception as a CPE first and, more recently, as a NPE deeply permeates and influences its external action, the way it implements its external policies and the way it carries out its external relations with other global actors within the broader international legal order. For instance, as a CPE the EU has for many years largely conducted international trade relations within the multilateral framework of the WTO. Like the EU, the former is considered as relying on a rules-based system rather than power-based diplomacy and, by promoting economic integration, it is seen a channel of democracy and peace.[113] Interestingly, it is in the WTO context that the EU has managed to act as a unitary actor[114] catalysing both a process of constitutionalization of WTO law[115] and judicialization of international trade.[116] The EU's self-projection as a NPE—as propounded by Orbie and Khorana-[117] is well-exemplified by the move towards bilateralism and deeper integration, namely, the so-called "new generation" of FTAs, which combine "deep trade agenda" objectives with normative goals, involving what have been defined as "WTO-plus" (WTO+) or "WTO-extra" (WTO-X) commitments. WTO+ provisions build upon commitments already existing in the WTO agreements but have deeper commitments. WTO-X provisions include commitments dealing with issues going beyond the current WTO mandate altogether, such as labour and environmental standards.[118]

The "new generation" of FTAs have come to encompass, on the one hand, trade-liberalizing aspects, such as services, public procurement, foreign direct investment (FDI), commercial aspects of intellectual property (IP) rights and competition and, on the other hand, normative commitments relating to human rights and sustainable development, including provisions on labour and environment.[119] Hence, "beyond-the-border" issues in trade agreements have extended to provisions on justice, education, health and science and can be considered therefore to be "WTO-plus" agreements.[120] In addition, the new generation of FTAs have focused on the promotion of international standard-setting and on designing provisions and mechanisms for

[112]Melo Araujo, above no. 104, at p. 4.

[113]Meunier and Nicolaïdis, above no. 17, at 912.

[114]Larik (2011), pp. 13–46; see also Streinz (2017), pp. 271–290, at p. 281.

[115]J. Larik, above no. 114.

[116]Krüger (2013), pp. 169–190.

[117]Orbie and Khorana, above no. 42, at 255–257.

[118]Horn, Mavroidis and Sapir (2009); see also Stoler (2011).

[119]The "new generation" of FTAs are the subject of analysis of Chapters 4 and 5; see Gstöhl and Hanf (2014), pp. 733–748, at 739–744.

[120]The 2014 EU-Canada Comprehensive Economic and Trade Agreement (CETA) is an example of the so-called "WTO-plus" agreements, Comprehensive Economic and Trade Agreement (CETA) between Canada, of the one part, and the European Union and its member states of the other part, Consolidate Text published 26 September 2014, available at http://trade.ec.europa.eu/doclib/docs/2014/september/tradoc_152806.pdf. Accessed on 23 March 2020; for further discussion, see Fahey (2017), pp. 293–302, at 294.

regulatory convergence and cooperation,[121] mutual recognition arrangements and common regulatory frameworks.[122]

With the TL the EU has acquired exclusive competence to negotiate and conclude trade agreements covering, among others, services, intellectual property rights (IPRs) and foreign direct investment (FDI).[123] The EU has since been pursuing further trade liberalization with the conclusion of "deep trade agreements" that encompass provisions increasingly touching upon issues traditionally within the remit of the member states while going beyond WTO commitments. All post-Lisbon FTAs include a trade and sustainable development (TSD) chapter, which goes beyond the mandate of the WTO. The 2011 EU-Korea FTA is the first new generation FTA featuring a TSD chapter and this format has been followed in subsequent trade agreements.[124] In so doing, the EU makes explicit reference to international conventions thus contributing to the development of "global standards".[125] Hence, the process of harmonization is taking place by promoting a commitment to international law rather than (solely) through the EU's internal market standards.[126] In particular, by concluding "deep trade agreements" with third countries, the EU is contributing to the development of new international standards that are also aligned or consistent with EU standards.[127]

At first, the EU's primary reason for advancing a "deep trade agenda" mainly derives from the experience with its internal market.[128] In particular, within the multilateral regime of the WTO the EU was keen to ensure that the "deep trade agenda" would be aligned with the EU's internal market rules. In this way, the multilateral context for the pursuit of the "deep trade agenda" would facilitate the 'spread of EU-type regulatory principles worldwide and provided EU firms with an important competitive advantage in the global marketplace'[129] and foster to some extent what Bradford has coined as the "Brussels effect",[130] that is unilateral regulatory globalization which 'occurs when a single state is able to externalize its laws and regulations outside its borders through market mechanisms, resulting in the globalization of standards.'[131] In addition, the pursuit of the "deep trade agenda" by the

---

[121] Cremona (2013), pp. 162–177, at p. 169.

[122] Melo Araujo, above no. 104, at p. 37.

[123] Article 207(1) TFEU; the changes introduced by the 2009 TL to the CCP are examined and discussed in Chapter 3.

[124] European Commission, 'Trade and Sustainable Development (TSD) chapters in EU Free Trade Agreements (FTAs)', non-paper, 11.07.2017, available at: http://trade.ec.europa.eu/doclib/docs/2017/july/tradoc_155686.pdf. Accessed on 14 June 2020.

[125] Cremona, above no. 121, at p. 170.

[126] Ibid., p. 176.

[127] Ibid; see also Gstöhl and Hanf, above no. 119, at 735.

[128] Orbie, Gistelinck and Kerremans, above no. 79, at p. 148.

[129] Melo Araujo, above no. 104, at p. 30.

[130] Bradford (2012), pp. 1–67 and Bradford (2020).

[131] Bradford, above no. 130, at 3.

EU is part of a broader trade policy goal of "managing globalization" to reap the benefits of globalization and, at the same time, limit its negative effects.[132]

The 2006 *Global Europe Strategy*[133] laid out a vision for Europe's place in the world and promoted greater coherence in the EU's external action.[134] As for trade, it continued the EU's process towards competitive liberalization albeit with a departure from multilateralism and a marked shift towards bilateralism and "commercially driven" FTAs.[135] Trade liberalization is not merely considered as a way of gaining access to foreign markets but also as a tool to expose EU firms to international competition thus emphasizing the need for implementing the structural reforms envisaged by the afore-mentioned *Lisbon Strategy*.[136] The EU approach, therefore, envisages a two-way process establishing a synergetic relationship between the EU's internal rules and international law. Specifically, through its external trade policy the EU exports its own rules and standards but, at the same time, it also incorporates international rules and standards into its legal framework.[137] Hence, as Melo Araujo posits:

> 'the *Global Europe Strategy* cannot be reduced to a mere change in the EU's choice of venue in which to pursue its "deep trade agenda". It also reformulates and adapts the substance of the "deep trade agenda" to reflect a new reality where multilateral trade liberalization no longer presents itself as a viable outlet for the EU's trade policy goals and where competition from other trading powers means that it must undertake an increasingly aggressive stance in terms of promoting its economic interests abroad.'[138]

Consequently, while focusing on the adoption of common disciplines on domestic regulation, the *Global Europe Strategy*'s remit covers a wider range of areas than those proposed in the multilateral context with a variety of more sophisticated tools employed for these disciplines, such as harmonization, mutual recognition and regulatory dialogue.[139]

From the above, it is plain to see why the *Global Europe Strategy* has been defined as being essentially a neo-liberal strategy. The EU *2020 Strategy*[140] and the EU *Single Market Act*[141] share the same objective of increasing the competitiveness of EU

---

[132]This concept is discussed further in Chap. 3 of this book.

[133]European Commission, Communication from the Commission to the Council, the European Parliament, the European Economic and Social Committee and the Committee of the Regions, *Global Europe: Competing in the World—A Contribution to the EU's Growth and Jobs Strategy*, COM(2006) 567 final.

[134]European External Action Service, *The European Union's Global Strategy. Three Years On, Looking Forward*, Brussels, 2019, available at: https://eeas.europa.eu/sites/eeas/files/eu_global_strategy_2019.pdf. Accessed on 14 June 2020, p. 5.

[135]Melo Araujo, above no. 104, at pp. 36–38; Bieler (2012), pp. 197–217, at p. 206.

[136]Hay (2007), pp. 25–43, at 32.

[137]Melo Araujo, above no. 104, at p. 36.

[138]Melo Araujo, above no. 104, at p. 37–38.

[139]Ibid, p. 38.

[140]European Commission, above no. 144, COM (2010) 612 final.

[141]European Commission, Communication from the Commission to the Council, the European Parliament, the European Economic and Social Committee and the Committee of the Regions,

business and industry both within the single market and in non-EU markets.[142] At the same time, these strategies also encompass many aspects of "managed globalization" and seek to meet broader objectives of EU foreign policy as outlined in Article 21(2) TEU, such as those concerning sustainable development goals, international labour standards and decent work.[143]

However, as the EU increasingly combines trade objectives with non-commercial values, tensions within the EU's "deep trade agenda"—as shown by the negotiations of the new generation of FTAs—have become particularly pronounced.[144] It is noteworthy that the EU's practice of including human rights conditionality clauses in its international trade agreements[145] has not been repeated in the "new generation" of FTAs concluded after the TL.[146]

2.5 Conclusion: The Role of the European Union as a Global Actor in the Age of Brexit and Anti-Globalism

'The trouble with our times is that the future is not what it used to be.'

Paul Valéry

The dynamics of the twenty-first century are quite different from those of the past 50 years in several important ways.[147] This is because 'what constitutes power, what constitutes influence, and how global actors behave with respect to each other' has changed dramatically even in the last decade.[148] Internal contestation in the EU as manifested by Euroscepticism and anti-globalism movements across (and outside) Europe,[149] securitization practices and systemic changes in the international system

Towards a Single Market Act. For a highly competitive social market economy 50 proposals for improving our work, business and exchanges with one another, COM (2010) 608 final/2, 11 November 2010, Sect. 1.6.

[142]Cremona, above no. 121, at p. 168.

[143]European Commission, Communication from the Commission to the Council, the European Parliament, the European Economic and Social Committee and the Committee of the Regions, *Trade, Growth and World Affairs. Trade Policy as a Core Component of the EU's 2020 Strategy*, COM (2010) 612 final, pp. 8, 9, 10, 15; see also the 2016 *Global Strategy* where the key components of managed globalisation remain a compass for EU action, European External Action Service, *Shared Vision, Common Action: A Stronger Europe—A Global Strategy for the European Union's Foreign and Security Policy*, Brussels, June 2016, available at: https://eeas.europa.eu/sites/eeas/files/eugs_review_web_0.pdf. Accessed on 14 June 2020.

[144]McKenzie and Meissner (2017), pp. 832–849, at 833.

[145]See Chap. 4 of this book.

[146]See Chap. 5 of this book.

[147]Howorth, above no. 43, at 459.

[148]Ibid, at 460.

[149]Larik (2017)

are altering the EU's self-perception in many domains, including its role as a global player in the world.[150]

In this uncertain climate the EU's "real comparative advantage" lies not so much in constituting a "model" to emulate but rather a "laboratory" where rather than outcomes what matters is the development of processes that enable it to 'manage enduring differences within a normative and institutional framework that reflects a commitment to democracy, the rule of law, and peaceful settlement of disagreements'.[151] Ultimately, the EU is less a "model" to be emulated than a "laboratory" where inter-state problems are addressed and notions of justice beyond the state are progressively and tentatively operationalized.[152]

Brexit[153] represents a momentous setback for the EU's *raison d'être*, inevitably impacting on the EU's credibility and legitimacy as a global actor, particularly in relation to its *Global Strategy* as revised in 2016. Moreover, the stance of the President in office of the United States (US), Donald Trump, towards international law and the international legal order, retracting back to protectionism and nationalism, as exemplified by his motto 'Americanism, not globalism, will be our credo',[154] challenges the central tenets of the EU's normative mission of preserving, strengthening and developing further a rules-based system of global governance.[155]

As much as these are challenging times for the EU they also constitute an opportunity for shedding renewed light on its role in the international legal order and conducting its external policies, including the CCP, within the legal framework of the Treaties and in accordance with international legal norms and procedures. The 2016 *Global Strategy* makes it unequivocally clear that promoting its values is a matter of law as well as of ethics and identity.[156] By enshrining the principles and values of EU external action in the Treaties the TL has thus made their promotion a constitutional mandate, which could only be abrogated by way of treaty amendment.[157]

With regard to the CCP, the TL has also provided the legal foundation for embedding a "managed globalization" approach within the EU's "deep trade agenda" with its two constituting logics—namely, a push for further liberalization to boost the EU's competitiveness and, at the same time, the promotion of a rule of law approach entailing the strict observance of international law and compliance with human rights and international labour standards—at the core of the EU's external action.

The challenges that lie ahead are linked to existing tensions between the two constituting logics mentioned above and the need to ensure more consistency in the implementation of different areas of EU external law and policy, which in turn will guarantee overall coherence of EU external action. As discussed in Sect. 2.2,

---

[150] Barbé and Morillas (2019), pp. 753–770, at 753–754.

[151] Nicolaïdis and Howse (2002), pp. 767–792, at 771.

[152] Ibid, at 783.

[153] Detailed information is provided in Chap. 3 of the book.

[154] Trump (2016).

[155] Larik, above no. 149, at 5.

[156] EEAS, above no. 108, at 15.

[157] Larik, above no. 149, at 12.

this requires a revised understanding of NPE, going beyond a "norms versus interests" approach. The 2016 *Global Strategy* acknowledges this and thus, unsurprisingly, aspires to transform rather than merely reiterating values and principles of EU external action or preserving the existing system.[158]

Subsequent chapters of the book focus on the way the EU attempts to conjugate the two constituting logics of the EU's "deep trade agenda" within the broader framework of the CCP, providing a detailed examination of EU human rights/social conditionality and the global normative reach of the EU.

References

EU Official Documents

EU Treaties

Treaty of Lisbon Amending the Treaty on European Union and the Treaty Establishing the European Community, 13 December 2007, 2007/C 306/01

EU International Agreements

CETA—EU-Canada Comprehensive Economic and Trade Agreement (2014) between Canada, of the one part, and the European Union and its member states of the other part, Consolidated Text published 26 September 2014. Available at http://trade.ec.europa.eu/doclib/docs/2014/september/tradoc_152806.pdf. Accessed on 23 March 2020

EU Institutions

European Council

European Council, Lisbon Presidency Conclusions, 23 and 24 March 2000. Available at: https://www.consilium.europa.eu/en/european-council/conclusions/. Accessed on 20 March 2020

European Council (2001) Laeken Declaration on the future of the European Union (15 December 2001), in Bulletin of the European Union. 2001, No 12. Luxembourg: Office for Official Publications of the European Communities. "Presidency Conclusions of the Laeken European Council (14 and 15 December 2001)", p. 19–23. Available at: https://www.cvce.eu/content/publication/2002/9/26/a76801d5-4bf0-4483-9000-e6df94b07a55/publishable_en.pdf. Accessed on 20 March 2020

158 EEAS, above no. 108, at 40; for further analysis of the EU's foreign policy (self-)identity, see Pishchikova and Piras (2017), pp. 103–120.

European Commission

European External Action Service

European Commission, 'Trade and Sustainable Development (TSD) chapters in EU Free Trade Agreements (FTAs)', non-paper, 11.07.2017. Available at: http://trade.ec.europa.eu/doclib/docs/2017/july/tradoc_155686.pdf. Accessed 14 June 2020
European Commission, Communication, *Working together for Growth and Jobs: A New Start for the Lisbon Strategy*, COM (2005) 24
European Commission, Communication on *Europe in the World—Some Practical Proposals for Greater Coherence, Effectiveness and Visibility* COM (2006) 278 final
European Commission, Communication from the Commission to the Council, the European Parliament, the European Economic and Social Committee and the Committee of the Regions, *Global Europe: Competing in the World—A Contribution to the EU's Growth and Jobs Strategy*, COM(2006) 567 final
European Commission, Communication from the Commission to the Council, the European Parliament, the European Economic and Social Committee and the Committee of the Regions, *Towards a Single Market Act. For a highly competitive social market economy 50 proposals for improving our work, business and exchanges with one another*, COM (2010) 608 final/2, 11 November 2010
European Commission, Communication from the Commission to the Council, the European Parliament, the European Economic and Social Committee and the Committee of the Regions, *Trade, Growth and World Affairs. Trade Policy as a Core Component of the EU's 2020 Strategy*, COM(2010) 612 final
European External Action Service, *Shared Vision, Common Action: A Stronger Europe—A Global Strategy for the European Union's Foreign and Security Policy* Brussels June 2016. Available at: https://eeas.europa.eu/sites/eeas/files/eugs_review_web_0.pdf. Accessed on 20 June 2020
European External Action Service, *The European Union's Global Strategy. Three Years On, Looking Forward*, Brussels, 2019. Available at: https://eeas.europa.eu/sites/eeas/files/eu_global_strategy_2019.pdf. Accessed on 14 June 2020

Table of Cases

Court of Justice of the European Union

Case C-366 10 *Air Transport Association of America*, ECR I-13755
Opinion 2/64 on the *Accession by the Communities to the Convention for the Protection of Human Rights and Fundamental Freedoms* ECR I-1759

Books and Chapters in Books

Bachmann V, Müller M (eds) (2015) Perceptions of the EU in Eastern Europe and Sub-Saharan Africa. Palgrave Macmillan, London
Bieler A (2012) The internal and external dimensions of neo-liberal restructuring. In: Nouisis P, Overbeck H, Tsolakis A (eds) Globalisation and European integration: critical appraisal. Routledge, New York, pp 197–217
Bradford A (2020) The brussels effect. How the European Union rules the World. OUP, Oxford, forthcoming
Casier T, De Bardeleben J (eds) (2018) EU-Russia relations in crisis. Understanding diverging perceptions. London: Routledge

Chaban N, Holland M (eds) (2011) The European Union and the Asia-Pacific media, public and elite perceptions of the EU. Routledge, Abingdon

Chaban N, Holland M (eds) (2013) Europe and Asia: perceptions from Afar. Baden-Baden, Nomos

Chaban N, Holland M (eds) (2018) Shaping the EU global strategy: partners and perceptions. Palgrave Macmillan, London

Cremona M (2008) Introduction. In: Cremona M (ed) Developments in EU external relations law. OUP, Oxford, pp 1–9

Cremona M (2008) Defining competence in EU external relations: lessons from the treaty reform process. In: Dashwood A, Maresceau M (eds) Law and practice of EU external relations—salient features of a changing landscape. CUP, Cambridge, pp 34–69

Cremona M (2013) Expanding the internal market: an external regulatory policy for the EU? In: Van Vooren B, Blockmans S, Wouters J (eds) The EU's role in global governance: the legal dimension. OUP, Oxford, pp 162–177, at p 169

Czuczai J, Naert F (eds) (2017) The EU as a global actor—bridging legal theory and practice. Liber amicorum in honour of Ricardo Gosalbo Bono. Leiden, Brill

Dashwood A, Maresceau M (2008) Introduction. In: Dashwood A, Maresceau M (eds) Law and practice of EU external relations—salient features of a changing landscape. CUP, Cambridge, pp 1–10

de Búrca G (2013) EU external relations: the governance mode of foreign policy. In: Van Vooren B, Blockmans S, Wouters J (eds) The EU's role in global governance. OUP, Oxford, pp 39–58

de Búrca G (2014) Europe's raison d'Être. In: Kochenov D, Amtenbrink F (eds) The European Union's shaping of the international legal order. CUP, Cambridge, pp 21–37

de Búrca G, Scott J (2001) The Impact of the WTO on EU decision-making. In: de Búrca G, Scott J (eds) The EU and the WTO. Legal and constitutional issues. Hart Publishing, Oxford, pp 1–30

de Witte B (2011) The EU and the international legal order: the case of human rights. In: Evans M, Koutrakos P (eds). Beyond the established legal orders: policy interconnections between the EU and the rest of the World. Hart Publishing, Oxford, pp 127–147

Duchêne F (1972) Europe's role in World peace. In: Mayne R (ed) Europe tomorrow: sixteen Europeans look ahead. Fontana, London, pp 32–47

Duchêne F (1973) The European community and the uncertainties of interdependence. In: Kohnstamm M, Hager W (eds) A nation writ large? Palgrave Macmillan, London, pp 1–21

Eliasson LJ (2010) America's perspective of Europe. Palgrave Macmillan, London

Foucault M (2008) The birth of biopolitics: lectures at the collège de France, 1978–79. Palgrave Macmillan, Basingstoke

Gasiorek M, Holmes P (2010) Globalisation and deep integration. In: Guimaraes MH, Faria AP (eds) Product market integration: a multifaceted approach. Emerald Group Publishing, Bingley, pp 139–156

Gerrits A (2009) Normative power Europe: introductory observations on a controversial notion. In: Gerrits A (ed) Normative power Europe in a changing World: a discussion. Institute of International Relations. The Hague, Netherlands, pp 1–8

Hillion C (2008) *Tous pour Un, Un Pour Tous!* Coherence in the external relations of the European Union. In: Cremona M (ed) Developments in EU external relations law, collected courses of the academy of European Law. OUP, Oxford, pp 10–36

Hoekman B, Kosteck M (2001) Towards deeper integration? the "trade and" Agenda. In: Hoekman B, Kostecki M (eds) The political economy of the world trading system: WTO and beyond. OUP, Oxford, pp 413–458

Khaliq U (2008) Ethical dimensions of the foreign policy of the European Union: a legal appraisal. CUP, Cambridge

Kochenov D, Amtenbrink F (2013) Introduction: the active paradigm of the study of the EU's place in the world. In: Kochenov D, Amtenbrink F (eds) The European Union's shaping of the international legal order. CUP, Cambridge, pp 1–18

Krüger T (2013) Shaping the WTO's institutional evolution: the EU as a strategic litigant in the WTO. In: Kochenov D, Amtenbrink F (eds) The European Union's shaping of the international legal order. CUP, Cambridge, pp 169–190

Laïdi Z (2009) European preferences and their reception. In: Laïdi Z (ed) European foreign policy in a globalized world: normative power and social preferences. Routledge, London, pp 1–20
Lamy P (2004) *La démocratie-monde: pour une autre gouvernance globale*. Seuil, Paris
Larik J (2011) Much more than trade: the common commercial policy in a global context. In: Evans M, Koutranos P (eds) Beyond the established legal orders. Hart Publishing, Oxford, pp 13–46
Larik J (2013) Shaping the international order as an EU objective. In: Kochenov D, Amtenbrink F (eds) The European Union's shaping of the international legal order. CUP, Cambridge, pp 62–86
Larik J (2013) Entrenching global governance: the EU's constitutional objectives caught between a sanguine world view and a daunting reality. In: Van Vooren B, Blockmans S, Wouters J (eds) The EU's role in global governance: the legal dimension. OUP, Oxford, pp 7–22
Lavranos N (2004) Legal interaction between decisions of international organizations and European law. Europa Law Publishing, Amsterdam
Lawrence RZ (1996) Regionalism, multilateralism and deeper integration. Brookings, Washington DC
Lucarelli S (2008) European political identity, foreign policy and the others image. In: Cerutti F, Lucarelli S (eds) The search for a European identity: values, policies and legitimacy of the European Union. Routledge, London and New York, pp 23–42
Lucarelli S (2006) Introduction: values, principles, identity and european union foreign policy. In: Lucarelli S, Manners I (eds) Values and principles in European foreign policy. Routledge, London, pp 1–18
Manners I (2009) The EU's normative power in changing world politics. In: Gerrits A (ed) Normative power Europe in a changing world: a discussion. Institute of International Relations, The Hague, Netherlands 2009, pp 9–24
Manners I (2011) The European Union's normative power: critical perspectives and perspectives on the critical. In: Whitman RG (ed) Normative power Europe: empirical and theoretical perspectives. Palgrave Macmillan, Basingstoke, pp 226–247
Melo Araujo BA (2016) The EU deep trade agenda. Law and policy. OUP, Oxford
Meunier S, Nicolaïdis K (2011) The EU as a trade power. In: Hill C, Smith M (eda) International relations and the European Union. OUP, Oxford, pp 275–298
Müller-Graff PC (2008) The common commercial policy enhanced by the reform of the treaty of Lisbon? In: Dashwood A, Maresceau M (eds) Law and practice of EU external relations. Salient features of a changing landscape. Cambridge University Press, Cambridge, pp 188–291
Orbie J, Gistelinck M, Kerremans B (2008) The social dimension of EU trade policies. In: Orbie J, Torrell L (eds) The European Union and the social dimension of globalisation: how the EU influences the world. Routledge, London, pp 148–165
Pardo S (2015) Normative power Europe meets Israel. Perceptions and realities. Rowman & Littlefield, New York
Pieterse JN (1995) Globalization as hybridization. In: Featherstone M et al (eds) Global modernities. Sage, London, pp 45–68
Polanyi K (1944) The great transformation. The political and economic origins of our time. Rinehart & Company, New York
Polanyi K (1957) The economy as instituted process. In: Polanyi K, Arensberg CM, Pearson HW (eds) Trade and market in the early empires. Economies in history and theory. Free Press, New York, pp 243–270
Sciarra S (2000) Global or renationalised? past and future of European labour law. In: Snyder F (ed) The Europeanisation of Law. Hart Publishing, Oxford, pp 269–292
Sicurelli D (2010) The European Union's Africa policies: norms, interests and impact. Ashgate Publishing, London
Twitchett K (ed) (1976) Europe and the world: the external relations of the common market. St. Martin's Press, New York
Van Vooren B, Blockmans S, Wouters J (eds) (2013) The EU's role in global governance. OUP, Oxford
Velluti S (2010) New governance and the European employment strategy. Routledge, London

Wetzel JE (ed) (2012) The EU as a "global player" in human rights?. Routledge, London
Zielonka J (2015) The uses and misuses of the imperial paradigm. In: Behr H, Stivachtis YA (eds) Revisiting the European Union as empire. Routledge, London, pp 45–58

Journal Articles and Working Papers

Aggestam L (2008) Introduction: ethical power Europe? Int Aff 84(1):1–11
Alston P, Weiler J (1999) An "ever closer union" in need of a human rights policy: the European Union and human rights. Harvard Jean Monnet Working Paper 1/99. Available at https://www.jeanmonnetprogram.org/archive/papers/99/990101.rtf. Accessed on 23 March 2020
Barbé E, Morillas P (2019) The EU global strategy: the dynamics of a more politicized and politically integrated foreign policy. Cambridge Rev Int Aff 32(6):753–770. https://doi.org/10.1080/09557571.2019.1588227
Bartels L (2014) The EU's human rights obligations in relation to policies with extraterritorial effects. EJIL 25(4):1071–1091
Bilal S, Hoekman B (2019) Perspectives on the soft power of EU trade policy, Vox, 31 July 2019. Available at https://voxeu.org/content/perspectives-soft-power-eu-trade-policy. Accessed on 14 June 2020
Bohnenberger F, Joerges C (2016) From trade liberalisation to transnational governance and TTIP: how Dani Rodrik, Karl Polanyi and the varieties of capitalism studies may help us to understand the present state of globalization. TLI Think! Paper 44/2016. https://doi.org/10.2139/ssrn.2862966, pp 1–38
Borzel TA, Van Hulle V (2014) One voice, one message, but conflicting goals: cohesiveness and consistency in the European neighborhood policy. J Eur Pub Policy 21(7):1033–1049
Bossuyt F (2009) The social dimension of the new generation of EU FTAs with Asia and Latin America: ambitious continuation for the sake of policy coherence. Eur Foreign Aff Rev 14(5):703–722
Bradford A (2012) Brussels effect. Northwest Univ Law Rev 5(1):1–67
Bull H (1982) Civilian power Europe: a contradiction in terms? J Common Mark Stud 21(2):149–164
Bungenberg M (2010) Going global? the EU common commercial policy after Lisbon. In: Hermann C, Terhechte JP (eds) European yearbook of international economic law, vol 1. Springer, Heidelberg, pp 123–151. https://doi.org/10.1007/978-3-540-78883-6_6
Cremona M (1998) The European Union as an international actor. The issues of flexibility and linkage. Eur Foreign Aff Rev 3(1):67–94
Cremona M (2004) The union as a global actor: roles, models and identity. Common Mark Law Rev 41(2):553–573
Cremona M (2008) Coherence through law: what difference will the treaty of Lisbon make? Hamburg RevSoc Sci 3(1):11–36
Crowe R (2008) The treaty of Lisbon: a revised legal framework for the organization and functioning of the European Union. ERA Forum 9:163–208
da Conceição-Heldt E, Meunier S (2014) Speaking with a single voice: internal cohesiveness and external effectiveness of the EU in global governance. J Eur Pub Policy 21(7):961–979
Damro C (2014) Market power Europe. J Eur Pub Policy 19(5):682–699
de Búrca G (2011) The road not taken: the EU as a global human rights actor. Am J Int Law 105:649–693
Del Sarto RA (2016) Normative empire Europe: the European Union, its borderlands, and the Arab Spring. J Common Market Stud 54(2):215–232
de Waele H, Kuipers JJ (eds) (2013) The European's emerging international identity. Views from the global arena. Brill-Nijhoff, Leiden
Dimopoulos A (2008) The common commercial policy after Lisbon. Croatian Yearbook Eur Law Policy 4:101–129

Dimopoulos A (2010) The effects of the Lisbon treaty on the principles and objectives of the common commercial policy. Eur Foreign Aff Rev 15:153–170
Dunne T (2008) Good citizen Europe. Int Aff 84(1):13–28
Egan A, Pech L (2015) Respect for human rights as a general objective of the EU's external action. Leuven centre for global governance studies. Working Paper No. 161. Available at https://ghum.kuleuven.be/ggs/publications/working_papers/2015/161eganpech. Accessed on 14 June 2020
Fahey E (2017) CETA and global governance law: what kind of model agreement is it really in law? Eur Papers Eur Forum Insight 2(1):293–302
Frunză R, Pascariu GC, Moga T (eds) (2013) The EU as a model of soft power in the eastern neighbourhood. Editura Universităţii "Alexandru Ioan Cuza", Iaşi. Available at http://www.cse.uaic.ro/Jean_Monnet/Volum%20EURINT%202013_oct_v2.pdf. Accessed on 14 June 2020
García M (2015) The European Union and Latin America: "transformative power Europe" versus the realities of economic interests. Cambridge Rev Int Aff 28(4):621–640
Gstöhl S, Hanf D (2014) The EU's post-Lisbon free trade agreements: commercial interests in a changing constitutional context. Eur Law J 20(6):733–748
Grevi G (2009) The interpolar world: a new scenario. Occasional paper No. 79, EU-ISS, Paris, June 2009. Available at https://www.iss.europa.eu/content/interpolar-world-new-scenario. Accessed on 28 October 2019
Hatzopoulos V (2007) Why the open method of coordination is bad for you: a letter to the EU. Eur Law J 13(4):309–342
Hay C (2007) Keynote article: what doesn't kill you can only make you stronger: the Doha development round, the services directive and the EU's conception of competitiveness. J Common Mark Stud 45(1):25–43
Herlin-Karnell E (2012) The EU as a promoter of values and the European global project. German Law J 13(11):1225–1246
Herlin-Karnell E, Konstadinides T (2012/13) The rise and expressions of consistency in EU law: legal and strategic implications for European integration. Cambridge Yearbook Eur Legal Stud 15:139–167. https://doi.org/10.1017/S1528887000003037
Hoekman B¸ Konan DE (1999) Deep integration, non-discrimination, and Euro-mediterranean free trade. (English), Policy, research Working Paper; No. WPS 2130, World Bank, Washington, DC. Available at http://documents.worldbank.org/curated/en/982521468773728458/Deep-integration-nondiscrimination-and-Euro-Mediterranean-free-trade. Accessed 14 June 2020
Hoffmeister F (2011) The European Union's common commercial policy one year after Lisbo—sea change or business as usual? In: Koutrakos P (ed) The European Union's external relations a year after Lisbon. CLEER Working Paper Series, 2011/3, The Hague, pp 83–95
Horn H, Mavroidis PC, Sapir A (2009) Beyond the WTO? an anatomy of EU and the US preferential trade agreements. Bruegel Blueprint Series, Available at https://bruegel.org/wp-content/uploads/imported/publications/bp_trade_jan09.pdf. Accessed 14 June 2020
Howorth J (2010) The EU as a global actor: grand strategy for a global grand bargain? J Common Mark Stud 48(3):455–474
Keene E (2013) Social status, social closure and the idea of Europe as a "normative power". Eur J Int Relat 19:939–956. https://doi.org/10.1177/1354066112437768
Keohane RO (2001) Governance in a partially globalized world. Am Polit Sci Rev 95(1):1–13
Kerremans B, Orbie J (2009) The social dimension of European Union trade policies. Eur Foreign Aff Rev 14(5):629–641
Kuijper PJ, Bronckers M (2005) WTO law in the European court of justice. Common Mark Law Rev 42:1313–1355
Ladrech R (1994) Europeanization of domestic politics and institutions: the case of France. J Common Mark Stud 32(1):69–88
Lamy P (1999) Hearings of commissioners-designate. European Parliament, Brussels
Langan M (2012) Normative power Europe and the moral economy of Africa-EU ties. New Polit Econ 7(3):243–270
Larik J (2017) The EU's global strategy in the age of Brexit and "America first"', Leuven centre for global governance studies. Working Paper No. 193, December 2017, pp 1–29. Available at

https://ghum.kuleuven.be/ggs/publications/working_papers/2017/193larik. Accessed on 14 June 2020
Larsen H (2014) The EU as a normative power and the research on external perceptions: the missing link. J Common Mark Stud 52(4):896–910. https://doi.org/10.1111/jcms.12109
Leeg T (2014) Normative power Europe? the European Union in the negotiations on a free trade agreement with India. Eur Foreign Aff Rev 19(3):335–356
Lisbonne-de Vergeron L (2012) Chinese and Indian views of Europe since the crisis: new perspectives from the emerging Asian giants. Fondation Robert Schuman, Brussels
Lucarelli S (2013) Seen from the outside: the state of the art on the external image of the EU. J Eur Integr 35(6):1–16
Lucarelli S, Fioramonti L (eds) (2010) External perceptions of the European Union as a global actor. Routledge, London
Maass M (2012) The European Union, Vietnam, and human rights as law: the case of the 1995 EU-Vietnam framework agreement and its human rights clause. Asia Europe J 10(4):215–231
Manners I (2002) Normative power Europe: a contradiction in terms? J Common Mark Stud 40(2):235–258
Manners I (2006) The European Union as a normative power: a response to Thomas Diez. Millenium J Int Stud 35(1):167–180. https://doi.org/10.1177/03058298060350010201
Manners I (2008) The normative ethics of the European Union. Int Aff 84:45–60
Manners I (2009) The social dimension of EU trade policies: reflections from a normative power perspective. Eur Foreign Aff Rev 14(5):785–803
Maull HW (1990) Germany and Japan: the new civilian powers. Foreign Aff 69(5):92–93
McKenzie L, Meissner KL (2017) Human rights conditionality in European Union trade negotiations: the case of the EU-Singapore FTA. J Common Mark Stud 55(4):832–849
Meunier S, Abdelal RE (2010) Managed globalisation: doctrine, practice and promise. J Eur Pub Policy 17(3):350–367
Meunier S, Jacoby W (eds) (2010) Europe and the management of globalization. J Eur Pub Policy 17(Special Issue):299–448
Meunier S, Nicolaïdis K (2006) The European Union as a conflicted trade power. J Eur Pub Policy 13:906–925
Nicolaïdis K, Howse R (2002) "This is my EUtopia…": narrative as power. J Common Mark Stud 40:767–792
Orbie J (2006) Civilian power europe: review of the original and current debates. Cooperation Confl 41(1):123–128
Orbie J, Kerremans B (2013) Introduction—theorizing European Union trade politics: contending or complementary paradigms? J Contemp Eur Res 9(4):493–500
Orbie J, Sangeta K (2015) Normative versus market power Europe? the EU-India trade agreement. Asia Eur J 13:253–264
Pishchikova K, Piras E (2017) The European Union global strategy: what kind of foreign policy identity? Int Spectator 52(3):103–120. https://doi.org/10.1080/03932729.2017.1339479
Portela C, Raube K (eds) (2008) Six authors in search of a notion: (In) Coherence in EU foreign policy and its causes. Hamburg Rev Soc Sci 3(1):1–10
Rosamond (2014) Three ways of speaking Europe to the world: markets, peace, cosmopolitan duty and the EU's normative power. Br J Polit Int Relat 16(1):133–148
Sicurelli D (2015) The EU as a promoter of human rights in bilateral trade agreements: the case of the negotiations with Vietnam. J Contemp Eur Res 11(2):230–245
Siles-Brügge G (2014) EU trade and development policy beyond the ACP: subordinating developmental to commercial imperatives in the reform of the GSP. Contemp Polit 20(1):49–62, at 50 and 58
Sjursen H (2006) The EU as a 'normative' power: how can this be? Eur Pub Policy 13(2):235–251
Sjursen H (2017) The EU's principles in world politics. In: Hill C, Smith M, Vanhoonacker S (eds) International relations and the European Union. Oxford University Press, Oxford, pp 443–462
Stivachtis YA (2008) The standard of civilization in contemporary international society: the case of the European Union. Contemp Polit 14(1):71–90

Stivachtis YA (2018) The "civilizing" empire: the European Union and the MENA neighborhood. Athens J Mediterr Stud 4(2):91–106

Stoler AL (2011) WTO-plus issues in the multilateral trading system. In: Trade and development symposium on perspectives on the multilateral trading system, A collection of short essays. International Centre for Trade and Sustainable Development, December 2011, on file with author

Streinz T (2017) Cooperative Brexit: giving back control over trade policy. In: Editorial ICON, vol 15, pp 271–290, at p 281

Thakur R, Van Langenhove L (2006) Enhancing global governance through regional integration. Global Gov 12(3):233–240

Velluti S (2016) The promotion and integration of human rights in EU external trade relations. Utrecht J Int Eur Law 83:41–68

Villalta Puig PG, Al-Haddab B (2011) The common commercial policy after Lisbon: an analysis of the reforms. Eur Law Rev 289–301

Weiler J (2002) A constitution for Europe? some hard choices. J Common Mark Stud 40(4):563–580. https://doi.org/10.1111/1468-5965.00388

Wessel RA, Takacs T (2017) Constitutional aspects of the EU's global actorness: increased exclusivity in trade and investment and the role of the European Parliament. Eur Bus Law Rev 28(2):103–117

Whitman RG (2013) The neo-normative turn in theorising the EU's international presence. Cooperation Conflict 48(2):171–193. https://doi.org/10.1177/0010836713485538

Wong R (2012) Model power or reference point? the EU and the ASEAN charter. Cambridge Rev Int Aff 25(4):669–682

Woolcock S (2017) Constitutional aspects of the EU's global actorness: increased exclusivity in trade and investment and the role of the european parliament. Eur Bus Law Rev 28(2):103–117

Woolcock S (2007) European Union policy towards free trade agreements. ECIPE Working Paper, No. 03/2007. Available at https://ecipe.org/publications/european-union-policy-towards-free-trade-agreements/. Accessed on 14 June 2020

Woolcock S (2008) The potential impact of the Lisbon treaty on European Union external trade policy. Eur Policy Anal 8:1–6. Swedish Institute for European Policy Studies (SIEPS)

Young A (2007) Trade politics ain't what it used to be: the European Union in the Doha Round. J Common Market Stud 45(4):789–811

Young A, Peterson J (2006) The EU and the new trade politics. J Eur Pub Policy 13(6):795–814

Zielonka J (2011) The EU as an international actor: unique or ordinary? Eur Foreign Affairs Rev 16:281–301

Zielonka J (2006) Europe as empire: the nature of the enlarged European Union. Oxford University Press, Oxford

Zielonka J (2013) Europe's new civilizing missions: the EU's normative power discourse. J Polit Ideologies 18(1):35–55

Other

Wolf M (2012) Why the Eurozone may yet survive: members remain absolutely committed to the idea of an integrated Europe. Financial times, 17 April 2012

On-line Resources

Trump D (2016) Speech at the republican convention, as prepared for delivery. CNN. 22 July 2016. Available at http://edition.cnn.com/2016/07/22/politics/donald-trump-rnc-speech-text/. Accessed on 14 June 2020

Chapter 3
The Legal Framework of the Common Commercial Policy After the Entry into Force of the Treaty of Lisbon

Samantha Velluti

3.1 Introduction: Aims and Structure

This chapter provides a detailed analysis of the main changes introduced by the 2009 Treaty of Lisbon (TL)[1] to the Common Commercial Policy (CCP), which are particularly significant for the conclusion of European Union (EU) international trade agreements. The key provisions concerning the CCP in the Treaty on the Functioning of the European Union (TFEU) are Articles 206 and 207 TFEU.[2] Together these articles form Title II on the "Common Commercial Policy" of Part V of the TFEU, which is entitled "External Action by the Union".

The main purpose of this chapter is to shed light on the significance of these changes with particular reference to the complex question of EU competence in the field of the CCP. In so doing, it takes into account other salient changes at global, European and domestic levels which impact directly on the further development of the CCP. The chapter examines three interrelated aspects about the TL reform. First, it shows how these changes reflect a broader conceptualization of trade and how they constitute a response to the challenges of the evolving international trading system and globalized markets. Linked to this, it shows how the reform contributes to a reconceptualization of the CCP, by departing from its narrower traditional role and covering new key economic areas. Effectively, the TL reform provides a legal basis

[1]Treaty of Lisbon Amending the Treaty on European Union and the Treaty Establishing the European Communities, Dec. 13, 2007, 2007 OJ (C 306) 1.

[2]Articles 206 and 207 TFEU amend and modify former Articles 131(1) and 133 Treaty of the European Community (TEC).

I am indebted to Roberto Bendini for reading an earlier draft of this chapter and for his invaluable comments. Any errors or omissions are my own. Parts of section 5.5. were presented at the ICON-S Annual Conference 2018 on *Identity, Security, Democracy: Challenges for Public Law*, Hong Kong, June 25–27, 2018.

S. Velluti, *The Role of the EU in the Promotion of Human Rights and International Labour Standards in Its External Trade Relations*,
https://doi.org/10.1007/978-3-030-56748-4_3

for EU external economic action[3] whilst ensuring, at the same time, the EU's single market competitiveness.

The chapter is structured as follows. It starts by examining the shift towards a global approach in-between the twentieth and the twenty-first centuries and the "new" context in which the CCP has to operate thus explaining the rationale of the TL reform. It then proceeds to the analysis of the principles and objectives of the CCP further to the changes introduced by the TL. The examination subsequently turns to the key substantive reforms of the CCP. In this context, it shows how the concept of trade has been significantly expanded. The other sections of the chapter focus on the most salient aspects of the EU competence question and, linked to this, the changes made to the decision-making system of the main EU legislative institutions, with a focus on the negotiation and ratification of international trade agreements. Particular attention is paid to the effects that the withdrawal of the United Kingdom (UK) from the EU—known as "Brexit"[4] has on the EU's international trade agreements as well as the increased powers of the European Parliament (EP), its democratizing function in the context of the CCP and the growing importance of the role of national parliaments, qua vox populi, in the negotiation and ratification of international trade agreements. The conclusion brings together the main findings of the chapter and puts forward some preliminary reflections about the CCP post-Lisbon in the broader context of the EU's "deep trade agenda" and overarching global changes.

3.2 The Shift Towards a Global Approach and the "New" Common Commercial Policy

The European Economic Community (EEC) Treaty did not contain a clear definition of the CCP. In particular, old Article 113(1) EEC did not provide a comprehensive definition of its *ratione materiae* but merely listed examples in a non-exhaustive manner as measures falling within the remit of the CCP.[5] The TL clarified and expanded at once the scope of EU external trade policy. Article 207(1) TFEU[6] includes policy areas, which already fell within the scope of the CCP, namely, trade in

[3]Dimopoulos (2008), 102.

[4]The term "Brexit" derives from the amalgamation of the words "British" or "Britain" and the word "exit", see further Sect. 5.5 in this chapter.

[5]Article 113(1) EEC provided that: 'The common commercial policy shall be based on uniform principles, particularly in regard to changes in tariff rates, the conclusion of tariff and trade agreements, the achievement of uniformity in measures of liberalization, export policy and measures to protect trade such as those to be taken in the event of dumping or subsidies.'

[6]Article 207(1) TFEU provides that: 'The common commercial policy shall be based on uniform principles, particularly with regard to changes in tariff rates, the conclusion of tariff and trade agreements relating to trade in goods and services, and the commercial aspects of intellectual property, foreign direct investment, the achievement of uniformity in measures of liberalisation, export policy and measures to protect trade such as those to be taken in the event of dumping or subsidies. The common commercial policy shall be conducted in the context of the principles and

services and the commercial aspects of intellectual property. However, by explicitly including them in the TFEU and by removing the distinction between trade in goods and trade in services the TL has broadened the concept of EU trade.[7] Another significant substantive reform is the inclusion of foreign direct investment (FDI) within the scope of the CCP.[8] It may be argued, therefore, that the TL extended the exclusive competence of the EU to all three "pillars" of the World Trade Organization (WTO)[9]: trade in goods (including GATT 1994),[10] General Agreement on Trade in Services (GATS)[11] and Agreement on Trade Related Aspects of Intellectual Property Rights (TRIPS).[12]

Hence, by reforming the CCP the TL reinforced the EU's external commercial competence.[13] In this context, it strengthened the role of the EP by raising it to co-legislator together with the Council of Ministers in many new areas of EU external relations and, in particular, with regard to external trade policy the EP has become jointly responsible with the Council for the implementation of the CCP.[14]

These changes introduced by the TL are particularly important because the CCP remains the most significant application of EU external economic relations.[15] Even though the CCP falls within the EU's exclusive competence[16] its precise scope has been the subject of a long legal, including jurisprudential, and political debate.[17]

---

objectives of the Union's external action.' It is noteworthy that Article 207 TFEU is identical to Article III-315 of the defunct Constitutional Treaty.

[7]The TL transferred these two areas from Article 133(5) Treaty Establishing the European Community (TEC) to Article 207(1) TFEU.

[8]See Article 207(1) TFEU.

[9]Eeckhout (2011), p. 59.

[10]General Agreement on Tariffs and Trade 1994, Apr. 15, 1994, Marrakesh Agreement Establishing the World Trade Organization, Annex 1A, 1867 U.N.T.S. 187, 33 I.L.M. 1153 (1994) [hereinafter GATT 1994].

[11]General Agreement on Trade in Services, Apr. 15, 1994, Marrakesh Agreement Establishing the World Trade Organisation, Annex 1B, 1869 U.N.T.S. 183, 33 I.L.M. 1167 (1994) [hereinafter GATS].

[12]Agreement on Trade-Related Aspects of Intellectual Property Rights, Apr. 15, 1994, Marrakesh Agreement Establishing the World Trade Organisation, Annex 1C, 1869 U.N.T.S. 299, 33 I.L.M. 1197 (1994) [hereinafter 'TRIPS Agreement'].

[13]Article 3(1)e TFEU and Articles 206 and 207 TFEU and 218 TFEU (in relation to the increased powers of the EU Parliament in the CCP); for critical commentary, see Dimopoulos (2010), 153, Müller-Graff (2008), p. 188, Hoffmeister (2011), p. 83, Villalta Puig and Al-Haddab (2011), 289.

[14]Article 207(2) TFEU provides that: 'The European Parliament and the Council, acting by means of regulations in accordance with the ordinary legislative procedure, shall adopt the measures defining the framework for implementing the common commercial policy.'

[15]Villalta Puig and Al-Haddab above no. 13, 289; Krajewski (2012), pp. 292–311; A. Dimopoulos, above no. 13, at 153.

[16]Article 3(1)(e) TFEU.

[17]Bourgeois (1998), pp. S149–173, Leal-Arcas (2007), pp. 305–399.

The reason is three-fold[18]: first, as seen above, the poor drafting of the original EEC Treaty Article on the CCP; second, the decades of resistance by the member states to accept the EU as a single actor in international trade that is empowered to conclude comprehensive international trade agreements without the need for separate member states' ratification; and third, the failure of the Court of Justice of the EU (CJEU) to give a logical and coherent follow-up to its initial broad definition of the CCP.

The CCP's long existence and gradual consolidation through successive Treaty amendments explain its centrality in the context of the Union's external action.[19] Unsurprisingly, the EU is one of the key players of the multilateral trading system and pursues bilateral and regional trade agreements with strategic partners throughout the world.[20] In addition, the CCP also functions as a vital instrument for the effective operation of the internal market and it builds on the economic constitution of the EU,[21] which has been largely developed by the jurisprudence of the CJEU. The linkage between the external and the internal sphere of EU trade policy explains why the CCP remains a dynamic area of EU external relations, which has rapidly developed in response to the challenges of the international trading system and globalization.[22] The TL has constitutionalized this complementarity and parallelism between the internal and external dimension of EU action first developed by the CJEU.[23] With regard to the scope of the CCP, this entails that when the EU exercises its powers under the CCP, it is subject to the same limitations on its competence that exist in its internal market, in relation to the same subject matter. However, as Dimopoulos aptly posits: 'this does not mean that the lack of exercise of Union internal competences poses a limitation on the existence or the exercise of external competence'.[24] As evidence of the fact that a lack of internal rules is of no impediment to the adoption of external action rules he refers to the absence in Article 207(4) TFEU of the requirement of unanimity for the adoption of commercial policy measures in cases where no internal measures have been adopted.[25]

---

[18]Devuyst (2011), pp. 639–661, at 641–42.

[19]Koutrakos (2015), p. 17; for an historical account, see P. Koutrakos, ibid., Ch. 2; P. Eeckhout, above no. 9, Ch. 2.

[20]Bungenberg (2010), 123, 126.

[21]Villalta Puig and Al-Haddab above no. 13, 289.

[22]Orbie et al. (2008), pp. 148–65.

[23]Joined Cases 3, 4 and 6/76, *Cornelis Kramer and Others* [1976] ECR 1279 and Opinion 1/76 *Draft Agreement establishing a European laying-up fund for inland waterway vessels* [1977] ECR 741. Article 21(3) TEU provides that the Union's general external policy objectives should be respected and pursued also in "the development and implementation of the external aspects of its other policies" and Article 207 (3)-(2) TFEU provides that the EU's CCP agreements shall be compatible with internal Union policies and rules; Article 207(6)(a) TFEU establishes explicit parallelism between internal and external EU competences. External powers cannot be used to override the limits of internal Union competence with regard to the same subject matter.

[24]A. Dimopoulos, above no. 3, at 118.

[25]Ibid.

Hence, new Article 207 TFEU somewhat differs from its predecessor.[26] It enables the EU to depart from a strict parallelism between internal and external economic relations[27] thus marking a new approach of the CJEU to the objectives of the EU in the context of the CCP, that is, from "evolutionary" to "global".[28] This interpretative approach of the CJEU can be seen in the *Daiichi Sankyo* case[29] where an act of the EU concerning intellectual property issues was in dispute.[30] The CJEU held that a distinction must be made between, on the one hand, the CCP—which according to Article 207 TFEU must be seen in the context of EU external action—and, on the other hand, the scope of Article 114 TFEU concerning the EU internal market. An EU act falls within the CCP if it relates specifically to international trade in that it is essentially intended to promote, facilitate or govern trade and has direct and immediate effects on trade.[31] The Court found that to be the case with the rules of the WTO TRIPS.[32]

The shift towards a "global approach" in its interpretation of Treaty provisions is particularly salient for the purposes of the present analysis as the CJEU's departure from the confines of the internal market can be of aid in broadening the scope of the EU's CCP provided that a given EU measure falls within the remit of international trade and, more generally, is also in line with post-Lisbon EU policy developments. Arguably, *Daiichi Sankyo*, cements together with other CJEU cases, a wide interpretation of the scope of the CCP following the TL reform.[33]

Another important change by the TL is the inclusion of consistency as one of the objectives of the CCP with the obligation for the Union to conduct its trade policy in the broader context of the principles and objectives of the Union's external action.[34]

---

[26]Former Article 133 EC.

[27]Dimopoulos, above no. 3.

[28]H. H. Voogsgeerd, 'The Nature of the Asymmetry between Trade and Labour Rights in Trade Agreements of the EU', paper presented at the European Union in International Affairs (EUIA) Biennial Conference, Brussels, Belgium, 11–13 May 2016. This interpretative approach of the CJEU can be seen in the *Daiichi Sankyo* case where an act of the EU concerning intellectual property issues was in dispute; Case C-414/11 *Daiichi Sankyo Co. Ltd and Sanofi-Aventis Deutschland GmbH v DEMO Anonymos Viomichaniki kai Emporiki Etairia Farmakon* ECLI:EU:C:2013:520.

[29]Case C-414/11 above no. 3.

[30]The case concerned the related issue of whether the Trade-Related Aspects of Intellectual Property Rights (TRIPS) agreement fell within the exclusive competence of the EU.

[31]Case C-414/11, para. 51. In para. 52. of the judgment the CJEU thus stated that '[i]t follows that, of the rules adopted by the European Union in the field of intellectual property, only those with a specific link to international trade are capable of falling within the concept of 'commercial aspects of intellectual property' in Article 207(1) TFEU and hence the field of the common commercial policy.'

[32]Agreement on Trade-Related Aspects of Intellectual Property Rights, Apr. 15, 1994, Marrakesh Agreement Establishing the World Trade Organisation, Annex 1C, 1869 U.N.T.S. 299, 33 I.L.M. 1197 (1994) [hereinafter 'TRIPS Agreement'].

[33]*E.g.* Case C-137/12, *European Commission v Council of the European Union (European Convention on the Legal Protection of Services Based on, Or Consisting of, Conditional Access)*, EU:C:2013:675.

[34]Articles 207(1) TFEU; 3(5) TEU.

In this context, the EU's CCP has evolved from being protectionist, inward-looking and reactive to one that is increasingly pursuing deep integration.[35] The reform of the TL facilitated this repositioning of the CCP. This change in focus represents in and of itself a significant paradigm shift in the international trading system.

The overarching changes brought about by the new globalization forces of the twenty-first century[36] has also led to a new conceptualization of EU trade policy, which was first envisioned in the 2010 *Trade, Growth and World Affairs* (TGWA) Strategy.[37] This Communication signalled a departure from EU trade policy largely based on trade in goods and customs tariffs to one based on the three pillars, of trade in goods, trade in services and investment with a focus on non-tariff barriers, standards, domestic taxation and competition. At the same time, the TGWA recognized that globalization processes impact negatively on certain sectors of the economy and specific categories of workers and cause environmental damage (thus suggesting the European Globalization Adjustment Fund (EGAF) as a means to provide some form of redress). This new approach to EU trade strategy was confirmed in *Trade for all—Towards a more responsible trade and investment policy*[38] where the aforementioned shift in focus has been further expanded in order to include a parallel concern for the environment, human rights, including social rights with explicit reference to the EGAF as a meaningful remedy for consumers, workers and small and medium enterprises (SMEs). In addition, there is explicit reference to using trade agreements and trade preference programmes as levers to promote around the world values such as sustainable development, human rights, fair and ethical trade and the fight against corruption as well as improving the responsibility of supply chains. In its Reflection Paper on *Harnessing Globalization*[39] the European Commission has once again confirmed the need to develop a balanced, rule-based and progressive trade and investment agenda, which is no longer exclusively concerned with the liberalization of markets.

Prior to this change the EU's deep trade agenda was linked to the more general trade policy objective of "managing globalization".[40] The term encompasses two key albeit conflicting objectives of EU trade policy: on the one hand, to maximize the benefits of globalization by promoting trade liberalization and, on the other hand, to develop mechanisms that minimize the negative effects of globalization.[41] In this

---

[35] Melo Araujo (2016).

[36] For a discussion on the complexity of twenty-first century regionalism and trade and for an argument in favour of a new theoretical and analytical framework departing from conventional thinking, see R. Baldwin, 'Filling the gap between twenty-first century trade and twentieth century trade rules', World Trade Organisation, Economic Research and Statistics Division, Staff Working Paper ERSD-2011-08, 23 May 2011, available at: https://www.wto.org/english/res_e/reser_e/ersd201108_e.pdf, accessed on 14 June 2020.

[37] COM(2010)612.

[38] Available at http://trade.ec.europa.eu/doclib/docs/2015/october/tradoc_153846.pdf, accessed on 14 June 2020.

[39] European Commission, Reflection Paper on *Harnessing Globalisation*, COM(2017) 240 final.

[40] Melo Araujo, above no. 35, p. 31.

[41] For further analysis, see Abdelal and Meunier (2010), pp. 350–367.

context there has been increasing attention on whether it is possible to develop a legitimate and effective CCP in a globalized economy.[42] Consequently, EU external trade policy remains beset by fundamental constitutional questions and disputes.[43]

With the exception of investment liberalization the TL did not introduce major substantive changes to the content of the CCP. However, it modified its addressees and the legal nature of its policy objectives. In this respect, Article 206 TFEU[44] refers to the EU rather than the member states. It thus increases the role of the EU thereby shifting the onus for the harmonious development of world trade and the progressive abolition of restrictions on international trade and FDI from the member states to the EU.[45]

The other EU external policies, such as development cooperation,[46] economic, financial and technical cooperation,[47] humanitarian aid[48] and restrictive measures[49] are included in the Union's external action under Part V of the TFEU. Moreover, the rules applying to the conclusion of international agreements[50] and the relations with third countries and international organizations[51] as well as the solidarity clause[52] are also included in Part V of the TFEU. With the TL all the provisions contained in this part of the TFEU unequivocally constitute the context of the CCP. The only exception is the Common Foreign and Security Policy (CFSP), which still has "special status",[53] However, the demarcation between CFSP and non-CFSP measures is not so clear-cut. Despite the "de-pillarization" of the EU,[54] the TL has maintained the institutional

---

[42]Burgoon (2009), pp. 643–661.

[43]See e.g. CJEU, Opinion 1/75 Local Costs ECLI:EU:C:1975:145; Opinion 1/78 Natural Rubber Agreement ECLI:EU:C:1979:224; Opinion 1/94 WTO ECLI:EU:C:1994:384; more recently see Opinion 2/15 on the EU-Singapore Free Trade Agreement ECLI:EU:C:2016:880; Opinion 3/15 on the Marrakesh Treaty ECLI:EU:C:2017:114.

[44]Article 206 TFEU provides that: 'By establishing a customs union in accordance with Articles 28 to 32, the Union shall contribute, in the common interest, to the harmonious development of world trade, the progressive abolition of restrictions on international trade and on foreign direct investment, and the lowering of customs and other barriers.'

[45]Villalta Puig and Al-Haddab above n 13, 291.

[46]Articles 208-211 TFEU.

[47]Articles 212-213 TFEU.

[48]Article 214 TFEU.

[49]Article 215 TFEU.

[50]Articles 216-219 TFEU.

[51]Articles 220 and 221 TFEU.

[52]Article 222 TFEU.

[53]The main provisions of the CFSP are to be found in Title V of the TEU, Articles 21-46. The CFSP competence has a specific nature and it is unclear whether the CFSP acts enjoy primacy and direct effect in the EU legal order; on this see further Wouters and Ramopoulos (2014), pp. 222–223.

[54]The Treaty of Lisbon abolished the 3-Pillar structure (namely, the 'supranational pillar' of the European Communities (1), the 'intergovernmental pillar' of the Common Foreign and Security Policy (2) and the 'intergovernmental pillar' of the Justice and Home Affairs (JHA) later renamed Police and Judicial Cooperation in Criminal Matters (PJCCM)), which made up the legal framework of the European Union set up by the 1992 Treaty of Maastricht. See Editorial (2005), pp. 325–329, Van Elsuwege (2010), pp. 987–1019.

and legal differences between the CFSP and the traditional external policies of the EU. The institutional provisions are split over the two Treaties: Parts I and II as well as sections of Parts VI and VII of the TFEU should have been placed into the TEU.[55] In addition, the CFSP has been inserted separately in the TEU.

Hence, notwithstanding the duty of consistency and the attempt to remove the traditional divide between "high" (that is, the EU's foreign policy) and "low" politics in EU external relations (that is, the EU's political, socio-economic and environmental aspects of its external action)[56] with, among others, the insertion of the so-called "mutual non-affectation clause" in Article 40 TEU,[57] the constitutional restructuring introduced by the TL has led to a number of systematic inconsistencies.[58] In particular, the TL failed to solve the complex dichotomy between CFSP and non-CFSP actions and arguably even increased the potential for inter-institutional conflicts, making the task of the CJEU of delineating the boundaries between the different components of EU external action extremely difficult.[59] The reason is that by removing the hierarchical delimitation rule of former Article 47 TEU[60] there is no longer a clear set of criteria to distinguish between CFSP and non-CFSP activities. As will be shown, these problems are particularly relevant to the "new" CCP and to the EU's attempt to inject a normative dimension into its international trade agreements.

3.3 Principles and Objectives of the CCP After Lisbon

The CCP is subject to two layers of principles and objectives. Article 206 TFEU[61] contains specific trade policy objectives and it can be considered as constituting the "inner layer" of objectives,[62] which are linked to the effective operation of the single market. The specific policy objectives of the CCP according to Article 206 TFEU are

---

[55] Schütze (2002), p. 42.

[56] On the distinction between "low" and "high" politics, see Allen (2012), p. 644.

[57] Former Article 47 TEU; Article 40 TEU provides that: 'The implementation of the common foreign and security policy shall not affect the application of the procedures and the extent of the powers of the institutions laid down by the Treaties for the exercise of the Union competences referred to in Articles 3 to 6 of the Treaty on the Functioning of the European Union.

Similarly, the implementation of the policies listed in those Articles shall not affect the application of the procedures and the extent of the powers of the institutions laid down by the Treaties for the exercise of the Union competences under this Chapter.'

[58] Schütze, above no. 55, p. 42.

[59] P. Van Elsuwege, above no. 54.

[60] Now Article 40 TEU.

[61] Based on former Article 131(1) TEC, which provided that: 'By establishing a customs union between themselves Member States aim to contribute, in the common interest, to the harmonious development of world trade, the progressive abolition of restrictions on international trade and the lowering of customs barriers.'

[62] Krajewski above no. 15, p. 294.

the harmonious development of world trade, the progressive abolition of restrictions on international trade, lowering of customs and other barriers and, further to the TL, the abolition of restrictions on FDI as per Article 207(1) TFEU.

Further to Article 205 TFEU the general objectives and principles of the Union's external policy as laid down in Chapter 1 of Title V TEU[63] also apply to the CCP[64] thereby forming an "outer layer" of principles and objectives of the CCP.[65] In a similar manner, Article 207(1) TFEU provides that the CCP shall be conducted 'in the context of the principles and objectives of the Union's external action.' Whereas the obligation contained in Article 207(1) TFEU, that the implementation of the CCP be conducted in the context of the general principles and objectives of the Union's external action, is phrased in general terms, the language used in Article 205 TFEU makes the latter obligation unequivocal.

Both the "inner" and "outer" layers of the principles and objectives of the CCP have legally binding nature and there is no hierarchy between the two layers of objectives and principles. This is well-illustrated by Article 3(3) and (5) TEU and Article 21(1) and (2) TEU where we find reference, among others, to the establishment of the internal market, a highly competitive social market economy, the progressive abolition of restrictions on international trade, free and fair trade, sustainable economic, social and environmental development, the promotion of scientific and technological advance and the protection of human rights. Nevertheless, the practice of linking trade and non-commercial objectives in the EU's international agreements with third countries suggests that a hierarchy between certain objectives and principles within each layer and between the two layers de facto exists.[66]

The novelty of the TL, in comparison with previous reforming treaties, is that it recognizes that trade policy may also pursue non-economic objectives and, in so doing, it lists those that are to be pursued by the Union through its external trade relations. Hence, by placing the CCP within the broader normative framework of such policy goals the TL departs substantially from previous reforms of trade policy.

With regard to the EU's external action's general principles and objectives,[67] Article 21 TEU explicitly includes the following: 'democracy, the rule of law, the universality and indivisibility of human rights and fundamental freedoms, respect for human dignity, equality and solidarity, and respect for the United Nations Charter and international law.' Furthermore, according to Article 21(2) TEU the Union shall define and pursue common policies among others to, 'foster the sustainable economic, social and environmental development of developing countries, with the primary aim of eradicating poverty, encourage the integration of all countries into

---

[63] Articles 21-22 TEU.

[64] Article 205 TFEU provides that: 'The Union's action on the international scene, pursuant to this Part, shall be guided by the principles, pursue the objectives and be conducted in accordance with the general provisions laid down in Chapter 1 of Title V of the Treaty on European Union.'

[65] Krajewski above no. 15, p. 294.

[66] This is examined further in Chap. 4.

[67] These principles and objectives also extend to the CCP via Article 207(1) TFEU where it provides that: 'the Common Commercial Policy shall be conducted in the context of the principles and objectives of the Union's external action.'

the world economy, including through the progressive abolition of restrictions on international trade and help develop international measures to preserve and improve the quality of the environment and the sustainable management of global natural resources, in order to ensure sustainable development.' Article 3(5) TEU refers to the Union upholding and promoting its values and, according to Article 2 TEU, the respect for human dignity and human rights features among the values of the EU.

From the wording and place in the TEU of the provisions contained in Articles 3(5) and 21(1) and (2)b and d TEU it can be argued that, following the TL, the EU recognizes economic and social rights as a matter of justice, which must be extended also to external trade relations. Moreover, Article 21(3) TEU refers to the external aspects of its other policies and thus extends the scope of application of the EU's external human rights obligations. This provision is also normatively stronger than Article 21(1) TEU because it employs the terms "shall respect" and "shall pursue" in comparison with the more nuanced term "shall be guided" employed in paragraph 1 of Article 21 TEU.[68] This argument finds further confirmation in *ATAA* where the CJEU held that Article 3(5) TEU establishes a positive duty for the EU to observe international law in its entirety.[69]

These goals reflect and reinforce the general objectives of the Union's relations with the "wider world" as per Article 3(5) TEU. As the pursuit of these general principles and objectives in the CCP is a legally binding obligation for the EU, its institutions, bodies and agencies must take them into consideration in the formulation and implementation of the EU's external trade policy.

However, the above provisions do not require the EU to pursue these objectives in any specific way and the EU is not formally bound by any multilateral or regional human rights treaty.[70] In addition, and linked to this, the EU does not have a general competence in the field of human rights.[71] At the same time, it should also be noted that both Articles 3(5) and 21 TEU contain references to classical trade policy objectives: Article 3(5) TEU refers to "free" and "fair" trade and Article 21 TEU calls for the encouragement of all countries' integration into the world economy, which shall be achieved, among others, 'through the progressive abolition of restrictions on international trade'. Hence, the Union's external trade policy still includes the gradual liberalization of trade among its general obligations and principles.

[68] Bartels (2014), pp. 1071–1091; cfr. Cannizzaro (2014), pp. 1093–1099.

[69] Case C-366/10 *Air Transport Association of America v Secretary of State for Energy and Climate Change* [2011] ECR I-13755, at paras. 101 and 123.

[70] The only exception being the 2008 UN Convention on the Rights of Persons with Disabilities (CRPD), which the EU ratified in 2010.

[71] For further discussion, see Velluti (2016), p. 182.

3.4 The Scope of the Common Commercial Policy After the Entry into Force of the Treaty of Lisbon: Substantive Reforms

3.4.1 New Fields of the Common Commercial Policy

3.4.1.1 Trade in Services and Commercial Aspects of Intellectual Property

Further to the changes made by the TL the CCP covers all aspects of trade in services and, in particular, all four GATS modes of supply are now entirely covered by the CCP[72] with the exception of transport services.[73] The CJEU relies on GATS for interpreting the scope of the CCP concept of trade in services, which gives it a dynamic nature given that the scope of the GATS may itself evolve overtime.[74]

The scope of the CCP with regard to trade in services has been the subject of a long-standing dispute between the member states and the EU institutions.[75] Post-Lisbon, the Union has exclusive competence to negotiate and implement trade agreements, which also contain provisions on services. Consequently, shared competence no longer applies to agreements relating to trade in cultural and audiovisual services, educational services and social and human health services.[76]

---

[72]Article 207(1) TFEU; the four modes of supplying services are as follows: cross-border trade, consumption abroad, commercial presence and presence of natural persons, see Article I:2 GATS. The pre-Lisbon Opinion 1/08 already established that trade in services was fully part of the CCP (except for transport services), Opinion 1/08, *GATS*, EU:C:2009:739.

[73]Article 207(5) TFEU refers to Title VI, Part III (and Article 218 TFEU), which establishes a *lex specialis* vis-à-vis trade in services. In particular, Article 91 TFEU—the main legal basis for the EU's Common Transport Policy- falls within shared competence. Here two scenarios can be envisaged. First, if the EU has covered a given field of transport services through internal legislation, this could create an exclusive competence under Article 3(2) TFEU; in the second case, if specific transport provisions in a trade agreement that is being negotiated do not mirror the EU's internal *acquis* then it will be left to the Council whether to exercise shared transport competence through the conclusion of said trade agreement or whether to opt for a mixed agreement, on this point see Hoffmeister (2017), pp. 307–336, at p. 311.

[74]Devuyst, above no. 18, at 654.

[75]Krajewski (2008), pp. 188–195.

[76]Shared competence was envisaged in Article 133(6) subparagraph 2 TEC. Following the TL reform, the CJEU has endorsed an expansive approach to the scope of the CCP as exemplified by Case C-137/12 *European Commission v Council of the European Union* (EU:C:2013:675), a case relating to the Council of Europe Convention on audio-visual services, European Convention on the Legal Protection of Services based on, or consisting of, Conditional Access (24 January 2001) CETS No 178. In this case it held that the main objective of the Convention was to extend the EU *acquis* on audio-visual services to states that were members of the Council of Europe and it fell therefore within the scope of the CCP and, in particular, that the Convention should be based on Article 207(4) TFEU (para. 81). Hence, the Court made it clear that as long as the subject-matter concerned services under Article 207(4) TFEU 'it is less relevant whether a trade provision

However, unanimity is still required in the Council for the conclusion of trade agreements concerning these services in particular circumstances. Subpara. 3 of Article 207(4) TFEU requires unanimity in the Council for the conclusion of agreements in the field of trade in cultural and audio-visual services, where the former risk prejudicing the Union's cultural and linguistic diversity and in the field of trade in social, education and health services, where the former risk seriously disturbing the national organisation of such services and prejudicing the responsibility of member states to deliver them.[77] In practice, this provision would require an assessment of the risk posed by an international agreement. A member state calling for a unanimous vote would need to rely on one of these subparagraphs and explain why and how the agreement concerned would pose a risk to the Union's cultural and linguistic diversity or to the provision of health, social and education services. If the other member states were to disagree it would be left to the CJEU to rule on the matter.

With regard to the scope of subparagraph 3, one question that arises is the type of services that it covers. In this context, the WTO standard classification of services (CPC) could be used.[78] Hence, audio-visual services would include motion picture, videotape production, distribution services, television and radio production and transmission services. Cultural services would cover services generally associated with literature, art, music and history, such as museums, archives and theatre services. Education services would include primary, secondary, higher and further education. Health services would cover hospital services, and possibly also medical services of doctors, nurses, midwives and physiotherapists, which are actually considered professional services. Social services are not further specified in the WTO classification, but arguably they would extend to social work, care and community services. The other term that will be subject to interpretation is that of "cultural and linguistic diversity", which is new in the context of the CCP. Even though there is reference to this term in Article 3(3) TEU subpara. 4 it is not defined.[79]

As to the extension of the CCP to the commercial aspects of intellectual property, the first point to raise about this field is the meaning of the concept of "commercial aspects" rather than "trade-related aspects", which is the one generally used by the WTO TRIPS Agreement. The latter effectively constitutes and attempt at worldwide harmonization of intellectual property laws. It is noteworthy that the former phrase is largely unused in international trade law and the WTO legal system. So it would have been preferable to maintain the phrase most commonly used in international trade law and known in the international trade system.

---

prohibits, authorizes or even requires civil, administrative or even criminal action from the parties to the agreement,' see Hoffmeister, above no. 73, p. 311.

[77] Krajewski argues that it only covers the conclusion and not the negotiation of agreements, which would therefore not be influenced by the unanimity rule of subparagraph 3, Krajewski, above no. 15, pp. 306–307.

[78] WTO, Services Sectoral Classification List, 10 July 1991, MTN.GNS/W/120, reproduced as part of the Guidelines for the Scheduling of Specific Commitments under the GATS of 23 March 2001, WTO-Document S/L/92.

[79] Article 3(3) TEU subparagraph 4, which provides that the Union 'shall respect its rich cultural and linguistic diversity, and shall ensure that Europe's cultural heritage is safeguarded and enhanced.'

The trade–related aspects of intellectual property rights are also included in treaties of the World Intellectual Property Organisation (WIPO).[80] Before the TL, the EU occupied the position of a permanent observer in the WIPO, in some organs as a special member without voting rights. With the acquisition of legal personality and the expansion of competences within the CCP, the EU can accede to all existing WIPO treaties and become a member of new WIPO–Administered Treaties. These treaties shall then be binding to all member states, even if they are not contracting parties to WIPO. These changes will gradually ensure a more harmonised regulation of commercial aspects of intellectual property rights and reduce the problems adverted to above.

Another problematic aspect about the changes introduced by the TL is the repeal of former Article 133(7) TEC,[81] which empowered the Council on the basis of certain conditions to broaden the competence of then European Community (EC) to act externally on certain aspects of intellectual property in so far as Article 133(5) TEC[82] did not cover them. This provision made it possible to connect "commercial aspects of intellectual property" to TRIPS and therefore constituted the legal basis for broadening the scope of the CCP to cover amendments to TRIPS that would affect the CCP's scope.[83]

However, a broader interpretation of "commercial aspects of intellectual property" allows for all trade-related aspects of intellectual property of the international trade and WTO legal system to fall within the scope of the CCP. By analogy to the inclusion of trade in services and GATS, TRIPs Agreements will most probably be used as a guide for the interpretation of Article 207(1) TFEU in relation to the commercial aspects of intellectual property. The CJEU seemed to confirm this in *Daiichi Sankyo* where it concluded that the EU is now exclusively competent to conclude the TRIPS

---

[80]For further information on the WIPO, visit: http://www.wipo.int/portal/en/index.html.

[81]Former Article 133(7) TEC provided that: 'Without prejudice to the first subparagraph of paragraph 6, the Council, acting unanimously on a proposal from the Commission and after consulting the European Parliament, may extend the application of paragraphs 1–4 to international negotiations and agreements on intellectual property in so far as they are not covered by paragraph 5.'

[82]Former Article 133(5) TEC provided that: 'Paragraphs 1 to 4 shall also apply to the negotiation and conclusion of agreements in the fields of trade in services and the commercial aspects of intellectual property, in so far as those agreements are not covered by the said paragraphs and without prejudice to paragraph 6.

By way of derogation from paragraph 4, the Council shall act unanimously when negotiating and concluding an agreement in one of the fields referred to in the first subparagraph, where that agreement includes provisions for which unanimity is required for the adoption of internal rules or where it relates to a field in which the Community has not yet exercised the powers conferred upon it by this Treaty by adopting internal rules.

The Council shall act unanimously with respect to the negotiation and conclusion of a horizontal agreement insofar as it also concerns the preceding subparagraph or the second subparagraph of paragraph 6.

This paragraph shall not affect the right of the Member States to maintain and conclude agreements with third countries or international organisations in so far as such agreements comply with Community law and other relevant international agreements.'

[83]Villalta Puig and Al-Haddab, above no. 13, at 293.

Agreement.[84] It follows that after *Daiichi* intellectual property rights provisions in a trade chapter fall within the EU's competence.

As Devuyst aptly observes the specific purposes of including trade in services and the commercial aspects of intellectual property in the CCP was to increase the EU's efficiency and effectiveness in the negotiation and conclusion of international agreements concerning both GATS and TRIPS. It is thus necessary to interpret Article 207(1) TFEU in a dynamic manner.[85] It should also be noted that a clear demarcation between "commercial aspects of intellectual property" and pure harmonization is difficult to draw as TRIPs Agreements are per se a way of harmonising intellectual property laws at international level.[86]

3.4.1.2 Foreign Direct Investment

While defining trade in services and commercial aspects of intellectual property presents relatively few challenges, circumscribing the ambit of FDI in the context of the "new" CCP has been far from straightforward and it has attracted considerable scholarly interest[87] triggering legislative and policy proposals from the Commission.[88] One of the reasons for this academic attention is that the inclusion of FDI within the scope of the CCP changes the distribution of power between the Union and the member states.[89] In addition, by removing the distinction between FDI, trade in goods, trade in services and the commercial aspects of intellectual property it also

---

[84] Case C-414/11, EU:C:2013:520.

[85] Devuyst, above no. 18, at 654.

[86] Eeckhout, above no. 9, at pp. 59–60.

[87] Weiss and Steiner (2013), pp. 355–374, Ortino and Eeckhout (2012), pp. 312–330; see also contributions in Bungenberg et al. (2011), Lavranos (2010), pp. 409–441, Karl (2005), pp. 413, Dimopoulos (2011), Herrmann (2010), p. 29, de Mestral (2009–2010), pp. 365–395, Moskvan (2016), pp. 241–262, Ziegler (2013), pp. 235–243; S. Woolcock, 'The EU Approach to International Investment Policy after the Lisbon Treaty', European Parliament, Directorate-General for External Policies of the Union, Directorate B, Policy Department, Brussels, October 2010, available at: http://www.europarl.europa.eu/RegData/etudes/etudes/join/2010/433854/EXPO-INTA_ET(2010)433854_EN.pdf, accessed on 14 June 2020; Eilmansberger (2009), pp. 383–429, Ceyssens (2005), pp. 259–291, Delgado Casteleiro (2016a).

[88] European Commission, 'Towards a comprehensive European investment policy' 7 July 2010, COM(2010) 343 final; European Commission, Proposal for a Regulation establishing transitional arrangements for bilateral investment treaties between EU Member States and third countries, 7 July 2010, COM(2010) 344 final; European Commission, Proposal for a Regulation of the European Parliament and of the Council establishing a framework for managing financial responsibility linked to investor-state dispute settlement tribunals established by international agreements to which the European Union is party, 21 June 2012, COM(2012) 335 final; Communication from the Commission to the European Parliament, the Council, the European Economic and Social Committee and the Committee of the Regions, *Trade for All—Towards a more responsible trade and investment policy*, 14 October 2015, COM(2015) 497 final.

[89] Villalta Puig and Al-Haddab, above no. 13, at 294.

contributes to the development of a common foreign investment policy.[90] Another reason for such academic interest is that the definition and scope of FDI is far from settled, with EU institutions holding different positions.[91] The absence of a clear definition means that the scope of EU exclusive competence remains a potentially contentious issue.[92] Opinion 2/15 on the 2013 Free Trade Agreement between the EU and Singapore (EUSFTA)[93] is a case in point. The agreement was one of the first "new generation" of bilateral FTAs [94] and the question the CJEU had to grapple with was whether the EU had exclusive competence to enter such agreements[95] or whether this competence was shared between the EU and the member states. In Opinion 2/15 the Court held that the EUSFTA could not be concluded by the EU alone[96] and that it had to be concluded by the EU and the member states acting together because some of the agreement's provisions fell within a competence that is shared between the EU and the member states.[97] In particular, for the purposes of the present chapter, it is in respect of two aspects of the agreement that, according to the CJEU, the EU did not have exclusive competence: the field of non-direct foreign investment, i.e. "portfolio" investments (i.e. the purchase of minority non-controlling shares of

[90] Ibid.

[91] For an analysis of the different positions of the EU Institutions, see F. Weiss and S. Steiner, above no. 87, pp. 361–367.

[92] Woolkock, above no. 87.

[93] Free Trade Agreement between the European Union and Singapore, (Authentic text as of May 2015) http://trade.ec.europa.eu/doclib/press/index.cfm?id=961, accessed on 14 June 2020.

[94] "New generation" of FTA refers to a trade agreement which contains, in addition to the classical provisions on the reduction of customs duties and non-tariff barriers in the field of trade in goods and services, provisions on various matters related to trade, such as intellectual property protection, investment, public procurement, competition and sustainable development. This type of FTA also included investor-state arbitration.

[95] This was the position of the European Commission and the EP.

[96] The CJEU had to examine whether the Union could have exclusive competence also on the basis of the doctrine of implied powers (developed through its case-law), in other words whether its exclusive external powers may derive from its internal powers. Article 3(2) TFEU provides that the Union shall also have exclusive competence to conclude an international agreement when its conclusion is provided for in a legislative act of the Union or is necessary to enable the Union to exercise its internal competence, or in so far as its conclusion may affect common rules or alter their scope. Opinion 2/15 concerned what Peers defines as the "legislative authorisation" ground and the "affect common rules" ground, see S. Peers, 'The EU's future trade policy starts to take shape: the Opinion on the EU/Singapore FTA', EU Law Analysis, 21 December 2016, available at: http://eulawanalysis.blogspot.co.uk/2016/12/the-eus-future-trade-policy-starts-to.html, accessed on 14 June 2020.

[97] The terminology used by the Court of "competence shared" (from the French language: "compétence partagée") is an alternative use of the notion of "shared competence" to indicate so-called "mandatory mixity" as opposed to "voluntary mixity", explained further below in the main text; see also no. 100. However, this semantic understanding of "shared competence" by the CJEU while not novel contradicts the constitutional meaning provided in Article 2(2) TFEU as introduced by the TL; on this point and further critical analysis, see D. Thym, 'Mixity after Opinion 2/15: Judicial Confusion over Shared Competences', Verfassungsblog, 31 May 2017, available at: http://verfassungsblog.de/mixity-after-opinion-215-judicial-confusion-over-shared-competences/, accessed on 14 June 2020.

a business),[98] and the regime governing dispute settlement between investors and states.[99] Consequently, these areas fell within the so-called "mixed competence" of the EU and its member states[100] and because it was an agreement that partly fell within the exclusive competence of the EU and partly within the exclusive competence of the member states, the EUSFTA was within the remit of so-called "mandatory" or "obligatory" mixed competence.[101] Opinion 2/15 has important consequences for future EU trade policy as it is likely that further to this judgment subsequent FTAs will remain mixed, thus requiring ratification of the member states.[102] Even so, as Larik rightly observes: 'whatever the member states do in what remains of their shared competence in mixed trade agreements, they will need to exercise it in a loyal way.'[103] The Court's judgment has a significant impact not only on the "*de jure* legitimacy of EU external action" in the area of trade and investment but also and significantly on the effectiveness, credibility and efficiency of multilevel governance of EU external economic relations[104]: on the one hand, 'the shape and strength of the Union's identity in its external commercial relations and [on the other hand][105] the reach of the member states in EU external economic relations conduct.'[106] The

[98]Portfolio investments are discussed further below in this section.

[99]Opinion 2/15, ECLI:EU:C:2016:880, paras. 226-243 and 244 concerning Section A of Chapter 9 and paras. 285-293 of Section B of Chapter 9 of the EUSFTA.

[100]Mixed agreements are agreements to which both the EU and its member states are a party and they require the joint ratification of the EU and each of the member states. Overall, this can be a cumbersome process which can take years and it is for this reason that the European Commission has often argued for a broad interpretation of the CCP in order to avoid the legal problems caused by the negotiation and conclusion of mixed agreements. Mixed agreements can be either bilateral agreements, namely agreements between EU/member states and a third party, or multilateral agreements, namely agreements between the EU, its Member States and other third parties; for detailed analysis see, Heliskoski (2001) and the contributions in Hillion and Koutrakos (2010), Van Der Loo and Wessel (2017), pp. 736–741.

[101]In contrast mixity is "optional" or "facultative" if it concerns exclusive as well as non-exclusive competence of the Union thus falling within an area of shared competence. In such cases there is a political choice as to who exercises said competence, either the Union or the member states; Rosas (2000), pp. 203–204 and Klamert (2013), Ch. 10.

[102]For further commentary and analysis, see among others, Kleimann (2017), Ankersmit (2017), available at: http://blogs.ucl.ac.uk/europe-and-the-world-journal/tag/opinion-215, accessed on 10 January 2019; Lenk (2017), pp. 357–382. On the effects of the Opinion on the withdrawal of the UK from the EU, i.e. "Brexit", see Sarmiento (2017).

[103]Larik (2015), pp. 779–800, at 797.

[104]D. Kleimann, above no. 102, p. 5

[105]Author's addition.

[106]D. Kleimann, above no. 102, p. 5. Compare this judgment with Opinion 3/15 of 14 February 2017 on whether the European Union has exclusive competence to conclude the 2013 WIPO Marrakesh Treaty to Facilitate Access to Published Works for Persons Who Are Blind, Visually Impaired, or Otherwise Print Disabled', ECLI:EU:C:2017:114. Here the CJEU ruled in favour of the EU's exclusive competence following the Commission in its argument that the Treaty is covered by the *ERTA* doctrine of implied powers. In particular the EU will have exclusive (implied) competence under Article 3(2) TFEU 'when the conclusion of an international agreement may affect common rules or alter their scope' (paras. 102-130 and specifically paras. 129–130). In this case the Court clarified the scope of Article 207(1) TFEU and, in particular, of the commercial aspects of intellectual

subsequent *OTIF* judgment[107] has somewhat qualified Opinion 2/15 insofar as the CJEU clarified that its position held in the former case was premised on the specific circumstances of that case. The Court explicitly made reference to its acknowledgment of a lack of voting majority within the Council that the Union would be able to exercise alone the external competence that it shares with the member states in the area of non-direct FI.[108] This seems to suggest that the CJEU did not intend to change in a significant manner its established case law by opting for mandatory mixity in Opinion 2/15.

While Article 207(1) and (4) TFEU refers specifically to FDI there is no definition of it to be found in the Treaty. The term "foreign" refers to investment from a member state to a third country or vice versa.[109] The term "direct" is more complex and difficult to define. The Explanatory Notes of Directive 88/361 on capital movement[110] define direct investment as 'investments of all kinds by natural persons or commercial, industrial or financial undertakings, and which serve to establish or to maintain lasting and direct links between the person providing the capital and the entrepreneur to whom or the undertaking to which the capital is made available in order to carry on an economic activity. This concept must therefore be understood in its widest sense.' According to the CJEU, direct investment is 'the form of participation in an undertaking through the holding of shares which confers the possibility of participating effectively in its management and control.'[111] Both definitions are in line with those of the Organisation for Economic Co-operation and Development (OECD)[112] and the International Monetary Fund (IMF).[113]

A key characteristic of FDI is that it generally refers to long-term investment in a foreign country. It is widely accepted that it is to be distinguished from foreign

---

property rights embracing a narrow interpretation, which explains why it relied instead on implied powers as per the last limb of Article 3(2) TFEU. According to the Court the mere cross-border exchange of goods or services is not enough to equate a measure with international trade for commercial purposes. A link with trade implies that the transaction or activity aims at fulfilling a commercial objective. Hence, using trade as a means to fulfil non-commercial objectives is not enough to bring a measure within the remit of the CCP.

[107]Case C-600/14 *Federal Republic of Germany v Council of the European Union* ECLI:EU:C:2017:935.

[108]Ibid., para. 68.

[109]Koutrakos, above no. 19, p. 46.

[110]Council Directive of 24 June 1988 for the implementation of Article 67 of the Treaty OJ L 178, 8.7.1988, pp. 5–18, at p. 11.

[111]Case C-35/11 *Test Claimants in the FII Group Litigation v Commissioners of Inland Revenue, The Commissioners for Her Majesty's Revenue & Customs*, ECLI:EU:C:2012:707, at para. 102. The CJEU provided this definition in the context of the free movement of capital; see Articles 63 and 64(1) and (2) TEU; see also Case C-81/09 *Idrima Tipou*, ECLI:EU:C:2010:622, at para. 48 and Case C-182/08 *Glaxo Wellcome GmbH & Co KG v Finanzamt München II*, ECLI:EU:C:2009:559, at para. 40.

[112]OECD (2008).

[113]International Monetary Fund (IMF) (2009).

portfolio investment (FPI),[114] which refers to 'the acquisition of shares on the capital market solely with the intention of making a financial investment without any intention to influence the management and control of the undertaking.'[115] This remains the position of the CJEU.[116] However, given the existence and increase of global value chains and production, it can be difficult to draw a clear distinction between FDI and FPI in practice.[117]

FPI is not covered by Article 207 TFEU. However, this does not exclude the existence of EU competence in this area.[118] Some maintain that the Union would have an implied external competence[119] relating to portfolio investments based on the provisions of the free movement of capital.[120] It is not very clear though how this competence could be exclusively implied given that free movement of capital is a shared competence and the EU has not exercised its competences under Articles 64(2) and 66 TFEU.[121] It follows that it would be difficult for the doctrine of implied powers to apply here given that there would be no legislation to be affected.[122] According to Krajewski, the express intention of the drafters of the TL was to limit the EU's competence to FDI. An implied external competence based on the free movement of capital would also cover FDI and would not explain the need for an express reference in Article 207 TFEU.[123] EU competence in this field thus remains a moot point.

Another open question is whether investment protection falls within the scope of FDI as Article 207 TFEU is silent on the specific substantive scope of FDI. Determining the scope of FDI requires a consideration of specific actions that the Union or the member states will carry out in the context of specific relationships with third countries or international organisations. Moreover, FDI is generally provided with other

[114] 'Foreign portfolio investment' consists of cross-border transactions and positions involving equity or debt securities, other than those included in direct investment or reserve assets, see IMF (2000), Appendix III, Glossary of Terms; Wolf (2008), pp. 71–105.

[115] Joined Cases C-282/4 and C-283/04 *Commission v Netherlands*, ECLI:EU:C:2006:608, para. 19.

[116] Opinion 2/15, ECLI:EU:C:2016:880, at para. 227.

[117] Woolcock, above no. 87, at p. 12.

[118] In this sense, see Hoffmeister, above no. 73, pp. 314–315.

[119] On the doctrine of implied powers, see above, infra no. 96; for detailed academic analysis including its relationship with the doctrine of parallelism, see Schütze (2014), Ch. 7.

[120] Articles 63-66 TFEU; European Commission, 'Towards a comprehensive European investment policy' above note no. 88, 8; A. Dimopoulos, above no. 3, pp. 104–05; De Luca (2012), pp. 182–195. The CJEU has held that such investments constitute movements of capital for the purposes of Article 63 TFEU, see, *inter alia*, Joined Cases C-282/04 and C-283/04, *Commission v Netherlands*, EU:C:2006:208, para. 19; C-81/09, *Idryma Typou*, EU:C:2010:622, para. 48; C-212/09, *Commission v Portugal*, EU:C:2011:717, para. 47.

[121] A. Delgado Casteleiro, 'Opinion 2/15 on the scope of EU external trade policy: some background information before next week's hearing', EU Analysis, 6 September 2016, available at: http://eulawanalysis.blogspot.co.uk/2016/09/opinion-215-on-scope-of-eu-external.html, accessed on 14 June 2020.

[122] Ibid.

[123] Krajewski, above no. 15, p. 302.

forms of foreign investment.[124] The majority view in the literature holds that Article 207 TFEU covers not only issues of investment liberalisation but also of investment protection. The underlying argument of this position is that, were it to be otherwise, it would undermine the effectiveness of the inclusion of FDI within the scope of the CCP.[125] In particular, the view of some scholars, which is shared by the Commission, is that this coverage should extend to all forms of investment protection including expropriation measures.[126] Others argue that the Union's investment competence should be limited to so-called "performance standards"[127] because the principle of neutrality vis-à-vis the member states' systems of property ownership[128] excludes an EU competence regarding expropriation.[129] In both cases, member states would lose the exclusive competence to negotiate, conclude and implement investment protection agreements and the Union would acquire the competence to negotiate new and re-negotiate old investment protection agreements. The member states would lose the competence to determine the scope, content and no longer be able to be partners of bilateral investment protection agreements should the CCP include investment protection.

Krajewski maintains that the term FDI included in Article 207 TFEU should only refer to those aspects of FDI, which concern investment liberalization and those, which have a close link to trade.[130] He argues that this reading of Article 207 TFEU is supported by context, object and purpose of the provision as well as its negotiating history[131] even though Article 206 TFEU refers to the Union's aims to contribute to 'the progressive abolition of restrictions on international trade and on foreign direct investment'. In this respect, the notion of "restrictions" in Article 206 TFEU concerns restrictive measures and not an investment-unfriendly environment. In addition, the phrase "foreign direct investment" appears in Article 207(1) and (4) TFEU where the provisions refer to trade agreements.[132] This suggests that only investment agreements, which have trade aspects are within the CCP. In addition, the interpretation of the phrase "foreign direct investment" relies on Article 206 TFEU.

Moreover, FDI is not a term to be found in international investment protection law and it is generally not used in bilateral investment treaties. Reference to FDI in the TFEU therefore seems to suggest that the drafters of the TL deliberately excluded

---

[124]Koutrakos, above no. 19, p. 47.

[125]Eeckhout, above no. 9, pp. 64–65.

[126]Bungenberg (2010), pp. 123–151, at 135 and Tietje (2009), p. 16; European Commission, above no. 88, at 5 and 8–9; for a detailed discussion about expropriation measures and whether EU investment agreements should cover compensation for expropriation, see Woolcock, above no. 87, at 36–38.

[127]Performance standards include non-discrimination, fair and equitable treatment and full protection and security.

[128]Article 345 TFEU provides that: 'The Treaties shall in no way prejudice the rules in Member States governing the system of property ownership.'

[129]For further discussion, Moskvan (2016), pp. 242–262, at 254–256.

[130]Krajewski, above no. 15, p. 303.

[131]Ibid.

[132]Villalta Puig and Al-Haddab, above no. 13, at 294.

investment protection from the substantive scope of the CCP and, more generally, that they did not want to cover all aspects of investment.

Consequently, agreements covering both FDI and portfolio investment like the majority of investment protection treaties do not fall within the exclusive competence of the EU as member states retain the competence over portfolio investments. In these cases, investment agreements, which cover both aspects of investment would need to be concluded as mixed agreements.[133]

The above analysis reveals that despite the broadening of the scope of the CCP by the TL there is a lack of legal certainty with regard to the inclusion of FDI as to its meaning and scope. 'The post-Lisbon external relations regime remains unclear as far as the exact competence division is concerned, leaving the CJEU to decide on the line of demarcation between EU and member states' external competences.'[134] The need for jurisprudential interpretation will not be devoid of problems given that although the CJEU 'has made broad statements of principle, it has been singularly reluctant to draw from them what may seem to be their logical consequences.'[135] More generally, a future Common Foreign Investment Policy will most probably be mixed as confirmed by the CJEU's Opinion 2/15.[136]

Member States' Bilateral Investment Treaties and the Development of the EU's Common Investment Policy

With FDI falling within the exclusive competence of the EU after the entry into force of the TL another question had to be addressed: the status under EU law of member states' Bilateral Investment Treaties (BITs) concluded with third countries, so-called—extra-EU" BITS—that existed before the entry into force of the TL.[137]

[133]Ibid; see analysis above.

[134]Van der Loo and Wessel, above no. 100, at 740.

[135]Tridimas and Eeckhout (1994), pp. 143–177, at 172.

[136]Opinion 2/15, ECLI:EU:C:2016:880.

[137]Since 1959 member states have concluded more than 1400 BITs with third countries, available at: http://ec.europa.eu/trade/policy/accessing-markets/investment/index_en.htm. There are also BITs concluded between EU member states, so-called "intra-EU" BITs, which have a different legal regime. The distinction of treatments between extra-EU and intra-EU BITs may lead to forum shopping particularly with regard to investment protection through corporate nationality planning. The EU's efforts to form a comprehensive investment policy (both intra-EU and extra-EU) has been affected by on-going horizontal and institutional incoherence, see Lenk (2015), pp. 6–20; for an analysis of the validity and applicability of intra-EU BITs, see F. Weiss and S. Steiner, above no. 87, pp. 367–373; see also the *Achmea* case, where the CJEU found that the CJEU found that the arbitration clause in the BIT between Slovakia and the Netherlands had an adverse effect on the autonomy of EU law because not only could disputes falling within the jurisdiction of the arbitral tribunal relate to the interpretation both of that agreement and of EU law but also because the possibility of submitting those disputes to a body which is not part of the judicial system of the EU is provided for by an agreement which was concluded not by the EU but by member states. As such, it called into question the principle of mutual trust between Member States and the preservation of the particular nature of EU law and was thus incompatible with the principle

As Koutrakos notes, the sheer number of member states' BITs compounds the lack of clarity that characterizes the scope of FDI under Article 207 TFEU.[138]

In particular, there are a number of significant problems concerning the emergence of the EU's common investment policy and existing BITs. First, there is the question of the continued validity of member states' obligations under existing agreements. The legal basis for the continued validity of member states BITs can be found in Article 30(4) Vienna Convention on the Law of Treaties (VCLT), which essentially establishes that a treaty between two parties will not be superseded by a subsequent treaty that one of the parties enters into with a third party.[139] Moreover, under public international law, a state cannot invoke violations of a provision of its internal law regarding competence to conclude treaties in order to waive its obligations under a validly concluded treaty.[140] However, from the perspective of EU law member states' obligations stemming from these existing BITs may not have valid legal effects. The CJEU has condemned member states for giving effect to International Treaty provisions that are found incompatible with the EU Treaties' competence rules. The *MOX Plant* case concerning an international environmental claim and, in particular radioactive waste pollution in the Irish Sea, is illustrative. The case concerned a conflict between Ireland and the UK about the construction and operation of the MOX Plant at Sellafield, on the Irish Sea. Both member states are parties to the United Nations Convention on the Law of the Sea (UNCLOS) and the Convention for the Protection of the Marine Environment of the North-East Atlantic (OSPAR Convention). In 2001, Ireland commenced dispute settlement proceedings under these International treaties. Furthermore, it also applied to the International Tribunal for the Law of the Sea (ITLOS) for provisional measures that would restrain the UK from commissioning the plant. In this context, while waiting for the final decision of the Arbitral Tribunal constituted under the UNCLOS, the ITLOS prescribed a provisional measure in December 2001, ordering the parties to co-operate and to engage in consultations, including the exchange of information, without further delay.

of sincere cooperation established in Article 4(3) TEU, Case C-284/16 *Slowakische Republik v Achmea BV*, ECLI:EU:C:2018:158, paras. 58–59.

[138] Koutrakos, above no. 19, at p. 48.

[139] Article 30(4) VCLT provides that: 'When the parties to the later treaty do not include all the parties to the earlier one: (a) As between States parties to both treaties the same rule applies as in paragraph 3; (b) As between a State party to both treaties and a State party to only one of the treaties, the treaty to which both States are parties governs their mutual rights and obligations.'

[140] Article 46(1) VCLT provides that: 'A State may not invoke the fact that its consent to be bound by a treaty has been expressed in violation of a provision of its internal law regarding competence to conclude treaties as invalidating its consent unless that violation was manifest and concerned a rule of its internal law of fundamental importance.'

When the case was brought before the CJEU, the Court for the first time explicitly determined the scope of its exclusive jurisdiction based on Article 344 TFEU. According to the Court, member states involved in a dispute that potentially raises issues of EU law, such as Ireland, cannot bring the case before a dispute settlement body other than the CJEU, without breaching the duty of sincere cooperation under Article 4(3) TFEU, as this might jeopardise the autonomy of the EU legal order largely because the Court's exclusive jurisdiction may adversely be affected by decisions of other international courts or tribunals in disputes which also concern aspects of EU law.[141] Moreover, there is no general exemption for pre-existing international obligations of member states that become incompatible with new rules created in the Treaty itself and Article 351(1) TFEU only refers to international agreements concluded before 1 January 1958.[142]

With the entry into force of the TL, member states are therefore required to re-negotiate or where necessary terminate their BITs in order to bring their international obligations in line with EU law.[143] With regard to existing BITs it is not clear whether an award of damages to an investor may be enforced against a member state on the basis of the BIT concerned without the risk of facing infringement procedures initiated by the Commission for a potential breach of EU law. Linked to this, there could be circumstances where a non-EU investor tries to enforce an international arbitral award made against the Member State. There is also the possible scenario of a third country questioning the continuing validity of their own obligations vis-à-vis European investors.

Transitional Arrangements for Member States' BITs and Regulation 1219/2012[144]

The TL did not insert any provisions on the transition from national BITs to the full implementation of EU investment agreements and thus the question of the continued validity of member states' BITs was left open after its entry into force.

There were thus two main challenges that the EU was confronted with during the transition from member state BITs to EU international agreements with third countries: first, ensuring that investors (both inward and outward) would continue to receive effective protection and, second, that existing BITs would conform with EU

---

[141] E.g., C-459/03, *Commission v. Ireland (Mox Plant)* ECLI:EU:C:2006:345.

[142] Article 351(1) TFEU provides that: 'The rights and obligations arising from agreements concluded before 1 January 1958 or, for acceding States, before the date of their accession, between one or more Member States on the one hand, and one or more third countries on the other, shall not be affected by the provisions of the Treaties.'

[143] Case C-205/06, *Commission v Austria* ECLI:EU:C:2009:118 and Case 249/06, *Commission v Sweden*, ECLI:EU:C:2009:119.

[144] Regulation (EU) No 1219/2012 of the European Parliament and of the Council of 12 December 2012 establishing transitional arrangements for bilateral investment agreements between member states and third countries, OJ L351/40 of 20 December 2012.

law, other EU international agreements and EU policies covering foreign investments. The solution was provided with the adoption of Regulation 1219/2012, which has been adopted to regulate transitional arrangements for national BITs.

The regulation addresses the status under EU law of national BITs that existed before the entry into force of the TL and establishes the terms, conditions and procedures under which member states can amend an existing BIT or conclude a new one with third countries.[145] In particular, Article 3 of the Regulation provides that: 'without prejudice to other obligations of the member states under Union law, bilateral investment agreements notified pursuant to Article 2 of this Regulation may be maintained in force, or enter into force, in accordance with the TFEU and this Regulation, until a bilateral investment agreement between the Union and the same third country enters into force.' The Commission has been given an important supervisory role as part of its central role of guardian of the EU Treaties during all main stages of the negotiations and must be notified also of a resulting agreement given that it will evaluate the text in accordance with criteria set out in the Regulation.[146] In particular, to open formal negotiations with a third country to amend or conclude a BIT member states must obtain the Commission's authorization.[147] This authorization is granted despite the Union's competence in the area and, as seen above, without prejudice to other EU law obligations that Member States have.

The Commission may decide to refuse the authorization on four grounds:

(a) be in conflict with Union law other than the incompatibilities arising from the allocation of competences between the Union and its member states;
(b) be superfluous, because the Commission has submitted or has decided to submit a recommendation to open negotiations with the third country concerned pursuant to Article 218(3) TFEU;
(c) be inconsistent with the Union's principles and objectives for external action as elaborated in accordance with the general provisions laid down in Chapter 1 of Title V TEU; or
(d) constitute a serious obstacle to the negotiation or conclusion of bilateral investment agreements with third countries by the Union.[148]

The first ground seeks to avoid the adoption of national BITs, which would result in a violation of EU law. For instance, BIT provisions on the free transfer of investment-related funds without any exceptions are incompatible with EU law because EU

[145] Article 1 of Regulation No. 1219/2012.
[146] Articles 9-11 of Regulation No. 1219/2012.
[147] Article 9 of Regulation No. 1219/2012.
[148] Ibid.

primary law provides for such exceptions.[149] The CJEU confirmed this incompatibility in various cases.[150] Incompatibilities may also arise with regard to the admission and the post-establishment treatment of foreign investments due to restrictions or limitations to the rights of foreign investors to enter or operate in the internal market. In addition, there may be incompatibilities due to the need for equal treatment of all EU nationals within the internal market as well as in third countries.[151] In particular, there could be a conflict when investors have recourse to an international arbitral tribunal in addition to courts of the host state.[152] Moreover, national BITs have to contain special clauses exempting third country investors from benefits and privileges conferred under EU law[153] However, these exemptions normally do not cover other standards such as fair and equitable treatment, full protection and security or full compensation for expropriation.[154] Investors can therefore use BIT arbitral proceedings to challenge any change in EU legislation or regulatory action in spite of the fact that, if interpreted properly, BIT standards should not afford any more protection than the European standards.[155] The extreme vagueness of BITs provisions combined with the lack of any binding and consistent case law makes the likelihood of these scenarios possible.[156] The second ground for the Commission to refuse an authorization is when the EU intends to open or has already started negotiations with the third country in question. In this context, the aim is to ensure the gradual development of a comprehensive EU investment policy and thus to replace member states' BITs with EU International Investment Agreements (IIAs). The third ground aims at ensuring consistency with

---

[149]Articles 64, 66 and 75 TFEU. E.g. see the Protocol of 26 August 2009 to the French-Turkish BIT of 15 June 2006: "The provisions of [Article 5 on the free transfer of capital] do not hinder the exercise in good faith by one Contracting Party of its international obligations as well as its right and obligations resulting from its participation or association in a free trade zone, a customs union, a common market, an economic and monetary union or any other form of regional co-operation or integration.' This example is taken from S. Woolcock, above n. 66, fn. 89, p. 57.

[150]Case C-205/06 *Commission v Austria* ECLI:EU:C:2009:118 and Case C-249/06 *Commission v Sweden* ECLI:EU:C:2009:119 and Case C-118/07, *Commission v. Finland* ECLI:EU:C:2009:715.

[151]For further analysis see A. Dimopoulos, above no. 87, pp. 310–318.

[152]Discussed above in Sect. 4.1.2.1.

[153]E.g. Article 7(a) of the UK-Argentina BIT of 11 December 1990; Article 4(2) of the Germany-India BIT of 10 July 1995; Article 3(4) France-Turkey BIT of 26 August 2009. These clauses are often referred to as Regional Economic Integration Organisation (REIO) clauses. These examples are taken from Woolcock, above no. 87, fn. 89, p. 57.

[154]Woolcock, above no. 87, p. 57.

[155]Ibid.

[156]In practice, member states may have to pay large damages awarded by arbitrators who owe no allegiance other than the BIT itself. E.g. *CME Czech Republic BV (The Netherlands) v Czech Republic* (Damages) (14 March 2003) 15(4) World Trade and Arbitration Material 83, where the Czech Republic was condemned to pay US$ 353 million for issuing regulatory advice (not involving EU law) that lead CME, a Dutch investment vehicle of Ronald Steven Lauder, a U.S. cosmetics billionaire, to divest itself of a popular TV station, despite the fact that another tribunal under the Czech-U.S. BIT had six months earlier found that the conduct of the Czech broadcast authority constituted no violation of any investment protection standards. This example is taken from Woolcock, above no. 87, fn. 91, p. 57.

the EU's principles and objectives which are meant to provide a normative framework for all EU external action, as per Articles 3(5) and 21 TEU and reproduced in Articles 205 and 207(1) TFEU. These principles and objectives provide the Commission with a significant amount of political discretion when deciding whether to grant an authorization. The fourth ground of refusal slightly overlaps with the second ground since obstacles are likely to occur when the EU itself has decided to open negotiations with the same third country. The question and degree of seriousness will be assessed on a case-by-case basis. It is noteworthy that the EU has negotiated international agreements with third countries that covered aspects of foreign investment even before the entry into force of the TL[157] and problems of overlap and/or incompatibility were already evident then.[158]

Despite some clarity introduced by the adoption of the Regulation the lack of legal certainty with regard to existing national BITs remains. Even if member states are to terminate their BITs most of the BITs contain clauses that provide for their continuation in force for 10–20 years after their termination.

3.5 The Expanding Competence of the EU in the Area of the Common Commercial Policy

3.5.1 Overview

As Krajewski aptly puts it 'the nature and scope of the Union's competence with regard to the CCP has been a "constitutional construction site" of growing complexity since the early days of the European Economic Community.'[159] The question of the scope of the CCP and its delimitation of competences is of constitutional salience for two key reasons: first, the EU must act on the basis of the principle of attributed powers[160]; second, the competence question has direct consequences for the EU decision-making procedure.

---

[157] E.g. Agreement establishing an Association between the European Community and its Member States, of the one part, and the Republic of Chile, of the other part, OJ L352/1, 30/12/2002, (2002 EU-Chile FTA); the Economic Partnership Agreement between the CARIFORUM States, of the one part, and the European Community and its Member States, of the other part [2008] OJ L289/3 (the 2008 EU-CARIFORUM EPA); 2013 EUSFTA.

[158] E.g. 2002 EU-Chile FTA. Article 195 EU-Chile FTA provides the contracting parties in case of 'serious balance of payments and external financial difficulties' to adopt 'restrictive measures with regard to trade in goods and in services and with regard to payment and capital movement, including those related to direct investments.' However, the national BITs concluded with Chile provide unqualified guarantees of free transfer of capital. Hence, if investors could challenge restrictions allowed by the FTA by invoking the BIT provision, this would undermine the overall balance of the FTA and could also raise questions of equal treatment between investors.

[159] Krajewski, above no. 15, p. 298.

[160] Article 5(1)-(2) TEU and Article 7 TFEU.

While the TL introduced some clarity, at the same time, it also raised new questions. For its implementation, the CCP relies on the use of autonomous regulatory and legislative measures adopted internally and the negotiation and conclusion of international agreements. Article 207 TFEU clarifies that the Union's exclusive competence in its external trade policy includes the negotiation and conclusion of agreements (external competence) as well as the implementation of these agreements (internal competence).[161] The analysis is going to focus on the EU's international agreements.

3.5.2 The European Union's Exclusive Competence in the Field of the Common Commercial Policy

Article 3(1)(e) TFEU explicitly provides that the Union shall have exclusive competence in the area of the CCP, effectively codifying the CJEU's case law[162] according to which member states do not have the power to enter into international agreements or legislate on matters of the CCP.

Article 3(2) TFEU provides that the exclusive competence of the EU also includes the conclusion of an international agreement 'when its conclusion is provided for in a legislative act of the Union or is necessary to enable the Union to exercise its internal competence, or insofar as its conclusion may affect common rules or alter their scope.' In a similar vein, Article 216(1) TFEU holds that the Union may conclude international agreements 'where the conclusion of an agreement is necessary in order to achieve, within the framework of the Union's policies, one of the objectives referred to in the Treaties, or is provided for in a legally binding Union act or is likely to affect common rules or alter their scope'. Both provisions are based on the doctrine of implied powers developed by the CJEU according to which the Union not only has external powers that are explicitly conferred to it by the Treaties, but also implicit powers deriving from its internal competences.[163]

---

[161] Article 207(3) TFEU refers to the negotiation and conclusion of international agreements and Article 207(2) TFEU refers to the implementation of the CCP.

[162] The Opinion 1/75 in the Low Cost Standard case denied Member States the power to enter into international agreements or to legislate matters related to commercial policy, even if the Community had not yet acted; see Case 1/75, *Low Cost Standard*, 1975 E.C.R. 1355; Case 41/76, *Suzanne Criel, nee Donckerwolcke and Henru Schou v. Procureur de la Republique*, 1976 E.C.R. 1921.

[163] See above, no. 96, 106 and 119.

3.5.3 The Negotiation, Signature, Provisional Application and Ratification of International Trade Agreements

Negotiations start with a mandate that is proposed by the European Commission and adopted by the Council.[164] The TL explicitly provides that the European Commission shall ensure the EU's entire external representation with the exception of the CFSP,[165] which should extend also to the negotiation of trade agreements that cover shared competences. No other legislative institution, either domestic or European, is involved at this stage. The EP will generally draft a resolution when the Council adopts a mandate to negotiate an agreement, which sets out a series of limitations that aim at circumscribing the action of the European Commission during the negotiations. In practice both the Council's mandate and the EP's resolution are meant to act as a "political compass" rather than as legally binding directives.[166] As Adriaensen and Neuhold rightly observe: 'a strict rule-based interpretation of the mandate not only affects the European Commission's room of manoeuvre during the negotiations, it also limits the Council (and the EP)'s ability to adjust their position over the course of the negotiations.'[167] The Council can adopt negotiating directives. However, it cannot define EU negotiating positions and impose them on the Commission. Moreover, most preferences are communicated directly to the European Commission.[168]

[164] Article 207(3) TFEU provides that: 'Where agreements with one or more third countries or international organisations need to be negotiated and concluded, Article 218 shall apply, subject to the special provisions of this Article.

The Commission shall make recommendations to the Council, which shall authorise it to open the necessary negotiations. The Council and the Commission shall be responsible for ensuring that the agreements negotiated are compatible with internal Union policies and rules.

The Commission shall conduct these negotiations in consultation with a special committee appointed by the Council to assist the Commission in this task and within the framework of such directives as the Council may issue to it. The Commission shall report regularly to the special committee and to the European Parliament on the progress of negotiations.'

[165] Article 17(1) TEU.

[166] In this provision the meaning of directive is to be distinguished from that found in Article 288(3) TFEU as a legislative instrument addressed to EU Member States.

[167] Adriaensen and Neuhold (2017).

[168] Adriaensen (2016), p. 47.

The European Commission is normally the main negotiator for EU international trade agreements.[169] During the negotiations, it has an obligation to keep both the Council and the EP informed[170] through an elaborated committee-structure, which is both formal and informal. With regard to the formal committees, the Council is informed through the Trade Policy Committee (TPC, the former "Committee 133") and the EP is informed through the Committee on International Trade (INTA).[171]

The other format of a more informal nature is represented by the Informal Technical Meetings (ITMs), which are attended solely by the European Commission and member state officials.[172] They constitute the informal counterpart of the TPC as they have a similar set-up and operate in a similar way as a control mechanism but allowing—in comparison with the TPC, which discusses the broad negotiation strategy—a more in-depth discussion about technical and regulatory aspects of EU trade policy, including international trade agreements that are in the process of being negotiated.[173] ITMs are organised entirely by the European Commission, also upon the request of any of its Directorates-General or Member State. Through the ITMs member states can increase their leverage and monitoring over the European Commission as well as receive further information about the way negotiations are going. The furthering of the EU's "deep trade agenda"[174] and the growing complexity of its international trade agreements - as exemplified by its Deep and Comprehensive Free Trade Agreements (DCFTAs) and "mega-regional trade agreements" such as CETA and TTIP—make ITMs a particularly valuable platform for question time and for providing the basis for establishing a common understanding of the issues at hand and thus for building consensus in the more formal TPC where only official positions of the parties involved are presented. It is for this reason that they have become increasingly important.[175]

Similarly, the EP has set up informal monitoring groups for each negotiation to enable a more detailed exchange with the European Commission. In practice, the European Commission informs the ad hoc groups that are part of the INTA Committee and takes into account majority views formulated there. If the latter are subsequently reflected in the EP's resolutions the European Commission will probably take them into account during the negotiations in order to increase the chance of getting the agreement accepted at approval stage.[176]

---

[169] Article 207(3) subpara. 2 TFEU.

[170] Article 207(3) subpara. 3 TFEU; Article 218(4) and (10) TFEU, respectively. The CJEU held that the Council can require the Commission to regularly report on the progress in the negotiations to a Committee or even the Council itself, see Case C-245/13 *Commission v Council* EU:C:483, paras. 60–73.

[171] Under para. 24 of the Framework Agreement on relations between the European Parliament and the European Commission, [2010] OJ L304/47, the European Commission informs either the responsible Committee of the EU Parliament or the plenary about the negotiations of an international agreement.

[172] Adriaensen and Coleman (2017), pp. 77–95.

[173] Ibid.

[174] Melo Araujo, above no. 35.

[175] J. Adriaensen and E. Coleman, above no. 172.

[176] Hoffmeister, above no. 73, p. 323; see also Hoffmeister (2014), pp. 145–146.

Once the negotiations are concluded, the European Commission will put forward a proposal to the Council to sign and provisionally apply the agreement. Under Article 218(5) TFEU no specific role is envisaged for the EP at this stage. However, two distinct scenarios can take place.[177] First, an agreement needs to be swiftly signed and provisionally applied. In this case, the Council will be able to safely make use of its prerogatives without any immediate involvement of the EP.[178] In the second scenario there is an important agreement to be concluded which will define the long-term relations with a given third country. In this case the EP will have the opportunity to express its view prior to the provisional application of the agreement.[179]

The Council and the EP will then ratify it. In particular, the Council takes the decision after formal approval of the EP.[180] If the scope of the agreement only covers the EU's exclusive competences, the Council ratifies it on the basis of a qualified majority voting (QMV). This will be followed by the EP's consent with a simple majority vote. Increasingly, trade agreements cover policy issues that are either of shared competence or that are of member state's exclusive competence. In the former case, the Council and the European Commission can decide on the applicable procedures. In the latter case, the procedure requires a unanimity vote in the Council and ratification by the legislatures of the member states. The next sections examine this in further detail.

3.5.4 The Decision-Making System in the Council of Ministers After the Entry into Force of the Treaty of Lisbon

Article 207(4) TFEU provides that the Council should use QMV to adopt decisions regarding the negotiation and conclusion of international agreements. QMV was already the main form of decision-making procedure before the TL. However, Article 207(4) subpara. 2 TFEU requires unanimity for the negotiation and conclusion of agreements regarding trade in services, commercial aspects of intellectual property

---

[177]Hoffmeister, above no. 73, p. 324.

[178]E.g. the so-called "Banana Agreement", Council Decision of 10 May 2010 on the signing and provisional application of the Geneva Agreement on Trade in Bananas between the European Union and Brazil, Colombia, Costa Rica, Ecuador, Guatemala, Honduras, Mexico, Nicaragua, Panama, Peru and Venezuela and of the Agreement on Trade in Bananas between the European Union and the United States of America, OJ L 141, 9.6.2010, pp. 1–2.

[179]E.g. 2011 EU-Korea FTA, Free Trade Agreement between the European Union and its Member States of the one part, and the Republic of Korea of the other part (EU-Korea FTA) [2011] OJ L127/6, 14 May 2011, p. 6. In the decision on this agreement the entry into force of a safeguard regulation was set as a precondition for provisional application of the agreement. The safeguard regulation was voted in the EU Parliament at the same time as the agreement itself. In practice, the Council effectively made the date of provisional application dependent on a positive vote of the EU Parliament on the agreement even if such condition is not provided for in Article 218(5) TFEU. This practice has been subsequently used for other EU international agreements, see Hoffmeister, above no. 73, pp. 324–326.

[180]Article 218(6) TFEU.

and FDI 'where such agreements include provisions for which unanimity is required for the adoption of internal rules.' Hence, with regard to trade in services, FDI and commercial aspects of intellectual property the provision, as drafted, applies the so-called "doctrine of *in foro interno-in foro externo*" or principle of "parallelism" or "complementarity"[181] to the decision-making procedure of the Council. Decisions concerning the negotiation and conclusion of international agreements shall thus be made according to the same majority requirements employed for internal legislation with the same content. The reason for such approach is that trade in services, commercial aspects of intellectual property and FDI are areas in which member states wish to retain regulatory control and autonomy. Same rationale applies to the unanimity rule applied to trade in cultural and audio-visual services, where these agreements risk prejudicing the Union's cultural and linguistic diversity and to trade in social, education and health services, where these agreements risk seriously disturbing the national organisation of such services and prejudicing the responsibility of member states to deliver them.[182] In circumstances where a trade agreement includes issues requiring unanimity and issues requiring only QMV the colloquially defined "Pastis" principle will apply. According to this principle, one single "drop" of unanimity in a proposal, otherwise covered by QMV, changes the entire agreement into unanimity agreement.[183]

[181]This principle of EU external relations has been developed further by the CJEU into two slightly distinct conceptualisations, that of complementarity and parallelism. With regard to the former, see the *Kramer* case (Cases 3, 4 & 6/76, *Kramer* ECLI:EU:C:1976:114). The principle of complementarity establishes that external competence is a necessary complement to the Union's internal competence. With regard to the principle of parallelism, see Opinion 1/76, Opinion given pursuant to Article 228 (1) of the EEC Treaty—'Draft Agreement establishing a European laying-up fund for inland waterway vessels' ECLI:EU:C:1977:63, paras. 3–4. According to the Court, the EU has competence to enter into an international agreement provided that: (a) the Treaty confers internal competence on the EU in a given area for the purpose of attaining a specific objective, and (b) participation of the EU in the agreement in question is necessary for the attainment of that objective. Most significantly, it is not necessary for the Union to have exercised its internal competence in that field as the very existence of such internal competence is sufficient; for academic analysis, see Dashwood and Heliskoski (2000), pp. 12–13; see also Cremona (1999), pp. 137–176 at p. 139.

[182]Article 207(4) subpara. 3 TFEU.

[183]This term was coined by Pascal Lamy, former Trade Commissioner of the EU Commission.

3.5.5 *Brexit, European Union International Agreements and the United Kingdom*

3.5.5.1 Why Brexit Matters for Future EU International Agreements and for the UK's Future Negotiations with Third Countries

This section examines the external relations implications of the UK's withdrawal from the EU.[184] As Michael Dougan aptly puts it[185]:

> the UK's decision to leave the European Union marks a fundamental reorientation in UK law and policy: both internally, when it comes to the structures, processes and outputs of our own domestic legal systems; and externally, as regards the UK's place in and relations with the broader European and international legal orders.

Understanding the impact of Brexit on the EU's international agreements and the UK's legal status in relation to these agreements is of particular importance as any final arrangement made with the UK will act as a precedent and will thus have significant implications for any future member state withdrawal from the EU. From the EU's perspective, the main concern is the impact of Brexit on the EU's relationship with third countries who are parties to its international agreements.[186] From the UK's perspective, the UK is bound by all of them even though it is not a party to all of the EU's international agreements, as they form an integral part of EU law.[187] Moreover, the EU has concluded agreements in many policy areas that are of particular salience to the UK and its economy. It is important, therefore, to identify and examine the possible scenarios with regard to the UK's status vis-à-vis the EU's international agreements as well as its position in the WTO after Brexit.

---

184 A detailed analysis of the withdrawal of the UK from the EU (or "Brexit") and the process(es) and procedures of disengagement from the EU is outside the scope of this chapter; for up-to-date information visit: https://ec.europa.eu/info/european-union-and-united-kingdom-forging-new-partnership_en, accessed on 20 March 2020; https://www.parliament.uk/brexit, accessed on 20 March 2020; https://ukandeu.ac.uk/, accessed on 20 March 2020; for academic discussion: Brexit Supplement 17 *German Law Journal* (2016), available at: http://www.germanlawjournal.com/brexit-supplement/; Craig (2016), pp. 447–468, Ahmed and Fahey (2019), Dougan (2017a), Eeckhout and Frantziou (2017), 695–734, Gee et al. (2016), pp. 51–56, Gormley (2017), pp. 1175–1210, Kostakopoulou (2017), pp. 339–352, Lazowski and Wessel (2016), pp. 623–638, Sif Tynes and Lian Haugsdal (2016), pp. 753–765, Wessel (2016), pp. 197–209, van der Wel and Wessel (2017)

185 Dougan (2017b), pp. 1–12, at p. 1.

186 Odermatt (2017), pp. 1052–1073, at 1055.

187 Case 181/73 *R & V Haegeman Spri v Belgium*, ECLI:EU:C:1974:41.

3.5.5.2 Certain Key Aspects About the Legal Status of the UK Under EU International Agreements Following Its Exit from the Union and the Need for Negotiation of New Trade Agreements

The EU has concluded more than a thousand bilateral and multilateral agreements with third parties.[188] Approximately three quarters of these agreements have relevance to the UK, covering by way of example trade in nuclear goods, customs, fisheries, trade, transport and regulatory co-operation in areas such as antitrust or financial services.

All of these agreements are being re-examined, revised and scoped out. As of 31 January 2020 the UK is no longer a member of the EU. The Withdrawal Agreement, signed by the UK and the EU and in force as of 1 February 2020,[189] sets out how the UK is able to continue to be covered by EU-third country trade agreements until 31 December 2020 (the end of the transition period). In general terms, during this time EU trade agreements continue to apply to the UK. The EU has notified third countries and international organizations about this arrangement. From 1 January 2021, EU trade agreements will no longer apply to the UK. At the time of writing, the British government is seeking to reproduce the effects of existing EU agreements for when they no longer apply to the UK. At this juncture, in order to fully understand the implications of Brexit on the legal status of the UK under these agreements, we need to distinguish between agreements, which fall within the Union's exclusive competence and have been concluded only by the Union[190] and "mixed agreements" where—as we have seen—the competence to conclude international agreements is shared between the EU and the member states. In the former case, the agreements only bind the UK as a matter of EU law.[191] Following its exit from the Union and, in particular, after the end of the transition period, "EU-only" international agreements, as mentioned above, are no longer applicable to the UK. In practice, this means that it needs to renegotiate its legal relationships with the third parties concerned.[192] Again, the EU has notified the parties to these EU-only agreements to inform them of the withdrawal of the UK and that the EU consists of 27 member states.[193] In the case of mixed agreements, even though the UK is a party

---

[188]EU treaty database, available at: http://ec.europa.eu/world/agreements/SimpleSearch.do, accessed on 10 March 2019.

[189]Full text of the Withdrawl Agreement can be found at: https://ec.europa.eu/info/european-union-and-united-kingdom-forging-new-partnership/eu-uk-withdrawal-agreement_en, accessed on 29 August 2020.

[190]As per Article 3 TFEU; e.g. the Agreement on Scientific and Technological Cooperation between the European Community and South Africa [1997] OJ L313/25.

[191]As per Article 216(2) TFEU, which provides that: 'Agreements concluded by the Union are binding upon the institutions of the Union and on its Member States.'

[192]Koutrakos (2016a), pp. 1–2; for a discussion as to whether the UK after leaving the EU would continue to be bound by the obligations under EU-only agreements by way of succession, see Odermatt, above no. 186, at 1057–1059.

[193]On the basis of a joint reading of Article 216(2) TFEU and Article 56 VCLT. Article 56 VCLT provides that:

to these agreements, the rights that it has enjoyed and the obligations it has assumed under their provisions will not continue to apply automatically.[194] In particular, with Brexit the UK is no longer bound by the "EU-only" elements of mixed agreements. On the other hand, if all the other parties agreed to it, the UK could remain bound by the "mixed" elements of these agreements because they were signed and ratified by the UK as a contracting party in its own right.[195] In practice, this may prove difficult as identifying a clear competence demarcation between "EU-only" and "mixed" elements of the agreement is a rather complex exercise. In addition, as posited by Van der Loo and Blockmans,[196] the extraction of the UK from a mixed agreement will have practical, economic and/or financial consequences and specific arrangements to tamper the effects of the UK's exit will need to be made and negotiated between the EU, its 27 remaining member states and the other contracting parties and laid down in a legally binding instrument such as a protocol to the agreement, an exchange of letters or a decision by the joint committee established by the said agreement, which may require ratification of all parties to the agreement.[197]

The great majority of mixed agreements would have to be renegotiated as they are mostly of bilateral nature: they are concluded *of the one part* by the EU and its member states and, *of the other part*, by the third country, and refer to the UK in its status as a member state of the EU.[198] In this regard, the CJEU held in the *European Development Fund* case that the Lomé Convention between the EU and its member states and African, Caribbean and Pacific states 'established an essentially bilateral ACP-EEC cooperation.'[199] In addition, most mixed agreements have clauses, which establish that with regard to the EU their territorial application is limited to the territories in which the TEU and the TFEU are applied and under

'1. A treaty which contains no provision regarding its termination and which does not provide for denunciation or withdrawal is not subject to denunciation or withdrawal unless:

(a) It is established that the parties intended to admit the possibility of denunciation or withdrawal; or

(b) A right of denunciation or withdrawal may be implied by the nature of the treaty.

2. A party shall give not less than twelve months' notice of its intention to denounce or withdraw from a treaty under paragraph 1.'

See in this sense, Van der Loo and Blockmans (2016), pp. 1–5.

194 Ibid.

195 Van der Loo and Blockmans, above no. 192, p. 2.

196 Ibid., pp. 2–3.

197 Article 39 VCLT provides that: '*A treaty may be amended by agreement between the parties*. The rules laid down in Part II apply to such an agreement except in so far as the treaty may otherwise provide.' [Emphasis added].

198 Koutrakos (2016b), pp. 475–478, at 475; e.g. Association Agreement between the European Union and its Member States, of the one part, and Ukraine of the other part [2014] OJ L161/3 (EU-Ukraine AA).

199 Case C-316/91 *Re European Development Fund*, ECLI:EU:C:1994:76; see Koutrakos, above no. 191, at 2.

the conditions laid down in those Treaties.[200] As Panos Koutrakos rightly points out,[201] the need for a renegotiation of mixed agreements is also supported by their context. As he puts it: 'third contracting states may well argue that the withdrawal of the UK will amount to a fundamental change of circumstances pursuant to Article 62 of the Vienna Convention on the Law of Treaties.'[202] As a matter of national law, and specifically from an internal constitutional law perspective, this means that the UK—in order to extract itself from mixed agreements- will need to repeal its approval act with which it ratified a given agreement and terminate or denounce the agreement according to the agreement's termination or suspension clauses.[203] This could be done by the procedure of making the coming into force of the repeal legislation effective through an Order in Council or a statutory instrument specifying the appropriate date.[204]

In light of these considerations, it is likely that the UK will need to renegotiate existing agreements with third countries from which the UK benefits due to its EU membership as well as mixed agreements. If the UK remains a party of existing trade agreements it would require the ratification of all the other 27 member states and the third countries. In practice, this would involve what Panos Koutrakos has termed as a "rolling over" argument, according to which the UK would simply agree with partner countries to "roll over" the provisions of existing agreements.[205] However, while at first sight this may seem like a pragmatic option, it would still require some degree

---

[200]E.g. Article 131, Stabilisation and Association Agreement between the European Communities and their Member States, of the one part, and Bosnia and Herzegovina, of the other part [2015] OJ L164/2.

[201]Koutrakos, above no. 197, at 476.

[202]Ibid; Article 62 VCLT provides that: '

1. A fundamental change of circumstances which has occurred with regard to those existing at the time of the conclusion of a treaty, and which was not foreseen by the parties, may not be invoked as a ground for terminating or withdrawing from the treaty unless:

(a) The existence of those circumstances constituted an essential basis of the con sent of the parties to be bound by the treaty; and

(b) The effect of the change is radically to transform the extent of obligations still to be performed under the treaty.

2. A fundamental change of circumstances may not be invoked as a ground for terminating or withdrawing from a treaty:

(a) If the treaty establishes a boundary; or

(b) If the fundamental change is the result of a breach by the party invoking it either of an obligation under the treaty or of any other international obligation owed to any other party to the treaty.

3. If, under the foregoing paragraphs, a party may invoke a fundamental change of circumstances as a ground for terminating or withdrawing from a treaty it may also invoke the change as a ground for suspending the operation of the treaty.

[203]Van der Loo and Blockmans, above no. 192, p. 2.

[204]This can be deducted *a contrario* from section 1(3) of the *European Communities Act* (ECA) 1972.

[205]Koutrakos, 'Brexit and International Trade Treaties: a complex, long, and expensive process', available at: http://lawyers-inforbritain.uk/briefings/brexit-and-international-trade-treaties-a-complex-long-and-expensive-process/, accessed on 20 March 2020.

of scoping out, review and changes to the provisions or clauses of the agreements. Most significantly, this option would still require a certain degree of renegotiation, given the new policy context of the UK as a non-EU member state. In this respect if the UK intends to remain a party to a given mixed agreement a legal instrument, such as a protocol, would be required stating that the UK (as a withdrawing member state) takes over the rights and obligations it previously had under the agreement as an EU member state and that it joins the agreement as a third party.[206] This legal instrument would have to be ratified by the EU, the 27 member states, the UK as a third party and as a withdrawing member state.[207] In this respect, Marise Cremona[208] uses the 2011 EU-Korea FTA[209] and the 2014 EU-Canada Comprehensive Economic Trade Agreement (CETA)[210] to illustrate this point. She maintains that the former could become an EU-Korea-UK FTA and the latter could become the EU-Canada-UK agreement. This "continuity strategy"—as she defines it—or "status quo" option would have the significant advantage of reducing the shock of suddenly ceasing to have FTA-status with many third countries that, in turn, may welcome the continuity and continued FTA access to the UK market.[211] In this context, attention should be paid to the fit between the EU-third country FTA, on the one hand, and the FTA that is eventually negotiated between the EU and the UK on the other.[212] To this end, the protocol to the third country agreement might have to include a clause ensuring that the EU-UK relations are covered by their bilateral agreement rather than by the EU-third country FTA.[213]

The other possible scenarios is the "renegotiation" option whereby the UK might consider the possibility of negotiating and concluding new trade agreements. The UK could model its trade agreements on the EU's trade agreements' structure and content. Hence, using the 2011 EU-Korea FTA as an example of this alternative scenario, Marise Cremona envisages the possibility of having a UK-Korea FTA that would be closely aligned to the existing EU-Korea FTA.[214]

The advantage of such approach is that the UK could build on the EU's extensive practice in the field of international trade. Moreover, the UK could tailor its trade agreements to the needs and specificities of the partner country concerned. Relying

---

[206]Van Der Loo and Wessel, above no. 100, at 748.

[207]Ibid., at 749; see also Lazowski and Wessel (2016), pp. 623–638.

[208]Cremona (2017), pp. 247–265, at p. 252.

[209]Free Trade Agreement between the European Union and its Member States of the one part, and the Republic of Korea of the other part (EU-Korea FTA) *OJ* [2011] L127/6, 14 May 2011, p. 6; see also Koutrakos, 'Global Britain: trade agreements with the rest of the world', paper presented at the UKLegalFuture, 'Brexit: The Future of International Trade', House of Commons, 9 February 2017.

[210]Comprehensive Economic and Trade Agreement (CETA) between Canada, of the One Part, and the European Union and its Member States of the Other Part, Consolidate Text published 26 September 2014, available at http://trade.ec.europa.eu/doclib/docs/2014/september/tradoc_152806.pdf, accessed on 14 June 2020.

[211]Cremona, above, no. 207, at p. 252.

[212]Ibid., pp. 252–253.

[213]Ibid.

[214]Cremona, above no. 207, at p. 253.

on the EU model with some adjustments could also help the UK in addressing its own economic interests and be of reassurance to businesses, firms and partner countries in terms of continuity as well as tackling legitimacy concerns both on the international and national plane. Linked to this, the UK cannot negotiate trade agreements with third countries until it has left the EU as it remains generally bound by the whole body of EU law during the whole period of negotiations.

At the same time, there is also a series of practical and policy issues that the UK will need to consider. First, the UK's capability to negotiate effectively given that it has not been negotiating trade deals "on its own" for over 40 years and thus the lack of experienced negotiators. Linked to this, in the case of new FTAs the UK will not be able to secure similar levels of reciprocal market access as the EU.[215] Second, the increasing emphasis on so-called "mega-regional" trade agreements and the concomitant reduction of state-to-state bilateral agreements. Third, the duration of negotiations as trade agreements can take a few years to conclude. The UK has been able to start negotiating trade agreements with non-EU countries only since its official departure from the EU on 31 January 2020. Until then, it remained generally bound by the whole body of EU law, in accordance with the principle of sincere cooperation under Article 4(3)[216] TEU as well as the doctrine of supremacy of EU law.[217]

In particular, the practical implications cannot be underestimated as post-Brexit the UK takes on the same trade policy tasks as the EU's Directorate-General for Trade. One of the main challenges, therefore, is the UK's ability to manage and complete the full transition from pre-Brexit trade arrangements to the new international trade landscape as a non-EU country. Given that the withdrawal from the EU is unprecedented uncertainty with regard to the negotiation of future trade agreements remains. Many of the aspects discussed above remain the focus of ongoing and complex negotiations between the EU-27 and the UK.[218] Amid much uncertainty, it

---

[215]The principle of sincere cooperation is discussed further below, sect. 3.5.6.1.

[216]For a discussion of the doctrine of supremacy of EU Law, see Capik (2016), pp. 379–420. The UK's Supreme Court confirmed the UK's obligation of being bound by the primacy of EU law until its exit from the Union in the *Miller* case, see *R (on the application of Miller) v Secretary of State for Exiting the European Union* [2017] UKSC 5. In particular, it held that 'Following the coming into force of the 1972 Act [ECA], the normal rule is that any domestic legislation must be consistent with EU law. In such cases, EU law has primacy as a matter of domestic law, and legislation which is inconsistent with EU law from time to time is to that extent ineffective in law' (para. 67).

[217]Cremona, above no. 207, at p. 253.

[218]An analysis of the possible future legal framework between the Union and the UK is beyond the scope of this chapter. On alternatives to EU membership, see among others, HM Government, 'The Future Relationship with the EU. The UK's Approach to Negotiations', February 2020, available at: https://assets.publishing.service.gov.uk/government/uploads/system/uploads/attachment_data/file/868874/The_Future_Relationship_with_the_EU.pdf, accessed on 20 March 2020; HM Government, 'Report on Alternatives to Membership: Possible Models for the United Kingdom Outside the European Union', March 2016, available at: https://www.gov.uk/government/uploads/system/uploads/attachment_data/file/504604/Alternatives_to_membership_-_possible_models_for_the_UK_outside_the_EU.pdf, accessed on 20 March 2020; Lazowski (2012), pp. 523–540; Tobler (2016), pp. 275–294; van der Wel and Wessel, above no. 184.

is clear that the UK needs to give further careful consideration to various timing and sequencing issues in the management of the transition from a situation of pre-Brexit in which it was an EU member state to the new post-Brexit scenario in which it has acquired the status of third country vis-à-vis the EU.

3.5.5.3 The United Kingdom and the World Trade Organization

A related and moot question is whether the UK will have to renegotiate key aspects of its WTO rights and obligations.[219] Answering this question is particularly important in consideration of the fact that since its withdrawal from the EU the great majority of its trading relations with most of its trading partners are to be regulated by WTO law. In general terms, after Brexit the EU will no longer be responsible for exercising the UK's rights and obligations as a WTO member. Achieving continuity of WTO protection is thus a priority for the British government to avoid that, among others, the EU-27 imposes prohibitive tariffs on UK exports or that they selectively discriminate against British firms particularly in the service sector.

Before Brexit some argued that the UK would be in the same position as a country that is seeking to accede the WTO for the first time,[220] and that it would have to sit down and negotiate its terms of membership with the other WTO members who would have a power of veto over the outcome of these negotiations.[221]

However, as Bartels correctly maintains, with regard to the multilateral WTO agreements the UK's rights and obligations are not contingent on its EU membership.[222] Hence, Brexit will not result in the UK losing its status as a WTO member and it will not need to accede again to the WTO. However, even though it is a WTO member as well as a founding member of the 1947 General Agreement on Tariffs and Trade (GATT; the WTO's predecessor),[223] the UK has not been conducting its independent trade policy at the WTO, as the EU has been a member of the WTO since the latter's entry into force and it has exclusive competence in the field of external trade policy via its CCP. Moreover, and linked to this, even though it is a member of the WTO the UK is in an irregular position because it does not have its

[219]For a detailed analysis, see I. Willemyns and M. Koekkoek, 'The legal consequences of Brexit from an international economic law perspective', Leuven Centre for Global Governance Studies, Working Paper No. 188, June 2017, pp. 5–21.

[220]P. Koutrakos, 'What does Brexit mean for the UK in WTO?', 12 July 2016, available at: www.monckton.com/brexit-mean-uk-wto/, accessed on 20 March 2020.

[221]P. Ungphakorn, 'Nothing simple about UK regaining WTO status post-Brexit,' 27 June 2016, http://www.ictsd.org/opinion/nothing-simple-about-uk-regaining-wto-status-post-brexit, accessed on 20 March 2020; C. Gammage, 'UK Trade after Brexit: Is the WTO a suitable alternative?', http://legalresearch.blogs.bris.ac.uk/2016/06/uk-trade-after-brexit-is-the-wto-a-suitable-alternative/, accessed on 20 March 2020.

[222]L. Bartels, 'The UK's status in the WTO after Brexit', University of Cambridge, Faculty of Law, Working Paper September 2016, http://papers.ssrn.com/sol3/papers.cfm?abstract_id=2841747, accessed on 20 March 2020.

[223]General Agreement on Tariffs and Trade, Oct. 30, 1947, 61 Stat. A-11, 55 U.N.T.S. 194 [hereinafter GATT].

own "schedules".[224] The WTO Agreements assume that every WTO member has its own "goods schedule" and its own "services schedule".[225] However, the UK's item-by-item commitments have been part of the consolidated EU-28 goods and services schedules. The UK does not have individual schedules, although the exercise of WTO rights is not explicitly conditioned on having fully valid individual schedules. That said, there has been a lack of clarity in relation to the UK's specific obligations in certain areas, which has been of some concern to other WTO members that export to the UK.[226] Bartels has always been of the view that even though the UK would need to submit a new schedule of commitments, objections to certification by other WTO members would not have any legal consequences, as certification is not required for a schedule, or a change in a schedule, to be legally effective.

Hence, in the summer of 2018 the UK presented its WTO schedule for goods as an outright amendment of the EU's schedule for goods, keeping its tariff on goods as they were while a member of the EU.[227] The UK has decided to keep the EU's Common External Tariff (CET) as its bound rate but is offering a zero applied rate on 87% of imported goods, in compliance with WTO rules. The remaining 13% of imported goods include vehicles which carry a 10% tariff. Some WTO members, most of whom were agricultural exporters, demanded renegotiation of the UK's share of agricultural tariff quotas within that schedule but the UK can trade on an uncertified schedule.[228] In December 2018 the UK submitted its draft schedule of commitments on services to the WTO.[229] As Collins posits, 'the UK services schedules should come into effect on an uncertified basis upon Brexit, regardless of whether objections are raised during the review period.'[230] In any event, post-Brexit UK exports are likely

[224] WTO negotiations produce general rules that apply to all members, and specific commitments made by individual member governments. The specific commitments are listed in documents called "schedules of concessions", which reflect specific tariff concessions and other commitments that they have given in the context of trade negotiations, such as the Uruguay Round.

[225] This assumption is reflected in Article II of the GATT and Articles XVI of the GATS.

[226] T. Sebastian, 'The WTO Option', paper presented at the UK Legal Future Event: Brexit: The Future of International Trade, House of Commons, 8 February 2017.

[227] WTO, 'United Kingdom submits draft schedule to the WTO outlining post-Brexit goods commitments', 24 July 2018, available at: https://www.wto.org/english/news_e/news18_e/mark_24jul18_e.htm, accessed on 20 March 2020.

[228] Collins (2019), pp. 238–252, at p. 243.

[229] WTO, Council for Trade in Services, Communication from the United Kingdom of Great Britain and Northern Ireland. Certification of Schedule of Specific Commitments, S/C/W/380, 3 December 2018, available at: https://docs.wto.org/dol2fe/Pages/FE_Search/FE_S_S009-DP.aspx?language=E&CatalogueIdList=259448,258652,255028,250414,250178,250169,249967,248583,248467,243365&CurrentCatalogueIdIndex=4&FullTextHash=&HasEnglishRecord=True&HasFrenchRecord=True&HasSpanishRecord=True, accessed on 20 March 2020; see also WTO, Council for Trade in Services, Communication from the United Kingdom of Great Britain and Northern Ireland. Certification of Schedule of Specific Commitments, Corrigendum, S/C/W/380, 13 December 2018, available at: https://docs.wto.org/dol2fe/Pages/FE_Search/FE_S_S009-DP.aspx?language=E&CatalogueIdList=259448,258652,255028,250414,250178,250169,249967,248583,248467,243365&CurrentCatalogueIdIndex=3&FullTextHash=&HasEnglishRecord=True&HasFrenchRecord=True&HasSpanishRecord=True, accessed on 20 March 2020. In January 2019, Russia, Taiwan and Costa Rica opposed the UK's draft schedule for GATS schedule.

[230] Collins, above no. 226, at p. 243.

to be protected under WTO rules even if the UK is unable to regularise its position in the WTO by establishing valid goods and services schedules by the end of the negotiation process. In addition, in February 2019 WTO members have confirmed that the UK will be able to rejoin the WTO plurilateral Government Procurement Agreement (GPA)[231] as an independent member. So, the position of the UK within the WTO after Brexit could remain the same as it is at present.[232]

This matter aside, and in more general terms, on withdrawal from the EU, the UK will have to adapt to a different institutional and legal framework in which the detailed regulatory framework of the EU consisting of common rules is absent and replaced with one where there are only general rules and a system largely based on complaints and retaliation between opposing members.[233]

3.5.6 The Democratising Role of the European Parliament and the Promotion of Non-commercial Objectives in the Common Commercial Policy

The TL reform has led to a parliamentarization and normalization of the negotiation and conclusion of international trade agreements whilst the over-all structure remains largely untouched. The European Commission retains the sole right to propose, conduct and conclude negotiations, with the Council's authorization but the EP has acquired a stronger role in relation to the conclusion of international agreements. This specific reform of the CCP is of great significance given that, at EU level, the EP represents a formally independent voice for EU citizens.[234] The procedure has been changed in relation to two key aspects. First, the EP has been given a right to be informed at all stages of the procedure for adopting international agreements.[235]

---

[231] The 1994 Agreement on Government Procurement (GPA) is available at: https://www.wto.org/english/docs_e/legal_e/gpr-94_01_e.htm, accessed on 20 March 2020; the 2012 revised GPA, is available at: https://www.wto.org/english/docs_e/legal_e/gpr-94_01_e.htm, accessed on 20 March 2020.

[232] For further discussion, see G. Messenger, 'Membership of the World Trade Organisation' in Dougan (2017b), pp. 225–245, at pp. 228–230. However, the situation is different with regard to the division of tariff-rate quotas and agricultural goods, see further pp. 230–231.

[233] Ibid, p. 244.

[234] On the powers of the EU Parliament in the external relations of the EU post-Lisbon, see C. Eckes, 'How the European Parliament's Participation in International Relations Affects the Deep Tissue of the EU's Power Structures', Jean Monnet Working Paper 12/14; K. Raube and J. Wouters, 'The Many Facets of Parliamentary Involvement and Interaction in EU External Relations', Leuven Centre for Global Governance Studies, Working Paper No. 174—April 2016.

[235] Article 218(10) TFEU which provides that: 'The European Parliament shall be immediately and fully informed at all stages of the procedure' and, specifically for international trade agreements, Article 207(3) subpara. 3 TFEU; the last limb provides that: 'The Commission shall report regularly to the special committee and to the European Parliament on the progress of negotiations'; see also the Framework Agreement on Relations between the European Parliament and the Commission, OJ [2010] L304/47, 20.11.2010, Annex 11, which goes beyond the strict wording of the Treaty on

Even though the European Commission already used to inform the EP on trade issues on the basis of an inter-institutional agreement,[236] the additional reference to the EP in Article 207(3) TFEU enhances its role because this provision makes the requirement of informing the EP legally binding. The provision requires the European Commission to inform the EP in the same way as the Council's TPC on trade negotiations. Given that the European Commission consults with this committee on a weekly basis, the inclusion of the EP in Article 207(3) TFEU goes beyond previous practice and it illustrates how the EP plays an active role in EU external trade policy post-Lisbon.

Second, with regard to the conclusion of international agreements the TL introduced other important changes. In particular, Article 218 TFEU includes two forms of parliamentary participation in the conclusion of international agreements. As a general rule, the EP needs to be consulted before the Council concludes an agreement.[237] The only exception to this rule concerns agreements relating exclusively to the CFSP. However, no exception exists for trade agreements. This distinguishes the TFEU from the TEC, which excluded trade agreements from parliamentary consultation. The EP has also acquired a general power of veto by either giving consent or rejecting international agreements.[238] Parliamentary consent is required in five specific categories.[239]

---

the Functioning of the EU thereby strengthening the European Parliament's role in the negotiations and conclusion of international agreements. It could be argued that this agreement is an expression of the duty of sincere cooperation under Article 4(3) TEU and the principle of inter-institutional balance as per Article 13(2) TEU; see also Case C-658/11 *European Parliament v Council* ECLI: EU:C:2014:2025 (the *Mauritius* case).

[236] See Framework Agreement on Relations between the European Parliament and the Commission, above no. 234.

[237] Article 218(6) subpara. 2(b) TFEU, which provides that: 'After consulting the European Parliament in other cases. The European Parliament shall deliver its opinion within a time-limit which the Council may set depending on the urgency of the matter. In the absence of an opinion within that time-limit, the Council may act.'

[238] Article 218(6)(a) (i)-(v) TFEU which provides that: 'The Council, on a proposal by the negotiator, shall adopt a decision concluding the agreement.

Except where agreements relate exclusively to the common foreign and security policy, the Council shall adopt the decision concluding the agreement:

(a) after obtaining the consent of the European Parliament in the following cases:

(i) association agreements;

(ii) agreement on Union accession to the European Convention for the Protection of Human Rights and Fundamental Freedoms;

(iii) agreements establishing a specific institutional framework by organising cooperation procedures;

(iv) agreements with important budgetary implications for the Union;

(v) agreements covering fields to which either the ordinary legislative procedure applies, or the special legislative procedure where consent by the European Parliament is required.'; compare with former Article 300(3) subpara. 2 TEC which provides that: 'By way of derogation from the previous subparagraph, agreements referred to in Article 310, other agreements establishing a specific institutional framework by organising cooperation procedures, agreements having important budgetary implications for the Community and agreements entailing amendment of an act adopted under the procedure referred to in Article 251 shall be concluded after the assent of the European Parliament has been obtained.'

[239] Article 218(6) subpara. 2(a) TFEU.

Among others, parliamentary consent is necessary for 'agreements covering fields to which either the ordinary legislative procedure applies, or the special legislative procedure where consent by the Parliament is required.'

It is noticeable, however, that the EP cannot introduce amendments to the text of the proposed agreement but only entirely approve it or entirely reject it. There is thus no *ex ante* formal control of the EP envisaged in Article 218 TFEU.[240]

In spite of this limitation, since the entry into force of the TL the EP has used its increased powers forcefully and it has refused to give its consent to various international agreements such as the Terrorist Finance Tracking Program (TFTP) with the US[241] to protect data protection rights of EU citizens[242] and the multilateral Anti-Counterfeiting Trade Agreement (ACTA)[243] for potential threat to civil liberties.[244] Similarly, the EP refused to give its consent to the EU-Morocco Fisheries Partnership Agreement[245] chiefly because further to the 2002 Opinion of the UN Legal Counsel Hans Corell there was no evidence in the agreement that the fishery activities were to the benefit of, and according to, the wishes of the people of Western Sahara.[246]

The EP's increased role and visibility in EU external relations has also contributed to furthering the social dimension of EU international trade agreements. In December 2011 the EP voted to block the textile agreement between the EU and Uzbekistan for

---

[240] Ripoll Servent (2014), pp. 568–586.

[241] Agreement between the European Union and the United States of America on the processing and transfer of Financial Messaging Data from the European Union to the United States for purposes of the Terrorist Finance Tracking Program, OJ [2010] L8/11, 13.1.2010.

[242] European Parliament, P7 TA(2010)0029 Legislative Resolution of 11 February 2010 on the proposal for a Council decision on the conclusion of the Agreement between the European Union and the United States of America on the processing and transfer of Financial Messaging Data from the European Union to the United States for purposes of the Terrorist Finance Tracking Program (05305/1/2010 REV 1—C7-0004/2010–2009/0190(NLE)).

[243] Council Decision on the Conclusion of the Anti-Counterfeiting Trade Agreement between the European Union and its Member States, Australia, Canada, Japan, the Republic of Korea, the United Mexican States, the Kingdom of Morocco, New Zealand, the Republic of Singapore, the Swiss Confederation and the United States of America, 12195/11, 2011.

[244] European Parliament, P7_TA-PROV(2012)0287. Legislative Resolution of 4 July 2012 on the draft Council decision on the conclusion of the Anti-Counterfeiting Trade Agreement between the European Union and its Member States, Australia, Canada, Japan, the Republic of Korea, the United Mexican States, the Kingdom of Morocco, New Zealand, the Republic of Singapore, the Swiss Confederation and the United States of America, 12195/11, 2011-C7-0027/2012-2011/0167(NLE)).

[245] European Parliament, P7_TA(2011)0569, Legislative Resolution of 14 December 2011 on the draft Council decision on the conclusion of a Protocol between the European Union and the Kingdom of Morocco setting out the fishing opportunities and financial compensation provided for in the Fisheries Partnership Agreement between the European Community and the Kingdom of Morocco (11226/2011-C7-0201/2011-2011/0139(NLE)).

[246] Letter dated 29 January 2002 from the Under-Secretary-General for Legal Affairs, the Legal Counsel, addressed to the President of the Security Council, United Nations Security Council, S/2002/161, 12 February 2022, available at: http://www.arso.org/UNlegaladv.htm, accessed on 20 March 2020.

the country's continuous use of a state-sponsored system of cotton production based on forced labour of children and adults.[247]

With the TL the EP has thus acquired renewed democratic legitimation and further monitoring control functions in relation to international agreements that it clearly intends to exercise together with its promotion of human rights generally.

3.5.6.1 The Involvement of National Parliaments in EU Trade Policy

When assessing the overall level of democratic legitimacy of EU external trade policy further to the changes introduced by the TL, there is also another important question, namely, whether the expansion of the scope of the CCP with the concomitant strengthening of the role of the EP has entailed a parallel reduction of the influence of national parliaments in trade negotiations and trade agreements generally. From a broader perspective, it raises the issue of whether the increased importance of the EP in the CCP reduces the need for additional parliamentary scrutiny by national parliaments.

The analysis carried out in the preceding sections showed how a clear demarcation of competencies has significant implications for the distribution of power among EU institutions and *a fortiori* for the distribution of power between EU and national institutions.

When negotiating international trade agreements, no direct role is explicitly envisioned for national parliaments. They will only be required to ratify an international agreement if it does not fall within the scope of the EU's exclusive competence and if it is thus a mixed agreement. Following this approach, it could be argued that the changes brought about by the TL have not substantially decreased the deficit of democratic legitimacy of the CCP despite the increased role of the EP.

However, problems with the ratification of the CETA agreement seem to suggest a more complex scenario. In 2014 the national parliaments of some member states started adopting a more pro-active role vis-à-vis international trade agreements by sending a joint letter to then EU Trade Commissioner, Karel de Gucht. This letter stated that FTAs should be considered as mixed agreements, since they contained provisions that concerned policy areas falling within the competence of the member states. This meant that national legislatures had to be involved in the ratification process of these international agreements thereby increasing the role of national parliaments in the democratic decision making process of the EU.

In October 2016 a small region of southern Belgium, Wallonia, stalled the ratification of CETA. In so doing, and not without drawing criticism from the main

[247]European Parliament Resolution of 15 December 2011 on the draft Council decision on the conclusion of a Protocol to the Partnership and Cooperation Agreement establishing a partnership between the European Communities and their Member States, of the one part, and the Republic of Uzbekistan, of the other part, amending the Agreement in order to extend the provisions of the Agreement to bilateral trade in textiles, taking account of the expiry of the bilateral textiles Agreement (16384/2010—C7-0097/2011–2010/0323(NLE)), P7_TA(2011)0586.

opposition party, the Walloon parliament declared its intention to scrutinize several ongoing as well as concluded negotiations of this agreement.[248]

The Walloon parliament's scrutiny of CETA trade negotiations began in 2014 with a parliamentary inquiry regarding the Investment-State Dispute Settlement (ISDS) Chapter. Subsequently, various resolutions were adopted by this parliament and one in particular contained a set of concrete demands for the Belgian federal government and the European Commission calling, among others, for binding commitments on social and environmental standards and adherence to International Conventions.[249] The resolution specifically instructed the Belgian federal government to vote against the agreement should the afore-mentioned demands not be met and respected. Noteworthy is the fact that almost all debates and questions on CETA contained references to the Transatlantic Trade and Investment Partnership Agreement (TTIP)[250] thus illustrating the politicized nature of the overall debate on CETA and such "mega-regional" trade agreements generally. Subsequently, even the Brussels Parliament as well as the German-speaking Community of Belgium (or Eastern Belgium)[251] weighed in on the CETA and TTIP negotiations with the aim of creating a broader platform against CETA and TTIP. These developments had significant effects on the process of ratification of CETA.

The Council was due to give its consent during a planned visit of Canadian Prime Minister Justin Trudeau. However, the Belgian Government was forced to abstain from giving its vote further to the refusal of the regional governments of Wallonia and Brussels to give their support to CETA. It was only after the intervention of then President of the European Commission Jean-Claude Juncker, then President of the European Council Donald Tusk and then EU Commissioner for Trade Karel de Gucht first and then Cecilia Malmström, and a political compromising solution - with the addition of a Joint Interpretative Instrument[252] and various declarations and

[248] Adriaensen and Neuhold, above no. 167.

[249] Parlement Wallon, 'Résolution sur l'Accord économique et commercial global (AECG)', Session 2015–2016, 25 Avril 2016, available at: http://nautilus.parlement-wallon.be/Archives/2015_2016/RES/212_4.pdf, accessed on 20 March 2020.

[250] Further information is available at: http://ec.europa.eu/trade/policy/in-focus/ttip/, accessed on 20 March 2020; for EU negotiating texts in TTIP, visit: http://trade.ec.europa.eu/doclib/press/index.cfm?id=1230, accessed on 20 March 2020; for further commentary and analysis, see D. Webb, 'The Transatlantic Trade and Investment Partnership', Briefing Paper, No. 06688, 4 December 2015, available at: https://commonslibrary.parliament.uk/research-briefings/sn06688/, accessed on 20 March 2020; Special Issue of Baetens et al. (2016), pp. 323–436, Fahey and Curtin (2014), Part II; de Ville and Siles–Brügge (2016), De Bième and Poletti (2017), pp. 1506–1521, Jančić (2017), pp. 202–221.

[251] In German *Deutschsprachigen Gemeinschaft Belgiens* (DG); in French *Communauté germanophone de Belgique.*

[252] Joint Interpretative Instrument on the Comprehensive Economic and Trade Agreement (CETA) between Canada and the European Union and its Member States, OJ 2017, L 11/3. It should be noted that this document does not change the text of the agreement but is mainly an interpretative tool. It does however provide 'in the sense of Article 31 VCLT, a clear and unambiguous statement of what Canada and the EU and its Member States agreed in a number of CETA provisions.'

statements to the agreement[253] that the stalemate was put to an end. The Council finally ratified the agreement on the 30th of October 2016 followed by the EP's consent on 15 February 2017.

Added to this, the former Minister-President of Wallonia, Paul Magnette, issued a new declaration for the EU's future trade policy, known as the "Namur Declaration". Amongst the many propositions of this declaration there was a call for greater involvement of national parliaments in the discussion of the negotiating mandate as well as the publication of interim results to facilitate parliamentary debate.[254]

Subsequently, in June 2016, more than 200 members of national parliaments once again submitted their request to the European Commission that CETA would have to be ratified by the legislatures of the member states.

Amid the uncertainty generated by the UK's withdrawal from the EU, the European Commission pragmatically conceded that CETA was a "mixed" agreement, thus making the approval of all national parliaments necessary.[255] This situation confirms that the choice for mixity is not always purely legal[256] as confirmed by then EU Trade Commissioner Cecilia Malmström who acknowledged that: 'from a strict legal standpoint, the Commission considers this agreement to fall under exclusive EU competence. However, the political situation in the Council is clear, and we understand the need for proposing it as a "mixed" agreement, in order to allow for a speedy signature.'[257]

Similar situations may arise also in relation to other future international agreements. On a more general note, such events seem to give a more complex picture

---

[253] G. Van der Loo, 'CETA's signature: 38 statements, a joint interpretative instrument and an uncertain future', CEPS Commentary, 31 October 2016, available at: https://www.ceps.eu/ceps-publications/cetas-signature-38-statements-joint-interpretative-instrument-and-uncertain-future/, accessed on 20 March 2020.

[254] The Namur Declaration of 5 December 2016 is available at: http://declarationdenamur.eu/en/index.php/namur-declaration/. The Namur Declaration contains key propositions for any EU negotiation of trade and economic agreements (particularly those forthcoming with the United States), stating that the EU should ensure that there is mandatory:

(1) respect for democratic procedures;

(2) compliance with socio-economic, sanitary, and environmental legislation; and

(3) guaranteed public interests in any dispute resolution mechanism.

This declaration has been signed also by many distinguished scholars, see further: https://www.ejiltalk.org/namur-declaration-of-5-december-2016-an-eu-values-driven-path-to-negotiating-and-concluding-economic-and-trade-agreements/.

[255] The Walloon compromise resulted in Belgium requesting the CJEU to decide on the compatibility of CETA's investor-state dispute settlement provisions (Chapter Eight, Section F) with EU Law, see Opinion 1/17, pending.

[256] Van der Loo and Wessel, above no. 100, at p. 737; in this respect Maresceau maintains that 'if there is political consensus among the Member States that an agreement ought to be mixed, they will almost certainly manage to impose the mixed procedure, particularly by adding provisions which stand on their own and need Member State involvement.' See Maresceau (2010), pp. 11–29, at p. 16.

[257] European Commission Press release, European Commission proposes signature and conclusion of EU-Canada trade deal, Strasbourg, 5 July 2016, available at: http://europa.eu/rapid/press-release_IP-16-2371_en.htm, accessed on 20 March 2020.

about the degree of involvement of member states' parliaments in EU trade policy, particularly when it concerns the conclusion of trade agreements which are highly contentious and where the debate is by nature highly politicized.

These events also force us to examine further the duties attached to the principle of sincere cooperation as per Article 4(3) TEU, particularly the last limb of this provision insofar as member states must 'refrain from any measure which could jeopardize the attainment of the Union's objectives.' In practice, the reality which the EU or a member state is presented with could be quite distant from that offered by the CJEU in its jurisprudence: rather than a mere refusal to ratify an international agreement it might concern a situation whereby it may prove extremely difficult for a member state to comply with said principle due to overwhelming "internal" impediments of a constitutional and institutional nature such as, for example, the outcome of parliamentary procedures or a referendum.[258] The case of Belgium and the ratification of CETA as well as the UK with Brexit are a case in point. This means that both the European Commission and the CJEU should be less stringent with regard to member states' defences in infringement proceedings under Article 258-260 TFEU. The duty of sincere cooperation[259] could be interpreted as entailing

---

[258]It should be noted that a member state's refusal to ratify an international agreement can also block the Union's ratification process if the mixed agreement requires a unanimous vote in the Council. Unanimity is required under one of the exceptions envisaged in Article 218(8) TFEU and in Article 207(4) TFEU. Article 218(8) TFEU provides that: 'The Council shall act by a qualified majority throughout the procedure. However, it shall act unanimously when the agreement covers a field for which unanimity is required for the adoption of a Union act as well as for association agreements and the agreements referred to in Article 212 with the States, which are candidates for accession. The Council shall also act unanimously for the agreement on accession of the Union to the European Convention for the Protection of Human Rights and Fundamental Freedoms; the decision concluding this agreement shall enter into force after it has been approved by the Member States in accordance with their respective constitutional requirements.' Article 207(4) TFEU provides that: 'For the negotiation and conclusion of the agreements referred to in paragraph 3, the Council shall act by a qualified majority.

For the negotiation and conclusion of agreements in the fields of trade in services and the commercial aspects of intellectual property, as well as foreign direct investment, the Council shall act unanimously where such agreements include provisions for which unanimity is required for the adoption of internal rules.

The Council shall also act unanimously for the negotiation and conclusion of agreements:

(a) in the field of trade in cultural and audio-visual services, where these agreements risk prejudicing the Union's cultural and linguistic diversity;

(b) in the field of trade in social, education and health services, where these agreements risk seriously disturbing the national organisation of such services and prejudicing the responsibility of Member States to deliver them.'

[259]This EU law principle can be considered to be a manifestation of the Public International Law obligation found in Article 18 VCLT "to refrain from acts which would defeat the object and purpose of a treaty." Article 18 VCLT entitled 'Obligation not to defeat the object and purpose of a Treaty prior to its entry into force' provides that: 'A State is obliged to refrain from acts which would defeat the object and pur pose of a treaty when: (a) It has signed the treaty or has exchanged instruments constituting the treaty subject to ratification, acceptance or approval, until it shall have made its intention clear not to become a party to the treaty; or (b) It has expressed its consent to be bound by the treaty, pending the entry into force of the treaty and provided that such entry into force is not unduly delayed.

an obligation to initiate the national ratification procedure through parliamentary approval.[260] It can also be read as including a "best efforts" obligation to try to ratify the agreement, in particular after the agreement has been signed.[261] During the negotiation process, and prior to its signature, member states have the possibility to express their concerns or objections with regard to (parts of) a given agreement: this may happen when authorizing the opening of the negotiations and during the adoption of the negotiating directives, in the TPC or when adopting the Council Decision signing the agreement.[262]

Implementing the principle of sincere cooperation may thus require a high degree of pragmatism on the part of EU institutions as well as creativity, in order to identify a satisfactory solution for all, for the purpose of ensuring unity in the international representation of the Union.[263]

3.6 Conclusion

The TL changed the constitutional and substantive landscape of the CCP in a number of significant ways and endorsed the EU as a "power in trade and through trade."[264] To some extent, it may be argued that, while these changes strengthen the EU's exclusive competence as regards the scope of the CCP *rationae materiae*, they also make the Union's external trade policy more federal. However, it remains to be seen whether they also ensure more in-put democracy particularly for the negotiation and ratification of international trade agreements.

The most salient aspect of this reform is that the EU, with the express reference to competence over trade in services and the commercial aspects of intellectual property enshrined in Article 207 TFEU, has acquired a comprehensive external competence, covering all fields of the multilateral trading system. The role of the EU in the formation of the international trading system has thus been significantly strengthened. The abolition of the distinction between trade in goods, trade in services and commercial aspects of intellectual property further integrates the internal market. In addition, the inclusion of FDI within the scope of the EU's competence enables the CCP not only to meet the external objectives of the internal market but also to develop an external economic policy,[265] enhancing the EU's "deep trade agenda".

However, the exact contours of the EU's competences regarding FDI and other new areas of the CCP, such as the commercial aspects of intellectual property rights,

---

[260] Van der Loo and Wessel, above no. 100, at p. 745.

[261] Ibid.

[262] Ibid.

[263] E.g. C-45/07 *Commission v Greece* (IMO) ECLI:EU:C:2009:81, where the CJEU considered the reciprocal nature of the duty of sincere cooperation meaning that also the Union has to cooperate loyally with its Member States (see para. 25).

[264] Meunier and Nicolaïdis (2011), at p. 277.

[265] Villalta Puig and Al-Haddab, above no. 13, at p. 3.

remain disputed and the CJEU will continue to have a pivotal role in shedding further light on the substantive scope of the CCP.

Furthermore, in spite of the expansion of the CCP's substantive scope, the post-Lisbon external relations regime remains unclear as to the exact demarcation of competence. The decision as to the precise division of competences between the EU and its member states' external competences is yet again left to the CJEU.[266] As the chapter showed, mixed agreements remain a 'viable and necessary *modus operandi* for the Union and its member states.'[267]

In addition, other legal questions will continue to arise in relation to the notions of trade in services, commercial aspects of intellectual property and FDI as well as in relation to the correct legal bases of the EU's international trade agreements, particularly with regard to the exact delimitation between trade matters and non-commercial aspects.

At the time of writing, it is not possible to make firm conclusions as to the new regime introduced by the TL and to a large extent much will depend on the further development and implementation of the arrangements introduced by the TL. In addition, the withdrawal of the UK from the EU is likely to have a significant impact on the negotiation and conclusion of future international agreements.

Undoubtedly, the TL represents a major breakthrough with regard to the EU's role as a key global trade negotiator, with the CCP clearly part of its broader external action. This has been achieved by extending non-trade objectives and principles to the EU's external trade policy, which will most probably continue to be ensured by a pro-active European Parliament and more vocal national parliaments. The dynamism that has been characterizing the CCP since its early days is set to remain.

References

Baetens F, Gruni G, Rijpma J (eds) (2016) Legal issues of economic integration, vol 43, issue 4, pp 323–436

IMF (2000) External debt statistics: guide for compilers and users (Draft). IMF, Washington DC

Jančić D (2017) TTIP and legislative-executive relations in EU trade policy. West Eur Polit 40(1):202–221

Documents from International Organisations

International Monetary Fund (IMF)

IMF (2009) Balance of payments and international investment position manual, 6th edn. International Monetary Fund, Washington, DC

[266] Van der Loo and Wessel, above no. 100, at p. 740.

[267] Larik, above no. 103, at 798.

Organisation for Economic Cooperation and Development (OECD)

OECD (2011) Benchmark definition of foreign direct investment, 4th edn, Paris

World Trade Organisation

Agreement on Government Procurement (GPA)

Agreement on Government Procurement (GPA) (1994) is available at https://www.wto.org/english/docs_e/legal_e/gpr-94_01_e.htm. Accessed 20 Mar 2020

Revised Agreement on Government Procurement (GPA) (2020), is available at https://www.wto.org/english/docs_e/legal_e/gpr-94_01_e.htm. Accessed 20 Mar 2020

Council for Trade in Services

WTO, Council for Trade in Services, Communication from the United Kingdom of Great Britain and Northern Ireland. Certification of Schedule of Specific Commitments, S/C/W/380, 3 December 2018. Available at https://docs.wto.org/dol2fe/Pages/FE_Search/FE_S_S009-DP.aspx?language=E&CatalogueIdList=259448,258652,255028,250414,250178,250169,249967,248583,248467,243365&CurrentCatalogueIdIndex=4&FullTextHash=&HasEnglishRecord=True&HasFrenchRecord=True&HasSpanishRecord=True. Accessed 20 Mar 2020

WTO, Council for Trade in Services, Communication from the United Kingdom of Great Britain and Northern Ireland. Certification of Schedule of Specific Commitments, Corrigendum, S/C/W/380/Corr.1, 13 December 2018. Available at https://docs.wto.org/dol2fe/Pages/FE_Search/FE_S_S009-DP.aspx?language=E&CatalogueIdList=259448,258652,255028,250414,250178,250169,249967,248583,248467,243365&CurrentCatalogueIdIndex=3&FullTextHash=&HasEnglishRecord=True&HasFrenchRecord=True&HasSpanishRecord=True. Accessed 20 Mar 2020

WTO, Sectoral Classification List, 10 July 1991, MTN.GNS/W/120, reproduced as part of the Guidelines for the Scheduling of Specific Commitments under the GATS of 23 March 2001, WTO-Document S/L/92

Under-Secretary-General for Legal Affairs

Under-Secretary-General for Legal Affairs, the Legal Counsel, Letter dated 29 January 2002 to the President of the Security Council, United Nations Security Council, S/2002/161, 12 February 2002. Available at: http://www.arso.org/UNlegaladv.htm. Accessed 20 Mar 2020

Press Releases

WTO, 'United Kingdom submits draft schedule to the WTO outlining post-Brexit goods commitments', 24 July 2018. Available at https://www.wto.org/english/news_e/news18_e/mark_24jul18_e.htm. Accessed 20 Mar 2020

Official Documents of the European Union

International Trade Agreements of the European Union

Comprehensive Economic and Trade Agreement (CETA) between Canada, of the One Part, and the European Union and its Member States of the Other Part, Consolidate Text published 26 September 2014. Available at http://trade.ec.europa.eu/doclib/docs/2014/september/tradoc_152806.pdf. Accessed 14 June 2020

Free Trade Agreement between the European Union and its Member States of the one part, and the Republic of Korea of the other part (EU-Korea FTA) *OJ* [2011] L127/6, 14 May 2011, p 6

Council of the European Union

Council Decision on the signing and provisional application of the Geneva Agreement on Trade in Bananas between the European Union and Brazil, Colombia, Costa Rica, Ecuador, Guatemala, Honduras, Mexico, Nicaragua, Panama, Peru and Venezuela and of the Agreement on Trade in Bananas between the European Union and the United States of America, OJ L 141, 9.6.2010, pp 1–2

Council Decision on the Conclusion of the Anti- Counterfeiting Trade Agreement between the European Union and its Member States, Australia, Canada, Japan, the Republic of Korea, the United Mexican States, the Kingdom of Morocco, New Zealand, the Republic of Singapore, the Swiss Confederation and the United States of America, No. 12195/11

European Commission

European Commission, 'Towards a comprehensive European investment policy' 7 July 2010, COM(2010) 343 final

European Commission, Proposal for a Regulation establishing transitional arrangements for bilateral investment treaties between EU Member States and third countries, 7 July 2010, COM(2010) 344 final

European Commission, Proposal for a Regulation of the European Parliament and of the Council establishing a framework for managing financial responsibility linked to investor-state dispute settlement tribunals established by international agreements to which the European Union is party, 21 June 2012, COM(2012) 335 final

European Commission, Communication to the European Parliament, the Council, the European Economic and Social Committee and the Committee of the Regions, *Trade for All—Towards a more responsible trade and investment policy*, 14 Oct 2015, COM(2015) 497 final

European Commission, Press release, 'European Commission proposes signature and conclusion of EU-Canada trade deal', Strasbourg, 5 July 2016, available at: http://europa.eu/rapid/press-release_IP-16-2371_en.htm. Accessed 20 Mar 2020
European Commission, Reflection Paper on *Harnessing Globalisation*, COM(2017) 240 final

European Parliament

European Parliament, Legislative Resolution of 11 February 2010 on the proposal for a Council decision on the conclusion of the Agreement between the European Union and the United States of America on the processing and transfer of Financial Messaging Data from the European Union to the United States for purposes of the Terrorist Finance Tracking Program (05305/1/2010 REV 1 – C7-0004/2010 – 2009/0190(NLE)) P7 TA(2010)0029
European Parliament, Legislative Resolution of 14 December 2011 on the draft Council decision on the conclusion of a Protocol between the European Union and the Kingdom of Morocco setting out the fishing opportunities and financial compensation provided for in the Fisheries Partnership Agreement between the European Community and the Kingdom of Morocco (11226/2011-C7-0201/2011-2011/0139(NLE)) P7_TA(2011)0569
European Parliament, Resolution of 15 December 2011 on the draft Council decision on the conclusion of a Protocol to the Partnership and Cooperation Agreement establishing a partnership between the European Communities and their Member States, on the one part, and the Republic of Uzbekistan, on the other part, amending the Agreement in order to extend the provisions of the Agreement to bilateral trade in textiles, taking account of the expiry of the bilateral textiles Agreement (16384/2010 – C7-0097/2011 –2010/0323(NLE)), P7_TA(2011)0586
European Parliament, Legislative Resolution of 4 July 2012 on the draft Council decision on the conclusion of the Anti-Counterfeiting Trade Agreement between the European Union and its Member States, Australia, Canada, Japan, the Republic of Korea, the United Mexican States, the Kingdom of Morocco, New Zealand, the Republic of Singapore, the Swiss Confederation and the United States of America, 12195/11, 2011-C7-0027/2012-2011/0167(NLE)) P7_TA-PROV(2012)0287

Table of cases

Cases of the Court of Justice of the European Union

Case 181/73 *R & V Haegeman Spri v Belgium*, ECLI:EU:C:1974:41
Case 1/75, *Low Cost Standard*, 1975 E.C.R. 1355
Case 41/76, *Suzanne Criel, nee Donckerwolcke and Henru Schou v. Procureur de la Republique*, 1976 E.C.R. 1921
Joined Cases 3, 4 and 6/76, *Cornelius Kramer and Others* ECR 1279
Joined Cases 3, 4 and 6/76, Kramer ECLI:EU:C:1976:114
Case C-316/91, *Re European Development Fund*, ECLI:EU:C:1994:76
Case C-459/03, *Commission v Ireland*, ECLI:EU:C:2006:345
Joined Cases C-282/04 and C-283/04, *Commission v Netherlands*, ECLI:EU:C:2006:608
Case C-205/06, *Commission v Austria* ECLI:EU:C:2009:118
Case 249/06, *Commission v Sweden*, ECLI:EU:C:2009:119
Case C-118/07, *Commission v. Finland* ECLI:EU:C:2009:715
Case C-45/07, *Commission v Greece* (IMO) ECLI:EU:C:2009:81
Case C-182/08, *Glaxo Wellcome GmbH & Co KG v Finanzamt München II*, ECLI:EU:C:2009:559

Case C-81/09, *Idryma Typou*, EU:C:2010:622
Case C-212/09, *Commission v Portugal*, EU:C:2011:717
Case C-366/10, *Air Transport Association of America v Secretary of State for Energy and Climate Change* [2011] ECR I-13755
Case C-35/11, *Test Claimants in the FII Group Litigation v Commissioners of Inland Revenue, The Commissioners for Her Majesty's Revenue & Customs*, ECLI:EU:C:2012:707
Case C-414/11, *Daiichi Sankyo Co. Ltd and Sanofi-Aventis Deutschland GmbH v DEMO Anonymos Viomichaniki kai Emporiki Etairia Farmakon* ECLI:EU:C:2013:520
Case C-658/11, *European Parliament v Council* ECLI: EU:C:2014:2025 (the *Mauritius* case)
Case C-137/12, *European Commission v Council of the European Union (European Convention on the Legal Protection of Services Based on, Or Consisting of, Conditional Access)*, EU:C:2013:675
Case C-137/12, *European Commission v Council of the European Union* (EU:C:2013:675)
Case C-600/14, *Federal Republic of Germany v Council of the European Union* ECLI:EU:C:2017:935

Opinions of the Court

Opinion 1/75 Local Costs ECLI:EU:C:1975:145
Opinion 1/76, 'Draft Agreement establishing a European laying-up fund for inland waterway vessels' ECLI:EU:C:1977:63
Opinion 1/78 Natural Rubber Agreement ECLI:EU:C:1979:224
Opinion 1/94 WTO ECLI:EU:C:1994:384
Opinion 2/15 on the EU-Singapore Free Trade Agreement ECLI:EU:C:2016:880
Opinion 3/15 on the Marrakesh Treaty ECLI:EU:C:2017:114

Official Documents of the United Kingdom

HM Government, 'The Future Relationship with the EU. The UK's Approach to Negotiations', Feb 2020. Available at https://assets.publishing.service.gov.uk/government/uploads/system/uploads/attachment_data/file/868874/The_Future_Relationship_with_the_EU.pdf. Accessed 20 Mar 2020
HM Government, 'Report on Alternatives to Membership: Possible Models for the United Kingdom Outside the European Union', March 2016. Available at https://www.gov.uk/government/uploads/system/uploads/attachment_data/file/504604/Alternatives_to_membership_-_possible_models_for_the_UK_outside_the_EU.pdf. Accessed 20 March 2020

Books and chapters in books

Adriaensen J (2016) National administrations in EU trade policy. Maintaining the capacity to control. Palgrave Macmillan, London
Adriaensen J, Coleman E (2017) Controlling covert integration in EU Politics. In: Bursens P et al (eds) Complex political decision-making: leadership, legitimacy and communication. Routledge, London, pp 77–95

Ahmed T, Fahey E (eds) (2019) On Brexit. Law, justices and injustices. Elgar Publishing, Cheltenham
Allen D (2012) The common foreign and security policy. In: Jones E, Menon A, Weatherill S (eds) The Oxford handbook of the European union. OUP, Oxford, pp 644–660
Collins D (2019) Brexit and international trade: the aspiration of global Britain. In: Ahmed T, Fahey E (eds) On Brexit. Law, justices and injustices. Elgar Publishing, Cheltenham, pp 238–252
Capik A (2016) Five Decades since Van Gend en Loos and Costa came to town: primacy, direct and indirect effect revisited. In: Łazowski A, Blockmans S (eds) Research handbook on EU institutional law. Elgar Publishing, Cheltenham, pp 379–420
Cremona M (1999) External relations and external competence: the emergence of an integrated policy. In: Craig P, de Búrca G (1999) The evolution of EU law. OUP, Oxford, pp 137–176
Cremona M (2017) UK trade policy. In: Dougan M (ed) The UK after Brexit. Legal and policy challenges. Intersentia, Cambridge, pp 247–265
Dashwood A, Heliskoski J (2000) The classic authorities revisited. In: Dashwood A, Hillion C (eds) The general law of EC external relations. Sweet & Maxwell, London, pp 3–19
Delgado Casteleiro A (2016) The international responsibility of the European Union: from competence to normative control. CUP, Cambridge, pp 195–223
De Luca A (2012) New developments on the scope of the EU common commercial policy under the Lisbon treaty. In: Sauvant KP (ed) Yearbook on international investment law and policy 2010–2011. OUP, Oxford, pp 182–195
de Mestral A (2009–2010) The Lisbon treaty and the expansion of EU competence over foreign direct investment and the implications for investor-state arbitration. In: Sauvant KP (ed) Yearbook on international investment law and policy. OUP, Oxford, pp 365–395
de Ville F, Siles-Brügge G (2016) TTIP—the truth about the transatlantic trade and investment partnership. Polity Press, Cambridge
Dimopoulos A (2011) EU foreign investment law. OUP, Oxford
Dougan M (ed) (2017) The UK after Brexit. Legal and policy challenges. Intersentia, Cambridge
Dougan M (2017) Editor's introduction. In: Dougan M (ed) The UK after Brexit. Legal and policy challenges. Intersentia, Cambridge, pp 1–12
Eeckhout P (2011) EU external relations law. OUP, Oxford
Fahey E, Curtin D (eds) (2014) A transatlantic community of law. CUP, Cambridge
Hillion C, Koutrakos P (eds) (2010) Mixed agreements in EU law revisited—the EU and its member states in the world. Hart Publishing, Oxford
Hoffmeister F (2014) The European Union as an international trade negotiator. In: Koops JA, Macaj G (eds) The European Union as a diplomatic actor. Palgrave MacMillan, London, pp 138–154
Hoffmeister F (2017) Of transferred competence, institutional balance and judicial autonomy—constitutional developments in EU trade policy seven years after Lisbon. In: Czuczai J, Naert F (eds) The EU as a global actor—bridging legal theory and practice. Brill Nijhoff, Leiden, pp 307–336
Klamert M (2013) The principle of loyalty in EU law. OUP, Oxford
Koutrakos P (2015) EU international relations law. Hart Publishing, Oxford
Krajewski M (2008) Of modes and sectors—external relations, internal debates and the special case of (trade in) services. In: Cremona M (ed) New developments in EU external relations law. OUP, Oxford, pp 188–195
Krajewski M (2012) The reform of the common commercial policy. In: Biondi A, Eeckhout P, Ripley S (eds) European Union law after the treaty of Lisbon. OUP, Oxford, pp 292–311
Maresceau M (2010) A typology of mixed bilateral agreements. In: Hillion C, Koutrakos P (eds) Mixed agreements in EU law revisited—the EU and its Member States in the World. Hart Publishing, Oxford, pp 11–29
Melo Araujo BA (2016) The EU deep trade agenda. Law and policy. OUP, Oxford
Messenger G (2017) Membership of the World Trade Organisation. In: Dougan M (ed) The UK after Brexit. Legal and policy challenges. Intersentia, Cambridge, pp 225–245

Müller-Graff PC (2008) The common commercial policy enhanced by the reform of the treaty of Lisbon? In: Dashwood A, Maresceau M (eds) Law and practice of EU external relations. Salient features of a changing landscape. CUP, Cambridge, pp 188–201
Meunier S, Nicolaïdis K (2011) The European Union as a trade power. In: Hill C, Smith M (eds) International relations and the European Union. OUP, Oxford, pp 276–298
Orbie J, Gistelinck M, Kerremans G (2008) The social dimension of EU trade policies. In: Orbie J, Tortilla L (eds) The European Union and the social dimension of globalisation: how the EU influences the World. Routledge, London, pp 148–165
Ortino F, Eeckhout P (2012) Towards an EU policy on foreign direct investment. In: Biondi A, Eeckhout P, Ripley S (eds) European Union law after the treaty of Lisbon. OUP, Oxford, pp 312–330
Rosas A (2000) The European Union and mixed agreements. In: Dashwood A, Hillion C (eds) The general law of EC external relations. Sweet & Maxwell, London, Ch. 13
Schütze R (2002) European constitutional law. CUP, Cambridge
Schütze R (2014) Foreign affairs and the EU constitution. CUP, Cambridge
Weiss F, Steiner S (2013) The investment regime under Article 207 of the TFEU—a legal conundrum: the scope of "foreign direct investment" and the future of intra-EU BITS. In: Baetens F (ed) Investment law within international law. CUP, Cambridge, pp 355–374
Wolf S (2008) The regulation of foreign direct investment under selected WTO agreements. In: Tietje C (ed) International investment protection and arbitration. Berliner Wissenschaftsverlag, Berlin, pp 71–105
Wouters J, Ramopoulos T (2014) Revisiting the Lisbon treaty's constitutional design of EU external relations. In: Rossi LS, Casolari F (eds) The EU after Lisbon: amending or coping with the existing treaties? Springer, Heildeberg, pp 215–239

Journal Articles and Working Papers

Abdelal R, Meunier S (2010) Managed globalisation: doctrine, practice and promise. J Eur Public Policy 17:350–367
Baldwin R (2020) Filling the gap between 21st century trade and 20th century trade rules. World Trade Organisation, Economic Research and Statistics Division, staff working paper ERSD-2011-08, 23 May 2011. https://www.wto.org/english/res_e/reser_e/ersd201108_e.pdf. Accessed 14 June 2020
Bartels L. The EU's human rights obligations in relation to policies with extraterritorial effects. Eur J Int Law 25:1071–1091
Bartels L (2016) The UK's status in the WTO after Brexit. University of Cambridge, Faculty of Law, working paper, Sept 2016. http://papers.ssrn.com/sol3/papers.cfm?abstract_id=2841747. Accessed 20 Mar 2020
Bourgeois JHJ (1998) External relations powers of the European Community. Fordham Int Law J 22(6):S149–173
Brexit Supplement (2016) Ger Law J 17. Available at http://www.germanlawjournal.com/brexit-supplement/
Bungenberg M (2010) Going global? The EU common commercial policy after Lisbon. In: Herrmann C, Terhechte J (eds) European yearbook of international economic law, vol 1, pp 123–151
Bungenberg M, Griebel J, Hindelang S (eds) (2011) Special issue 'International Investment Law and EU Law'. In: European yearbook of international economic law. Springer, Heidelberg
Burgoon B (2009) The distinct politics of "Fair Trade" linkage to labour standards. Eur Foreign Aff Rev 14:643–661

Cannizzaro E (2014) The EU's human rights obligations in relation to policies with extraterritorial effects: a reply to Lorand Bartels. Eur J Int Law 25:1093–1099
Ceyssens J (2005) Towards a common foreign investment policy? Foreign investment in the European Constitution. Legal Issues Econ Integr 32:259–291
Craig P (2016) Brexit: a drama in six acts. Eur Law Rev 4:447–468
De Biève D, Poletti A (2017) Why the transatlantic trade and investment partnership is not (so) new, and why it is also not (so) bad. J Eur Public Policy 10:1506–1521
Devuyst Y (2011) The European Union's competence in international trade after the treaty of Lisbon. Georgia J Int Comp Law 39:639–661
Dimopoulos A (2008) The common commercial policy after Lisbon. Croatian Yearb Eur Law Policy 4:102–131
Dimopoulos A (2010) The effects of the Lisbon treaty on the principles and objectives of the common commercial policy. Eur Foreign Aff Rev 15(2):153–170
Eilmansberger T (2009) Bilateral investment treaties and EU law. Common Mark Law Rev 46(2):383–429
Eckes C. How the European Parliament's Participation in International Relations Affects the Deep Tissue of the EU's Power Structures. Jean Monnet working paper 12/14
Editorial (2005) The CFSP under the EU constitutional treaty—issues of depillarisation. Common Mark Law Rev 42:325–329
Eeckhout P, Frantziou E (2017) Brexit and Article 50 TEU: a constitutionalist reading. Common Mark Law Rev 54:695–734
Gee G, Rubini L, Trybus M (2016) Leaving the EU? The legal impact of "Brexit" on the United Kingdom. Eur Public Law 22:51–56
Gormley L (2017) Brexit—nevermind the whys and wherefores? Fog in the channel, continent cut off! Fordham Int Law J 40:1175–1210
Heliskoski J (2001) Mixed agreements as a technique for organising the international relations of the European Community and its member states. Brill, Martinus Nijhoff Publishers, Leiden
Herrmann C (2010) The treaty of Lisbon expands the EU's external trade and investment powers. ASIL Insights 14:29
Hoffmeister F (2011) The European Union's common commercial policy one year after Lisbon—sea change or business as usual? In: Koutrakos P (ed) The European Union's external relations a year after Lisbon CLEER working paper series, 2011/3, pp 83–96
Karl J (2005) The competence for foreign direct investment: new powers for the European Union? J World Investment Trade 5:413–444
Kleimann D (2017) Reading opinion 2/15: standards of analysis, the Court's discretion, and the legal view of the advocate general. EUI working paper RSCAS 2017/23
Kostakopoulou D (2017) What fractures political Unions? Failed Federation, Brexit and the importance of political commitment. Eur Law Rev 42:339–352
Koutrakos P (2016) Brexit and international treaty-making—editorial. Eur Law Rev 41:1–2
Koutrakos P (2016) Negotiating international trade treaties after Brexit. Eur Law Rev 41:475–478
Koutrakos P (2017) Global Britain: trade agreements with the rest of the world. Paper presented at the UK Legal Future, 'Brexit: The Future of International Trade', House of Commons, 9 Feb 2017
Koutrakos P (ed) The European Union's external relations a year after Lisbon. CLEER working paper series, 2011/3, The Hague
Larik J (2015) No mixed feelings: the post-Lisbon Common Commercial Policy in *Daiichi Sankyo* and *Commission v. Council (Conditional Access Convention)*. Common Mark Law Rev 52:779–800
Lavranos N (2010) New developments in the interaction between international investment law and EU law. Law Pract Int Courts Tribunals 9:409–441
Lazowski A (2012) Withdrawal from the European Union and alternatives to membership. Eur Law Rev 37(5):523–540

Lazowski A, Wessel RA (2016) The external dimension of withdrawal from the European Union. Rev Aff européennes 4:623–638
Leal-Arcas R (2007) Is EC trade policy up to par? A legal analysis over time—Rome Marrakesh, Amsterdam, Nice, and the Constitutional Treaty. Columbia J Eur Law 13:305–399
Lenk H (2015) Challenging the notion of coherence in EU foreign investment policy. Eur J Legal Stud 8:6–20
Lenk H (2017) Mixity in EU foreign trade policy is here to stay: advocate general Sharpston on the allocation of competence for the conclusion of the EU-Singapore Free trade Agreement. Eur Pap 2:357–382
Moskvan D (2016) The European Union's competence on foreign investment: "New and Improved"? San Diego Int Law J 18:241–262
Odermatt J (2017) Brexit and international law: disentangling legal orders. Emory Int Law Rev 31:1052–1073
Parlement Wallon, 'Résolution sur l'Accord économique et commercial global (AECG)', Session 2015–2016, 25 Avril 2016. Available at http://www.meco.lu/wp-content/uploads/2016/04/resolution-wallonisches-Parlament.pdf. Accessed 20 Mar 2020
Raube K, Wouters J (2016) The many facets of parliamentary involvement and interaction in EU external relations. Leuven Centre for Global Governance Studies, working paper No. 174, Apr 2016
Ripoll Servent A (2014) The role of the European parliament in international negotiations after Lisbon. J Eur Public Policy 21:568–586
T. Sebastian, 'The WTO Option', paper presented at the UK legal future event: Brexit: the future of international trade, House of Commons, 9 Feb 2017. Available at: https://www.monckton.com/wp-content/uploads/2017/02/TS-handout-as-sent-for-printing-v2.pdf. Accessed 20 Mar 2020
Sif Tynes D, Lian Haugsdal E (2016) In, out or in-between? The UK as a contracting party to the agreement on the European Economic Area. Eur Law Rev 41:753–765
Tietje C (2009) Die Außenwirtschaftsverfassung der EU nach dem Vertrag von Lissabon. In: Tietje C, Kraft G (eds) Beiträge zum Transnationalen Wirtschaftsrecht 9:16
Tobler C (2016) One of many challenges after "Brexit": the institutional framework of an alternative agreement—lessons from Switzerland and elsewhere? Maastricht J Eur Comp Law 23:275–294
Tridimas T, Eeckhout P (1994) The external competence of the community and the case-law of the court of justice: principle versus pragmatism. Yearb Eur Law 14:143–177
Ungphakorn P (2016) Nothing simple about UK regaining WTO status post-Brexit, 27 June 2016. Available at http://www.ictsd.org/opinion/nothing-simple-about-uk-regaining-wto-status-post-brexit. Accessed 20 Mar 2020
Van der Loo G (2016) CETA's signature: 38 statements, a joint interpretative instrument and an uncertain future. CEPS Commentary, 31 Oct 2016. Available at https://www.ceps.eu/ceps-publications/cetas-signature-38-statements-joint-interpretative-instrument-and-uncertain-future/. Accessed 20 Mar 2020
Van der Loo G, Blockmans S (2016) The impact of Brexit on the EU's international agreements. Centre for European Policy Studies (CEPS), Friday 15 July 2016. Available at https://www.ceps.eu/ceps-publications/impact-brexit-eus-international-agreements/. Accessed 20 Mar 2020
Van Der Loo G, Wessel RA (2017) The non-ratification of mixed agreements: legal consequences and solutions. Common Mark Law Rev 54:735–770
Van der Wel M and R. A. Wessel, 'The Brexit Roadmap: Mapping the Choices and Consequences during the EU/UK withdrawal and Future Relationship Negotiations', CLEER 2017/5 available at: http://www.asser.nl/cleer/publications/, accessed on 20 March 2020
Van Elsuwege P (2010) EU External Action after the Collapse of the Pillar Structure: in search of a new balance between delimitation and consistency. Common Mark Law Rev 47:987–1019
Velluti S (2016) The promotion and integration of human rights in EU external relations. Utrecht J Int Eur Law 32(82):41–68. https://doi.org/10.5334/ujiel.342
Villalta Puig PG, Al-Haddab B (2011) The common commercial policy after Lisbon: an analysis of the reforms. Eur Law Rev 36:289–301

Webb D (2015) The transatlantic trade and investment partnership. Commons Briefing Paper, No. 06688, 4 Dec 2015. Available at https://commonslibrary.parliament.uk/research-briefings/sn06688/. Accessed 20 Mar 2020
Wessel RA (2016) You can check out any time you like, but can you really leave? On "Brexit" and leaving international organisations. Int Organ Law Rev 2:197–209
Willemyns I, Koekkoek M (2017) The legal consequences of Brexit from an international economic law perspective. Leuven Centre for Global Governance Studies, working paper No. 188, June 2017
Woolcock S (2010) The EU approach to international investment policy after the Lisbon treaty. European Parliament, Directorate-General for External Policies of the Union, Directorate B, Policy Department, Brussels, Oct 2010. Available at http://www.europarl.europa.eu/RegData/etudes/etudes/join/2010/433854/EXPO-INTA_ET(2010)433854_EN.pdf. Accessed 14 June 2020
Ziegler AR (2013) The new competence of the European Union in the area of Foreign Direct Investment (FDI): a third country perspective. In: Bungenberg M, Hermann C (eds) Common commercial policy after Lisbon special issue, European yearbook of international economic law. Springer, Heidelberg, pp 235–243

Other

Blogposts

Ankersmit L (2017) Opinion 2/15 and the future of mixity and ISDS. Europe and the World: a law review, 5 June 2017. Available at http://blogs.ucl.ac.uk/europe-and-the-world-journal/tag/opinion-215. Accessed 20 Mar 2020
Delgado Casteleiro A (2016) Opinion 2/15 on the scope of EU external trade policy: some background information before next week's hearing, EU Analysis, 6 Sept 2016. Available at http://eulawanalysis.blogspot.co.uk/2016/09/opinion-215-on-scope-of-eu-external.html. Accessed 14 June 2020
Gammage C (2016) UK trade after Brexit: is the WTO a suitable alternative? University of Bristol Law School Blog, 21 June 2016. Available at http://legalresearch.blogs.bris.ac.uk/2016/06/uk-trade-after-brexit-is-the-wto-a-suitable-alternative/. Accessed 20 Mar 2020
Koutrakos P (2016) What does Brexit mean for the UK in WTO? 12 July 2016. www.monckton.com/brexit-mean-uk-wto/. Accessed 20 Mar 2020
Peers S (2016) The EU's future trade policy starts to take shape: the Opinion on the EU/Singapore FTA. EU law analysis, 21 Dec 2016. Available at http://eulawanalysis.blogspot.co.uk/2016/12/the-eus-future-trade-policy-starts-to.html. Accessed 14 June 2020
Sarmiento D (2017) The Singapore Silver Bullet. Verfassungsblog, 17 May 2017. Available at http://verfassungsblog.de/the-singapore-silver-bullet/. Accessed 14 June 2020
Thym D (2017) Mixity after Opinion 2/15: judicial confusion over shared competences. Verfassungsblog, 31 May 2017. Available at http://verfassungsblog.de/mixity-after-opinion-215-judicial-confusion-over-shared-competences/. Accessed 14 June 2020

Conference Papers

Adriaensen J, Neuhold C (2017) Shaking the institutional foundations: national parliamentary involvement in EU trade negotiations. Paper presented at the UACES 47th annual conference, 4–6 Sept 2017

Voogsgeerd HH (2016) The nature of the asymmetry between trade and labour rights in trade agreements of the EU. Paper presented at the European Union in International Affairs (EUIA) Biennial conference, Brussels, Belgium, 11–13 May 2016

Online sources

On Brexit

European Commission

https://ec.europa.eu/info/european-union-and-united-kingdom-forging-new-partnership_en

UK Parliament Research Analysis

https://www.parliament.uk/brexit

The UK in a Changing Europe

https://ukandeu.ac.uk/

Chapter 4
EU Political Conditionality as a Tool for the Promotion and Protection of Non-trade Values in Non-EU Countries

Francesca Martines

4.1 Introduction: Unpacking the Notion of External Conditionality

Conditionality has different meanings in different situations. Conditionality is applied in different policy areas such as lending or investment programmes, trade agreements and development cooperation aid.[1] In international economic relations, for example, it indicates a performance-based aid allocation by international organizations such as the World Bank or the International Monetary Fund (IMF).[2] In this financial and economic context, conditionality requires governments seeking aid to agree to economic policy adjustments defined by the donors. Conditionality can also refer to the process of tying aid to a specific use or it can describe projects and programmes aimed at supporting democracy or human rights protection.[3]

This chapter intends to examine "political" conditionality to distinguish it from economic conditionality[4] and, in particular, the European Union (EU)'s toolkit in the

---

[1] See Velluti (2016), referring to a form of conditionality provided for in agreements with Eastern Partners whereby they can gain additional access to the EU single market should they successfully implement their legislative approximation commitments. This is an example of positive conditionality, which differs from non-trade values conditionality.

[2] Buira (2003), Koeberle et al. (2005), Santiso (2001)), Alexander (2005).

[3] The European Instrument for Democracy and Human Rights (EIDHR), for example, was created to support projects in areas of human rights, fundamental freedoms and democracy in non-EU countries. Regulation (EU) No 235/2014 of the European Parliament and of the Council of 11 March 2014 establishing a financing instrument for democracy and human rights worldwide OJ [2014] L77/85. Dobreva 2015).

[4] Economic conditionality is the linking of benefits to the fulfilment of macro-economic conditions or the adoption of certain economic policies by the recipient state. Political conditionality is an expression that refers to different values such as democracy, human rights, rule of law. The reference to human rights alone seems reductive and does not take into account the complexity of conditionality tools. The expression 'political conditionality' is also used by Koch (2015).

S. Velluti, *The Role of the EU in the Promotion of Human Rights and International Labour Standards in Its External Trade Relations*,
https://doi.org/10.1007/978-3-030-56748-4_4

framework of its external trade policy,[5] which is used to promote non-trade values[6] with a focus on human rights, democracy, rule of law, in EU agreements and in the General System of Trade Preferences (GSP). Reference will also be made to financial aid instruments for the benefit of third countries.[7]

In Sect. 4.1 the chapter defines conditionality in general terms, clarifying its structure and rationale, explaining the difference between positive and negative conditionality and highlighting the relevance and difficulties of establishing monitoring mechanisms. This provides a basis for examining EU political conditionality tools.

---

[5]Conditionality is also applied within the EU, the Economic and Monetary Union (EMU) being a good example of how economic conditionality is applied. In the EMU context, criteria of convergence must be fulfilled for states wishing to join. Another example is in relation to European structural and investment (ESI) Funds, see Regulation (EU) n. 1303/2013 of the European Parliament and of the Council of 17 December 2013 laying down common provisions on the European Regional Development Fund, the European Social Fund, the Cohesion Fund, the European Agricultural Fund for Rural Development and the European Maritime and Fisheries Fund and laying down general provisions on the European Regional Development Fund, the European Social Fund, the Cohesion Fund and the European Maritime and Fisheries Fund and repealing Council Regulation (EC) No 1083/2006 in OJ [2013] L 347/340. Recently, a new form of conditionality can be detected in the proposed regulation on the protection of the Union budget in case of generalized deficiencies as regards the rule of law in the member states. Proposal for a regulation of the European Parliament and the Council on the protection of the Union's budget in case of generalised deficiencies as regards the rule of law in the Member States, COM (2018) 324 final. Whereas EU spending is conditional upon its proper use, requiring consistency with the objectives of the programs, and administrative soundness, the mechanism proposed is based on the 'necessity to respect the rule of law as a precondition for ensuring compliance with the principle of sound financial management of EU funds', see Court of Auditors, Opinion 1/2018 concerning the proposal of 2 May 2018 for a regulation of the European Parliament and of the Council on the protection of the Union's budget in case of generalised deficiencies as regards the rule of law in the Member States, paragraph 10. Whereas payments could be suspended in the case of the excessive deficit procedure and *ex-ante* conditionality was introduced for the 2014–2020 funding period, the new mechanism centres on respect for the rule of law. Heinemann (2018).

[6]On non-trade values see Chap. 2 of this book and in particular Sect. 2.3. Human rights conditionality is the most widespread expression but by using conditionality tools the EU intends to promote democracy, rule of law besides human rights. The wording non-trade values conditionality will also be employed in this paragraph to underline the scope of these tools.

[7]The rules for external financial assistance are contained in several EU financial instruments. These are: Instrument for Pre-accession Assistance; the European Neighbourhood Instrument; the Development Cooperation Instrument; the Partnership Instrument for cooperation with third countries; the European Instrument for Democracy and Human Rights. With the exception of the Partnership Instrument, they provide for unilateral suspension in cases of non-compliance with fundamental rights principles. For example, Article 21 of the Pre-accession instrument (IPA I) established: 'Respect for the principles of democracy, the rule of law and for human rights and minority rights and fundamental freedoms is an essential element for the application of this Regulation and the granting of assistance under it'. Council Regulation (EC) (2006). The new pre-accession regulation does not contain the same condition, but see preamble, paragraph 7 of Regulation (EU) No 231/2014 of the European Parliament and of the Council of 11 March 2014 establishing an Instrument for Pre-accession Assistance (IPA II) OJ [2014] L77/11. The European Commission has proposed to merge eight existing financial instruments into a single instrument called Neighbourhood, Development and International Cooperation Instrument (NDICI) to avoid gaps and overlaps. COM (2018). Immenkamp (2020).

After an overview of EU unilateral and conventional conditionality mechanisms (Sect. 4.2), the analysis focuses on the behaviour required from recipient countries in conditionality clauses contained in trade agreements (Sect. 4.3) and in unilateral trade arrangements (Sect. 4.4), respectively. Section 4.5 examines certain aspects and problems associated with the application of EU conditionality, whereas Sect. 4.6 looks at monitoring and enforcement mechanisms. The conclusions (Sect. 4.7) bring together the main points and findings of the chapter and offer some general reflections on the function and limits of conditionality clauses.

4.1.1 Structure and Rationale of Conditionality Mechanisms

External conditionality is defined here as the granting of an advantage, or the withdrawal of a benefit, by an international subject (an international organization or a state) made contingent upon a pre-defined behaviour by another state (not a member of the international organization).

Conditionality thus requires: (i) two subjects: the donor and the recipient or beneficiary; (ii) a benefit (such as financial aid, trade advantages, visa facilitation, access to the donor's market) or a disadvantage (withdrawal of a benefit, like trade preferences, suspension of a treaty in force) connected to (iii) a required behaviour, defined unilaterally or by mutual agreement between the donor and the recipient. The triggering of conditionality requires (iv) the setting up of monitoring procedures by the donor country.

As far as its rationale is concerned, conditionality is considered a leverage mechanism[8] to orientate behaviour: 'pro-social behaviour is rewarded and anti-social behaviour is punished.'[9]

Conditionality is founded on the assumption that the recipient country makes a cost-benefit calculation: for example the benefit that derives from the incentive (trade preferences, financial aid) is balanced with the cost of compliance (application of labour standards, economic reforms); conversely, the cost of punishment (the withdrawal of benefits) is balanced with the cost of compliance. When non-compliance is more costly than compliance, conditions are respected, or criteria fulfilled.

Any political choice is based on a cost-benefit analysis. However, conditionality 'is a means to "manipulate" cost-benefit calculations through creating incentives (positive and negative).'[10] Thus, in order to work, conditionality needs to offer a benefit constituting sufficient pull for behavioural change by the recipient, or to provide a sanction more costly than non-compliance.

---

[8]The structure followed in this paragraph is inspired by S. Koch, above n. 4; for a definition see also Dorussen (2001).

[9]Schimmelfennig et al. (2003).

[10]Börzel and Risse (2004), available http://www.atasp.de/downloads/tandt_stanford_final.pdf. Accessed 13 June 2020.

Conditionality usually works well when the donor is stronger (from an economic and/or political point of view) than the recipients. For example, with reference to the United States (US) GSP (a unilateral trade instrument), it was remarked: 'workers' rights conditionality works reasonably well in the GSP program because the target countries are mostly small and they perceive that denying US demands will have higher costs than complying with them'.[11]

Costs and benefits have to be interpreted broadly. They are not measured only in economic terms, but also in terms of participation,[12] political or coordination gains.[13] For example, the benefits of EU membership (going well beyond a mere economic gain), outweigh the costs for complying with the Copenhagen criteria and the required domestic reforms for candidate countries.[14]

The cost of non-compliance with the required behaviour can also be reputational when the (sanctioned) conduct consists in the violation of international law. In this case, however, the reputational cost is generated by non-compliance and not by the "sanction" triggered by the negative conditionality mechanism, namely, suspension of benefit, withdrawal of aid, suspension or termination of agreement. However, the sanction certifies non-compliance and thus contributes to the loss of reputation.[15] The ensuing possible termination of the relationship would (further) affect the reputational standing of the recipient state.[16]

Conversely, positive conditionality, which might consist in becoming a member of an organization, can be valued in terms of improvement of the beneficiary's global standing and reputation. Conditionality can be measured according to a cost-benefit analysis or can be the expression of an actor identity or beliefs.[17] For instance in the

---

[11]Elliott and Freeman (2003).

[12]Gustafsson (2017).

[13]Gustafsson, ibid. 1213, For the Author coordination gains are understood as the "efficiency gains arising from cooperation and agreement". See also Guzman.

[14]Political conditions of accession are defined in Article 49 TEU, with reference to Article 2 TEU. The Copenhagen criteria were established by the Copenhagen European Council (21–22 June 1993) and by the Madrid European Council (15–16 December 1995). In order to be admitted to the EU, a state, besides *political criteria*, must satisfy a set of economic criteria (the existence of functional market economies and the capacity to compete with the economies of the EU member countries), *legal criteria* (adoption of *acquis communautaire*, that is the capacity of the country to transpose the EU legislation into the national one), and *administrative criteria*, (a candidate state is required to ensure the functionality of the public administrations and judicial systems). For an examination of the evolution of the accession criteria see Hillion (2004), Janse (2018), Dimitrova (2002, 2004).

[15]Keohane (1984); according to the Keohane: 'Regimes rely not only on decentralized enforcement through retaliation but on government desires to maintain their reputations", at 108. See also Guzman (n. 13) 71. Critically see Downs and Jones(2002). Downs and Jones maintain that: "reputational implications of non-compliance are narrower than much of the literature suggests. A reputation for unreliability might hinder cooperation because promises appear non-credible. Reputation is important for predicting future behavior, not for punishing past actions'.

[16]Gustafsson, above n. 12.

[17]States are moved by rational choice assumption but also norm-based considerations. Guzman, above n. 13. See also Saltnes (2013).

case of the EU, political conditionality criteria contribute to the EU (self)definition as a normative actor.[18]

The use of conditionality presupposes that the donor is also motivated by a benefit-cost calculation in prompting the recipient state to adopt a certain conduct, to change its behaviour or to maintain the *status quo*. For example, in the case of economic conditionality behavioural change can be functional for the *effectiveness* of the donor's aid (or to ensure the donor is repaid).[19] Since some political choices are hard to make, conditionality is a way of incentivizing reforms that can benefit both the recipient and the donor. For example, within the EU GSP,[20] the Special Incentive Arrangement for Sustainable Development and Good Governance, scheme (GSP+) providing for extended tariff benefits conditional to the adoption of labour standards,[21] can be considered as a way to offset social dumping and unfair competition for European industries.[22] The donor's interest in having a stable and democratic neighbouring country, enlarging its market, and increasing its international influence is also an important factor.

Conditionality may also imply a cost for the donor. In this case, the donor might decide not to trigger conditionality or even not to use it with countries with which it has relevant economic or strategic relationships.[23] On the contrary, if conditionality is applied, the costs[24] might be high in economic, security and financial terms. When the mechanism is set up but seldom or never applied or applied selectively on the basis of disputable criteria, the donor's credibility may be undermined.

On the other hand, political, especially human rights or democratic conditionality, may entail reputational benefits for the donor country: it shows the donor's commitment to those values, implicitly confirming its willingness to question its relationship with a state which violates human rights.

---

[18]Manners (2002). For Manners the capacity of the EU to influence the behaviour of other actors by exporting its values makes it a very distinct kind of actor in international relations.

[19]Donno and Neureiter (2018); the scholars note: "we know surprisingly little about the effectiveness of the EU's strategy of embedding human rights commitments within economic partnerships. Do human rights clauses reduce repression? Exploring this question will shed light, beyond the EU, on important debates in international relations, namely, whether economic conditionality can (and should) be used to promote political change, as well as the conditions under which international law influences state behavior".

[20]See Regulation (EU) No 978/2012 of The European Parliament and of the Council of 25 October 2012 applying a scheme of generalised tariff preferences and repealing Council Regulation (EC) No 732/2008, OJ [2012] L303/1. This regulation, based on Article 207 of the TFEU, will expire on 31 December 2023.

[21]See further below for a more detailed analysis.

[22]See further, Chap. 5 of this book; see also de Wet. This connection had been made in a forward-looking manner by See Article 7 of the Havana Charter: 'unfair labour conditions, particularly in production for exports, create difficulties in international trade'. Havana Charter for an International Trade Organization, Final act of the United Nations Conference on Trade and Employment, 24 March 1948.

[23]See De Bardeleben (2008); De Bardeleben argues that the EU declined using conditionality leverage in its relations with Russia with whom a politics of interests takes precedence over a politics of values, not only for the refusal of Russia to accept conditionality but also for the economic and stronger geopolitical position of this country.

[24]Barrett (2007).

The reasons for the choice of a positive rather than a negative mechanism of conditionality should also be considered; the use of positive conditionality tools avoids possible confrontation generated by the application of coercive measures and overcomes the limits of sanctions in terms of effectiveness and human rights concerns. Likewise, there is a need to reflect on the use of conditionality instruments and consider alternative tools (such as technical assistance, financing projects) and methods (negotiation and persuasion) that could be used. The choice depends on the interests, values and aims of the donor.

4.1.2 The Standard of Behaviour Required by the Donor as a Condition for Granting Benefits or Avoiding Punishment

Criteria to be fulfilled or behaviour required are usually unilaterally defined by the donor. When conditionality takes the form of a contractual relationship, it is usually the stronger partner that define the terms of conditionality.[25]

The behaviour can be *positive*, that is the recipient is required to act in a specific manner: for example, accede to a specific agreement, readmit illegal migrants, or *negative* when it is required to abstain from a conduct: for example not to make reservations to a specific agreement.

Political conditionality mechanisms may establish a problematic issue linkage when the behaviour required (such as the respect for human rights, the rule of law and democracy) and the benefit/sanction applied (trade preferences or loss of market access) are related to different areas or regimes. The linkage consists of a de facto connection established by the donor and may be contested by the recipient. Indeed, the relationship between regimes (trade and human rights; trade and environment, labour rights and trade) can be perceived as unfair or raise opposition as regards the degree of connection between the norms of the two regimes and can even inhibit the establishment of the relationship.[26]

---

[25]Fierro defines conditionality as an asymmetrical relationship between a donor (the stronger party) and a recipient (the weaker one), see Fierro (2003). In most cases the donor is in a stronger contractual position than the recipient and it can impose the incorporation and the terms of conditionality. However, when the parties' interests in the relationship are more balanced, reciprocal conditionality can be substantial and have consequences for both parties. This is not always the case, however, as we shall see, in the case of the agreements recently concluded by the EU with some developed countries. This more balanced relationship in economic, political and institutional terms can affect the elements of the clause. See further below on this point.

[26]In a seminal article, Leebron provides an in-depth analysis of the types of linkage. He distinguishes between *substantial* and *strategic* linkages. In the first category he includes coherence based and consequentialist linkage. In the first case the linkage norm reconciles conflicting norms: for example, sustainable development in the trade and environment area. *Consequential linkage* is when the norms of one regime affects the realization of the goals of the other regime (competition regime and worker's rights is the example that he uses, but one could add child labour prohibition and the competitive advantage of some exporting industries). Linkage is *strategic* when it aims at enhancing

Another question is the transparency and clear definition of the criteria to be fulfilled or the conduct demanded to enable the recipient to comply with it. There are instances where this is not the case. For example in the US African Growth and Opportunity Act (AGOA),[27] to be eligible for duty-free benefits, a country shall not "engage in activities that undermine US national security or foreign policy interests" or "has established, or is making continual progress toward establishing a market-based economy," "the rule of law" and "the elimination of barriers to US trade and investment". The decision that those criteria are met is clearly established by the donor which enjoys a broad margin of discretion. This poses the problem of monitoring, as will be explained later in this chapter.

4.1.3 Positive and Negative Conditionality

Conditionality is *positive* (providing for incentives or rewards) when the benefit is received (or increased) in exchange for a (previously defined) action or behaviour to be encouraged. Positive conditionality can be designed in the form of pre-conditions: defined criteria are to be fulfilled by the recipient *before* receiving the benefit (for example entering into an agreement or be part of an aid programme).

Conditionality is *negative* when a previously enjoyed benefit is withdrawn if the recipient fails to comply with the required behaviour or the criteria formerly defined. The "sanction" in negative conditionality is the withdrawal of a benefit or advantage previously granted and can be considered as a reversal of the benefit. For instance, if the benefit is the conclusion of the agreement, the "sanction" may be the suspension or termination of the agreement concluded between the parties. Although the negative/positive features of conditionality have to be distinguished, it is also clear that when pre-conditions are not fulfilled the failure to obtain the promised benefit can be perceived as a punishment by the potential recipient.

Benefits can be material and specific, this is the case for example of granting financial aid,[28] trade preferences, market access, technical assistance, visa facilitations; benefit can also be general or not well defined, such as the benefits deriving from

---

bargaining power or when sanctions from one issue area are applied to enforce norms from another issue area. For an example of the first scenario he mentions the case of a state (the US) having overwhelming bargaining power on economic issues in a trade agreement, that "might seek to link other issues (e.g., human rights) to the trade negotiations in the hope of obtaining an agreement that the state would not be able to obtain in isolation." (this might be the case for positive conditionality). *Sanction linkage* is to be found when coercive measures from one issue area are applied to enforce norms from another issue area. Leebron (2002); As for the *tools of linkage*, he refers, *inter alia*, to the *negotiating linkage*. Positive conditionality and political conditionality such as political clauses can be qualified as a negotiating linkage: trade, cooperation and human rights are connected during negotiations, the linkage then continues during the relationship.

[27]The AGOA was enacted on 18 May 2000 as Public Law 106 and was renewed to 2025 on the 6 January 2015, public law 114–27.

[28]Foreign aid has been considered as having "added a new dimension to the realm of international economic persuasion". See *Comment. The Use of Nonviolent Coercion: A Study in Legality under*

institutional ties, for example becoming member of an organization can strengthen the legitimacy of a government vis-à-vis its citizens.

States employ different means and instruments to influence other states' behaviour and, more generally, policies. The main distinction is between cooperative (to act through persuasion) and coercive means (with the use of sanctions).[29] The choice to adopt a negative or a positive conditionality tool defines the paradigm of the relationship the donor intends to establish with the recipient. Positive conditionality denotes the intention of creating a cooperative model whereas negative conditionality seems to indicate a punitive approach. However, this clearly demarcated distinction of the use of conditionality does not reflect standard practice, which often sees the combined use of both typologies. As will be discussed later in this chapter, negative conditionality tools, such as the political clauses incorporated into EU agreements with third countries and withdrawal of benefits in EU GSP, also contemplate a phase of dialogue and positive constructive interrelations between the parties. It should be noted that incentives and punitive measures have different effects and results. Incentives are usually less controversial and easier to accept than punitive measures. The choice between negative and positive conditionality is the result of the donor's political preference or depends on the relationship between the donor and the recipient.[30] The implementation of punitive measures (withdrawal of the benefit) may be considered a second-choice solution since it might cut off or make dialogue more difficult. The donor country loses leverage over the recipient.

4.1.3.1 Negative Conditionality as a Coercive Tool. The Distinction with Sanctions and Countermeasures

Negative conditionality is characterized by a coercive element.[31] In this respect Ronzitti maintains that 'coercion may assume various forms that have in common the will of a state to force another state into taking a particular action'.[32] As seen above, negative conditionality imposes a cost for non-compliance[33] on the recipient and although there is also a cost in the case of positive conditionality, that is, the loss of a potential benefit, positive conditionality does not imply an *extra* cost. Thus, negative

---

Article 2(4) of the Charter of the United Nations, in *University of Pennsylvania Law Review*, vol. 122, no. 4, 1974, pp. 983–1011. *JSTOR*, www.jstor.org/stable/3311418.

[29]Farer (1985), Raponi (2015).

[30]According to Viță, 'The closer the partnership with third countries or closer the candidate to the accession, the more conditionality becomes positive and dynamic, pursuing a behavioural and effectiveness function. In the case of far-away partners, the conditionality is mainly negative and static, exercising a punitive function in case of non-compliance with fundamental rights'. Viță (2014), at 36.

[31]Portela (2007).

[32]Ronzitti (2016).

[33]Joyner (2020); defines coercion as follows: 'Coercion in inter-state relations involves the government of one State compelling the government of another State to think or act in a certain way by applying various kinds of pressure, threats, intimidation or the use of force'.

conditionality has a stronger coercive feature if compared with positive conditionality. In contemporary international law, coercion[34] may be legal or illegal, according to the means used,[35] the objectives pursued[36] or when its use deprives a state of a benefit to which it is legally entitled.[37] In the latter case, coercive measures (short of the use of force) might lose their illegal character only if they can be correctly qualified as countermeasures.[38]

Countermeasures are actions taken by the injured state that are per se violations of international law but become legal because they are a reaction to a previous internationally wrongful act by the targeted state.[39] Their goal is to compel the wrongful state to comply with its obligation to make amends towards the injured state. For this reason, they must be adopted only by the latter and be directed exclusively against the wrongdoer and will end only when the wrongful act has been remedied.

Sanctions[40] are coercive measures which are adopted by international organizations.[41] Even though they are usually triggered by actions of the targeted state that

[34]The threat or use of force is illegal unless authorized by the United Nations (UN) Security Council; the use of force may be justified in self-defence. Economic coercion, defined as the 'threat to use, measures of an economic—as contrasted with diplomatic or military—character taken to induce [a target State] to change some policy or practices or even its governmental structure' it is usually not prohibited by international law. Carter (2020).

[35]McDougal and Feliciano (1958), categorized strategies of coercion according to the means employed and according to the particular ends that are sought. These authors distinguish between diplomatic, ideological, economic and military instruments of coercion.

[36]For example the 1965 *Declaration on the Inadmissibility of Intervention in the Domestic Affairs of States and the Protection of their Independence and Sovereignty*, UNGA Resolution 2131 (XX) of 21 December 1965 proclaimed that 'No state may use or encourage the use of economic, political or another type of measures to coerce another State in order to obtain from it the subordination of the exercise of its sovereign rights or to secure from it advantages of any kind' (para. 2). The Organization of American State (OAS) Charter proclaims in its Article 20 that no state 'may use or encourage the use of coercive measures of an economic or political character in order to force the sovereign will of another State and obtain from it advantages of any kind'.

[37]See, for example, International Court of Justice, *Military and Paramilitary Activities in and against Nicaragua (Nicaragua v. United States of America)* I.C.J Rep 1986, 14, para. 205.

[38]Countermeasure have to satisfy procedural and substantial condition to be lawful. See Articles 49 to 54 of Articles on responsibility of states for internationally wrongful acts. Text adopted by the Commission at its fifty-third session, in 2001, and submitted to the General Assembly as a part of the Commission's report covering the work of that session. Yearbook of the International Law Commission, 2001. These applies by analogy to countermeasures adopted by an International organisation against a state. The 2011 draft Articles on the responsibility of international organizations (DARIO) is concerned only with countermeasures taken by an international organization against another international organization. Yearbook of the International Law Commission, 2011. Article 22.

[39]Countermeasures 'must be taken in response to a previous international wrongful act of another state and must be directed against that state', *Hungary v. Slovakia* (Gabcikovo-Nagymaros Project), Judgment, I.C.J. Reports 1997, par. 83.

[40]The definition is controversial. Alexander defines sanctions as 'the withholding of a benefit or the imposition of a penalty'. The relationship between sanctions and countermeasures has not been fully clarified as noted by Ronzitti, n. 32, at 1.

[41]The term refers to a variety of measures, ranging from embargos, freezing of transport connections, measures against specific person (e.g. travel bans, asset freezes). Ruys refers to sanctions taken by

qualify as breaches of international law, unlike countermeasures, they do not necessarily consist in actions that infringe the international organization's international obligations towards the sanctioned state.

This is a feature present in negative conditionality instruments: the "punishment" might be the withdrawal of a benefit not legally due by the donor to the recipient. In other words, by activating negative conditionality, the donor state is not necessarily breaching a previously assumed obligation towards the recipient (for example, the suspension of unilateral economic aid or limitation of trade interests not protected by law). On the contrary, if the withdrawal of a benefit consists of an international obligation due to the recipient, this has to be justified according to international law. When sanctions consist of actions qualifying as breaches of international law, they must be based on international law.[42] EU sanctions are legal if they are adopted and applied to ensure implementation of UN sanctions, or as countermeasures.[43] However, if autonomous EU sanctions do not violate any international law obligations towards the targeted states, no justification under international law is required.

The purpose of conditionality and sanctions is to force the recipient state to change its behaviour. Sanctions may also have a punitive purpose: in fact, they are not necessarily conditional on compliance, even if it is usually implied that they will be lifted if the targeted state puts an end to the contested behaviour. They also signal or express condemnation for a certain type of conduct.

If conditionality is provided for in a unilateral instrument such as the GSP, the benefit (e.g. duty free market access) is at the disposal of the donor country that can decide whether to grant it or withdraw it without violating international law. However, there might be international obligations that might limit choices, or affect the design of the incentive/sanction provided for. This will be examined further below, with reference to the EU unilateral conditionality tools (the GSP) and the World Trade Organization (WTO) provisions. As regards non-trade clauses, the analysis will look at the possible violation of international law that their application might entail (in terms of suspension of the treaty obligations), with reference to international law of treaties.

---

single states, with reference, for example, to Russia's intervention in Ukraine in 2014, see Ruys (2017) at 19. 'The term "sanctions" has been used for measures taken in accordance with the constituent instrument of some international organization, in particular under Chapter VII of the Charter of the United Nations—despite the fact that the Charter uses the term "measures", not "sanctions"', Crawford (2002) at 168.

[42]In more general terms, EU sanctions must comply with international law: 'introduction and implementation of restrictive measures must always be in accordance with international law. They must respect human rights and fundamental freedoms, in particular due process and the right to an effective remedy. The measures imposed must always be proportionate to their objective'. See Council of the EU, *Guidelines on implementation and evaluation of restrictive measures (sanctions)*, 15 June 2012. On EU sanctions see Gestri (2016).

[43]There are different models of EU Sanctions: those adopted to implement UN sanctions, those that provide for additional restrictive measures as compared to the UN sanctions and autonomous sanctions. Sossai (2017), Morviducci (2019), White (2018).

4.1.4 Monitoring Compliance with the Conditions Established by the Donor

Monitoring is essential for the application of conditionality, for the reputation of the donor and effectiveness of the instrument. It helps in verifying the preconditions for applying benefits in positive conditionality or trigger sanctions in negative conditionality.

As seen above, in case of positive *ex ante* conditionality, the benefit is not provided for until compliance by the recipient is verified. In case of negative conditionality, the benefit is withdrawn when the donor attests that the behaviour triggering the sanction has taken place. It is clear that in both hypotheses checking compliance with the previously defined criteria is crucial for the correct application and efficiency of the conditionality tool.

The application of positive or negative measures (benefits, sanctions) requires a benchmark for behaviour. This issue is connected with the transparency of conditions. Another important element of conditionality is definition of the actors designated to perform control and the setting up of monitoring instruments for verifying behaviour. This is usually the donor competent to attest whether conditions of conditionality are satisfied, but the recipient country may also be involved in the process, or an institutionalized dialogue may be set up between donor and recipient as in the above-cited United States AGOA program; the evaluation may be carried out by other subjects, such as International Labour Organization (ILO) in the case of the EU GSP. Other instruments such as monitoring missions, the involvement of stakeholders and civil society may be used.

For example, the eligibility designation process in the US GSP involves a dialogue between the United States and potential AGOA beneficiary countries. The 2015 AGOA Act[44] also provides for the private sector or 'any interested person, at any time' to file a petition with respect to the failure of a country's "compliance" "with eligibility requirements" and to petition the United States Trade Representative (USTR) in this regard.

The task is particularly difficult, at least in principle, where criteria are not defined (rule of law, democracy, human rights) or may provide for a margin of flexibility in their interpretation.

---

[44] n. 27.

4.2 The European Union's Conditionality Tool-Kit to Promote Non-trade Values

4.2.1 Conditionality in the EU GSP Schemes

EU conditionality tools can be classified according to the legal instruments used and to their positive or negative structure.

The EU unilateral conditionality tools are contained in the GSP regulation and in financial instruments. The EU GSP regulation offers tariff preferential access for some products[45] originating from developing countries.[46] EU GSP includes three schemes: the General Arrangement, the Special Incentive Arrangement for Sustainable Development and Good Governance, (GSP+)[47] and the "Everything but Arms".[48] The EU GSP+ provides for positive and negative mechanism of conditionality. Positive conditionality consists of a reward mechanism in terms of further tariff concessions (as specifically defined in the GSP+) provided that the recipient state satisfies a number of conditions (see infra for further details). Negative conditionality consists in the temporary withdrawal of preferences offered in the GSP schemes (General GSP, EBA) for all or certain products in case of serious and systematic violations of principles laid down in core human and labour rights. In the Special Incentive Arrangement (GSP+), negative conditionality consists in the return of trade conditions to the less-preferential scheme (that is the GSP General Arrangement) in case the recipient state does not effectively implement the mentioned conventions.

GSP was first adopted by the EU in 1971 and reformed several times.[49] It is worth remembering that GSP was the product of a different approach to international trade strongly sponsored by developing countries in UNCTAD and then codified in Part IV of GATT ("Enabling Clause"). The idea was to replace aid by trade which, through a preferential access to industrialized country markets of products originating from developing countries, would have contributed to the latter's development. More precisely generalized, non-reciprocal and non-discriminatory preferences were offered to developing countries to respond positively to their 'development, financial and trade needs'.

---

[45]A distinction is made between sensitive products that are exempted from all duties and non-sensitive products that receive a tariff reduction compared to the standard most favoured nation (MFN) treatment. Some agricultural goods and arms and ammunition are excluded from the schemes. (see art. 7).

[46]A country can no longer be a GSP beneficiary when the World Bank classifies it as a high-income or an upper-middle income country during three consecutive years immediately preceding the update of the list of beneficiary countries (Article 3 of GSP regulation). There are separate lists of countries eligible for preferences, least developed countries (LDC) and a list of countries entitled to GSP Plus preferences. The lists can be amended by the Commission by way of delegated legislation.

[47]This Special Arrangement is applied only to vulnerable countries (as defined by the regulation).

[48]Only for Least developed countries.

[49]See for a comprehensive analysis, Chap. 5, Sect. 5.3 in this book.

Both positive and negative conditionality were introduced[50] in the EU GSP in 1994 and confirmed by subsequent regulations.[51]

4.2.2 *Conditionality in Financial Instruments*

Another form of conditionality can be found in financial aid instruments, providing for a performance-based allocation approach. For example, Regulation establishing a European Neighbourhood Instrument (ENI)[52] provides in Article 4.1 that 'Union support under this Regulation provided to each partner country ... shall be incentive-based and differentiated in form and amounts, taking into account all the elements listed below...' Among these elements one finds "commitment to and progress in building deep and sustainable democracy".[53] However, according to the European

[50]See Council Regulation (EC) No 1256/96 of 20 June 1996 applying multiannual schemes of generalized tariff preferences from 1 July 1996 to 30 June 1999 in respect of certain agricultural products originating in developing countries OJ[1996] L160/1 and Council Regulation (EC) No 3281/94 of 19 December 1994 applying a four-year scheme of generalized tariff preferences (1995 to 1998) in respect of certain industrial products originating in developing countries OJ [1994] 348/1. Special incentives for countries that have adopted and actually apply domestic legal provisions incorporating the substance of standards laid down in some International Labour Organization Conventions (art. 7). Punitive mechanism (withdrawal of preferences) was provided for countries practicing any form of slavery or exporting goods made by prison labour (punitive social clause: Article 9 of Council Regulations Nos. 3281/94 and 1256/96). The punitive clause was applied for the first time in 1997 against the Union of Myanmar about the forced labour. See European Parliament report on the Communication from the Commission to the Council on the trading system and internationally recognised labour standards, 11 November 1998, PE 228.265/fin. In this Report it is stated: "this type of procedure must not be limited to the least powerful third countries at international level" and that the Union's GSP incentive scheme "does not provide for any link between the trade incentive and action programmes to promote the education of children as proposed in the 1994 Sainjon report.".

[51]This was confirmed by Council regulation (EC) 2820/98 of 21 December 1998 applying a multi-annual scheme of generalised tariff preferences for the period 1 July 1998 to 31 December 2001, OJ [1998] 357/1; Council regulation (EC) 2501/2001 of 10 December 2001 applying a scheme of generalised tariff preferences for the period from 1 January 2002 to 31 December 2004, OJ [2001] 346/1-and further reinforced by Council regulation (EC) 980/2005 of 27 June 2005 applying a scheme of generalised tariff preferences OJ [2005] 169/1. Conditionality was applied against Belarus. Regulation 1933/2006 temporarily withdrawing access to the generalised tariff preferences from the Republic of Belarus OJ [2006] L405/35. The incentive mechanism was applied in favour of Bolivia, Colombia, Costa Rica, Ecuador, Georgia, Guatemala, Honduras, Sri Lanka and Moldova. See 2005/924/EC: Commission Decision of 21 December 2005 on the list of the beneficiary countries which qualify for the special incentive arrangement for sustainable development and good governance, provided for by Article 26(e) of Council Regulation (EC) No 980/2005 applying a scheme of generalised tariff preferences OJ [2005] 337/50.

[52]Regulation (EU) No 232/2014 of the European Parliament and of the Council of 11 March 2014 establishing a European Neighbourhood Instrument OJ [2014] L77/27.

[53]In its COM (2011), the Commission clearly stated: "Increased EU support to its neighbours is conditional. It will depend on progress in building and consolidating democracy and respect for the rule of law. The more and the faster a country progresses in its internal reforms, the more support

Parliament (EP),[54] financial instruments[55] "do not contain any explicit reference to the possibility of suspending assistance in cases where a beneficiary country fails to observe the basic principles enunciated in the respective instrument and notably the principles of democracy, rule of law and the respect for human rights.".[56] To put it differently, these regulations provide for a positive rather than a negative mechanism of conditionality.

More recently, the regulation on the financial rules applicable to the general budget of the Union[57] establishes, that the European Commission will provide payment only if a number of economic and financial conditions are satisfied. However, Article 236(3) specifies that the European Commission 'shall support the respect for the rule of law, the development of parliamentary control and audit and anti-corruption capacities and the increase of transparency and public access to information.' It then provides that: 'the financial arrangement concluded with third countries shall contain also a right for the European Commission to suspend the financing agreement if the third country breaches an obligation relating to respect for human rights, democratic principles and the rule of law and in serious cases of corruption.' Therefore, positive conditionality is reserved to financial and economic criteria, while negative conditionality is provided in case of non-economic values violations.

On the contrary, Article 32 of the financial regulation applicable to the 11th European Development Fund[58] establishes that budget support shall be based on mutual

---

it will get from the EU. This enhanced support will come in various forms, including increased funding for social and economic development, larger programmes for comprehensive institution-building (CIB), greater market access, increased European Investment Bank financing in support of investments; and greater facilitation of mobility".

[54]See the European Parliament statement annexed to Regulation 232/2014, OJ L 77 15.3.2014, p. 77.

[55]Such as Regulation 234/2014 establishing a Partnership Instrument for cooperation with non-EU countries OJ [2014] L77/77 and Regulation (EU) No 231/2014 establishing an Instrument for Pre-accession Assistance (IPA II), at n. 7.

[56]Previous regulation such as regulation (EC) No 1638/2006 of the European Parliament and of the Council of 24 October 2006 laying down general provisions establishing a European Neighbourhood and Partnership Instrument OJ [2006] L310/1 provided in Article 28: "Without prejudice to the provisions on the suspension of aid in partnership and cooperation agreements and association agreements with partner countries and regions, where a partner country fails to observe the principles referred to in Article 1, the Council, acting by a qualified majority on a proposal from the Commission, may take appropriate steps in respect of any Community assistance granted to the partner country under this Regulation". TACIS regulation—applied to eastern European countries (before accession)-affirms: "this regulation is based on respect for democratic principles and the rule of law and also for human rights and fundamental freedoms, which constitute an essential element thereof, the violation of which element will justify the adoption of appropriate measures".

[57]Regulation (EU, Euratom) 2018/1046 of the European Parliament and of the Council of 18 July 2018 on the financial rules applicable to the general budget of the Union, amending Regulations (EU) No 1296/2013, (EU) No 1301/2013, (EU) No 1303/2013, (EU) No 1304/2013, (EU) No 1309/2013, (EU) No 1316/2013, (EU) No 223/2014, (EU) No 283/2014, and Decision No 541/2014/EU and repealing Regulation (EU, Euratom) No 966/2012 OJ [2018] L193/1. See 236 paragraphs 1 and 2.

[58]Regulation 2018/1877 of 26 November 2018 on the financial regulation applicable to the 11th European Development Fund (EDF) and repealing Regulation (EU) 2015/32 OJ [2018] L307/1.

accountability and shared commitments to universal values, and shall aim at strengthening contractual partnerships between the Union and African, Caribbean and Pacific Group of States (ACP) states or Overseas countries and territories (OCTs) in order to promote democracy, human rights and the rule of law, to support sustainable and inclusive economic growth and to eradicate poverty. According to the same provision: 'any decision to provide budget support shall be based on an assessment of the commitment, record and progress of ACP States and OCTs with regard to democracy, human rights and the rule of law'.

The new proposal for a Neighbourhood, Development and International Cooperation Instrument, which intends to merge all Union's external action instruments[59] into a single regulation, based on Articles 209, 212 and 322 TFEU,[60] contains a positive conditionality mechanism.[61] The proposed regulation links budget support to an assessment of the commitment, record and progress of partner countries with regard to democracy, human rights and the rule of law.[62] The performance-based allocation is maintained in the Neighbourhood pillar of the regulation proposal: Article 17 provides that: 'The performance-based allocations shall be decided on the

---

The EDF, one of the major external funding instruments, will expire at the end of 2020. It aims to ensure cooperation with African, Caribbean and Pacific States, contracting parties to the Cotonou Partnership Agreement, and with the Overseas Countries and Territories.

[59]Regulation (EU) No 230/2014 of the European Parliament and of the Council of 11 March 2014 establishing an instrument contributing to stability and peace OJ [2014] L77/1; Regulation (EU) No 231/2014 of the European Parliament and of the Council of 11 March 2014 establishing an Instrument for Pre-accession Assistance (IPA II) OJ [2014] 77/11; Regulation (EU) No 232/2014 of the European Parliament and of the Council of 11 March 2014 establishing a European Neighbourhood Instrument OJ [2014] L77/27; Regulation (EU) No 233/2014 of the European Parliament and of the Council of 11 March 2014 establishing a financing instrument for development cooperation for the period 2014–2020 OJ [2014] L77/44; Regulation (EU) No 234/2014 of the European Parliament and of the Council of 11 March 2014 establishing a Partnership Instrument for cooperation with third countries OJ [2014] L77/77; Regulation (EU) No 235/2014 of the European Parliament and of the Council of 11 March 2014 establishing a financing instrument for democracy and human rights worldwide OJ [2014] L77/85; regulation (EU) No 236/2014 of the European Parliament and of the Council of 11 March 2014 laying down common rules and procedures for the implementation of the Union's instruments for financing external action OJ [2014] L77/95.

[60]According to the European Commission proposal for a regulation of the European Parliament and the Council establishing the Neighbourhood, Development and International Cooperation Instrument: 'The objective of the Neighbourhood, Development and International Cooperation Instrument is to uphold and promote the Union's values and interests worldwide in order to pursue the objectives and principles of its external action, as laid down in Article 3(5), Articles 8 and 21 of the Treaty on European Union'. COM (2018) 460.

[61]This is not new. For example. the European Neighbourhood Instrument contains positive conditionality mechanism, "more for more" whereby the partner countries are rewarded with more investment if they make progress with reforms such as improving the functioning of the Judiciary and fight against corruption. See Communication from the Commission, *Eastern Partnership*, COM (2008) 823.

[62]Article 4.2. "Any decision to provide the general or sector budget support shall be based on budget support policies agreed by the Union, a clear set of eligibility criteria and a careful assessment of the risks and benefits. One of the key determinants of that decision shall be an assessment of the commitment, record and progress of partner countries with regard to democracy, human rights and the rule of law".

basis of their progress towards democracy, human rights, rule of law, cooperation on migration, economic governance and reforms. The progress of partner countries shall be assessed annually'.[63] The EP in its first reading proposed the inclusion of a provision establishing the possibility for the Commission to suspend assistance in case of persistent failure by one of the beneficiary countries 'to observe the principles of democracy, the rule of law, good governance, respect for human rights and fundamental freedoms, or nuclear safety standards'.[64]

It seems that the inclusion of a negative conditionality mechanism in the financial instrument would make this more consistent with the generalized system of preferences or the conditionality clause and would send a strong message to beneficiaries of EU funds where these are states and government authority.[65] Shared commitment to "universal values" such as democracy, human rights, rule of law, leaves a wide margin of flexibility to the European Commission, but does not provide the Union with enough teeth to react to serious violations of those values. Even if negative conditionality would seldom be triggered (as it happened in the case of GSP suspension or in the activation of the essential element and non-execution clause) its inclusion would prove that the EU is ready to act for the protection of its values in non-member states.

4.2.3 Conditionality Clauses in EU International Agreements

Conditionality incorporated into the EU's international agreements takes the form of a provision that defines respect for human rights, and for other non-trade values (democratic principles, rule of law, good governance) as an "essential element"[66] of the agreement. This provision is complemented[67] by a "non-execution" clause, which provides for a reaction in the hypothesis of a violation of an essential element of the agreement. The "essential element" clause is not, per se, a conditionality tool. Indeed, the (negative) conditional aspect of the clause only comes to the fore with the

[63] It is interesting to note that this methodology applies only to central government. In fact, the same provision specifies: 'The performance-based approach shall not apply to support to civil society, people-to-people contacts, including cooperation between local authorities, support for the improvement of human rights, or crisis-related support measures. In the event of serious or persistent degradation of democracy, human rights or rule of law, support to these actions may be increased'.

[64] European Parliament legislative resolution of 27 March 2019 on the proposal for a regulation of the European Parliament and of the Council establishing the Neighbourhood, Development and International Cooperation Instrument (COM(2018)0460–C8-0275/2018–2018/0243(COD)).

[65] This was the position assumed by the European Parliament, The European Parliament and the new external financing instrument, EP/EXPO/B/AFET/2018/06, November 2018, PE603.468.

[66] The main focus here is on the clause as a conditionality mechanism, but it is important to take into account that the clause also functions as a positive value promoting tool. See Martines (2016).

[67] In the European Community early practice, only the essential element clause was included, see for example, the Cooperation Agreement between the European Community and the Republic of India on partnership and development—OJ [1994] L 223/24.

"non-execution" clause. It should also be noted that acceptance by EU partners of the inclusion of such provisions is a condition for the conclusion of the agreement.[68]

The EU has made it clear that it intends to include non-trade clauses in all agreements with third countries (although sectoral agreements do not contain such a provision, and some partnership agreements constitute an exception, as will be shown later). The start of the negotiations and the conclusion of the agreements depend upon the respect for human rights and other values by the EU partner. It should be noted that the two conditions (acceptance of the inclusion of non-trade values and non-execution provisions) and respect for human rights and other values raise different questions. A partner country can have a positive record of respect for those values, but it might nevertheless oppose the inclusion of non-trade clauses for other reasons.[69]

4.2.3.1 The Origin and the Evolving Practice of the Clauses

The reason that first prompted the EU to incorporate negative conditionality into its international agreements was to provide the organisation with an instrument to be deployed in cases of human rights violation committed by a non-EU (partner) country. For instance, in order to counter serious and widespread human rights abuses in Uganda in 1977,[70] the EU suspended financial aid granted under Lomé I Convention,[71] which did not, however, contain a reference to human rights. The then European Economic Community (EEC) adopted the so-called "Uganda guidelines"[72] where it was stipulated that aid disbursement under the Lomé Convention would not contribute to serious violations of human rights in Uganda. As posited by Borchert et al., 'what originated as a mere "escape clause", enabling the EU to suspend its treaty relations with other states in cases of human rights violations, developed into a practice of conditioning the financial and trade benefits the EU grants to third countries on compliance with a range of non-trade policy objectives'.[73] However, the elaboration of conditionality mechanisms was done 'reluctantly and in small steps.'[74]

---

[68] The incorporation of an essential element clause into agreements concluded by the EU has blocked or made negotiations more difficult with some countries. For example, India refused to accept the inclusion of the clause in the new Partnership and Cooperation Agreement. Japan was rather displeased by the request of the EU, although it was explained as a move to make the EU stance stronger in the request of incorporating a HRC into a future agreement with China. Okano-Heijmans (2014).

[69] During the negotiations with Mexico, the reference in the essential elements clause to external relations was problematic due to the traditional non-intervention doctrine of Mexico. See E. Fierro, *The EU's Approach*, above n. 25, at 303–304. As for India the perception is that the EU insistence on labour rights is inspired by protectionist motivations, see Orbie and Khorana (2015).

[70] Fierro, *European Union's Approach to Human Rights Conditionality in Practice*, above n. 25.

[71] See First ACP-Eu Convention, Lomé 28th February 1975.

[72] EC Bulletin 1977, 6, 2.2.59.

[73] Borchert et al. (2019).

[74] E. Fierro, *European Union's Approach* above n. 25, at 45.

The EU practice relates to two aspects of the clause: one is the incorporation of the clause into EU agreements and the decision to make it a qualifying element of the relationship, the second issue concerns the scope of the clause and the linkage with the mechanisms to enforce it.

With regard to the inclusion of the clause in EU agreements, the first conditionality clause referring to human rights and democracy was included[75] in an agreement with non-EU countries in Latin America.[76] A reference to human rights was incorporated in Article 5 of the IV Lomé Convention.[77]

A first reference by the Commission to the possibility of providing for a negative response to serious and systematic human rights violations was made in a Communication back in 1991.[78] On May 11, 1992 the Council declared[79] that respect for democratic principles formed an essential part of agreements between the European Community (EC) and the Conference on Security and Cooperation in Europe (CSCE), following which an essential elements clause had to be included in all association agreement with CSCE partners. The practice was then extended to other areas and countries[80] and formalized by the Commission Communication,[81] followed by a full endorsement of the Council.[82]

Subsequently, the clause was incorporated into sectoral agreements through a linkage or "passerelle clause".[83]

With regard to the formulation of the clauses, namely the essential element and non-execution clauses, the practice started with the incorporation of the clause into the EU's agreements with Latin American countries. By way of example, the cooperation agreement with Argentina,[84] established that 'ties between the Community and

---

[75] The Lomé V Convention between the EEC, its member states and the ACP countries contained a provision on human rights which was not formulated in terms of conditionality, see Fourth ACP-EEC Convention signed at Lomé on 15 December 1989 OJ [1991] L229/3, Article 5.

[76] Framework Agreement for Trade and Economic Cooperation between the European Economic Community and the Argentine Republic, Article 1 (democratic basis for Cooperation), OJ [1990] L 295/67. The clause was included in the Framework Agreement for Cooperation between the European Community and the Republic of Chile OJ [1991] L 79/2), Framework Agreement for Cooperation between the European Community and the Republic of Uruguay OJ [1992] L 94/2 and Framework agreement for cooperation between the European Community and the Republic of Paraguay, OJ [1992] L 313/72.

[77] Fourth ACP-EEC Convention, signed in Lomé on 15 December 1989, OJ L[1991] 229/3.

[78] Commission Communication to the Council and Parliament on Human Rights, Democracy and Development Cooperation Policy, SEC(91) 61 Final, at 6.

[79] Bull. EC 1992, 5. 1.2.13.

[80] See Communication of the Commission on the inclusion of respect for democratic principles and human rights in agreements between the Community and third countries, COM (95) 216 final, at 11 for a list of countries.

[81] Ibid. See also the Resolution of the European Parliament endorsing such a proposal OJ [1996] C 320/261.

[82] Conclusions of 29 May 1995, Bulletin 1995-5, point 1.2.3.

[83] See Sect. 5.3.

[84] Framework Agreement for trade and economic cooperation between the European Economic Community and the Argentine Republic OJ [1990] L295/67, Article 1.

Argentina and this Agreement in its entirety are based on respect for democratic principles and human rights'. These agreements did not contain a non-execution clause, but the agreement[85] authorized either party to take appropriate measures when it considers that the other party has failed to fulfil an obligation under the agreement.

An essential elements clause was then included in agreements concluded with Baltic states, ("Baltic clause").[86] The formulation changed in two respects. First, as regards the content, reference was made to democratic principles and human rights, established by the Helsinki Final Act[87] and in the Charter of Paris for a New Europe,[88] as well as the principles of market economy'; second, as regards the qualification, respect for these values constituted an "essential element" of the agreement. The right to suspend the agreement, in whole or in part, was provided for in cases of a serious violation of its essential provisions.[89] The inclusion of a non-execution provision was crucial because it established—in connection with the essential element clause—a justification for the parties to resort to suspension or termination of the agreement.

As discussed further below,[90] the qualification of respect for non-trade values as "essential" seems, in fact, to refer to the content of Article 60 of the Vienna Convention on the Law of Treaties (VCLT), the *inadimplenti non est adimplendum* rule[91] allowing a party to suspend or terminate a treaty in case of a material breach by another contracting party. A material breach consists in the violation of a provision that is "essential" to the accomplishment of the object or purpose of the treaty. According to a different interpretation, the clause was considered as the application of the *rebus sic stantibus* principle codified in Article 62(1) VCLT. However, this ground of suspension and termination is only admitted for situations that were unforeseen at the time of the conclusion of the agreement and thus does not seem applicable in the hypothesis of human rights violations.[92]

---

[85] See Article 44.

[86] See, for example, the Agreement between the European Economic Community and the Republic of Estonia, on trade and commercial and economic cooperation OJ L 403 31.12.1992 1992 p. 3.

[87] Helsinki Act 1975.

[88] Charter of Paris for a New Europe, Conference of Security and Co-operation in Europe (CSCE 19–21 November 1990), available at: https://www.osce.org/files/f/documents/0/6/39516.pdf. Accessed on 14 June 2020.

[89] see Article 21 of the Europe Agreement establishing an association between the European Communities and their Member States, of the one part, and the Republic of Estonia, OJ [1998] L68/3.

[90] See Sect. 5.1 of this chapter.

[91] See Bartels (2014b). The EC referred to the application of the *rebus sic stantibus* principle in the case of the suspension of the Agreement with Yugoslavia. The ECJ confirmed the soundness of this measure in Judgment of the Court of Justice Case C-162/96 *Racke* ECLI:EU:C:1998:293.

[92] Bartels, *A modern human rights clause for the EU's International Trade agreement*, above, n. 91.

The non-execution clause contained in agreements with Baltic states[93] was later replaced by the so-called "Bulgarian clause".[94] The essential elements clause[95] remained unaltered but the non-execution clause was formulated as follows: 'If either party considers that the other party has failed to fulfil an obligation under the agreement, it may take appropriate measures. Before so doing, except in cases of special urgency, it shall supply the Association Council with all relevant information required for a thorough examination of the situation with a view to seeking a solution acceptable to the parties'.[96]

Therefore, according to this provision, infringement of human rights obligations would not automatically lead to a suspension of the agreement since the reacting party was allowed to resort to other measures, giving priority to those that least disturb the functioning of the agreement. These measures have to be notified immediately to the Association Council and are subject of consultations within the Association Council if the other Party so requests except in cases of special urgency. An interpretative declaration, contained for example in the Cooperation Agreement with Georgia[97] spells out that "cases of special urgency" refer to a repudiation of the agreement not sanctioned by the general rules of international law or to a violation of the essential elements of the agreement.

The Baltic clause, adopted on the wake of the suspension of the agreement with Yugoslavia after the outburst of the civil war,[98] was clearly more rigid in comparison to the Bulgarian model, as the former did not leave space for alternatives to the immediate suspension of the agreement and without a prior consultation procedure. On the contrary, the Bulgarian clause requires a conciliation procedure, and provides for the possibility to adopt, after consultation, other measures alternative to suspension.[99] The latter was to be used only as a measure of last resort.

It is clear that the Bulgarian clause was more in tune with the line of action defined in the 1991 Commission Communication,[100] where there was a preference

[93] See Europe Agreement establishing an association between the European Communities and their Member States, of the one part, and the Republic of Estonia, above n. 88; Europe Agreement establishing an association between the European Communities and their Member States, of the one part, and the Republic of Latvia OJ [1998] L 26/ 3.

[94] See Europe Agreement establishing an association between the European Communities and their Member States, of the one part, and the Republic of Bulgaria, of the other part in OJ [1994] L 358/1; see Commission Communication on the inclusion of respect for democratic principles and human rights in agreements between the Community and third countries, COM (95) 216 final, 23.5.1995, at 7.

[95] See, for instance, Article 6 of the Agreement with Bulgaria, Europe Agreement establishing an association between the European Communities and their Member States, of the one part, and the Republic of Bulgaria, of the other part OJ [1994] L 368/3.

[96] Article 118.

[97] Partnership and Cooperation Agreement between the European Communities and their Member States, of the one part, and Georgia, of the other part, OJ [1999] L205/3, Joint Declaration concerning Article 98.

[98] Fierro, above n. 25, at 220.

[99] See Annex 2 of the Commission Communication on the inclusion of respect, cit. COM (95) 216.

[100] Fierro, above n. 25, at 219.

for positive measures. The suspension of an agreement was too rigid a measure: 'A system which automatically triggers a particular reaction to human rights violations would not be able to deal with all the various situations that might arise. Reactions will therefore be determined by the case in question'.[101] The Bulgarian version of the clause has been used since as it allows more flexibility and it also facilitates its inclusion by demonstrating a more accommodating attitude to EU partners unwilling to accept the clause.

Moreover, suspension might be a blunt tool because it deprives the EU of the possibility of recurring to other measures or exercising other forms of more effective pressure towards the human rights violator.[102]

4.2.4 The EU's Competence to Include Conditionality Clauses in Its External Agreements and in Unilateral Acts

The inclusion of conditionality mechanisms[103] in unilateral instruments and in EU agreements raises the question of their legal justification. This is to be distinguished from the problem of the legal foundation of EU competence to adopt secondary legislation or to conclude international agreements whose content and primary purpose is the protection of human rights.[104] In other words, although the member states did not confer a general competence in the field of human rights on the EU,[105] it does possess a legislative competence for concluding agreements based on a conferred competence, such as development cooperation or trade, incorporating human rights conditionality mechanisms.

The incorporation of such clauses[106] into the EU's international agreements has no longer been disputed by member states since the Court of Justice of the European

[101] Commission Communication on human rights, democracy and development cooperation policy, SEC (91) 61.

[102] See the Decision of the European Ombudsman on complaint 933/2004/JMA against the European Commission, decision of 25 June 2005. According to the EU Ombudsman 'the Commission's reasoning for its decision not to trigger the suspension of the cooperation agreement, but instead to make use of measures that it considers to be more proportionate, in accordance with the criteria set out in its 1995 Communication, appeared to be reasonable'.

[103] The term mainstream is often used to indicate the process of "deliberately incorporating human rights considerations into processes or organisations which are not explicitly mandated to deal with human rights", McCrudden (2005).

[104] Reid (2015). The conclusion by the EU of the United Nations Convention on the Rights of Persons with Disabilities (Marrakesh agreement), concerning human rights and copyrights was based on Article 13 TEC (now Article 19 of the TFEU) and Article 95 TEC (now 114 TFEU approximation of Laws) and 300.2 and 3 (now 218.2 and 3 TFEU).

[105] With the exception of the EU accession to the ECHR, based at present on Article 6 of the TEU.

[106] For the origin of this practice see E. Fierro, *European Union's Approach,* above, n. 25.

Union's (CJEU) judgment in *Portugal v. Council*.[107] The Court considered that the inclusion of human rights in development cooperation agreement found its legal justification in the Treaty development cooperation provision.[108] The latter established that development cooperation 'shall contribute to the general objective of developing and consolidating democracy and the rule of law, and to that of respecting human rights and fundamental freedom.' This expression has been modified by the 2009 Treaty of Lisbon (TL), but the protection of human rights is still one of the components of EU development cooperation and of external relations more generally.[109] Article 209 TFEU refers to the objectives of Article 21(3) TEU[110] which establishes that: 'the Union shall respect the principles and pursue the objectives set out in paragraphs 1 and 2 in the development and implementation of the different areas of the Union's external action covered by this Title and by Part Five of the Treaty on the Functioning of the European Union, and of the external aspects of its other policies.'[111] Here it is necessary to distinguish between the duty of the EU to respect human rights, that is, the obligation to refrain from adopting any act that can either violate or that can negatively affect individuals' human rights within member states' jurisdiction (including those measures with extraterritorial effects),[112] and a duty to protect individuals in non-EU states' territories or, more precisely, jurisdiction.

This duty to protect finds its legal basis in EU primary law.[113] The instruments applied to protect the principles laid down in Article 21 TEU are not defined by the EU Treaties although the inclusion of the conditionality clause in its international agreements could be one of the instruments employed to comply with Article 21 TEU. However, the EU could also make recourse to other tools.[114]

The conclusion reached by the CJEU in *Portugal v. Council*, according to which the agreement with India would have had to be based on a different Treaty provision than Article 130U TEC to allow the inclusion of human rights as a specific field of cooperation,[115] seems *mutatis mutandis* still valid. In other words, the integration

---

[107]Case C-268/94, *Portugal v. Council* ECLI:EU:C:1996:461; Portugal argued that the Agreement with India should have been based on Article 235 TEC (at present Article 352 TFEU).

[108]At the time of the judgment Article 130u TEC, later 177 TEC and now 208 TFEU.

[109]Bulterman (2005), at 270 also considers that the conclusion of the ECJ in case C-268/94 applies to all external policy areas.

[110]Nakanishi (2014) at 20.

[111]Velluti, 'The Promotion and Integration', above n. 1; Broberg (2011). Ioannides 2017). Study. Reference No: PE 558.764, European Parliamentary Research Service, European Parliament, Brussels, February 2017. Available at SSRN: https://ssrn.com/abstract=2916198. Accessed on 13 June 2020.

[112]See Sect. 4 of Chap. 6 of this book.

[113]Articles 3 paragraph 5 and 21 TEU.

[114]According to Van Elsuwege the clause is the expression of a 'constitutional obligation to ensure that the EU's external action respects [Article 21 TUE] principles', see Van Elsuwege (2019). Prickartz and Staudinger (2019).

[115]For Portugal a correct legal basis would have been former Article 235 TEC (now Article 352 TFEU) (para. 15 of *Portugal v. Council*. See, however, the limits set up by the Court for the use of this provision as legal basis to extend the EU competences. In alternative the lack of Community

of objectives of human rights protection,[116] sustainable development, democracy and the rule of law in EU association or cooperation agreements is distinct from considering Article 217 TFEU on association agreements and Article 208 TFEU on development cooperation agreements[117] as valid legal bases for specific actions to protect human rights of individuals from violations committed by other subjects when the EU or its member states are not directly or indirectly involved.[118]

As for unilateral trade measures that contain provisions aimed at contributing to the protection of human rights, it is necessary to consider that the regulation[119] establishing the GSP schemes, has been adopted on the basis of Article 207 TFEU, the key Common Commercial Policy (CCP) Treaty provision. The GSP is thus an instrument of EU external trade policy. Article 207 TFEU, therefore, must be read in conjunction with Article 3(5) TEU which clearly conceives human rights as a key horizontal objective of EU external action, and Article 21(1) TEU.

Conditionality can be incorporated into EU agreements or in GSP regulations, on the basis of Article 3(5) and Article 21 TEU. The CJEU recently stated in Opinion 2/15 that 'one of the features of that development [of the CCP] is the rule laid down in the second sentence of Article 207(1) TFEU that 'the Common Commercial Policy shall be conducted in the context of the principles and objectives of the Union's external action'. Those principles and objectives are specified in Article 21(1) and (2) TEU and, as is stated in Article 21(2)(f) TEU, relate *inter alia* to sustainable development linked to preservation and improvement of the quality of the environment and the sustainable management of global natural resources. The obligation for the EU to integrate those objectives and principles into the conduct of its CCP is apparent from the second sentence of Article 207(1) TFEU read in conjunction with Article 21(3) TEU and Article 205 TFEU.[120]

It has been argued above that conditionality is a mechanism to guide or influence behaviour or to reward the virtuous conduct of other subjects. This consideration applies also to EU conditionality mechanisms. The question is to understand the underlying reason for the EU's use of such tools aimed at inducing non-EU countries (and possibly also non-state actors established or located in these countries) to

---

competence would be compensated by the participation of Member States as contracting parties to the (mixed) agreement. Mixed agreements are agreements concluded by the EU and its member states as contracting parties with one or more non-EU states. *Ex multis* see Hillion and Koutrakos (2010).

[116]It is necessary to distinguish the obligation to respect human rights abroad in the case of a direct or indirect conduct of public authority abroad or with extraterritorial effect (Cannizzaro 2014) with the obligation to protect human rights from actions of other actors.

[117]See Case C 377/12 *Commission v. Council* ECLI:EU:C:2014:1903, para 37.

[118]For a direct or indirect conduct of public authority abroad. See Cannizzaro (2014). https://doi.org/10.1093/ejil/chu085.

[119]Regulation 978/2012, *above* n. 21.

[120]Opinion of the Court of Justice 2/15 *Free Trade Agreement between the European Union and the Republic of Singapore* ECLI:EU:C:2017:376, paras. 142 and 143, Article 21(1) TEU principles are: democracy, the rule of law, the universality and indivisibility of human rights and fundamental freedoms, respect for human dignity, the principles of equality and solidarity, and respect for the principles of the United Nations Charter and international law.

modify their behaviour or to discourage them from acting illegally. As mentioned above, it is necessary to consider that the reason that first prompted the EU to incorporate negative conditionality into its international agreements was to provide the organisation with an instrument of immediate and strong reaction in cases where the EU's partner country violated human rights or other fundamental values. However, subsequently negative conditionality has become a means to give these normative values centre stage within EU external relations. This is confirmed by the wording of the current version of the clause and by its limited application. The clause thus provides for a coercive instrument that could induce the human rights violator to put an end to its illegal behaviour in certain cases[121] but equally helps the EU to reaffirm the core of its identity values that the Union intends to "export" through its external relations and foreign policy.[122]

Article 21(1) subparagraph 2 TEU provides that: 'The Union shall seek to develop relations and build partnerships with third countries, and international, regional or global organisations which share the principles referred to in the first subparagraph.' Some scholars argue that this provision codifies the conditionality policy of the EU.[123] Taking this point further, we can see that conditionality is based on the same overarching objective and guiding principle of all EU external action, namely, that relations with non-EU countries are (or should be) based on the sharing of common values. However, this does not mean that the EU cannot enter into relations with countries that do not share or that infringe those values, as demonstrated by EU practice. The Union acts also to further its own interests that are considered a legitimate objective to pursue as per Article 21(2) (a).[124] The EU's relationship with Azerbaijan is illustrative.[125] This is a country that does not share common values with the EU but ties with this country are very important for EU energy security.[126]

[121]For a list of cases up to 2015, see the answer given by the High Representative the Union for Foreign Affairs and Security Policy Mogherini on behalf of the European Commission, on the 5th August 2015, to a Member of the European Parliament on the number of EU agreements, containing human rights clauses, suspended in response to human rights violations. Doc. E-008626/2015, (26th may 2015). Available at http://www.europarl.europa.eu/sides/getAllAnswers.do?reference=E-2015-008626&language=EN. Accessed on 13 June 2020.

[122]See above, paragraph 2.1 and Chap. 2 of this book.

[123]See Bartoloni and Cannizzaro (2014).

[124]"The Union shall define and pursue common policies and actions, and shall work for a high degree of cooperation in all fields of international relations, in order to: (a) safeguard its values, fundamental interests, security, independence and integrity" (Article 21, paragraph 2).

[125]99/614/EC, ECSC, Euratom: Council and Commission Decision of 31 May 1999 on the conclusion of the Partnership and Cooperation Agreement between the European Communities and their Member States, of the one part, and the Republic of Azerbaijan, OJ [1999] L246/1. On 14 November 2016, the Council adopted a mandate to negotiate a comprehensive agreement with Azerbaijan, press release available https://www.consilium.europa.eu/en/press/press-releases/2016/11/14/azerbaijan/.

[126]On this issue, see Poli.

In general terms, the EU often adopts a realist approach, whereby it considers that the conclusion of treaty relationships with a partner might improve the situation in the country by exerting pressure[127] rather than strictly scrutinising its partner.[128]

The reason for including positive conditionality in the GSP scheme is to encourage developing countries to ratify and implement a number of international conventions and treaties as well as compensating them for the costs that they might incur for complying with these international treaties. It should be recalled that, through this unilateral trade instrument, the EU also exports the values incorporated into those conventions.

After the entry into force of the TL the EU uses an array of coercive measures at its disposal, such as sanctions and conditionality tools, to promote its founding values as per Article 2 TEU and Article 21(2) TEU. This provision refers to democracy to be "supported and consolidated", which implies a proactive attitude[129] by the EU, rule of law, human rights, that is the same values mentioned in conditionality clauses and in unilateral instruments. The use of positive and negative conditionality mechanisms to prompt third countries to change their behaviour in order to promote EU values overseas, strongly supported by Article 21 TEU, implies some form or degree of extraterritorial effect, which is to be exercised within the limits of international law and the EU legal order.[130] The EU shall promote the respect for human rights, democracy and the rule of law beyond its borders without relying exclusively on the use of conditionality tools but together with or solely on the recourse to other instruments such as political dialogues or consultations involving both non-EU governments and civil society.[131]

---

[127] For example, the Council gave its assent to the provisional application of the agreement with Syria as it is considered that the agreement could lead to improvements in the human rights position in Syria. See Draft Council Decision on the signature and provisional application of certain provisions of a Euro-Mediterranean Association Agreement between the European Community and its Member States and the Syrian Arab Republic 17 August 2009, doc. 9921/. However, as a consequence of extremely serious violations of human rights the Council partially suspended the Association Agreement with Syria in 2011, Council Decision 2011/523 of 2 September 2011 partially suspending the application of the Cooperation Agreement between the European Economic Community and the Syrian Arab Republic OJ [2011] L 228/ 19.

[128] However, the European Parliament urged the Commission 'not to propose free trade agreements and/or association agreements—even containing human rights clauses—to governments of countries where, according to reports by the Office of the High Commissioner for Human Rights of the United Nations, massive human rights violations' take place. Report on the evaluation of EU sanctions as part of the EU's actions and policies in the area of human rights, dc. 2008/2031, 15.7.2008, para 20. More recently the European Parliament's Committee on Foreign Affairs recommended the European Parliament to subordinate its consent to the conclusion of the FTA with Vietnam to the release of political prisoners. See EP Committee on Foreign Affairs, 'Opinion on the draft Council decision on the conclusion of the Free Trade Agreement' (2018/0356 M(NLE), 5 February 2019 between the European Union and the Socialist Republic of Viet Nam, para 15.

[129] Ghazaryan (2014), p. 17. See the observations of the same author on the distinction between principles, objectives and values.

[130] On the issue of extraterritoriality, see Chap. 6 of this book.

[131] E.g. the consultations envisaged under the Trade and Sustainable Development Chapters (TSD) in the new generation of free trade agreements (FTAs), see further Chap. 5 of this book.

4.2.4.1 The Essential Clause as a Basis for the Adoption of Positive Measures

The political clause, made up of the essential element provision together with the non-execution clause, is one of the conditionality mechanisms applied by the EU. It should be recalled that the essential element clause also 'makes human rights the subject of common interest, part of the dialogue between the parties and an instrument for the implementation of positive measures.[132] The essential element clause has an autonomous and separate function, as it can act as the basis for the adoption of positive measures.[133]

These can be measures of support such as financial and technical cooperation or financial aid instruments. For Fierro there is a potential positive entitlement deriving from the essential element clause on the basis of the political and legal statements "shaping" the clause. In particular she refers to a 1991 Council resolution which gave priority to a "positive cooperative approach".[134] In particular, according to the Council, the Union can choose an active promotion of human rights or a negative response to serious and systematic violations, and that before making a decision 'it will wherever possible give preference to the positive approach of support and encouragement'. In one of its most important communications on human rights clauses,[135] in addition to highlighting its function of enabling the parties to adopt restrictive measures, the Commission considered that the clause makes human rights a subject of common interests and instrument for the implementation of positive measures.

Thus far, it is plain to see that the positive scope of the essential element clause has certainly been endorsed by all the main EU institutions.[136] The key issue then is understanding how the EU translates theory into action. It has been clarified above that the competence to include the clause in all EU agreements finds its legal basis in EU primary law. This does not necessarily mean, however, that the material competences of the Union are extended beyond its conferred powers. The clause can be the basis

---

[132]Commission Communication on the inclusion of respect for democratic principles and human rights in agreements between the Community and third countries, COM (95)216, at 7. According to some authors 'EU's essential policies clauses are "aspirational" and aimed at fostering dialogue', Chauffour and Maur (2011).

[133]Fierro (2001). Gazaryan (2015). Bartels underlined the function of the clause 'as a means to force "positive" measures (political dialogue and the funding of initiatives) onto recalcitrant third countries', Bartels (2005). He rightly notes that financial aid to non-governmental organizations, for example under the European Initiative for Democracy and Human Rights (EIDHR), does not need the consent of the government. Bartels (2004).

[134]Resolution of the Council and of the Member States, meeting in the Council, on human rights, democracy and development of 28 November 1991 (Bulletin of the European Communities, No 11/1991 para 2.3.1).

[135]Communication of the European Commission on the inclusion of respect for democratic principles and human rights in agreements between the Community and third countries, COM (95) 216 final, paras. 7/8.

[136]See also as regards the position of the European Parliament 'Resolution on human rights in the world in 2003 and the European Union's policy on the matter', P5_TA-PROV(2004)0376, 22 April 2004.

only for those positive measures that have a legal basis in the EU treaty. For example, the EU can adopt technical measures, financial aid and economic incentives on the basis of Article 209 TFEU for developing countries and on the basis of Article 212 TFEU for non-developing countries. It is clear that this could be done unilaterally, in the absence of the clause, but the incorporation of the essential element provision into the agreement would affect the attitude of EU partners. In fact, in terms of the relationship with its partner(s), the added value of the essential element clause—which certifies the shared commitment of the parties to human rights—is that it clearly sets the normative boundaries within which the cooperation shall be developed, and in more substantive terms, it prevents the EU partner state to oppose or contest positive measures claiming a violation of the principle of non-intervention in internal affairs.[137]

There is nothing surprising in a government's rejection of technical or economic assistance if it is not the beneficiary of these measures and if the assistance is directed towards a civil society association, human rights defenders' groups etc., especially if they oppose the current government.

Finally, the essential elements clause could be the basis for dialogue with the partner country. EU human rights dialogue refers to several forms of relationship between the EU and its partners in the world. For the purpose of our discussion, we mainly focus on structured human rights dialogues, exclusively dedicated to discussing human rights concerns with countries such as with China, Uzbekistan and Kyrgyzstan, and with the African Union,[138] as well as human rights dialogues provided for in agreements such as those concluded within the framework of the Cotonou Partnership agreement.[139] The essential elements clause can be the basis for initiating a dialogue with the partner country in the eventuality that the agreement containing the clause does not provide for such a dialogue or that the country in question is not part of an independent human rights dialogue instrument. It is clear that dialogues require in principle the willingness of both parties to engage into such ad hoc dialogues.

4.3 The Type of Behaviour Required in Conditionality Clauses

The conditionality tools of the EU define, to different degrees and levels of specification, the behaviour required by the recipient.

The "essential element" provision refers to respect for democratic principles, human rights and fundamental freedoms and (in some cases) rule of law and good governance. In the EU, human rights, democracy and the rule of law are conceived

---

[137]See further below on this point, Sect. 5.1.

[138]Council of the European Union EU Guidelines on Human Rights Dialogues with Third Countries, 16526/08, 22 December 2008.

[139]Partnership agreement between the members of the African, Caribbean and Pacific Group of States of the one part, and the European Community and its Member States, of the other part, signed in Cotonou on 23 June 2000, OJ [2000] L317/3, Article 8.

as closely connected and mutually reinforcing. This is confirmed by EU Financing instruments which contain conditionality mechanisms, and which do not specifically define democracy, human rights and the rule of law. For example, the financing instruments for democracy and human rights states: "Democracy and human rights are inextricably linked and mutually reinforcing, as recalled in the Council Conclusions of 18 November 2009 on democracy support in the EU's external relations. The fundamental freedoms of thought, conscience and religion or belief, expression, assembly and association are the preconditions for political pluralism, democratic process and an open society, whereas democratic control, domestic accountability and the separation of powers are essential to sustain an independent judiciary and the rule of law which in turn are required for effective protection of human rights."[140]

Even though the above principles are referred to in most EU documents as if they constituted a single concept,[141] for analytical purposes they will each be examined individually.

4.3.1 Human Rights

The essential elements clause refers to respect for human rights without making any specific reference to their content. The EU stance is clear: human rights are indivisible and universal. There is no space given to cultural, ethnic or religious relativism. Human rights in the clause extend to political, social, cultural, economic, labour, minority rights.

The clause often refers to both legally binding and non-legally binding international law instruments. The most common reference is to the 1948 General Assembly Universal Declaration on Human Rights (UDHR). The test of the "essential element" clause contained in partnership agreements with Eastern European states, such as

---

[140]Regulation (EU) (2014), preamble, indent 11. See also article 2.

[141]See for instance Regulation 235/2014 of the European Parliament and of the Council of 11 March 2014 establishing a financing instrument for democracy and human rights worldwide, *OJ* [2014] L 77/85, 15.3.2014. The eleventh indent of the preamble reads: 'Democracy and human rights are inextricably linked and mutually reinforcing, as recalled in the Council Conclusions of 18 November 2009 on democracy support in the EU's external relations. The fundamental freedoms of thought, conscience and religion or belief, expression, assembly and association are the preconditions for political pluralism, democratic process and an open society, whereas democratic control, domestic accountability and the separation of powers are essential to sustain an independent judiciary and the rule of law which in turn are required for effective protection of human rights.' See also Article 1 ('Subject matter and objective') and the Annex to the regulation, point 3 on actions in support of democracy. It is submitted that this understanding of democracy—which is clearly stated in unilateral EU external policy instruments—cannot but affect the EU perspective and approach in bilateral agreements. For another example of the connection between democracy and the rule of law, see *European Neighbourhood Policy. Fact Sheet*, (Brussels 19 March 2013), according to the EU 'Deep and sustainable democracy includes judicial independence and democratic control over armed forces'.

the agreement with Georgia,[142] which specifies that: 'Respect for the democratic principles, human rights and fundamental freedoms, as proclaimed in the United Nations Universal Declaration of Human Rights of 1948 and as defined in the European Convention for the Protection of Human Rights and Fundamental Freedoms of 1950, the Helsinki Final Act of 1975 of the Conference on Security and Cooperation in Europe and the Charter of Paris for a New Europe of 1990 shall form the basis of the domestic and external policies of the Parties and constitutes an essential element of this Agreement'.[143]

What is the legal significance of such references? The UDHR symbolizes the principle of interrelation, universality, inter-independency and indivisibility of human rights. The Helsinki Final Act[144] or the Charter of Paris[145] have a clear symbolic meaning. The first instrument established, inter alia, a definition of security that is also based on human rights and the second one put an end to an era of confrontation and division in Europe, establishing the grounds for a relationship among states on the basis of human rights, democracy and rule of law (the First Principle). It is to be reminded that those documents are explicitly mentioned in Article 21 TEU.

It has been argued[146] that reference to the soft law documents in the essential element clause transformed them into hard law obligations. As regards the UDHR, one can argue that its content corresponds to customary international law and as such it binds all states. By ratifying an agreement defining respect for human rights as an essential element of the agreement, the parties do not seem to assume new obligations but to reinforce their existing legal commitments. One can doubt that the transformation of soft law commitments into hard law obligations was the intention of the parties. It is interesting to note that in a Joint declaration on Articles 2 and 107 the Partnership and Cooperation Agreement with Russia[147] it is specified that

---

[142]See above n. 97.

[143]The second sentence of the provision specifies: 'Countering the proliferation of weapons of mass destruction, related materials and their means of delivery also constitute essential elements of this Agreement'. The Helsinki Final Act adopted at the end of a three year round of negotiations within the Conference on Security and Cooperation (CSCE which became the OSCE in 1994), has a very important symbolic significance in the relationship between the West and the East during the cold war and that comprises three "baskets" (security and disarmament; economics, science, technology and the environment; the human dimension). The Charter of Paris (1990) contains a part titled: human rights democracy and rule of law. These documents still "represent the cornerstones of a peaceful European continent;" see European Parliament resolution of 12 March 2019 on the state of EU-Russia political relations (2018/2158(INI).

[144]Above n. 87.

[145]Above n. 88.

[146]Cannizzaro (2002); the same is argued by L. Bartels (2005). It is argued that the clause does not transform a soft law instrument in a binding one but it transforms the obligation of the EU partner vis-à-vis the EU (and vice versa) within the context of the agreement itself.

[147]Agreement on partnership and cooperation establishing a partnership between the European Communities and their Member States, of one part, and the Russian Federation, of the other part, OJ [1997] L327/3. The reference to the ECHR was not possible because Russia became a contracting party of the Convention only in 1998 while the agreement with the EU entered into force in December 1997.

the inclusion of the essential element clause in the EU-Russia agreement follows, inter alia: 'from the attachment of both Parties to the relevant obligations, arising in particular from the Helsinki Final Act and the Charter of Paris for a new Europe.' In this case it can be argued that the parties intend to consider the content of the above-mentioned documents as legally binding.[148]

Another example is provided by the essential elements clause contained in the partnership Agreement with African Caribbean and Pacific countries (Cotonou[149]): it does not refer to specific international law instruments but states: "The Parties refer to their international obligations and commitments concerning respect for human rights". A list of those acts is to be found in the Preamble.[150] These instruments perform an interpretative function of the obligations of the parties.

In principle the EU partner country is thus expected to maintain the status quo, that is to continue to apply human rights treaties to which it is a party at the time of negotiation.[151]

In other Partnership agreements with countries outside Europe, such as the one with the Philippines,[152] the essential element sclause is formulated as follows: 'Respect for democratic principles and human rights, as laid down in the Universal Declaration of Human Rights,[153] and other relevant international human rights instruments to which the Parties are contracting parties, and for the principle of the rule of law, underpins the internal and international policies of both Parties and constitutes

---

[148]In the Resolution of February 2019, on the state of EU-Russia political relations (2018/2158(INI)), the European Parliament declared: "... under the present circumstances, Russia can no longer be considered a 'strategic partner'; it is of the view that the principles of Article 2 of the Partnership and Cooperation Agreement (PCA) are no longer being met, and that the PCA should therefore be reconsidered; believes that any framework for the EU-Russia relationship should be based on the full respect of international law, the Helsinki OSCE principles, democratic principles, human rights and the rule of law, and allow for dialogue on managing global challenges, the strengthening of global governance and ensuring enforcement of international rules, particularly with a view to guaranteeing European peace order, and security in EU's neighbourhood and the Western Balkans" (point 3).

[149]Above n. 138.

[150]See Cotonou Agreement Preamble, seventh indent referring to: "Charter of the United Nations, and recalling the Universal Declaration of Human Rights, the conclusions of the 1993 Vienna Conference on Human Rights, the Covenants on Civil and Political Rights and on Economic, Social and Cultural Rights, the Convention on the Rights of the Child, the Convention on the Elimination of all forms of Discrimination against Women, the International Convention on the Elimination of all forms of Racial Discrimination, the 1949 Geneva Conventions and the other instruments of international humanitarian law, the 1954 Convention relating to the status of stateless persons, the 1951 Geneva Convention relating to the Status of Refugees and the 1967 New York Protocol relating to the Status of Refugees".

[151]The assumption is that human rights obligations are complied with by EU partners before concluding the agreement.

[152]Framework Agreement on Partnership and Cooperation between the European Union and its Member States, of the one part, and the Republic of the Philippines, of the other part OJ [2017] L343/3.

[153]The reference to the General Assembly Universal Declaration on Human Rights, not a binding instrument, symbolizes the universality and indivisibility of human rights.

an essential element of this Agreement'. This latter reference makes it clear that these 'other agreements' are the sources[154] of human rights obligations for the parties. It could be noted that this provision is drafted to cover also the legal instruments that the parties might ratify after the conclusion of the EU agreement.[155]

At this juncture, it is necessary to consider that the essential element provision is not only part of a negative instrument (the "essential element" part) but is a guiding principles of the action ("shall form the basis of the domestic and external policies of the parties and constitute an essential element of this Agreement").[156] The reference to those sources of law, therefore, also serve as an interpretative supportive tool within the framework of intensified political dialogues. Indeed, the question of interpretation is more likely to arise in the context of political dialogue where more specific issues of human rights violations may be discussed. When a negative conditionality measure is applied, usually a sanction in the form of aid suspension, there is little scope for interpretation as it follows from a serious and widespread violation of democratic principles, such as flawed elections and coups d'état.

The issue of interpreting the scope of a human rights clause is also likely to arise in the context of negotiations. For example, Singapore opposed the inclusion of the clause in the Partnership and Cooperation Agreement (ESPCA)[157] that was being negotiated with the EU and its member states, because it feared that this could affect its legislation on the death penalty. This is an interesting case because it highlights the problems pertaining to the interpretation of the human rights clause during the negotiations. A compromise was reached by the parties who signed a side letter to the ESPCA declaring that 'neither party are aware (…) of any of each other's domestic laws, or their application, which could lead to the invocation of the non-execution mechanism. Both sides confirm their understanding that …. they are not aware of any of each other's domestic laws, or their application, which could lead to the

---

[154]In other agreements reference is made to the United Nation Covenants of 1966, that is the International Covenant on Civil and Political Rights of 16 December 1966, available at: https://www.ohchr.org/en/professionalinterest/pages/ccpr.aspx, and the International Covenant on Economic, Social and Cultural Rights of 16 December 1966, available at: https://www.ohchr.org/en/professionalinterest/pages/cescr.aspx. Accessed both on 13 June 2020.

[155]This obviously applies to the Convention against Torture and Other Cruel, Inhuman or Degrading Treatment or Punishment and the UN Convention on the Rights of Persons with Disabilities, ratified by Vietnam after singing of the Framework Agreement on Comprehensive Partnership and Cooperation with the EU and its Member States and thus before the entry into force of the agreement.

[156]See, for example, the Association Agreement between the European Union and the European Atomic Energy Community and their Member States, of the one part, and Georgia, of the other part OJ [2014] L261/4.

[157]Proposal for a Council decision on the signing, on behalf of the Union, of the Partnership and Cooperation Agreement between the European Union and its Member States, of the one part, and the Republic of Singapore, of the other part COM (2014) 070 final. The EU-Singapore Free Trade Agreement (FTA) entered into force on November 21, 2019. The Partnership and Cooperation Agreement is linked to the FTA as far as the human rights clause is concerned (see *infra*).

invocation of Article 44 of the Agreement"[158] (i.e. the non-execution mechanism). This is a recognition made in advance by Singapore that it complies with the human rights clause and that the EU will not challenge this.[159] This compromising solution is of concern because in this way the EU is explicitly accepting that the human rights protection standards in Singapore are the same as the level of protection of human rights in the EU. Another question that might arise is the extension of the scope of the human rights so as to include within it the commitment to respect for lesbian, gay, bisexual, and transgender LGBT rights.[160]

In any event, a general reference to human rights without further specification as to their content gives room for more flexibility. The extension of the clause to cover human trafficking is a clear example of the potentiality of the clause and its interpretation.[161]

4.3.2 Democratic Principles

Democracy[162] is clearly related to human rights, as can be inferred from the human rights conventions mentioned in some of the essential element clauses or in the preamble of the partnership agreement, examined above. For example, individual rights 'to vote and to be elected at genuine periodic elections which shall be by universal and equal suffrage and shall be held by secret ballot, guaranteeing the free expression of the will of the electors participation in democratic election' is established in Article 25 of the 1966 International Covenant on Civil and Political Rights (ICCPR).[163] All Contracting parties to the ICCPR[164] are under an obligation to respect such rights. The UN Convention on the Elimination of All Forms of

---

[158] Proposal for a Council decision on the signing, on behalf of the Union, of the Partnership and Cooperation Agreement between the European Union and its Member States, of the one part, and the Republic of Singapore, of the other part, above n. 156, Explanatory Memorandum.

[159] Meissner and Mckenzie (2017). Meissner and Mckenzie (2018).

[160] F. Martines, above n. 66 on this question, considering that those rights are included.

[161] According to the European Commission 'trafficking in human beings will continue to be covered under the Human Rights Clauses in the EU's agreements with third countries, including the Free Trade Agreements', Commission Communication, EU Strategy Towards the Eradication of Trafficking in Human Beings 2012–2016, COM (2012), at 12.

[162] In the European Commission Communication on *Human rights and democracy at the heart of the EU external action Towards a more effective approach* ' it was stated: " Democracy is a universal value based on the freely expressed will of people to determine their own political systems. Human rights and democracy go hand in hand with the empowering freedoms—freedom of expression, association and assembly—which underpin democracy", COM(2011) 886 final, p. 7.

[163] See also Article 13 African Charter on Human and Peoples Rights, 1981.

[164] With the exception of South Sudan, Saudi Arabia (no action) and China (signature) all states are contracting parties of the ICCP. See https://indicators.ohchr.org/. Accessed on 13 June 2020.

Racial Discrimination (CERD),[165] and the 1979 UN Convention on the Elimination of All Forms of Discrimination against Women[166] (CEDAW), contain provisions on participation and elections.

As with human rights, democracy is also not defined in the clause, which usually contains the expression "democratic principles". This highlights the fact that there are some fundamental elements of democracy in the EU partner's legal order that have to be respected, whatever the choice of its political regime. In a Communication dating back to 1998 the Commission clarified that: 'By opting for the phrase 'democratic principles' rather than 'democracy', Article 5 of Lomé IV sought to emphasise the universally recognized principles that must underpin the organisation of the State and guarantee the enjoyment of rights and fundamental freedoms, while leaving each country and society free to choose and develop its own model'.[167]

The concept of "democratic principles" also serves to accentuate the dynamic process leading to democracy. Democratization is a gradual and ongoing process which must take account of a country's socio-economic and cultural context. The above mentioned 1998 Commission Communication contains a list of democratic principles: legitimacy, legality and effective application, including, for example, elements of participatory democracy but also recognition of local democracy and the principle of the free administration of the people, which may lead to administrative decentralization and recourse to consultations on certain key issues.

In the Charter of Paris[168]—mentioned in the essential element clauses contained in association agreements with former Soviet republics—democracy refers to the will of the people, regularly expressed through free and fair elections, representativeness and pluralism; it also entails accountability to the electorate, the obligation of public authorities to comply with the law and justice administered impartially.

Even though there is no definite conception of democracy, on the basis of the instruments mentioned in some of the essential elements clauses, it can be argued that the contracting parties agree on some of the fundamental features of the liberal notion of democracy, such as representation, participation, human rights, liberties, rights to free elections.[169]

---

[165]International Convention on the Elimination of All forms of Racial Discrimination of 21 December 1965, https://www.ohchr.org/en/professionalinterest/pages/cerd.aspx. Accessed on 13 June 2020. On elections see Article 5.

[166]Convention on the Elimination of All Forms of Discrimination against Women of 18 December 1979, available at: https://www.ohchr.org/en/professionalinterest/pages/cedaw.aspx. Accessed on 13 June 2020. On elections see Article 7.

[167]Communication Democratization, the rule of law, respect for human rights and good governance: the challenges of the partnership between the European Union and the ACP States, COM (1998), at 5.

[168]Above n. 88.

[169]Wetzel and Orbie (2015). Wetzel et al. (2017). See also European Parliament, *Annual Report on Human Rights and Democracy in the World 2013 and the European Union's policy on the matter* (2014/2216(INI)), which specifies at point E: "whereas democratic regimes are defined not only by the organisation of elections but also by respect for the rule of law, freedom of speech, respect for human rights, an independent judiciary and impartial administration". In a previous resolution the European Parliament affirmed that "although democratic systems may vary in form

If we are to consider the limited application of the clause, what emerges is that it has been triggered mostly for very serious attacks on democracy: such as coups d'états[170] or the interruption of democratic process,[171] as in the case of flawed elections,[172] that is in cases where there was a clear breach of democratic principles. This does not mean that the EU adopts a minimalist conception of democracy[173] and electoral democracy[174] but rather that so far it has decided to trigger the clause only in exceptional circumstances, when there has undoubtedly been a violation of democratic principles.[175]

The Strategic Partnership Agreement concluded with Canada[176] is also telling in this respect. Article 28 of the Agreement establishes: 'The Parties consider that, for a situation to constitute a "particularly serious and substantial violation" of Article 2(1), its gravity and nature would have to be of an exceptional sort such as a *coup d'état*[177] or grave crimes that threaten the peace, security and well-being of the international

---

and shape, as is the case within the EU, democracy is a universal value and its essential principles or elements are enshrined in numerous international declarations and conventions". It also refers to the UN resolution of 2000 and 2004 A/RES/55/96 and A/RES/59/201. See Democratic Building in External Relation, P7_TA(2009)0056. In the Annual Report on Democracy and Human Rights (doc. 9431/13), it is affirmed: "Genuine elections are an essential basis for a functioning democracy and a key element of sustainable development", p. 45.

[170]The African Union seems more determined in suspending member states in case of coups d'états. Egypt was suspended after the deposition of Mohamed Morsi by General Abdel Fattah el-Sisi while the EU did not define this event as a *coup d'état* and invited Egypt to the EU-Africa summit.

[171]See Commission Communication on the Inclusion of Respect for Democratic Principles and Human Rights in Agreements between the Community and Third Counties, COM (95) 216, Annex II for a list of measures to be taken I this case.

[172]Portela (2007), available at http://ink.library.smu.edu.sg/soss_research/1698. See also Saltnes.

[173]Del Biondo (2011).

[174]See Norberto Bobbio's concept of *political democracy*, based on the control of the ruled over the rulers guaranteed by the electoral process where parties compete, and *societal democracy* which refers to societal control over different policy processes. The notion of democracy inferred from the essential elements clause seems to refer to this concept. A similar distinction is made by Pridham (2000) who uses the notion of *formal and substantive* democracy. Bobbio (1989).

[175]This does not prevent the EU from adopting autonomous sanctions in the case of violations of democratic principles, rule of law and human rights. See, for example, the sanctions against Venezuela. See Council Decision (CFSP) 2017/2074 and Council Regulation (EU) 2017/2063 of 13 November 2017 concerning restrictive measures in view of the situation in Venezuela. This provides for, *inter alia*, a ban on the export of arms and equipment which might be used for internal repression, a ban on the export of surveillance equipment and the freezing of funds and economic resources of certain persons, entities and bodies responsible for serious human rights violations or abuses or the repression of civil society and democratic opposition and persons, entities and bodies whose actions, policies or activities otherwise undermine democracy or the rule of law in Venezuela, as well as persons, entities and bodies associated with them. It is to be recalled that Venezuela was suspended from Mercosur in 2017 and that the country has no treaty relationship with the EU. Venezuela was removed from the EU GSP when it qualified as an upper middle income country.

[176]Strategic Partnership Agreement between the European Union and its Member States, of the one part, and Canada, of the other part OJ [2016] L 329/45.

[177]Aid was suspended in response to the presidential coups in Guatemala in 1993 and 1999. In the Democratic Republic of the Congo, the EU adopted targeted sanctions against members of the

community.' These seem exceptional circumstances, which can actually be explained by the difficult negotiating process with Canada as regards the inclusion of a clause in the Partnership Agreement. In a similar vein, the Cooperation Agreement with New Zealand[178] contains an essential element clause traditionally formulated with reference to commitment to democratic principles, human rights and fundamental freedoms, and the rule of law and good governance[179] and non-proliferation of weapons of mass destruction,[180] but the provision on non-execution (Article 54, paragraphs 3 and 4) is formulated as follows: 'Reaffirming their strong and shared commitment to human rights and non-proliferation, the Parties agree that if either Party considers that the other Party has committed a particularly serious and substantial violation of any of the obligations described in Articles 2(1) and 8(1) as essential elements, which threatens international peace and security so as to require an immediate reaction, it shall immediately notify the other Party of this fact and the appropriate measure(s) it intends to take under this Agreement. The notifying Party shall advise the Joint Committee of the need to hold urgent consultations on the matter.'

In addition, the particularly serious and substantial violation of the essential elements could serve as grounds for appropriate measures under the common institutional framework.[181]

4.3.3 Rule of Law

The other non-trade value usually mentioned in the essential element clause is the rule of law, one of the guiding principles of the EU external relations incorporated into Article 21 of the TEU.[182]

The notion of rule of law is hard to define and a diversity of qualifications exists in the literature. In very broad terms it signifies the submission of the government and of all components of society to the law. Supremacy of the law, accountability to the law, public promulgation, equal enforcement by an independent judiciary are

government who were seeking to exert control over the December 2018 presidential and parliamentary elections. In November 2018, the EU froze support to the government of Tanzania in response to negative political developments in the country.

[178] Partnership Agreement on Relations and Cooperation between the European Union and its Member States, of the one part, and New Zealand, of the other part, OJ [2016] L 321/3.

[179] See Article 2, paragraph 1.

[180] See Article 8, paragraph 1.

[181] As referred to in Article 52(1).

[182] Pech (2012). The EU Court of Auditors, in Opinion 1/18, summarized rule of law as including: "legality, which implies a transparent, accountable, democratic and pluralistic process for enacting laws; legal certainty; prohibition of arbitrariness of the executive powers; independent and impartial courts; effective judicial review including respect for fundamental rights; and equality before the law".

frequent elements that one finds in any rule of law definition. As argued elsewhere, the notion can also extend to the *international* rule of law.[183]

A common distinction is made between so-called *thin* and *thick* conceptions of the rule of law. A *thin* concept of the rule of law emphasizes formal and procedural aspects (how the law is formulated and applied); a *thick* notion of the rule of law is concerned with the substantive aspects of the law, which incorporates human rights. It is clear that the EU promotes a *thick* rule of law. In a Communication dating back to 1991[184] the Commission specified that the rule of law requires that "governments guarantee the enjoyment of human rights, primarily through an independent judiciary, is a particularly significant indicator. Great importance will therefore be attached to the main civil liberties and political freedoms, in keeping with the desire for democracy and efficient economic machinery". Another provision that can be referred to which helps define the rule of law concept as adopted by the EU and its partners is contained in the Cotonou agreement.[185] Article 9 of the Partnership Agreement specifies, inter alia: "The structure of government and the prerogatives of the different powers shall be founded on rule of law, which shall entail in particular effective and accessible means of legal redress, an independent legal system guaranteeing equality before the law and an executive that is fully subject to the law."

On the basis of what has been observed above, it is safe to suggest that the clause is sufficiently clear as to the "hard content" of the behaviour required by the donor to avoid triggering the negative conditionality. It might be a problem for specific rights or aspects of the rule of law. The lack of definition leaves some flexibility to the EU and its partners that can be clarified in the framework of political dialogue[186] where suggestions may be made over measures to be taken and directions to be followed.[187]

---

[183] Martines, 'Human rights clauses in EU Agreements', above n. 66. See the example reported by Bartels (2014a). Respect for international rule of law is reiterated in the preamble of the Declaration on Principles of International Law Concerning Friendly Relations and Cooperation Among States in Accordance with the Charter of the United Nations, 25 GAOR, Supp (No 28), U.N. Doc. A/5217 (1970); see also the UN Millennium Declaration, Resolution adopted by the UN General Assembly A/Res/55/2. (18 September 2000), para. 9.

[184] 1991s (91) 61 final, Commission Communication to the Council and Parliament, Human Rights, Democracy and Development Cooperation Policy, Brussels, 25 March 1991, at 6.

[185] Above n. 138.

[186] See also for a quite detailed definition of the rule of law Commission Communication, Democratization, the rule of law, respect for human rights and good governance: the challenges of the partnership between the European Union and the ACP States, COM(98) 146, at 4.

[187] The case of Colombia and Peru is illustrative in this respect. The European Union signed a Trade Agreement with Colombia and Peru in June 2012, provisionally applied since August 2013. EU Trade Agreement with Colombia, Peru OJ [2012] 354/3. As explicitly recognized by the European Parliament 'both Colombia and Peru have made enormous efforts in recent years to improve the general condition of their citizens' lives, including human and labour rights', however, 'despite these enormous efforts, in order to fully achieve the high standards set out and demanded by individual citizens, civil society organisations, the opposition parties and the government, there is still substantial work to be done'. The EP suggested a road map for legislative reforms in the field of human rights and in particular labour rights. European Parliament resolution of 13 June 2012 on the EU trade agreement with Colombia and Peru (2012/2628 (RSP).

During negotiation, discussions[188] concerning the incorporation of the clause and its specific content make the EU's policy priorities and interests clear for its partners. As mentioned, the inclusion of the clause makes it impossible for the parties to claim that human rights, democratic principles, the rule of law, and other values are matters of national concern.[189]

4.3.4 Other Non-trade Values as Standards of Behaviour

Other non-trade values are mentioned in some of the agreements the EU and its member states concluded with third countries. Although a basic model of the political clause[190] exists and a standard formulation can be detected, there are some differences that are justified by regional differences and that highlight EU interests and concerns.

The Association Agreement with Ukraine,[191] which creates quite a unique form of economic integration, includes, for example, as an essential element, together with the traditional ones: 'Promotion of respect for the principles of sovereignty and territorial integrity, inviolability of borders and independence as well as countering the proliferation of weapons of mass destruction.'

These are corollaries of state sovereignty and general principles of international law and are referred to as a component of the prohibition of the use of force in the United Nations (UN) Charter[192]: a unilateral change of territory by coercive

---

[188] There are various reasons why the EU partners object to the inclusion of non-economic values in trade agreements. A common reason concerns the contested link between human rights and trade. For example, Australia contended that human rights protection would be better guaranteed within a multilateral context. See Fierro, above, n. 25, pp. 28–300. Non EU-countries consider that the clause impinges upon their sovereignty and that the clause could be abused. For example Australia feared that trade unions could lobby the EU for action against Australia on the basis of the Universal Declaration's recognition of everybody's right to form and join trade unions, available at www.hartford-hwp.com/archives/24/121.html. Accessed on 13 June 2020. On the contrary, the inclusion of a human rights clause can be accepted by a non-EU country (especially new democracy) as a way of proving its commitments to human rights and democracy and as a means to increase its international reputation and to attract foreign investments.

[189] Although the principle of non-interference cannot be invoked in case of gross violations of human rights, the issue of sovereignty and identity values has been invoked by EU partners to object to the inclusion of the clause. See the example concerning Mexico reported above n. 70.

[190] The content of the clause was first spelled out by the Commission in its communication COM (95) 216.

[191] Association Agreement between the European Union and its Member States, of the one part, and Ukraine, of the other part OJ [2014] L161/3, in force since September 2017.

[192] Article 2.4 of the Charter of the United Nations of 26 June 1945, available https://www.un.org/en/charter-united-nations/. Accessed on 12 June 2020. In the Association Agenda to prepare and facilitate the implementation of the Association agreement, there is a reference to the intensification of "consultations and coordination through available diplomatic and military channels to address international issues of common concern, including and especially challenges to commonly shared principles of international peace and security, as established by the UN Charter, the OSCE Helsinki Final Act". Joint Proposal for a COUNCIL DECISION on the Union position within the Association

means amounts to a violation of international law.[193] It is clear that (the unlikely) violation of the partner's territorial integrity by one of the contracting parties of the EU-Ukraine association agreement can trigger the suspension or termination of the agreement. A consequence that does not need to be provided for in a treaty but that would unquestionably find a justification in international law. However, it seems clear that this provision intends to indicate the relevance for the Union of the territorial integrity of Ukraine that could be threatened by other countries. When Ukraine's territorial integrity was violated by the annexation of Crimea by Russia,[194] sanctions against the latter were adopted as part of the Common Foreign and Security Policy (CFSP).[195]

In the Association Agreement with Georgia[196] the parties 'agree to promoting respect for the principles of sovereignty and territorial integrity, inviolability of borders and independence.' But these values are not qualified as essential elements. The Association Agreement with Moldova does not contain such a reference at all.[197]

The inclusion of the non-proliferation of weapons of mass destruction in the essential element provision dates back to the 'European Strategy against the proliferation of Weapons of Mass Destruction'[198] and in particular to a Council Document[199]

Council established by the Association Agreement between the European Union, the European Atomic Energy Community and its Member States, of the one part and Ukraine, of the other part with regard to the adoption of a Recommendation on the implementation of the EU-Ukraine Association Agenda, Join 2015 004 final.

[193]On this issue, with reference to Crimea, see Marxsen (2015).

[194]The process took place between the 20 February 2014 and 26 March 2014.

[195]Council decision 2014/145/CFSP concerning restrictive measures in respect of actions undermining or threatening the territorial integrity, sovereignty and independence of Ukraine OJ [2014] L78/16 (asset freezes and visa bans on persons and entities responsible for actions against Ukraine's territorial integrity); Council decision 2014/386/CFSP of 23 June 2014 concerning restrictions on goods originating in Crimea or Sevastopol, in response to the illegal annexation of Crimea and Sevastopol OJ[2014] L183/70 (prohibition to provide, directly or indirectly, financing or financial assistance, as well as insurance and reinsurance, related to the import of goods originating in Crimea or Sevastopol).

[196]Association Agreement with Georgia, above n. 156.

[197]Association Agreement between the European Union and the European Atomic Energy Community and their Member States, of the one part, and the Republic of Moldova, of the other part OJ [2014] L 260/4.

[198]See the Council 'EU strategy against Weapons of Mass Destruction', (WMD) doc. 15708 (Brussels 10 December 2003, at 13). In the framework of its CFSP, since 2003, the EU has developed a strategic framework to identify new threats to security and to define the common interests and objectives of EU foreign and security policy. WMD are one of the challenges identified by the European Security Strategy (12 December 2003), For an analysis of the origin of the strategy, see Grip (2009a; 2009b).

[199]Council of the EU, Fight against the proliferation of weapons of mass destruction. Mainstreaming non-proliferation policies into the EU's wider relations with third countries', doc.14997/03 Brussels, 19 November 2003. In this document the Council contemplates different hypothesis: the inclusion of the clause in future mixed agreements, the insertion of the clause on occasion of amending agreement in force or the conclusion of a separate agreement linked to the overall agreement.

providing for the introduction of such a reference.[200] The integration of the EU's non-proliferation strategy into its external trade and cooperation policy raises the question of whether the structure of the essential element clause, conceived as an incentive for the protection of human rights and other values mostly in the EU's partners' domestic legal order, is an appropriate tool to attain the external policy strategy objective in a global context. Moreover, there is a serious risk of undermining the EU's credibility in the case of non-compliance.

Other non-trade values clause are the International Criminal Court (ICC) Clause,[201] the anti-terrorism[202] and the small arms clauses.[203] Since they are non-essential elements,[204] the non-execution clause cannot be triggered. This does not exclude recourse to other forms of reaction by the EU in case of violation of those

---

[200]The first EU agreement including a WMD clause was the EU Partnership and Cooperation Agreement (PCA), with the Republic of Tajikistan signed in 2004, OJ [2009] L 350/1, 29.12.2009.

[201]According to the EU the International Criminal Court (ICC) 'is an essential means of promoting respect for international humanitarian law and human rights, thus contributing to freedom, security, justice and the rule of law' Council Decision 2011/168/CFSP of 21 March 2011 on the International Criminal Court and Repealing Common Position 2003/444/CFSP, *OJ* L 76/56, 22.3.2011, EU's Reply to Information request of paragraph 6, sub-paragraph h) of the Plan of Action for Achieving Universality and Full Implementation of the Rome Statute, June 2013, available at https://www.icc-cpi.int. The ICC clause formulation differs according to the status of non-EU countries as Members or non-Members of the ICC Statute. For the list of agreements containing the ICC clause, see the European Union's reply to the information request in paragraph 6, sub-paragraph h) of the Plan of Action for achieving universality and full implementation of the Rome Statute, available at www.sipri.org. Accessed on 12 June 2020.

[202]The inclusion of anti-terrorism clauses in EU agreements dates back to the Plan of Action to Combat Terrorism (European Council 21 September 2001). Council doc. 6898/02). The European Declaration on Combating Terrorism of 25 March 2004 provided for the inclusion of effective anti-terrorism clause in all EU agreements (Objective 1) as a key element of the EU relations with priority countries (European Council, EU Counter-terrorism Coordinator, 'EU Counter Terrorism Clauses: an assessment', doc. 14458/02/04/, 18.11.2004. See the Association agreement with Syria (finalised the 9th December 2003); Cooperation agreement with Vietnam. The clause establishes a commitment of the parties to engage in co-operation and establish the reference parameters of such a cooperation taking place in the framework of international relations. It is interesting to note that these clauses provide the EU with much clearer benchmark to evaluate the EU's partners' behaviour than the human rights clauses. For example, the anti-terrorism clause refers to the (binding) UN Security Council Resolution 1373, which requires, *inter alia*, the freezing of terrorist assets or the signing of a number of anti-terrorist Conventions by States.

[203]The provision addresses the illicit accumulation and trafficking of small arms and light weapons (SALW), and complements the WMD clause as part of an integrated approach to disarmament and arms control. The inclusion of this clause is part of the EU strategy to combat the illicit trafficking of SALW and their ammunition. See for the model SALW clause, Council of the European Union, Council Conclusion on the inclusion of a SALW Article in agreements between the EU and third Countries, Brussels, Doc. 17186, 17.12.2008.

[204]Even if the ICC clause is not an essential element and cannot not trigger the adoption of appropriate measures in the case of non-ratification of the Rome Statute by the EU partner, the inclusion of the clause in the Cotonou Agreement has prompted Sudan not to ratify the revised Cotonou agreement in 2011. This prevented Sudan from having access to the 10th European Development Fund. The Commission continued to finance essential services to the Sudanese population through the 9th European Development Fund and other financial instruments such as for example the European Initiative for Human Rights (EIDHR), and the Development Cooperation Instrument (DCI)

provisions. Similar arguments could be made about good governance which in the Cotonou Agreement is qualified as a fundamental element.[205] Good governance is defined[206] as ‘the transparent and accountable management of human, natural, economic and financial resources for the purposes of equitable and sustainable development.’[207] It entails clear decision-making procedures at the level of public authorities, transparent and accountable institutions, the primacy of law in the management and distribution of resources and capacity building for elaborating and implementing measures aiming in particular at preventing and combating corruption”. Serious cases of corruption[208] (in relation to programmes supported by the EU, but not exclusively)[209] constitute a violation of good governance that might trigger Article 97 (consultation) and also the application of “appropriate measures”.[210] It thus seems that the qualification of *fundamental* element provides for the possibility that—after consultation according to Article 97—punitive measures can be adopted.

The (very poor) practice does not clarify the issue. In the case of measures against Liberia, the Council decision was adopted on the basis of Articles 96 and 97 Cotonou Agreement but no distinction was made between human rights violations and corruption.[211]

---

thematic programmes. See Parliamentary Questions, 4 February 2010, Answer given by M. De Gucht on behalf of the Commission.

[205] Hilpold (2000); Ibid, Hilpold (2017).

[206] In more general terms ‘good governance is the process whereby public institutions guarantee the realisation of human rights in a manner essentially free of abuse and corruption, and with due regard for the rule of law. Moreover, the true test of ‘good’ governance is the degree to which it also delivers on the promise of economic and social rights’. United Nations High Commissioner for Human Rights (OHCHR), Good Governance and Human Rights, November 2016.

[207] Sustainable development is defined “as the use of natural resources in a manner that meets the needs of the present without compromising the ability of future generation to their own needs”. The World Commission Development on Environment and Development (WCED) Report, also known as “Brundtland Commission”, 1987 (Report para 27) https://sustainabledevelopment.un.org/milestones/wced. Accessed on 13 June 2020.

[208] It is debatable whether there is an international customary law obligation upon states to fight against corruption. According to some: ‘it is certainly a norm of general international law that obliges states to fight corruption offences, since the structure of the current international community attaches to them individually and collectively the responsibility of ensuring the orderly and legal pursuit of international relations including with and between private parties.’ Parisi (2019). The European Parliament in a resolution adopted on 13 September 2017 on corruption and human rights in third countries calls ‘on the EU to include an anti-corruption clause alongside human rights clauses in agreements with third countries that should require monitoring and consultations and, as a last resort, to impose sanctions or suspend such agreements in the event of serious and/or systemic corruption leading to serious human rights violations’, see doc P8_TA-PROV(2017)0346, point 19.

[209] See COM (2003) 615 final.

[210] Broberg (2010).

[211] Council decision 2002/274 of 25 March 2002 concluding consultations with Liberia under Articles 96 and 97 of the ACP Partnership Agreement OJ [2002] L96/23.

Another agreement containing a reference to good governance is the EU-Chile Association Agreement[212] where good governance is not part of the essential element clause (the parties "reaffirm their attachment to the principle of good governance").[213] This raises the question of whether and how the EU can react to the violation of such principle where the content of the obligation is not defined.

4.3.5 Sustainable Development as a New Form of Conditionality?

This section considers whether the provisions of sustainable development included in agreements concluded with third states, especially the so-called "new generation" trade agreements,[214] to be a new form of conditionality. The idea put forward is summarized as follows: "the legal architecture of Trade and Sustainable Development (TSD) chapters (enforceability; monitoring and civil society consultation and dispute settlement) constitutes an improved model of conditionality".[215]

Firstly, it must be noted that the chapter on sustainable development aims at, *inter alia*, promoting the effective implementation of multilateral labour and environmental agreements to which the EU and its partner are parties. Promoting ratification of other labour and environmental protection conventions is not excluded, as specified, for instance, in the Free Trade Agreement with Korea[216] where the list of objectives includes "promoting the ratification of fundamental and other ILO Conventions and multilateral environmental agreements with an impact on trade".[217] Other provisions require the parties not to lower their level of protection.[218]

---

[212] Agreement establishing an association between the European Community and its Member States, of the one part, and the Republic of Chile, of the other part OJ [2002] L 352/3, Art. 2.

[213] 'According to the United Nations Office of the High Commissioner for Human Rights (OHCHR), good governance is tightly linked to human rights. It is seen as encompassing, among other issues: full respect of human rights; rule of law; effective participation; multi-actor partnerships; political pluralism; transparent and accountable processes in institutions; an efficient and effective public sector; legitimacy; political empowerment of people; equity; sustainability; and tolerance'. https://www.ohchr.org/EN/Issues/Development/GoodGovernance/Pages/GoodGovernanceIndex.aspx. Accessed on 13 June 2020. See also Ioannides, above n. 111.

[214] The first agreement to include a TSD was the EU Cariforum economic partnership agreement (EPA). Council Decision of 15 July 2008 on the signature and provisional application of the Economic Partnership Agreement between the CARIFORUM States, of the one part, and the European Community and its member states, of the other part; OJ [2008] L 289/1.

[215] Laugier (2018).

[216] Free Trade Agreement between the European Union and its Member States, of the one part, and the Republic of Korea, of the other part OJ [2011] L 127/1, Korea FTA.

[217] Annex 13, paragraph 1, (c).

[218] Article 13.7, paragraph, 2 As noted by Bartels "It is quite conceivable that a measure may reduce the level of domestic protection in these areas without this amounting to a violation of the norms set out in the human rights clause, or indeed in any applicable multilateral environmental agreement." Bartels (2013), at 308.

As regards the monitoring of the chapter's provisions, a special body—the Committee on Trade and Sustainable Development—has been established[219] with the task of overseeing the implementation of the TSD chapter. Moreover, the agreement provides for the setting up of Domestic Advisory Group(s) on sustainable development (environment and labour)—composed of independent representative organisations of civil society in the fields of environment, labour and business—with the task of advising on the implementation of the TSD Chapter. The Members of Domestic Advisory Group(s) of each Party meet at a Civil Society Forum in order to conduct a dialogue encompassing sustainable development aspects of trade relations between the Parties.[220] A consultation procedure is provided for any matters of mutual interest arising under the TSD chapter.[221] It is possible that the question is considered by Committee on Trade and Sustainable Development at the request of one of the parties. If the government to government consultations has not led to satisfactory results, a Panel of experts may be convened.[222] The panel report is public and neither party can block it.

From these characteristics of the TSD chapter, it emerges that this chapter cannot be equated to the essential elements clause (conditionality mechanism) contained in EU agreements with third countries. The approach is clearly one of cooperation and dialogue. No punishment or appropriate measures are provided for specifically in the case of infringement of the TDS chapter, although appropriate measures in accordance with international law can be adopted in case of denunciation of the agreement not sanctioned by the general rules of international law.[223]

Another problem concerns the effect of the TSD chapter on the essential element clause as regards its content. As discussed above, the clause covers all human rights including labour rights. At the same time labour rights are protected under the ILO conventions that are mentioned in the TSD chapter and whose effective implementation is the object of a specific commitment and cooperation procedure. It is argued that the inclusion of the TDS chapter does not affect the scope of the clause. The tools applied are different: the essential element and non-execution provisions can be triggered in case of serious violations of labour rights,[224] which are treated as human rights, although the clause has never been activated by human rights violations. Dialogue, monitoring and cooperation in the TSD Chapter are meant to address the structural difficulties in applying labour conventions or issues of interpretation of labour rights. Unilateral enforcement of TSD is not contemplated.

---

[219]Korea FTA, Article 15.2, paragraph 1.

[220]Korea FTA, Article 13.13.

[221]Korea FTA, Article 13.14.1.

[222]Korea FTA, Article 13.15.

[223]Korea FTA, Article 15.12.2.

[224]ILO Declaration on Fundamental Principles and Rights to Work, 1998, available https://www.ilo.org/declaration/lang--en/index.htm.

4.4 Behaviour Required in GSP Arrangements

In the case of the GSP the behaviour required changes according to the different schemes.[225] The general GSP scheme provides for the suspension of tariff preferences in cases of violation of the ILO's core labour and human rights standards. To be eligible for the GSP+ scheme (special incentive arrangement for sustainable development and good governance) a country is required to have previously ratified, and to undertake effective implementation of a number of international conventions; it also has to accept monitoring mechanisms provided for by those conventions and to cooperate with GSP+ monitoring led by the European Commission, as explained below. The list of conventions is contained in an Annex to the GSP regulation and it is determined by the EU alone.[226] Those conventions concern human rights, labour standards (eight core ILO labour standard conventions) but also environmental protection and climate change (for example the Cartagena Protocol on Biodiversity, The Kyoto Protocol[227]), Good Governance (UN Convention on Narcotic Drugs), (Part B Conventions.).[228] The fulfilment of this requirement does not create problems of interpretation. The list of ratifications has to be presented by the State that is applying for inclusion in the scheme.

A rather different question concerns implementation. Currently, Article 9(1) specifies as a condition that 'the most recent available conclusions of the monitoring bodies under those conventions (the 'relevant monitoring bodies') do not identify a serious failure to effectively implement any of those conventions'. One can observe that the EU relies exclusively on external evaluation to check implementation by a beneficiary country.[229] It is clear that the idea conveyed by this provision is that the GSP+ aims at promoting sustainable economic development in beneficiary countries. Therefore, not all implementation problems lead to exclusion from the GSP+, provided that there is a concrete commitment by the beneficiary country to remedy a critical situation.

This can be illustrated by the case of Sri Lanka. In its Report on assessment of the application for GSP+ by Sri Lanka'[230] the European Commission clarified that:

---

[225]See, this chapter, Sect. 2.1 and Chap. 5, Sect. 3.1.

[226]Shaffer and Apea (2005).

[227]As compared with the previous GSP Scheme the new regulation has added the Framework Convention on Climate Change (UNFCCC), and removed the International Convention on the Suppression and Punishment of the Crime of Apartheid.

[228]See Cherubini (2017).

[229]In Resolution of 5 July 2016 on Implementation of the 2010 Recommendations of Parliament on Social and Environmental Standards, Human Rights and Corporate Responsibility, Reference no P8_TA-PROV(2016)0298, Strasbourg, 5 July 2016, the European Parliament asked the European Commission and the Council to clarify the criteria of serious failure to effectively implement' an international convention and 'serious and systematic violation of principles' either through a delegated act or through the forthcoming revision of Regulation 978/2012, above n. 21.

[230]Commission Report on assessment of the application for GSP+ by Sri Lanka'SWD(2016) 474 final.

'for the purposes of GSP, a serious failure to effectively implement ILO conventions occurs when the tripartite International Labour Conference (ILC) Committee of Application of Standards, in the context of the yearly meetings of the International Labour Conference, notes the existence of a serious failure to implement a convention and introduces a "special paragraph" to that effect in its Report'. Thus, an infringement of the listed conventions is tolerated and does not impede eligibility for GSP+ arrangement unless it reaches a certain degree (serious violation).

Another requirement imposed on the (potential) recipient is that of not formulating reservations prohibited by the convention or incompatible with its object and purpose.[231] If the first condition is objective, since it is based on the text of the convention, the second one requires a more specific and institutionalized procedure (as defined in Article 9 of the Regulation).

The beneficiary is also required to commit to maintaining ratification of the GSP+ Conventions, accepting regular monitoring, respecting the reporting obligations under the conventions and to fully cooperate with the European Commission in the GSP+ monitoring procedure referred to in Article 13 of the GSP regulation. These conditions clearly aim at ensuring effective implementation in order to avoid merely formal compliance. The undertaking to implement the conventions is however more future oriented. On the basis of Article 13 of the GSP Regulation, the European Commission verifies the ratification status of the relevant conventions and monitors their effective implementation. It cooperates with the relevant monitoring bodies by examining the conclusions and recommendations of those monitoring bodies.

The removal of a country from GSP+ depends (in addition to where a beneficiary no longer satisfies vulnerability criteria) on whether it has made reservations incompatible with the ratified convention (Article 9.1.c) or withdrawn the undertakings referred to in points (d), (e) and (f) of Article 9(1).[232]

Negative conditionality concerning non-trade values applies to all GSP arrangements. Preferences are withdrawn on a number of grounds such as unfair trading practices and serious shortcomings in customs controls and in the event of 'serious and systematic violation of principles' contained in the conventions listed in Part A of Annex VIII, that are considered core human rights and labour conventions.

The GSP conditionality mechanisms respond to criteria of transparency and precision as far as the behaviour required is concerned. The margin of flexibility in evaluating behaviour is rather restricted since it is based on objective criteria (ratification, prohibited reservations). Flaws in implementation are to be verified by external monitoring and by specialized bodies.

---

[231] For example, Pakistan ratified the Convention against Torture and the International Covenant on Civil and Political Rights in 2010 and removed reservations to certain human rights conventions in October 2011. Pakistan gained GSP+ status as of 2014. See Commission Joint staff working document The EU Special Incentive Arrangement for Sustainable Development and Good Governance ('GSP+ ') assessment of Pakistan covering the period 2016–2017 SWD(2018) 29 final.

[232] The difference is clear: in one scenario the country has withdrawn its undertakings and has been removed, in the other case the undertakings have not been respected.

4.5 EU Conditionality Tools and International Law

Conditionality tools might raise some problems of compatibility with international law, in particular, the adoption of appropriate measures in the case of serious violation of one of the values the respect of which is qualified as an essential element of the agreement, the asymmetry that can be present within conditionality when it affects the intention of a state to conclude an international agreement (e.g. the GSP+ scheme); the compatibility of non-reciprocity and non-discrimination in the GSP Scheme.

4.5.1 Conditionality Clauses and International Law

In case of non-compliance with the essential element provision of the agreement, the "non-execution clause"[233] provides for the application of "appropriate measures" by either party.

Formally, the clause can be activated by the EU partner in the case of violation of essential elements by the EU or one of its member states. The European Commission has stressed that the discussion on human rights 'should be a two-way one, with the EU also agreeing to discuss human rights and democracy within its borders'.[234] The bilateral character of the clause makes it easier, in principle, for EU partners to accept it.

To date, the clause has been activated only by the EU since the contracting parties of the agreements containing this negative conditionality instrument have been, until recently, developing countries that do not have the economic and political strength to threaten the activation of the clause or of sanctions in general. It is noteworthy that in recent times the clause has also been included in agreements with developed (and thus stronger) countries.

Ultimately, it is in the power of each party to unilaterally qualify a situation as a violation, or as a serious violation of an essential element. Parties enjoy a broad margin of discretion in deciding whether to invoke the clause and, in this case, which measures they considers appropriate.[235] It is clear, but often underestimated, that the clause, although formulated in legal terms, has a strong political character.

---

[233]The expression used in EU agreements to refer to the clause varies: "Fulfilment of obligations" or "Settlement mechanism" or "non-execution of the agreement". The non-execution clause has a general application since it can be triggered in the case of a violation of other provisions of the agreement. See Bartels, *Human Rights Conditionality in EU's International Agreements* above n. 133.

[234]Communication from the Commission to the Council and the European Parliament—The European Union's role in promoting human rights and democratisation in third countries, COM (2001) 252 final, 8.5.2001, p. 9.

[235]See case T-292/09 *Mugraby* v. *Council of the European Union and European Commission*, ECLI:EU:T:2011:418.

The "punishment"—may translate into a suspension[236] or termination of the agreement or suspension of financial aid.[237] In principle, other measures might be adopted, such as the so called "smart sanctions", that is visa bans or travel limitation or freezing the assets of persons involved inhuman rights violations.[238]

The suspension or termination of any agreement provisions shall find justification in international law. Unilateral suspension or termination of treaties is possible only in a defined number of cases. One of these is a material breach of the agreement. The combined effect of the essential element and the non-execution provisions seems to reproduce the international customary rule codified in the Vienna Convention of the Law of Treaties,[239] that is the *inadimplenti non est adimplendum* principle.[240] Instead, it is posited that the combined effect of the "essential element" and the "non execution" clauses is not the application of the *inadimplenti* rule but rather the setting up of a *self-contained regime* regulating the parties' response to a breach of the treaty. In fact, in the case of a material breach of the treaty,[241] the above-mentioned international customary law allows the parties only to suspend or terminate the agreement[242] that has been breached, whereas the non-execution clause allows the parties to apply "appropriate measures", leaving the hypothesis of suspension of the agreement as a measure 'of last resort'.[243] The two provisions (essential element

---

[236]The Council decision of 11 March 1999 on the procedure for implementing Article 366a of the fourth ACP-EC Convention (no longer in force) established that: 'If, on expiry of the deadline set in Article 366a for the consultations and despite all efforts, no solution has been found, or immediately in a case of urgency or refusal to hold consultations, the Council may, pursuant to that Article, decide, on a proposal from the Commission, to take appropriate steps including partial suspension acting by a qualified majority. The Council shall act unanimously in case of a full suspension of application of the Convention in relation to the ACP State concerned'.

[237]This might create a problem of compatibility between development cooperation goals on the one hand, and democracy promotion on the other. Del Biondo (2015a).

[238]Portela (2018).

[239]Vienna Convention on the Law of Treaties, concluded in Vienna on 23 May 1969, United Nations, Treaty series, Vol. 1155, I-18232, 1980 (VCLT).

[240]Whereby a material breach of an agreement can be invoked as a cause of suspension or extinction of a treaty. According to the International Court of Justice, Article 60 VCLT is declaratory of international customary law. See the ICJ (1997). See also Arbitral Tribunal *Rainbow Warrior* case, *New Zealand* v. *France*, Judgment 30.4.1990, U.N.R.I.A.A., Vol XX, at 251. See E. Fierro, *European Union's Approach to Human Rights Conditionality in Practice*, cit. at 221; Hachez at 24. The Court of Justice also referred to the essential element clause as 'an important factor for the exercise of the right to have a development cooperation agreement suspended or terminated where the non-member country has violated human rights' (C-268/94, *Council* v. *Portugal*, para. 27), but it should be reminded that the essential element clause in the agreement was not accompanied by a non-execution provision.

[241]That is a repudiation of the treaty or violation of a provision 'essential to the accomplishment of the object or purpose of the treaty'. See Article 60 3(a) and 3(b) of the VCLT.

[242]See, above on the Baltic and Bulgarian version of the clause, Sect. 2.3.1.

[243]The reference to measures which 'least disrupt the functioning of the agreement', as a formula that is usually applied, confirms that the suspension of the agreement is a measure of last resort. See for example the Framework Agreement between the EU, its Member States and Korea, Joint Interpretative Declaration concerning Article 45 and 46. In the case of Partnership agreement with

and non-execution) include the violation of non-trade values within the framework of the Law of Treaties as a contractual obligation.

As for the legality of adopting measures other than suspension and termination,[244] one has to envisage two scenarios. Firstly, there are measures that are not a violation of an international obligation perpetrated by the "sanctioning" state, such as for example, the suspension of financial aid if it is unilaterally granted, that is if it is not provided for in an agreement with the targeted state. These measures can be adopted even if the clause was not included in the agreement. On the contrary, if the measure adopted amounts to a violation of an obligation previously assumed by the EU,[245] the clause constitutes the legal basis of those measures. In this case, proportionality[246] and compatibility with international law, that is the standards usually required by international customary law for countermeasures, must be respected.

The relevance of the clause, as regards international law, can be appreciated when comparison is made with a hypothetical agreement that does not contain the essential element clause-suspension provisions (as it was in earlier EU practice). If an EU partnership or association agreement did not include a political clause, suspension or termination of the agreement (or any other coercive measure) by the EU could be contested by the other party because violation of democratic principles or the rule of law would not amount to a breach of the agreement.[247] In this scenario, the suspension of the agreement by the EU could be resorted to as a countermeasure, which presupposes that the targeted state has violated an international obligation qualified as *erga omnes*.[248] However, the question whether a non-injured state can

Canada, it is specified that the 'unlikely event' of the serious violation of the essential element clause would lead to the termination of the relationships, leaving no space to recourse to other measures.

[244]As regards the content of those measures, one can find some examples in the list provided by the European Commission in 1995. See Commission Communication on the Inclusion of Respect for Democratic Principles and Human Rights in EC Agreements with Third Countries, COM (95) 216 final, 23.05.1995, Annex II, at 17, mentioning reduction of cultural, scientific, and technical cooperation programmes; postponement of a Joint Committee meeting; suspension of high-level bilateral contacts; postponement of new projects; refusal to follow up partner's initiatives; trade embargoes; suspension of arms sales, suspension of military cooperation; suspension of cooperation.

[245]The association agreement between the European Union, its member states and Georgia, above n. 156, establishes (Article 422) that appropriate measures do not include the suspension of trade provisions with the exception of the violation of the essential element clause.

[246]As specified in the Framework Agreement between the EU, its Member States and Korea, 'proportionate to the failure to implement obligations under this Agreement'. See also Sect. 5.2 of this chapter.

[247]It should be recalled that the only case of suspension of an agreement which did not actually incorporate an essential element clause concerned the EEC—Yugoslavia association agreement which was suspended as a consequence of the civil war. According to the Court of Justice, the Council regulation suspending trade concession provided for in the agreement had been correctly based on the customary international law rule of fundamental change of circumstances. The peculiarity of the case cannot thus provide a useful example except for the reference to 'customary international law concerning the termination and the suspension of treaty relations which binds the EU institutions and form part of the EU legal order'. (point 46 of the judgment Case C-162/96).

[248]An *erga omnes* obligation is one that is owed to the international community as a whole. See ICJ Judgment (1970), ICJ Report 1970, recently, ICJ Advisory Opinion (2019), para 180.

adopt countermeasures targeted at the state responsible for the human rights violations is contentious.[249] It is true that the 1977 Cooperation Agreement with Syria[250] was partially suspended in 2011 by the EU[251] which motivated the measure by the 'extreme seriousness of the violations perpetrated by Syria in breach of general international law and the principles of the United Nations Charter'. It should be noted that the agreement does not contain an essential elements clause, but a reference in the preamble to the UN principles.[252]

If it is no longer disputed that international law requires respect by states for at least some fundamental standard of protection of its own citizens, the question of the extent to which one state can intervene in the definition of the regime of another state is instead more debatable. A measure incompatible with EU obligations adopted in case of violation of democratic principles and of the rule of law would be critical, since there is no customary international obligation to be a democratic state and to respect the rule of law, even if most cases of serious violation of democratic principles (for example, seriously flawed electoral process) would infringe human rights as well.[253]

The conditionality clause can thus provide the solution as far as the binding character of the democracy and rule of law principles are concerned. It would be difficult for a non-EU member state to claim that democratic principles are an issue of non-concern for the EU if it has qualified their respect as essential in the relationship

[249]Article 54 of the State Responsibility Report (International Law Commission, Commentaries to the ILC Articles on State responsibility Report of the International Law Commission on the Work of its Fifty-third Session, UN GAOR, 56th Sess., Supp. No. 10, at 43, UN Doc. A/56/10, at 139 (2001)) is quite ambiguous on the legality of the adoption of countermeasures by a non-injured State when it specifies that "This chapter does not prejudice the right of any State, entitled under Article 48, paragraph 1, to invoke the responsibility of another State, to take lawful measures against that State to ensure cessation of the breach and reparation in the interest of the injured State or of the beneficiaries of the obligation breached". See also D. Hovell, *Unfinished Business of International Law: The Questionable Legality of Autonomous Sanctions*, American Society of International Law, available online (visited 19 October 2019) See also RUYS, *Sanctions, Retorsions and countermeasures*, cit. Kokott and Hoffmeister argued, 'If there is no special reference to the protection of human rights in Community development agreements, their suspension because of human rights violations is lawful only if the formidable conditions for invoking *clausula rebus sic stantibus* or a right to take countermeasures against the gross violation of *erga omnes* human rights is satisfied. If, on the other hand, respect for human rights and democratic principles is an essential element of the agreement, the Community can suspend the agreement for material breach of its provisions', Kokott and Hoffmeister (1998).

[250]Cooperation agreement between the European Economic Community and the Syrian Arab Republic OJ [1978] L269/2.

[251]Council Decision 2011/523 of 2 September 2011 partially suspending the application of the Cooperation Agreement between the European Economic Community and the Syrian Arab Republic OJ[2011] L 228/ 19.

[252]European Commission, *Using EU Trade Policy to Promote Fundamental Human Rights—Current Policies and Practices*, Non-Paper, Brussels.

[253]See comments in Sect. 3.2 of this chapter.

entered into with the former.[254] The principle of non-intervention in internal affairs of the state could not be invoked in this case.[255]

In a similar vein, the non-execution clause can provide the EU with an enforcement mechanism in cases of violations of those principles, whose application cannot be contested by the other party that has consented to it by ratifying the agreement.

In cases of violations, human rights, the rule of law or the democratic principle by a third country that fall outside the remit of the essential elements clause, the EU can resort to autonomous sanctions, as defined under EU law.[256]

To sum up, the added value of the clause is to provide the EU (and its partners) with an enforcement mechanism that the parties can apply in cases of serious violations of human rights, democratic principles, rule of law or other non-trade values[257] that are included in the clause.

By ratifying the agreement, the parties give their consent to the possible application of "appropriate measures" which do not require a further source of authority. Such a clause also makes "it impossible for both parties to claim that human rights are a purely internal matter"[258] and that the party adopting the measures is interfering in the other party's reserved domain.

4.5.2 The Adoption of "Appropriate Measures"

In some agreements, there is preference for measures that least disturb the functioning of the agreement.[259] This can be interpreted as a preference for a suspension

[254]Cuba expressed its interest to accede to the Cotonou agreement but later it withdrew its application due to alleged interference in internal affairs on the issue of human rights. See Nwobike (2005), at 1393–1406.

[255]The dictum of the Permanent Court of International Justice (PCIJ) in Nationality Decrees in Tunis and Morocco according to which 'The question whether a certain matter is or is not solely within the jurisdiction of a State is an essentially relative question; it depends upon the development of international relations' is still valid. Permanent Court of International Justice, Advisory Opinion, Nationality decrees issued in Tunis and Morocco November 8th, 1921 (1923) P.C.I. J. Rep. Series B, No. 4, para 40.

[256]Although it is in principle possible that the human rights measures are adopted as a reaction to the same events, this does not seem to be the case. The two types of tools are separated and used rather independently. On the coincidence of CFSP sanctions and GSP withdrawal see Portela and Orbie (2014).

[257]The Cotonou agreement provides in Article 97 for a procedure that can lead to the adoption of restrictive measures for serious violation of corruption (good governance).

[258]Human Rights and Sustainable Development in the EU-Vietnam Relations with specific regard to the EU-Vietnam Free Trade Agreement. Commission Staff Working Document SWD (2016) 21 final. (21 January 2016).

[259]For example this limit is contained in the Cotonou Agreement ('least disrupt') Article 96, above n. 151. In the association agreement with Georgia (Article 419), above n. 158; Korea Article 45. This caveat is to be found in Articles providing emergency safeguard and anti-dumping measures Bartels (2014).

with a limited scope. For example, Article 96 of the Cotonou Agreement established that 'suspension or termination of the Agreement must be a measure of last resort'. A suspension limited to some of the agreement provisions make resumption of cooperation easier.

The adopted measures shall also conform to international law standards (in particular those applying to counter-measures) and to the principle of proportionality or to obligations of other agreements binding the EU.[260] Particular attention to the most vulnerable groups of the population and humanitarian considerations also determine the choice of measures and can be considered as the manifestation of the EU's obligation to respect human rights.

As to the Cotonou agreement, which constitutes the framework of EU practice concerning the political clause, the adoption of appropriate measures is the outcome of the consultation procedure as per Article 96. If the EU contracting partner does not respond to the EU's concern, and if no progress is detected in improving the situation, consultations, opened under Article 96, are terminated and the EU will adopt measures under Article 96(2)(c).[261] The EU practice shows that appropriate measures have mainly been taken in the form of suspension and reorientation of financial aid. The suspension (or redirection in favour of non-governmental organisations[262]) of financial aid is a measure of coercion signaling EU disapproval of the government's failure to comply with basic democratic principles.

The suspension of financial aid or budget support has been described as follows by Clara Portela: 'EU aid sanctions operate differently from the classical trade embargo. The EU does not intend to extort the population—on the contrary, it makes a dedicated

[260] A trade embargo was considered in the case of the Haiti crisis, but it was discarded because it would run contrary to the EU obligations within GATT. See written question No 593/92 by Mr Gijs de Vries (LDR) to European Political Cooperation (19 March 1992), 92/C 274/99. The General Affairs Council had also considered denunciation of the Lomé Convention with respect to Haiti, but was at the time not convinced of the practicality of this proposal. Ibid.

[261] It is possible that cooperation is suspended during consultation. For example, in the case of Niger it was decided that cooperation activities would have been confined to payments relating to contracts already being implemented, humanitarian measures or those that directly benefit the population. All other elements of the development cooperation framework with Niger were suspended until an acceptable solution to the crisis was found. Communication from the Commission to the Council on the opening of consultations with Niger under Article 96 of the Cotonou Agreement, COM(2009) 529 final.

[262] A principle established in 1991 in a Council Resolution on human rights democracy and development, Council and Member States, meeting within the Council, 28 November 1991). 'The Community's response to violations of human rights will avoid penalizing the population for governmental actions. Rather than simply discontinuing development cooperation, the Community and the Member States may adjust cooperation activities with a view to ensuring that development aid benefits more directly the poorest sections of the population in the country, for example through non-governmental or informal networks, while at the same time establishing a certain distance vis-à-vis the government concerns.', para 7. http://archive.idea.int/lome/bgr_docs/resolution.html. Accessed on 12 June 2020.

effort to spare it from deprivation. Humanitarian aid is maintained,[263] and often even increased, notably through the redirection of the funds withheld to projects in support of the population. The disutility that the EU expects to inflict on the target arises from a series of interlinked considerations: the absence of new infrastructure projects creates a negative business environment in the country, thereby failing to attract foreign investment. Moreover, given that donors co-ordinate their policies, the EU's withdrawal is often accompanied by that of the international financial institutions and other EU member states. In the absence of donor support and private foreign investment, economic performance worsens. As a result, the government becomes increasingly unpopular in domestic circles.'[264]

The suspension of direct budgetary aid and the withholding of future aid from the European Development Fund (EDF) were adopted against Haiti,[265] but remaining funds of the first tranche of the eighth EDF to projects were redirected to the benefit of the Haitian people, to strengthen civil society and the private sector. The same happened in the case of Guinea.[266] The suspension of financial budgetary support under the EDF National Indicative Programmes and the freezing of financial support for EU funded projects were also adopted against Zimbabwe.[267] Since consultations with the Central African Republic under Article 96 were unsuccessful, the EU partially suspended cooperation applying to infrastructural investment operations concerning the Bouar-Garoua Boulai roads, the upgrading of Bangui's roads and macroeconomic support.[268]

The renewal of measures is justified by the EU for lack of progress in reform processes, while it restores cooperation if progress is made.[269] From this perspective, it is interesting to note that the application of the measures by the EU is inspired,

---

[263]Economic sanctions may have detrimental human rights impacts. "Human rights law does not ever demand that a state enforce its norms by imposing general economic sanctions on a delinquent state" Vazquez (2003), at 825.

[264]Portela (2007), at 43.

[265]2001/131/EC: Council Decision of 29 January 2001 concluding the consultation procedure with Haiti under Article 96 of the ACP-EC Partnership Agreement OJ [2001] L 48/31.

[266]Council Decision 2005/321/EC of 14 April 2005 concluding consultations with the Republic of Guinea under Article 96 of the Cotonou Agreement, OJ L 104, 23.4.2005, p. 33 provides for the implementation of 'programmes directly aimed at improving the living conditions of the most disadvantaged sections of the population or victims of the sub-regional political crisis'. Other form of financial cooperation would be resumed 'once sufficient progress has been noted in the implementation of the undertakings given by Guinea'.

[267]With the exception of financing in direct support of the population, in particular in the social sectors and to operations of humanitarian nature. See Council Decision EC/148/2002 (Zimbabwe) under Article 96.2 of the Cotonou agreement. OJ [2002] L 50/ 64.

[268]2003/837/EC: Council Decision of 24 November 2003 concluding the consultation procedure opened with the Central African Republic and adopting appropriate measures under Article 96 of the Cotonou Agreement OJ [2003] L 319/1.

[269]The measures against Zimbabwe, adopted as a consequence of serious human rights violations (refusal of free elections) were partially lifted in 2012 as a consequence of the creation of a process leading to free elections. See also Council of the EU, Council Decision of 25 June 2001 Concluding Consultations With C.te d'Ivoire Under Article 96 of The ACP-EC Partnership Agreement, Council Decision 2001/510/EC, OJ [2001] L183/41.

under some circumstances, by a positive conditionality approach. The practice is as follows: the consultations lead to the adoption of a road map and undertakings made by the partner. The "positive" measures are a list of commitments made by the EU to assist the targeted state towards transition and to assist in the establishment of a constitutional framework.[270] The resumption of the suspended cooperation is thus conditional on a number of criteria that, according to the specific situation, are defined by the EU in the decision adopting Article 96(2)(c) measures. In this case the letter addressed to the targeted country authorities and annexed to the Council decision, lists a number of steps that the partner shall undertake, such as the organisation of elections, the repeal of specific pieces of legislation. The EU commits itself to adopting measures (e.g. the implementation of the Country Strategy Paper and National Indicative Programme, the allocation of an incentive tranche of the EDF) that are subject to the respect for the commitments made with regard to human rights and the rule of law. The decision details all the measures that will be gradually adopted by the EU corresponding to the full commitment of the EU partner. For example, partial resumption of suspended cooperation might be envisaged once an electoral plan has been adopted laying down the steps and procedures for the organisation of the various elections, while full and complete resumption of cooperation depends on the re-establishment of democracy and the rule of law following the elections.[271]

Outside the Cotonou framework, Uzbekistan ought to be mentioned as an example of (very limited) suspension of an agreement containing a non-trade values conditionality clause. This country concluded a partnership and cooperation agreement with the EU and its member states.[272] Sanctions were adopted as a consequence of the Andijon massacre and the country's refusal of an independent international

[270] 2010/588/EU: Council Decision of 27 September 2010 concerning the conclusion of consultations with the Republic of Niger under Article 96 of the ACP-EU Partnership Agreement OJ [2010] L 260/6.

[271] See for Fiji Island: 2001/334/EC: Council Decision of 9 April 2001 concluding consultations with the Republic of the Fiji Islands under Article 96 of the ACP-EC Partnership Agreement—Draft Letter to the President of the Republic of the Fiji Islands OJ [2001] L 120/33; 2007/641/EC: Council Decision of 1 October 2007 on the conclusion of consultations with the Republic of the Fiji Islands under Article 96 of the ACP-EC Partnership Agreement and Article 37 of the Development Cooperation Instrument OJ [2007] L 260/15; 2010/589/EU: Council Decision of 27 September 2010 amending and extending the period of application of Decision 2007/641/EC concluding consultations with the Republic of the Fiji Islands under Article 96 of the ACP-EU Partnership Agreement and Article 37 of the Development Cooperation Instrument, OJ [2010] L 260/10. 2009/618/EC: Council Decision of 27 July 2009 concerning the conclusion of consultations with the Republic of Guinea under Article 96 of the Cotonou agreement OJ [2009] L 214/34. 2011/465/EU: Council Decision of 18 July 2011 amending the appropriate measures laid down by Decision 2009/618/EC concerning the conclusion of consultations with the Republic of Guinea under Article 96 of the Cotonou Agreement and repealing that Decision, OJ [2011] L 195/2. 2009/618/EC: Council Decision of 27 July 2009 concerning the conclusion of consultations with the Republic of Guinea under Article 96 of the Cotonou agreement OJ [2009] L 214/34 positive measures 2011/465/EU: Council Decision of 18 July 2011 amending the appropriate measures laid down by Decision 2009/618/EC concerning the conclusion of consultations with the Republic of Guinea under Article 96 of the Cotonou Agreement and repealing that Decision, OJ [2011] L 195/2.

[272] OJ [1999] L 229.

investigation.[273] Sanctions were adopted in the form of visa bans and restriction on arms sale but also a suspension of the technical meetings scheduled in accordance with the partnership and cooperation agreement.[274]

4.5.3 The Application of Conditionality in the Framework of Agreements not Incorporating the Clause: The **Passerelle Clause**

In this section we examine the scenario of a trade (or sectoral) agreement between the same parties that does not contain an essential elements clause.[275] In order to establish a clearer ground for the possible adoption of trade-related measures,[276] the EU is following the practice[277] of linking a Free Trade Agreement (FTA), that generally

[273]Conclusions of the Council of General Affairs and External Relations of 23/24 May 2005; doc. 1888/05.

[274]Common position 2005/792/PESC 14.1.2005, restrictive measures against Uzbekistan OJ [2005] L 299/ 7. On the 17 November 2006 this technical meeting were reinstated. See Axyonova, at 67.

[275]See European Parliament resolution of 5 July 2016 on implementation of the 2010 recommendations of Parliament on social and environmental standards, human rights and corporate responsibility (2015/2038(INI): the EP reiterates its support for human rights conditionality in trade agreements and recalls the importance of respecting and implementing human rights clauses; welcomes the Commission and Council's efforts to insert such legally binding HR clauses into all trade and investment agreements in accordance with the common approach and requests the publication of the Council's common approach; notes that HR clauses have not been included in all EU agreements and calls for the ongoing trade negotiations with the EU's other partners, particularly those on TTIP, to ensure the inclusion of a legally binding human rights clause. The EP it is no longer prepared to give its assent to new international agreements that do not contain a human rights and democracy clause.

[276]Interestingly, the 2014 Association Agreements with Moldova, Ukraine and Georgia, establish that the appropriate measures the parties may adopt in the case of non-fulfilment of the agreement may not include suspensions of provisions contained in the Trade Title of the Agreement, but an exception is carved out in the case of violation of essential elements of the Agreements. See, for example, Moldova Association Agreement, Art. 455.3.b.

[277]See a partially derestricted document of the Council, 'Reflection Paper on Political Clauses in Agreements with third Countries', (Doc. 7008/09 of 27 February 2009) which provides for a linkage between EU agreements and free trade agreements. It specifies that 'in order to have a comprehensive framework with third countries covering the main areas of cooperation including political cooperation the EU has a preference to enter into framework agreements prior to concluding sector agreements which in principle do not include political clauses'. Cited by Bartels (2014), at 6. See the reference to the practice in the Council of the European Union, EU Annual Report on Human Rights and Democracy in the World in 2014, doc. 10152/15, (Luxembourg, 22.06.2015).

This approach, for example, has been followed in East Asia but also with Canada. The Cotonou agreement could be considered a model: the Cotonou agreement defines the general relationships between the EU, its Member States and the ACP countries. Leaving the definition of economic (free trade areas and investment) and development cooperation to Economic Partnership Agreement to be concluded between the EU and groups of countries engaged in a regional integrating process.

does not contain human rights clauses, to the corresponding political framework agreement,[278] which includes human rights clause (passerelle clause).

If there is no Association or Framework Agreement in force, a separate human rights clause is inserted in the FTA with the same partner country.[279] The EU has been following this approach since the conclusion of the 2012 trade agreement with Colombia and Peru.[280]

The passerelle clause is also contained in the 2013 Protocol of the fisheries partnership agreement between the EU and Morocco.[281] Article 1 specifies that the Protocol is implemented in accordance with Article 1 of the EU-Morocco Association Agreement (on developing dialogue and cooperation) and Article 2 of the same

[278]The EU does not seem to follow pre-established criteria for choosing the title of the general agreement. In any case these framework and cooperation agreements aim 'to bring together, under a single framework, a holistic and coherent vision of relations with a given partner and to identify policies and instruments that will be used to advance bilateral relations', Commission Staff Working Document. The framework political agreement sets out values and standards on which the cooperation is to be built.

[279]The linking (or *passerelle*) clause can also be included in the Trade Agreement. For example, Article 15.14.2 of the EU-Korea specifies that: 'the present Agreement shall be an integral part of the overall bilateral relations as governed by the Framework Agreement. It constitutes a specific Agreement giving effect to the trade provisions within the meaning of the Framework Agreement.' The Framework agreement with Korea was signed in 2010 and entered into force in 2014. The FTA was signed in 2010 and was provisionally applied in the same year (OJ [2010] L 127/3). It should also be considered that framework agreements with some countries are not accompanied by a trade agreement but are supplemented by the GSP system, which provides for its own mechanism of (unilateral) suspension in the case of violation of human rights. This is the case for example of Mongolia, which signed an EU-Mongolia Partnership and Cooperation agreement in 2013 (ratification still pending) containing a human rights clause The text of the Agreement is available at the EU Treaties Office Database http://ec.europa.eu/world/agreements/default.home.do. The Association agreement with Ukraine (above n. 192) provides (Article 478) that the suspension of the entire agreement, including the part on Trade and Trade-related measures, is only possible in case of violation of the essential elements or in accordance with the general rules of international law. EU-Vietnam Trade and investment agreement OJ [2019] L175/1, Article 17, paragraph 18: 'If a Party considers that the other Party has committed a material breach of the Partnership and Cooperation Agreement, it may take appropriate measures with respect to this Agreement in accordance with Article 57 of the Partnership and Cooperation Agreement. The Cooperation agreement with New Zealand (above n. 179) in Article 52 established that: specific agreements and arrangements concluded after the signature of the Cooperation agreement " shall be an integral part of the overall bilateral relations as governed by this Agreement and shall form part of a common institutional framework.". In May 2018 the Council approved negotiating directives for a free trade agreement with New Zealand, doc. 7661/18, 25 June 2018. The same applies to the EU-Australia Framework Agreement (FA), initialed in March 2015 which includes the respect of human rights as one of essential elements of the bilateral framework agreement. future EU-Australia FTA "will become an integral part of the overall bilateral relations as governed by this FA". Commission Staff Working Documents Recommendation for a Council Decision authorising the opening of negotiations for a Free Trade Agreement with Australia SWD/2017/0293 final at 38.

[280]Trade agreement between the European Union and its member states on the one part and Colombia and Peru on the other, OJ [2012] L 354/3, Article 1.

[281]Protocol between the European Union and the Kingdom of Morocco setting out the fishing opportunities and financial contribution provided for in the Fisheries Partnership Agreement between the European Union and the Kingdom of Morocco OJ [2013] L 328/1.

Agreement concerning the respect for democratic principles and fundamental human rights. Article 8(1)(c) provides for the suspension of the Protocol in cases of a breach of these principles. In the fisheries agreement between the EU and the Ivory Coast[282] parties may suspend the Protocol, *inter alia*, in the event of 'activation of the consultation mechanisms laid down in Article 96 of the Cotonou Agreement owing to one of the essential and fundamental elements of human rights and democratic principles as provided for the Cotonou Agreement'.[283] This linkage clause is a practice applied to all Sustainable Fisheries Partnership Agreements (SFPAs)[284]

In the Caribbean Forum (CARIFORUM) European Partnership Agreement (EPA)[285] it is established that: 'nothing in this Agreement shall be construed so as to prevent the adoption by the EC Party or a CARIFORUM State Signatory of any measures deemed appropriate, including trade-related measures under this Agreement, as provided for under Articles 11(b), 96 and 97 of the Cotonou Agreement and according to the procedures set forth in these Articles'.[286] The non-execution clause can thus constitute the basis for the adoption of restrictive trade measures in breach of the agreement.

An analogous connection has been provided for in sectoral agreements such as fisheries protocols, which traditionally did not include an essential element clause.[287] Thus, Protocols 'setting out the fishing opportunities and the financial contribution' signed by some African countries with the EU have been connected to the essential element and non-execution clauses of the Cotonou Agreement.[288]

---

[282]Protocol on the implementation of the Fisheries Partnership Agreement between the European Union and the Republic of Côte d'Ivoire (2018–2024) OJ [2018] L 194/3.

[283]Article 9, paragraph 1, letter (c).

[284]Question E-000823/2018 Answer given by Mr Vella on behalf of the Commission, 25.5.2018.

[285]Council Decision of 15 July 2008 on the signature and provisional application of the Economic Partnership Agreement between the CARIFORUM States, of the one part, and the European Community and its member states, of the other part; OJ [2008] L 289/1. Article 241(2).

[286]The same formula was proposed by the EU in the Economic Partnership Agreement (EPA) between the EU West African States (ECOWAS) of the one part, and the European Union and its Member States, of the other part. The EPA Article 105 reads: 'Nothing in this Agreement may be interpreted as preventing the European Union Party or any of the West African States taking any measure deemed appropriate concerning this Agreement in accordance with the relevant provisions of the Cotonou Agreement' The text of the agreement is available at http://trade.ec.europa.eu/doclib/docs/2015/october/tradoc_153867.pdf. See also the EPA with East African Community Partner States, Article 136. The text of the agreement was finalized on the 16th of October 2014, and is available at http://ec.europa.eu/trade/policy/countries-and-regions/regions/eac/. For the EPA with Southern Africa Development Community (negotiations were concluded on the 15th of July 2014), see Article 110, text available at http://trade.ec.europa.eu/doclib/docs/2015/october/tradoc_153915.pdf.

[287]It has been reported that sectoral agreements are not considered a suitable context for the inclusion of political clauses. See Thematic evaluation of the European Commission support to respect of Human Rights and Fundamental Freedoms, Evaluation for the European Commission, Final Report Consortium PARTICIP-ADE–DIE–DRN-ECDPM-ODI, Ref.: EuropeAid/122888/C/SER/Multi, October 2011.

[288]The provisions contained in the Fishing Protocols establish the suspension of financial contribution by the EU if the European Union ascertains a breach of essential and fundamental elements on

The connection between the two types of agreement raises the question of the expiry of the Partnership Cooperation agreement (Cotonou) in 2020. It is likely that the new agreement, which is being negotiated at the time of writing, will incorporate an "essential element" clause similar if not identical to Article 9 of the Cotonou Agreement. In the hypothesis that no agreement is concluded in time, the EU would not be able to suspend the FTA provisions following a violation of one of the principles contained in the essential element clause.[289]

It is, however, possible, for the EU to resort to unilateral measures, as explained above, where we have considered the hypothesis of human rights violations in the absence of an essential element clause.

The next question to be considered concerns the consequences of the suspension of a trade agreement under WTO rules.[290] Trade restrictive measures adopted by a state member of the WTO against another state member constitute a violation of the non-discrimination principle enshrined in the GATT MFN provision, since a sanctioned state receives a less favourable treatment as compared with a non-sanctioned state. Trade bans would also be in violation of Article XI GATT (prohibition of quantitative restrictions) and also—but this depends on how the restriction is designed in the first place-with Article III (national treatment). If this is the case, they have to be justified either under Article XX or Article XI.[291] In the case of a human rights clause, however, the parties agreed in advance that the serious violations of one of the non-trade values might trigger the adoption of restrictive measures. Thus, they accept the

---

human rights as laid out by Article 9 of the Cotonou Agreement or as a consequence of the activation of the consultation mechanisms laid down in Article 96 of the Cotonou Agreement owing to a violation of one of the essential and fundamental elements of human rights and democratic principles as provided for in Article 9 of the Cotonou Agreement Protocol setting out the fishing opportunities and the financial contribution provided for by the Fisheries Partnership Agreement between the European Union and the Republic of Seychelles, OJ [2014] L 4/3, 9.1.2014, (Arts. 7 and 8.1.f). Similar provisions (Arts. 7 and 8) are contained in the Protocol Between the European Union and the Republic of Cape Verde, OJ [2014] L 369/3, 24.12.2014, in the Protocol with Comoros (Arts. 8 and 9), OJ [2010] L 335/2, 18.12.2010 and in the Protocol with the Republic of Côte d'Ivoire (Arts. 8 and 9) OJ [2013] L170/2, 22.6.2013.

[289] Bartels distinguishes the possible outcome according to the formula used in FTAs. Bartels (2017).

[290] The introduction of this link, however, can be contentious during the negotiations of an FTA. The inclusion in European Partnership Agreements of a provision linked to the Cotonou non-execution clause, let alone the inclusion of a complete human rights clause, has been one of the contentious issues that have delayed for several years the conclusions of full European Partnership Agreements; for further analysis see section of Chap. 5.

[291] Article XX provides for General Exceptions. In a number of specific cases WTO members may be exempted from GATT rule. Article XXI provides for security exceptions. According to Howse and Genser, on the basis of US Gambling: 'There is ample support for the inclusion of human rights standards in the definition of "public morals." And "Human rights standards are clearly" standards of right and wrong conduct maintained by or on behalf of 'member states, as most Members maintain statutory and customary bans on human rights abuses.' In the event of the most serious violation of human rights abuses (the Author was discussing sanctions against Myanmar, or Burma) the Chapeau test of Article XX would be satisfied. Howse and Genser (2008), Joseph (2011). On the compatibility of trade sanctions against Russia by the US and the EU, see Lekhadia (2015), Mitchell (2017).

outcome and cannot object that the restrictive measures undermine their advantages under WTO.

4.5.4 GSP Conditionality and the Conclusion of International Agreements

States are free to conclude international agreements or to accede to agreements in force. The conclusion of a treaty is founded on the free consent of a state as expression of its sovereignty. The international law of the treaties envisages invalidity for treaties for lack of proper consent: violation of a provision of internal law regarding competence to conclude treaties, error, fraudulent conduct, corruption and use and threat of use of force.[292] None of these hypotheses is relevant in the case of positive conditionality, which applies economic or financial tools to prompt a state to conclude an agreement. Economic force is not contemplated as a ground for invalidity of treaties However, soft law instruments condemn economic and political coercion as undue interference in internal affairs.[293] This might be so when one party of the agreement is particularly weaker in comparison with the other party, as is the case of developing countries vis-à-vis the EU and its member states. Could positive conditionality be equated to economic coercion? The answer seems to be in the negative because the GSP+ scheme, for example, does not contemplate the withdrawal of preferences in case of non-ratification of listed conventions—which could negatively affect important economic sectors of a developing country. This scheme only foresees extra benefits in case of compliance. If the country does not ratify

[292]Guzman refers to the Trade and investment framework Agreement between the US and Afghanistan as an example of coercive agreement because "the decision to sign an agreement presented by the United States can hardly be construed as a free choice" Guzman *How international Law Works*, n. 14, at 60. The same author affirms that: "One might seek a definition under which consensual agreements are those that (at least in expectation) lead to a Pareto improvement (i.e., make all parties better off), but there is no reliable way to determine when an agreement satisfies this definition". Ibid.

[293]See Vienna Convention Declaration final decision of the Vienna Conference to condemn 'the threat or use of pressure in any form, whether military, political, or economic, by any State in order to coerce another State to perform any act relating to the conclusion of a treaty. See preamble: 'The United Nations Conference on the Law of Treaties, Upholding the principle that every treaty in force is binding upon the parties to it and must be performed by them in good faith, Reaffirming the principle of the sovereign equality of States, Convinced that States must have complete freedom in performing any act relating to the conclusion of a treaty, Deploring the fact that in the past States have sometimes been forced to conclude treaties under pressure exerted in various forms by other States, Desiring to ensure that in the future no such pressure will be exerted in any form by any State in connection with the conclusion of a treaty'. McDougal and Feliciano. It is not because the type of coercion prohibited would be one that is intended to obtain from the coerced state subordination of its sovereignty will or to secure an advantage of any kind (resolution 1965 inadmissibility intervention internal affairs of a state and 1971 declaration on friendly relations ("Permissible intervention" "impermissible coercion". See, for economic boycotts in international law, Y. Z. Blum (2016), 'Will "Justice" bring peace?' (Leiden, Boston: Brill, 2016), pp. 178 et seq.

the listed conventions, it can still benefit from the general GSP scheme. The extra benefits are lost only if the country seriously violates its conventional obligations, in the terms described above.

4.5.5 GSP Positive and Negative Conditionality and WTO Law

WTO law is relevant in the case of unilateral measures providing for the withdrawal of preferences and tariff advantages to countries that satisfy the conditions provided for in the GSP scheme. The GSP scheme is a unilateral measure and there is no obligation for a developed country to grant such benefits. Thus, if the EU decides to adopt GSP it can also decide not to grant such preferences. But it is also clear that if the EU (and the same applies to other donors) sets up a mechanism to promote developing countries' trade through tariff preferences it must abide by the WTO rules which allows states to derogate from the MFN principle.

In fact, the GSP is justified in the international law of trade (WTO) on the basis of the Enabling Clause. The Enabling Clause authorizes tariff preferences (that is positive measures) to the benefit of developing countries in order to contribute to their trade and consequently to their economic development.[294] The question is whether the EU GSP scheme and, in particular, the GSP Plus arrangement comply with the Enabling Clause. More specifically, the GSP lawfulness under the WTO depends on the interpretation of the conditions provided for in the enabling clause whereby tariff preferences have to respect the principle of non-discrimination, non-reciprocity and respond to development needs of beneficiary countries.

Developing states that are members of the WTO but not beneficiaries of the GSP scheme may claim that they are being discriminated. This question was discussed by the WTO Dispute Settlement bodies (Panel and Appellate Body (AB) in *EC—Tariff Preferences*.[295] The AB declared the Drug Arrangement illegal as not being justified by the Enabling Clause. The Appellate Body also considered that conditions required under the EU GSP drug arrangement can be admitted provided that extra preferences represented a "positive response" to an objective "development, financial or trade need".

The lawfulness of the GSP+ and in particular the conditionality mechanisms (both positive and negative) are to be analysed according to these criteria. The idea behind the GSP Special arrangement is as follows: the donor (the EU) considers that development needs are the same for all developing countries. There is no space in the GSP+[296] for a differentiation of conditions according to different needs of the

---

[294] The issue is examined in detail in Chap. 5, par. 3.1 of this book.

[295] Appellate Body Report (2004).

[296] In accordance with the eligibility criteria for GSP+ as set out in Article 9(1) of regulation 978/2012 GSP+ preferences may be granted to a country which: (a) is considered to be vulnerable; (b) has ratified all the conventions listed in Annex VIII to the GSP Regulation (hereafter the 'relevant

beneficiaries, a point that has been criticized.[297] However, the differentiation would probably run contrary to the requirement of non-discrimination between developing countries. Conditions in the GSP+ scheme (ratifications of conventions, acceptance of mechanism to verify compliance etc.) can be satisfied in principle by any developing country.

The issue is whether it is possible to consider that tariff preferences constitute a positive answer to the needs of beneficiary countries. It is clear that development is not to be conceived only in economic terms,[298] but extends to the protection of human rights, labour rights, protection of the environment and good governance as well as biodiversity. Thus, the ratification of the conventions listed in the GSP would contribute to the fulfilment of those needs and more specifically to sustainable development. The GSP tariff preferences would positively contribute to those needs in two ways. First, the prospective of being granted a (further) tariff gain would encourage developing countries to ratify conventions; second, since extra preferences are granted after the ratification has taken place, the reward for developing countries in terms of further tariff concessions would support them to assume the burden deriving from effective implementation of the conventions.[299] This objective affects the interpretation of the conditions for inclusion of vulnerable countries in the GSP+ scheme: no implementation problem would lead to exclusion from the scheme. Determination of the "serious failure" of implementation is also based on the practice of the ILO, and it takes into account the objective of the GSP+ and the general principles elaborated by the EU.[300] Although ratification of a convention can be a long and difficult process for several reasons, such as lack of capacity-building, will and political opposition, it is likely to be a less costly exercise than effective implementation from an economic, social, cultural and political point of view. In its report on Sri Lanka the European Commission argued: 'The general approach is

---

conventions') and the most recent available conclusions of the monitoring bodies under those conventions do not identify a serious failure to effectively implement any of those conventions; (c) in relation to any of the relevant conventions, has not formulated a reservation which is prohibited by any of those conventions or which for the purposes of Article 9 of the GSP Regulation is considered to be incompatible with the object and purpose of that convention; (d) accepts without reservation the reporting requirements imposed by each convention and gives binding undertakings referred to in points (d), (e) and (f) of Article 9(1) of the GSP Regulation.

297 Wardhaugh (2013).

298 The Enabling clause seems to refer only to economic side of development, but this is not a convincing argument to exclude it as a legal basis for GSP schemes as argued by Jayasinghe (2015). Actually, development has undergone important changes in conceptualization. See the 1986 United Nations (UN) Declaration on the Right to Development, the 1992 Rio Declaration on Environment and Development, the 1998 International Labour Organisation (ILO) Declaration on Fundamental Principles and Rights at Work, the 2000 UN Millennium Declaration, and the 2002 Johannesburg Declaration on Sustainable Development. (referred to in recital 11 of Regulation 978/2012).

299 "to help vulnerable developing countries assume the special burdens and responsibilities resulting from the ratification and effective implementation of the relevant conventions", regulation 978/2012, recital 11, above n. 21.

300 See Report on assessment of the application for GSP Plus by Sri Lanka, SWD(2016) 474 final, point 3.

that, as developing countries, all applicants experience problems of implementation. However, not every implementation problem should lead to the exclusion of countries from the scheme—even developed countries have a number of shortcomings—but only serious failures to implement. GSP+ recognizes that developing countries have special needs in this respect and provides additional incentives. The ILO has an established practice for the application of the benchmark of "serious failure" to effectively implement.'

Moreover, the "advantage" or the "carrot" is not so palatable due to the so-called "preference erosion", that is, the diminishing value of preferences deriving from the progressive lowering of trade barriers via the multilateral system (WTO) and other regional or bilateral FTAs.[301] In the framework of a general trend of tariff reductions, GSP+ preferences might not be so advantageous. As for the non-discrimination principle the Special arrangement is open to all developing countries that meet the established criteria. Contrary to what was provided for in the previous EU regulation, the new provisions do not establish a fixed date for application and a country which satisfies the conditions can file application at any time. The benefits may be granted after verification by the European Commission.

As mentioned above, the 2012 regulation also provides for negative conditionality to be applied to all schemes (GSP, GSP+, EBA[302]): the benefits may be temporarily withdrawn for all or certain products in case of serious and systematic violations of principles laid down in core human and labour rights (standard GSP and EBA) or in case of a failure to maintain the ratification or effectively implement the conventions, or if it introduces reservations to the GSP+ Conventions that are prohibited or incompatible with the Conventions[303] (GSP+).

---

[301] Countries that became contracting parties to other preferential trade agreements cannot benefit from GSP any longer. Beneficiary Countries of the GSP+ arrangement are Armenia, Bolivia, Cape Verde, Kyrgyzstan, Mongolia, Pakistan, Philippines, Sri Lanka. Sri Lanka re-entered GSP+ in May 2017, after having been removed in 2010. Paraguay has left the GSP+ since it has been classified for three consecutive years by the World Bank as an upper middle-income country. Costa Rica, El Salvador, Guatemala, Panama and Peru will cease to be GSP+ 11 beneficiaries from January 2016 because they joined other trade agreements. (Report Commission on the GSP covering the period 2016/2017, COM (2018) 36, 19.1.2018. In the past Venezuela lost its GSP+ preferences for failure to ratify the UN convention against corruption. Commissin Decision of 11 June 2009 amending Decision 2008/938/EC on the list of the beneficiary countries which qualify for the special incentive arrangement for sustainable development and good governance, provided for in Council Regulation (EC) No 732/2008 applying a scheme of generalised tariff preferences for the period from 1 January 2009 to 31 December 2011 OJ [2009] L149/78. Sri Lanka preferences were withdrawn because of massive and systematic human rights violations committed during the final stages of the civil war in 2008 and 2009. See Report on Sri Lanka meets eligibility criteria: shortcoming but progress. Brussels, 11.1.2017 SWD(2016) 474 final.

[302] EBA (Everything but arms) It provides for completely duty free access to the EU market for all exports, except arms and ammunition, from the Least Developed Countries. See Article 17 of regulation 978/2012.

[303] For example, reservations such as those made by some Arabic states concerning Islamic Shariah law in relation to the Convention on the Elimination of All Forms of Discrimination against Women. One can seriously have doubts about the compatibility of such reservations with the object and purpose of the Convention.

The question is whether withdrawal of preferences conforms to the Enabling Clause as interpreted by the WTO dispute settlement bodies, that is, if it responds to the development need of the country.[304] The compatibility with the Enabling Clause of a decision of withdrawing preferences granted under the GSP+ scheme is hard to assess because the former has been established to make *more favourable* tariff treatment compatible with the MFN principle. One cannot judge the lawfulness of tariff preferences withdrawal under the same criteria used to evaluate the granting of tariff preferences. The exclusion of a country from the GSP+ would send it back to regular GSP, which may in turn be suspended.[305] Although the effect of a withdrawal on exports, and thus on the economic situation of the developing country affected, depends on a number of factors, it has been pointed out that removal of the country from the list of beneficiaries may not only have serious consequences on its exports[306] but also on the workers employed in the export sectors.[307] According to a study, the 'empirical results of this study demonstrate that poverty and income inequality are expected to be exacerbated in Sri Lanka as a result of the removal of GSP+ by the EU using non-economic reasons such as human rights violation'.[308] At the same time, one cannot see how less preferences would contribute to the effective implementation of the conventions listed in the regulation.

The AB stressed that: 'We do not rule on whether the Enabling Clause permits ab initio exclusions from GSP schemes of countries claiming developing country status, or the partial or total withdrawal of GSP benefits from certain developing countries under certain conditions'. There are thus serious doubts on the effectiveness of the withdrawal of the GSP in addressing developing countries' specific needs. According to Howse 'the AB has in mind a rational connection and, as it emphasized in the *Shrimp-Turtle* ruling, there would be no requirement of empirical proof of effectiveness'.[309]

---

[304] Bartels.

[305] If a country is a standard GSP member its exclusion may entail a MFN treatment if it is a WTO member or standard non-preferential tariffs, if it is not a WTO member. This happened to Belarus when it was suspended from the GSP in 2006.

[306] Gruszczyński (2006–2008); The Author cites a report from University of Sussex, whereby the losing of GSP Plus status by Sri Lanka would have led to a 4% cut in its garment exports and overall it would cost approx. 2% of Sri Lanka's gross domestic product ('Not Many Pluses' in The Economist (14 August 2008).

[307] Bartels (2008).

[308] Jayatillake and Athula (2014).

[309] Howse (2014). See also, Trebilcock and Howse (2005, 3rd edition, p. 526): "My own view of state practice is that donor states never accepted that their ability to modify or withdraw GSP preferences would be subject to such a 'hard' legal constraint. At most, they considered 'non-discriminatory' as an aspirational, soft law norm.".

4.6 Monitoring and Enforcement in EU Conditionality Tools

4.6.1 Monitoring and Enforcement in EU Conditionality Clauses

The application of both positive and negative conditionality requires the donor to verify whether the criteria indicated are fulfilled in order to apply benefits or to have proof of the behaviour that would trigger the withdrawal of the benefits. This issue raises different problems: the setting up of monitoring tools, the identification of actors that are involved in the monitoring process and that guarantee the enforcement of conditionality instruments, as well as cooperation with recipient countries. The definition of thresholds might also constitute a problem.

As regards the threshold that triggers the clause, so far this has been set by EU practice at a rather high level. The high benchmark can be established by the agreement that contains the clause. For example, in the Framework agreement with Australia[310] the provision on dispute settlement (Article 57) specifies that "case of special urgency" means a particularly serious and substantial violation of the obligations described in Articles 2(2) and 6(2) of this Agreement by one of the Parties leading to a situation which requires an immediate reaction by the other. The parties consider that a particularly serious and substantial violation of Article 2(2) or Article 6(2) would have to be of an exceptional sort that threatens international peace and security. The setting up of a high threshold for activating the non-execution clause made the EU partner willing to accept the inclusion of the essential element clause. The same technique was used in the Partnership Agreement with Canada.[311] A very similar solution was applied with Japan. The negotiations for the Strategic Partnership Agreement concluded in 2018 with Japan were delayed also because of the issue of including a human rights clause.[312] The formulation of the provision referring to human rights and democracy differs from the traditional one, without using the expression "essential element". In fact, the reference to democracy, human rights and fundamental freedom put emphasis on the sharing of values.[313] The same

---

[310] Joint Proposal for a COUNCIL DECISION on the signing, on behalf of the European Union, and provisional application of the Framework Agreement between the European Union and its Member States, of the one part, and Australia, of the other part, JOIN/2016/08 final.

[311] As seen above n. 176, McKenzie (2018).

[312] One of the possible causes was the reticence of Japan, which feared criticism for its legislation providing for the death penalty. See Parliamentary question for written answer to the Commission (Hilde Vautmans), 21 December 2015 E-016047-15 and answer given by Vice-President Mogherini on behalf of the Commission, 16 March 2016.

[313] Article 2 provides that: 'The Parties shall continue to uphold the shared values and principles of democracy, the rule of law, human rights and fundamental freedoms which underpin the domestic and international policies of the Parties. In this regard, the Parties reaffirm the respect for the Universal Declaration of Human Rights and the relevant international human rights treaties to which they are parties. 2. The Parties shall promote such shared values and principles in international fora.

can be said on the cooperation for the prevention of the proliferation of weapons of mass destruction. The expression "essential element" is, on the contrary, to be found in Article 43 (Dispute settlement) where it is specified: 'The Parties consider that a particularly serious and substantial violation of the obligations described in paragraph 1 of Article 2 and paragraph 1 of Article 5, which respectively constitute an essential element of the basis of the cooperation under this Agreement, with its gravity and nature being of an exceptional sort that threatens peace and security and has international repercussion, may be addressed as a case of special urgency.' It is clear that the conditionality function of the essential element- non-execution clause is watered down.[314]

EU international agreements usually provide for instruments to monitor the implementation of the agreement[315] and for procedures of consultation and dispute settlement mechanisms, which can also be applied also in relation to the application of the political conditionality clause. The bodies established by the agreements, such as the Association Councils, have the task of monitoring and supervising the application and implementation of the agreement and periodically review its functioning in the light of its objectives.[316] No specific sub-committees have been created with competences over human rights clauses.[317]

Some agreements provide for a consultation procedure that has the effect of suspending the application of the measure for a rather short pre-established period of time,[318] but this is not the rule applicable to all clauses.

The Parties shall cooperate and coordinate, where appropriate, in promoting and realising those values and principles, including with or in third countries.'.

[314]Bartels (2017).

[315]E.g. in the EC-Mexico Global Cooperation Agreement, a Joint Committee is established to "examine any major issues arising from within the framework of [the] Agreement and any other bilateral or international issues of mutual interest" OJ [2000] L276/3 (Article 45).

[316]See, for example, Article 461 of the Association Agreement with Ukraine, above n. 191.

[317]See Bartels. Note that in some agreements sub-committees with specific competences are created. For example, Article 300 of the Association with Ukraine establishes a Trade and Sustainable Development Sub-committee.

[318]E.g. 21 days, in the Agreement with Singapore, COM/2014/70 final 17.2.2014. See also the Joint Declaration on Article 57 of the Cooperation Agreement with Vietnam, at n. 11. The agreement with Korea also provides (Article 46) for an arbitration procedure, which can be initiated at the request of the party addressee of the "measure". The Cotonou Agreement provides for a consultation procedure if a Party has failed to fulfil an obligation stemming from respect for human rights, democratic principles and the rule of law referred to in paragraph 2 of Article 9, however, in case of a particularly serious and flagrant violation of one of the essential elements, immediate reaction is allowed after notification to the other party.

As seen above, prior to the adoption of "appropriate measures"[319] a consultation procedure is provided for. In the scenario of 'special urgency',[320] which consists in the 'violation of the essential elements of the agreement',[321] or of a 'particularly serious and substantial violation of an essential element',[322] the other party is allowed to immediately[323] adopt 'appropriate measures'.[324]

---

[319]As a general rule the measures are notified to the other party and a consultation procedure is activated before the adoption of those measures. A Joint or Cooperation Committee set up by the agreement examines the situation and is provided with all information required. See for example Article 107 of the Agreement with Russia, or Article 45 of the EU Korea Framework Cooperation Agreement, above n.

[320]See the 2012 Framework Agreement on Comprehensive Partnership with Vietnam. In the Joint Declaration on Article 57 it is specified that a material breach covers the violation of an essential element of the agreement as contained in Articles 1.1, 1.2 and 8. Article 57(4) provides for 'measures taken in accordance with international law which are proportionate to the failure to implement obligations under this Agreement', but suspension is not mentioned.

[321]For example this is specified in the Framework Agreement with Korea, in a Joint Interpretative Declaration concerning Article 45 and 46. The Parties agree that for the purpose of the correct interpretation and practical application of this Agreement, the term "cases of special urgency" in Article 45 (4) means a case of a material breach of this Agreement by one of the Parties. A material breach consists in 'either repudiation of this Agreement not sanctioned by the general rules of international law or a particularly serious and substantial violation of an essential element of the Agreement.' The Parties shall assess a possible material breach of Article 4 (2), taking account of the official position, where available, of the relevant international agencies'. It is thus clear that the "urgency" is a case of serious material breach and not a temporal urgency. Bartels (2013), p. 297, at 302.

[322]Respect for democratic principles and human rights, as laid down in the Universal Declaration of Human Rights, and other relevant international human rights instruments to which the Parties are contracting parties, and for the principle of the rule of law, underpins the internal and international policies of both Parties and constitutes an essential element of this Agreement' See Korea Framework Agreement, Joint Interpretative Declaration Concerning Articles 45 and 46.

[323]See the 2012 Partnership Cooperation Agreement with Iraq (not yet in force), Article 122: 'any Party may immediately take appropriate measures in accordance with international law in case of violation by the other Party of the essential elements of this Agreement referred to in Articles 2 and 5'. *OJ* [2012] L 204/50, 31.7.2012. In the early practice of the EEC, the so-called Baltic clause was included, authorising immediate partial or total suspension of the agreement in case of serious breach of essential elements of the agreement. This was then replaced by the present general non-execution clause (so-called Bulgarian clause). See Commission Communication on the inclusion of respect for democratic principles and human rights in agreements between the Community and third countries, COM (95) 216 final, 23.5.1995, at 7.

[324]Some agreements provide, even in this case, for a consultation procedure that has the effect of suspending the application of the measure for a rather short pre-established period of time. E.g. 21 days, in the Agreement with Singapore, COM/2014/70 final. See also the Joint Declaration on Article 57 of the Cooperation Agreement with Vietnam, above n. 11. The Cooperation agreement with Korea also provides (Article 46) for an arbitration procedure, which can be initiated at the request of the party addressee of the 'measure'. The Cotonou Agreement provides for a consultation procedure if a Party has failed to fulfil an obligation stemming from respect for human rights, democratic principles and the rule of law referred to in paragraph 2 of Article 9. However, in the case of a particularly serious and flagrant violation of one of the essential elements, immediate reaction is allowed after notification to the other party.

Here it is necessary to distinguish between the mechanisms aimed at establishing a dialogue on the issues covered by the clause and those that may be resorted to in case of situations that can trigger the reaction in the form of appropriate measures.

The more sophisticated model of institutionalized dialogue and monitoring mechanism is established in the Cotonou Partnership Agreement. In short, the Cotonou agreement provides for a regular political dialogue[325] or an intensified political dialogue as a prerequisite[326] before initiating consultation in case of violation of human rights, democracy or the rule of law. However, as an exception, in the case of special urgency consultations start immediately without previous political dialogue. Consultations aim at reaching a solution acceptable to the parties. If consultations do not succeed, the party which launched them can adopt "appropriate measures". Article 96 of the Cotonou agreement may be perceived as a form of punitive measure.

Other agreements provide for political dialogue overseen by joint management bodies (such as Association Councils and sub-committees).[327] A recent interesting example of the strong relationship between the essential element clause and political dialogue is provided by the Association agreement with Ukraine.[328] The aim of political dialogue is, inter alia, 'to strengthen respect for democratic principles, the rule of law and good governance, human rights and fundamental freedoms, including the rights of persons belonging to national minorities, non-discrimination of persons belonging to minorities and respect for diversity, and to contribute to consolidating domestic political reforms".[329] The cooperation in the fields of justice, freedom and security attaches "particular importance to the consolidation of the rule of law and the reinforcement of institutions at all levels in the areas of administration in general and law enforcement and the administration of justice in particular'.[330] The violation of an essential element clause constitutes an exceptional rule as regards the procedure for dispute settlement (for example the three-month consultation period in the association agreement with Ukraine) and the type of measures that can be applied. Monitoring is ensured by the Association Council and by the Association Committee.

The general question which arises for all existing monitoring mechanisms is whether they suffice in terms of ensuring compliance, as argued by the European Commission,[331] or whether new and more specific instruments would improve control and compliance.

---

[325]Article 8, Cotonou agreement, above n.

[326]Cotonou provides also for political dialogue as an 'ongoing process', Bartels (2017)Study commissioned by the European Parliament, Brussels, doc. PE 578.011.

[327]Bartels (2012), Del Biondo.

[328]Above n. 192.

[329]Article 6 of the Association agreement with Ukraine.

[330]Article 14 of Association Agreement with Ukraine.

[331]This institution considered that human rights committees would duplicate existing bodies. According to the Commission, institutional bodies established under the agreements "provide for a comprehensive and structured channel to discuss with partner countries any human rights issue, including those that may emerge in connection to trade". Ioannides, above n. 111, at 46.

Possible alternative monitoring mechanisms—as suggested by Bartels[332]—are periodic human rights assessments, civil society petition for investigations, permanent human rights committees. The Association Agreement with Ukraine provides for a Civil Society Platform to facilitate monitoring of the implementation of the Association Agreement, including civil society monitoring of the human rights area.[333] The involvement of civil society in monitoring the application of the agreement combines the top-down approach characterising conditionality mechanisms (the donor exercises its leverage on governments of the recipient State) with the bottom-up approach of support to civil society.

The EP has also made some suggestions to modify the existing monitoring tools. It has suggested regular monitoring of the implementation of human rights clauses in trade and association agreements. In particular, this scrutiny should take place through the publication of regular joint reports from the Commission and the European External Action Service (EEAS) to the EP on partner countries' respect for human rights and through the establishment of inter-institutional committees. The EP has proposed that the inclusion of a specialized committee for human rights in all EU trade agreements be considered in order to ensure serious and systematic follow-up on human rights issues; it has also underlined the importance of involving the public in negotiations to ensure transparency, and one very interesting part of the proposal concerns the establishment of a domestic legal remedies system for the submission of complaints in cases of non-compliance with trade agreements and human rights clauses.[334]

As regards monitoring by private parties, the activation of the non-execution provision, that is, the suspension of the agreement in the case of violation of the essential element clause, is precluded to individuals and rests exclusively on the discretionary power of the EU institutions. This has been clearly established by the General Court (GC) in *Mugraby* where the applicant criticised the Council and the European Commission for having failed to suspend the Association Agreement as provided for in Article 86.[335]According to the GC, the EU was not obliged to adopt such a measure, nor does that measure represent the only avenue available to deal with an infringement of the obligations in the Association Agreement. [336]The Council and the European Commission enjoy a wide margin of discretion in the management of the external relations of the EU with respect to development in so far as that management involves complex political and economic assessments.[337] However,

[332]Bartels (2014b).

[333]Rácz and Ghazaryan.

[334]European Parliament resolution of 5 July 2016 on implementation of the 2010 recommendations of Parliament on social and environmental standards, human rights and corporate responsibility (2015/2038(INI)).

[335]Conclusions upheld by the European Court of Justice Case C-581/11 Mugraby v. Council and Commission, ECLI:EU:C:2012:466.

[336]See para. 59.

[337]In a recent case concerning a Commission's alleged failure to initiate a temporary withdrawal procedure from the EU's GSP against Bangladesh the EU Ombudsman rejected the complaint arguing that "The decision as to whether or not to launch a withdrawal procedure involves complex

the applicant has not established that the Council and the European Commission have manifestly and gravely disregarded the limits of the broad discretion they have with regard to a possible suspension of the Association Agreement. (point 60) Even assuming that those institutions have manifestly and gravely exceeded the limits of their discretion and have thereby infringed Article 86, that article does not, in any event, give rights to individuals (point 61).

4.6.2 Monitoring in the GSP Scheme

The GSP+ monitoring process[338] is based on two instruments: the scorecard and the dialogue. In order to assess whether the beneficiaries implement the international conventions they have ratified, the EU relies on information provided by competent ILO and other UN bodies or rapporteurs for the relevant conventions. On the basis of this information, the European Commission prepares a scorecard, that is a list of shortcomings to be addressed by the recipient to comply with the conventions, and a progress list made by the country. The first scorecard is prepared when the country applies to become a beneficiary of the GSP+ scheme and constitutes the baseline of the beneficiary situation.

After the inclusion of the country in the scheme, monitoring takes place every two years and is ensured by two instruments. The first one is the preparation of a scorecard which highlights issues to be addressed, shortcomings and progress. The second monitoring tool is dialogue with beneficiary country which comprises regular on-site monitoring missions to each GSP+ beneficiary (at least once during each monitoring cycle). Since the responsibility of implementation lies on beneficiaries, they must cooperate with the European Commission. Scorecards are confidential[339] Civil society organizations are involved in open consultations organised by the Commission at different stages of the monitoring process. Civil society is encouraged to provide the European Commission with information, but the confidentiality of the scorecards makes the involvement of civil society organizations less effective.[340] Every two years the Commission draws up a report on the status of implementation and compliance with the obligations provided for by those conventions. The GSP+ report summarises a beneficiary country's performances over the monitoring period

policy judgments. The Commission has a broad margin of discretion in determining when to do so. The Ombudsman took the view that the explanations the Commission had provided for its chosen course of action were reasonable." Decision in cases 1056/2018/JN and 1369/2019/JN on the European Commission's actions regarding the respect for fundamental labour rights in Bangladesh in the context of the EU's Generalised Scheme of Preferences.

[338] See Chap. 5 of this book for detailed analysis of the GSP monitoring process.

[339] Regulation 978/2012, Articles 14 and 15.

[340] Portela (2018).

(2 years). A country may be suspended and GSP+ preferences withdrawn,[341] when the European Commission[342] identifies shortcomings in the application of the listed Conventions on the basis of information gathered and reports from competent international bodies[343]; if the European Commission considers that there are sufficient grounds for an investigation, it adopts a decision which formally initiates the withdrawal procedure.[344] A six-month period for investigation follows. The Commission invites the interested parties to send relevant information and reports. In the event that the tariff preferences are withdrawn, the burden of proof is on the beneficiaries.[345] In fact, after a further six-months the European Commission submits a report on its findings.[346] The beneficiary country has the right to submit its comments on the report.

The GSP Regulation does not provide an assessment procedure for Standard GSP and EBA beneficiaries. The European Commission and EEAS have developed a monitoring process built on the methodology of the GSP+.[347] A monitoring process was initiated for Bangladesh and Cambodia. This enhanced monitoring process is based on intensified dialogue and monitoring and a fact-finding mission in Cambodia (July 2018). The procedure for withdrawal of Cambodia under the EBA GSP Scheme

[341] See European Commission delegated regulation 1083/2013 rules related to the procedure for temporary withdrawal of tariff preferences and adoption of general safeguard measures under Regulation (EU) No 978/2012.

[342] Enforcement can be "stimulated" by the EP. See human rights abuses in Cambodia: EP Subcommittee Chair calls for EU measures 30-07-2018. See resolution of 13 September on Cambodia, notably the case of Kem Sokha, P8_TA(2018)0346, point 9.

[343] For example reports and statements form Special Rapporteur on Extrajudicial Executions, the Special Advisor to the Special Representative for Children and Armed Conflict of 13 November 2006 and the Special Rapporteur on torture and other cruel, inhuman or degrading treatment. See Report on the findings of the investigation with respect to the effective implementation of certain human rights conventions in Sri Lanka. C(2009) 7999, 19 October 2009, 2.

[344] See for example Commission Implementing Decision of 11 February 2019 on the initiation of the procedure for temporary withdrawal of the tariff preferences provided to the Kingdom of Cambodia under Article 19 of Regulation (EU) No 978/2012 C/2019/896, in OJ [2019] C 55/11.

[345] Regulation 758/2012, Article 15. Sri Lanka refused to be subject to an investigation and refused to collaborate with the Commission. See doc. C(2009) 7999, cit. However, delegated regulation 1083/2013 provides for the obligation for the country under an investigation to cooperate, it is in the interest of the recipient country do to do. The Commission will in fact proceed and its "findings, affirmative or negative, may be made on the basis of the facts available". Commission Delegated Regulation (EU) No 1083/2013 of 28 August 2013 establishing rules related to the procedure for temporary withdrawal of tariff preferences and adoption of general safeguard measures under Regulation (EU) No 978/2012 of the European Parliament and the Council applying a scheme of generalised tariff preference, OJ [2013] L 293/16, Article 3).

[346] For example, the preliminary report outlining the findings of the investigation triggered in February 2019 was sent to Cambodian authorities on the 12 November 2019. It has been pointed out that suspension of EBA would directly affect people's livelihoods by putting textile workers (most of them women) out of work. Russell, at 2.

[347] Trade for all—Towards a more responsible trade and investment policy October 2015.

was launched on February 2019[348]; a preliminary report outlining the findings of the investigation was sent to Cambodia on 12 November 2019.[349]

The Council asked the European Commission to monitor the situation in Myanmar due to the violations of human rights in order to verify its eventual position on EBA and to step-up engagement with Myanmar in light of the provisions of Regulation. 978/2012.[350]

Readmission is likewise based on the evaluation of the European Commission.[351] In both cases the EU relies on the assessment by other international organisations competent in the field, in particular on ILO. Decisions on temporary withdrawal are adopted by delegated act.

The performance-based approach or positive conditionality raises the problem of ascertaining whether the conditions have been fulfilled (see later paragraph on control). Although in the case of ratification the fulfilment of the convention is easily ascertain, in the case of implementation the regulation on GSP refers to "competent bodies".

It also seems that a process for the improvement of a critical situation is sometimes considered sufficient. For example, although in a different context, in the case of Moldova,[352] the proposal for the macro financial assistance regulation (where respect for human rights, democracy and the rule of law, is a precondition, that is a positive conditionality) specifies that: 'While Moldova still faces concerns regarding its human rights record as well as governance and rule of law issues, the Moldovan authorities are demonstrating a renewed commitment to addressing the country's governance challenges and to moving forward with the necessary political reforms. However, delivering on key reforms remains indispensable for a successful implementation of the macro financial assistance and will be monitored closely'. Article 2 of the regulation establishes that the European Commission and EEAS would monitor the fulfilment of the pre-condition throughout the life-cycle of the Union's macro-financial assistance.

[348]Commission Press Release, 11 February 2018 *EU triggers procedure to temporarily suspend trade preferences for Cambodia*.

[349]Available at: https://trade.ec.europa.eu/doclib/press/index.cfm?id=2080. Accessed on 12 June 2020.

[350]Myanmar/Burma—Council conclusions (26 February 2018, doc. 6428/18, 25 February 2018.

[351]For example, Sri Lanka was re-admitted in 2017, although the implementation of international conventions was not fully satisfactory, readmission was clearly based on improvement of the situation. See press Release, 11 January 2017, at https://ec.europa.eu/commission/presscorner/detail/en/IP_17_34. Accessed on 12 June 2020. See also doc. SWD (2018) 31 final.

[352]COM (2017).

4.7 Conclusion

This chapter examined the external conditionality tools adopted by the EU to promote the respect for values such as human rights, democracy and the rule of law by non-member states. The most common instruments are unilateral such as the GSP scheme and financial aid regulations or bilateral such as the political conditionality clause contained in most EU external cooperation and partnership agreements.

The chapter started by deconstructing and analyzing, in general terms, the various components of conditionality tools which follow a common pattern whereby a donor tries to influence a recipient's behaviour by using benefits if it complies with pre-established standards or by punishing it in case it diverges from them. This first part highlighted some of the main problems that might arise as regards these aspects of the conditionality tools. These are, in particular, the definition of the behaviour required—since a clear benchmark allows for a correct application of the tool and facilitates effective monitoring control- and the legal foundation that must be found in international law when the application of the conditionality tool implies a violation of the donor's obligations.

The above-defined conditionality pattern has been used as a reference for a thorough examination of EU conditionality tools, especially conditionality clauses included in EU international agreements and the GSP positive and negative conditionality mechanisms. Particular attention has been given to the question of competence, the definition of the behaviour required by the EU partners and their compatibility with international law. The issue of competence to include non-trade values clauses in EU international agreements is no longer problematic after the TL entered into force. The definition of the standard might be contentious as it is not well defined, at least in the non-trade values clauses whereas it is clearer in the GSP. However, this feature of the clause has the advantage of leaving the parties a certain flexibility in applying the tool. In fact, the analysis seems to highlight that the political clause performs different functions. The reason that first prompted the EU to incorporate negative conditionality into its international agreements was to provide the organization with an instrument that allowed for an immediate and strong reaction in the case of an EU partner country seriously violating human rights or other values. This is also confirmed by the (limited) practice of the application of the clause in cases of gross human rights violations. This is not surprising if one considers the undeniable political character of the tool. From an international law perspective, the clause allows the EU to react to human rights violations with particular regard to the infringement of democratic principles. In this way the EU avoids possible reactions by its partner country that could, in the absence of the clause, invoke the principle of non-intervention in internal affairs to contest the adoption of sanctioning measures (as a form of coercion).

However, the clause also has another function, namely, to put the values at the centre of EU external action and to reaffirm the core of EU identity values that the Union intends to export through its external relations and foreign policy. However, from this point of view, the insistence by the EU of including the conditionality clause in all of its agreements requires not only some creative solutions, for example the establishment of a connection clause linking sectoral agreements with cooperation or partnership agreements to overcome the opposition of its partners, but also the watering down of the scope and meaning of the principles contained in the clause, as the agreement with Singapore and the 2019 EU-Canada Comprehensive Economic and Trade Agreement (CETA) clearly illustrate.

Ultimately, it is difficult to strike a balance between the actions of the EU as an international power pursuing its own (and member states') interests and the EU as a normative power. The scope of the political clause and EU practice illustrate the problems that political conditionality raises and it constitutes the litmus test for the EU's external action, straddling between "realpolitik" and its normative aspirations. As suggested in earlier parts of the book, a revisited notion of Normative Power Europe (NPE), which seeks to remove the divide between values and interests, needs to be embedded into EU political conditionality, thus strengthening the EU's credibility and legitimacy as a good global actor on the international plane.

References

International Law

Treaties and Conventions

Council of Europe

European Convention on Human Rights and Fundamental Freedoms as amended by Protocols No. 11 and 14, 4 November 1950. Available https://www.echr.coe.int/Pages/home.aspx?p=basictexts&c=. Accessed on 13 June 2020

United Nations Treaties

Charter of the United Nations of 26 June 1945. Available https://www.un.org/en/charter-united-nations/. Accessed 13 June 2020

Convention against Torture and Other Cruel, Inhuman or Degrading Treatment or Punishment of 10 December 1984. Available https://www.ohchr.org/en/professionalinterest/pages/cat.aspx. Accessed on 13 June 2020

Convention on the Rights of Persons with Disabilities New York, 13 December 2006. Available at https://treaties.un.org/pages/ViewDetails.aspx?src=IND&mtdsg_no=IV-15&chapter=4&clang=_en. Accessed on 13 June 2020

Convention on the Elimination of All Forms of Discrimination against Women of 21 December 1979. https://www.ohchr.org/en/professionalinterest/pages/cedaw.aspx. Accessed on 13 June 2020

International Convention on the Elimination of All forms of Racial Discrimination of 21 December 1965. https://www.ohchr.org/en/professionalinterest/pages/cerd.aspx. Accessed on 13 June 2020

International Covenant on Economic, Social and Cultural Rights of 16 December 1966. Available https://www.ohchr.org/en/professionalinterest/pages/cescr.aspx. Accessed on 13 June 2020
International Covenant on Civil and Political Rights of 16 December 1966. Available at https://www.ohchr.org/en/professionalinterest/pages/ccpr.aspx. Accessed on 13 June 2020
United Nations, Vienna Convention on the Law of Treaties, 23 May 1969, United Nations, Treaty Series, vol 1155, p 331
1979 UN Convention on the Elimination of All Forms of Discrimination against Women (CEDAW)

Documents from International Organizations

Havana Charter for an International Trade Organization, Final act of the United Nations Conference on Trade and Employment, 24 March 1948, www.wto.org. Accessed on 13 June 2020
The World Commission Development on Environment and Development (WCED) Report, also known as "Brundtland Commission", 1987. Available https://sustainabledevelopment.un.org/milestones/wced. Accessed on 13 June 2020

Conference on Security and Cooperation in Europe

Charter of Paris for a New Europe, Conference of Security and Co-operation in Europe (CSCE 19-21 November 1990). Available at https://www.osce.org/files/f/documents/0/6/39516.pdf. Accessed on 13 June 2020
Helsinki Act (1975) The Final Act of the conference on security and cooperation in Europe. Organization for Security and Co-operation in Europe. August 1, 1975. Helsinki. https://www.osce.org/mc/39501?download=true. Accessed on 13 June 2020

United Nations

General Assembly
UN General Assembly, Universal Declaration of Human Rights, 10 December 1948, 217 A (III). Available at https://www.ohchr.org/EN/UDHR/Documents/UDHR_Translations/eng.pdf. Accessed on 13 June 2020
1965 Declaration on the Inadmissibility of Intervention in the Domestic Affairs of States and the Protection of their Independence and Sovereignty, UNGA Resolution 2131 (XX) of 21 December 1965, https://www.unescwa.org/declaration-inadmissibility-intervention-domestic-affairs-states-and-protection-their-independence. Accessed on 13 June 2020
Declaration on Principles of International Law Concerning Friendly Relations and Cooperation Among States in Accordance with the Charter of the United Nations, 25 GAOR, Supp (No 28), U.N. Doc. A/5217 (1970)
Millennium Declaration, Resolution adopted by the UN General Assembly A/Res/55/2, 18 September 2000

Organization of American State (OAS)

Charter of the Organization of American States signed in Bogotá in 1948

International Labour Organization

ILO Declaration on Fundamental Principles and Rights to Work, 1998. Available https://www.ilo.org/declaration/lang–en/index.htm. Accessed on 13 June 2020

International Law Commission (ILC)

Draft articles on the responsibility of international organizations adopted by the International Law Commission at its sixty-third session, in 2011, and submitted to the General Assembly as a part of the Commission's report covering the work of that session (A/66/10, para. 87). Yearbook of the International Law Commission, 2011, vol II, Part Two

Responsibility of States for Internationally Wrongful Acts Articles on responsibility of States for internationally wrongful acts. Text adopted by the Commission at its fifty-third session, in 2001, and submitted to the General Assembly as a part of the Commission's report covering the work of that session. Yearbook of the International Law Commission, 2001, vol II (Part Two)

Table of Cases

International Court of Justice (ICJ)

ICJ Judgment (1970) Case concerning the Barcelona traction, light and power company, limited, 5 February 1970, ICJ Report 1970

ICJ (1986) Judgment on the military and paramilitary activities in and against Nicaragua (Nicaragua v. United States of America) (Merits) 27 June 1986, ICJ Reports 1986, p 14

ICJ (1997) Judgment on the *Gabčikovo-Nagymaros Project* of 25 September 1997, ICJ Reports Reports 1997, p 7

ICJ Advisory Opinion (2019) *Legal Consequences of the Separation of The Chagos Archipelago From Mauritius In 1965*, 25 February 2019, ICJ Report 2019

International Arbitral Awards

Arbitral Tribunal *Rainbow Warrior* case, *New Zealand* v. *France*, Judgment 30 April 1990, U.N.R.I.A.A., XX, at 251

WTO Reports

Appellate Body Report, European communities—conditions for the granting of tariff preferences to developing countries, WT/DS246/AB/R, adopted 20 April 2004, DSR 2004:III, 925

European Union Official Documents

Treaties

International Agreements of the European Union

Agreement on partnership and cooperation establishing a partnership between the European Communities and their Member States, of one part, and the Russian Federation, of the other part, OJ [1997] L327/3

Agreement establishing an association between the European Community and its Member States, of the one part, and the Republic of Chile, of the other part OJ [2002] L 352/3

Association Agreement between the European Union and its Member States, of the one part, and Ukraine, of the other part OJ [2014] L161/3

Association Agreement between the European Union and the European Atomic Energy Community and their Member States, of the one part, and the Republic of Moldova, of the other part OJ [2014] L 260/4

Association Agreement between the European Union and the European Atomic Energy Community and their Member States, of the one part, and Georgia, of the other part OJ [2014] L261/4

Cooperation Agreement between the European Community and the Republic of India on partnership and development—OJ [1994] L 223/24

Council Decision of 15 July 2008 on the signature and provisional application of the Economic Partnership Agreement between the CARIFORUM States, of the one part, and the European Community and its member states, of the other part; OJ [2008] L 289/1

Europe Agreement establishing an association between the European Communities and their Member States, of the one part, and the Republic of Bulgaria, of the other part in OJ [1994] L 358/1

Europe Agreement establishing an association between the European Communities and their Member States, of the one part, and the Republic of Estonia, OJ [1998] L68/3

Europe Agreement establishing an association between the European Communities and their Member States, of the one part, and the Republic of Latvia OJ [1998] L 26/3

EU partnership and Cooperation agreement (PCA), with the Republic of Tajikistan signed in 2004, OJ [2009] L 350/1, 29

EU Trade Agreement with Colombia, Peru OJ [2012] 354/3

Economic Partnership Agreement (EPA) between the EU West African States (ECOWAS) of the one part, and the European Union and its Member States, of the other part, 2015. Available at http://trade.ec.europa.eu/doclib/docs/2015/october/tradoc_153867.pdf. Accessed on 13 June 2020

Economic Partnership Agreement EPA between Southern Africa Development Community of the one part, and the European Union and its Member States, of the other part. Available at http://trade.ec.europa.eu/doclib/docs/2015/october/tradoc_153915.pdf. Accessed on 13 June 2020

Economic Partnership Agreement (EPA) between East African Community Partner States of the one part, and the European Union and its Member States, of the other part, The text of the agreement was finalized on the 16th of October 2014, and is available at http://ec.europa.eu/trade/policy/countries-and-regions/regions/eac/. Accessed on 13 June 2020

Framework Agreement for trade and economic cooperation between the European Economic Community and the Argentine Republic, article 1 (democratic basis for Cooperation), OJ [1990] L 295/67
Framework agreement for cooperation between the European Community and the Republic of Chile OJ [1991] L 79/2
Framework agreement for cooperation between the European Community and the Republic of Uruguay, OJ [1992] L 94/2
Framework agreement for cooperation between the European Community and the Republic of Paraguay, OJ [1992] L 313/72
Free Trade Agreement between the European Union and its Member States, of the one part, and the Republic of Korea, of the other part OJ [2011] L 127/1
Partnership and Cooperation Agreement between the European Communities and their Member States, of the one part, and Georgia, of the other part, OJ [1999] L205/3
Partnership and Cooperation Agreement between the European Communities and their Member States, of the one part, and the Republic of Azerbaijan, OJ [1999] L246/1
Partnership Agreement on Relations and Cooperation between the European Union and its Member States, of the one part, and New Zealand, of the other part, OJ [2016] L 321/3
Protocol between the European Union and the Kingdom of Morocco setting out the fishing opportunities and financial contribution provided for in the Fisheries Partnership Agreement between the European Union and the Kingdom of Morocco OJ [2013] L 328/1
Protocol on the implementation of the Fisheries Partnership Agreement between the European Union and the Republic of Côte d'Ivoire (2018–2024) OJ [2018] L 194/3
Strategic Partnership Agreement between the European Union and its Member States, of the one part, and Canada, of the other part OJ [2016] L 329/45

Table of Cases

Cases of the Court of Justice of the European Union

General Court

T-292/09 *Mugraby* v. *Council of the European Union and European Commission*, ECLI:EU:T:2011:418

European Court of Justice

C-162/96 *Racke* ECLI:EU:C:1998:293
C-268/94, *Portugal v. Council* ECLI:EU:C:1996:46
C 377/12 *Commission v. Council* ECLI:EU:C:2014:1903
C-581/11 *Mugraby v. Council and Commission*, ECLI:EU:C:2012:466
Opinion of the Court of Justice 2/15 Free Trade Agreement between the European Union and the Republic of Singapore ECLI:EU:C:2017:376

European Ombudsman

Decision of the European Ombudsman on complaint 933/2004/JMA against the European Commission, decision of 25 June 2005
Decision in cases 1056/2018/JN and 1369/2019/JN on the European Commission's actions regarding the respect for fundamental labour rights in Bangladesh in the context of the EU's Generalised Scheme of Preferences

Official Documents of the EU Institutions and Bodies

European Commission

Commission Communication to the Council and Parliament on Human Rights, Democracy and Development Cooperation Policy, SEC (91) 61 final
Communication of the Commission On the inclusion of respect for democratic principles and human rights in agreements between the Community and third countries, COM (95) 216 final,
Communication Democratisation, the rule of law, respect for human rights and good governance: the challenges of the partnership between the European Union and the ACP States, COM (1998) 146 final
Commission Decision 2005/924/EC of 21 December 2005 on the list of the beneficiary countries which qualify for the special incentive arrangement for sustainable development and good governance, provided for by Article 26(e) of Council Regulation (EC) No 980/2005 applying a scheme of generalised tariff preferences OJ [2005] 337/50
Commission Implementing Decision of 11 February 2019 on the initiation of the procedure for temporary withdrawal of the tariff preferences provided to the Kingdom of Cambodia under Article 19 of Regulation (EU) No 978/2012 C/2019/896, in OJ [2019] C 55/11
Communication Eastern Partnership, COM (2008) 823
COM (2011) Communication, A new response to a changing Neighbourhood, p 303
COM (2012) Communication, EU Strategy Towards the Eradication of Trafficking in Human Beings 2012–2016, COM (2012) 286 final
Decision of 11 June 2009 amending Decision 2008/938/EC on the list of the beneficiary countries which qualify for the special incentive arrangement for sustainable development and good governance, provided for in Council Regulation (EC) No 732/2008 applying a scheme of generalised tariff preferences for the period from 1 January 2009 to 31 December 2011 OJ [2009] L149/78
Joint staff working document The EU Special Incentive Arrangement for Sustainable Development and Good Governance ('GSP+') assessment of Pakistan covering the period 2016–2017 SWD (2018) 29 final
Proposal for a Council decision on the signing, on behalf of the Union, of the Partnership and Cooperation Agreement between the European Union and its Member States, of the one part, and the Republic of Singapore, of the other part COM (2014) 070 final
Proposal for a decision of the European Parliament and of the Council providing macro-financial assistance to the Republic of Moldova, COM (2017) 14 final
Proposal for a regulation of the European Parliament and the Council on the protection of the Union's budget in case of generalized deficiencies as regards the rule of law in the Member States, COM (2018) 324 final
Proposal for a regulation of the European Parliament and the Council establishing the Neighbourhood, Development and International Cooperation Instrument. COM (2018) 460 final
Report on assessment of the application for GSP+ by Sri Lanka' SWD(2016) 474 final

Staff Working Documents Recommendation for a Council Decision authorising the opening of negotiations for a Free Trade Agreement with Australia SWD (2017) 293 final
Trade for all—Towards a more responsible trade and investment policy October 2015

Council of the European Union

Basic Principles on the Use of Restrictive Measures (Sanctions), Doc. 10198/1/04, 7 June 2004
Council Regulation (EC) No 3281/94 of 19 December 1994 applying a four-year scheme of generalized tariff preferences (1995 to 1998) in respect of certain industrial products originating in developing countries OJ [1994] 348/1
Council Regulation (EC) No 1256/96 of 20 June 1996 applying multiannual schemes of generalized tariff preferences from 1 July 1996 to 30 June 1999 in respect of certain agricultural products originating in developing countries OJ [1996] L160/1
Council regulation (EC) 2820/98 of 21 December 1998 applying a multiannual scheme of generalised tariff preferences for the period 1 July 1998 to 31 December 2001, OJ [1998] 357/1
Council Decision (EC) 2001/131 of 29 January 2001 concluding the consultation procedure with Haiti under Article 96 of the ACP-EC Partnership Agreement OJ [2001] L 48/31
Council decision 2002/274 of 25 March 2002 concluding consultations with Liberia under Articles 96 and 97 of the ACP Partnership Agreement OJ [2002] L96/23
Council Decision EC/148/2002 (Zimbabwe) under article 96.2 of the Cotonou agreement. OJ [2002] L 50/ 64
Council regulation (EC) 2501/2001 of 10 December 2001 applying a scheme of generalised tariff preferences for the period from 1 January 2002 to 31 December 2004, OJ [2001] 346/1
Council Decision (EC) 2003/837 of 24 November 2003 concluding the consultation procedure opened with the Central African Republic and adopting appropriate measures under Article 96 of the Cotonou Agreement OJ [2003] L 319/1
Council regulation (EC) 980/2005 of 27 June 2005 applying a scheme of generalised tariff preferences OJ [2005] L 169/1
Common position 2005/792/PESC 14.1.2005, restrictive measures against Uzbekistan OJ [2005] L299/ 7
Council Regulation (EC) No 1085/2006 of 17 July 2006 establishing an Instrument for Pre-Accession Assistance (IPA), OJ [2006] L210/86
Council regulation (EC) 1933/2006 temporarily withdrawing access to the generalised tariff preferences from the Republic of Belarus OJ [2006] L405/35
Council of the European Union EU Guidelines on Human Rights Dialogues with Third Countries, 16526/08, 22 December 2008
Council Conclusions of 18 November 2009 on democracy support in the EU's external relations Towards Increased Coherence and Effectiveness
Council Decision 2011/523 of 2 September 2011 partially suspending the application of the Cooperation Agreement between the European Economic Community and the Syrian Arab Republic OJ [2011] L 228/ 19
Council Decision 2011/168/CFSP of 21 March 2011 on the International Criminal Court and Repealing Common Position 2003/444/CFSP, OJ L 76/56, 22.3.2011
Council decision 2014/145/CFSP concerning restrictive measures in respect of actions undermining or threatening the territorial integrity, sovereignty and independence of Ukraine OJ [2014] L78/16
Council decision 2014/386/CFSP of 23 June 2014 concerning restrictions on goods originating in Crimea or Sevastopol, in response to the illegal annexation of Crimea and Sevastopol OJ [2014] L183/70
Council Decision (CFSP) 2017/2074 and Council Regulation (EU) 2017/2063 of 13 November 2017 concerning restrictive measures in view of the situation in Venezuela

EU strategy against Weapons of Mass Destruction (WMD) doc. 15708, Brussels 10 December 2003
Guidelines on implementation and evaluation of restrictive measures (sanctions) 15 June 2012
Fight against the proliferation of weapons of mass destruction. Mainstreaming non-proliferation policies into the EU's wider relations with third countries', doc.14997/03 Brussels, 19 November 2003
Resolution of the Council and of the Member States, meeting in the Council, on human rights, democracy and development of 28 November 1991, Bulletin of the European Communities, No 11/1991 para 2.3.1

European Parliament

European Parliament resolution of 13 June 2012 on the EU trade agreement with Colombia and Peru (2012/2628 (RSP)
European Parliament resolution of 5 July 2016 on implementation of the 2010 recommendations of Parliament on social and environmental standards, human rights and corporate responsibility (2015/2038(INI)
European Parliament legislative resolution of 27 March 2019 on the proposal for a regulation of the European Parliament and of the Council establishing the Neighbourhood, Development and International Cooperation Instrument (COM(2018)0460–C8-0275/2018–2018/0243(COD)
Resolution of 13 September 2017 on corruption and human rights in third countries doc P8_TA-PROV(2017)0346
Report on the Communication from the Commission to the Council on the trading system and internationally recognised labour standards, 11 November 1998, PE 228.265/fin
Resolution on human rights in the world in 2003 and the European Union's policy on the matter, P5_TA-PROV(2004)0376, 22 April 2004
Report on the evaluation of EU sanctions as part of the EU's actions and policies in the area of human rights, dc. 2008/2031, 15.7.2008

European Parliament and Council of the European Union

Regulation (EC) No 1638/2006 of the European Parliament and of the Council of 24 October 2006 laying down general provisions establishing a European Neighbourhood and Partnership Instrument OJ [2006] L310/1
Regulation (EU) No 978/2012 of The European Parliament and of the Council of 25 October 2012 applying a scheme of generalised tariff preferences and repealing Council Regulation (EC) No 732/2008, OJ [2012] L303/1
Regulation (EU) n. 1303/2013 of the European Parliament and of the Council of 17 December 2013 laying down common provisions on the European Regional Development Fund, the European Social Fund, the Cohesion Fund, the European Agricultural Fund for Rural Development and the European Maritime and Fisheries Fund and laying down general provisions on the European Regional Development Fund, the European Social Fund, the Cohesion Fund and the European Maritime and Fisheries Fund and repealing Council Regulation (EC) No 1083/2006 in OJ [2013] L 347/340
Regulation (EU) No 231/2014 of the European Parliament and of the Council of 11 March 2014 establishing an Instrument for Pre-accession Assistance (IPA II) OJ [2014] L77/11
Regulation (EU) No 230/2014 of the European Parliament and of the Council of 11 March 2014 establishing an instrument contributing to stability and peace OJ [2014] L77/1

Regulation (EU) No 231/2014 of the European Parliament and of the Council of 11 March 2014 establishing an Instrument for Pre-accession Assistance (IPA II) OJ [2014] 77/11
Regulation (EU) No 232/2014 of the European Parliament and of the Council of 11 March 2014 establishing a European Neighbourhood Instrument OJ [2014] L77/27
Regulation (EU) No 233/2014 of the European Parliament and of the Council of 11 March 2014 establishing a financing instrument for development cooperation for the period 2014–2020 OJ [2014] L77/44
Regulation (EU) No 234/2014 of the European Parliament and of the Council of 11 March 2014 establishing a Partnership Instrument for cooperation with third countries OJ [2014] L77/77
Regulation (EU) No 235/2014 of the European Parliament and of the Council of 11 March 2014 establishing a financing instrument for democracy and human rights worldwide OJ [2014] L77/85
Regulation (EU) No 236/2014 of the European Parliament and of the Council of 11 March 2014 laying down common rules and procedures for the implementation of the Union's instruments for financing external action OJ [2014] L77/95
Regulation (EU, Euratom) 2018/1046 of the European Parliament and of the Council of 18 July 2018 on the financial rules applicable to the general budget of the Union, amending Regulations (EU) No 1296/2013, (EU) No 1301/2013, (EU) No 1303/2013, (EU) No 1304/2013, (EU) No 1309/2013, (EU) No 1316/2013, (EU) No 223/2014, (EU) No 283/2014, and Decision No 541/2014/EU and repealing Regulation (EU, Euratom) No 966/2012 OJ [2018] L193/1
Regulation 2018/1877 of 26 November 2018 on the financial regulation applicable to the 11th European Development Fund, and repealing Regulation (EU) 2015/32 OJ [2018] L307/1

Court of Auditors

Opinion 1/2018 concerning the proposal of 2 May 2018 for a regulation of the European Parliament and of the Council on the protection of the Union's budget in case of generalised deficiencies as regards the rule of law in the Member States

Books and Chapters in Books

Alexander K (2005) Global governance of financial systems: the international regulation of systemic risk. OUP, Oxford
Bartels L (2005) Human rights conditionality in the EU's International Agreements. OUP, Oxford
Barrett S (2007) Why cooperate? The incentive to supply global public goods. OUP, Oxford
Bartels L (2008) The application of human rights conditionality in the EU's Bilateral Trade Agreements and Other Trade Arrangements with third countries. European Parliament, Doc EXPO-B-INTA-2008-57 PE 406.991
Bartels L (2014, February) The European Parliament's role in relations to human rights in trade and investment agreements study for the European Parliament, Directorate-General for External Policies of the Union, Directorate B, Policy Department, 2014 433.751
Bartels L (2017) Human rights provisions in Economic Partnership Agreements in light of the expiry of the Cotonou Agreement. Study commissioned by the European Parliament, Brussels, doc. PE 578.011
Blum YZ (2016) Will "Justice" bring peace? (Leiden, Boston: Brill, 2016), pp. 178
Bobbio N (1989) Democracy and dictatorship. The nature and limits of state power. Polity Press, Cambridge

Buira A (2003) An analysis of IMF conditionality. In: Buira A (ed) Challenges to the World Bank and IMF developing country perspectives. Anthem Press, Cambridge
Bulterman M (2005) The contribution of the agency to the external policies of the European Union. In Alston P, De Schutter O (eds) Monitoring fundamental rights in the EU: the contribution of the fundamental rights agency. Bloomsbury Publishing, London, pp 253–278
Cadilhac MC, Jones A (2018, November) The European Parliament and the new external financing instrument. Study Requested by the AFET committee EP/EXPO/B/AFET/2018/06, November 2018, PE603.468
Cherubini F (2017) I valori dell'Unione europea nella politica di cooperazione allo sviluppo. In: Sciso E, Baratta ER, Morviducci C (eds) I valori dell'Unione europea e l'azione esterna. Giappichelli, Torino, pp 120–141
Crawford J (2002) The international law commission's articles on state responsibility. Introduction text and commentaries. CUP, Cambridge
De Bardeleben J (2008) Public attitudes towards EU Russian relations: knowledge, values and interests. In: De Bardeleben J (ed) The boundaries of EU enlargement: finding a place for neighbours. Palgrave, London
Dimitrova AL (2004) Enlargement driven change and post-communist transformations: a new perspective. In Dimitrova AL (ed) Driven to change: the European Union's enlargement viewed from the east. Manchester University Press, Manchester
Dobreva A (2015) European instrument for democracy and human rights. European Parliament Research Service 2015
Elliott KA, Freeman RB (2003) Can Labor Standards Improve Under Globalization. Harvard University, Wasington DC
Fierro E (2003) European Union's Approach to Human Rights Conditionality in Practice, Kluwer. Kluwer Law International, The Hague
Gestri M (2016) Sanctions imposed by the European Union, legal and institutional issues. In: Ronzitti N (ed) Coercive diplomacy, sanctions and international law. Brill Nijhof, Leiden, pp 70–102
Ghazaryan N (2014) The European neighbourhood policy and the democratic values of the EU: a legal analysis. Hart Publishing, Oxford
Hillion C (2004) The Copenhagen criteria and their progeny. In: Hillion C (ed) EU enlargement: a legal approach. Hart Publishing, Oxford
Hillion C, Koutrakos P (eds) (2010) Mixed agreements revisited, the EU and its member states in the world. Hart Publishing, Oxford
Immenkamp B (2020) *A new neighbourhood, development and international cooperation instrument* Study. EU Legislation in Progress Reference PE 628.251, European Parliamentary Research Service February 2020
Ioannides I (2017, February 10) The effects of human rights related clauses in the EU-Mexico Global Agreement and the EU-Chile Association Agreement: ex-post impact assessment. Study. Reference No: PE 558.764, European Parliamentary Research Service, European Parliament, Brussels, February 2017. Available at SSRN https://ssrn.com/abstract=2916198. Accessed on 13 June 2020
Joseph S (2011) Blame it on the WTO? A human rights critique. Oxford Scholarship online, Oxford
Koeberle S, Bedoya H, Silarsky P, Verheyen G (eds) (2005) Conditionality revisited. The World Bank, Washington
Keohane RO (1984) After hegemony: cooperation and discord in the world political economy. Princeton UP, Princeton
McCrudden C (2005) Mainstreaming Human Rights. In: Harvey C (ed) Human rights in the community: rights as agents for change. Hart Publishing, Oxford. Research network electronic paper collection at: http://ssrn.com/abstract=568642. Accessed on 13 June 2020
Mitchell AD (2017) Sanctions and the World Trade Organization. In van den Herik L (ed) Research handbook on UN sanctions and international law. Edward Elgar, Cheltenham, pp 283–303

Okano-Heijmans M (2014) Trade diplomacy in EU asia relations time for a rethink The Hague Clingendale report, Netherlands Institute of International Relations
Reid E (2015) Balancing human rights, environmental protection and international trade. Hart Publishing, Oxford
Parisi N (2019) The international and European model to prevent corruptio. In: AA.VV., Temi e questioni di diritto dell'Unione europea. Cacucci, Bari, pp 465–480
Portela C (2018, December) How to promote human rights trough the EU's GSP plus? Exploring the role of civil society, businesses and beneficiary countries. Briefing paper
Portela C (2018, September) Enforcing respect for labour standards with targeted sanctions. https://www.researchgate.net/publication/329449719. Accessed on 13 June 2020
Pridham G (200) The dynamics of democratization. A comparative approach. Continuum, London
Ronzitti N (2016) Coercive diplomacy, sanctions and international law. Brill Nijhoff, Leiden
Ruys T (2017) Sanctions, retorsions and countermeasures: concepts and international legal framework. In van den Herik L (ed) Research handbook on un sanctions and international law. Edward Elgar Publication, Cheltenham, pp 19–51
Sossai M (2017) UN sanctions and regional organizations: an analytical framework. In: van den Herik L (ed) Research handbook on UN sanctions and international law. Edward Elgar, Cheltenham, pp 395–417
Trebilcock MJ, Howse R (2005) The regulation of international trade. Routledge, London
Van Elsuwege P (2019) The nexus between Common Commercial Policy and Human Rights: implications of the Lisbon Treaty. In: Van der Loo G, Hahn M (eds) The law and practice of the Common Commercial Policy: the first 10 years after the Treaty of Lisbon. Brill/Martinus Nijhoff, Leiden
Wetzel AJ, Orbie J (2015) Substance of EU democracy promotion: concepts and cases. Palgrave Macmillan, London
Wetzel AJ, Orbie J, Bossuyt F (2017) Comparative perspectives on EU democracy promotion. Routledge, London

Journal Articles

Bartels L (2004) A legal analysis of human rights clauses in the European Union's Euro-Mediterranean Association Agreements. Mediterranean Polit 9(3):368–395
Bartels L (2012) Human rights and sustainable development obligations in EU free trade agreements. University of Cambridge legal studies research paper series 24
Bartels L (2013) Human rights and sustainable development obligations in EU free trade agreements. Legal Issues Econ Integr 40(4):297–313
Bartels L (2014a) The EU's human rights obligations in relation to policies with extraterritorial effects. Eur J Int Law 25:1071–1091
Bartels L (2014b) A model human rights clause or the EU's international trade agreements. German Institute for Human Rights, Belin
Bartels L (2017) Human rights, labour standards and environmental standards in CETA. Legal studies research paper series. University of Cambridge
Bartoloni ME, Cannizzaro E (2014) Articolo 21 TUE. In: Tizzano A (a cura di) Trattati dell'Unione europea. Giuffrè, Milano, pp 221–226
Broberg M (2010) Much ado about nothing? On the European Union's fight against corruption in developing countries under Articles 9(3) and 97 of the Cotonou Agreement. DIIS Working Pap
Borchert I, Conconi P, Di Ubaldo M, Herghelegiu C (2019) Trade conditionality in the EU and WTO Legal regimes. RESPECT Working Pap

Börzel TA, Risse TA (2004) One size fits all! EU policies for the promotion of human rights, democracy and the rule of law. https://www.researchgate.net/publication/228768742_One_Size_Fits_All_EU_Policies_for_the_Promotion_of_Human_Rights_Democracy_and_the_Rule_of_Law. Accessed on 13 June 2020
Broberg M (2011) Don't mess with the missionary man! On the principle of coherence, the missionary principle and the European Union's development policy. In: Cardwell PJ (ed) EU external relations law and policy in the post-Lisbon Era. TMC Asser Press, The Hague, pp 181–196
Cannizzaro E (2002) Is the EC competent to conclude agreements with third states including human rights clauses? In: Id. The EU as an actor in international relations. Kluwer Law International, The Hague, London New York, pp 297–320
Cannizzaro E (2014) The EU's human rights obligations in relation to policies with extraterritorial effects: a reply to Lorand Bartels. Eur J Int Law 25(4):1093–1099. https://doi.org/10.1093/ejil/chu085
Chauffour JP, Maur JC (2011) Overview. In: Chauffour JP, Maur JC (eds) Preferential trade agreement policies for development: a handbook. World Bank, Washington DC, p 16
Del Biondo K (2011) EU aid conditionality in ACP countries: explaining inconsistency. EU Sanctions Practice. J Contemp Eur Res 380. Available at http://www.jcer.net/ojs/index.php/jcer/article/view/294/290. Accessed on 12 June 2020
Del Biondo K (2015) Donor interests or development performance? Explaining sanctions in EU democracy promotion in sub-Saharan Africa. World Dev 75:74–84
Dimitrova AL (2002) Governance by enlargement? The case of the administrative capacity requirement in the EU's Eastern enlargement. West Eur Polit 25(4):171–190
Donno D, Neureiter M (2018) Can human rights conditionality reduce repression? Examining the European Union's economic agreements. Rev Int Organ 335–357
Dorussen H (2001) Mixing carrots with sticks: evaluating the effectiveness of positive incentives. J Peace Res 38(2):251–262
Downs GW, Jones MA (2002) Reputation, compliance and international law. J Legal Stud 31(1):95–114
Farer FTJ (1985) Political and economic coercion in contemporary international law. AJIL 79(2):405
Fierro E (2001) Legal basis and scope of the human rights clauses in EC bilateral agreements any room for positive interpretation? Eur Law J 41–68
Gazaryan N (2015) A new generation of human rights clauses? The case of association agreements in the Eastern neighbourhood. Eur Law Rev 391–410
Grip L (2009a, November) The EU non-proliferation clause: a preliminary assessment. SIPRI Background Pap. Available at https://www.sipri.org/sites/default/files/files/misc/SIPRIBP0911.pdf. Accessed on 13 June 2020
Grip L (2009b) The European Union's Weapons of Mass Destruction Non-Proliferation Clause: a Ten Year Assessment, EU Non-Proliferation Consortium, *Non Proliferation Papers*, (40, April 2014), available at www.sipri.org. Accessed on 13 June 2020.
Grip L (2014) The European Union's weapons of mass destruction non-proliferation clause: a ten year assessment, EU non-proliferation consortium. Non Prolif Papers (40 Apr 2014). https://www.sipri.org/publications/2014/eu-non-proliferation-papers/european-unions-weapons-mass-destruction-non-proliferation-clause-10-year-assessment. Accessed 13 June 2020
Gruszczyński Ł (2006–2008) EC incentive arrangements for sustainable development and good governance (GSP Plus) and WTO law—critical analysis. Polish J Int Law 216
Gustafsson MPL (2017) Compliance and membership value in international economic law. Georgetown J Int Law 1201–1222
Heinemann (2018) Going for the wallet? Rule-of-law conditionality in the next EU multiannual financial framework. Inter Econ 53(6):297–301
Hilpold P (2000) EU development cooperation at crossroads: the Cotonou Agreement of 23 June 2000 and the principle of good governance. Eur Foreign Aff Rev 7(1):53–72

Hilpold P (2017) The politicization of the EU development policy. Trade Law Dev IX(2):206–231
Howse R (2014) Appellate body ruling saves the GSP, at least for now. Bridges 8(4):5–6
Howse R, Genser JM (2008) Are EU trade sanctions on Burma compatible with WTO law? Mich J Int Law 29(2):165–197
Janse R (2018) The evolution of the political criteria for accession to the European community 1957–1973. Eur Law J 24(1):57–76
Janse R (2019) Is the European Commission a credible guardian of the values? Int Const Law J 17(1):43–65
Jayasinghe V (2015) The legality of the European Union's special incentive arrangement. J Int Econ Law 18(3):555–575
Jayatillake B, Athula N (2014) Garment Industry in Sri Lanka and the removal of GSP plus by EU. World Econ 1438–1461
Koch S (2015) A typology of political conditionality beyond aid: conceptual horizons based on lessons from the European Union. World Dev 75:97–108
Kokott J, Hoffmeister K (1998) Portuguese Republic v. Council, case 268/94. Am J Int Law 292–295
Laugier R (2018) Conditionality 2.0: an improved legal framework to protect sustainable development through EU free trade agreements. Trans Eur Policy Stud Assoc Briefs 1
Leebron DW (2002) Linkages. AJIL 96(5):25–27
Lekhadia R (2015) Can the west justify its sanctions against Russia under the world trade law? India J Int Econ Law VII :151–176
Manners I (2002) Normative power Europe: a contradiction in terms? J Market Stud 40:235–258
Martines F (2016) Human rights clauses in EU agreements. Cleer Pap 5:37–62
Marxsen C (2015) Territorial integrity in international law: its concept and implications for crimea. ZaöRV 75:7–26
McDougal M, Feliciano F (1958) International coercion and world public order: the general principles of the law of war. Yale Law J 771–792
McKenzie L (2018) Overcoming legacies of foreign policy (dis)interests in the negotiation of the European Union–Australia free trade agreement. Aust J Int Aff 72(3):255–271
Meissner KL, Mckenzie L (2017) Human rights conditionality in European Union trade negotiations: the case of the EU-Singapore FTA. J Common Market Stud 55(4):832–849
Meissner KL, Mckenzie L (2018) The paradox of human rights conditionality in EU trade policy: when strategic interests drive policy outcomes. J Eur Pub Policy 1–19
Mitchell AD (2017) Sanctions and the World Trade Organization. In: van den Herik L (2017) Research handbook on UN sanctions and international law. Edward Elgar, Cheltenham, pp. 395–417
Morviducci C (2019) Le misure restrittive dell'Unione europea e il diritto internazionale: alcuni aspetti problematici. Eurojus 77–96
Nakanishi Y (2014) Political principles in Article 21 TEU and constitutionalism. Hitotsubashi J Law Politics 42(2):11–40
Nwobike J (2005) Application of human rights in ACP-EU partnership. Ger Law J 1381–1406
Orbie J, Khorana S (2015) Normative versus market power Europe? The EU-India trade agreement. Asia Eur J 13:253–26
Pech L (2012) Rule of law as guiding principle of the European Union's external action. Cleer Papers 3
Portela C (2007) Aid suspensions as coercive tools? The European Union's experience in the African-Caribbean-Pacific (ACP) context. Rev Eur Russ Aff 3(2):38–53
Portela C, Orbie J (2014) Sanctions under the EU generalised system of preferences and foreign policy: coherence by accident? Contemp Politics 20(1):63–76
Prickartz A-C, Staudinger I (2019) Policy vs practice: the use, implementation and enforcement of human rights clauses in the European Union's international trade agreements. Eur World Law Rev 3(1):2–23

Raponi S (2015) Is coercion necessary for law? The role of coercion in international and domestic law. Wash U Jur Rev 8:35–58. Available at https://openscholarship.wustl.edu/law_jurisprudence/vol8/iss1/2 visited 18 October 2019
Saltnes JD (2013) The EU's human rights policy. Unpacking the literature on the EU's implementation of aid conditionality. Arena Working Paper, vol 2
Santiso C (2001) Good governance and aid effectiveness: the World Bank and conditionality. Georgetown Pub Policy Rev 7(1):1–22
Schimmelfennig F, Engert S, Knobel H (2003) Costs, commitment and compliance: the impact of EU democratic conditionality on Latvia, Slovakia and Turkey. JCMS 41(3):495–496
Shaffer G, Apea Y (2005) Institutional choice in the generalized system of preferences case: who decides the conditions for trade preferences? The Law and Politics of Rights. J World Trade 5:977–1008
Vazquez CM (2003) Trade sanctions and human rights—past, present, and future. J Int Econ Law 797–839
Velluti S (2016) The promotion and integration of human rights in EU external trade relations. Utrecht J Int Eur Law 32(83):41–68
Wardhaugh B (2013) GSP+ and human rights: Is the EU's approach the right one? J Int Econ Law 16(4):827–846
White N (2018) Autonomous and collective sanctions in the international legal order. Italian Yearb Int Law 3

Encyclopedia

Carter BE (2020) 'Economic coercion' Max Planck Encyclopedias of International Law
Joyner CC (2020) Coercion' in Max Planck encyclopedias of international law. OUP, Oxford

Doctorate or Master Dissertations

Viţă V (2014) Ex ante fundamental rights conditionalities—a novel fundamental rights tool in the European Structural and Investment Funds architecture. Locating it in the broader EU fundamental rights conditionality landscape. Master Thesis, European University Institute, Florence

Chapter 5
The Promotion of Social Rights and Labour Standards in EU External Trade Relations

Samantha Velluti

5.1 Introduction—The Role of the EU as a Global Social Actor

In the past decade the European Union (EU) has been at the forefront of attempts to strengthen and promote the social dimension of globalization, focusing chiefly on the promotion of labour standards internationally, through increased cooperation with the International Labour Organization (ILO) and through its external trade policies.[1]

The EU's social ambition continues to grow exponentially as exemplified by the increasing number of trade agreements containing social conditionality clauses.[2] To varying degrees and with mixed success, many of the EU's trade agreements (both bilateral and regional) to date include an element of social conditionality, namely social incentive clauses that condition trade concessions and market access on the respect and implementation of internationally recognized human rights, social and environmental standards.[3]

Since the entry into force of the 2009 Treaty of Lisbon (TL), and chiefly through Articles 3(5) and 21 Treaty on European Union (TEU), the EU has constitutionalized its commitment to human rights obligations to the extent that non-commercial objectives are now clearly within the remit of EU internal and external action.

The EU constitutes a formidable platform for developing an integrated system to further diverse goals through the coordinated action of various institutions. As a

[1]European Commission (2017a).

[2]Velluti (2016c).

[3]ILO (2016), Velluti (2015), Velluti and Van den Putte (2018), Harrison et al. (2019), Ebert (2015), and Campling et al. (2015).

[4]Cremona (2001).

The chapter incorporates some material previously published in journals and edited volumes, as follows: Velluti (2015, 2016b) and Velluti and Van Den Putte (2018).

S. Velluti, *The Role of the EU in the Promotion of Human Rights and International Labour Standards in Its External Trade Relations*,
https://doi.org/10.1007/978-3-030-56748-4_5

regional entity with a "global vocation"[4] to promote global human rights, the EU now has a regulatory framework enabling it to mobilize various instruments of governance in a social perspective.[5] In this context, the EU stands as a model of a highly competitive social market economy[6] 'reflecting the ambition of furthering diverse economic and social aims simultaneously, however much that model is both incomplete and under threat'.[7] The TL has refocused attention on a holistic approach to European integration and the goals of full employment, social progress and cohesion have been relaunched in the context of a new 'highly competitive social market economy'.[8]

The methods used as conditionality are made up of two elements: the "stick", i.e. a punitive method in order to punish proven breaches of human rights standards with the elimination of trade preference, by imposing trade sanctions against third countries that do not observe them (negative conditionality) and the "carrot", i.e. an incentive method that provides for additional preferential treatment through reduced tariffs and market access, to reward achievements in respecting and promoting human rights and social and environmental standards (positive conditionality).

The reconceptualization of EU trade policies[9] are evidence of a growing support in the EU's internal and external policies and actions for ILO labour standards and reflect the increasing importance in the EU of decent job creation, social dialogue and social protection for ensuring inclusive growth and sustainable development in the broader context of the global economic crisis. The promotion of ILO labour standards is mostly visible in the EU's trade arrangements, at the unilateral, regional and bilateral levels.

The strong normative connotation that the trade-labour linkage has come to acquire within the EU can be explained by various interrelated factors. First, with the TL the European Parliament (EP)—a strong advocate of the inclusion of labour in trade arrangements—has gained increased competences in external trade policy.[10] All the main political groups in the EP, while having different motivations, agree on the need for trade arrangements to include labour provisions.[11]

The inclusion of labour provisions makes it easier to find public support, given that they act as a counterweight to the market liberalizing provisions of the EU's trade agreements. In addition, the framing of labour (and environmental) provisions

[5]Perulli (2014), at 37.

[6]Article 3(3) TEU.

[7]Reddy (2015), at p. xv; for further analysis, see Damjanovic (2013); for an account of EU social and employment law and policy, see Velluti (2010), Chaps. 4 and 5.

[8]Perulli, above 5, 34.

[9]European Commission (2017b).

[10]Raube and Wouters (2016).

[11]Van den Putte (2015a).

as part of "sustainable development",[12] to be found particularly in the so-called "new generation of free trade agreements (FTAs)",[13] reduces their objection.[14]

5.1.1 Labour Rights, Labour Standards and Social Clauses

It should be noted from the outset that the distinction between "rights" and "standards" is no mere formality or a simple semantic question rather it is one of substance, which in turn has a direct impact on issues of universality and enforceability. The argument that social and labour rights are not human rights at all no longer finds general consensus and has been widely confuted.[15] This notwithstanding, it is the nature and content of the right that determines its status rather than assuming that its classification as a "right" entails an obligation. As posited by Reid,[16] such distinction 'has tangible implications in the way in which a balance may be sought between the protection of these rights and the interests of free trade, as compared with the balance that may be held between the enforcement of labour standards and free trade.' It follows that, while a

[12]Sustainable development is a concept that has been present in EU law since 1997 when the Treaty of Amsterdam referred to it as an overarching objective of EU Policies, which encompasses, among others, labour rights. Article 3(3) TEU provides that: 'The Union shall establish an internal market. It shall work for the *sustainable development* of Europe based on balanced economic growth and price stability, a highly competitive social market economy, aiming at full employment and social progress, and a high level of protection and improvement of the quality of the environment. It shall promote scientific and technological advance;' [Highlighted by the author] it is also a principle guiding the external action of the EU, see Article 3(5) TEU, which provides that: ' In its relations with the wider world, the Union shall contribute to peace, security, the *sustainable development* of the Earth, solidarity and mutual respect among peoples, free and fair trade, eradication of poverty and the protection of human rights, [...] as well as to the strict observance and the development of international law, including respect for the principles of the United Nations Charter' [Highlighted by the author]; Article 21(1) and (2)(d) TEU externalize the EU's commitment to sustainable development where it states that: 'The Union's action on the international scene shall be guided by the principles which have inspired its own creation, development and enlargement, and which it seeks to advance in the wider world [...] and 'foster the sustainable economic, social and environmental development of developing countries, with the primary aim of eradicating poverty'; the European Commission started to develop the idea that sustainable development should be mainstreamed in all relevant EU policies including external trade and that the EU trade policy should equally support economic growth, social development and environmental protection. The EU has long had a Sustainable Development Strategy, which it regularly reviews and assesses, see Communication from the Commission A Sustainable Europe for a Better World: A European Union Strategy for Sustainable Development (Commission's proposal to the Gothenburg European Council) /* COM/2001/0264 final */; further information can be found at: https://ec.europa.eu/environment/sustainable-development/strategy/index_en.htm, accessed on 14 June 2020. For an analysis of the legal concept of sustainable development, see Cordonnier Segger and Khalfan (2004), Barral (2012), and Grosse Ruse-Khan (2010).

[13]These agreements are examined in Sect. 5.3 of this chapter.

[14]Van den Putte and Orbie (2015).

[15]Mantouvalou (2012).

[16]Reid (2015).

human rights discourse is generally more persuasive than that of standards because of its inbuilt deontological nature, nevertheless it remains necessary to establish what substantive rights are at issue before proceeding to any taxonomy of rights. Consequently and unsurprisingly, 'discussions concerning a social clause are often confused and the terminology employed is often unclear'.[17] In this chapter the definition of "social clauses"—as and when they are generically referred to—is that found in the *Dictionnaire de Droit International Public*, namely 'provisions included in regional trade agreements or the agreement establishing the World Trade Organization (WTO) providing for the use of restrictive measures such as trade restrictions or the withdrawal of trade preferences, where fundamental rights at work are not respected.'[18] More specifically, social clauses aim 'at improving labour conditions in exporting countries by allowing sanctions to be taken against exporters who fail to observe minimum standards. A typical social clause in an international trade arrangement makes it possible to restrict or halt the importation or preferential importation of products originating in countries, industries or firms where labour conditions are inferior to certain minimum standards.'[19] For the purposes of the present chapter, the term "social clause" includes both the unilateral application of trade measures and clauses in bilateral and regional agreements.

5.1.2 Thematic Scope, Aims and Structure of the Chapter

The focus of analysis of this chapter is on the EU's increased practice of promoting social rights and international labour standards in its external trade relations, unilaterally through the Generalised System of Preferences (GSP; and largely under its incentive scheme, namely the GSP+), and at regional and bilateral levels via international agreements, which encompass reciprocal or non-reciprocal preferential trade links with third countries. In this context, the chapter unpacks and addresses the tensions in and limitations of the discourse and practice of the EU's promotion of social rights in its external trade relations, putting forward recommendations to strengthen the effectiveness of the operationalization of EU social conditionality. The normative framework for developing these recommendations is largely based on the capabilities approach.[20] In particular, it draws on Sen's writings according to which sustainable economic development will be achieved provided the capabilities

[17] Leary (1996), at p. 178.

[18] Salmon (2001).

[19] van Liemt (1989), at 434.

[20] Sen (1999) and Nussbaum (2011); for a detailed account of the capabilities approach, see Barnard et al. (2001), at 465–467; Langille (2019); see also Supiot (2001); this is the English version of what is known as the "Supiot Report", A. Supiot (general rapporteur) et al., *Transformation of Labour and Future of Labour Law in Europe, Final Report* (European Commission, Luxembourg, 1999) where the central thesis is the need to develop forms of economic security which are not confined to the traditional or standard employment relationship but need to consider the wider significance of employment in terms of people's well-being and living conditions.

of individuals, organisations and public institutions in less developed countries are fostered and placed on a path towards continuous improvement. Situated within a capability metric, international labour standards should focus on devising a set of public policy measures, which is not limited to labour regulation but also extends to education and training, in order to advance the living and working conditions of people in less developed countries.

EU external social trade has received much praise and much criticism. The European Commission has claimed that it provides the greatest possible contribution to strengthening the social dimension of development cooperation.[21] In a similar vein, some have argued that there is evidence showing an improvement in labour rights in the signatory countries of EU preferential trade agreements, which is exhibited *ex post* as a result of learning by civil society actors during the implementation phase of labour provisions.[22] At the other end of the spectrum, it has been argued that the GSP programme has allowed the EU to provide significant trade benefits to countries that have abhorrent human and labour rights records[23] and that the GSP+ scheme and its conditionality has not yet resulted in significant changes in the situation "on the ground" in beneficiary countries.[24]

The above diverse if not opposing views about EU social conditionality immediately present us with the controversy surrounding the trade-labour linkage and a certain degree of scepticism in relation to the effectiveness of any policy, agreement, measure or arrangement aimed at linking non-commercial objectives to trade. It also brings to light issues of legitimacy and credibility of EU external action particularly in relation to the EU's normative mission as a global human rights actor, which has been reinforced by the TL. Despite the major changes introduced by this Treaty in relation to the constitutional design of EU external relations,[25] particularly in relation to the EU external commercial competence,[26] the EU's authority to act on external matters of trade and labour is all but clear. Even though the scope of the EU's Common Commercial Policy (CCP) has been interpreted broadly by the EU Court of Justice (CJEU),[27] labour issues in trade agreements are not part of the EU's exclusive competence and remain within member states' competence giving rise to the phenomenon of mixed agreements.[28]

---

[21]European Commission—ILO, Memorandum of Understanding concerning the establishment of a strategic partnership between the International Labour Organisation and the Commission of the European Communities in the field of Development, 17 July 2004, Brussels and 16 July 2004, Geneva, available at https://www.ilo.org/brussels/ilo-and-eu/european-commission/WCMS_169299/lang--en/index.htm, accessed on 23 March 2020.

[22]Postnikov and Bastiaens (2014).

[23]Vogt (2015a).

[24]CARIS (2010).

[25]Ramopoulos and Wouters (2015).

[26]Articles 3(1)e TFEU, 206, 207 and 218 TFEU; for further detailed analysis, see Chapter 3 of this book.

[27]Ibid.

[28]Hillion and Koutrakos (2010) and Timmermans (2013).

When it comes to issues that go beyond trade, as most international agreements of the EU do, potential conflicts are not limited to the content of the agreements but also extend to the very objectives pursued by these agreements. To put it shortly, is linking trade to labour a way of protecting domestic industries or promoting EU values? In this context other questions arise concerning the way the EU furthers the trade-labour linkage and, chiefly, what are the reasons for the EU's reluctance to include a legally enforceable social clause in trade agreements?[29]

For the above reasons, EU discourse and practice in relation to social conditionality in trade offer a rather complicated picture. On the one hand, they seem to indicate that the EU utilises the trade-labour linkage as an invaluable development tool. On the other hand, the absence of a uniform and coherent understanding and approach to the trade-labour linkage and the reticence to rely on hard conditionality in certain cases of serious labour violations seems to suggest that the EU utilises the trade-labour linkage instrumentally and in a carefully planned manner as part of broader strategic geo-political, economic and foreign policy objectives. In the latter instance, this reluctance seems to demonstrate that the EU is not willing to go beyond the realm of rhetoric.

Against this background, the chapter intends to investigate whether a deeper analysis of the EU's social conditionality discourse and practice shows a strong commitment towards the promotion of social rights and labour standards in its external trade relations, in spite of what appears to be reticence to take social trade more seriously. With the changes introduced by the TL, social clauses in trade agreements are not mere EU foreign policy instruments but rather mechanisms that the EU should use to comply with its obligations under the EU Treaties, particularly in the light of Articles 3(5) and 21(1) TEU which recognize economic and social rights as a matter of justice that must be extended to external trade relations.

The chapter is structured as follows: it starts by examining the foundations and history of the trade-labour linkage, followed by a critical evaluation of social conditionality in EU external trade relations, drawing examples from previous and current EU practice at unilateral, regional and bilateral levels. The conclusion brings together and reflects on the main findings of the chapter.

5.2 The Foundations of the Trade-Labour Linkage

> The Members recognize that the avoidance of unemployment or underemployment, through the achievement and maintenance in each country of useful employment opportunities for those able and willing to work and of a large and steadily growing volume of production and effective demand for goods and services, is not of domestic concern alone, but is also a necessary condition for the achievement of the general purpose and the objectives set forth

[29]The only exceptions are the GSP scheme and the 2008 EU-CARIFORUM Economic Partnership Agreement (EPA) with Caribbean countries (CARICOM and the Dominican Republic), where a weak form of conditionality is envisaged.

in Article 1, including the expansion of international trade, and thus for the well-being of all other countries.

Article 1 of the Havana Charter for an International Trade Organization[30]

5.2.1 The Debate on the Trade-Labour Linkage

Discussions concerning the nature of the relationship between labour and trade and, in particular, the role played by social policies in the furthering of trade liberalization and what type of trade should be promoted (i.e. should we ensure "fair" and not only "free" trade?) both at multilateral and regional levels, has been with varying degrees at the centre stage of political and legislative agendas since the early nineteenth century.[31] And yet, to this day, it remains a contentious and divisive question. There is no agreement as to whether the WTO should be involved in labour issues and if so to what extent, nor is there clear conceptual guidance as to how the various labour provisions may or should interact with trade regulation.[32]

As Cottier and Caplazi[33] put it:

> there is ample consensus that labour standards are required. Yet, there is ample disagreement on how they should be implemented and enforced in international law. Labour standards apparently touch upon domestic regulations on labour relations. They are mainly part of internal affairs. And it can be readily seen that this aspect has disabled powerful implementation and supervision by international instruments, so far.

In short, the lack of coercive authority and weak international solidarity are the key determinants that explain the absence of a global floor of labour regulation.[34]

5.2.1.1 Attempts to Establish a Social Clause at the WTO

Attempts to establish the connection between trade liberalization and labour rights during the Uruguay Round (1986–1994), which resulted in the creation of the World Trade Organization (WTO), failed. In 1987, the US made an attempt with the support of the EU to gain consensus on the creation of a GATT working party to review the inclusion of labour standards into the GATT.[35] The quest for a social clause at the WTO had been driven by ethical and unfair competition concerns between

[30]United Nations Conference on Trade and Employment, Havana Charter for an International Trade Organization, Havana, Cuba, 24 March 1948. A full text is available at: https://www.wto.org/english/docs_e/legal_e/havana_e.pdf, accessed on 14 June 2020.

[31]Hepple (2005), Sapir (1995), Charnovitz (1987), Leary (1996), Kaufmann (2007), Ch. 3 and Cottier and Caplazi (2007).

[32]Cottier and Caplazi, above n. 31, p. 551.

[33]Ibid., p. 552.

[34]Teague (2002), at 326.

[35]The proposal made by the US for the terms of reference of the working party was:

industrialized and developing countries as well as concerns for the ILO limited ability in enforcing its Conventions.[36] Unsurprisingly, the ILO has been described as being akin to a "Kantian" international organization with the role of setting a set of moral benchmarks to assess the democratic legitimacy and credentials of national governments.[37]

As to the insertion of a social clause in the WTO legal regime, it is noteworthy that the 1994 EP's Sainjon report paved the way for a common EU position, which called for a social clause in the GATT/WTO as well as in unilateral trade policies.[38] Since then, the EP has expressed the view that social rights are to be considered as human rights and has been a strong advocate for the inclusion of enforceable labour provisions in EU trade agreements.

It is now well-documented that the majority of developing countries have fiercely opposed the proposal of the insertion of a "social" clause because of the latter being perceived as an expression of veiled protectionism undermining their comparative advantage in terms of labour costs.[39] Renewed attempts in favour of a trade-labour linkage were made at the first WTO Ministerial Conference in Singapore in 1996 without receiving any consensus. Nevertheless, delegates committed themselves to a declaration to observe internationally recognized core labour standards (CLS) and accepting that the ILO would be the competent body to set and supervise such standards.[40] In addition, and despite the lack of consensus for inserting a social clause

> To examine the possible relationship of internationally recognised labour standards to international trade and to the attainment of the objectives of the General Agreement. In the light of this examination, to consider any proposals and suggestions that may be put forward with respect to issues relating to trade and the observance of internationally recognized labour standards; and to report its findings and conclusions to the Council

GATT (1987) quoted in Addo (2015), at p. 148; see also Sutherland (1998), at 92.

[36] Kenner (2013a).

[37] Teague, above no. 34, at 326 citing Hongiu Koh, see Hongju Koh (1997).

[38] Burgoon (2004); European Parliament, Resolution of 9 February 1994 on the Introduction of a Social Clause in the Unilateral and Multilateral Trading System (OJ C 61, 28.2.1994, p. 89). The European Parliament's approach in favour of a code of basic social standards was based on two inseparable principles clearly laid down in the Sainjon report: (a) the observance of labour rights, in particular certain minimum social standards, was considered an essential requirement of natural justice, which should always govern international trade; (b) the possible introduction of a social clause in agreements regulating international trade should never be an excuse for increasing protectionism against developing countries. On the contrary, the instrument of the social clause should enable the objectives of social justice and fair competition to be achieved in the context of the increasing interdependence between national economies and the of globalisation of the economy and trade.

[39] Hepple, above note 31, Ch. 10.

[40] WTO, Ministerial Conference, Singapore, WT/MIN(96)/DEC/Ministerial Conference Singapore: Declaration, § 4, 13 December 1996.

in a multilateral trade agreement, a social clause was inserted in various international commodity agreements.[41]

At the third WTO Ministerial Conference in Seattle in 1999 the need for a link between trade and labour was once again raised with some suggesting the use of sanctions against those countries violating international labour standards. The EU strongly advocated the promotion of CLS in its trade policy while rejecting the use of labour rights for protectionist reasons.[42] In addition, it also favoured an increased cooperation between the WTO and the ILO and proposed in this context ILO observership at the WTO and the creation of a joint ILO-WTO standing working forum on trade, globalization and labour issues. The strong interventionist approach advocated at this conference led to its failure. At the 2001 Doha Ministerial Conference the trade-labour linkage had lost momentum and the Singapore Declaration was merely confirmed. Further, the Council and the Commission became increasingly reluctant to favour a "social" clause at the WTO because of fears that such a position would hinder the Doha Development Round.

Besides the political dimension to it, the debate on the social clause in the WTO should also be examined from an international trade perspective. The GATT 1994 has always permitted that legitimate state policies may justify the adoption of measures that in principle are contrary to basic GATT rules. As discussed further below, in certain circumstances, non-trade values can prevail over trade rules, provided that the national policies in question fall within the remit of one of the exceptions listed in Article XX of GATT and they are applied in good faith.[43] The question of whether trade can be subject to labour standards conditions should also be examined in relation to another related question, namely whether a trade regulation can introduce distinctions on the basis of *criteria unrelated to the products themselves*, namely the process and production method (PPM).[44] The reliance on PPMs is particularly important for the trade-labour linkage as any such measure, which conditions trade to labour standards will be about work and workers and not about the product itself. Hence, it is not so clear cut that labour standards or rights considerations in a trade regulation are explicitly prohibited under WTO law.[45]

5.2.1.2 Labour Standards and Decent Work at the ILO

While the introduction of a "social" clause in the WTO context failed, the ILO has proven to have more than certain standard-setting powers to ensure compliance with

---

[41] E.g. Article 45 of the 1982 Sixth International Tin Agreement; Article 28 of the 1987 International Sugar Agreement; Article 53 of the 1987 International Natural Rubber Agreement and Article 42 of the 2010 International Cocoa Agreement.

[42] Council Conclusions on the third Ministerial Conference of the WTO, 26 October 1999.

[43] See infra Sect. 5.2.1.2.

[44] Marceau (2009), at p. 545; for further analysis, see Conrad (2011), Howse and Regan (2000), and Jackson (2000).

[45] Marceau, above n 44, p. 549.

its own conventions' obligations.[46] In particular, the ILO's constitution foresees the setting up of a Commission of Inquiry where an ILO member state does not fulfil its obligations and in cases of continued non-compliance the ILO's governing body may recommend the imposition of sanctions against the state concerned under Article 33 of the ILO constitution. The procedure was invoked for the first time against Myanmar (formerly Burma) in 2000.[47]

Outside the WTO context, the prominence of the labour dimension to international trade received increased support.[48] In 1995, the Copenhagen World Summit for Social Development[49] defined a set of fundamental workers' rights, based on International Labour Conventions.[50]

This led to the adoption of the 1998 Declaration on Fundamental Principles and Rights at Work with which ILO member states committed themselves to the respect and promotion of four CLS embodied in eight ILO Conventions: (i) freedom of association and the right to collective bargaining (Conventions 87 and 98); (ii) the elimination of all forms of forced or compulsory labour (Conventions 29 and 105); (iii) the effective abolition of child labour (Conventions 138 and 182); and (iv) the elimination of discrimination in respect of employment and occupation (Conventions 100 and 111). Pursuant to Article 2 of the 1998 Declaration, all ILO members must respect these conventions, even when they have not actually ratified them, by virtue of their membership.[51]

The 1998 ILO Declaration was important insofar as it increased the visibility of CLS conceiving them as fundamental rights, thus providing a key point of reference for their action.[52] The recognition of CLS as human rights was in line with other key international instruments such as the UN Charter, the 1948 Universal Declaration of Human Rights (UDHR), the 1996 International Covenant on Economic, Social and Cultural Rights (ICESCR, Pact I) and the 1996 International Covenant on Civil and Political Rights (ICCPR, Pact II). At the same time, the above CLS are not controversial in the same way that other labour standards such as wages, working hours and annual leave are, which in some countries are also considered to be social rights.[53] With CLS, therefore, it was much easier to reach a satisfactory level of multinational consensus. In addition, freedom of association and collective bargaining have 'the advantage of being rights to a process' and are not associated only with a particular substantive result and outcome.[54]

---

[46]Maupain (2005a).

[47]Maupain (2005b).

[48]Organization for Economic Cooperation and Development (OECD) (1996, 2000).

[49]Further information is available at: https://www.un.org/development/desa/dspd/world-summit-for-social-development-1995.html, accessed on 20 March 2020.

[50]Granger and Siroën (2006), at p. 4.

[51]All EU member states have ratified the relevant conventions.

[52]For further analysis, see Kenner, above n 36, pp. 309–310.

[53]Cottier and Caplazi, above n 31, p. 557.

[54]Langille (1997), at 32; Cottier and Caplazi, above n 31, p. 557.

As stated by Kenner 'the more distinguishing characteristic of the CLS is that they have come to be regarded, through a process of meta-institutional iteration, as an élite set of higher human rights norms to be applied under international law irrespective of the traditional method of ratification or an individual country's level of development. […] The adoption of CLS has revived the notion that labour rights are capable of having a transformative emancipating effect on the lives of individuals and therefore should be promoted centre stage as freestanding universal and indivisible human rights.[55] Furthermore, the adoption of the 1998 ILO Declaration also contributed to the idea that the implementation of WTO rules must be read in the light of public international law including human rights law.[56] In particular, it could be argued that Article XX GATT,[57] which enumerates the general exceptions that a WTO member may invoke to restrict access to its market, should be interpreted as allowing the restriction of trading goods produced in a manner that violates human rights, including CLS, in order to protect the public morals applicable in the importing country.[58] In addition, parts of the WTO Treaty could be interpreted as allowing references to be made to labour treaties, including ILO instruments.[59] The Preamble of the WTO Agreement itself refers to '[…] increasing standards of living, ensuring full employment' as goals of the WTO. Similarly, reference is also made to 'sustainable development',[60] which incorporates also economic development and social justice.[61] As posited by Marceau, this very language of the Preamble 'could lead to an evolutionary interpretation of WTO provisions that would take social or labour-related principles into account in relevant circumstances.'[62] More generally, WTO provisions should be read in the light of other relevant international rules,

[55] Kenner, above n 36, p. 310.

[56] Breining-Kaufmann (2005), p. 116.

[57] The corresponding provisions for the General Agreement on Trade in Services (GATS) is Article XIV GATS.

[58] Bartels (2002, 2009); see also Vásquez (2003). It should be noted that Article XX GATT on General Exceptions comprises two cumulative requirements. In particular, for a GATT-inconsistent measure to be justified under Article XX, a WTO member must prove: first, that its measure falls under at least one of the exceptions (e.g. paragraphs (b)–(g), two of the ten exceptions under Article XX) and, then, that the measure satisfies the requirements of the so-called "Chapeau" of Article XX, namely that it is not applied in a manner which would constitute 'a means of arbitrary or unjustifiable discrimination between countries where the same conditions prevail', and is not 'a disguised restriction on international trade'; for an analysis of the "Chapeau" of Article XX GATT, see Bartels (2015).

[59] Marceau, above no. 44, 543.

[60] WTO, Marrakesh Agreement Establishing the World Trade Organization, 15 April 1994, 1867 U.N.T.S 154, Preamble, available at: https://www.wto.org/english/docs_e/legal_e/04-wto.pdf, accessed on 20 March 2020.

[61] E.g. relevant United Nations (UN) General Assembly Sustainable Development Goals (SDGs or Global Goals for Sustainable Development) targets related to labour standards, 8.8, 16.3, 16.5 and 16.b. further information is available at: https://sustainabledevelopment.un.org/?menu=1300, accessed on 20 March 2020.

[62] Marceau, above no. 44, p. 543, citing the Appellate Body Report, *United States—Import Prohibition of Certain Shrimp and Shrimp Products*, WT/DS58/AB/R, adopted 6 November 1998, paras 153–55 and 130.

including those that impose certain obligations and provide for the respect for certain rights contained in other treaties, covenants and conventions.[63] This normative argument does not find unanimous consensus and even when there is some level of agreement in favour of it there are still questions concerning the way and the extent to which the WTO provisions should be read and interpreted in the light of other international rules.

At the same time, the 1998 ILO Declaration has been subject to criticism, among others, because of its "promotional" character and its limited scope.[64] In particular, the CLS are narrower in scope than the labour rights of the EU Charter of Fundamental Rights (EUCFR),[65] which explicitly recognizes freedom of association and collective bargaining,[66] the prohibition of child labour, forced labour and slavery[67] as well as the equality between women and men in all areas, including employment, work and pay.[68]

Soon after the ILO's 2000 Decent Work Agenda (DWA) was adopted, which is based on four pillars: employment, creation and enterprise development; standards and rights at work: social protection and labour market governance and social dialogue. Hence the DWA goes beyond the promotion of CLS. Further to the 2004 recommendation of the World Commission on the social dimension of globalization to make "decent work for all" a global goal,[69] the agenda has spread to the main international and regional organizations such as the EU. The formation of a strategic partnership between the EU and the ILO in 2004[70] was a necessity not only as a form of defensive collaboration to prevent the retrogression of transnational labour standards but also as a positive engagement to promote an alternative approach to policies of deregulation and privatization that tended to dominate the discourse of globalization.[71] Since then, the ILO's twin agenda for the promotion of its CLS and DWA has been entwined with the EU's approach to promoting labour rights and social

---

[63] Marceau, above no. 44, p. 543; for further discussion, see Van Damme (2009).

[64] McCrudden and Davies (2000).

[65] Alston (2004, 2005).

[66] Articles 12 and 28 EUCFR.

[67] Articles 5 and 32 EUCFR.

[68] Article 23 EUCFR.

[69] World Commission on the Social Dimension of Globalization, Report on *A Fair Globalization: Creating Opportunities for All*, https://www.ilo.org/public/english/wcsdg/docs/report.pdf, accessed 14 June 2020.

[70] European Commission—ILO, Memorandum of Understanding concerning the establishment of a strategic partnership between the International Labour Organization and the Commission of the European Communities in the field of Development, 17 July 2004, Brussels and 16 July 2004, Geneva, https://www.ilo.org/brussels/ilo-and-eu/european-commission/WCMS_169299/lang--en/index.htm accessed 14 June 2020; ILO, *The ILO and the EU, partners for decent work and social justice. Impact of Ten Years of Cooperation*, Brussels, November 2012, http://www.ilo.org/wcmsp5/groups/public/---europe/---ro-geneva/---ilo-brussels/documents/publication/wcms_195135.pdf accessed 14 June 2020.

[71] Kenner (2013b).

dialogue with reference both to ILO standards and the European social model.[72] The EU's GSP+ special incentive arrangement, examined further below, is illustrative of this EU-ILO collaboration. Recent developments at EU level, such as the Europe 2020 Strategy on Smart, Inclusive and Sustainable Development (*in tandem* with the ILO's 2009 Global Jobs Pact),[73] the 2012 EU Strategy on Promoting Human Rights and Democracy[74] and the 2011 EU Agenda for Change for Development Policy[75] are evidence of a growing support in the EU's internal and external policies and actions for ILO standards and reflect the increasing importance in the EU of decent job creation, social dialogue and social protection for ensuring inclusive growth and sustainable development in the broader context of the global economic crisis.[76]

5.2.2 The Trade-Labour Linkage Rationales

These developments are premised on the idea that 'trade liberalization and the improvement of labour and social conditions are not "two solitudes",[77] they can find expression and operate coherently and consistently with each other.'[78]

Various rationales for including labour provisions in trade agreements have thus been put forward, namely, a social, economic and human rights rationale.[79] The overarching reason is the existence of interdependence between different set of problems and objectives.[80] Following on from this is the other equally important rationale

---

[72]Interview with Marco Ferri, First Counsellor in Social Affairs of the Permanent Delegation to the United Nations Office and other International Organizations in Geneva, 24 May 2013, Geneva, Switzerland.

[73]Information on the Europe 2020 Strategy is available at: http://ec.europa.eu/europe2020/index_en.htm accessed 25 July 2014; for the ILO's Global Jobs Pact: http://www.ilo.org/jobspact/lang--en/index.htm accessed 25 July 2014.

[74]Council of the European Union, EU Strategic Framework and Action Plan on Human Rights and Democracy, Luxembourg, 25 June 2012.

[75]European Commission, Communication from the Commission to the European Parliament, the Council, the European Economic and Social Committee and the Committee of the Regions, *Increasing the Impact of EU Development Policy: an Agenda for Change* COM(2011) 637 final.

[76]ILO (2011a, b).

[77]Langille (1997), at 27.

[78]Marceau, above no 44, at p. 540.

[79]ILO, Report on *The Social Dimensions of Free Trade Agreements*, 6 November 2013, 6–7, available at http://www.ilo.org/global/research/publications/WCMS_228965/lang--en/index.htm, accessed on 20 March 2020; see also European Commission, Final report on *The Use, Scope and Effectiveness of Labour and Social Provisions and Sustainable Development Aspects in Bilateral and Regional Free Trade Agreements*, 15 September 2008, Chapter 2, available at http://ec.europa.eu/social/main.jsp?catId=89&furtherNews=yes&langId=en&newsId=480, accessed 10 December 2014. For an engaging discussion and proposal for a linkage between international trade and labour standards, see Barry and Reddy (2008); see also Addo, above no. 35, Ch. 2; Arnold (2005); Melo Araujo (2018), at 234–237.

[80]Reddy, above no. 7, at vi–xi.

of creating incentives for actors and, in particular, states to take actions which are desirable or to refrain from taking actions which are undesirable in terms of labour standards.[81] In the EU context three broad forces have maintained and increased the demand for EU social measures linked to globalization and transnational trade processes: the pace of globalization itself; the risk of trade policy failure, and associated adjustment measures combined with proposals advocating for a reconceptualization of the governance and institutional setting of key international organizations such as the International Monetary Fund (IMF) and the ILO.

The *social rationale* aims at providing redress against the negative social effects of globalization processes. Trade liberalization is not only associated with job creation but also with job destruction.[82] The idea of trade and market exchange automatically directing self-interest towards socially desirable ends that guarantee the common good—what Adam Smith famously coined "an invisible hand of the market"—[83] combined with the ability and resilience of the economic system to reinvent and regenerate itself after an economic crisis[84]—what Joseph Schumpeter referred to as the tendency of a capitalist economic system for "creative destruction"—[85] remains pervasive.[86] From this perspective, liberalized markets break down barriers with a series of what may be termed "trickle-down of positive effects", including the improvement of the standards of labour and social rights. As posited by Cottier and Caplazi, 'while the argument that economic growth will be a powerful indirect means of raising labour standards might be right, growth in countries without a democratic system and which are hostile to labour issues will not lead to any improvement on working conditions'.[87] The same may be said about countries with high inequality in the distribution of wealth and income.[88] Moreover, there is no agreement on how to design appropriate redistribution policies in the current system of globalized trade given that they can potentially introduce distortions in market processes.

Labour and social policies will thus be required to redistribute some of the trade gains from winners to losers whenever trade liberalization affects parts of the labour force negatively.[89] This argument is made even more compelling by the fact that there is a disjuncture between the legal frameworks governing trade relations, which are no longer underpinned by a territorial principle of jurisdiction, and labour which to a large extent has not managed to free itself from national regulation. Hence, while

---

[81] Ibid., at ix–xi.

[82] Jansen and Lee (2007), p. 2.

[83] Smith (1976), p. 456.

[84] Schmidt and Thatcher (2013).

[85] Schumpeter (1942), p. 83.

[86] Taking this further it is possible to argue that 'while neoliberal political rationality is based on a certain conception of the market, its organization of governance and the social is not merely the result of leakage from the economic to other spheres but rather of the explicit imposition of a particular form of market rationality on these spheres,' see Brown (2006), at 693.

[87] Cottier and Caplazi, above n 31, p. 566.

[88] Lee (1997), at 12.

[89] Jansen and Lee, above n 82, p. 2.

markets have become global, decision-making authorities remain largely national creating a tension between the economic and legal rules employers and firms have to abide by. In these circumstances, trade and labour/social policies should interact as 'greater policy coherence in the two domains can help to ensure that trade reforms have significantly positive effects on both growth and employment.'[90] In this context, the social-trade linkage is meant to ensure the enforcement of domestic labour laws concerning the protection of workers in the sphere of trade in compliance with common international labour standards. It thus reflects a broader concern for safeguarding social protection and for counteracting the threat of a "race-to-the-bottom" whereby international competition to attract trade and investment may trigger countries to lower labour standards in order to regain a cost-based competitive advantage vis-à-vis those countries with lower labour standards, rather than spurring a "race to the top".[91] The quality and quantity of labour standards has thus become an international public policy issue and, in this context, the respect for CLS helps to ensure good governance such as the rule of law, transparency and social security.[92]

The *economic rationale* is premised on the idea of using labour provisions as tools to prevent unfair competition by ensuring a "level playing-field" in international trade to encourage labour standards in the exporting country that are comparable with those in the importing country.[93] The adoption and application of a social clause would act as a necessary regulatory measure.[94] In this context, fair trade conceived as fair competition becomes a means to implement free trade.[95] The ILO Constitution Preamble provides that: 'the failure of any nation to adopt humane conditions of labour is an obstacle in the way of other nations which desire to improve the conditions in their own countries.'[96] Arguably, any WTO member could claim that another member's failure to respect social rights impedes its ability to uphold social rights within its own territory.[97] The reason would be that a state's tolerance of labour violations could significantly undermine another state's protection of labour by increasing the pressure on that state to tolerate similar labour abuses or risk losing investments to the violation.[98] In the 2008 ILO Declaration on Social Justice for a Fair Globalization[99] it is stated that: 'the violation of fundamental principles and rights at work cannot be invoked or otherwise used as a legitimate comparative advantage.' The Declaration recognized the impact of

---

[90] Jansen and Lee, above no. 82, p. 10; see also pp. 14 and 90.

[91] Peels and Fino (2015), at 191; Barton et al. (2008), p. 144; Hepple, above n 31, p. 272.

[92] Cottier and Caplazi, above no. 31, p. 565.

[93] Lee, above n 88, at 6.

[94] Cottier and Caplazi, above no. 31, p. 565.

[95] Perulli, above no 5, at 31; see also Martens and Orbie (2018), at pp. 286–287; Cremona and Marín Durán (2012).

[96] International Labour Organisation (ILO), Constitution of the International Labour Organisation (ILO), 1 April 1919.

[97] Thomas (2009), Ch. 10, at p. 257.

[98] Ibid.

[99] Available at http://www.ilo.org/wcmsp5/groups/public/---dgreports/---cabinet/documents/genericdocument/wcms_371208.pdf, accessed on 20 March 2020.

trade and financial policies on employment and social rights and referred to the need to develop and employ an integrated approach in the promotion of decent work, through the cooperation with other international and regional organizations.[100] This argument is interpreted differently by developed and developing countries, respectively.[101] The aim of creating a "level playing field" where everyone that participates in international trade plays by the same set of rules is mainly pursued by developed countries. Developing countries have generally opposed the inclusion of social clauses in trade agreements for fear of protectionist misuse by developed countries, which could jeopardize their comparative advantage in international trade.[102] The case of the EU-India Free Trade Agreement (FTA) negotiations is illustrative. While the inclusion of human rights provisions and CLS in the ongoing EU-India FTA negotiations has been actively pursued by the EU on the basis of the so-called "domestic analogy" thesis[103] the Indian government has rejected it.[104] India has opposed the incorporation of social clauses in the FTA as its constitution foresees the protection of labour standards. The EU's insistence on including human rights in the agreement is considered to be patronizing given India's tradition of democracy and also to have potentially negative implications for India's sovereignty.[105] In addition, the Indian business sector views the pursuit of social trade in the proposed FTA as inspired by protectionist motives with negative effects on India's exports in labour intensive industry sectors such as the garment industry.[106] Similarly, civil society and non-governmental organisations (NGOs) in India have also expressed concerns about the FTA. The EU has addressed these concerns and most trade agreements, particularly the new generation of FTAs, make it explicit that labour standards should not be used for protectionist trade purposes.[107]

A persuasive argument in favour of guaranteeing harmonized labour standards in trade is for developing countries to use the protection of CLS as a means to defend their interests against aggressive foreign investment policies given that competition for investment has the potential effect of increasing a "race to the bottom".[108] From

[100]Perulli, above n 5, at 31.

[101]For a critical and philosophical analysis of the development and anti-development debate, see Rabbani (2011). By unpacking and deconstructing the main tenets of each discourse and examining the key conceptions as well as the underlying requirements and implications of the claims raised in each debate Rabbani maintains that beyond the seemingly apparent differences and opposing claims and goals there are important and fundamental similarities.

[102]Peels and Fino, above no. 91, 191; Montserrat Garibay (2009).

[103]The "domestic analogy" thesis embraces the idea that as the EU is becoming a global player it should pursue normative goals not only at home but also outside its borders; see European Commission, Communication from the Commission to the Council, the European Parliament, the European Economic and Social Committee and the Committee of the Regions, *Global Europe: Competing in the World—A Contribution to the EU's Growth and Jobs Strategy,* COM(2006) 567 final, at p. 5.

[104]Orbie and Khorana (2015), at 260.

[105]Krishna (2009).

[106]Orbie and Khorana, above no. 104.

[107]e.g. Article 50 of the 2000 Cotonou Partnership Agreement (CPA), Article 13(2) subpara. 2 of the 2011 EU-Korea FTA; these agreements are examined in Sects. 5.3.2.2 and 5.3.4 of this chapter.

[108]Cottier and Caplazi, above no. 31, p. 565.

this perspective, harmonized labour standards would act as a discipline on domestic and foreign employers and, therefore, assist governments in enforcing minimal standards.[109] Here we can see that the *economic rationale* would have the same purpose as the *social rationale* of preventing a "race to the bottom". While it is true that the social clause would mainly be applicable to the exporting sector of countries' economies and it would not tackle the problems affecting internal markets or the informal sector (which is prevalent in some developed and many developing countries)[110] this argument still has its cogency. If all countries world-wide operate in the context of an international harmonized legal framework of labour standards, it follows that the incentive for foreign investment firms or multinational enterprises to transfer production to a more favourable country, that is a country which does not have a set of minimal labour standards in place, would diminish.[111]

The *human rights rationale* is associated with moral and legitimacy arguments on the basis of which it is considered normatively unacceptable to trade with countries that are violators of basic labour rights. It uses labour provisions as a means for ensuring respect for labour-related human rights that reflect values universally accepted by the international community and also for improving labour standards generally. However, as Cottier and Caplazi observe: 'we cannot ask less developed countries to observe fundamental human rights and take their political problems or lack of a democratic system as an opportunity to ignore our historically developed ethics related to working conditions and exploit its human resources.'[112] It is thus important to avoid any double standards in the application of this rationale.

From the above we can see that the EU's rationales are mostly attributable to the social and human rights motivations and are not to be associated with protectionist sentiments.[113] This strongly contrasts with the United States' (US) discourse where both Congress and government advocate the trade-labour linkage largely to prevent third countries from having comparative advantage.[114]

The existence of such diverse rationales underlying the labour-trade linkage requires us to acknowledge that there isn't a single, privileged form of justification for rights. To date there has been a tendency to believe that engaging philosophically with human rights equates to engaging with them as a by-product of some commitment to a broader moral theory.[115] As Tasioulas aptly points out, this is a limitative and privileged vision of how to conceive a philosophical account of human rights' justification and such an approach must be challenged, precisely because there may be overlapping strands that go towards justifying each right.[116] What matters is

---

[109]Ibid.

[110]Jansen and Lee, above no. 82, p. 16.

[111]Cottier and Caplazi, above no. 31, p. 565.

[112]Cottier and Caplazi, above no. 31, p. 578.

[113]Van den Putte and Orbie, above no. 14, at 274–278.

[114]Ibid.

[115]Tasioulas (2020).

[116]Ibid.

that we attempt to make sense of human rights[117] and abandon the philosophical mistake to reduce everything to a system where every part follows from an orderly set of given principles.[118] In a similar vein, we should avoid the prevailing discursive practice of constructing development as a "science"[119] 'functioning on the basis of a universal economic rationality and a linear, consequential reading of history, [which] has operated since the end of the colonial period.'[120] This discursive practice is a manifestation in Foucauldian terms[121] of the dynamics of discourse and power within development seen in this sense as the outcome of a system of hierarchical relations perpetuating domination by systematically relating forms of knowledge and techniques of power.[122] A way to break this pattern is through what Bhambra defines as a "recognition of connected histories" challenging the insularity of historical narratives and historiographical traditions emanating from Europe.[123] This requires setting in motion a process of reconstruction of history at global level in order to 'acknowledge a sociology of connections that takes seriously the histories of interconnection that have enabled the world to emerge as a global space.'[124] In particular, 'any transformation of understandings would require a reconstruction "backwards" of our historical accounts of modernity, as well as "forwards" in terms of constructing a sociology adequate for our global (postcolonial) age.'[125] It is necessary, therefore, to develop and apply a notion of inclusion 'founded on the recognition of human unity or the

[117]Nickel (2007).

[118]Tasioulas, above no. 111.

[119]The expression "science of development" has been coined by Anghie, see Anghie (2000), at 281.

[120]Alessandrini (2010), Ch. 2; as Alessandrini tells us (p. 4): 'this framework relies on three normative assumptions, namely: the establishment of an unquestionable dichotomy between advanced and backward societies; the reliance on a supposedly neutral economic rationality through which to bridge this gap; and the invocation of the help and expertise of the so-called advanced members of the international community and the specialized international economic and financial institutions in order to facilitate the development process.' At the basis of this discourse is the idea of "failure" on the part of developing countries to develop their trade as fast as that of developed countries and the consequential need to seek the help of industrialised countries in order to redress this "failure" (p. 42). In this context, the author also acknowledges that the distinction between "developed countries" and "developing countries" is limitative and problematic and some scholars have replaced such distinction with terms such as the "Global North" and "Global South". The latter used by the World Bank to refer to countries located in Asia, Africa, Latin America and the Caribbean and considered to have low and middle income compared to the Global North, which generally comprises the G8 countries, the United States, Canada, all member states of the European Union, Israel, Japan, Singapore, South Korea, as well as Australia and New Zealand and four of the five permanent members of the UN Security Council, excluding China. For further discussion and analysis, see Global South Studies Centre (2015) and Dados and Connell (2012).

[121]Foucault (1981).

[122]The conceptualization of development as discursive practice leads to its "professionalization" and "institutionalization", which in turn creates an apparatus that organizes the production of forms of knowledge and the deployment of forms of power, relating to one another; Escobar (1995), pp. 5–6, 10, 32–39 and 41, 45–46.

[123]Bhambra (2014).

[124]Ibid., p. 156.

[125]Ibid., p. 117.

interdependency of *all* peoples and individuals, [which] cannot exclude any one person or collectivity from the validation of other's choices.'[126]

In this context, Rabbani argues that:

> Development policies conceived according to these lines can alone accomplish the practical goals of development and antidevelopment discourses, respectively, namely the unfolding of individuals and community's unique and socially relevant qualities and capacities. Similarly, the recognition of human unity in their search for self-understanding demands respect to the other not in terms of everyone's right to decide on their own, but in terms of the equal and irreplaceable value that everyone holds in giving meaning to everyone else's choices.

5.3 Social Trade as an "Unobjectionable Norm"[127] and the EU's Promotion of Social Rights and Labour Standards Through Its External Trade Instruments

The analysis carried out in the preceding sections helps us to understand the reasons for the widening and deepening of labour provisions in EU trade agreements and why social trade has rapidly become an "unobjectionable norm" in the EU context,[128] which has also been used to find public support in the face of criticism against FTAs.[129]

The status of "unobjectionable norm" acquired by social trade has become embedded in EU discourse and practice not only externally but also internally. The EU is integrating social, labour and environmental standards in important areas of the internal market, such as public procurement, as illustrated by Directive 2014/24/EU.[130] The Directive links public procurement with sustainable development and injects an approach based on social responsibility and solidarity. In comparison with previous public procurement regulations this Directive places considerably more importance on the protection of human rights and labour standards, particularly with regard to global supply chains. In addition, it significantly expands the array of social and labour policies that can be legitimately achieved through public procurement paying particular attention to enforcement along the entire production and supply chain.[131] With the transnationalization of supply chains, the respect for human rights and labour standards has become a priority also in the domestic regulation of public procurement.[132]

---

[126] Rabbani, above n 101, p. viii.

[127] This term is borrowed from Van den Putte and Orbie, above no. 14.

[128] The rising trend in the number of trade arrangements with labour provisions has steadily become a global phenomenon and it is not limited to the EU context; see Ebert and Posthuma (2011).

[129] Van den Putte and Orbie, above no 14, 263–283.

[130] Directive 2014/24/EU of the European Parliament and of the Council of 26 February 2014 on public procurement and repealing Directive 2004/18/EC, OJ [2014] L94/65, 28.3.2014; see E. Van den Abeele, 'Integrating social and environmental dimensions in public procurement: one small step for the Internal Market, one giant leap for the EU?' ETUI Working Paper 2014.08, available at http://www.etui.org/Publications2/Working-Papers, accessed on 20 March 2020.

[131] Corvaglia (2017), pp. 174–180; Wiesbrock (2016).

[132] Ibid. 1.

At all stages of the procedure there is now an obligation for member states and contracting authorities to comply with social and environmental legislation and labour law and to combat excessively low tenders.[133] This obligation provided by the Directive is particularly significant because, as noted by Corvaglia and Li, this Directive 'extends its regulatory influence outside the EU territorial jurisdiction and directly impacts the behaviour of firms, suppliers and subcontractors linked by supply chains across different jurisdictions.'[134]

The next section maps out and assesses the relevant labour provisions provided under selected EU trade arrangements, including international agreements, and the key monitoring and enforcement mechanisms put in place to ensure their compliance.

5.3.1 Unilateral Trade Arrangements: The GSP Scheme

The GSP scheme's concept was first adopted internationally in 1968 by the United Nations Conference on Trade and Development (UNCTAD), at the UNCTAD II Conference in New Delhi, India.[135]

The EU's GSP is an autonomous non-contractual and non-reciprocal trade arrangement which was first set up in 1971 (and since then subject to periodical revision) through which the EU provides preferential access to the EU market to a certain number of developing countries and territories, in the form of reduced tariffs for their goods when entering the EU market. In particular, the standard GSP arrangement accords tariff preferences to developing countries that are classified by the World Bank as lower or lower-middle income countries and that do not have equal preferential access to the EU market through another arrangement or measure—for example an Association Agreement (AA), FTA or Economic Partnership Agreement (EPA).[136] Social considerations, however, were inserted in the scheme only in January 1995 when the new GSP scheme for industrial products entered into force. The first objective pursued by the GSP is to contribute to the growth of developing countries' economies by helping them reduce poverty. Secondly, it also aims at improving their political and social situation by promoting good governance and sustainable development.

---

[133] Article 18(2) and Recital 37; Annex X which lists the International Social and Environmental Conventions mentioned in Article 18(2), Article 69; see also Article 71 which is aimed at preventing subcontracting chains; for further discussions, see Corvaglia and Li (2018).

[134] Corvaglia and Li, above no. 133, 2.

[135] UNCTAD, 'About GSP', available at: https://unctad.org/en/Pages/DITC/GSP/About-GSP.aspx, accessed on 23 March 2020.

[136] The list of these countries which fulfil certain economic criteria in terms of poverty and non-diversification of exports is reviewed on a yearly basis. If beneficiaries no longer meet the requirements set out above, they will no longer be granted trade preferences under the standard GSP.

Under international trade law, the GSP operates as an exception to the WTO Most Favoured Nation (MFN) principle,[137] which requires that any member country that extends a preferential trade concession to any other country is subsequently bound to extend precisely the same concession to all member countries. The MFN non-discrimination principle, however, does allow a few exceptions. For example, Article XXIV GATT authorizes the creation of regional trading blocs in the form of customs unions or free-trade areas, which is what allows regional trade agreements (RTAs) such as the EU to be WTO compliant and thus to lawfully exist.

The GSP exception was adopted back in the early seventies, via the "WTO waiver"[138] then replaced in 1979 by the "Enabling Clause,"[139] to take into account the structural disadvantages of developing countries in the world trade system.[140] The Enabling Clause allows developed countries to extend non-reciprocal trade concessions to them. In this way it is possible for Article I(1) GATT not to be applied to generalized tariff preferences that are granted to developing countries. However, any GSP arrangement has to fulfil a number of conditions in order to be protected by the Enabling Clause.[141] Specifically, only generalized, non-reciprocal and non-discriminatory preferences beneficial to the developing countries are admissible. Hence, trade preferences must be *generalized i.e.* they must be made available to certain classes of countries and not specific countries; they must be *non-reciprocal i.e.* the granting country must not expect any trade or other concessions in return; they must be applied in a *non-discriminatory* manner and, they must be of demonstrable *benefit* to the developing countries they target.

In addition to the general GSP scheme there is also the special incentive arrangement for sustainable development and good governance ("GSP+"), which was adopted in response to a WTO Appellate Body decision against one of the EU's special arrangements under the GSP scheme.[142] The case concerned a dispute between India and the then European Community (EC) regarding the consistency of the EC's Drug Arrangements, a GSP programme which made a system of additional trade preferences available to developing countries confronted with a higher need to control the production and trafficking of narcotics, with WTO law. The EC appealed against the Panel's

[137] Article I(1) GATT: 'With respect to customs duties and charges of any kind […] any advantage, favour, privilege or immunity granted by any contracting party to any product originating in or destined for any other country shall be accorded immediately and unconditionally to the like product originating in or destined for the territories of all other contracting parties.'

[138] WTO Waiver on the Generalized System of Preferences Decision of 25 June 1971, BISD 18S/24.

[139] Decision of 28 November 1979, *Differential and More Favourable Treatment, Reciprocity and Fuller Participation of Developing Countries* (the "Enabling Clause"), GATT BISD, 26th Supp, 203, GATT Doc L/4903.

[140] Michalopoulos (2001).

[141] These conditions are contained in Article 2 (a) footnote 3 of the Enabling Clause, which itself refers to the Waiver of 1971.

[142] *European Communities—Conditions for the Granting of Tariff Preferences to Developing Countries*, WTO Doc WT/DS246/R (2003) [7.161] (Report of the Panel) ('*Tariff Preferences Panel Report*'); WTO Doc WT/DS246/AB/R, AB-2004-1 (2004) (Report of the Appellate Body) ('*Tariff Preferences Appellate Body Report*'); Marceau, above no. 44, pp. 565–566; Harrison (2003) and Howse (2003).

finding at first instance that developed countries must provide *identical* tariff preferences to *all* developing countries under their GSP schemes (except when implementing a narrow range of a priori limitations). The Panel's finding was based on its interpretation of the non-discrimination requirement in the Enabling Clause. Contrary to the Panel, the Appellate Body held that the non-discrimination requirement did not preclude developed countries from granting different tariffs to products originating in different GSP beneficiaries. Instead, it considered that developed countries can differentiate between beneficiaries of their GSP schemes based on their different 'development, financial and trade needs', provided that identical treatment is available to all 'similarly-situated' GSP beneficiaries. Such need must be assessed in accordance with a sufficiently objective standard and the preferences accorded must have a sufficient nexus with that need. Despite the different interpretation of the non-discrimination requirement by the WTO Appellate Body, the EC's Drug Arrangements still failed to comply with WTO law because it operated on a closed list and was found not to be available to all 'similarly-situated' GSP beneficiaries.[143]

Following this WTO ruling the EU set up the GSP+ scheme.[144] The incentive scheme offers additional benefits under certain conditions to support vulnerable countries in their ratification and implementation of international conventions, including ILO Conventions. The purpose of the "vulnerability" requirement is to limit the GSP+ to those countries that have significant difficulties complying with the international Conventions due to their economic situation.[145] However, the application of some of the requirements for a country to be considered as being "vulnerable" ends up excluding stronger exporting countries like China and Brazil, which from a human rights perspective is highly questionable as the 'mere fact that a country has decent economic performance does not imply that it has no problems with regard to human

[143] *European Communities—Conditions for the Granting of Tariff Preferences to Developing Countries*, WTO Doc WT/DS246/R (2003) [7.161] (Report of the Panel) ('*Tariff Preferences Panel Report*'); WTO Doc WT/DS246/AB/R, AB-2004-1 (2004) (Report of the Appellate Body) ('*Tariff Preferences Appellate Body Report*').

[144] Bartels (2007).

[145] These are the vulnerability criteria, which have been partly amended further to the reform of the GSP Scheme. A vulnerable country means a country:

- which is not classified by the World Bank as a high-income or upper-middle income country during three consecutive years (in other words, is a beneficiary of the standard GSP);
- whose imports into the EU are heavily concentrated in a few products (the 7 largest sections of its GSP-covered imports into the EU represent more than 75% in value of its total GSP-covered imports);
- and with a low level of imports into the EU (its GSP-covered imports into the EU represent less than 6,5% in value of the EU's total GSP-covered imports from all GSP beneficiaries).

See Commission Delegated Regulation (EU) No 155/2013 of 18 December 2012 establishing rules related to the procedure for granting the special incentive arrangement for sustainable development and good governance under Regulation (EU) No 978/2012 of the European Parliament and of the Council applying a scheme of generalised tariff preferences, OJ L48/5, 21.2.2013; Commission Delegated Regulation (EU) 2015/602 of 5 February 2015 amending Regulation (EU) No 978/2012 of the European Parliament and the Council as regards the vulnerability threshold defined in point 1(b) of Annex VII to that Regulation, OJ L100/8, 17.4.2015.

rights.'[146] To qualify for GSP+, countries must ratify and effectively implement international standards in the field of human rights, CLS, sustainable development and good governance.[147] In particular, since 2005 GSP+ beneficiaries need to ratify and effectively implement all eight ILO fundamental conventions that together make up the four CLS,[148] which enhances the legitimacy of the ILO labour standards laid down in these conventions. The preferences granted by the GSP+ may be withdrawn from the beneficiary if the latter fails to implement the necessary Conventions. It is not clear whether the GSP+ scheme is fully WTO-compliant and it is possible that a WTO member in the future might challenge such a scheme in a WTO dispute.[149]

There is also the Everything But Arms (EBA) scheme set up in 2001, a permanent arrangement pursuant to which the Least Developed Countries (LDCs) as classified by the United Nations (UN) receive full duty and quota-free access to the EU market with the exception of arms and armaments listed in the World Customs Organisation (WCO) Harmonised Commodity Description and Coding System.[150] Unlike other GSP beneficiary countries, LDCs are not excluded from the scheme if they benefit from other preferential arrangements. This makes tariffs treatment and product coverage more advantageous for LDCs in comparison with other arrangements such as the Cotonou Agreement.[151] In addition, further to the reformed graduation criteria under Regulation (EU) 978/2012,[152] less countries benefit from the GSP and GSP+ schemes. This has reduced the competitive pressure for LDCs providing these countries with increased export opportunities. In this respect, the reform of 2012 discussed further below has also made the EBA arrangement more effective.

The EU pursues a two-fold objective with these unilateral trade reference schemes: on the one hand, it rewards countries that are vulnerable but willing to ratify and

---

[146]Ebert (2009), at 9.

[147]To be eligible all "vulnerable" developing countries must have 'ratified and effectively implemented' 16 human rights conventions, including the 8 fundamental ILO Conventions, and at least 7 (out of 11) conventions on environment and governance; for a list of the 27 core conventions, see Annex VIII of Regulation (EU) No 978/2012 of the European Parliament and of the Council of 25 October 2012 applying a scheme of generalised tariff preferences and repealing Council Regulation (EC) No 732/2008, OJ L303/1, 31.10.2012, p. 1. For further information visit: http://trade.ec.europa.eu/tradehelp/gsp, accessed on 14 June 2020.

[148]The eight ILO Conventions are: (i) freedom of association and the right to collective bargaining (Conventions 87 and 98); (ii) the elimination of all forms of forced or compulsory labour (Conventions 29 and 105); (iii) the effective abolition of child labour (Conventions 138 and 182); and (iv) the elimination of discrimination in respect of employment and occupation (Conventions 100 and 111).

[149]Marceau, above n 44, p. 567.

[150]Chapter 93; the Harmonized Commodity Description and Coding System, generally referred to as the "Harmonised System" is a multipurpose international product nomenclature developed by the WCO.

[151]Partnership agreement between the members of the African, Caribbean and Pacific Group of States of the one part, and the European Community and its Member States, of the other part, signed in Cotonou on 23 June 2000, OJ L317, 15/12/2000, p. 3.

[152]Regulation (EU) No. 978/2012 of the European Parliament and of Council of 25 October 2012 applying a scheme of generalised tariff preferences and repealing Council Regulation (EC) No 732/2008 *OJ* [2012] L303/1, 31.10.2012.

implement key International Conventions on sustainable development, including human rights and CLS, with additional tariff reductions under GSP+; on the other hand, it will temporarily withdraw GSP preferences in case of serious and continued violations of these Conventions.

5.3.1.1 The Nature of EU Unilateralism: A Comparison with the US' Unilateralism

Before proceeding to the detailed analysis of the operation and implementation of the EU GSP scheme it is necessary to examine its nature and key features by analyzing comparatively the US GSP scheme. This examination together with the findings of the study of the functioning of the EU GSP scheme in the next subs-section will enable us to better assess the effectiveness and impact of the EU GSP scheme.

The EU's approach is generally referred to as "soft unilateralism" in contrast with that of the US, which is often defined as being "aggressive unilateralism".[153] The US GSP programme came into effect on 1 January 1976.[154] The first US GSP was authorized in Title V of the Trade Act of 1974,[155] which aimed at providing developing countries with 'fair and reasonable access' in the US for specified products. It provides non-reciprocal, duty-free tariff treatment to certain products imported from designated beneficiary developing countries.[156]

The petition process within the US GSP scheme allows organizations to request the US government to review a country's treatment of workers to determine whether or not GSP benefits should be suspended for lack of progress in respecting worker rights. Petitions are filed with the office of the United States Trade Representative (USTR), which decides whether to dismiss them or accept them for review. Review essentially puts a country on probation. After a review period, the USTR can end the country's review, suspend duty-free treatment on one or more products or suspend the country from the programme in its entirety. Changes to GSP country eligibility or product coverage are made at the discretion of the President, drawing on the advice of the USTR.

---

[153] The case of Bangladesh, discussed in Sect. 5.3.1.2, is illustrative of this underlying difference in approach between the EU and the US. The latter decided that after the Rana Plaza tragedy, Bangladesh had made insufficient progress on factory safety reform to justify a reinstatement of its preferential status under the GSP programme. Hence in June 2013 the US suspended GSP status for Bangladesh. In the EU context, Bangladesh continues to be a beneficiary of the Everything But Arms (EBA) arrangement and generally the EU finds that there has been some progress resulting from the Bangladesh Sustainability Compact.

[154] For detailed analysis, see Jones (2015).

[155] US Public Law 93-617, 88 Stat. 1978, enacted January 3, 1975; 19 U.S.C Ch. 12.

[156] For detailed analysis, see Addo, above no. 35, pp. 154–156.

This unilateral trade arrangement is subject to periodic renewal by Congress.[157] In recent years, GSP renewal has become controversial. Some issues have included whether or not to continue to include emerging developing countries, such as India or Brazil, as beneficiaries or to open the programme to LDCs only. Particular products given duty-free access have also caused controversy, as well as the country practices of certain beneficiaries. Russia is a case in point. Many in the US Congress were critical of Russia's status as a GSP beneficiary following its invasion of Crimea. In May 2014, US President Obama notified Congress that he intended to graduate Russia from the GSP programme because he had determined that 'it is appropriate to withdraw Russia's designation as a beneficiary developing country under the GSP programme because Russia is sufficiently advanced in economic development and improved in trade competitiveness that continued preferential treatment under the GSP is not warranted'.[158] In October 2014, the President officially terminated Russia's GSP status, which became effective on the same date.

Since 1980s the promotion of labour rights in developing countries has become an important component of the US trade policy further to pressure from US labour and human rights activists.[159] The labour rights provision prohibits access to US markets to any country 'that is not taking steps to afford internationally recognized rights to its workers.'[160] The way this provision has been drafted is problematic as it does not require full compliance with labour standards and thus allows for significant discretion to be applied when using the 'taking steps' criterion. For example, the application of the labour provisions of the US GSP can be waived for reasons of national economic interest.[161]

In addition, it is noteworthy, that the US GSP legislation does not use the ILO concept of CLS. Instead it applies to "internationally recognized worker rights". The first four of these rights correspond almost entirely to those of the ILO Declaration. However, the right against all forms of discrimination, which is included in the ILO Declaration, is excluded. This important omission was the result of a political compromise on the labour rights amendment in 1984.[162] In practice monitoring officials regularly base themselves on ILO assessments.[163]

Arguably the US is demanding standards from other countries that it has not accepted as part of its own international obligations[164] as the US has ratified only 14

---

[157] The US GSP programme has been extended until 31 December 2017. The inclusion of conditional labour provisions into the US' GSP dates back to 1984 and has not undergone fundamental reforms since then.

[158] The US Government, Proclamation 9188 of 3 October 2014, 'To Modify the List of Beneficiary Developing Countries Under the Trade Act of 1974', 79 *Federal Register* 60945, October 8, 2014.

[159] A labour rights clause in the GSP was adopted by the US Congress and signed by the US President Ronald Reagan on 30th of October 1984, taking effect in the GSP Renewal Act of 1984, see US GSP Renewal Act of 1984. Pub. L. No. 98-573, 98 Stat. 3019 (1984).

[160] 19 U.S.C.A. § 2462(b)(2)(G).

[161] Greven (2005).

[162] Compa and Vogt (2001), at 203–204.

[163] Siroën (2013a), at 94.

[164] Hepple, above no. 31, 94.

of 189 ILO Conventions including two of the ILO's CLS on forced labour (Convention 105) and the worst forms of child labour (Convention 182), but not any of the other 'core' ILO Conventions, nor those relating to wages, hours of work or occupational safety and health, with the exception of safety and health in mines (Convention 176). Moreover, Hepple points out that the US' claim that it is enforcing customary international law is not correct as there is no general consensus to maintain that the ILO Conventions can be said to be part of customary international law apart from those relating to slave and forced labour.[165] Furthermore, some of the Executive branch's decisions to suspend benefits from certain countries and not others,[166] demonstrates the political nature of the decisions made under the GSP programme and that foreign policy reasons and the US economy's competitiveness globally are a key drivers in the way decisions are made under the US GSP programme.[167]

5.3.1.2 Assessing the Effectiveness of the Trade-Labour Linkage in EU Unilateral Trade Arrangements

Criticisms have been made in relation to the choice of the Conventions that beneficiary countries have to respect (both under the regular GSP and GSP+ schemes). Bartels notes that not all member states have ratified the 1948 Genocide Convention.[168] Similarly, Valette points out that when the 2005 Regulation for GSP+ scheme was adopted, the UN Convention against Corruption had not entered into force and it had not even been ratified by all member states.[169] This state of affairs seems to contrast with the rhetoric of the European Commission to the effect that the human and labour rights Conventions 'incorporate universal standards and reflect rules of customary international law and form the core basis of the concept of sustainable development' and that the Conventions on good governance and environmental protection reflect "basic global norms" for sustainable development.[170]

Moreover, the fact that some of the ILO Conventions are not fully implemented by EU member states raises concerns and undermines the credibility of the EU.[171] Germany, for instance, has been breaching ILO Convention No. 87 on Freedom of

[165] Ibid. 95.

[166] E.g. such as in the case of Bangladesh, above, no. 141 or Russia, discussed in this section. Both countries have been suspended from the US GSP scheme.

[167] As the analysis will go on to show foreign policy reasons can also underlie benefits withdrawal decisions in the EU GSP scheme.

[168] Bartels, above no 144, at 878.

[169] Valette (2007).

[170] European Commission, *Proposal for a Council Regulation applying a scheme of generalized tariff preferences* COM(2004) 699.

[171] Novitz (2005), at p. 214.

Association by failing to grant civil servants the right to strike.[172] Similarly, the United Kingdom has been found to be in breach of the same Convention, as well as of Convention No 98, several times.[173] As noted by Ebert, 'while it is true that even European trade unions and ILO officials do not view infringements committed by the Member States as comparable to those of many developing countries, it seems that Member States do not attribute as much importance to international standards as they would expect from developing countries.'[174] This leads to a double standard, which undermines the credibility of the EU GSP scheme. As adverted to above, it is necessary to break from a pattern of what Foucault calls 'hierarchical relations perpetuating domination' and thus decolonize EU external action, particularly in the field of social trade.[175] Consequently, and in practice, this would mean the removal of any double standard vis-à-vis EU trading partners.

Moreover, and significantly, the ILO's Committee of Experts on the Application of Conventions and Recommendations (CEACR) has found the CJEU landmark decisions in the *Viking* and *Laval* cases,[176] in which the Court held that trade union action violated the employers' right to freedom of establishment and freedom to provide services, to violate ILO Convention No. 87 on freedom of association and protection of the right to organise.[177]

In addition, some of the countries that have been admitted to the GSP scheme still have a fairly poor track record of human rights and labour rights protection

---

[172]Committee of Experts on the Application of Conventions and Recommendations (hereafter CEACR), Individual Observation Concerning Convention Nr. 87 (Germany) 1991, CEACR Individual Observation Concerning Convention Nr. 87 (Germany) 2003. CEACR Individual Observation Concerning Convention Nr. 87 (Germany) 2005 and 2006.

[173]E.g. Committee of Experts on the Application of Conventions and Recommendations (hereafter CEACR), Individual Observation Concerning Convention Nr. 87 (UK) in 2003 and 2007 and Concerning Convention Nr. 98 in 2002. In addition, in 2016 (while the TTIP negotiations were taking place), the ILO Committee of Experts held that the British government that proposed trade union legislation would if enacted violate ILO Convention No. 87, see CEACR, Observation on the Freedom of Association and Protection of the Right to Organise Convention, 1948 (No 87), 105th ILC sess (2016, adopted 2015) ('United Kingdom'). The legislation was adopted with the Trade Union Act 2016 (c.15) and CEACR has made other observations in relation to specific aspects concerning the right to strike, see CEACR, Report of the Committee of Experts on the Application of Conventions and Recommendations, International Labour Conference, 106th Session, 2017, ILC.106/III(1A), available at: https://www.ilo.org/wcmsp5/groups/public/---ed_norm/---relconf/documents/meetingdocument/wcms_543646.pdf, accessed 14 June 2020. A study conducted on compliance with ILO Conventions showed that 22 out of 28 EU Member States are in breach of the freedom of association ILO Conventions, see Ewing and Hendy (2015).

[174]Ebert, above note 146, 12–13.

[175]See above infra Sect. 5.2.2 of this chapter.

[176]C-438/05 *International Transport Workers' Federation v Viking Line ABP* ECLI:EU:C:2007:772 and C-341/05 *Laval un Partneri Ltd v Svenska Byggnadsarbetareförbundet* ECLI:EU:C:2007:772; for critical commentary of these judgments and the implications for Member States' domestic labour market regulation, see Freedland and Prassl (2016).

[177]CEACR, Observation (CEACR)—adopted 2012, published 102nd ILC session (2013) Freedom of Association and Protection of the Right to Organise Convention, 1948 (No. 87)—Sweden (Ratification: 1949).

and clearly, in some instances, the decisions of the Commission to admit a given country are not in line with the findings of the international supervisory bodies. Colombia, and its breaches of ILO Conventions No. 87 and 98 on the freedom of association and collective bargaining, is a case in point. ILO and UN supervisory bodies have severely criticised the acts of violence, including murder, perpetrated against trade union members and leaders as 'preventing the free exercise of trade union rights guaranteed.'[178] In addition, a number of elements of the Colombian labour legislation are not in line with ILO Convention No. 87[179] and progress made by the Colombian government to remedy the situation remains insufficient.

The preferences granted by the GSP+ may, following a procedure, be temporarily withdrawn from a certain beneficiary country if the latter fails to implement the necessary Conventions.[180] The preferential arrangements under the regular GSP programme can also be temporarily withdrawn for 'serious and systematic violation' of principles contained in the core international human rights and labour rights Conventions.[181] Hence, regular GSP beneficiaries not only do not have any obligation with regard to the additional international instruments of the GSP+, but they are not even bound by the requirement of continuing ratification and effective implementation of the core human rights and labour instruments—they only need to avoid 'serious and systematic violations'. Hence, 'within the EU's GSP programme there are not only multiple layers of preferences but also multiple layers of policy conditionalities.'[182]

A particular problem arises in the context of the withdrawal procedure: it is at the complete discretion of the Commission and the Council, and the EP is excluded from the procedure.[183] The Commission is at complete liberty to refrain from opening an investigation even if there is sufficient information documenting human rights violations, which could justify a withdrawal. Similarly, the Council decides upon the proposal of the Commission without having to take into account any factual or normative criteria. This implies that it may decide not to withdraw the preferences

[178] E.g. CEACR: Examination of individual case concerning Convention No. 87, Freedom of Association and Protection of the Right to Organise, 1948 Colombia (ratification: 1976), published: 2005, Conclusions; Case No. 1787 (Colombia), Report No. 343 (Vol. LXXXVIX, 2006, Series B, No. 3), para. 422; United Nations High Commissioner for Human Rights (UNCHR) (2011), 'Report of the United Nations High Commissioner for Human Rights on the Situation of Human Rights in Colombia' A/HRC/16/22 of 3 February 2011, available at: http://www.ohchr.org/Documents/HRBodies/HRCouncil/RegularSession/Session19/A-HRC-19-21-Add3_en.pdf, accessed on 20 March 2020.

[179] CEACR, Individual Observation concerning Freedom of Association and Protection of the Right to Organise Convention, 1948 (No. 87) Colombia (ratification: 1976), published: 2006.

[180] Article 15 of Regulation (EU) No. 978/2012.

[181] Article 19 of Regulation (EU) No. 978/2012.

[182] Yap (2013), at 289.

[183] European Commission, Commission Delegated Regulation (EU) No 1083/2013 of 28 August 2013 establishing rules related to the procedure for temporary withdrawal of tariff preferences and adoption of general safeguard measures under Regulation (EU) No 978/2012 of the European Parliament and the Council applying a scheme of generalized tariff preferences.

even in the case of compelling evidence of the most flagrant violations of the relevant Conventions. The Commission has used its power to withdraw access from beneficiary countries very rarely, and only in response to grave violations of ILO labour standards rather than human rights more generally. Two countries have been suspended from access to the GSP scheme (including the EBA): Myanmar/Burma and Belarus.

With regard to the former, the investigation against Myanmar/Burma followed a joint complaint filed by the European Trade Union Confederation (ETUC) and the International Confederation of Free Trade Unions (ICFTU) in 1995. The Commission was unable to obtain permission from Myanmar/Burma to dispatch a fact-finding mission. The investigation was thus based on hearings with NGOs and experts and it led to the conclusion that forced labour existed. In 1996 also an ILO Commission of Inquiry had been established on forced labour in Myanmar/Burma. Hence, in 1997 the Council withdrew GSP/EBA beneficiary status from Myanmar/Burma for forced labour practices,[184] which was then reinstated in June 2012 after the ILO dropped its restrictions on the country following evidence of an on-going reform process, including government agreement to end forced labour.[185]

Since May 2015, the EU has participated in the "Initiative to promote fundamental labour rights and practices in Myanmar" with the Governments of Myanmar, the US, Japan, Denmark and the ILO. The initiative aims to:

(1) improve Myanmar/Burma's labour rights system through a multi-year labour law reform and capacity building plan;
(2) and foster strong relations among businesses, workers, civil society organizations and Myanmar/Burma through a stakeholder consultative mechanism.

The labour reform plan developed under this initiative intends to serve as a basis for fostering legal change, coordinating donor assistance and strengthening government capacity to implement those reforms together with civil society representatives.[186]

Despite significant progress and wide-ranging reforms in the country, there is evidence of ongoing and severe human rights violations including discrimination against ethnic and religious minorities such as the Rohingya people, conflict-related violence and repression of the freedoms of expression, speech, assembly and association.[187] Myanmar/Burma has been seemingly cooperating with the UN Special Rapporteur on the situation of human rights in Myanmar, Ms Yanghee Lee. However,

---

[184]Council Regulation (EC) No 552/97 temporarily withdrawing access to the generalized tariff preferences from Myanmar/Burma, OJ L 85, 27.3.1997, p. 8.

[185]Regulation (EU) No 607/2013 of the European Parliament and of the Council of 12 June 2013 repealing Council Regulation (EC) No 552/97 temporarily withdrawing access to the generalized tariff preferences from Myanmar/Burma, OJ L 181/13.

[186]For further information see, https://www.ilo.org/yangon/press/WCMS_615269/lang--en/index.htm; https://www.ilo.org/yangon/speeches/WCMS_319811/lang--en/index.htm, accessed on 23 March 2020.

[187]United Nations General Assembly, Report of the Special Rapporteur on the situation of human rights in Myanmar, A/73/332, 20 August 2018, available at: http://undocs.org/A/73/332, accessed on 23 March 2020.

her full access to areas to discharge her mandate in an appropriate manner have been problematic. Moreover, a 2019 report of the Independent International Fact-Finding Mission on Myanmar, which was established by the UN Human Rights Council (HRC) in March 2017,[188] details the persistence of alleged violations by the military against the Rohingyas (including killings, rapes and gang rapes, torture, forced displacement and other grave rights violations) and states that the conditions that prompted them to flee to neighbouring Bangladesh are still present.[189] The Fact-Finding Mission also said that Myanmar incurred state responsibility under the prohibition against genocide and crimes against humanity, as well as other violations of international human rights law and international humanitarian law. On the basis of these findings, it has been submitted that the human rights violations occurring in Myanmar/Burma qualify for temporary withdrawal under Article 19 of the GSP Regulation.[190] To date the European Commission has been reluctant to withdraw the EBA beneficiary preferences.[191] An evaluation report of the GSP scheme suggests that the previous withdrawal might have had little impact on enhancing compliance with human rights and labour rights.[192] An explanation of this decision could be the relatively low levels of trade that Myanmar/Burma has had with the EU prior to withdrawal, which may have limited the EU's leverage in the country.[193] As things stand, the EU has taken a more cautious approach. A high-level mission of the European Commission and the European External Action Service (EEAS) has been set up to monitor progress in relation to compliance with human rights, as part of a broader engagement under the EBA.

It has also been suggested that the eligibility criteria of the GSP+ incentive scheme, which condition trade preferences to effective compliance with international human

[188] Human Rights Council, Report of the Special Rapporteur on the situation of human rights in Myanmar, A/HRC/31/71, 1 March 2016, available at: https://www.ohchr.org/EN/HRBodies/HRC/RegularSessions/Session37/Documents/A-HRC-37-70.docx, accessed on 23 March 2020.

[189] UN HRC, Report of the independent international fact-finding mission on Myanmar, Forty-second session, 16 September 2019, A/HRC/42/50; UN News, 'Genocide threat for Myanmar's Rohingya greater than ever, investigators warn Human Rights Council', 16 September 2019, available at: https://news.un.org/en/story/2019/09/1046442, accessed on 23 March 2020.

[190] European Commission, Mid-Term Evaluation of the EU's Generalised System of Trade Preferences (GSP), Final Interim Report, prepared by DEVELOPMENT Solutions for the Directorate-General for Trade Directorate D—Sustainable Development; Economic Partnership Agreements—Africa Caribbean and Pacific; Agri-food and Fisheries Unit D1—Trade and Sustainable Development, Generalised system of Preferences, Brussels, Belgium, 21 September 2017, p. 237, available at: https://trade.ec.europa.eu/doclib/docs/2018/october/tradoc_157434.pdf, accessed on 23 March 2020.

[191] In October 2018 the EU has given notice of its intention to send an emergency, high-level EU mission to the country to assess the situation on the ground. It was further stated that this high-level mission would be within the framework of a potential withdrawal of Myanmar from the EBA arrangement and there would be a clear possibility that a withdrawal could be the outcome, see Michael O'Kane, 'EU imposes trade sanctions on Cambodia and notifies Myanmar of potential similar action', https://europeansanctions.com/category/burmamyanmar/, accessed on 23 March 2020.

[192] Ibid.

[193] Ark et al. (2016).

rights and labour standards conventions, should be extended to EBA countries such as Myanmar/Burma.[194]

As to Belarus, in 2003, the Commission initiated an investigation against alleged violations of the ILO Conventions on freedom of association and the right to collective bargain, triggered by a joint request of the ICFTU, ETUC, and the World Confederation of Labour (WCL).[195] At the same time, the ILO appointed a Commission of Inquiry to investigate the freedom of trade unions in Belarus, which urged the country to implement 12 recommendations in July 2004. In June 2005, in view of the lack of implementation, the European Commission announced that it intended to submit a proposal for withdrawal to the Council unless Belarus 'made a commitment to take the measures necessary to conform with the principles referred to in the 1998 ILO Declaration on Fundamental Principles and Rights at Work'.[196] Subsequently, all attempts by Belarus to comply were considered by the Commission as lacking any 'indication of effective implementation of ILO Conventions Nos 87 and 98'.[197] After almost 4 years of the start of the withdrawal process and the lack of tangible progress the Council decided to suspend Belarus access to the EU GSP as of June 2007, further to ILO and European Commission investigations, which revealed serious and persistent violations of the rights of freedom of association and collective bargaining in Belarus.[198] The withdrawal of EU trade preferences from Belarus did not change the authorities' attitude towards independent trade unions and, in general terms, the situation with regard to freedom of association has not improved. Since the 2012 reform of the GSP,[199] the reinstatement of the GSP for Belarus is no longer possible as upper-middle-income countries are no longer eligible under the revised GSP.[200] The maintenance of the suspension may thus be considered a purely political gesture on the part of the EU.[201] As for Myanmar, reports seem to indicate that more than ten years after the withdrawal of EU trade preferences no progress towards the abolition of forced labour has been recorded.[202] In each case the main answer relates to the low commercial leverage exerted by the EU: in the case of Belarus, Russia is the main economic partner and in the case of Myanmar/Burma it is China and the Association of Southeast Asian Nations (ASEAN) trading bloc.[203]

It is noteworthy that both in the case of Belarus and Myanmar/Burma, the procedure leading to GSP sanctions chronologically followed the adoption of restrictive

[194]International Federation for Human Rights (FIDH) (2017), p. 2.

[195]Portela and Orbie (2014), at 68.

[196]European Commission, *Proposal for a council regulation temporarily withdrawing access to the generalised tariff preferences from the Republic of Belarus* COM (2006)0438 final, p. 37.

[197]Ibid., at p. 39.

[198]Council Regulation (EC) No 1933/2006 of 21 December 2006 temporarily withdrawing access to the generalized tariff preferences from the Republic of Belarus, OJ L 4056/2006, p. 35.

[199]Discussed further below, see Sect. 5.3.1.3.

[200]Portela (2018), p. 5.

[201]Ibid.

[202]Cuyvers and Zhou (2011).

[203]Ibid.

measures under the Common Foreign and Security Policy (CFSP).[204] Various factors explain the coherence between these two spheres of EU external action.[205] First, an authoritative condemnation by the ILO seems to have facilitated the imposition of GSP sanctions. Both Myanmar/Burma and Belarus had been heavily condemned by the relevant ILO Commission of Inquiry, which was established for each of these countries in parallel to the EU procedure leading to GSP withdrawal. Linked to this, in both Myanmar/Burma and Belarus the labour rights violations had been perpetrated by the public authorities rather than private actors such as employers and firms.[206]

At this juncture, another EBA beneficiary country, which should be examined for the way it illustrates the nature of the problems concerning the enforcement of GSP sanctions, is Bangladesh. At the time of writing, no withdrawal procedure has been launched by the Commission against its government. Bangladesh is the main beneficiary of the EBA arrangement as most of the EBA preferential imports into the EU come from this beneficiary country and through this GSP scheme the EU remains Bangladesh's largest trading partner.[207] Bangladesh relies heavily on the EBA arrangement in terms of preferential trade as almost all of Bangladesh's exports to the EU come from the Ready-Made Garment (RMG) industry.[208] Following the collapse of the Rana Plaza factory building in Dhaka in 2013,[209] there has been a joint effort at international level to improve labour, health and safety conditions for workers in the garment industry in Bangladesh.[210]

Only 10% of garment factories in Bangladesh have registered unions[211] and in 2017 it was estimated that only 4% of RMG workers were union members.[212] One

[204] For detailed analysis and discussion, see Portela and Orbie, above no. 195, 67–68 and 70–72.

[205] Ibid., 71–72.

[206] Ibid., 73; for further discussion, see Kryvoi (2008).

[207] For further information visit: http://ec.europa.eu/trade/policy/countries-and-regions/countries/bangladesh/index_en.htm, accessed on 23 March 2020.

[208] *Id.* A large amount of workers are employed in the RMG sector of whom mostly women; see further: http://www.worldbank.org/en/news/feature/2017/02/07/in-bangladesh-empowering-and-employing-women-in-the-garments-sector, accessed on 20 March 2020.

[209] On 24 April 2013, the five-story Rana Plaza building collapsed killing more than 1000 people and seriously injuring more than 2000 people, see https://ranaplaza-arrangement.org, accessed on 20 March 2020. Despite large cracks were discovered the day before and the building evacuation the day before, factory owners threatened to withhold wages of those garment workers who would not return for work. On this point Phil Robertson, then Asia Deputy Director of Human Rights Watch (HRW), commented that had the garment workers more of a voice, they might have been able to resist managers who ordered them to work in the doomed building a day after large cracks appeared in it', see Human Rights Watch, 'Bangladesh: Garment Worker's Union Rights Bleak' (21 April 2016) https://www.hrw.org/news/2016/04/21/bangladesh-garment-workers-union-rights-bleak, accessed on 23 march 2020.

[210] For a detailed study of labour standards in Bangladesh, see Hossain et al. (2018). The authors argue that while trade arrangements such as the EU GSP scheme have made significant contributions to the economic upgrading of the country, but have failed to upgrade its social development.

[211] Human Rights Watch (2016).

[212] See further information at: http://www.dhakatribune.com/tribune-supplements/business-tribune/2017/04/23/garment-workers-rights-still-far-cry/, accessed on 20 March 2020.

of the main barriers to the formation of trade unions is to be found in the Bangladesh Labour Act (BLA), which includes a 30% minimum membership requirement to form trade unions.[213] The government also has significant power to cancel any registration that might cause 'serious hardship to the community' or is 'prejudicial to the national interest', terms that are undefined and therefore subject to abuse.[214] Further barriers to unionization include the factory owners' negative attitude towards unionism, a lack of trust between factory owners and workers as well as the workers' lack of knowledge regarding their rights.[215] Few steps to guarantee a respect for the rule of law, particularly in the areas of freedom of association, collective bargaining and workplace safety have been taken by Bangladesh since the Rana Plaza tragedy.[216] In addition, systemic abuses continue, such as the Bangladeshi authorities' repression of a strike in Ashulia in 2016 during which garment workers called for living wages[217] and following which employers responded by making thousands of workers redundant.[218]

In response to the Rana Plaza tragedy, the EU has made a commitment to work with Bangladesh to improve labour rights and ensure safety in the garment industry.[219] The EU has been reluctant to trigger a withdrawal process or impose sanctions on Bangladesh in consideration of the fact that the RMG sector makes up a majority of the country's gross domestic product (GDP) and that the EBA trade terms have assisted Bangladesh in reducing extreme poverty.[220] Instead the EU has chosen to adopt the "Sustainability Compact for Continuous Improvement in Labour Rights and Factory Safety in Ready-made Garment and Knitwear Industry in Bangladesh" (known as "Sustainability Compact").[221] The Sustainability Compact is a partnership between the EU, the ILO, and the Government of Bangladesh aimed at improving

[213] European Commission (2017c).

[214] Ark et al., above no. 193.

[215] Ibid.

[216] The 2006 Bangladesh Labour Act, which was amended in 2013 and its 2015 implementing rules still fall short of ILO standards. The law continues to be prejudiced against unions by making founding, registering and operating a union very difficult. While there was an initial increase in trade union registrations after the Compact was adopted, the 2013 legislation gives the government great discretion to refuse to register trade unions and many unions have since been busted or are now inactive.

[217] Bangladeshi authorities arrested or detained at least 34 union leaders and worker rights advocates, see further information at: https://www.hrw.org/news/2017/02/15/bangladesh-stop-persecuting-unions-garment-workers, accessed on 20 March 2020.

[218] Visit: https://www.solidaritycenter.org/bangladesh-living-wage-strike-sparks-government-crackdown/, accessed on 20 March 2020.

[219] European Commission DG Trade (2013).

[220] Ahmad (2015).

[221] European Commission, 'Staying Engaged: The Sustainability Compact for the Bangladesh Ready Made Garment Sector', available at: http://trade.ec.europa.eu/doclib/docs/2018/june/tradoc_157065.27"%20x%2011.69"_%2019.06.2018_Te….pdf, accessed on 23 March 2020.

labour, health and safety conditions for workers as well as to encourage responsible businesses in the ready-made garment industry in Bangladesh.[222] Bangladesh's progress under the Compact is monitored by a high-level group, referred to as the 3 + 5 + 1 Group, which regularly reviews the progress Bangladesh has made on the implementation of the Compact.[223]

In April 2016, an ILO high level tripartite mission visited Bangladesh and published a highly critical report about the violations of the freedom of association occurring in the country.[224] In June 2016, further to the government's continuing failure to comply with Convention 87 on the freedom of association, the ILO's Committee on the Application of Standards (CAS) wrote a special paragraph in their report to the ILO stating that it 'noted with deep concern that the government has failed to make progress on the repeated and consistent conclusions of this Committee despite the substantial technical assistance and financial resources provided by donor countries.'[225]

In a report submitted to the 107th Session of the International Labour Conference the ILO CEACR continued to express concerns over Bangladesh's progress.[226] In response to Bangladesh's proposed amendments to the BLA, the ILO noted that, 'many of the changes [the CEACR] has been requesting for a number of years have either not been addressed or addressed only partially.'[227] The CEACR concluded in urging Bangladesh 'to continue to review and amend the relevant provisions of the BLA in order to ensure that any restrictions on the exercise of the right to freedom of association are in conformity with the Convention.'[228]

The EU has repeatedly requested the Bangladeshi government to redress such violations in the garment industry identified and condemned by the ILO. In a letter of March 2017, the European Commission and the EEAS warned Bangladesh that failure to take 'concrete and lasting measures' to ensure respect for fundamental human and labour rights might trigger the launch of a formal investigation that could

---

[222]The US and Canada joined as partners in 2013 and 2016, respectively; the Compact is built on short- and long-term commitments related to three main pillars: (1) respect for labour rights; (2) the structural integrity of buildings and occupational safety and (3) responsible business conduct. For further analysis, see Kenner and Peake (2017) and Vogt (2017).

[223]This group is comprised of three secretaries of Labour, Commerce and Foreign Affairs of the Government of Bangladesh, as well as the ambassadors of the EU, the US, Canada, plus two other Member States, together with the ILO.

[224]Further information available at: http://www.ilo.org/wcmsp5/groups/public/---ed_norm/---relconf/documents/meetingdocument/wcms_488339.pdf, accessed on 23 March 2020.

[225]Further information available at: http://www.ilo.org/wcmsp5/groups/public/---ed_norm/---relconf/documents/meetingdocument/wcms_489124.pdf, accessed on 23 March 2020.

[226]"Report of the Committee of Experts on the Application of Conventions and Recommendations", 2018, available at: http://www.ilo.org/wcmsp5/groups/public/---ed_norm/---relconf/documents/meetingdocument/wcms_617065.pdf, accessed on 23 March 2020.

[227]Ibid.

[228]Ibid.

result in the temporary withdrawal of preferences.[229] In spite of the government's lack of progress the European Commission failed to act upon this warning. This led the ITUC, the Clean Clothes Campaign (CCC) and the École des Hautes Études Commerciales (HEC)—New York University (NYU) EU Public Interest Clinic to lodge a complaint with the European Ombudsman alleging maladministration in the European Commission's failure to launch an investigation into Bangladesh's status under the GSP Regulation.[230] The European Commission enjoys broad discretion under the provisions of the GSP Regulation. However, that discretion is not unfettered. The European Commission is bound to conduct its international and trade policy in line with the principles and values, which govern EU action, including universal human rights and respect for human dignity.[231] The European Commission's process for determining whether to investigate a GSP beneficiary country is not transparent or clear. The European Commission's position is that the trigger for an investigation is two consecutive special paragraphs in ILO reports.[232] It appears that the Commission seeks to avoid enforcing the GSP partly because it does not intend to start investigating until a second special paragraph is published in spite of the fact that the GSP Regulation does not support the idea that two special paragraphs are necessary for initiating an investigation.[233] Most importantly, using these as 'the only triggering mechanism improperly insulates the Commission from its responsibility to determine whether an investigation is necessary under all of the circumstances.'[234]

Other countries such as Uzbekistan[235] and Turkmenistan, which have been found to be breaching labour rights, continue to have access to the EU's GSP scheme.[236] This "selective human rights conditionality" has led many to question the legitimacy of the EU's role in promoting human rights and ILO labour standards. A study conducted on the impact of the withdrawal of GSP benefits also seems to indicate an inherent contradiction: the general economic situation of the target country worsens by reverting to less favourable terms of trade, which in turn is likely to translate into

---

[229]European Commission and European External Action Service, Letter sent by Trade Director of the European Commission Sandra Gallina, Director of Labour Mobility at the Directorate-General for Employment, Social Affairs and Inclusion of the European Commission Jordi Curell and Managing director of Human Rights, Global and Multilateral Issues at the European External Action Service Lotte Knudsen, Brussels, Belgium, 31 May 2017.

[230]ITUC-CCC, Complaint to the European Ombudsman. Alleging maladministration by the European Commission in its failure to investigate the status of Bangladesh under the GSP, Brussels, Belgium, 6 June 2018, available at: https://www.ituc-csi.org/IMG/pdf/bangladesh_ombudsman_complaint_nal_2018_06_06_clean.pdf. The present author was part of the HEC-NYU EU Public Interest Clinic team that prepared the complaint filed to the European Ombudsman.

[231]Article 21 TEU.

[232]Vogt, above no. 222.

[233]Ibid.

[234]ITUC-CCC, above no. 230.

[235]Under the Uzbekistan Partnership and Cooperation Agreement technical meetings were suspended in response to the Andjan massacre. However, in the Council Common Position there was no reference to the human rights clause, see Council Common Position 2005/792/CFSP concerning restrictive measures against Uzbekistan [2005] OJ L 299/72.

[236]Bartels (2013).

an increasing deterioration of labour and human rights.[237] Many observers argue that the EU not only applies the GSP scheme at its own discretion, but also that it uses it instrumentally in order to pursue foreign policy objectives rather than for ensuring the protection of labour rights.[238] More generally, it would seem that despite its purported development goals, and in particular as an effort to improve the value of preferences for the "neediest", the GSP scheme is used as a tool to improve the EU'S leverage in trade negotiations with emerging economies.

With regard to the GSP+, benefits are seldom withdrawn and only in response to grave violations of ILO labour standards rather than human rights more generally. Where they are withdrawn this is temporary reflecting the EU's intention to use GSP conditionality as a "carrot", namely, an incentive to make progress on human rights, sustainable development and good governance.

The effects of withdrawal of GSP+ benefits have varied. For example, in 2008 the Commission opened an investigation into El Salvador, following a judgment of the El Salvador Supreme Court that El Salvador's ratification of ILO Convention No 87 on freedom of association and the right to organise was unconstitutional.[239] The prospect of loss of access to GSP+ benefits appears to have been instrumental in persuading the El Salvadorian government to amend the Constitution so as to render ratification of the Convention constitutional and the Commission therefore terminated the investigation as it found that there was no longer reason for justifying the temporary withdrawal of the GSP+.[240] Similarly, the Commission initiated an investigation into Bolivia concerning the effective implementation of the United Nations Single Convention on Narcotic Drugs[241] following Bolivia's decision to withdraw from the said Convention as of 1 January 2012. However, Bolivia continued to give effect to the Convention and on 10 January 2013 Bolivia's request to re-accede was accepted. Consequently, the Commission stopped its investigation in March 2013.

The case of Sri Lanka differs from those of El Salvador and Bolivia. Sri Lanka, which had access to the GSP+ since 2004, is the only beneficiary country to have been suspended from this scheme to date. It is noteworthy that Sri Lanka's compliance with labour standards has never been contested.[242] Instead an investigation launched by the Commission in October 2008, drawing on UN reports and statements as well

---

[237] Sykes (2006), at p. 69.

[238] For a discussion of these issues, see Orbie and De Ville (2010).

[239] European Commission, Decision 2008/316/EC of 31 March 2008 providing for the initiation of an investigation pursuant to Article 18(2) of Council Regulation (EC) No 980/2005 with respect to the protection of the freedom of association and the right to organize in El Salvador OJ [2008] L 108/29, 18 April 2008.

[240] European Commission, Report of the Investigation pursuant to Article 18(2) of the Council Regulation (EC) No 980/2005 with respect to the protection of the freedom of association and the right to organize in El Salvador, C(2009) 7934 (2009).

[241] European Commission, Implementing Decision 2012/161/EU of 19 March 2012 providing for the initiation of an investigation pursuant to Article 17(2) of Council Regulation (EC) No 732/2008 with respect to the effective implementation of the United Nations Single Convention on Narcotic Drugs in Bolivia OJ [2012] L 80, 20.3.2012, p. 30.

[242] Portela, above no. 200, p. 5.

as findings of human rights NGOs, found widespread violations of the ICCPR, the 1984 Convention against Torture (CAT) and the 1989 Convention on the Rights of the Child (CRC). Independent experts were tasked to conduct an investigation, which included interviews with NGO representatives and officials of international organisations as well as a field visit to Sri Lanka. It was concluded that the Sri Lankan national legislation did not effectively implement the above human rights conventions, in addition to the lack of co-operation from the Sri Lankan government, which was condemned.[243]

The Commission proposal to withdraw access to the GSP+ from Sri Lanka in October 2009 was not sufficiently persuasive to convince the Sri Lankan government to take adequate measures to address the violations identified by the investigation. Sri Lanka was then temporarily suspended from the GSP+ scheme in August 2010.[244] The regulation stated that the withdrawal would last until it was decided that 'the reasons justifying the temporary withdrawal no longer prevailed.'[245] Prior to this the Commission had offered to delay the entry into force of the withdrawal by six months (decision was made in January 2010) in exchange of 'tangible and sustainable progress on a number of outstanding issues'.[246] The suspension of GSP+ preferences had a negative impact on the Sri Lankan garment industry and the closing of many garment factories in the three years following the temporary withdrawal resulted in the loss of thousands of jobs.[247] This illustrates that the degree of leverage of the GSP+ conditionality is also determined by the level of importance of the EU market for the beneficiary country's exports.[248]

In May 2017, the EU granted GSP+ status to Sri Lanka in light of its improved governance and human rights conditions, including re-establishing the independence of the National Human Rights Commission and re-engaging with the UN system.[249] Nevertheless, the EU acknowledges what remains an unsatisfactory situation of labour rights and standards in the country. Sri Lanka's reinstatement constitutes

[243] European Commission, Report on the findings of investigation with respect to the effective implementation of certain human rights conventions in Sri Lanka, Brussels, Belgium, 19 October 2009, C(2009) 7999, available at: https://reliefweb.int/sites/reliefweb.int/files/resources/9501F5EFE0C4F6C449257655000EECA5-Full_Report.pdf, accessed on 14 June 2020.

[244] European Commission, Implementing Regulation (EU) No 143/2010 of 15 February 2010 temporarily withdrawing the special incentive arrangement for sustainable development and good governance provided under the Regulation (EC) No 732/2008 with respect to the Democratic Socialist Republic of Sri Lanka, OJ [2010] L 45/2010, 22.7.2010, p.1.

[245] Ibid., Article 2.

[246] European Commission, Press release, 'EU regrets silence of Sri Lanka regarding preferential import regime' of 5 July 2010, IP/10/888, available at https://ec.europa.eu/commission/presscorner/detail/en/IP_10_888, accessed on 14 June 2020.

[247] Democracy Reporting International, 'GSP+ and Sri Lanka' August 2017, available at: http://democracy-reporting.org/wp-content/uploads/2018/04/GSP-English_August-2017.pdf, p. 10, accessed on 20 March 2020.

[248] European Commission, above no. 171, p. 241.

[249] Commission Delegated Regulation (EU) 2017/836 of 11 January 2017 amending Annex III to Regulation (EU) No 978/2012 of the European Parliament and of the Council applying a scheme of generalised tariff preferences, OJ 18.5.2017 L 125/1.

'a vote of confidence from the European Union that the Sri Lankan Government will maintain the progress it has made in implementing the international conventions.'[250]

While it is not clear whether the EU's GSP+ scheme is fully WTO compliant—particularly with the Most-Favoured Nation (MFN) principle (Article I:1 GATT) on the basis of the exceptions provided under Article XX GATT-[251] questions have arisen concerning the lack of transparency in the decision-making process pursuant to which third countries are granted GSP+ preferences, as well as issues of selective conditionality and double standards.[252] There have also been questions concerning the review of implementation of the relevant Convention requirements for the granting of GSP+ benefits. In particular, the monitoring of the GSP+ has been subject to criticism due to various GSP+ beneficiary countries having a particularly poor record as regards one or more CLS. Infringements of CLS have often been reported[253] and the EP has continuously called upon the Commission to monitor more strictly the compliance with ILO labour standards and asked for the suspension of preferences in respect of countries that breach fundamental rights. A 2016 European Commission report on the GSP+ arrangement shows that several countries still lack full compliance with the conventions' requirements, which are insufficiently implemented in domestic laws or lack adequate reporting.[254] In addition, according to a study conducted by CARIS[255] the GSP+ scheme and its conditionality has not yet resulted in significant changes in the situation "on the ground" in beneficiary countries.

There is also another related problem: although suspensions are directed against a given government, they end up having negative effects on the country as a whole, including its population.[256] For example, we have seen in the case of Sri Lanka that suspension from the GSP+ forced many garment industries to close down with many job losses. Hence, the scheme ends up harming those who it purports to help.[257]

---

[250] European Commission, 'EU Grants Sri Lanka Improved Access to Its Market as Incentive for Reform', Press Release IP/17/1363, Brussels, Belgium, May 17, 2017, available at: http://trade.ec.europa.eu/doclib/press/index.cfm?id=1663, accessed on 20 March 2020.

[251] See above, *infra* Sect. 5.3.1.

[252] Velluti (2016a), at pp. 358–361.

[253] European Parliament, Report on the external dimension of social policy, promoting labour and social standards and European corporate social responsibility (2010/2205(INI)), Committee on Employment and Social Affairs, A7-0172/2011, of 20 April 2011.

[254] European Commission, *Joint Staff Working Document on the EU Special Incentive Arrangement for Sustainable Development and Good Governance (GSP+) covering the period 2014–2015,* Brussels, 28.01.2016, SWD (2016) 8 final; European Commission, *GSP + Report on Sustainability, Human Rights and Good Governance.* Questions and Answers', Brussels, Belgium, 28.01.2016, available at: trade.ec.europa.eu/doclib/docs/2016/january/tradoc_154179.pdf, accessed on 23 March 2020.

[255] CARIS, 'Mid-term Evaluation of the EU's Generalized System of Preferences', Report commissioned by the EC, Brighton: Centre for the Analysis of Regional Integration at Sussex, University of Sussex, 2010, available at: http://www.sussex.ac.uk/caris/projects, and the final report is available at: http://trade.ec.europa.eu/doclib/docs/2010/may/tradoc_146196.pdf, accessed on 23 March 2020.

[256] Portela, above no. 200, p. 7.

[257] Ibid., p. 8.

Linked to this, the rules do not distinguish between public and private actors and, in particular, they do not envisage the possibility of penalising non-state actors when they commit a breach.[258] In addition, the withdrawal of GSP privileges is non-discriminating as it is the same list of products that ceases to receive benefits without foreseeing any mechanisms to allow that the preferences remain in place for those not complicit with the wrongdoing concerned, in the event of a suspension.[259] Similarly, with regard to the incentives under the GSP+ there is no link between the products given additional preferences and the relevant international standards.[260]

From the above analysis, it may be argued that the GSP scheme is only a modest success as a development policy instrument for developing countries.[261] We can also see why the European Commission is generally reluctant to suspend the GSP privileges. While a mid-term review shows that the GSP has increased LDCs exports and welfare, that a significant share of the gain accrues to the exporting country and that countries seeking to benefit from the GSP+ attempt to ratify various conventions,[262] its impact has been limited, in part because most of the exports from GSP beneficiaries are goods which would not pay any tariff even if there were no GSP since the EU's MFN tariff is zero and it is thus difficult to have an effective preferences for these goods.[263] However, in this regard it should also be pointed out that MFN tariffs faced by exporters differ depending on the particular composition of their exports to the EU under a given GSP scheme. For some exported goods, therefore, particularly those products from GSP+ or EBA beneficiaries the preferential treatment under the scheme does provide a certain level of economic benefit.[264]

In addition, the GSP+ scheme does not empower the Commission to ensure more effective implementation of all the international Conventions. Furthermore, export-led growth strategies might encourage developing countries to curb the process of standard improvement.[265] For these reasons, the GSP is best seen as a "development safety net"[266] and, in more general terms, the causality between improved labour standards and economic growth remains controversial and difficult to establish.[267]

Some of these problems have been addressed by the revised GSP which entered into force in 2014, examined below.

---

[258] Ibid., p. 7.

[259] Ibid., p. 7.

[260] Ibid., p. 7.

[261] CARIS, above no. 255.

[262] Ibid.

[263] Stevens and Kennan (2011).

[264] I am grateful to Lorand Bartels for raising this-point to me.

[265] Siroën (2013b).

[266] Ibid.

[267] Hepple, above no 31, pp. 13–23.

5.3.1.3 The Reform of the GSP

In 2012 the EU adopted a reformed GSP law with the aim of strengthening the overall effectiveness of the GSP scheme.[268] The reform tackled some of the above problems.

Firstly, it changed the eligibility criteria for GSP so that all high-income and upper-middle-income countries—namely, those which meet the World Bank definitional criteria for the most recent three consecutive years—are no longer entitled to preferences.[269] Another significant change concerns the so-called "product graduation" for GSP imports.[270] It also removed those countries and territories with a trade agreement with the EU 'which provides the same tariff preferences as the scheme, or better, for substantially all trade' from the list of beneficiaries of the scheme.[271] In addition, the reform reduced the number of beneficiaries focusing on those developing countries "most in need" and reinforcing the incentives in respect of core human and labour rights, and environmental and good governance standards.[272] Siles-Brügge questions the European Commission's claim that with the 2012 reform it is 'aiming at improving the value of non-reciprocal preferences for those "most in need"—LDCs and "vulnerable economies" in receipt of GSP+—as he considers it not to be 'entirely consistent with its general preference for contractually enshrined free trade'[273] and sees it more as part of a broader "reciprocity" and "exporter-driven" trade agenda of the EU's CCP being pursued in the context of the current economic crisis to ensure that the EU possesses sufficient leverage in ongoing trade negotiations with third countries.[274]

Others have also found changes made to the revised labour criteria for the GSP+ to be particularly problematic. According to Article 9(1) of the 2012 GSP Regulation a beneficiary country can benefit from the enhanced preferences if:

(1) it has ratified all the conventions listed in Annex VIII and the most recent available conclusions of the relevant monitoring bodies do not identify a 'serious failure' to effectively implement any of these conventions;
(2) it gives a binding undertaking to maintain ratification of the conventions listed in Annex VIII and to ensure their effective implementation;

---

[268] Regulation (EU) No. 978/2012 of the European Parliament and of Council of 25 October 2012 applying a scheme of generalised tariff preferences and repealing Council Regulation (EC) No 732/2008 *OJ* [2012] L303/1, 31.10.2012.

[269] This is defined as "income graduation", see, Stevens et al. (2011).

[270] Ibid., pp. 6–19.

[271] Article 4 of Regulation (EU) No. 978/2012.

[272] The list of beneficiaries has been modified several times to reflect the exit from and the entry of countries newly meeting the eligibility conditions for each of the three types of arrangements since the first modifications effected with the 2012 reform, which at the time of writing is as follows: 30 GSP, 13 GSP+ and 49 EBA beneficiaries; European Commission, Report from the Commission to the European Parliament and the Council, Report on the Generalised Scheme of Preferences Covering the Period 2014–2015, COM(2016) 29 final, Brussels, 28.1.2016.

[273] Siles-Brügge (2014), at 53.

[274] Ibid.

(3) it accepts without reservation the reporting requirements imposed by each convention and gives a binding undertaking to accept regular monitoring and review of its implementation record in accordance with the provisions of the conventions listed in Annex VIII; and
(4) it gives a binding undertaking to participate in and cooperate with the monitoring procedure referred to in Article 13.

The revised eligibility criteria are a step back from the previous labour criteria as an applicant country could be deemed eligible for the GSP+ so long as the relevant monitoring bodies have not identified a "serious failure" to effectively implement the Conventions.[275] Vogt argues that the standard of "serious failure" is too low and reference to most recent reports of monitoring bodies is limitative. Specifically, the Commission will consider whether there is a "serious" violation for purposes of entry into the GSP+ only if there is a "special paragraph" in the report of the ILO Committee on Application of Standards (CAS) to the International Labour Conference. There is no textual support in the 2012 GSP Regulation for such a narrow interpretation and reference is made only in staff working documents of the Commission. Moreover, the restrictive interpretation of the entry criteria for the GSP+ does not take into account the overall supervisory system of the ILO which is made up of various committees of experts. This constitutes a significant limitation of the GSP+ scheme as it allows countries that do not comply with the ILO Conventions to become or remain GSP+ beneficiaries.

For example, in 2014 Pakistan and Guatemala—two notorious labour rights violators—were granted GSP+. While the decision to include Pakistan in the GSP+ may have justification on humanitarian grounds further to the devastating flooding of 2010 thus showing a willingness on the part of the EU to support the economy of this country through trade measures,[276] the inclusion of Guatemala in the GSP+ is more difficult to justify. It is particularly disconcerting considering that this country has appeared before the CAS more than any other country (including Myanmar which was suspended from the standard GSP scheme in 1997 for forced labour practices and reinstated only in 2012) and is faced with the continuous threat of a Commission of Inquiry at the ILO for serious and systematic violations of the Freedom of Association and Protection of the Right to Organize Convention (No. 87).[277]

In 2011, the US initiated arbitration against Guatemala under Article 16(2)a of the 2004 Dominican Republic—Central America—United States Free Trade Agreement

[275] Vogt, above no. 222.

[276] For an examination of the legal and political problems that this gave rise to, see Orbie et al. (2014), at 163.

[277] Further information is available at http://www.ilo.org/dyn/normlex/en/f?p=1000:50012:0::NO:50012:P50012_COMPLAINT_PROCEDURE_ID,P50012_LANG_CODE:3088000,en:NO and http://www.ilo.org/wcmsp5/groups/public/---ed_norm/---relconf/documents/meetingdocument/wcms_419599.pdf, accessed 4 January 2016.

(CAFTA-DR).[278] The US v Guatemala arbitration should have been a fairly expedited process further to Chapter 20 of the CAFTA-DR which provides for a fast-track arbitration procedure. However, after initiating this punitive approach the US subsequently moved to a more cooperative approach further to a series of enhanced labour enforcement measures that Guatemala agreed to pursue. These measures included the hiring of significant numbers of new labour inspectors and the creation of fast-track processes for labour courts to adopt fines recommended by Guatemala's Ministry of Labor for labour law violations. Hence, the filing of a CAFTA state-to-state arbitration used as a "stick" clearly led to the diplomatic "engagement" between the US and Guatemala. In September 2014 the USTR announced that it would finally proceed to arbitration against Guatemala[279] marking the first time that the US government has proceeded to the arbitration phase for a complaint alleging violations of the labour chapter of a FTA.[280] The first hearing before the arbitration panel took place in June 2015 and the panel's final decision was delivered two years later.[281]

Trade unions and NGOs submitted extensive and widely-known evidence of violence against trade unionists. However, the USTR took the position that such violence was a matter of criminal law, not labour law, and was not covered by labour chapters of the earlier trade agreements calling for effective enforcement of labor law.[282] The USTR therefore did not submit such evidence to the arbitration panel. This precluded its consideration, since the scope of the panel's mandate was limited to issues presented by the complaining government, not by third parties.[283] In the words of Compa, Gottwald and Vogt: 'this was a fundamental flaw in the entire proceeding: it was treated primarily as a trade dispute and handled like a WTO case. Trade considerations, not workers' rights, drove the dynamic of the Panel's deliberations and analysis.'[284] In particular, the arbitration panel relied on WTO rulings without taking into account the reports and decisions by the ILO, UN human rights bodies, international trade unions, and international human rights NGOs, which all

[278] Further information is available at https://ustr.gov/issue-areas/labor/bilateral-and-regional-trade-agreements/guatemala-submission-under-cafta-dr, accessed 14 June 2020.

[279] Office of the United States Trade representative, 'Standing Up for Workers: Ensuring that the Benefits of Trade are Broadly-Shared', 18 September 2014, available at: https://ustr.gov/about-us/policy-offices/press-office/fact-sheets/2014/September/Standing-Up-for-Workers-Ensuring-that-the-Benefits-of-Trade-are-Broadly-Shared, accessed on 23 March 2020.

[280] For further critical analysis, see Goldhammer and Gottwald (2014) and Compa et al. (2018).

[281] Dominican Republic—Central America—United States Free Trade Agreement Arbitral Panel Established Pursuant to Chapter 20, Final Report of the Panel in the Matter of Guatemala—Issues Relating to the Obligations Under Article 16.2.1(a) of the CAFTA-DR, 14 June 2017, available at: https://www.trade.gov/industry/tas/Guatemala%20%20%E2%80%93%20Obligations%20Under%20Article%2016-2-1(a)%20of%20the%20CAFTA-DR%20%20June%2014%202017.pdf, accessed on 23 March 2020.

[282] Compa, Gottwald and Vogt, above no. 280, p. 5.

[283] Ibid.

[284] Compa, Gottwald and Vogt, above no. 280, p. 6.

provided detailed information about labour law violations in the country as well as governmental failure to enforce labour laws.[285]

The Labour Chapter of the CAFTA-DR agreement contains a specific provision prohibiting the parties to the agreement from failing to effectively enforce its labour law through a sustained or recurring course of action or inaction in a manner affecting trade between the parties.[286] The panel read this provision as requiring parties to ensure that their domestic labour laws are enforced by their respective legal systems and applied among employers. Violations of such rules would have to demonstrate a trend of poor or failed enforcement efforts together with giving some competitive advantage to domestic employers vis-à-vis their foreign competitors, such as for instance lowering their costs in practice.[287] The panel found that Guatemala failed to enforce court orders and fines concerning eight employers who were cited for their dismissal of workers who had attempted to engage in union activities.[288] These findings also raised concerns over whether employers believed they would be held accountable for labour law violations. The panel looked at specific examples in assessing the relationship between labour rights enforcement and trade. It found that one employer's violations of workers' rights to freedom of association, together with how this was handled by domestic labour courts, amounted to poor enforcement that effectively did give that employer a competitive advantage. At the same time, the panel found that this advantage was not consistent across the board when looked at other cases where labour law enforcement was lacking and therefore did not prove that this was 'a sustained or recurring course of action or inaction' that was also 'in a manner affecting trade.'[289]

The arbitration panel then concluded that it had no jurisdiction over other claims advanced by the US in these proceedings, as they had not been included in the panel request.[290] In addition, it held that the US had failed to prove that Guatemala had not conformed to its obligations under the Labour Chapter of the CAFTA-DR agreement. The dispute took more than nine years to conclude. Moreover, the arbitration panel's report still leaves key questions about the basic meaning of labour and other non-trade provisions in FTAs open.[291] In relation to the specific legal matter raised in this

[285]Ibid., p. 8.

[286]Chapter Sixteen, Article 16.2 'Enforcement of Labour Laws', para. 1(a) provides that: 'A Party shall not fail to effectively enforce its labor laws, through a sustained or recurring course of action or inaction, in a manner affecting trade between the Parties, after the date of entry into force of this Agreement.'

[287]CAFTA-DR Arbitral Panel, above no. 281, paras. 165, 190–191 and 196.

[288]Those cases spanned several years and together involved seventy-four workers. However, the Panel found that these instances did not constitute a course of inaction that was in a manner affecting trade, CAFTA-DR Arbitral Panel, above no. 281, para. 594.

[289]CAFTA-DR Arbitral Panel, above no. 281, para. 505.

[290]CAFTA-DR Arbitral Panel, above no. 281, para. 594.

[291]In this regard, see Compa, Gottwald and Vogt, above no. 280, pp. 29-31; the authors put forward specific recommendations to be applied to the negotiation or renegotiation of labour provisions in future or current (in the case of renegotiation) trade agreements to ensure the effective enforcement of the labour provisions contained therein.

dispute, it remains to be seen whether anti-union violence will be actionable under later trade agreements that incorporate stronger minimum labor obligations. More generally, it remains to be seen whether this panel report will lead to the strengthening of the labour provisions of US trade agreements so as to make their enforcement easier. It is not unlikely that this panel report might have some effects also in the EU context, giving rise to a very similar debate with regard to the enforcement (or lack of) labour provisions contained in EU trade agreements.

Guatemala has ceased to be a GSP+ beneficiary country from January 1, 2016. However, the reason for this is that it benefits from preferential market access under the 2012 EU-Central America trade agreement and not because of a decision of the Commission to withdraw GSP+ preferential treatment for labour rights abuses.

More generally, a 2017 Mid-Term Evaluation shows that the positive impact of the GSP+ on labour and human rights is limited and that the majority of the new GSP+ beneficiaries had already ratified the fundamental international conventions long before their admission to the special arrangement.[292]

The monitoring of GSP+ compliance has been enhanced and the Commission has a key monitoring function in relation to the status of ratification and effective implementation of the Conventions as well as ensuring that the beneficiaries cooperate with the Conventions' monitoring bodies. Together with the European External Action Service ('EEAS'), the Commission has set up a structured monitoring process: an ongoing "GSP+ dialogue" with the beneficiary authorities, formalised through annual lists of issues known as "scorecards". Every two years the Commission reports to the EU Parliament and the Council on the fulfillment status of those conditions using scorecards for each GSP+ recipients.[293] These scorecards are an important source of information for the Commission as it enables it not only to establish a form of cooperation with beneficiary countries through the so-called "GSP+ dialogue" but also to constructively discuss beneficiaries' commitments to the ILO Conventions within the relevant international organisations, such as the ILO Tripartite Committee on the Application of Standards or the ILO Governing Body.[294] The limitation of this monitoring system is that it lacks transparency as the evaluation contained in these scorecards is not publicly available. In addition, since it involves only state actors, it is difficult to know whether these scorecards actually lead to government consultations.[295]

---

[292] European Commission, above no. 190, p. 238.

[293] Article 14(1) of Regulation (EU) No. 978/2012.

[294] European Commission, Joint Staff Working Document 'The EU Special Incentive Arrangement for Sustainable Development and Good Governance ('GSP + ') covering the period 2014–2015. Accompanying the document Report from the Commission to the European Parliament and the Council Report on the Generalised Scheme of Preferences during the period 2014–2015 (COM(2016) 29 final), Brussels, 28.1.2016 (SWD(2016) 8 final).

[295] Van den Putte et al. (2015).

In its 2016 report on the revised GSP scheme to the EP and the Council,[296] which also includes an analysis of the GSP+, the Commission emphasised the importance of strengthening the EU's engagement with other international organisations, and their local offices in the beneficiary countries, such as the ILO and the UN, to ensure that GSP+ monitoring and evaluation by the EU continuously takes into account their views and experiences. It also recognised the significance of a wide range of sources for gathering information including civil society, social partners, the EP and the Council. GSP+ monitoring visits by the Commission, together with the assistance of EU delegations, have also proven to be beneficial in this respect. The Commission has also stressed the importance of beneficiary countries taking ownership of the monitoring process and becoming more proactive in addressing the issues in the scorecards. In addition, the Commission has been funding cooperation projects in beneficiary countries such as the GSP+ pilot project on capacity building in partnership with the ILO in Pakistan, Mongolia, Guatemala and El Salvador to support local administrations to put administrative structures in place so as to facilitate the effective implementation of international conventions.[297] This illustrates how the EU still prefers and relies on a cooperative, dialogue-based method to increase the GSP's impact on labour rights.[298]

With regard to the withdrawal of beneficiary status, the GSP+ status shall be withdrawn temporarily in respect of all or certain products originating in the beneficiary country if the beneficiary country does not respect its binding undertakings.[299] The burden of proof of compliance with the Conventions is now on the beneficiary country. If the Commission has a 'reasonable doubt' that the country is not respecting its binding undertakings, it shall adopt a decision to initiate the procedure for withdrawal and shall inform the European Parliament and the Council of the EU. The Commission shall state grounds for the reasonable doubt and specify a time not greater than six months for beneficiary country to submit its observations, during which the Commission will give every opportunity to cooperate. The Commission shall seek all information it considers necessary, *inter alia*, the conclusions and recommendations of the relevant monitoring bodies and in drawing its conclusions, it shall assess all relevant information.

However, as a 2017 Mid-Term Evaluation demonstrates 'the GSP is at most a facilitator and for it to have a positive social and human rights impact, the governments must have enacted effective legislation, social policies and actively support

---

[296]European Commission, Report from the Commission to the European Parliament and the Council, Report on the Generalised Scheme of Preferences Covering the Period 2014–2015, COM(2016) 29 final, Brussels, 28.1.2016.

[297]As part of its on-going collaboration and cooperation with the ILO, the European Commission has provided a grant to the ILO for a 2-year pilot-project *Sustaining GSP-Plus Status by Strengthened National Capacities to Improve ILS Compliance and Reporting* to strengthen the capacity of public administrations to apply the eight Fundamental ILO Conventions. The project was launched on 1 October 2015 and consists of ILO technical assistance, workshops, trainings, as well as awareness-raising activities, see ILO (2013b).

[298]European Commission, above no. 190, p. 235.

[299]As referred under Article 9, see Article 15 of Regulation (EU) No. 978/2012, *supra* note 96.

institutions and legal reforms focusing on the promotion and protection of human and labour rights.'[300] The same report also shows that a full analysis of the social impact of the GSP scheme is hindered by an overall lack of or outdated data on social indicators as well as long delays before statistics become available.[301] The reason for this state of affairs might be the lack of or insufficient financial, institutional and human capacities necessary for monitoring and collecting such data in developing countries.[302] Many GSP+ and standard GSP beneficiary countries also encounter problems in relation to their reporting obligations under the relevant international conventions.[303]

To sum up, the reform has addressed some of the concerns previously raised by reducing the number of beneficiaries and by strengthening the monitoring of compliance. That said, the revised eligibility criteria, particularly those for the GSP+, are problematic as they can allow a country with a record of serious labour rights abuses to become eligible for the GSP+ scheme.

5.3.2 *Regional and Bilateral Trade Agreements*

5.3.2.1 The Rise of Regionalism and Bilateralism and the Increasing Growth of the Social Dimension of Trade Agreements

From the mid-1990s to the present days there has been a growing rise of regionalism and bilateralism which—albeit not homogenous-[304] has had a seismic effect on the "sedate world of economics,"[305] calling into question the overall effectiveness of the multilateral trading system.[306] Various factors explain this spread such as, for example, the central focus on trade liberalization with the non-discrimination principle representing its cornerstone,[307] the excessive length of time to negotiate new agreements within the WTO context and the fact that often the clauses of these agreements constitute the lowest common denominator.[308] Conversely, regional or bilateral agreements can be used to achieve market access gains and deeper market

---

[300] European Commission, above no. 190, p. 234.

[301] Ibid.

[302] Ibid.

[303] Ibid., pp. 238–239.

[304] E.g. for an interesting comparative analysis of the differences between the legal environments of regional trade agreements, see Duina (2006).

[305] This expression is taken from Urata (2002), at 21.

[306] Addo, above no. 35, p. 176.

[307] This principle is known as the most-favoured-nation (MFN) treatment; see GATT Article I, GATS Article II and Agreement on TRIPS Article 4.

[308] Addo, above no. 35, pp. 176–177.

integration as well as to promote specific political, strategic objectives or pursuing non-trade concerns.[309]

From the time of GATT until the 1990s, there was no trade agreement with a labour provision. However, since the 1994 North American Free Trade Agreement (NAFTA)[310] and in particular one of its side agreements, namely, the North America Agreement on Labour Cooperation (NAALC),[311] labour provisions have become increasingly common in trade agreements. The number of trade agreements with labour provisions has increased from three in 1995 to 77 in 2016.[312]

NAALC—the labour standard-setting arrangement for NAFTA—is of particular salience because it created a multinational enforcement and review system via a trade agreement that allows each party to monitor how they each enforce their respective national labour laws.[313] At the time of its adoption, it was the first trade agreement of its kind to provide an avenue for employers, workers, trade unions and governments to promote and protect workers' rights and labour standards creating mutual labour-related obligations and responsibility and, in certain cases, establishing sanctions for failure to fulfill these obligations.[314] However, critics have pointed out that its objectives are mostly aspirational and bland as they focus largely on the promotion of cooperation and innovation on labour market methods and pursuing higher living standards.[315] Moreover, NAALC does not constitute a fully-fledged form of

---

[309] Ibid.

[310] The North American Free Trade Agreement (NAFTA), 32 I.L.M. 289 and 605 (1993); see also http://www.naftanow.org/, accessed on 23 March 2020.

[311] The North American Agreement on Labour Cooperation (NAALC), 32 I.L.M. 1499 (1993).

[312] International Labour Organisation (ILO) (2017); for information regarding the regional patterns of labour provisions in trade agreements as well as their normative content and scope, see pp. 12–14.

[313] Addo, above no. 35, p. 217; for critical commentary, see Hepple, above no. 31, pp. 108–114 and 118–121.

[314] Article 49 and Annex 1 of NAALC contain the eleven labour principles that the parties have to adhere to: 1. Freedom of association and protection of the right to organize; 2. The right to bargain; 3. The right to strike; 4. The prohibition of forced labour; 5. The labour protection for children and young persons; 6. Minimum employment standards such as minimum wages and overtime pay, covering wage earners, including those not covered by collective agreements; 7. Elimination of employment discrimination on the basis of grounds such as race, religion, age, sex, or other grounds as determined by each Party's domestic laws; 8. Equal pay for men and women; 9. Prevention of occupational injuries and illnesses; 10. Compensation in cases of occupational injuries and illnesses; 11. Protection of migrant workers.

These principles go far beyond the CLS embodied in the 1998 ILO Declaration on Fundamental Principles and Rights at Work. The NAALC not only defines labour laws as laws and regulations that are directly related to the eleven rights but also requires that these rights provide for "high labour standards" to be harmonized among the three parties and that they should be improved over time (see Article 2 of NAALC; see also Article 3 of NAALC subject to Article 42 of NAALC). The side agreement allows any person with a recognized interest under the law to submit complaints or petitions to any of the three parties in relation to occupational safety and health, child labour, minimum wage or technical labour standards (see Articles 3(2) and 4 of NAALC as well as Article 27 of NAALC; the more controversial areas of freedom of association, right to bargain collectively and forced labour are excluded).

[315] Teague, above no. 34, at 338–345; for a similar position in relation to the renegotiated NAFTA, see also the US Labour Advisory Committee for Trade Negotiations and trade Policy (LAC),

deliberative supranational governance and its institutional setting remains essentially intergovernmental. Significantly, the agreement does not have the purpose of tying any of the member countries to international labour standards and, linked to that, it does not have the capacity to adopt and impose supranational labour market provisions. In addition, because NAALC is only a side agreement to NAFTA, the link between labour standards and the main trade and investment elements of the accord are weak.

The 2001 US-Jordan Free Trade Agreement (USJFTA)[316] went a step further by way of including a set of enforceable workers' rights provisions[317] in the main body of the agreement rather than in a side agreement such as in the case of NAFTA,[318] and allowing either party the right to take 'any appropriate and commensurate measure' if the dispute procedures do not lead to a resolution.[319] Like NAALC the key labour rights obligation is effective enforcement of domestic labour law. However, in the USJFTA there is a major difference, namely, an express linkage between ILO and domestic standards.[320] Studies on the impact of the agreement in Jordan[321] show that the 2001 USJFTA has prompted Jordan to adopt important labour reforms as of 2006, developing partnerships with organizations such as the ILO, the International Finance Corporation (IFC), the World Bank, the EU, and US Agency for International Development (USAID), even though the changes were not the immediate consequence of the FTA's labour provisions.[322] The labour measures enacted included a workplace inspection reform and a set of action plans to fight against human trafficking. With regard to companies, two examples warrant attention: the so-called "Golden List" project and the ILO "Better Work Jordan" project.[323] The former is essentially a special legal status that companies and factories, largely in the garment sector, can acquire provided they follow a voluntary code of conduct containing criteria derived

Report on the Impacts of the Renegotiated North American Free Trade Agreement, 27 September 2018, pp. 7, 19–22 and Appendix, Section 10, available at: https://ustr.gov/sites/default/files/files/agreements/FTA/AdvisoryCommitteeReports/Labor%20Advisory%20Committee%20on%20Trade%20Negotiations%20and%20Trade%20Policy%20%28LAC%29.pdf, accessed on 23 March 2020.

[316] Agreement Between the United States of America and the Hashemite Kingdom of Jordan on the Establishment of a Free Trade Area, 41 I.L.M. 63 (2002).

[317] The labour provisions of the USJFTA are in line with both the ILO's CLS and with the US 1974 Trade Act (Trade Act of 1974, 19 U.S.C. §§ 2111-2462 (Suppl. 2 1976), as amended).

[318] Key provisions are found in Articles 6 and 17 of the 2001 USJFTA; as illustrated by the language used in Article 6 of the agreement, namely the words "shall strive to" or "exercise discretion", the obligations entered into are more one of effort rather than result.

[319] Article 17(2) (b) of the 2001 USJFTA.

[320] Article 6(1) of the 2001 USJFTA.

[321] Sibbel (2010).

[322] It should be noted that the process of reform followed a report published in May 2006 by the Jordanian National Labor Committee (NLC—now Institute for Global Labour and Human Rights) alleging serious worker rights violations in Jordan's garment sector, including trafficking, forced labour, and non-payment of wages. The work force in Jordan's garment sector is made up mostly of migrant workers; see, Kernaghan (2006).

[323] Kernaghan, above no. 322, at 4–5.

from Jordanian labour law, international labour standards and best practice.[324] The incentive for these companies is that, once included in the Golden List, they are exempted from the obligation of having to acquire a bank guarantee for the recruitment of temporary workers. In addition, factory conditions are regularly assessed against the set of criteria and in cases of non-compliance companies can be removed from the list.

The ILO Better Work Jordan project was launched in 2008 with the partnership of the IFC and funded by the Government of Jordan and USAID.[325] Initially it was a voluntary programme, which subsequently became mandatory for factories. The key aim of this all-encompassing programme is to bring different stakeholders from the garment industry to promote decent working conditions of workers and advocate for labour rights in the local apparel industry through a range of activities such as, for example, advising, assessing and training.[326]

While the 1994 NAALC and the 2001 USJFTA do not act as precedents *stricto sensu* for the social trade link in the EU's international agreements they have undoubtedly confirmed the insertion of labour provisions in international trade agreements.

5.3.2.2 The Case of the EU

Introduction

The EU has been linking the respect for labour rights with trade arrangements via regional trade agreements and, increasingly, bilateral trade agreements. In particular, after the failure at multilateral level to include a social clause in the WTO, the EU has been steadily including labour provisions in its bilateral and regional agreements.

Since the 1990s, most EU preferential agreements contain provisions on labour standards and cooperation in social affairs.[327] In the early agreements social norms have been taken up as issues for cooperation between the EU and its trading partners. In subsequent agreements social norms have been raised to the status of human

---

[324]These criteria covered a range of aspects such as working hours, workers' legal status and wages and other issues such as, for example, dormitory conditions.

[325]The ILO Better Work Programme now operates in eight countries, namely, Bangladesh, Cambodia, Ethiopia, Haiti, Indonesia, Jordan, Nicaragua and Vietnam. The programme has started to be piloted in Egypt; further information can be found at: https://betterwork.org/, accessed 14 June 2020.

[326]These activities covered issues such as child labour, forced labour, trafficking, wages, working hours, occupational safety and health, and dormitory conditions; for an assessment of the programme's impact, see the Better Work Jordan Annual Report 2018: An Industry and Compliance Review, available at: https://betterwork.org/blog/portfolio/better-work-jordan-annual-report-2018-an-industry-and-compliance-review/, accessed 14 June 2020.

[327]Full text access to European FTAs and their labour provisions can be found at http://ilo.org/global/standards/information-resources-and-publications/free-trade-agreements-and-labour-rights/WCMS_115822/lang--en/index.htm#P4_728, accessed 14 June 2020.

rights.[328] This social commitment has become visibly stronger since the 2008 EU-CARIFORUM economic partnership agreement (EPA)[329] and subsequent agreements based on the EU's *Global Europe Strategy*.[330] As the next sections will go on to show, the EU approach largely relies on cooperation and dialogue with a reluctance to use sanctions and a preference for civil society involvement.

The Widening and Deepening of the Trade-Labour Linkage in EU Trade Agreements

Introduction

Since the mid-2000s there has been a "widening and deepening" of the trade-labour linkage in EU trade agreements, particularly in relation to the content, governance and legal status of social clauses.[331] The content of social clauses has become more detailed and their scope has been expanded. In addition to technical cooperation in social policy, the so-called "new generation of trade agreements" include a commitment to respect CLS as human rights. Moreover, social clauses are included in a specific chapter or title dealing with labour and environmental norms under the heading of 'Trade and Sustainable Development'. With regard to the governance of these social clauses, a wide range of actors, including high level labour officials, civil society and business actors are involved in monitoring and promoting social clauses. Trade agreements envisage the setting up of a (Sub-)Committee/Board on Trade and Sustainable Development in which senior government officials regularly meet to oversee the implementation of the labour (and environmental) commitments of the agreement. In addition, civil society actors have a formal role in monitoring the implementation of sustainable development provisions. As to the judicialization of labour provisions, social clauses have been drafted in more legally binding terms in comparison with those inserted in earlier EU trade agreements and their enforceability has increased given that labour violations are subject to scrutiny via the dispute settlement system envisaged in these agreements. However, the EU's approach to social conditionality remains largely promotional in nature and it is

---

[328]For example, the Preambles of the 1997 EU's Cooperation Agreements with Cambodia and Laos, Yemen and the Former Yugoslav Republic of Macedonia refer to the need to complement economic with social development as well as the respect for basic social rights. The 1999 EU-South Africa Trade, Development and Cooperation Agreement with South Africa and the 2005 EU-Algeria Association Agreement also refer to the need to respect fundamental social rights and provide for dialogue and cooperation in social matters.

[329]The regional group comprises 15 Caribbean countries: Antigua and Barbuda, Bahamas, Barbados, Belize, Dominica, Dominican Republic, Grenada, Guyana, Haiti, Jamaica, St Lucia, St Vincent and the Grenadines, St Kitts and Nevis, Suriname, Trinidad and Tobago; Economic Partnership Agreement between the CARIFORUM States, of the one part, and the European Community and its Member States, of the other part [2008] OJ L289/3.

[330]European External Action Service (EEAS) (2016); Van den Putte and Orbie, above no 14, at 265.

[331]Van den Putte and Velluti, above no. 3, at pp. 232–233; see also Raess and Sari (2018).

based on cooperation, also because social clauses are not trade issues and, as such do, not fall within the remit of the Trade Chapters' dispute settlement mechanism. In the chapter on Trade and Sustainable Development labour provisions together with the environmental provisions are conceived as aspirations. In particular, they are regarded as part of sustainable development, which is to be guaranteed through the implementation of the trade agreement itself, rather than being considered as a fundamental basis for trade relations.

In addition, these social clauses mainly require the parties to the trade agreement to uphold and not lower their existing labour commitments and thus do not contain an obligation to increase the respect for labour norms. In particular, the new generation of trade agreements require the parties to uphold their commitments to the respect for ILO's CLS, which they should already adhere to via their ILO membership.[332] They also provide that the level of protection of domestic labour regulation shall not be lowered to encourage trade or attract investment.[333] It seems that these agreements do not provide for an increase respect for labour rights: arguably the parties can still lower the level of labour protection in their own country provided that the aim is not to increase trade or investment.

As mentioned earlier, the EU approach can be described as one based on cooperation. In the case of a labour dispute arising, EU trade agreements include a cooperative approach, which relies on dialogue and cooperation between the parties, namely government officials and civil society. If the issue cannot be resolved in this way, a panel of experts can be established.[334] However, the recommendations of this panel lack enforceability. The overall governance of the new generation of trade agreements is based on cooperation and they foresee regular dialogue between high level officials in a (sub)committee/board on trade and sustainable development where, the parties update each other on key labour and environmental developments and discuss the possibility of further cooperation. In addition, the agreements foresee social dialogue both at domestic and transnational levels.

As to their content and level of judicialization, social clauses included in EU trade agreements refer to the labour provisions of other international agreements, particularly the ILO. Labour norms always include a commitment to the ILO's CLS as well as a commitment to productive employment and decent work as agreed upon in the 2006 Ministerial Declaration of the UN Economic and Social Council on Full Employment and Decent Work.[335] In addition, the dispute settlement provisions envisage the possibility or the need to involve the ILO.[336]

---

[332]E.g. Article 13.4 subpara. 3 and Article 13.7 subpara. 2 of the 2011 EU-Korea FTA.

[333]E.g. Article 13.7 subpara. 2 of the 2011 EU-Korea FTA.

[334]E.g. Article 13.15 of the 2011 EU-Korea FTA.

[335]Office for the Economic and Social Council (ECOSOC) Support and Coordination, Department of Economic and Social Affairs of the United Nations, 'Full and Productive Employment and Decent Work Dialogues at the Economic and Social Council' United Nations, New York, 2006, available at: https://www.un.org/en/ecosoc/docs/pdfs/ecosoc_book_2006.pdf, accessed 14 June 2020; see Article 13(4) of the 2011 EU-Korea FTA.

[336]Article 13(4) of the 2011 EU-Korea FTA.

The promotional and cooperative approach of the EU differs quite significantly from that of the US[337] as the latter not only relies on a more punitive approach[338] but its position towards and compliance with the ILO differs quite notably. In particular, US trade agreements generally require compliance with the CLS as found in the 1998 ILO Declaration on Fundamental Principles and Rights at Work, which represent minimum labour protection standards.[339] The reason for this is that the US has ratified 14 ILO Conventions out of which only two are 'core' ILO Conventions,[340] namely, on forced labour and the worst forms of child labour.[341] This also explains why US trade agreements do not envisage a central role for the ILO in the monitoring of labour standards implementation.

Social Clauses in EU Trade Agreements at the Turn of the Twenty-First Century

The 2000 Cotonou Partnership Agreement (CPA)[342] occupies a particularly prominent position as it is the most comprehensive partnership agreement between developing countries. The CPA, which provides the framework for Economic Partnership Agreement (EPA) negotiations, reflects a policy shift in EU development policy

---

[337] Van den Putte and Velluti, above no. 3, at p. 234. For further analysis on the differences between the EU and the US approaches, see Oehri (2015); Melo Araujo, above no. 79, at 239–245; De Ville et al. (2016a, b), at 290–292; Vogt (2015b); for a mapping of the key differences between the EU and the US, see Tham and Ewing (2016), Tables 4 and 5 at 14–16.

[338] The dispute settlement mechanism in US trade agreements allows the suspension of benefits against a party if it can be shown that non-enforcement resulted from a sustained or recurring course of action or inaction and has occurred in a manner affecting trade or investment between the parties; e.g. Articles 17(4)(5) and 20(6) of the 2004 US-Singapore Free trade Agreement (USSFTA), January 2004, full text is available at: https://ustr.gov/sites/default/files/uploads/agreements/fta/singapore/asset_upload_file708_4036.pdf, accessed on 23 March 2020.

[339] Conversely, EU trade agreements often extend beyond CLS by also requiring parties to maintain laws, regulations and practices in accordance with the ILO Decent Work Agenda; e.g. Article 13(1) of the Free Trade Agreement between the European Union and its Member States, of the one part, and the Republic of Korea OJ L 127; Article 191(2) of the Economic Partnership between the CARIFORUM States, of the one part, and the European Community and its Member States, of the other part OJ L289/I/3, 30.10.2008. Article 23(3) of the Comprehensive Economic and Trade Agreement (CETA) between Canada, of the One Part, and the European Union and its Member States of the Other Part, Consolidate Text published 26 September 2014, available at http://trade.ec.europa.eu/doclib/docs/2014/september/tradoc_152806.pdf, accessed on 20 March 2020.

[340] Detailed information about the Conventions ratified by the US can be found at: https://www.ilo.org/dyn/normlex/en/f?p=NORMLEXPUB:11200:0::NO::P11200_COUNTRY_ID:102871, accessed on 20 March 2020.

[341] ILO Convention C105 on the Abolition of Forced Labour, 1957 (No. 105), 25 September 1991 and ILO Convention C182 on the Worst Forms of Child Labour, 1999 (No. 182), 2 December 1999.

[342] The CPA was concluded for a 20-year period from 2000 to 2020 between the EU and 79 ACP countries. Partnership agreement between the members of the African, Caribbean and Pacific Group of States of the one part, and the European Community and its Member States, of the other part, signed in Cotonou on 23 June 2000, OJ L317, 15/12/2000, p. 3. It has been revised twice: in Luxembourg on 25 June 2005 (*OJ* [2005] L 209, 11/08/2005, p. 27) and in Ouagadougou on 22 June 2010 (*OJ* [2010] L 287, 04/11/2010, p. 3).

from preferential market access to mutual free trade between the EU and African, Caribbean and Pacific (ACP) regions, in which development is the overriding goal. However, this shift to differentiated reciprocity is partially based on the EU's own commitment to make its trade agreements compatible with the WTO rules. Hence, this change is guided, to a certain extent, by self-interest. Nevertheless, it is still noteworthy that both the EU and the ACP countries have equally committed themselves to respect CLS and to enhance cooperation in this area, for example, through the adoption and enforcement of legislation and, at the same time, rejecting the use of labour standards for protectionist purposes, as provided in Article 50, which is the key labour clause of the agreement. The latter is mainly promotional in nature, reaffirming standards that do not create binding obligations and which, according to Alston, may undermine ILO's supervision.[343] Kenner maintains that Article 50 should not be viewed in isolation but within the broader context of the agreement's trade and development regime.[344] In particular, the labour clause 'entrenches the CLS within the partnership as recommended by the World Commission on the Social Dimension of Globalization (WCSDG).' In particular, it is based on the view that the objectives of the ILO can be best achieved with the cooperation of regional actors and through transposition into the CPA of those obligations stemming from the 1998 ILO's Declaration, which in in turn are 'subject to the oversight of the parties and coordinated action under the EU-ILO strategic partnership.'[345] This is reflected in Article 8 which clearly states that priority is given to political dialogue in relation to the essential elements (Annex VII) to avoid scenarios in which a party might deem it justified to activate the non-execution clause provided in Article 96. The latter foresees the holding of consultations, excepted in the cases of 'special urgency', in circumstances where a Party considers that the other Party has failed to fulfill an obligation stemming from the essential elements clause. It is only when these consultations between the parties fail that appropriate measures may be taken. In any event, these measures shall be revoked as soon as the reasons for taking them have disappeared.

Article 9 envisages several features which link development and human rights to labour standards and social policies.[346] First, development is 'centred on the human person', who is seen as the protagonist and beneficiary for development, entailing 'respect for and promotion of all human rights.' Respect for human rights is regarded as integral to sustainable development.[347] Second, the definition of human rights includes respect for fundamental social rights. In addition, the CPA provides for the use of dispute settlement in relation to the interpretation and application of their human rights clauses, including appropriate measures adopted under these clauses.[348]

---

[343] Alston, above no. 65, at 511.

[344] Kenner, above no. 36, at p. 316.

[345] Ibid.

[346] Kenner, above no. 36, at p. 315.

[347] Ibid.

[348] Cfr. with the EU-Central America Association Agreement, which provides that an affected party can request that an urgent meeting be called to bring the Parties together within fifteen days for a

However, what is problematic is that the essential elements clause in Article 9(2) has been invoked to initiate a consultation procedure mainly for coups d'état or flawed election processes with a reluctance to use it in relation to social and economic rights.[349] Besides these more technical legal aspects of the agreement, the CPA seems to have had a negative impact on local communities as tariff liberalization has led to an increase in unemployment levels in certain key agriculture sectors and, in some instances, to their collapse such as in the case of poultry meat production.[350] The CPA, therefore, seems to be instrumental to the EU's need to have access to the markets of emerging economies rather than to the development needs of third countries.

In addition, with the exception of Article 50 of the CPA, social norms in EU agreements seem to have been included as objectives to be achieved under the umbrella term of "sustainable development" rather than enforceable legal commitments as they do not provide for genuine enforcement mechanisms. As Bartels points out 'it is notable that the principle of sustainable development has never been treated as a concrete obligation in itself: none of the agreements admit the possibility of violating the principle of sustainable development.'[351] This is because 'the exact implications of sustainable development for trade agreements are far from clear due to the normative uncertainty surrounding the concept of sustainable development, which has played out differently in varied contexts and is still subject to evolution.'[352] The agreements contain provisions on cooperation and obligations to respect and "strive" to improve multilateral and domestic labour and environmental standards.[353] In particular, a first set of obligations contain minimum obligations to implement certain multilateral obligations and other obligations which require the parties to the agreement not to reduce their levels of protection and encouraging them to raise their levels of protection, subject to a proviso that this is not done for protectionist purposes.[354] With the turn in the 1990s to social trade at the regional and bilateral levels, sustainable development has become increasingly important in the EU's trade policy[355] and the Treaty of Lisbon has elevated it to one of the key principles underlying EU external action.[356]

This overarching legal commitment has been given further effect with the adoption of so-called "new generation" of trade agreements mentioned earlier, containing

thorough examination of the situation with a view to seeking a solution acceptable to the Parties, see Article 355(5).

[349] E.g. The coup d'état in Guinea Bissau in 2003, the coup d'état in Central African Republic in 2003 and flawed elections in Togo in 2003, for further analysis, see Mbangu (2005).

[350] Kwa et al. (2014) and Gathii (2013).

[351] Bartels, above no 236, 306.

[352] Durán (2013).

[353] For further analysis, see Bartels, above no. 58, at p. 342.

[354] Bartels, above no. 236, at 307–309.

[355] The first of the EU's agreements to make reference to the principle of sustainable development was the 1993 EU-Hungary Europe Agreement, Bartels, above no. 236, 306.

[356] Article 21(2)d and (3) TEU.

a "trade and sustainable development" chapter, which includes provisions for the respect of labour and environmental standards. Examples of such agreements are the 2011 EU-Korea FTA,[357] the 2012 EU-Central America Agreement[358] and the 2012 EU-Colombia/Peru Agreement.[359] Specifically, in relation to labour issues the agreements require the effective implementation in law and practice of CLS. Notably, before it ratified the trade agreement of the EU with these countries, the European Parliament demanded a road map for legislative reform in the field of human rights, particularly for labour rights from Colombia and Peru.[360] One of the main objectives of this agreement was to maintain the provisions contained in the GSP Regulation while making access of Colombian and Peruvian products to the EU market easier.[361] According to the Commission the objective has been met since the agreement has GSP+ equivalent content or above, depending on the specific issue concerning labour and the environment. Arguably, the sustainable development chapter of the agreement goes beyond the GSP+ in some respects.[362] For example, it contains obligations on the effective implementation of, and non-derogation from, domestic labour laws, recognition of the ILO decent work principles and their relevance for trade and labour. It also includes a provision on equality of treatment as regards working conditions with a focus on migrant workers legally employed in the Parties' respective territories.[363] There is also an "implementation" clause such as the one contained in the 2012 EU-Central America Agreement providing that 'the Parties shall adopt any general or specific measures required for them to fulfil their obligations under this Agreement.' The exact meaning of this clause is unclear. According to Bartels 'it could have the effect of imposing on the parties not only a negative duty to ensure that human rights and democratic principles are *respected* but also a positive duty to ensure that these norms are ensured and *fulfilled*.'[364]

In addition, the EU-Colombia and Peru trade agreement has provided a formal platform where civil society actors annually meet to discuss the implementation of the sustainable development aspects of the trade agreement. These civil society

---

[357] Free Trade Agreement between the European Union and its Member States of the one part, and the Republic of Korea of the other part (EU-Korea FTA) *OJ* [2011] L127/6, 14 May 2011, p. 6. It entered into force in July 2011 and it is the EU's first trade agreement with an Asian country. It is also the first completed agreement in a new generation of FTAs launched by the EU in 2007 as part of its strategy to create "deep and comprehensive" free trade agreements (DCFTA) with selective partners following the Doha round stand-still at the WTO. On this point see, Hoffmeister (2014).

[358] Agreement establishing an Association between the European Union and its Member States, on the one hand, and Central America on the other (EU-CAAA) *OJ* [2012] L346/3, 15 December 2012, p. 3.

[359] Trade Agreement between the European Union and its Member States, of the one part, and Colombia and Peru, of the other part *OJ* [2012] L354/3, 21 December 2012, p. 3.

[360] European Parliament Resolution of 13 June 2012 on the EU Trade Agreement with Colombia and Peru, Doc 2012/2628 (RSP), 13.6.2012.

[361] Bendini and Delaunay (2011).

[362] Ibid.

[363] E.g. Article 276.

[364] Bartels, above no. 236, 301. Cfr. With Article 8(1) of the EU-Colombia and Peru Agreement which makes explicit reference to all authorities and government levels of the Parties.

meetings could provide a first step to strengthen social dialogue and could bring about empowerment of trade unions. Another significant aspect of the agreement is that it provides a forum for enhanced information exchange and cooperation on labour-matters between the Colombian government and the European Commission.

The 2019 EU-Singapore (EUSFTA) also contains such chapter.[365] The 2008 CARIFORUM-EU agreement is worthy of mention as it is the first EPA concluded with a regional group.[366] Since the conclusion of this agreement, the inclusion of a specific chapter setting out cooperation and commitments in relation to sustainable development has become systematic. It includes a reference to the ILO Decent Work Agenda (DWA) and CLS and the clauses are worded in such a manner suggesting that there is also reference to labour rights rather than merely standards or principles. For example, Article 72 provides that investors are required to act in accordance with ILO CLS and Article 73 provides that promotion of foreign direct investment (FDI) does not take place by lowering domestic environmental, labour or occupational health and safety legislation and standards.[367] It also has a separate chapter on social aspects of trade.[368] Another innovative feature of this EPA is, firstly, the setting up of the Joint Council, which has 'the power to take decisions in respect of all matters covered by the Agreement.'[369] Secondly, the EPA provides for a consultation and monitoring process, under which each party may request consultations on the interpretation and application of the social clauses in the agreement, with an advisory role for the ILO.[370] The agreement also envisages that in the event of continued disagreement a Committee of Experts may be convened.[371]

The 2011 EU-Korea FTA and the 2012 FTA Columbia and Peru include a reference to decent work and four CLS; in addition to the latter agreements, the 2012 EU-Central American Association Agreement (EU-CAAA) refers to the need to implement fundamental ILO Conventions, contained in the 1998 ILO Declaration of Fundamental Principles and Rights at Work. These three agreements all exemplify the

---

[365] It is the first bilateral agreement concluded by the EU with an Association of Southeast Asian Nations (ASEAN) country and it has provided the blueprint for future bilateral agreements with other ASEAN countries; Free Trade Agreement between the European Union and Singapore, 17 October 2014, Authentic text as of May 2015 available at http://trade.ec.europa.eu/doclib/press/index.cfm?id=961, accessed on 20 March 2020. Member states endorsed the trade agreement on 8 November 2019. It entered into force on 21 November 2019. The investment protection agreement is awaiting ratification by all member states.

[366] The regional group comprises 15 Caribbean countries: Antigua and Barbuda, Bahamas, Barbados, Belize, Dominica, Dominican Republic, Grenada, Guyana, Haiti, Jamaica, St Lucia, St Vincent and the Grenadines, St Kitts and Nevis, Suriname, Trinidad and Tobago; Economic Partnership Agreement between the CARIFORUM States, of the one part, and the European Community and its Member States, of the other part (OJ [2008] L289, 30/10/2008, p. 3).

[367] For commentary on the investment provisions of the 2008 CARIFORUM-EU EPA, see Cardwell and French (2011).

[368] 2008 CARIFORUM-EU EPA, Articles 191–196.

[369] 2008 CARIFORUM-EU EPA, Article 229(1).

[370] 2008 CARIFORUM-EU EPA, Article 195.

[371] Ibid.

EU predilection for soft conditionality. In particular, the Trade and Sustainable Development Chapter (Chapter 13) of the 2011 EU-Korea FTA has served as a model for other FTA negotiations,[372] following the adoption of the *Global Europe Strategy*.[373] Even though South Korea is a member of the Organisation for Economic Cooperation and Development (OECD), not all fundamental labour rights are respected.[374] Within the framework of the FTA, labour issues are discussed annually both between government officials (in the 'Committee on Trade and Sustainable Development') as well as between civil society actors in a domestic context (in the 'Domestic Advisory Group') and between both sides (in 'the Civil Society Forum').[375] The 2011 EU-Korea FTA exemplifies a new trend in the EU's regulatory approach to the integration of trade and environmental/labour issues at the bilateral level according to which 'trade-labour and trade-environmental linkages are no longer conceived as exception clauses that are permissive and conditional in nature, but are further elaborated through positive commitments, as well as cooperative measures.'[376] These fora have paved the way for South Korea to consider ratifying certain ILO standards fostering regular dialogue between the European Commission and the South Korean government.[377] In addition, they have increased the exchange of information

---

[372]See G. M. Durán, above no. 352, 124–145. For a legal critique of the 2011 EU-Korea FTA, see Gruni (2017).

[373]Communication from the Commission to the Council, the European Parliament, the European Economic and Social Committee and the Committee of the Regions of 4 October 2006 'Global Europe: Competing in the world' COM(2006) 567 final.

[374]South Korea became the 152nd country to join the ILO in 1991, but it has only ratified four of what the ILO General assembly has identified as its eight core conventions. The still unratified conventions are No. 87 and No. 98, which concern the freedom of association, and No. 29 and No. 105, which concern the abolition of compulsory labour; in addition, South Korea has been heavily criticised by the ILO supervisory bodies on freedom of association, e.g. ILO, Committee on Freedom of Association, Case No 2602 (Republic of Korea) (Interim Report No 359, March 2011).

When South Korea joined the OECD in 1996 and also when it became a member of the UN Human Rights Council (UNHRC) in 2006, the government had pledged to ratify these conventions, but so far it hasn't followed through on that promise. Among the 35 member states of the OECD, South Korea and the US are the only countries that haven't ratified conventions No. 87 and No. 98. Public servants are being discriminated against and prevented from joining or establishing trade unions. The case of the Korean Teachers and Education Workers Union (KTU) is illustrative. In 2018 the KTU's application for establishing a trade union was rejected because terminated workers are enrolled as members. Hence, not all fundamental labour rights that the ILO core conventions protect are being guaranteed in South Korea; e.g. the International Trade Union Confederation's (ITUC) condemnation in 2019 of South Korea's delay in bringing its own labour legislation in line with international labour standards, available at: https://www.ituc-csi.org/fundamental-labour-rights-under; accessed on 14 June 2020.

[375]These meetings take place in Seoul (South Korea) and Brussels (Belgium) on an alternate basis.

[376]See G. M. Durán, above no. 344, at 135; the EU-Japan Economic Partnership Agreement, which entered into force on 1 February 2019, includes all the key elements of the EU approach on sustainable development and is in line with most EU trade agreements adopted since the 2011 EU-Korea FTA; see Agreement between the European Union and Japan for an Economic Partnership, OJ L 330/3 27.12.2018, Chapter 16.

[377]Van den Putte and Velluti, above no. 3, at p. 237.

on labour issues between Korean and European civil society organisations thereby involving also the ILO.[378]

In July 2019 the EU requested a panel of experts, corresponding to the second phase of the arbitration procedure envisaged under the 2011 EU-Korea FTA, to address its long-standing concerns on labour standards in South Korea.[379] When the EU signed a trade agreement with South Korea both sides committed to respect international labour standards. The commitments included the ratification and effective implementation of a number of fundamental conventions of the ILO, including setting domestic legal guarantees on the freedom of association and the right to collective bargaining. The EU considered that the actions taken by South Korea to implement this part of the agreement remained insufficient. The decision of the European Commission was based on a 15 action-points plan unveiled in February 2018 to monitor more effective the implementation of the clauses included in the Trade and Sustainable Development Chapter of the trade agreement.[380] This second phase of the arbitration procedure was triggered after formal government consultations held in January 2019 and efforts on the part of the South Korean government to introduce labour regulations in line with international labour standards failed.

The 2016 EU-Vietnam FTA[381] is also noteworthy. The FTA makes an institutional and legally binding linkage to the 2012 EU-Vietnam Partnership and Cooperation Agreement (PCA).[382] Significantly, in the latter agreement the commitment of both parties to the respect for human rights through the human rights clause and the promotion of sustainable development have been included in one article, which seems to suggest that sustainable development has gained further prominence.[383] The FTA contains a Trade and Sustainable Development Chapter, which includes obligations for both the EU and Vietnam with regard to a core set of multilateral standards and agreements on labour and environment, ensuring the respect by both parties of fundamental workers' rights as well as furthering environmental governance.[384] With regard to labour provisions, there is reference to specific commitments on the

---

[378] Ibid.

[379] European Commission (2019).

[380] European Commission (2018b).

[381] Free Trade Agreement between the European Union and the Socialist Republic of Vietnam, Agreed Text as of January 2016, available at http://trade.ec.europa.eu/doclib/press/index.cfm?id=1437, accessed on 14 June 2020; see also European Commission, 'Human Rights and Sustainable Development in the EU-Vietnam Relations with specific regard to the EU-Vietnam Free Trade Agreement', Commission Staff Working Document, Brussels, 26.1.2016, SWD(2016) 21 final; the EU and Vietnam signed the agreement (comprising also an Investment Protection Agreement) on 30 June 2019.

For academic commentary see Hoang et al. (2014).

[382] E.g. Preamble, Articles X. 17 and 21 of the Chapter on Institutional, General and Final Provisions (CIGF), Ch. 17, 2016 EU-Vietnam FTA; Framework Agreement on Comprehensive Partnership and Cooperation between the European Union and its Member States, of the one part, and the Socialist Republic of Viet Nam, of the other part of 27 June 2012, available at http://eur-lex.europa.eu/resource.html?uri=cellar:e9d99d61-6897-11e3-a7e4-01aa75ed71a1.0011.01/DOC_2&format=PDF.

[383] 2012 EU-Vietnam PCA, Article 1(1) and (3).

[384] 2016 EU-Vietnam FTA, Ch. 15.

effective implementation of each of the four ILO CLS and of all the ratified ILO Conventions (not only the fundamental ones), as well as progress towards ratification of non-ratified fundamental ILO Conventions.[385] Overall, these new provisions clearly indicate a stronger domestic political commitment to labour reforms that will ensure a more developed domestic labour legal framework, improvement of the enforcement of domestic labour law system. It is noticeable however that a legally binding language is absent and the more nuanced terms of 'recognize', 'reaffirm its commitment' or 'will make continued and sustained efforts' are used as opposed to the stronger term of 'shall ensure.'[386]

In general terms, while there is some variation between the provisions contained in the different agreements, there seems to be some level of commonality as to the substantive standards and the institutional set-up envisaged. Indeed we can identify a common core of the new generation of trade agreements such as a reaffirmation by the parties of their general commitment to promote trade in a way that fosters sustainable development; a reaffirmation that countries have the freedom to define their own level of social and environmental protection, and that social and environmental standards should not be used for protectionist purposes; a commitment to "strive" towards high levels of social and environmental protection by: a) implementing the ILO Conventions and other multilateral instruments applicable to the parties and b) respecting, promoting and realizing in their laws and practice the CLS and associated ILO Conventions proclaimed in the ILO Declaration of Fundamental Principles and Rights at Work of 1998; a commitment to cooperate to develop trade schemes and trade practices favouring sustainable development; and a commitment not to lower or fail to apply social and environmental standards with a view to encouraging trade or attracting investment.

Mega-Regional Trade and Investment Agreements: The Case of CETA and TTIP

The 2014 EU-Canada Comprehensive Economic and Trade Agreement (CETA)[387] stands out for its detailed provisions on labour issues.[388] This is to be expected given that it is the first comprehensive economic agreement with a highly industrialised developed country, which shares a similar set of values and principles as well similar political and legal traditions with EU member states. At the same time, there have

[385] 2016 EU-Vietnam FTA Article 3, Ch. 15.

[386] Ibid.

[387] Comprehensive Economic and Trade Agreement (CETA) between Canada, of the one part, and the European Union and its Member States of the other part, Consolidate Text published 26 September 2014, available at http://trade.ec.europa.eu/doclib/docs/2014/september/tradoc_152806.pdf. The Agreement was signed in October 2016 and parts of the Agreement have been provisionally applied as of 21 September 2017, following the European Parliament's approval on 15 February 2017; see Council Decision of 26 Oct. 2016 on the signing on behalf of the European Union of the Comprehensive Economic and Trade Agreement (CETA) Between Canada, of the one hand, and the European Union and its Member States, of the other (2016/0206 (NLE)).

[388] For a detailed analysis of the provisions of CETA, see Bartels (2017).

been growing concerns about the social impact of so-called "mega-regional trade and investment agreements"[389] giving rise to heated debates among the public and within the academic community. In the words of Ebert, 'CETA has thus turned into a crystallization point for the debate on possible adverse social effects of trade and investment agreements and the strategies to counter them.'[390] One of the reasons specifically concerning labour rights was that, at the time of the signing of the agreement, Canada had yet to ratify ILO Convention No. 98 on the right to organize and collective bargaining.[391] This explains why the EU and Canada decided to issue also a joint interpretative instrument of the agreement.[392]

In the 2014 EU-CETA there are separate chapters on Trade and Sustainable Development (TSD),[393] Trade and Labour[394] and also Trade and Environment.[395] The Chapter on Trade and Labour is far more detailed than the one of the 2011 EU-Korea FTA and the degree of legal obligation is phrased in stronger terms. The focus is on the effective enforcement of labour provisions as can be seen by the binding language used, such as "shall ensure".[396] In particular, it is stated that the Parties 'shall ensure' that their labour laws embody and provide protection for the eight ILO CLS fundamental Conventions.[397] However, a careful reading of the provision shows that CETA makes reference to the ILO's 1998 Declaration on Fundamental Principles and Rights at Work rather than directly to the ILO's Fundamental Conventions. This reference has significant implications in practice because although those instruments concern the same set of labour standards the ILO Declaration's commitments are not only less detailed than those under the relevant conventions but, as opposed to ILO conventions, they are also not directly subject to the ILO supervisory mechanisms.[398] Hence, reference to the labour standards in the Declaration could lead to more legal uncertainty, which would be quite problematic in the case of a dispute between the parties.

---

[389]The term 'mega-regional trade agreements' was adopted by the World Bank to refer to 'regional agreements that have systemic, global impact. […] They are sufficiently large and ambitious to influence trade rules and trade flows beyond their areas of application; World Bank Group, 'Global Economic Prospects, January 2016: Spillovers Amid Weak Growth', Washington DC: World Bank, p. 221, available at: https://openknowledge.worldbank.org/handle/10986/23435, accessed on 20 March 2020.

[390]Ebert (2017), at 297.

[391]Canada has since ratified this convention (14 June 2017), see the ILO's NORMLEX database, available at: https://www.ilo.org/dyn/normlex/en/f?p=NORMLEXPUB:11200:0::NO::P11200_COUNTRY_ID:102582, accessed on 14 June 2020.

[392]Joint Interpretative Instrument on the Comprehensive Economic and Trade Agreement (CETA) Between Canada and the European Union and its Member States, OJ 14.1.2017, L11/3.

[393]2014 EU-CETA, Chapter 22.

[394]2014 EU-CETA, Chapter 23.

[395]2014 EU-CETA, Chapter 24.

[396]E.g. 2014 EU-CETA, Articles 23.3 and 23.5 para. 2.

[397]2014 EU-CETA, Article 23.3, par. 1.

[398]Ebert, above no. 390, at 304.

This limitation is to some extent compensated by Article 23.3, para. 4, which provides that:

> each Party reaffirms its commitment to effectively implement in its law and practices in its whole territory the fundamental ILO Conventions that Canada and the Member States of the European Union have ratified respectively. The Parties shall make continued and sustained efforts to ratify the fundamental ILO Conventions if they have not yet done so. The Parties shall exchange information on their respective situations and advances regarding the ratification of the fundamental as well as priority and other ILO Conventions that are classified as up to date by the ILO.[399]

The 2014 EU-CETA also refers to specific labour law rights related to the ILO's 2000 DWA and the ILO's 2008 Declaration on Social Justice for a Fair Globalization,[400] namely, health and safety at work and the prevention of occupational injuries; acceptable minimum employment standards for wage earners and non-discrimination of working conditions, including for migrant workers, occupational safety and health.[401] Other requirements are encouraging public debate and promoting public awareness of their labour standards and their enforcement.[402]

In addition, a party is not allowed to waive or derogate from its labour law and standards in order to promote trade or investment and through a sustained or recurring course of action or inaction, fail to effectively enforce its labour law and standards for the same reasons.[403] Furthermore, CETA includes a list of cooperative and collaborative activities,[404] envisages a 'Committee on Trade and Sustainable Development' as a platform for dialogue between the parties on labour matters,[405] domestic advisory groups and a civil society forum to ensure dialogue for civil society.[406] A difference with the other EU trade agreements is the provision of a mechanism for submissions from civil society on the implementation of the labour provisions,[407] although it remains unclear how these submissions will be considered and dealt with.

The labour chapter's dispute settlement procedure includes arrangements for consultations as well as a possible review of the dispute by a Panel of Experts.[408] Breaches of the labour chapter's provisions, as established in the Panel's final report, are to be addressed through discussions between the parties, which need to inform

---

[399]The inclusion of this provision is particularly significant given that at the time of signing the agreement Canada had only ratified six of the eight Fundamental Conventions (Conventions No. 29, No. 87, No. 100, No. 105, No. 111 and No. 182).

[400]ILO Declaration on Social Justice for a Fair Globalisation, adopted by the International Labour Conference at its Ninety-seventh Session, Geneva, Switzerland, 10 June 2008, available at: https://www.ilo.org/wcmsp5/groups/public/---dgreports/---cabinet/documents/genericdocument/wcms_371208.pdf, accessed on 20 March 2020.

[401]2014 EU-CETA, Article 23.3 para. 2.

[402]2014 EU-CETA, Article 23.5 and 23.6.

[403]2014 EU-CETA, Article 23.4, paras. 2 and 3.

[404]2014 EU-CETA, Article 23.7.

[405]2014 EU-CETA, Article 22.4.

[406]2014 EU-CETA, Article 22.5 and 23.8(4).

[407]2014 EU-CETA, Article 23.8(5).

[408]2014 EU-CETA, Article 23.9 and 23.10.

the advisory groups and are to be monitored by the TSD Committee.[409] As in the case of other EU trade agreements, access to CETA's trade dispute settlement mechanism is expressly excluded.[410]

The 2014 EU-CETA, therefore, appears to contain a fairly robust labour-related chapter which combines promotional with more binding elements. However, a problem with these provisions is their legal design, which makes their effective application difficult. A significant number of civil society groups have voiced concerns that CETA may result in adverse effects, among others, on labour standards and workers generally.[411] It is telling that the EP Committee on Employment and Social Affairs advised against the adoption of CETA because of its negative social effects and insufficient safeguards for labour standards.[412]

One example are the lengthy procedures in place under Chapter 23 and the difficulty in showing a link between the lowering of domestic labour standards and the intention to encourage trade or investment. Other concerns relate to CETA rules dealing with public procurement,[413] which could be used to challenge clauses requiring contractors to abide by certain statutory labour standards or collective agreements.[414] In addition, CETA's investment chapter, particularly the investment protection provisions such as those on expropriation and fair and equitable treatment, may be used to challenge domestic legislation, including that on labour issues.[415] In a similar vein, the CETA chapter on regulatory cooperation does not contain any specific labour standards-related exceptions as its scope extends to matters concerning the TSD and Labour Chapters.[416] These concerns are further corroborated

[409]2014 EU-CETA, Article 23.10(12).

[410]2014 EU-CETA, Article 23.11(1).

[411]Over 450 public interest groups from across Europe and Canada published an open letter, dated 28 November 2016, urging legislators to vote against CETA; see Corporate Europe Observatory, 'European and Canadian Civil Society Groups Call for Rejection of CETA', 28.11.2016, available at: https://corporateeurope.org/en/international-trade/2016/11/european-and-canadian-civil-society-groups-call-rejection-ceta, accessed on 14 June 2020. In August 2016 a group of German NGOs, namely Campact, Foodwatch and Mehr Demokratie, filed a complaint to the Constitutional Court arguing that certain elements of the agreement were unconstitutional and breached the rule of law under the German Constitution. The German Constitutional Court rejected the legal challenge on 13 October 2016; the text of the judgment is available here (in German): https://www.bundesverfassungsgericht.de/SharedDocs/Entscheidungen/DE/2016/10/rs20161013_2bvr136816.html, accessed on 14 June 2020.

[412]Opinion of the Committee on Employment and Social Affairs for the Committee on International Trade on the draft Council decision on the conclusion of the Comprehensive Economic and Trade Agreement (CETA) Between Canada, of the one part, and the European Union and its Member States, of the other part (10975/2016—C8-0438/2016—2016/0205(NLE)) of 8 Dec. 2016, 3.

[413]2014 EU-CETA, Chapter 19.

[414]Some exception clauses can be found in CETA's Chapter on Procurement such as the one found in Article 19.2(3)(d), which provides that public employment contracts are excluded from the scope of the Chapter. However, aspects concerning labour standards in public contracts have not been taken into account among the evaluation criteria for the notice of intended procurement or tender documentation, see 2014 EU-CETA Article 19.9(9).

[415]2014 EU-CETA, Chapter 8.

[416]2014 EU-CETA Article 21.1.

by the fact that CETA's labour provisions do not regulate the relationship between the labour provisions and the agreement's other provisions to prevent adverse effects on domestic labour labour standards, as they mainly deal with the parties' conduct in relation to labour standards in general.[417] They only have broad references to matters concerning cooperation on the trade and labour linkage.[418]

From the above, it appears that because of the way they have been designed the provisions in CETA do not provide a sufficient level of protection of domestic labour standards. Ebert puts forward various suggestions to address these limitations.[419] One idea would be to increase the exception clauses contained in the agreement by expanding CETA's general exception clauses. Moreover, ad hoc provisions could be inserted to exempt existing and future labour laws and collective agreements from the obligations under the agreement, incorporating them directly into the relevant chapters.[420] These substantive changes could be combined with specific institutional arrangements to increase the involvement of civil society in monitoring the application of these clauses also under the other chapters of the agreement.[421]

Another "mega-regional trade and investment agreement", which warrants attention for the purpose of the present analysis, is the EU-US Transatlantic Trade and Investment Partnership (TTIP).[422] The latter was considered by both sides to be more

[417]Ebert, above no. 390, at 313.

[418]E.g. 2014 EU-CETA Article 23.7(1)b.

[419]Ebert, above no. 390, at 327.

[420]Ibid. Ebert gives specific examples. With regard to CETA's investment protection provisions, he suggests having clauses providing that labour law-related measures cannot be considered an expropriation or a breach of the fair and equitable treatment standard. Such clauses would also have the purpose of reducing the chilling effects of the investment protection provisions vis-à-vis labour regulation. In a similar vein, CETA's Procurement Chapter could contain a clause to provide that the agreement does not prevent the inclusion of labour standards-related conditions in public contracts.

[421]Ebert, above no. 390, at 328–329.

[422]Detailed information can be found at: https://trade.ec.europa.eu/doclib/press/index.cfm?id=1230, accessed 14 June 2020; TTIP is also known as the Transatlantic Free Trade Area (TAFTA), see Fung (2014). The initiative to establish TTIP was taken in November 2011 during an EU–US summit. A High Level Working Group on Jobs and Growth was set up soon after, chaired by the European Trade Commissioner Karel De Gucht and the US Trade Representative Ron Kirk. The purpose of the Group was to identify ways to increase trade and investment between the EU and the US. Its final report of February 2013 included a recommendation to enter into negotiations aimed at a wide agreement in the field of trade and investment. Negotiations were launched at the G8 summit at Lough Erne, Northern Ireland, in June 2013 and the first negotiation round began on July 8, 2013. After 15 negotiating rounds the negotiations ended without conclusion in November 2016. A Council Decision of 15 April 2019 states that the negotiating directives for TTIP have become obsolete, see Council of the European Union, Council Decision authorising the opening of negotiations with the United States of America for an agreement on the elimination of tariffs for industrial goods, No. 6052/19, Brussels, 9 April 2019, Article 3. TTIP together with CETA has been the subject of much opposition, see the European Citizen's' Initiative (ECI) "STOP TTIP" (aimed at preventing negotiations on TTIP and CETA, for reasons relating to the procedures of the investors-states dispute resolution and the provisions on regulatory cooperation seen as a threat to democracy and the rule of law), which the EU Commission refused to register. This decision was challenged successfully before the General Court, which annulled the Commission's decision, see Case T-754/14 *Efler and Others v Commission* ECLI:EU:T:2017:323; for case commentary, see

than just an economic agreement. It was part of the EU and the US normative trade agenda and thus instrumental to the promotion of global standards and their shared commitment to fundamental values of democracy and the rule of law. In particular for the EU, TTIP provided the avenue not only for guaranteeing existing labour standards but also to 'go further than ever before in a bilateral trade agreement to promote these standards at home and abroad.'[423] Even though at the time of writing the negotiations of this agreement seem to have come to a halt, the negotiating drafts of TTIP published by the EU and, in particular, the EU's 2015 proposal for a legal text of the TTIP's TSD Chapter[424] as well as the EP's recommendations to the European Commission on the negotiations of TTIP[425] provide a valuable insight into the "grand vision"[426] embraced by the EU for the future direction of labour standards in its trade agreements. With regard to the EU's textual proposal, the focus was on

Fahey (2017); for academic discussion and critique of TTIP, see Special Issue on TTIP, Baetens et al. (2016).

[423]Malmström (2015).

The US equivalent is the Trans-Pacific Partnership Agreement (TPP), signed on 4 February 2016, between Australia, Brunei, Canada, Chile, Japan, Malaysia, Mexico, New Zealand, Peru, Singapore, Vietnam, and the United States (a copy is available at: https://ustr.gov/trade-agreements/free-trade-agreements/trans-pacific-partnership/tpp-full-text, accessed on 20 March 2020). It never entered into forced because of the withdrawal of the US from the agreement on 23 January 2017. Like most US FTAs, the TPP includes a comprehensive chapter on labour issues, Chapter 19, which among others requires parties to generally adopt laws and regulations on ILO core labour rights, that no party shall encourage trade or investment by weakening or reducing labour laws; that labour laws shall be effectively enforced; that no party shall eliminate all forms of forced or compulsory labour domestically as well as discourage importation of goods from other sources produced with compulsory labour. With regard to the agreement's institutional and procedural rules, the TPP foresees the possibility of public submissions, cooperative activities, a cooperative labour dialogue, a labour council, contact points and public engagement. To enforce these commitments, it foresees a procedure for labour consultations with clear deadlines. Significantly, all provisions of the Labour Chapter are subject to the TPP's dispute settlement procedure and a dispute may result in sanctions, see Chapter 28 of TPP. The novelty of TPP in comparison to current US FTA practice is represented by a number of bilateral side agreements negotiated between the US and Vietnam, Malaysia and Brunei, namely, those TPP parties, which are considered as having low labour standards and are slow or reluctant in ratifying ILO labour conventions. These side agreements provide that the countries concerned must put in place a number of ad hoc domestic reforms in order to benefit from duty free access to the US. These side agreements constitute the US pre-ratification conditionality practice, which to date has been used quite effectively by the US, see further Hornbeck (2009); Vogt, above no. 337, 836–842.

[424]European Commission, 'EU textual proposal: Trade and sustainable development in TTIP', Brussels, Belgium, available at: https://trade.ec.europa.eu/doclib/docs/2015/november/tradoc_153923.pdf; this textual proposal is the European Union's initial proposal for legal text on "Trade and Sustainable Development" in TTIP. It was tabled for discussion with the US in the negotiating round of 19–23 October 2015 and made public on 6 November 2015; for detailed analysis, Gruni (2016).

[425]European Parliament, Resolution of 8 July 2015 containing the European Parliament's recommendations to the European Commission on the negotiations for the Transatlantic Trade and Investment Partnership (TTIP). Strasbourg: European Parliament, available at http://www.europarl.europa.eu/sides/getDoc.do?pubRef=-//EP//TEXT+TA+P8-TA-2015-0252+0+DOC+XML+V0//EN, accessed 14 June 2020.

[426]This term has been borrowed from Melo Araujo, above no. 79, at 234.

substantive international labour provisions rather than on civil society participation and dispute settlement. At the time, the Commission stated that it wanted to agree with the US on the substantive provisions before proceeding to the negotiation of the institutional provisions and dispute settlement. The textual proposal was based on the existing format of the EU's new generation of FTAs and was also in line with US FTA practice, as seen from Art 4(2), where there is a requirement to comply with CLS.[427] However, the textual proposal also provided details of the principles that were to be considered as part of these CLS and had to be complied with by each party, together with a list of measures that had to be adopted in order to ensure the protection of these CLS.[428] This approach was intended to promote the adoption and compliance with CLS as well as ensuring that the labour rights enshrined therein would be put into practice.[429]

In the textual proposal there was also reference to the trade-labour linkage, as found in most current EU FTAs.[430] As can be seen, the textual proposal largely

---

[427] Article 4(2) of the Textual Proposal provides that: provides that:

'In accordance with the obligations of all ILO members and the ILO Declaration on Fundamental Principles and Rights at Work, adopted by the International Labour Conference at its 86th Session in 1998 and its Follow-up, each Party shall:

(a) ensure that its laws and practices respect, promote, and realise within an integrated strategy, in its whole territory and for all, the internationally recognised core labour standards, which are the subject of the fundamental ILO Conventions, namely:
    (i) the freedom of association and the effective recognition of the right to collective bargaining;
    (ii) the elimination of all forms of forced or compulsory labour;
    (iii) the effective abolition of child labour; and
    (iv) the elimination of discrimination in respect of employment and occupation;
(b) in this context, continue to make sustained efforts towards ratifying the fundamental ILO Conventions and their Protocols, and regularly exchange information on its respective situation and advancements as regards the ratification of these as well as of priority and other ILO Conventions that are classified as up to date by the ILO and their Protocols.'

[428] E.g. Articles 5–9 of the Textual Proposal.

[429] As to working conditions, the Textual Proposal is not as detailed in that it provides a broad obligation—in accordance with the ILO Decent Work Agenda, as expressed in the ILO Declaration on Social Justice for a Fair Globalisation of 2008, and in accordance with its other international commitments—to guarantee the protection of health and safety at work and decent working conditions for all. There is no detailed description of how such standards can be implemented in practice, and only a short and open-ended list of areas and issues that must be covered by domestic legislation, such as decent working conditions being ensured in relation to wages and earnings, working hours and other conditions in order to guarantee a minimum living wage, see Article 4(3) of the Textual Proposal.

[430] E.g. Article 17 of the Textual Proposal, which provides that:

1. The Parties recognise that it is inappropriate to weaken or reduce the levels of protection afforded in domestic environmental or labour laws in order to encourage, or in a manner affecting, trade or investment.
2. A Party shall not waive or derogate from, or offer to waive or derogate from, its environmental or labour laws as an encouragement for, or in a manner affecting, trade or investment.

followed standard EU FTA practice, going beyond the US' minimalist FTA practice. The EP resolution on TTIP of 8 July 2015 is also of particular salience as it contains specific recommendations on the labour provisions that the agreement should have included,[431] which are here reproduced:

- to ensure that the sustainable development chapter is binding and enforceable and aims at the full and effective ratification, implementation and enforcement of the eight fundamental ILO conventions and their content, the ILO's DWA and the core international environmental agreements; provisions must be aimed at further improving levels of protection of labour and environmental standards; an ambitious trade and sustainable development chapter must also include rules on corporate social responsibility based on OECD Guidelines for Multinational Enterprises and clearly structured dialogue with civil society;
- to ensure that labour and environmental standards are not limited to the trade and sustainable development chapter but are equally included in other areas of the agreement, such as investment, trade in services, regulatory cooperation and public procurement;
- to ensure that labour and environmental standards are made enforceable, by building on the good experience of existing FTAs by the EU and US and national legislation; to ensure that the implementation of and compliance with labour provisions is subjected to an effective monitoring process, involving social partners and civil society representatives and to the general dispute settlement which applies to the whole agreement;
- to ensure, in full respect of national legislation, that employees of transatlantic companies, registered under EU member state law, have access to information and consultation in line with the European works council directive;
- to ensure that the economic, employment, social, and environmental impact of TTIP, is also examined by means of a thorough and objective ex-ante trade sustainability impact assessment (SIA) in full respect of the EU Directive on SIA,

---

3. A Party shall not, through a sustained or recurring course of action or inaction, fail to effectively enforce its environmental or labour laws as an encouragement for, or in a manner affecting, trade or investment.

The first paragraph reproduces the provision found in Article 73 of the 2008 EU-CARIFORUM EPA with the difference that it is not drafted in legally binding terms as the latter, which is clearly termed as a legal obligation of the parties to the agreement, cfr. 'recognise that' found in the former with 'shall ensure' found in the EPA. Paragraphs 2 and 3 are meant to prevent parties from resorting to social dumping. However, the way they are drafted makes it difficult to understand which labour provisions/rights are covered and to determine the causal link between derogation from labour standards and trade and/or investment. There is also no reference to enforcement mechanisms. See further Gruni, above no. 424.

[431] European Parliament, above no. 406, Section d, points (ii)–(vi); on similar positions, see also European Trade Union Confederation (ETUC) and the American Federation of Labor and Congress of Industrial Organizations (AFL/CIO), 'TTIP must work for the people or it won't work at all', Declaration of Joint Principles ETUC/AFL-CIO, 10.07.2014, Brussels, Belgium, available at: https://www.etuc.org/sites/default/files/document/files/afl-cio_ttip_report_uk_1.pdf, accessed on 14 June 2020.

with clear and structured involvement of all relevant stakeholders, including civil society; asks the Commission to conduct comparative in-depth impact studies for each Member State and an evaluation of the competitiveness of EU sectors and their counterparts in the US with the aim to make projections on job losses and gains in the sectors affected in each Member State, whereby the adjustment costs could be partly taken up by EU and Member State funding.

When comparing it with the EP's resolution the first noticeable difference is the lack of reference in the textual proposal of the enforceability and monitoring of labour provisions given the decision to postpone the discussion of any matters concerning institutional aspects of the agreement and the setting up of a dispute settlement to a later stage. As to the eight core ILO Conventions the textual proposal did not mandate their ratification and the language used was less strong. Instead, it provided that each party shall, among others, 'make sustained efforts towards ratifying the fundamental ILO Conventions and their Protocols, and regularly exchange information on its respective situation and advancements as regards the ratification'[432] as well as 'effectively implement in its laws and practices and in its whole territory the ILO Conventions it has ratified.'[433] The EP's resolution also recommended mainstreaming labour provisions across all chapters of TTIP, rather than having only a dedicated chapter on labour provisions. In this regard, the textual proposal contained provisions on a trade-labour linkage.[434] However, the textual proposal did not contain more specific provisions on how to support labour standards in other areas or on the relationship between the agreement's labour provisions and, for example, investment or public procurement to avoid that the measures adopted in these areas could be used to undermine labour protection or, more generally, to the detriment of labour standards. Finally, the reliance on SIAs to assess the impact of TTIP followed current practice, although the EU Parliament explicitly envisaged an important and structured role for civil society and other relevant stakeholders.

The above confirms how the EP also pursues an unequivocal normative trade agenda and is generally a stronger advocate of clearly enforceable labour protection provisions in trade agreements compared to the EU Commission, which opted for adhering largely to the EU's standard FTA practice.[435]

The use of "mega-regional trade agreements" is a way of the EU and the US to maintain or strengthen their role as global actors on the international scene rather than a way to depart substantially from current FTA practice.

---

[432] Article 4(2)(b) of the Textual Proposal.

[433] Article 4(4) of the Textual Proposal.

[434] E.g. Article 17 of the Textual Proposal.

[435] It is noteworthy that Business Europe has presented its position on TTIP's Trade and Sustainable Development Chapter along similar lines as the EU Commission calling for a more conservative approach in relation to the ILO Conventions and for a softer approach focused on consultation and cooperation, see Business Europe, 'TTIP: the sustainability chapter', Position Paper, Brussels, Belgium, May 2015, available at: https://www.businesseurope.eu/sites/buseur/files/media/imported/2015-00382-E.pdf, accessed 14 June 2020.

In the words of Melo Araujo[436]:

> the mega-regionals can be viewed as the latest instalment in the ongoing attempts of large industrialized powers to use their increased bargaining powers in the context of bilateral or regional trade agreements to impose regulatory positions that were rejected at the multilateral level, with the aim of incrementally raising labour standards whilst reducing the ability of countries to lower the application and enforcement of such standards to gain a competitive advantage in trade.

Even though both the EU and the US have been promoting the trade-labour linkage in their FTAs for some time, albeit in different ways *de jure*, they have been reluctant to enforce the labour provisions of these trade agreements *de facto*.[437] Before the demise of TTIP (and TPP), Tham and Ewing had already argued, somewhat presciently, that both in the case of the US and the EU there would be a general orientation to non-application of the labour clauses.[438] There are several convincing reasons for this argument. First, is the issue about power relations between the parties to the agreement. Given that this would classify as an agreement of equals—although probably not in relation to all EU member states—the US would be reluctant to require compliance to EU Member States that are not fulfilling their labour standards commitment under the agreement, particularly because the US might also be in breach of certain labour standards.[439] Even though the US has not ratified the core ILO Conventions 87 and 98 concerning freedom of association, it has been found by the ILO's Committee on Freedom of Association to be in breach of the fundamental constitutional principle of freedom of association.[440] In addition, the US is arguably in breach of the ILO 1998 Declaration[441] and its full compliance by the US might be difficult due to domestic political constraints.[442] The EU and the EU member states are in a similar position as the US[443] and so are or will be equally reluctant to submit a complaint for breach of labour clauses.

---

[436] Melo Araujo, above no. 79, at 250.

[437] Melo Araujo, above no. 79, at 234.

[438] Tham and Ewing, above no. 337, at 24.

[439] Ibid.

[440] E.g. Case No 2460 (United States)—Complaint date: 07-DEC-05—The United Electrical, Radio and Machine Workers of America (UE) supported by Public Services International (PSI); Case No 2524 (United States)—Complaint date: 20-OCT-06 American Federation of Labor and Congress of Industrial Organizations (AFL-CIO); Case No 2547 (United States)—Complaint date: 26-FEB-07 United Automobile, Aerospace and Agricultural Implement Workers of America International Union (UAW) and American Federation of Labor and Congress of Industrial Organizations (AFL-CIO).

[441] International Labour Organization, 'Your Voice at Work: Global Report under the Follow-Up to the Declaration on Fundamental Principles and Rights at Work' (Report, 2000) https://perma.cc/AT8W-ATAF, accessed on 22 March 2020, paras. 74, 103–104, concerning restrictions in agriculture, strike restrictions on state employees and the use of replacement labour in all strikes.

[442] Tham and Ewing, above no. 337, at 25.

[443] Various EU Member States have been found to breach ILO Convention No. 87, see further above, infra Sect. 5.3.1.2. of this chapter; for detailed analysis, see Novitz (2017).

Governance and Implementation of the Social Clauses in the New Generation of Free Trade Agreements

The governance and implementation of the labour provisions has been expanded so as to include a wide range of actors, including high-level labour officials, civil society and business actors of the partner countries to a given trade agreement who are involved in monitoring and promoting social clauses.[444] In principle, the "new generation" of EU trade agreements enable third countries—as legal subjects qua partner countries—to acquire a renewed role: from one of mere public power recipients to one of co-shapers.

In particular, they provide for the setting up of a Sub-Committee/Board on Trade and Sustainable Development in the context of which senior government officials regularly meet to oversee the implementation of the labour (and environmental) commitments of the agreement.[445] In addition, civil society actors officially have a role in monitoring the implementation of sustainable development provisions,[446] although their role and the key features of civil society meetings vary significantly from agreement to agreement.[447]

With regard to the institutional provisions, at government level, ministerial contact points, specialized committees and/or boards of senior officials for the purpose of implementing the trade and sustainable development chapter have been set up. Government officials meet annually with labour and environmental experts in the Committee on Trade and Sustainable Development, which has been established to oversee the implementation of the Trade and Sustainable Development chapter.

As regards civil society and social partners, the 2011 EU-Korea agreement provides for Domestic Advisory Groups for each party made up of civil society, business, social partners and other experts from relevant stakeholder groups, which meet at an annual Civil Society Forum.[448] Similarly, the 2012 EU-Colombia/Peru[449] and EU-CAAA[450] agreements mandate each party and the subcommittee/board to meet with existing national advisory groups (or to create new ones) and civil society on a regular basis.

---

[444]For further analysis, Orbie et al. (2016).

[445]W. T. Douma, 'The Promotion of Sustainable Development through EU Trade Instruments' in L. Pantaleo, and M. Andenas (eds) *The European Union as a Global Model for Trade and Investment*, University of Oslo Faculty of Law Legal Studies Research paper Series No 2016-02, 86; F. de Andrade Correa, 'The Integration of Sustainable Development in Trade Agreements of the European Union' in D. Kleimann, 'EU Preferential Trade Agreements: Commerce, Foreign Policy and Development Aspects', International Trade Observatory and Relex Working Group, European University Institute, Robert Schuman Centre for Advanced Studies, 141, available at: cadmus.eui.eu/handle/1814/27661, accessed 20 March 2020.

[446]L. Bartels, 'The Role of Civil Society in Monitoring Free Trade Agreements', Report for the EU European Economic and Social Committee, EESC/COMM/16/2012.

[447]Orbie, Martens and Van den Putte, above no. 444, 12–25.

[448]2011 EU-Korea FTA, Article 13.12(3)-(5) and Article 13.13.

[449]2012 EU-Colombia/Peru, Article 282.

[450]2012 EU-CAAA, Part III.

While the inclusion of these actors is meant to ensure better input democratic legitimacy, the lack of clarity as to their role means that it is difficult to evaluate their effective contribution to the objectives of the Trade and Sustainable Development chapter.[451] Some argue that their involvement is purely instrumental to the "real" economic purpose of the agreement: they are used to forge broad support by 'helping the parties to "sell" the agreement to their constituencies and can thus be reduced to a public relations stunt to improve the reputation of the trading partners'.[452] Taking this further, it is argued that, through direct involvement in the governance of the social clauses, civil society organizations and social partners are 'being co-opted and their opposition is being neutralized'[453] despite being assigned the role of legal subjects in the operationalization of the agreement. Hence there is a risk of 'meta-injustice' in the form of 'meta-political misrepresentation'.[454] Specifically, where a political community or system frames questions of justice so as to exclude individuals from consideration 'the consequence is a special kind of meta-injustice, in which one is denied the chance to press first-order justice claims in a given political community.'[455] By becoming institutionalized as such it becomes more difficult to oppose the instrumental nature of the TSD chapter. On a more positive note, and in spite of the limited enforceability of labour provisions in the short term, their inclusion may nevertheless have important policy learning effects in the longer term, such as providing the ground for transnational advocacy building or facilitating the functioning of existing transnational networks.[456] This form of experimentalist governance which is emerging in the context of these new trade agreements[457] may provide a better understanding of the challenges faced by a given third country, thus reducing negative externalities on affected stakeholders and communities.[458]

The Impact of the Trade-Labour Linkage in the "New Generation" of Trade Agreements

By its very nature, and to some extent due to a lack of transparency of what happens in practice, any evaluation concerning the results that the promotional approach of the EU's social conditionality has achieved so far cannot be definitive. It is difficult to establish a causal link between the implementation of measures and the results yielded, also due to the significant degree of variation between the *de jure* and the *de*

---

[451] For further analysis of alternative forms to representative democracy, their legal force and the credibility of the EU's meaningful use in decision-making and implementation processes, particularly in relation to Art.11 TEU, see Korkea-aho (2017).

[452] Orbie, Martens and Van den Putte, above no 444, 28.

[453] Ibid.

[454] For further discussion on issues of (political) injustice, misrepresentation and mis-framing, see Fraser (2005); see also Wheatley (2010).

[455] Ibid., at p. 77.

[456] Keck and Sikkink (2002).

[457] In this sense, see Orbie, Martens and Van den Putte, above 444, 47–48; for an analysis of experimentalist governance in the context of EU external action, see Zeitlin (2015).

[458] Velluti, above no. 2, at 110.

facto configurations of the plurality of actors, and thus subjects, that can be involved. Second, it is not possible to make generalized conclusions as to the effects of promotional labour provisions due to the differences between the new trade agreements and the way they are operationalized in practice. Third, there are significant cultural, political and socio-economic differences between the partner countries with which the EU signs these agreements. More specifically, the fact that new subjects such as civil society organizations and social partners are envisaged in promoting social trade may be insufficient in terms of results because much will depend on the domestic context. In particular, the reliance upon cooperation and dialogue to enforce labour standards shows how pivotal political will is in the case of the EU's promotional provisions, as key power rests with governments rather than other institutions or civil society.[459]

For example, empirical studies of the 2012 EU-Colombia agreement show that, despite the country putting in place a fairly robust legal and institutional framework to protect labour rights, to date it has not yielded much impact. This is due to shortcomings in the way the TSD chapter of this agreement has been designed in the first place and then applied.[460] This unsatisfactory state of affairs is explained by the fact that there are still deeply rooted political and social inequalities in the country and institutionalized anti-union practices continue in spite of the new labour laws that have been put in place in the country.

Another example is the EU-South Korea FTA. There is no process beyond continued dialogue insofar as there are no provisions if dialogue fails and the broad language used in relation to the Domestic Advisory Group (DAGs) has enabled the government of South Korea to cherry pick those who sit in those committees.[461]

A textual analysis of these new trade agreements also shows that social clauses are not given the same importance as its counterpart, the trade provisions of these trade agreements.[462] Hence, we can see a difference in the weight that each of the main objects of these agreements has with the trade provisions carrying more weight than the social clauses. Furthermore, the latter do not strive for increased compliance but rather aim at preserving what is already in place, requiring the parties to the trade agreement to uphold and not lower their already existing labour commitments; they are conceived as aspirations together with the environmental provisions. Labour provisions are conceived as an element of sustainable development to be

[459] Moore and Scherrer (2017).

[460] Marx et al. (2016).

[461] FES Korea (2016); see also European Commission, Evaluation of the Implementation of the Free Trade Agreement between the EU and its Member States and the Republic of Korea Interim Technical Report Part 1: Synthesis Report, prepared by Civic Consulting and the Ifo Institute June 2017, available at https://trade.ec.europa.eu/doclib/docs/2017/june/tradoc_155673.pdf, accessed on 14 June 2020, pp. 174–177.

[462] A study on labour provisions in EU trade agreements with South Korea, Moldova and CARIFORUM, shows that labour provisions were not considered as a natural part of trade agreements by these countries' negotiators, see Harrison et al. (2019), at 265.

pursued through the trade agreement itself. They are not considered as having conditioning force on which to base trade relations.[463] This is well illustrated in the 2011 EU-Korea FTA agreement, which requires the parties to uphold their international commitments, namely the four CLS, which they should already adhere to automatically via their ILO membership.[464] It is thus a formal reaffirmation by the parties to uphold these labour standards within their own territory, in law and in practice.[465] It also contains a commitment by the signatory parties that they will not lower their domestic labour standards to attract trade and FDI.[466] This provision seems to weaken rather than strengthen the parties' commitment to the respect for labour rights as it still enables them to lower the standards of labour protection in their countries if no causal link with increased trade or investment can be found. In addition, the commitment is loose: none of the agreements sets out specific steps that should be undertaken by the signatory parties to increase respect for social clauses. In the case of a labour dispute, EU trade agreements foresee a cooperative approach, which relies on dialogue and cooperation between the parties and between government officials and civil society. If the issue cannot be resolved in this way, a panel of experts can be established.[467] However, the recommendations of this panel lack enforceability.

While these promotional features of the "new generation" of trade agreements contribute to injecting a social dimension into the EU's trade policy through cooperation and social dialogue, it remains to be seen whether they entail an effective improvement of the implementation-capacity of developing countries to respect and protect social clauses and thus lead to an effective improvement of labour standards internationally. The EU approach to social conditionality is to a large extent promotional in nature and based on cooperation. The promotional approach combines binding and non-binding commitments to labour standards, domestic or international, with provisions on cooperation, knowledge sharing, technical assistance, dialogue and monitoring, with the purported objective of allowing third countries to strengthen their capacity-building to address labour concerns.[468] To date whether the EU soft conditionality works remains an open question. When countries adopt a clear resistant and/or obstructionist approach particularly towards full compliance with ILO Conventions, this approach tends to be ineffective. The substantive norms that this new type of agreements introduces to achieve the sustainability objectives are 'formulated in such manner that it often seems hard or even impossible to prove that a party is not meeting its obligations.'[469] According to a study by Harrison, Barbu, Campling,

---

[463] Van Den Putte (2016).

[464] eg Art.13.4 subpara.3 and Art.13.7 subpara.2 of the 2011 EU-Korea FTA.

[465] Marx, Brecht and Brando, above no. 460, 5.

[466] eg Art.13.7 subpara.2 of the 2011 EU-Korea FTA.

[467] eg Art.13.15 of the 2011 EU-Korea FTA.

[468] ILO, Report on *Social Dimensions of Free Trade Agreements*, International Institute for Labour Studies, Geneva, Switzerland, 2013, Ch. 3.

[469] Douma, above no. 445, p. 101; the analysis focuses specifically on the 2012 EU-Colombia/Peru Trade Agreement as an example of the new generation of EU trade agreements. For a critical analysis of the meaning of sustainable development and sustainability also in the light of the UN

Richardson and Smith[470] there is no evidence to suggest that the existence of TSD chapters has led to improvements in labour standards governance nor do they find any evidence that 'the institutionalization of opportunities for learning and socialization between the parties has created[471] a significant prospect of longer-term change.'

Enforcement remains weak as any dispute concerning the trade and sustainable development chapters should be resolved solely through the specific dispute settlement procedure provided therein, as recourse to the general dispute settlement procedures available under the FTAs is explicitly excluded for matters falling under the chapter. In most cases there is a tendency to delegate disputes to a more neutral Panel of Experts. In some instances, there are no provisions in case of non-compliance and there is a lack of representativity of the social partners such as in the case of the EU-South Korea agreement where some trade unions and organized civil society representatives have been excluded from the Korean DAG. In this regard, Van den Putte's research shows that none of the civil society groups perceive the EU's social trade as 'providing them with a strong tool to improve their labour situation'[472] and there is little information and awareness among civil society groups of governments' obligations under the labour provisions of a given trade agreement or of the tools available to them in the agreement.[473]

In addition, there is a risk of overlap between the implementation of the TSD chapter provisions and the obligations that arise from the human rights clauses. ILO's CLS are also human rights and the Commission itself considers that they are covered by the standard human rights clauses.[474] This is not a mere theoretical issue: whether a labour violation falls within the scope of the TSD chapter or that of a human rights clause has significant implications in terms of enforceability.[475]

In essence, there are two parallel co-existing systems: on the one hand, human rights and democratic principles with a strong monitoring and enforcement mechanism, which is seldom applied and, on the other hand, the TSD chapter with a weak monitoring and enforcement mechanism, which impedes any form of effective enforceability of the labour provisions. These different approaches of the EU are problematic because they undermine the EU's obligation to respect the indivisibility of all human rights. Moreover, including labour provisions under the TSD chapter weakens their human rights connotation because labour rights as fundamental rights cannot be questioned whereas sustainable development as such leaves more room for

Sustainable Development Goals (SDGs) 2015, see Gammage and Novitz (2019); on the SDGs and the UN's 2030 Agenda, for Sustainable Development see, UN General Assembly, Resolution on Transforming our world: the 2030 Agenda for Sustainable Development, Seventieth session, 25 September 2015, available at: https://www.un.org/ga/search/view_doc.asp?symbol=A/RES/70/1&Lang=E, accessed on 14 June 2020; see also the dedicated website on the SDGs at: https://www.un.org/sustainabledevelopment/sustainable-development-goals/, accessed on 14 June 2020.

[470] Harrison et al., above no. 462, at 273.

[471] In the original text 'was creating.'.

[472] Van den Putte, above no. 463, at p. 101.

[473] Ibid.

[474] Bartels, above no. 236, at 312.

[475] Ibid.

interpretation.[476] At EU level, it also causes confusion as to the competent department in terms of responsibility, expertise and interpretation, particularly within the Commission, namely, should it be the Directorate-General (DG) for Trade to deal with issues or complaints concerning labour provisions, which is responsible for the whole FTA, or should it be the DG for International Cooperation and Development (DG DEVCO) or the DG for Employment, Social Affairs and Inclusion, or coordination among all of these DGs?[477]

Despite the limited enforceability of labour provisions in the "new generation" of trade agreements in the short term, their inclusion may nevertheless have an impact in the longer term, such as, promoting transnational advocacy building and, linked to this, a better understanding of the challenges faced by a given third country, thus reducing negative externalities on affected stakeholders and communities.

5.3.3 An Overview of Selected Proposals for Strengthening EU Social Conditionality

Various proposals to improve the effectiveness and enforcement of labour provisions in EU trade instruments have been put forward. As Moore and Scherrer point out: 'critically, enforcement goes beyond the ratification of new standards. It is about the response of the trading partners when a violation of those agreed-to standards occurs, the development of the necessary conditions for implementation and the political will to follow through such processes.'[478] In the analysis that follows, these factors will be taken into consideration in order to assess the viability of the proposals put forward to strengthen social conditionality, both in cases where what is provided in an agreement (and also unilateral trade arrangements) is either rarely enforced and in cases where there is no effective enforcement process outlined.

With regard to social conditionality in EU unilateral trade arrangements and, in particular the GSP+, it is suggested that the Commission should adopt a more comprehensive and cohesive approach in the way that it utilizes the documents of ILO's supervisory bodies to ensure that it always intervenes in cases of blatant labour rights violations. In particular, this means that it should aim at reducing its selective conditionality by giving more weight to ILO reports and its supervisory bodies' findings and exercise more pressure on beneficiary countries in cases where there is strong evidence of labour rights abuses.

---

[476] Moore and Scherrer, above no. 459, p. 3; Novitz argues that 'there may be benefits to supplementing bare human rights compliance with a richer and more nuanced SD perspective, but that we have yet to see trade instruments which realize that ambition', see Novitz (2018).

[477] Moore and Scherrer, above no. 459, p. 3.

[478] Moore and Scherrer, above no. 459, p. 1.

With regard to bilateral trade agreements, the 3-year US-Cambodia Textile Agreement[479] is often mentioned as an effective model for including labour provisions in FTAs and, in particular, as providing an incentive mechanism for so-called "positive sanctions".[480] The agreement established that US textile and apparel import quotas would be increased annually by 14 percent in correlation with progress on improving labour practices.[481] Companies that fulfilled their undertakings, therefore, would be rewarded fairly quickly. This provided incentives for the private sector and the Cambodian authorities to make an effort to improve labour standards in the textile sector. The US and Cambodia also requested ILO's technical assistance, which led to an ILO project (largely funded by the US), directed by a Chief Technical Adviser appointed by the ILO and guided by a tripartite Project Advisory Committee, to monitor factories in the textile and apparel sector in Cambodia and to improve the capacity of government, employers and workers to improve working conditions. This ILO programme not only provided a mechanism to report on labour conditions in factories but significantly also served as a form of replacement for Cambodia's inadequate and weak domestic regulatory system, which did not have the capacity to enforce labour standards, whether international or national.[482] Kolben maintains that this textile agreement constituted a remarkable experiment for two principal reasons. First, it used trade-related incentives to enforce workers' rights in a trade agreement. Second, it harnessed the power of factory level monitoring of labour rights compliance.[483] Unsurprisingly, Siroën argues that such a system of positive or "smart" sanctions could be introduced and applied more generally in trade agreements targeting companies, not the industry or country concerned as a whole. Incentive mechanisms in the form of additional preferences or privileges should promote improved practices and prevent undesirable effects such as companies or workers moving into the informal economy.[484] The US-Cambodia Textile Agreement certainly offers some useful and helpful pointers for future EU agreements, particularly because it also addresses the concerns of many third countries that see the EU as using the trade-labour linkage instrumentally, largely for disguised protectionist purposes.

---

[479] Signed on 20 January 1999 for a three-year period, and then extended for a further three years, the textile agreement between the US and Cambodia expired in January 2005; see Agreement Relating to Trade in Cotton, Wool, Man-made Fiber, Non-Cotton Vegetable Fiber and Silk Blend Textiles and Textile Products Between the Government of the United States of America and the Royal Government of Cambodia, available at: https://photos.state.gov/libraries/cambodia/231771/PDFs/uskh_texttile.pdf, accessed on 14 June 2020.

[480] For detailed analysis, see Kolben (2004).

[481] In particular, Article 10(D), to be read in combination with the other paragraphs A-C, referred to working conditions in the Cambodian textile and apparel sector substantially complying with Cambodian labour law and internationally recognized core labour standards. In the amended version, the agreement offered a possible 18 percent annual increase provided that Cambodia would support the implementation of a programme to improve working conditions including internationally recognized core labour standards, through the application of Cambodian labour law.

[482] Kolben, above no. 480, at 81.

[483] Ibid., at 80-81.

[484] J.-M. Siroën, above no. 163, 98.

Specifically, with regard to the new generation of trade agreements, one solution could be the amendment of the provisions of the TSD Chapter so as to tailor them to the specificities of the third country that is party to the agreement.[485] This could be along similar lines as those already proposed by Bartels in relation to the adoption of a new human rights clause.[486] Other proposals for improving the effectiveness of social conditionality in bilateral and regional agreements are: the development of time-bound labour-related objectives to trade agreements, greater involvement and consultation of social partners and civil society in the negotiations and implementation of labour provisions, to ensure better coherence in the way that ILO instruments are included in the various trade agreements,[487] and to improve current mechanisms for reviewing the impact of international agreements such as *ex ante* 'trade sustainability impact assessments' (hereafter "trade SIAs"), which the EU has been conducting prior to the conclusion of each trade agreement as part of the EU's sustainable development policy (focusing in particular on economic

[485] In this sense the new agreement that the EU and Mexico have agreed in principle in April 2018 seems to go in right direction. The text of the agreement is available at: https://trade.ec.europa.eu/doclib/press/index.cfm?id=1833, accessed on 14 June 2020. The agreement will be part of a broadened and revised 'Global Agreement', which entered into force in 2000, see Economic Partnership, Political Coordination and Cooperation Agreement between the European Community and its Member States, of the one part, and the United Mexican States, of the other part, 28.10.2000 OJ L 276/45. It is the first of its kind to include provisions to tackle corruption in the private and public sector. These set of anti-corruption provisions are particularly salient for labour protection in Mexico. Prior to this agreement, the EU has addressed corruption under a different type of trade agreement, namely, the Deep and Comprehensive Free Trade Agreement ('DCFTA'). Significantly, its TSD Chapter includes a provision on the responsible management of supply chains, which makes explicit reference to corporate social responsibility and lists various documents that the Parties must 'promote' 'disseminate' or 'use', namely, the Organisation for the Economic Cooperation and Development (OECD) (2011), the ILO Tripartite Declaration of Principles concerning Multinational Enterprises and Social Policy, adopted by the Governing Body of the International Labour Office at its 204th Session (Geneva, November 1977) and amended at its 279th (November 2000), 295th (March 2006) and 329th (March 2017) Sessions, the International Labour Office, Geneva, Switzerland, available at: https://www.ilo.org/wcmsp5/groups/public/---ed_emp/---emp_ent/---multi/documents/publication/wcms_094386.pdf, accessed on 14 June 2020, and the UN Global Compact and the UN Guiding Principles on Business and Human Rights, see Article 9 of the EU-Mexico, text available at: https://trade.ec.europa.eu/doclib/docs/2018/april/tradoc_156822.pdf, accessed on 5 September 2019.

[486] Bartels (2014b). In particular, see p. 30, where Bartels suggests adding a clause to 'the general exceptions that are included in every trade agreement, permitting a party to adopt measures taken to respect, promote or fulfil human rights as defined in the essential elements clause. Importantly, it would need to be clear that measures may be adopted with respect to human rights domestically as well as extraterritorially' and p. 31 where he suggests having more 'specificity as to the human rights aspects of the monitoring process.' The same rationale could be extended to social clauses in the "new generation" of free trade agreement.

[487] ILO (2013), Chapter 4; see also European Parliament, Resolution on implementation of the 2010 recommendations of Parliament on social and environmental standards, human rights and corporate responsibility of 5 July 2016 (2015/2038(INI)), para 22(b), where the EU Parliament suggests granting civil society and, in particular, Domestic Advisory Groups the right to complain about labour standards breaches before the European Commission.

development, social development and environmental protection).[488] Three types of evaluation can be conducted during the life of a trade initiative[489]: an Impact Assessment (IA) at the initial design stage, a SIA during the trade negotiations,[490] and an evaluation after implementation.

The EU has been systematically conducting *ex ante* trade SIAs to establish what the impact of a given international agreement could be, particularly the likely changes and trade-offs caused by trade liberalization, and to identify certain measures which may reduce its negative effects.[491] Once the Council gives a mandate to conduct trade negotiations, the Commission initiates the process of a trade SIA.[492] The scope of the impact is broad so as to cover a variety of objects, namely third countries and within countries, regions, businesses, firms, different categories and status of citizens, services, goods, the environment and the overall ecological system.[493]

---

[488]European Commission (2016a); a list of completed and ongoing assessments is available at http://ec.europa.eu/trade/policy/policy-making/analysis/sustainability-impact-assessments/assessments/; the 2011 Joint Communication of the European Commission and High Representative of the European Union for Foreign Affairs and Security Policy on Human Rights and Democracy at the Heart of EU External Action—Towards a More Effective Approach, COM(2011)886 final. (2011) explicitly refers to the importance of impact assessments; see also the 2012 EU Strategic Framework and Action Plan on Human Rights and Democracy, of 25 June 2012. Luxembourg, Luxembourg. 11855/12 which expressly calls for the insertion of human rights in Impact Assessment, as and when it is carried out for trade agreements that have significant economic, social and environmental impacts. The new generation of trade SIAs reflect this goal; for further analysis, see Cote (2014).

[489]Further information is available at *ec.europa.eu/trade/policy/policy-making/analysis/index_en.htm#_bilateral-regional*, accessed 6 February 2017.

[490]There are also economic assessments of the negotiated outcome (EANOs). Once the negotiations are concluded, and before the trade agreement is signed, an economic analysis of the proposed agreement for the EU is prepared by the services of the Directorate-General (DG) Trade of the Commission for the European Parliament and the Council. The analysis assesses the impact of the actual outcome of the negotiations with regard to the reduction of trade barriers. This economic assessment is distinct from SIAs in which estimation of the likely impact of a proposed trade agreement is based on assumptions about the level of such reductions that will be achieved. It should also be noted that the economic assessment of the negotiated outcome is a trade-specific instrument and relates only to negotiations conducted by DG Trade: Nilsson, Lars, 'EU Trade Policy: Recent Progress and Analytical Advances' (GIFTA Workshop on 'Social and Labour Impacts of Free Trade Agreements', German Marshall Fund, Brussels, July 2016).

[491]See above infra no. 488.

[492]The EU trade SIAs are outsourced to competitive agencies and experts selected by the Commission who will employ a specific methodology, deliver economic analysis, carry out a preliminary assessment, provide detailed sector studies and a final synthesis report. Potentially these agencies and experts have a role as legal subjects in carrying out these SIAs. Economic, social and environmental impacts outside the EU are explicitly part of the analysis. European Commission, Better Regulation Guidelines, COM(2015) 215 final; European Commission, Better Regulation Toolbox Toolbox 16, Identification/Screening of Impacts, available at: ec.europa.eu/smart-regulation/guidelines/docs/br_toolbox_en.pdf, accessed 6 February 2017.

[493]The relevant type of object will depend on the specific sector and/or nature of the issue addressed, as SIAs are generally highly contextualized.

These trade SIAs have been increasingly subject to criticism by many non-governmental organizations (NGOs) as they have failed to provide a proper assessment of how a given trade agreement will impact on human rights.[494] In particular, it is argued that they do not adequately consider the real problems that developing countries (particularly Least Developed Countries (LDCs)) have. This is mainly because not all sectors are assessed as illustrated by the SIAs carried out in relation to the EU–ACP EPAs, which have not fully taken into account the impact that market integration has on small-scale farmers. A 2007 study on EPAs for the UN Human Rights Council concluded that the treaties would 'result, at least in the short run, in huge losses in revenue and restricted access to the EU market, making it highly likely that the social and economic human rights of millions will be adversely affected'.[495] The European Commission's own SIA's of EPAs warned that, without adequate safeguards, ACP countries could be negatively exposed to lost tariff revenue and increased competition from EU exports, resulting in a damage to the local production that could disproportionately threaten the livelihoods and food security of rural populations.[496]

It has to be added that trade SIAs involve highly complex studies concerning a wide spectrum of sectors, stakeholders and economic, social and political variables that, as some IAs recognize, are very difficult to disaggregate and measure. To some extent, therefore, trade SIAs have inherent limitations, which explains why they can only provide a limited perspective on a given trade agreement and its potential impact.

In light of these limitations, it has been argued that these *ex ante* trade SIAs should be increasingly informed by human rights considerations[497] and combined with *ex post* evaluations to assess the human rights impact and review the implementation of trade agreements.[498] In this regard, the U.N. Special Rapporteur on the Right to

[494]Oxfam (2008); Office of the United Nations High Commissioner for Human Rights (2010).

[495]Human Rights Council (2007).

[496]PricewaterhouseCoopers (2007); see also Bilal et al. (2009) and CEPII-CIREM (2008).

[497]Harrison and Goller suggest the setting up of a mechanism for reviewing the implementation of agreements in accordance with human rights norms, on the basis of a human rights impact assessment, see Harrison and Goller (2008). The 2008 EU-CARIFORUM EPA includes a procedural framework for carrying out human rights impact assessments and for reviewing the agreement. Article 5 states that: 'The Parties undertake to monitor continuously the operation of the Agreement through their respective participative processes and institutions, as well as those set up under this Agreement, in order to ensure that the objectives of the Agreement are realised, the Agreement is properly implemented and the benefits men, women, young people and children deriving from their Partnership are maximised. The Parties also undertake to consult each other promptly over any problem that may arise'; on this point see Bartels, above no. 465, at 31.

[498]With the 2009 Treaty of Lisbon there has been growing emphasis on the need to develop tailor-made approaches to human rights–relevant policies, including trade policy, the use of impact assessments to ensure human rights consistency and, linked to the former, the importance of inserting human rights in impact assessments. Since 2012, and in line with Article 21 TEU, a new generation of EU trade SIAs has thus started to integrate, albeit partially, human rights considerations into their research methodologies; see European Commission (2011); see also Council of the European Union (2012), 2.

Food has recommended that trade agreements be adopted provisionally with sunset clauses, namely a provision that it shall automatically cease to have effect after a specific date unless further action is taken to extend it, so as to allow for modifications in case their implementation is found by independent assessments to be generating human rights violations.[499]

Hence, "human rights impact assessments" (HRIAs) have increasingly been developed and conducted outside of the EU covering specific aspects of public policy, including the impact of government programmes for developing countries, trade negotiations, intellectual property and domestic legislation on human rights protection.[500] HRIAs can examine a number of activities of different actors such as government measures, multinationals and NGOs, the overall aim being to determine the degree of impact on human rights.[501] This is achieved by measuring specific human rights impacts through an evidence-based analysis, of particularly vulnerable and potentially disadvantaged groups.

As posited by Harrison, HRIAs must be based on an clear evaluation of the impact of trade law obligations on relevant, codified human rights obligations that apply to a given country avoiding that the inclusion of human rights in the assessment becomes a mere window dressing exercises.[502] However, the problem with HRIAs is that it is often difficult to translate human rights obligations contained in international treaties and national laws into analytical tools that can be used to measure the impact of trade agreements.[503] Despite much talk about using indicators there is not much evidence of their use in practice. Again, this is explained by the difficulty of developing appropriate human rights indicators that have the required contextual specificity, which is tailored to the problems of the country concerned. Despite these shortcomings, HRIAs constitute an invaluable process to systematically identify, predict and respond to the potential human rights impact of trade agreements particularly in consideration of the fact that the EU is increasingly establishing trade relationships with countries that are either notoriously human rights violators or that cannot prevent or stop human rights abuses from taking place in their own territory because they do not have the adequate governance and capacity-building to do so. Given that increasingly non-state actors perpetrate human rights breaches within states' territories, *ex ante* HRIAs could also assist states to fulfill due diligence obligations.[504]

---

[499] Human Rights Council (2008), para. 37.

[500] United Nations (UN) (2011) (known as "Guiding Principles on HRIA"); UN Guiding Principles on Business and Human Rights (United Nations Guiding Principles on Business and Human Rights: Implementing the United Nations "Protect, Respect and Remedy" Framework. Final Report of the Special Representative of the Secretary-General on the Issue of Human Rights and Transnational Corporations and other Business Enterprises, John Ruggie. 21 March 2011, A/HRC/17/31 (known as the "Ruggie Principles").

[501] For a detailed list and analysis of HRIAs, see Harrison (2010); for academic commentary, see Harrison (2011).

[502] Ibid.

[503] Ibid.

[504] Joseph (2011), at p. 272.

In the Joint Communication on *Human Rights and Democracy at the Heart of EU External Action—Towards a More Effective Approach*[505] there is an emphasis on the need to develop tailor-made approaches to human rights—relevant policies, including trade policy and the use of IAs to ensure human rights consistency.[506] Similarly, the EU Strategic Framework and Action Plan on *Human Rights and Democracy* emphasises the importance of inserting human rights in IAs.[507]

Since 2012, and in line with Article 21 TEU, a new generation of EU trade SIAs has thus started to integrate, albeit partially, human rights considerations into their research methodologies.[508] While trade HRIAs focus on state obligations, trade SIAs generally look at policy goals and the outcome of economic processes. For these EU trade SIAs of new generation (which in part derive their legitimacy from human rights obligations) to be credible they must be employed to draft international agreements with third countries or regions. However, studies show that this is not always the case.[509] Moreover, if potential negative impacts are expected the Trade SIA Handbook provides that consultants conducting the trade SIA should make recommendations to prevent or minimise them and make proposals for the adoption of flanking measures to maximise the benefits of the proposed agreement. Generally, EU trade SIAs tend to focus on so-called "mitigation" measures, which deal with negative impacts after the relevant agreement has come into force rather than amendments to the agreement to prevent negative impacts, or recommendations that the agreement should not come into force as currently constituted. From a human rights perspective the predilection for "mitigation" measures may not be an optimal way, however, of dealing with negative impact particularly in light of the fact that impact assessments are not fully accurate or do not consider all sectors of the economy where human rights abuses may potentially occur. As pointed out by Bürgi Bonanomi 'this limited set of responses available for trade SIAs reflects the assumptions underlying trade SIA processes: that FTAs are, in general, favourable to sustainable development, and that negative impacts can be adjusted. In contrast to trade HRIAs, which focus on risks, trade SIAs concentrate on opportunities and seek ways to optimally capture the opportunities provided by a new trade agreement'.[510]

According to the Guiding Principles on HRIA states have human rights obligations to both individuals on their territory and to individuals on the territory of the states with which they conclude a trade or an investment agreement.[511] The EU Trade SIA

---

[505] European Commission (2011).

[506] Ibid., pp. 11–12 and 19.

[507] Council of the European Union, above note 4, Action 1, p. 6.

[508] E.g. SIA of the EU–Georgia and EU–Moldova DCFTAs; European Commission, 'Guidelines on the analysis of human rights impacts in impact assessments for trade-related policy initiatives', Directorate-General for Trade, Brussels, July 2015, http://trade.ec.europa.eu/doclib/docs/2015/july/tradoc_153591.pdf, accessed on 20 March 2020; for detailed analysis of this new generation of trade SIAs, how they measure human rights impact of the trade agreements and the extent to which they are informed by human rights considerations, see Bürgi Bonanomi (2016).

[509] George and Kirkpatrick (2008).

[510] Bürgi Bonanomi (2014).

[511] UN Guiding Principles on HRIA 2011, Part II, 2.6, p. 6.

Handbook is in line with this approach but SIA practice reveals a different picture. Firstly, there is a problem of lack of consistency. The EU trade SIAs, such as the EU–ACP EPAs, have focused exclusively on the EU trade partners whereas on the other side of the spectrum the SIA of the EU–India FTA resulted in a comprehensive report on the overall economic, social, and environmental impacts on both partners.[512] An additional problem, as seen above, is that *ex ante* impact assessments may lack accuracy for a variety of reasons. Hence, more consistency is required in the EU SIA practice ensuring the assessment of human rights impacts is made in the EU and in the partner country concerned. The former, therefore, should always be combined with *ex post* assessments after implementation, which should also include human rights considerations. With the new generation of trade SIAs *ex post* evaluations are conducted to analyse the observed economic, social, environmental and human rights impacts. These evaluations are prepared by Commission services.[513] It is pivotal that the EU responds adequately to the findings of the *ex post* evaluation.

However, EU practice reveals that the EU does not always respond adequately to SIAs, which show the adverse impact of trade measures on human rights. The EU-ACP EPAs, examined above, are a case in point.[514] Without adequate safeguards the resultant damage to local production could disproportionately threaten the livelihoods and food security of rural populations, with the most affected being the Economic Community of West African States (ECOWAS) region, even though imports from other regions of the world would continue to provide tariff revenues. By the same token, Oxfam has also reported that the real winners of these EPAs would be EU member states and not ACP countries.[515]And yet the EU has insisted on the inclusion of a Most-Favoured Nation (MFN) provision in EPAs (encapsulating the WTO principles of reciprocity and non-discrimination), which reinforces the historical dependence of former colonies on the EU based on the ACP exporting primary low-cost goods and importing high-value goods.[516] This explains why to date there has been only one EPA finalised with ACP countries, namely the 2008 EU-Cariforum EPA, discussed above.

The foregoing shows that the combined use of *ex ante* trade SIAs and *ex post* evaluations could significantly contribute to strengthening the EU's practice of human rights conditionality in trade agreements, provided the methodologies employed in the *ex ante* trade SIAs and *ex post* evaluations increasingly take into consideration

---

[512]Bürgi Bonanomi, above no. 510, 14.

[513]Detailed information is available at: https://ec.europa.eu/info/law/law-making-process/evaluating-and-improving-existing-laws/evaluating-laws_en#:~:text=The%20Commission%20evaluates%20if%20specific,should%20be%20continued%20or%20changed, accessed on 14 June 2020.

[514]PricewaterhouseCoopers (2007); see also B. Sanoussi et al., above no. 496; CEPII-CIREM (2008).

[515]Oxfam (2008).

[516]Ibid. A study conducted for the EU Parliament clearly recommends that EPAs with ACP countries should not contain an MFN provision; European Parliament, 'African, Caribbean and Pacific (ACP) countries' position on Economic Partnership Agreements (EPAs)', EP Directorate-General for External Policies, Policy Department, EXPO/B/DEVE/2013/30, April 2014 at p. 7.

the human rights impact of EU trade agreements and, most importantly, that the EU acts upon their findings in a way which is not limited to maximising the benefits of trade agreements and minimising their potential negative impact.

Portela has put forward the idea of developing a targeted enforcement mechanism for TSD chapters of the new generation of FTAs, for cases concerning systematic and persistent violations of labour provisions, namely, the same type of violations of the principles of the ILO core Conventions that are envisaged for activating the enforcement mechanism under the GSP scheme.[517] In particular, this proposed enforcement mechanism draws inspiration from certain features of the EU's CFSP targeted restrictive measures or sanctions[518] and from the procedures of the enforcement mechanism under the GSP scheme. From a governance perspective, this enforcement mechanism would see the involvement of the European Council at the preliminary stage of the enforcement procedure, in an advisory capacity.[519] Allegations of severe breaches would be brought to the attention of the Commission by the EP, the EU member states and civil society actors from both the EU and the partner country, while the Commission would also act of its own accord. As for those who can be held responsible for the above violations, Portela foresees the application of sanctions at four levels, namely, individual, company, sector and country economy.[520] This is a significant feature of the proposed enforcement mechanism as it would see the application of sanctions not only to government actors but also to private actors. This is important insofar as corporate actors and economic operators generally commit many of the violations. Linked to that, the advantage of relying on targeted sanctions, as opposed to blanket sanctions, is that it reduces the negative externalities or effects on those who have not committed the violations and, in particular, on the partner country at large. Another added value of this enforcement mechanism is the gradualist approach in the application of the sanctions, which would foresee escalation, de-escalation and termination stages thus embracing the necessary flexibility required to take into account any changes in the initial situation, which led to the imposition of sanctions. The latter provides a further key benefit in that the availability of a workable sanction mechanism would act as a deterrent making its activation unnecessary. In the words of Portela: 'the critical implication is not that sanctions ought to be wielded more frequently but that a higher ease of employment may enhance its deterrent effect, persuading partners to comply with labour standards.'[521] This proposal would be in

---

[517] Portela, above no. 200, pp. 10–14. The proposed enforcement mechanism would also be applicable to the GSP scheme.

[518] For a detailed examination of CFSP sanctions, see Portela (2011); for critical analysis of the use of restrictive measures see, Poli (2017); on the use of targeted sanctions and human rights, see Happold (2016).

[519] At this stage the EU Commission would be deciding whether or not to proceed after consulting with the European Council. It is also noteworthy how this proposed enforcement mechanism draws on the overall enforcement procedure of the GSP scheme with an improved "targetability", Portela, above no. 200, at 10, citing Charnovitz (2005), at p. 161.

[520] Portela, above no. 200, at 12.

[521] Ibid., at 16.

line with the position of the EP, which has been calling for better enforcement of labour (and environmental) provisions of EU FTAs for several years.[522]

The above enforcement mechanism would certainly have many benefits and advantages not only for the reasons examined earlier but also because it would be based on the principle of reciprocity meaning that the EU would have to be prepared to be held responsible from its partner countries for breaches of labour standards.[523] However, this benefit also constitutes a limitation of the proposed enforcement mechanism because, as the analysis carried out in this chapter has shown, both in relation to the GSP scheme and bilateral agreements, the EU would probably remain reluctant to initiate any such enforcement mechanism. Many of its member states have been found by the ILO supervisory bodies to have violated certain ILO's core Conventions. In particular, in relation to trade agreements it may be questioned whether 'the EU's model is actually designed to be a two-way process of dialogue, or if it rather represents a form of "sophisticated unilateralism" wherein more powerful states negotiate provisions that reflect their own unilateral agenda, embedding them within a formally reciprocal structure.'[524] In a similar vein, it has been argued that the 'EU's discourse towards "soft power" [and its refusal to date to apply a fully-fledged sanction-based regime to enforce compliance with labour standards][525] should be seen as stemming both from the pursuit of international credibility and from a cost-effectiveness analysis'[526] which have been shaped and constrained by the internal and external context where decisions on labour standards have been taken.[527] At the internal level, the combined effect of decision-making rules and disagreement among EU member states 'have sometimes directed trade-labour linkage policies to a "lowest common denominator". At the external level, the EU's decisions have been shaped by the perceptions and market power of negotiating partners.'[528] Hence, a potential weakness of this proposal lies not in its very-well thought and elaborated design but in the "realpolitik" of labour standards in EU member states, which does not make it politically palatable. This explains why the European Commission while recognizing the need for change and envisaging several improvements to the implementation of the TSD chapter is not in favour of applying trade sanctions in cases of infringements of FTAs Sustainability chapters.[529]

Bronckers and Gruni[530] have put forward a proposal to allow labour standards to be enforced via a private complaint procedure before the European Commission,

---

[522] European Parliament (2010) para 22(a); European Parliament (2015) paras 22(c) and (d).

[523] Portela, above no. 200, at 13.

[524] Harrison et al., above no. 3, at 12.

[525] Author's addition.

[526] Adriaensen and González-Garibay (2013), at 553, and 549–555.

[527] Ibid., at 543.

[528] Ibid.

[529] European Commission (2017a, 2018a).

[530] Bronckers and Gruni (2018).

under the Trade Barriers Regulation (TBR).[531] Under the TBR, companies can file a complaint to the European Commission when a member state is not respecting an obligation set out in the agreement. The European Commission can then initiate an investigation and a number of actions can follow against the country concerned. This precedes the enforcement procedure of the FTA's dispute settlement mechanism. However, labour and environmental provisions are excluded from the set of rights which can be enforced under the TBR. The strength of Bronckers 'and Gruni's proposal consists in providing representative social partners[532] with the legal standing for filing a complaint whenever a member state is breaching labour standards protection provisions of an FTA. A system of financial penalties and trade sanctions is also envisaged for cases of persistent violations, as a measure of last resort.[533] The main limitation of their proposal is that it would add another layer to the dispute settlement mechanism (DSM) of a trade agreement, in what would probably be a lengthy and cumbersome process.

5.3.4 Recommendations

Sengenberger—[534] formerly Director of the ILO's Employment Strategy Department and the ILO's Working Group on the Social Dimensions of Globalization and Liberalization of Trade—has listed what he considers to be the necessary (and interlinked) conditions for international labour standards (ILS) to be respected. First, there has to be an understanding of and respect for ILS in the political arena and

---

[531] European Parliament and European Council (2015). For a proposal extending the model of Investor-State Dispute Settlement (ISDS) to the provisions of the Trade and Sustainable Development Chapter, see Gött (2018).

[532] As per the recognition procedure of Article 154 TFEU. Their proposal—as suggested—would address the so-called "insider-outsider dilemma" of civil society representatives, including social partners who are often reluctant to take part in an enforcement mechanism of a trade agreement that they seldom approve of. This dilemma is exacerbated by the lack of transparency of the negotiation process that typifies the adoption of EU trade agreements. For instance, the meetings of the Civil Society Dialogue on Trade have largely acted as an informative session rather than providing the forum for active participation and real dialogue, see further Moore and Scherrer, above no. 459, at 13. This state of affairs also extend to domestic organized labour, see Harrison et al., above no. 462, at 266.

[533] In this sense, see the Free Trade Agreement between the United States and Chile (USCFTA), signed on 6 June 2003 and entered into force on 1 January 2004, see the U.S.-Chile Free Trade Agreement Implementation Act ("the Act"; Public Law 108-77; 117 Stat. 909; 19 U.S.C. 3805 note). The final text is available at: https://ustr.gov/archive/Trade_Agreements/Bilateral/Chile_FTA/Final_Texts/Section_Index.html, accessed on 14 June 2020. It is the first FTA between the United States and a South American country. The 2004 USCFTA is an example of best practice, specifically for including an enforcement mechanism which combines sanction and incentive-based procedures thereby including the payment of fines into a fund for improving the specific labour rights violations that occurred, alongside the removal of trade preferences as a last resort; see Article 22.16 subpara. 4. of the 2004 USCFTA.

[534] Sengenberger (2009).

institutional setting and for this to take place there has to be strong economic performance and political will. The former are pre-conditions for a set of conditions, which will then determine the respect for ILS. Specifically, adequate and effective regulatory and legal frameworks with strong labour institutions, domestic civil society and social partners (particularly independent trade unions), as well as policy coherence at national and international levels.

Drawing on Sengenberger's key conditions for respecting ILS, we outline various recommendations on certain important aspects of social conditionality that, at the time of writing, present deficiencies and limitations. With regard to monitoring mechanisms the EU could strengthen them by making the relevant committee and/or institution a more fully-fledged body with a clear and common structure and composition across all of its trade agreements and operating on a permanent basis. This would allow for more consistency across the EU's trade agreements. By way of example, the DAG, which is becoming the main formal body to monitor the implementation of trade agreements, particularly since the 2008 EU-CARIFORUM EPA,[535] could become the standard form of monitoring the implementation of all future EU trade agreements with a complaints mechanism via public submissions attached to the DAGs.[536] In this context, the inclusion of civil society should be institutionalized and made compulsory rather than being left to governments' discretion with regular meetings taking place rather than on an annual basis.[537] In this regard, Bartels[538] suggests the setting up of national contact point and establishing a well-defined public submission process, which is common in other jurisdictions outside of the EU.[539] Significantly, the EU Commission has indicated how Global Aid for Trade funding, and the G7's Vision Zero Fund could be utilized to develop projects to deliver on TSD chapter objectives.[540] It is notable that the EU Commission has also

---

[535]The 2008 EU-CARIFORUM EPA provided the blueprint for a new monitoring mechanism that envisages changes to the agreement whenever problems arise during the implementation process. A number of institutions and bodies play a pivotal role in implementing the agreement. The Joint CARIFORUM-EU Council, the highest organ at ministerial level (Article 227), which is supported by the Trade and Development Committee (Article 230), meeting annually at senior official level. These institutions discuss all questions concerning the EPA. The Parliamentary Committee (Article 231) draws on the Lomé and the Cotonou agreements and foresees the involvement of parliaments. The most innovative body of the EPA is the Consultative Committee, which is composed of representatives of civil society, academics, and the social and business partners, and is entitled to make recommendations to the EPA Council and the Trade and Development (Article 232). This institution could play a key role in identifying the implementation problems and ways forward to address them. However, the meetings should be held more than once a year with better funding, see Schmieg (2015), at 26.

[536]To date only the EU-South Korea DAG meets on a regular basis.

[537]Van Den Putte (2015b), at 225.

[538]Bartels (2014a), at 18.

[539]E.g. the 1993 NAALC provides for the establishment of national administrative offices in the Ministry of Labour (NAOs, e.g. Articles 15-16). It also provides for any person or group (the "submitter") in a NAFTA country may file a submission with a NAO, not in the country to which the dispute relates, alleging that one or other of the governments has failed effectively to enforce its labour laws (Article 16(3), namely, public complaints referred to in the text as "public communications").

[540]EU Commission, above no. 529, at p. 7.

been using its Partnership Instrument to fund projects concerning the TSD chapter.[541] In addition, other development cooperation financial mechanisms could be employed to finance further projects to improving the impact of the TSD on domestic labour standards, such as the Development Cooperation Instrument, European Instrument for Democracy and Human Rights, and the European Development Fund.[542] Moreover, consultation processes should have stipulations on the time needed to consider complaints or submissions and the panel of experts' composition could include social partners from both trading partners.

With regard to improving the enforcement of labour provisions, the EU could follow the US' steps and incorporate pre-ratification conditions to the signing of trade agreements, as they are most likely to be complied with or enforced given the clarity and measurability of the conditions to be met.[543] These *ex-ante* conditions could demand the signing of new ILO conventions, followed by the adoption of implementing domestic legislation; require the setting up of labour inspectorates or develop capacity-building programmes combined with *ex-post* monitoring processes in collaboration with the ILO. Moreover, these programmes could be linked to aid and training programmes. The EU Commission has opened up to this possibility in one of its non-papers, where it proposes to 'encourage early ratification of core international agreements' (including the eight core ILO Conventions) during the negotiation of new trade agreements.[544]

In addition, there should be a formal role for civil society, including social partners, in the DSM of trade agreements, which should be extended to the whole agreement including the TSD Chapter.[545] In this context, the ILO could play an important consultative role as a last resort for particularly complex disputes. This change not only ensures consistency in the way the DSM is applied but also ensures overall coherence and credibility of the EU's normative mission vis-à-vis the trade-labour linkage by further integrating ILS into economic trade concerns. There should also be rules in place that require the trading partners to ensure that the trade, public

---

[541] E.g. to improve the involvement and activities of civil society and to foster responsible supply chains.

[542] Harrison et al., above no. 3, at p. 17.

[543] E.g. the 2006 US-Morocco Free Trade Agreement, final text available at: https://ustr.gov/trade-agreements/free-trade-agreements/morocco-fta/final-text, the 2006 US-Bahrain Free Trade Agreement, available at: https://ustr.gov/trade-agreements/free-trade-agreements/bahrain-fta/final-text, the 2009 US-Oman Free Trade Agreement, available at: https://ustr.gov/trade-agreements/free-trade-agreements/oman-fta/final-text, the 2012 US-Colombia Trade Promotion Agreement, available at: https://ustr.gov/trade-agreements/free-trade-agreements/morocco-fta/final-text, all accessed on 14 June 2020; for detailed analysis, see ILO (2013a).

[544] European Commission (2018a), above no. 529, p. 2.

[545] E.g. the 2009 US-Peru Trade Promotion Agreement, final text available at: https://ustr.gov/trade-agreements/free-trade-agreements/peru-tpa/final-text, Article 21.2 entitled 'Scope of Application' of the DSM of the agreement, which provides that: '1. Except as otherwise provided in this Agreement, the dispute settlement provisions of this Chapter shall apply with respect to the avoidance or settlement of all disputes between the Parties regarding the interpretation or application of this Agreement [...],' accessed on 23 March 2020.

procurement and investment protection provisions of an agreement do not impact negatively on labour protection.[546]

Moreover, there should be rules to ensure more transparency in the way the DSM functions and provide timelines, particularly in relation to decisions concerning public submissions and the settlement of disputes.[547]

For labour violations, as evidenced by the ILO's supervisory bodies, international and national NGOs reports, there should be a combined punitive and incentive-based system whereby sanctions (imposed as a last resort) work alongside incentives, tied with capacity-building and cooperation programmes and aid through the technical assistance and monitoring of the ILO and local NGOs and trade unions.[548]

The above changes should also be made by taking into consideration the specificities and peculiarities of the trading partner concerned, which has also been recognized by the EU Commission in relation to TSD issues.[549] In the words of Harrison, Barbu, Campling, Richardson and Smith: 'In the same way that the EU has addressed context-specific commercial issues in a bespoke manner (such as in the annex to deal with non-tariff barriers in auto-mobile parts under the Korea FTA), it ought to extend the same treatment to fundamental labour rights by designing provisions that articulate with the most pressing labour issues in each trade partner.'[550] In broader terms, it is also equally important for developing an effective design of the TSD chapters, that the EU makes the purposes of the insertion of labour provisions in trade agreements

[546]E.g. Article 10(1) and (2)a and c, of the new agreement between the EU and Mexico entitled 'Other Trade- and Investment-related Initiatives Favouring Sustainable Development' provides that:

1. The Parties confirm their commitment to enhance the contribution of trade and investment to the goal of sustainable development in its economic, social and environmental dimensions.
2. Pursuant to paragraph 1, the Parties shall promote:

   (a) trade and invest ent policies that support the objectives of the Decent Work Agenda, consistent with the 2008 ILO Declaration on Social Justice for a Fair Globalisation, including policies in regard to wages, earnings and working hours, inclusive social protection, health and safety at work, and other aspects related to working conditions;
   (b) trade in goods that contribute to enhanced social conditions and environmentally sound practices, including goods that are the subject of voluntary sustainability assurance schemes such as fair and ethical trade schemes and eco-labels;

3. Each Party should cooperate with the other Party bilaterally, regionally and in international fora on issues in this article.

[547]In their draft Sustainability Chapter, Lukas and Steinkellner suggest specific time frames. In particular, they suggest that submissions should be considered by a panel of experts within 90 days after the delivery of the request for consultations (Article 15); they also suggest that the parties to an agreement should within 180 days after the entry into force of the agreement, enter into discussions to adopt rules of procedure, which should be the role of the Committee on the Trade and Sustainable Development (Article 16(11), see Lukas and Steinkellner (2010), p. 20.

[548]In particular for sanctions the monetary fine should go into a fund that would specifically target the labour violation under consideration, e.g. 2004 US-Chile FTA.

[549]EU Commission, above no. 529, at p. 2.

[550]Harrison et al. above no. 462, at 273.

more explicit, addressing the key questions of 'for who?' and 'to achieve what?' For this reason, it is important to combine the use of *ex ante* trade SIAs with *ex post* evaluations of trade agreements.[551]

The design and application of these recommendations are in need of further development and should be carefully explored and elaborated further, on the basis of future empirically grounded research.

5.4 Conclusion

> But although the opening up of markets produces benefits to many, it also creates adjustments costs, which we cannot ignore. These adjustments must not be relegated to the future: they must be an integral part of the opening-up agenda. This is what I call the "Geneva consensus": a belief that trade opening works for development but only if we address the imbalances it creates between winners and losers, imbalances that are all the more dangerous the more fragile the economies, societies or countries. This is the only way to ensure that the opening up of markets will produce real benefits to all people in their everyday lives. [...]
>
> We need to remember that trade is only a tool to elevate the human condition; the ultimate impact of our rules on human beings should always be at the centre of our consideration. We should work first for human beings and for the well-being of our humanity. I want to believe that the new "Geneva consensus" has the potential to succeed in contributing to the process of humanising globalization and establishing further justice and equity.'[552]
>
> Pascal Lamy,
>
> Santiago de Chile,
>
> January 2006

The words of Pascal Lamy, former Director-General of the WTO, forcefully remind us of the normative nature and cogency of the interconnectedness between trade and labour in the context of new and more complex globalization and transnational forces. Like Sen, Lamy emphasizes the centrality of humanity's well-being and dignifying standards of living. However, the relationship between trade and labour remains complex, partly because the liberalization and de-territorialization of trade has progressed much further, in terms of depth and political commitment, than labour which has remained "relatively immobile",[553] with little progress on enforceable global labour standards. Whilst in the context of a globalized economy, questions of workers' rights have increasingly been elevated to the global stage, transnational labour regulation has been developing at a slow pace and not in a consistent manner, with domestic regulation still remaining the main tool for protecting workers' rights.

The chapter illustrated and critically examined this state of affairs by tracing the historical developments of the trade-labour linkage at international and EU levels,

---

[551] As outlined in detail in Sect. 5.3.5.

[552] Lamy (2006a); see also Lamy (2006b).

[553] Hepple, above no. 31, at p. 5.

its foundations and the reasons for its promotion. In this context, it analyzed the partnership of the EU and the ILO, together with other international organizations, local civil society organizations and (to a lesser extent) social partners, in promoting the social dimension of international trade agreements and instruments.

In spite of these EU-ILO joint efforts, and the combined use of hard and more experimentalist forms of governance and implementation, problems concerning the enforceability (and thus credibility) of social conditionality in EU external trade policy remain. There is a growing body of evidence showing that EU practice does not always reflect the objectives set out in EU discourse on social trade. In particular, the chapter showed how the EU still devotes relatively little attention to the actual implementation and continued enforcement of labour provisions included in its external trade instruments. This is particularly the case for the EU's FTAs, which have become the main modus operandi of the EU's external trade relations. Once the agreements enter into force, their impact on domestic labour conditions in the partner-countries remains limited.

The reasons for the EU's continuous reluctance to rely on a more punitive and less cooperative or promotional approach are many and, in some instances legitimate. Indeed, there are valid explanations for refraining from adopting a sanction-based approach. However, we have seen that the EU's own inability to develop a robust and cohesive social dimension to its internal market is also a decisive factor in explaining the limited impact of EU social trade externally, which is compounded by the EU's reluctance to invest more in resources to ensure the monitoring and implementation of the labour provisions in FTAs.

Clearly, more consideration must be given to removing the inconsistencies in EU practice, adding more clarity to the nature of the labour provisions' obligations contained in EU external trade instruments. Stronger mechanisms—such as pre-ratification conditionality, combined negative and positive social conditionality with increased participation of organized civil society, and investment in monitoring and capacity building—need to be developed to strengthen the impact of EU social conditionality on domestic labour conditions.

References

International Law

Documents from International Organizations

Organisation for Economic Co-operation and Development (OECD)

OECD (1996) Trade, employment and labour standards: a study of core workers' rights and international trade. OECD Publishing
OECD (2000) International Trade and Core Labour Standards. OECD Publishing
OECD (2011) Guidelines for multinational enterprises. OECD Publishing. Available at: http://dx.doi.org/10.1787/9789264115415-en. Accessed 5 Sept 2019

International Labour Organisation (ILO)

ILO, Constitution of the International Labour Organisation, 1 Apr 1919
ILO, Tripartite Declaration of Principles concerning Multinational Enterprises and Social Policy, adopted by the Governing Body of the International Labour Office at its 204th Session (Geneva, November 1977) and amended at its 279th (November 2000), 295th (March 2006) and 329th (March 2017) Sessions. The International Labour Office, Geneva, Switzerland. Available at: https://www.ilo.org/wcmsp5/groups/public/---ed_emp/---emp_ent/---multi/documents/publication/wcms_094386.pdf. Accessed 14 June 2020
ILO Convention C105 on the Abolition of Forced Labour, 1957 (No. 105), 25 September 1991
ILO Convention C182 on the Worst Forms of Child Labour, 1999 (No. 182), 2 December 1999
ILO 'Your Voice at Work: Global Report under the Follow-Up to the Declaration on Fundamental Principles and Rights at Work'. Available at: https://perma.cc/AT8W-ATAF. Accessed 22 Mar 2020
ILO, Declaration on Social Justice for a Fair Globalisation, adopted by the International Labour Conference, at its Ninety-seventh Session, Geneva, 10 June 2008. Available at: https://www.ilo.org/wcmsp5/groups/public/---dgreports/---cabinet/documents/genericdocument/wcms_371208.pdf. Accessed 20 Mar 2020
ILO, The Impact of EU Development on Agenda for Change (COM(2011) 637 final
ILO (2011a) Towards a greener economy: the social dimensions. International Institute for Labour Studies, Geneva
ILO (2011b) Building a Sustainable Job-Rich Recovery. Geneva
ILO, Committee on Freedom of Association, Case No. 2602 (Republic of Korea) (Interim Report No 359, March 2011)
ILO (2013a) Social dimensions of free trade agreements. Studies on growth with equity. International Institute for Labour Studies, 6 Nov 2013. Available at: http://www.ilo.org/global/research/publications/WCMS_228965/lang–en/index.htm. Accessed 14 June 2020
ILO (2013b) The ILO and the EU, partners for decent work and social justice. Impact of ten years of cooperation. Report, ILO, Geneva, Switzerland. Available at: https://www.ilo.org/wcmsp5/groups/public/---europe/---ro-geneva/---ilo-brussels/documents/publication/wcms_195135.pdf. Accessed 14 June 2020

ILO (2016) Assessment of labour provisions in trade and investment arrangements. Geneva, Switzerland. Available at: www.ilo.org/global/about-the-ilo/newsroom/news/WCMS_499348/lang–en/index.htm. Accessed 6 Feb 2017
ILO (2017) Handbook on assessment of labour provisions in trade and investment arrangements. Geneva. Available at: https://www.ilo.org/wcmsp5/groups/public/---dgreports/---inst/documents/publication/wcms_564702.pdf. Accessed 23 Mar 2020
ILO, Better work, Jordan annual report: an industry and compliance review. Available at: https://betterwork.org/blog/portfolio/better-work-jordan-annual-report-2018-an-industry-and-compliance-review/. Accessed 14 June 2020

ILO Committee on Freedom of Association

Case No. 2460 (United States)—Complaint date: 07-DEC-05—The United Electrical, Radio and Machine Workers of America (UE) supported by Public Services International (PSI)
Case No. 2524 (United States)—Complaint date: 20-OCT-06 American Federation of Labor and Congress of Industrial Organizations (AFL-CIO)
Case No. 2547 (United States)—Complaint date: 26-FEB-07 United Automobile, Aerospace and Agricultural Implement Workers of America International Union (UAW) and American Federation of Labor and Congress of Industrial Organizations (AFL-CIO)

Committee of Experts on the Application of Conventions and Recommendations (CEACR)

CEACR, Individual Observation concerning Freedom of Association and Protection of the Right to Organise Convention, 1948 Nr. 87 Colombia (ratification: 1976), published: 2006
CEACR, Observation on the Freedom of Association and Protection of the Right to Organise Convention, 1948 (No. 87), 105th ILC sess (2016, adopted 2015) ('United Kingdom')
CEACR, Individual Observation Concerning Convention Nr. 87 (Germany), 1991
CEACR, Individual Observation Concerning Convention Nr. 87 (Germany), 2003
CEACR, Individual Observation Concerning Convention Nr. 87 (UK) in 2003 and 2007 and Concerning Convention Nr. 98 in 2002
CEACR, Individual Observation Concerning Convention Nr. 87 (Germany), 2005 and 2006
CEACR, Observation (CEACR)—adopted 2012, published 102nd ILC session (2013) Freedom of Association and Protection of the Right to Organise Convention, 1948 (No. 87)—Sweden (Ratification: 1949)
CEACR, Report of the Committee of Experts on the Application of Conventions and Recommendations, International Labour Conference, 106th Session, 2017, ILC.106/III(1A)
CEACR, Examination of individual case concerning Convention No. 87, Freedom of Association and Protection of the Right to Organise, 1948 Colombia (ratification: 1976), published: 2005, Conclusions; Case No. 1787 (Colombia), Report No. 343 (Vol. LXXXVIX, 2006, Series B, No. 3)
CEACR, Report of the Committee of Experts on the Application of Conventions and Recommendations, International Labour Conference, 106th Session, 2017, ILC.106/III(1A). Available at: https://www.ilo.org/wcmsp5/groups/public/---ed_norm/---relconf/documents/meetingdocument/wcms_543646.pdf. Accessed 14 June 2020

United Nations

United Nations (2011) Guiding Principles on Human Rights Impact Assessments of Trade and Investment Agreements, Report of the Special Rapporteur on the Right to Food, Olivier de Schutter, 19 December 2011. A/HRC/19/59/Add.5

United Nations General Assembly, Resolution on Transforming our world: the 2030 Agenda for Sustainable Development, Seventieth session, 25 September 2015. Available at: https://www.un.org/ga/search/view_doc.asp?symbol=A/RES/70/1&Lang=E. Accessed 14 June 2020

United Nations General Assembly, Report of the Special Rapporteur on the situation of human rights in Myanmar, A/73/332, 20 August 2018. Available at: http://undocs.org/A/73/332. Accessed 23 Mar 2020

United Nations Conference on Trade and Employment, Havana Charter for an International Trade Organization, Havana, Cuba, 24 March 1948. A full text is available at: https://www.wto.org/english/docs_e/legal_e/havana_e.pdf. Accessed 14 June 2020

United Nations Economic and Social Council (ECOSOC)

ECOSOC, Office for the Economic and Social Council (ECOSOC) Support and Coordination, Department of Economic and Social Affairs of the United Nations, 'Full and Productive Employment and Decent Work Dialogues at the Economic and Social Council' United Nations, New York. Available at: https://www.un.org/en/ecosoc/docs/pdfs/ecosoc_book_2006.pdf. Accessed 14 June 2020

Human Rights Council

Human Rights Council, 'Application of the criteria for periodic evaluation of global development partnerships—as defined in Millennium Development Goal 8—from the right to development perspective: the Cotonou Partnership Agreement between the European Union and ACP Countries (Report by Professor James Thuo Gathii), UN doc. A/HRC/8/WG.2/TF/CRP.6 (21 December 2007), 2

Human Rights Council, Report of the Special Rapporteur on the situation of human rights in Myanmar, A/HRC/31/71, 1 March 2016. Available at: https://www.ohchr.org/EN/HRBodies/HRC/RegularSessions/Session37/Documents/A-HRC-37-70.docx. Accessed 14 June 2020

Human Rights Council, 'Report of the Special Rapporteur on the Right to Food, Olivier De Schutter: Mission to the World Trade Organisation', UN doc. A/HRC/10/5/Add.2 (25 June 2008)

United Nations Human Rights Office of the High Commissioner (OHCHR)

Office of the United Nations High Commissioner for Human Rights, Human Rights Impact Assessments for Trade and Investment Agreements, Report of the Expert Seminar, 23–24 June 2010, Geneva, Switzerland, accessed 6 February 2017. Available at: www2.ohchr.org/english/issues/food/docs/report_hria-seminar_2010.pdf. Accessed 14 June 2020

United Nations High Commissioner for Human Rights on the Situation of Human Rights in Colombia' A/HRC/16/22 of 3 February 2011. Available at: http://www.ohchr.org/Documents/HRBodies/HRCouncil/RegularSession/Session19/A-HRC-19-21-Add3_en.pdf. Accessed 14 June 2020

World Trade Organisation (WTO)

World Trade Organisation, Marrakesh Agreement Establishing the World Trade Organization, 15 April 1994, 1867 U.N.T.S 154, Preamble. Available at: https://www.wto.org/english/docs_e/legal_e/04-wto.pdf. Accessed 14 June 2020

WTO, Ministerial Conference, Singapore, WT/MIN(96)/DEC/Ministerial Conference Singapore: Declaration, § 4, 13 December 1996

World Trade Organisation, WTO Waiver on the Generalized System of Preferences Decision of 25 June 1971, BISD 18S/24

WTO/GATT Decision of 28 November 1979, *Differential and More Favourable Treatment, Reciprocity and Fuller Participation of Developing Countries* (the "Enabling Clause"), GATT BISD, 26th Supp, 203, GATT Doc L/4903

World Trade Organisation, Appellate Body Report, *United States – Import Prohibition of Certain Shrimp and Shrimp Products*, WT/DS58/AB/R, adopted 6 November 1998

World Bank Group

World Bank Group, 'Global Economic Prospects, January 2016: Spillovers Amid Weak Growth', World Bank, Washington, DC. Available at: https://openknowledge.worldbank.org/handle/10986/23435. Accessed 14 June 2020

World Commission on the Social Dimension of Globalization

World Commission on the Social Dimensions of Globalization, Report on *A Fair Globalization: Creating Opportunities for All*. https://www.ilo.org/public/english/wcsdg/docs/report.pdf. Accessed 14 June 2020

European Union Official Documents

International Agreements of the European Union

Partnership Agreement between the members of the African, Caribbean and Pacific Group of States of the one part, and the European Community and its Member States, of the other part, signed in Cotonou on 23 June 2000, OJ L317, 15/12/2000, p 3

Economic Partnership Agreement, between the CARIFORUM States, of the one part, and the European Community and its Member States, of the other part (OJ [2008] L289, 30/10/2008, p 3)
Free Trade Agreement between the European Union and its Member States of the one part, and the Republic of Korea of the other part (EU-Korea FTA) *OJ* [2011] L127/6, 14 May 2011, p 6
Trade Agreement between the European Union and its Member States, of the one part, and Colombia and Peru, of the other part (2012) *OJ* [2012] L354/3, 21 December 2012, p 3
Framework Agreement on Comprehensive Partnership and Cooperation between the European Union and its Member States, of the one part, and the Socialist Republic of Viet Nam, of the other part of 27 June 2012. Available at: https://eur-lex.europa.eu/legal-content/EN/TXT/?uri=CELEX%3A22016A1203%2802%29. Accessed 14 June 2020
Agreement establishing an Association between the European Union and its Member States, on the one hand, and Central America on the other (2012) (EU-CAAA) *OJ* [2012] L346/3, 15 December 2012, p 3
Comprehensive Economic and Trade Agreement (CETA) (2014) between Canada, of the one part, and the European Union and its Member States of the other part, Consolidate Text published 26 September 2014. Available at: http://trade.ec.europa.eu/doclib/docs/2014/september/tradoc_152806.pdf. 14 June 2020
Free Trade Agreement between the European Union and Singapore, 17 October 2014, Authentic text as of May 2015. Available at: http://trade.ec.europa.eu/doclib/press/index.cfm?id=961. Accessed 14 June 2020
Free Trade Agreement between the European Union and the Socialist Republic of Vietnam, (2016) Agreed Text as of January 2016. Available at: http://trade.ec.europa.eu/doclib/press/index.cfm?id=1437. Accessed 14 June 2020
Joint Interpretative Instrument on the Comprehensive Economic and Trade Agreement (CETA) Between Canada and the European Union and its Member States, OJ 14.1.2017, L11/3
Agreement between the European Union and Japan for an Economic Partnership, OJ L 330/3 27.12.2018, Chapter 16

Table of cases

Cases of the Court of Justice of the European Union

General Court

Case T-754/14, *Efler and Others v Commission*, ECLI:EU:T:2017:323

European Court of Justice

C-438/05 *International Transport Workers' Federation v Viking Line ABP* ECLI:EU:C:2007:772
C-341/05 *Laval un Partneri Ltd v Svenska Byggnadsarbetareförbundet* ECLI:EU:C:2007:772
Opinion 2/15 Request for an opinion submitted by the European Commission pursuant to Article 218(11) TFEU, *OJ* [2015] C 363/22, 3.11.2015

Official Documents of the EU Institutions and BodiesOfficial Documents of the EU Institutions and Bodies

European Commission

European Commission, Communication from the Commission, A Sustainable Europe for a Better World: A European Union Strategy for Sustainable Development (Commission's proposal to the Gothenburg European Council) /* COM/2001/0264 final */; further information can be found at: https://ec.europa.eu/environment/sustainable-development/strategy/index_en.htm. Accessed 14 June 2020

European Commission, *Proposal for a Council Regulation applying a scheme of generalized tariff preferences* COM(2004) 699

European Commission, *Proposal for a council regulation temporarily withdrawing access to the generalised tariff preferences from the Republic of Belarus* COM (2006) 438 final

European Commission, Communication from the Commission to the Council, the European Parliament, the European Economic and Social Committee and the Committee of the Regions of 4 October 2006 'Global Europe: Competing in the world' COM(2006) 567 final

European Commission, Decision 2008/316/EC of 31 March 2008 providing for the initiation of an investigation pursuant to Article 18(2) of Council Regulation (EC) No. 980/2005 with respect to the protection of the freedom of association and the right to organize in El Salvador OJ [2008] L 108/29, 18 Apr 2008

European Commission, Report of the Investigation pursuant to Article 18(2) of the Council Regulation (EC) No. 980/2005 with respect to the protection of the freedom of association and the right to organize in El Salvador, C(2009) 7934 (2009)

European Commission, Report on the findings of investigation with respect to the effective implementation of certain human rights conventions in Sri Lanka, Brussels, Belgium, 19 October 2009, C(2009) 7999. Available at: https://reliefweb.int/sites/reliefweb.int/files/resources/9501F5EFE0C4F6C449257655000EECA5-Full_Report.pdf. Accessed 14 June 2020

European Commission, Implementing Regulation (EU) No. 143/2010 of 15 February 2010 temporarily withdrawing the special incentive arrangement for sustainable development and good governance provided under the Regulation (EC) No 732/2008 with respect to the Democratic Socialist Republic of Sri Lanka, OJ [2010] L 45/2010, 22.7.2010, p 1

European Commission, Press release, 'EU regrets silence of Sri Lanka regarding preferential import regime' of 5 July 2010, IP/10/888. https://ec.europa.eu/commission/presscorner/detail/en/IP_10_888. Accessed 14 June 2020

European Commission, Communication from the Commission to the European Parliament, the Council, the European Economic and Social Committee and the Committee of the Regions, Increasing the Impact of EU Development Policy: an Agenda for Change COM(2011) 637 final

European Commission, Implementing Decision 2012/161/EU of 19 March 2012 providing for the initiation of an investigation pursuant to Article 17(2) of Council Regulation (EC) No. 732/2008 with respect to the effective implementation of the United Nations Single Convention on Narcotic Drugs in Bolivia OJ [2012] L 80, 20.3.2012

European Commission, Commission Delegated Regulation (EU) No. 155/2013 of 18 December 2012

European Commission, Commission Delegated Regulation (EU) No. 1083/2013 of 28 August 2013 establishing rules related to the procedure for temporary withdrawal of tariff preferences and adoption of general safeguard measures under Regulation (EU) No. 978/2012 of the European Parliament and the Council applying a scheme of generalized tariff preferences

European Commission, DG Trade, 'Joint Statement by EU Trade Commissioner Karel De Gucht and Bangladesh Foreign Minister Dr Dipu Moni following recent disasters in the Bangladeshi garment manufacturing industry' (Brussels, 28 May 2013). Available at: https://ec.europa.eu/commission/presscorner/detail/es/IP_13_667. Accessed 14 June 2020

European Commission Final report on 'The Use, Scope and Effectiveness of Labour and Social Provisions and Sustainable Development Aspects in Bilateral and Regional Free Trade Agreements', 15 September 2008, Chapter 2. Available at: https://ec.europa.eu/social/BlobServlet?docId=2111&langId=en. Accessed 14 June 2020

European Commission, Trade for All—Towards a More Responsible Trade and Investment Policy, 6 February 2017. Available at: trade.ec.europa.eu/doclib/docs/2015/october/tradoc_153846.pdf. Accessed 14 June 2020

European Commission, EU textual proposal: trade and sustainable development in TTIP. Brussels, Belgium. Available at: https://trade.ec.europa.eu/doclib/docs/2015/november/tradoc_153923.pdf. Accessed 14 June 2020

European Commission, Better Regulation Guidelines, COM(2015) 215 final

European Commission, Better regulation toolbox. Available at: ec.europa.eu/smart-regulation/guidelines/docs/br_toolbox_en.pdf. Accessed 14 June 2020

European Commission, Commission Delegated Regulation (EU) 2015/602 of 5 February 2015 amending Regulation (EU) No 978/2012 of the European Parliament and the Council as regards the vulnerability threshold defined in point 1(b) of Annex VII to that Regulation, OJ L100/8, 17.4.2015

European Commission, *Joint Staff Working Document on the EU Special Incentive Arrangement for Sustainable Development and Good Governance (GSP+) covering the period 2014–2015*

European Commission, GSP+ *Report on Sustainability, Human Rights and Good Governance*. Questions and Answers. Brussels, Belgium, 28.01.2016. Available at: trade.ec.europa.eu/doclib/docs/2016/january/tradoc_154179.pdf. Accessed 14 June 2020

European Commission, 'Human Rights and Sustainable Development in the EU-Vietnam Relations with specific regard to the EU-Vietnam Free Trade Agreement', Commission Staff Working Document, Brussels, 26.1.2016, SWD(2016) 21 final

European Commission, Joint Staff Working Document on the EU Special Incentive Arrangement for Sustainable Development and Good Governance (GSP+) covering the period 2014–2015, Brussels, 28.01.2016, SWD (2016) 8 final

European Commission, Report from the Commission to the European Parliament and the Council, Report on the Generalised Scheme of Preferences Covering the Period 2014–2015, COM(2016) 29 final, Brussels, 28.1.2016 (SWD2016) 8 final)

European Commission (2016a) Handbook for trade sustainability impact assessment. Available at: http://trade.ec.europa.eu/doclib/docs/2016/april/tradoc_154464.PDF. Accessed 14 June 2020

European Commission (2016b) DG trade, Nilsson L, EU trade policy: recent progress and analytical advances. In: GIFTA workshop on social and labour impacts of free trade agreements, German Marshall Fund, Brussels, July 2016

European Commission, 'Reflection Paper on Harnessing Globalisation' 10 May 2017, pp 14–15, COM(2017) 240

European Commission (2017a) Trade and sustainable development chapters in EU free trade agreements, non-paper, 11 July 2017. Available at: http://trade.ec.europa.eu/doclib/docs/2017/july/tradoc_155686.pdf. Accessed 14 June 2020

European Commission, Mid-Term Evaluation of the EU's Generalised System of Trade Preferences (GSP), Final Interim Report, prepared by DEVELOPMENT Solutions for the Directorate-General for Trade Directorate D—Sustainable Development; Economic Partnership Agreements—Africa Caribbean and Pacific; Agri-food and Fisheries Unit D1—Trade and Sustainable Development, Generalised system of Preferences, Brussels, Belgium, 21 September 2017. Available at: https://trade.ec.europa.eu/doclib/docs/2018/october/tradoc_157434.pdf. Accessed 14 June 2020

European Commission (2017b) Implementation of the Bangladesh compact: technical status report. Available at: http://trade.ec.europa.eu/doclib/docs/2017/october/tradoc_156343.pdf. Accessed 14 June 2020

European Commission (2017c) Commission Delegated Regulation (EU) 2017/836 of 11 January 2017 amending Annex III to Regulation (EU) No 978/2012 of the European Parliament and of the Council applying a scheme of generalised tariff preferences, OJ 18.5.2017 L 125/1

European Commission, 'EU Grants Sri Lanka Improved Access to Its Market as Incentive for Reform', Press Release IP/17/1363, Brussels, Belgium, May 17, 2017. Available at: http://trade.ec.europa.eu/doclib/press/index.cfm?id=1663. Accessed 14 June 2020

European Commission, Evaluation of the Implementation of the Free Trade Agreement between the EU and its Member States and the Republic of Korea Interim Technical Report Part 1: Synthesis Report, prepared by Civic Consulting and the Ifo Institute, June 2017. Available at: https://trade.ec.europa.eu/doclib/docs/2017/june/tradoc_155673.pdf. Accessed 14 June 2020

European Commission (2018a) Feedback and way forward on improving the implementation and enforcement of trade and sustainable development chapters in EU free trade agreements, non-paper, 26 February 2018. Available at: http://trade.ec.europa.eu/doclib/docs/2018/february/tradoc_156618.pdf. Accessed 14 June 2020

European Commission, 'Staying Engaged: The Sustainability Compact for the Bangladesh Ready Made Garment Sector'. Available at: https://trade.ec.europa.eu/doclib/docs/2018/june/tradoc_157065.pdf. 14 June 2020

European Commission (2018b) Feedback and way forward on improving the implementation and enforcement of Trade and Sustainable Development chapters in EU Free Trade Agreements. Directorate General for Trade, Brussels, Belgium, 26 February 2018. Available at: https://trade.ec.europa.eu/doclib/docs/2018/february/tradoc_156618.pdf. Accessed 14 June 2020

European Commission, 'EU moves ahead with dispute settlement over workers' rights in Republic of Korea', News, Directorate for Trade, Brussels, Belgium, 6 July 2019. Available at: http://trade.ec.europa.eu/doclib/press/index.cfm?id=2044. Accessed 14 June 2020

European Commission and European External Action Service, Letter sent by Trade Director of the European Commission Sandra Gallina, Director of Labour Mobility at the Directorate-General for Employment, Social Affairs and Inclusion of the European Commission, Jordi Curell and Managing director of Human Rights, Global and Multilateral Issues at the European External Action Service Lotte Knudsen, Belgium, Brussels, 31 May 2017

European Commission and High Representative of the European Union for Foreign Affairs and Security Policy, Joint Communication to the European Parliament and the Council, *Human Rights and Democracy at the Heart of EU External Action—Towards a More Effective Approach*, of December 12, 2011 (COM(2011)886 final

European Commission, High Representative of the European Union for Foreign Affairs and Security Policy (2011) Joint Communication to the European Parliament and the Council, *Human Rights and Democracy at the Heart of EU External Action—Towards a More Effective Approach*, of December 12, 2011 (COM(2011)886)

European Commission—ILO, Memorandum of Understanding concerning the establishment of a strategic partnership between the International Labour Organisation and the Commission of the European Communities in the field of Development, 17 July 2004, Brussels and 16 July 2004, Geneva. Available at: https://www.ilo.org/brussels/ilo-and-eu/european-commission/WCMS_169299/lang–en/index.htm. Accessed 14 June 2020

Council of the European Union

Council Regulation, Council Regulation (EC) No. 552/97 temporarily withdrawing access to the generalized tariff preferences from Myanmar/Burma, OJ L 85, 27.3.1997

Council Conclusions on the third Ministerial Conference of the WTO, 26 October 1999

Council Common Position 2005/792/CFSP concerning restrictive measures against Uzbekistan [2005] OJ L 299/72

Council Regulation, Council Regulation (EC) No. 1933/2006 of 21 December 2006 temporarily withdrawing access to the generalized tariff preferences from the Republic of Belarus, OJ L 4056/2006
Council of the European Union, EU Strategic Framework and Action Plan on Human Rights and Democracy, Luxembourg, 25 June 2012
Council of the European Union (2012), 'EU Strategic Framework on Human Rights and Democracy', Luxemburg 25 June 2012, 11855/12
Council of the European Union (2016) Council Decision of 26 Oct. 2016 on the signing on behalf of the European Union of the Comprehensive Economic and Trade Agreement (CETA) Between Canada, of the one hand, and the European Union and its Member States, of the other (2016/0206 (NLE))
Council of the European Union (2019) Council Decision authorising the opening of negotiations with the United States of America for an agreement on the elimination of tariffs for industrial goods, No. 6052/19, Brussels, 9 April 2019

European Parliament and Council of the European Union

European Parliament and European Council, Regulation (EU) No. 978/2012 of the European Parliament and of the Council of 25 October 2012 applying a scheme of generalised tariff preferences and repealing Council Regulation (EC) No. 732/2008 OJ [2012] L303/1, 31.10.2012
European Parliament and European Council, Regulation (EU) No. 607/2013 of the European Parliament and of the Council of 12 June 2013 repealing Council Regulation (EC) No. 552/97 temporarily withdrawing access to the generalized tariff preferences from Myanmar/Burma, OJ L 181/13
European Parliament and European Council, Directive 2014/24/EU of the European Parliament and of the Council of 26 February 2014 on public procurement and repealing Directive 2004/18/EC, OJ [2014] L94/65, 28.3.2014
European Parliament and European Council (2015) Regulation (EU) 2015/1843 of the European Parliament and of the Council of 6 October 2015, OJ L 272/1

European Parliament

European Parliament (1994) Resolution of 9 February 1994 on the Introduction of a Social Clause in the Unilateral and Multilateral Trading System (OJ C-61, 28.2.1994, p 89)
European Parliament (2010) Resolution on human rights and social and environmental standards in international trade agreements of 25 November 2010 (2009/2219(INI))
European Parliament (2011) Report on the external dimension of social policy, promoting labour and social standards and European corporate social responsibility (2010/2205(INI)), Committee on Employment and Social Affairs, A7-0172/2011, of 20 April 2011
European Parliament, Resolution of 13 June 2012 on the EU Trade Agreement with Colombia and Peru, Doc 2012/2628 (RSP), 13.6.2012
European Parliament (2014) 'African, Caribbean and Pacific (ACP) countries' position on Economic Partnership Agreements (EPAs)', EP Directorate-General for External Policies, Policy Department, EXPO/B/DEVE/2013/30, April 2014
European Parliament, Resolution of 8 July 2015 containing the European Parliament's recommendations to the European Commission on the negotiations for the Transatlantic Trade and Investment

Partnership (TTIP). Strasbourg: European Parliament. Available at: http://www.europarl.europa.eu/sides/getDoc.do?pubRef=-//EP//TEXT+TA+P8-TA-2015. Accessed 14 June 2020
European Parliament, Resolution on implementation of the 2010 recommendations of Parliament on social and environmental standards, human rights and corporate responsibility of 5 July 2016 (2015/2038(INI))

Committee on Employment and Social Affairs

Committee on Employment and Social Affairs (2016) 'Opinion for the Committee on International Trade on the draft Council decision on the conclusion of the Comprehensive Economic and Trade Agreement (CETA) Between Canada, of the one part, and the European Union and its Member States, of the other part (10975/2016—C8-0438/2016—2016/0205(NLE)) of 8 Dec. 2016

European External Action Service

European External Action Service (EEAS), *A Global Strategy for the European Union's Foreign and Security Policy—Shared Vision, Common Action: A Stronger Europe*, June 2016. Available at: https://eeas.europa.eu/sites/eeas/files/eugs_review_web_0.pdf. Accessed 14 June 2020

United States of America

US Trade

Agreement between the United States of America and the Hashemite Kingdom of Jordan on the Establishment of a Free Trade Area, 41 I.L.M. 63 (2002)
U.S.-Chile Free Trade Agreement Implementation Act ("the Act"; Public Law 108-77; 117 Stat. 909; 19 U.S.C. 3805 note). The final text is available at: https://ustr.gov/archive/Trade_Agreements/Bilateral/Chile_FTA/Final_Texts/Section_Index.html. Accessed 14 June 2020
US-Morocco Free Trade Agreement, final text available at: https://ustr.gov/trade-agreements/free-trade-agreements/morocco-fta/final-text. Accessed 14 June 2020
US-Bahrain Free Trade Agreement. Available at: https://ustr.gov/trade-agreements/free-trade-agreements/bahrain-fta/final-text. Accessed 14 June 2020
US-Oman Free Trade Agreement. Available at: https://ustr.gov/trade-agreements/free-trade-agreements/oman-fta/final-text. Accessed 14 June 2020
US-Peru Trade Promotion Agreement, final text available at: https://ustr.gov/trade-agreements/free-trade-agreements/peru-tpa/final-text. Accessed 14 June 2020
US-Colombia Trade Promotion Agreement. Available at: https://ustr.gov/trade-agreements/free-trade-agreements/morocco-fta/final-text. Accessed 14 June 2020
Agreement Relating to Trade in Cotton, Wool, Man-made Fiber, Non-Cotton Vegetable Fiber and Silk Blend Textiles and Textile Products Between the Government of the United States of America and the Royal Government of Cambodia. Available at: https://photos.state.gov/libraries/cambodia/231771/PDFs/uskh_texttile.pdf. Accessed 14 June 2020

Dominican Republic—Central America—United States Free Trade Agreement Arbitral Panel Established Pursuant to Chapter 20, Final Report of the Panel in the Matter of Guatemala—Issues Relating to the Obligations Under Article 16.2.1(a) of the CAFTA-DR, 14 June 2017. Available at: https://www.trade.gov/industry/tas/Guatemala%20%20%E2%80%93%20Obligations%20Under%20Article%2016-2-1(a)%20of%20the%20CAFTA-DR%20%20June%2014%202017.pdf. Accessed 14 June 2020

NAALC, The North American Agreement on Labour Cooperation, 32 I.L.M. 1499 (1993)

NAFTA, The North American Free Trade Agreement, 32 I.L.M. 289 and 605 (1993); see also http://www.naftanow.org/. Accessed 23 Mar 2020

US GSP Renewal Act of 1984. Pub. L. No. 98-573, 98 Stat. 3019 (1984)

US Labour Advisory Committee for Trade Negotiations and trade Policy (LAC) Report on the Impacts of the Renegotiated North American Free Trade Agreement, 27 Sept 2018. Available at: https://ustr.gov/sites/default/files/files/agreements/FTA/AdvisoryCommitteeReports/Labor%20Advisory%20Committee%20on%20Trade%20Negotiations%20and%20Trade%20Policy%20%28LAC%29.pdf. Accessed 20 Mar 2020

Office of the United States Trade Representative, 'Standing Up for Workers: Ensuring that the Benefits of Trade are Broadly-Shared', 18 Sept 2014. Available at: https://ustr.gov/about-us/policy-offices/press-office/fact-sheets/2014/September/Standing-Up-for-Workers-Ensuring-that-the-Benefits-of-Trade-are-Broadly-Shared. Accessed 20 Mar 2020

Books and chapters in books

Alessandrini D (2010) Developing countries and the multilateral trade regime. The failure and promise of the WTO's development mission. Hart, Oxford

Barry C, Reddy S (2009) International trade and labour standards. Columbia University Press, New York

Bartels L (2009) Social issues: labour, environment, and human rights. In: Lester S, Mercurio B (eds) Bilateral and regional trade agreements: commentary, analysis and case studies. Cambridge University Press, Cambridge, pp 342–366

Bartels L (2017) Human rights, labour standards and environmental standards in CETA. In: Griller S, Obwexer W, Vranes E (eds) Mega-regional trade agreements: TTIP, CETA, TiSA: new orientations for EU external economic relations. OUP, Oxford, pp 202–215

Barton JH et al (1976) The evolution of the trade regime: politics, law, and economics of the GATT and the WTO. Princeton University Press, Woodstock

Bhambra GK (2001) Connected sociologies. Bloomsbury, London

Breining-Kaufmann C (2005) The legal matrix of human rights and trade law: state obligations versus private rights and obligations. In: Cottier T, Pauwelyn J, Bürgi E (eds) Human rights and international trade. Oxford University Press, Oxford, pp 95–136

Bronckers M, Gruni G (2018) Improving the enforcement of labour standards in the EU's free trade agreements. In: Prévost D, Alexovičová I, Hillebrand Pohl J (eds) Restoring trust in trade: Liber Amicorum in Honour of Peter Van den Bossche. Hart Publishing, Oxford, pp 157–172

Cardwell PJ, French D (2013) The European Union as a global investment partner: law, policy and rhetoric in the attainment of development assistance and market liberalisation? In: Brown C, Miles K (eds) Evolution in investment treaty law and arbitration. Cambridge University Press, Cambridge, pp 201–222

Charnovitz S (2005) The World Trade Organisation: sanctions for non-compliance. In: Wallensteen P, Staibano C (eds) International sanctions. Between words and wars in the global system. Frank Cass, London, pp 159–164

Conrad CR (2015a) Processes and production methods (PPMs) in WTO law. Interfacing trade and social goals. Cambridge University Press, Cambridge

Cordonnier Segger M-C, Khalfan A (2004) Sustainable development law. Oxford University Press, Oxford
Corvaglia MA (2015) Public procurement and labour rights: towards coherence in international instruments of procurement regulation. Hart, Oxford
Cottier T, Caplazi A (2016a) Labour standards and world trade law: interfacing legitimate concerns. In: Cottier T (ed) The challenge of WTO law: collected essays. Cameron May, London, pp 551–586
Cremona M, Marin Duran G (2012) Fair trade in the European Union: regulatory and institutional aspects. In: Granville B, Dine J (eds) The processes and practices of fair trade: trust, ethics and governance. Routledge, London, pp 122–196
Durán GM (2013) Innovations and implications of the trade and sustainable development chapter in the EU–Korea free trade agreement. In: Harrison J (ed) The European Union and South Korea. The legal framework for strengthening trade, economic and political relations. Edinburgh University Press, Edinburgh, pp 124-145
Escobar A (2016) Encountering development: the making and unmaking of the third world. Princeton, Princeton
Foucault M (2015) The history of sexuality, vol 1. Penguin, Harmondsworth, pp 92–102
Freedland MR, Prassl J (eds) (xxxb) Viking, laval and beyond. Hart, Oxford
Gammage C, Novitz T (2019) The concept of sustainability and its application in international trade, investment and finance. In: Gammage C, Novitz T (eds) Sustainable trade, investment and finance: toward responsible and coherent regulatory frameworks. Edward Elgar Publishing, Cheltenham, pp 3–12
Gathii JT (2013) The Cotonou agreement and economic and partnership agreements. In: United Nations Human Rights, Office of the High Commissioner. Realizing the right to development: essays in commemoration of 25 years of the United Nations declaration on the right to development. United Nations, New York, Geneva, pp 259–273
Gött H (2018) An internationalised individual labour complaint procedure for workers, trade unions, employers and NGOs in future free trade agreements. In: Gött H (ed) Labour standards in international economic law. Springer, Heidelberg, pp 185–210
Happold M (2016) Targeted sanctions and human rights. In: Happold M, Eden P (eds) Economic sanctions and international law. Hart Publishing, Oxford, pp 87–112
Heliskoski J (2005) Mixed agreements as a technique for organising the international relations of the European Community and its member states. Brill, Martinus Nijhoff Publishers, Leiden
Hepple B (2005) Labour laws and global trade. Hart Publishing, Oxford
Hillion C, Koutrakos P (eds) (2001) Mixed agreements revisited—the EU and its member states in the world. Hart Publishing, Oxford
Hoffmeister F (2014) The European Union as an international trade negotiator. In: Koops JA, Macaj G (eds) The European Union as a diplomatic actor. Palgrave MacMillan, London, Ch 9
Joseph S (2002) Blame it on the WTO? A human rights critique. OUP, Oxford
Kaufmann C (2007) Globalisation and labour rights. The conflict between core labour rights and international economic law. Hart, Oxford
Kenner J (2013) Economic partnership agreements: enhancing the labour dimension of global governance? In: Van Vooren B, Blockmans S, Wouters J (eds) The EU'S role in global governance: the legal dimension. OUP, Oxford, pp 306–321
Korkea-aho E (2015) Evolution of the role of third countries in EU law—towards full legal subjectivity? In: Bardutzky S, Fahey E (eds) Framing the subjects and objects of contemporary EU law. Elgar, Cheltenham, pp 206–226
Krishna P (2009) The economics of PTAs. In: Lester S, Mercurio B (eds) Bilateral and regional trade agreements. CUP, Cambridge, pp 11–27
Langille B (ed) (2004) The capability approach to labour law. OUP, Oxford
Leary V (1996) Workers' rights and international trade: the social clause (GATT, ILO, NAFTA, US laws). In: Bhagwati J, Hudec R (eds) Fair trade and harmonization: prerequisites for free trade? Legal analysis, vol 2. MIT Press, Cambridge, pp 177–230

Marceau G (2009) Trade and labour. In: Bethlehem D, Van Damme I, McRae D, Neufeld R (eds) The Oxford handbook of international trade law. Oxford University Press, Oxford, pp 539–570
Martens D, Orbie J (2018) The European Union and fair trade: hands off? In: Sangeeta Khorana S, Garcia M (eds) Handbook on the EU and international trade. Elgar, Cheltenham, pp 281–295
Maupain F (2005) Is the ILO effective in upholding workers' rights?: reflections on the Myanmar experience. In: Alston P (ed) Labour rights as human rights. OUP, Oxford, pp 85–142
Michalopoulos C (2014) Developing countries in the WTO. Palgrave, London
Nickel J (2001) Making sense of human rights. Wiley, Oxford
Novitz T (2005) The European Union and international labour standards: the dynamics of dialogue between the EU and the ILO. In: Alston P (ed) Labour rights as human rights. Oxford University Press, Oxford, pp 214–241
Novitz T (2012) Labour standards and trade: need we choose between "human rights" and "sustainable development?". In: Gött H (ed) Labour standards in international economic law. Springer, Heidelberg, pp 113–134
Nussbaum M (2013) Creating capabilities. Harvard University Press, Cambridge, MA
Orbie J, De Ville F (2010) Core labour standards in the GSP regime of the European Union: overshadowed by other considerations. In: Fenwick C, Novitz T (eds) Human rights at work. Perspectives on law and regulation. Hart Publishing, Oxford, pp 487–508
Poli S (2017) The turning of non-state entities from objects to subjects of EU restrictive measures. In: Bardutzky S, Fahey E (eds) Framing the subjects and objects of contemporary EU law. Elgar, Cheltenham, pp 158–181
Portela C (2015) European Union sanctions and foreign policy. Routledge, London
Rabbani MJ (2017) The development and anti-development debate. Critical reflections on the philosophical foundations. Ashgate, Farnham
Reddy S (2015) Foreword. International trade as a means to diverse ends: development, workers, the environment and global public goods. In: De Schutter O (ed) Trade in service of sustainable development. Hart, Oxford, pp v–xvi
Reid E (2015) Balancing human rights, environmental protection and international trade. Hart, Oxford
Salmon J (ed) (2001) Dictionnaire de Droit International Public. Bruylant, Bruxelles, pp 41–68
Schmidt VA, Thatcher M (eds) (2014) Resilient liberalism in Europe's political economy. Cambridge University Press, Cambridge
Sengenberge W (2009) International labour standards in the globalized economy: obstacles and opportunities for achieving progress. In: Craig JDR, Lynk SM (eds) Globalisation and the future of labour law. CUP, Cambridge, pp 331–355. https://doi.org/10.1017/CBO9780511495304.013
Schumpeter JA (2009) Capitalism, socialism and democracy. Harper and Row, New York
Sen A (2010) Development as freedom. Oxford University Press, Oxford
Smith A (1976) An inquiry into the nature and causes of the wealth of nations, vol 1. Liberty Classics, Indianapolis
Supiot A (2017) Beyond employment—changes in work and the future of labour law in Europe. Oxford University Press, Oxford
Sykes AO (2006) International trade and human rights: an economic perspective. In: Abbott FM, Breining-Kaufmann C, Cottier T (eds) International trade and human rights: foundations and conceptual issues. University of Michigan Press, Ann Arbor, pp 69–92
Thomas, C (2009) The WTO and labour rights: strategies of linkage. In: Joseph S et al (eds) The world trade organisation and human rights. Interdisciplinary perspectives. Elgar, Cheltenham, p 257
Timmermans C (2013) The court of justice and mixed agreements. In: Rosas A, Levits E, Bot Y (eds) The court of justice and the construction of Europe: analyses and perspectives on sixty years of case-law. TMC Asser Press, The Hague, pp 659–674
Van Damme I (2009) Jurisdiction, applicable law and interpretation. In: Bethlehem D, Van Damme I, McRae D, Neufeld R (eds) The Oxford handbook of international trade law. Oxford University Press, Oxford, pp 298–343

Van den Putte L (2018) Divided we stand—the European parliament's position on social trade in the post-Lisbon era. In: Marx A et al (eds) Global governance of labour rights. Elgar, Cheltenham, UK and Northampton, MA, pp 63–82
Velluti S (2010) New governance and the European employment strategy. Routledge, London
Velluti S (2015) The EU's social dimension in its external trade relations. In: Marx A, Wouters J, Rayp G (eds) Global governance of labour rights. Elgar, Cheltenham, UK and Northampton, MA, pp 42–62
Velluti S (2016a) Human rights conditionality in the EU GSP scheme: "a focus on those in need or a need to refocus?" In: Ferreira N, Kostakopoulou D (eds) The human face of the European Union: is EU law and policy humane enough? CUP, Cambridge, pp 342–366
Velluti S, Van den Putte L (2018) The promotion of social trade by the European Union in its external trade relations. In: Khorana S, Garcia M (eds) Handbook on the EU and international trade. Edward Elgar Publishing, Cheltenham, pp 224–242
Wheatley S (2000) The democratic legitimacy of international law. Hart Publishing, Oxford, pp 311–331
Wiesbrock A (2016) Socially responsible public procurement. European value or national choice? In: Sjåfjell B, Wiesbrock A (eds) Sustainable public procurement under EU law: new perspectives on the state as stakeholder. CUP, Cambridge, pp 75–98
Zeitlin J (ed) (2017) Extending experimentalist governance? The European Union and transnational regulation. OUP, Oxford

Journal Articles

Adriaensen J, Gonzalez-Garibay M (2013) The illusion of choice: the European Union and the trade-labour linkage. J Contemp Eur Res 9(4):549–559
Alston P (2004) Core labour standards" and the transformation of the international labour rights regime. Eur J Int Law 15(3):457–521
Alston P (2005) Facing up to the complexities of the ILO's core labour standards. Eur J Int Law 16(3):467–480
Anghie A (2000) Time present and time past: globalisation, international financial institutions, and the third world. N Y Univ J Int Law Polit 32:243
Arnold LL (2005) Labour and the World Trade Organization: towards a reconstruction of the linkage discourse. Deakin Law Rev 10(1):83–119
Baetens F, Gruni G, Rijpma J (eds) (2016) Legal Issues of Econ Integr 43(4):323–343
Barnard C et al (2001) Capabilities and rights: an emerging agenda for EU social policy. Ind Relat J 32(5):464–479
Barral V (2012) Sustainable development in international law: nature and operation of an evolutive legal norm. Eur J Int Law 23(2):377–400
Bartels L (2002) Article XX of GATT and the problem of extraterritorial jurisdiction: the case of trade measures for the protection of human rights. J World Trade 36(2):353–403
Bartels L (2007) The WTO legality of the EU's GSP+ arrangement. J Int Econ Law 10:869–886
Bartels L (2013) Human rights and sustainable development obligations in EU free trade agreements. Legal Issues Econ Integr Law 40(4):297–313
Bartels L (2015) The chapeau of the general exceptions in the WTO GATT and GATS agreements: a reconstruction. Am J Int Law 109:95–125
Brown W (2014) American nightmare: neoliberalism, neoconservatism, and de-democratization. Polit Theory 34(6):690–714
Burgoon B (2015) The rise and stall of labour linkage in globalisation politics. Int Polit 41:196–220
Campling L et al (2015) Can labour provisions work beyond the border? Evaluating the effects of EU free trade agreements. Int Labour Rev 155(3):357–382

Charnovitz S (2014) The influence of international labour standards on the world trading system: an historical overview. Int Labour Rev 126:565–584
Compa L, Vogt J (2001) Labour rights in the generalized system of preferences: a 20 year review. Comp Labour Law Policy J 22:199
Corvaglia MA, Li K (2018) Extraterritoriality and public procurement regulation in the context of global supply chains' governance. In: Velluti S, Tzevelekos V (eds) Special issue on Extraterritoriality of EU law and human rights after Lisbon: the case of trade and public procurement in Europe and the World: A Law Review 2(1):6 [16]. https://doi.org/10.14324/111.444.ewlj.2018.06
Cote K (2014) European Union trade sustainability impact assessments: developing coherence between trade agreements and labour standards. In: Wouters J, Rayp G, Beke L, Marx A (eds) Special issue on 'Protecting labour rights in a multi-polar supply chain and mobile global economy'. Bull Comp Labour Relat 89, Ch. 6
Cremona M (2001) Rhetoric and reticence: EU external commercial policy in a multilateral context. Common Market Law Rev 38:359
Cuyvers L, Zhou W (2011) Linking international trade and labour standards: the effectiveness of sanctions under the European Union GSP. J World Trade 45:63–85
Dados N, Connell R (2012) The global south. Contexts 12–13. Available at: https://journals.sagepub.com/doi/pdf/10.1177/1536504212436479. Accessed 14 June 2020
Damjanovic D (2013) The EU market rules as social market rules: why the EU can be a social market economy. Common Market Law Rev 50(6):1685–1718
De Ville F, Orbie J, Van den Putte L (2016b) Sustainable development in TTIP: a highest common denominator compromise? Eur J Risk Regul 2:290–294
Duina F (2006) Varieties of regional integration: the EU, NAFTA and Mercosur. J Eur Integr 28(3):247–275. https://doi.org/10.1080/07036330600744456
Ebert FC (2015) Labour provisions in EU trade agreements: what potential for channeling labour standards related capacity building? Int Labour Rev 155(3):407–433
Ebert FC (2017) The Comprehensive Economic and Trade Agreement (CETA): are existing arrangements sufficient to prevent adverse effects on labour standards? Int J Comp Labour Law Ind Relat 33(2):295–329
Ewing KD, Hendy J (2015) The eclipse of the rule of law: trade union rights and the EU Revista Derecho Social y Empresa 4:80–112
Fahey E (2017) European citizens' initiative can proceed says general court. Eur J Risk Regul 8(4):787–790
Fraser N (2005) Reframing justice in a globalizing world. New Left Rev 36:69–88
Fung ST (2014) Negotiating regulatory coherence: the costs and consequences of disparate regulatory principles in the Transatlantic Trade and Investment Partnership agreement between the United States and the European Union. Cornell Int Law J 47(2):445–471
George C, Kirkpatrick C (2008) Sustainability impact assessment of trade agreements: from public dialogue to international governance. J Environ Assess Policy Manag 10:67–89
Montserrat Garibay G (2009) Trade-labour linkage from the eyes of the developing countries: a euphemism for protectionist practices. European Foreign Affairs Review 14(5):763–784
Grosse Ruse-Khan H (2010) A real partnership for development? Sustainable development as treaty objective in European economic partnership agreements and beyond. J Int Econ Law 13(1):139–180
Gruni G (2016) Law or aspiration? The European Union proposal for a labour standards clause in the transatlantic trade and investment partnership. Legal issues Econ Integr 43(4):399–405
Gruni G (2017) Labor standards in the EU-South Korea free trade agreement. Pushing labour standards into global trade law? Korean J Int Comp Law 5:100–121
Harrison J (2003) GSP conditionality and non-discrimination. Int Trade Law Regul 9:159
Harrison J, Goller A (2008) Trade and human rights: what does "impact assessment" have to offer? Hum Rights Law Rev 8:587–615

Harrison J (2010) Human rights impact assessments of trade agreements: reflections on practice and principles for future assessments, 1–24, Geneva, Switzerland. Available at: https://warwick.ac.uk/fac/soc/law/research/centres/chrp-old/projects/humanrightsimpactassessments/trade/hr_impact_background_paper.pdf. Accessed 14 June 2020

Harrison J (2011) Human rights measurement: reflections on the current practice and future potential of human rights impact assessment. J Hum Rights Pract 3:162–187

Harrison J et al (2018) Labour standards provisions in EU free trade agreements: reflections on the European Commission's reform agenda. World Trade Rev 1–23

Harrison J et al (2019) Governing labour standards through free trade agreements: limits of the European Union's trade and sustainable development chapters. J Common Market Stud 57(2):260–277

Hongju Koh H (1997) Why do nations obey international rules? Yale Law J 106:2579–2658

Howse R (2003) 'India's WTO challenge to drug enforcement conditions in the European community generalized system of preferences: a little known case with major repercussions for "political" conditionality in US trade policy. Chicago J Int Law 4:385–405

Howse R, Regan D (2000) The product/process distinction—an illusory basis for disciplining "unilateralism" in trade policy. Eur J Int Law 11(2):249–290

Jackson JH (2000) Comments on shrimp/turtle and the product/process distinction. Eur J Int Law 11(2):303–307

Keck M, Sikkink K (2002) Transnational advocacy networks in international and regional politics. Int Soc Sci J 51:89–101

Kenner J, Peake K (2017) The Bangladesh sustainability compact: an effective exercise of global experimentalist EU governance? Camb Yearb Eur Legal Stud 19:86–115

Kernaghan C (2006) US-Jordan free trade agreement descends into human trafficking and involuntary servitude. NLC, New York. Available at: https://issuu.com/iglhr/docs/0605-iglhr-usjordanfreetradeagreeme. Accessed 14 June 2020

Kolben K (2004) Trade, monitoring and the ILO: working to improve conditions in Cambodia's garment factories. Yale Hum Rights Dev Law J 7(1):79–107

Kryvoi Y (2008) Why European Union trade sanctions do not work. Minn J Int Law 12(2):209–246

Langille B (1997) Eight ways to think about international labour standards. J World Trade 31(4):27–53

Lee E (1997) Globalization and labour standards: a review of issues. Int Labour Rev 136(2):1–16

Mantouvalou V (2011) Are labour rights human rights? Eur Labour Law J 3:151–172

Marx A, Brecht L, Brando N (2016) The protection of labour rights in trade agreements. the case of the EU-Colombia agreement. J World Trade 50:587–610

Maupain F (2005) Revitalization not retreat: the real potential of the 1998 ILO declaration for the universal protection of workers' rights. Eur J Int Law 16:448

McCrudden C, Davies A (2000) A perspective on trade and labour rights. J Int Econ Law 3(1):43, 51–52

Melo Araujo BA (2018) Labour provisions in EU and US mega-regional trade agreements: rhetoric and reality. Int Comp Law Q 67(1):233–253

Novitz T (2017) The restricted right to strike: "far-reaching" ILO jurisprudence on the public sector and essential services. Comp Labor Law Policy J 38(3):353–374

Oehri M (2015) Comparing the US and EU labour governance "near and far"—hierarchy vs network? J Eur Public Policy 22(5):731–749

Orbie J, Khorana S (2015) Normative versus market power Europe? The EU-India trade agreement. Asia Europe J 13:253–264

Orbie J, Van Elsuwege P, Bossuyt F (2014) Humanitarian aid as an integral part of the European Union's external action: the challenge of reconciling coherence and independence. J Conting Crisis Manag 22(3):158–165

Peels R, Fino M (2015) Pushed out the door, back in through the window: the role of the ILO in EU and US trade agreements in facilitating the decent work agenda. Global Labour J 6(2):189–202

Perulli A (2014) Fundamental social rights, market regulation and EU external action. Int J Comp Labour Law Ind Relat 30:37
Portela C, Orbie J (2007) Sanctions under the EU generalised system of preferences and foreign policy: coherence by accident? Contemp Polit 20(1):63–76. https://doi.org/10.1080/13569775.2014.881605
Postnikov E, Bastiaens I (2014) Does dialogue work? The effectiveness of labor standards in EU preferential trade agreements. J Eur Public Policy 21:923–940
Raess D, Sari D (2016) Labor Provisions in Trade Agreements (LABPTA): introducing a new dataset. Global Policy 4:451–466
Sapir A (1995) The interaction between labour standards and international trade policy. World Econ 18(6):791–803
Siles-Brügge G (2014) EU trade and development policy beyond the ACP: subordinating developmental to commercial imperatives in the reform of GSP. Contemp Polit 20(1):49–62. https://doi.org/10.1080/13569775.2014.881604
Siroën JM (2013) Labour provisions in preferential trade agreements: current practice and outlook. Int Labour Rev 152(1):85
Sutherland J (1998) International trade and the GATT/WTO social clause: broadening the debate. Qld Univ Technol Law J 14:83–107
Teague P (2002) Standard-setting for labour in regional trading blocs: the EU and NAFTA compared. J Public Policy 22(3):325–348
Tham J-C, Ewing KD (2016) Labour clauses in the TPP and the TTIP: a comparison without a difference? Melb J Int Law 17(2):1–35
Urata S (2002) Globalization and the growth in free trade agreements. Asia-Pac Rev 1:20–32
Valette MF (2007) Le Nouveau schéma Européen de Préférences Tarifaires Généralisées: Sous le Signe du Développement Durable et de la Bonne Gouvernance. Revue du Marché Commun et de l'Union Européenne 163–171
Van den Putte L (2015) Involving civil society in social clauses and the decent work agenda. Global Labour J 6(2):221–235
Van den Putte L, Orbie J (2015) EU bilateral agreements and the surprising rise of labour provisions. Int J Comp Labour Law Ind Relat 31:263–283
van Liemt G (1989) Minimum labour standards and international trade: would a social clause work? Int Labour Rev 128(4):433–448
Vásquez CM (2003) Trade sanctions and human rights: past, present and future. J Int Econ Law 6(4):797–839
Velluti S (2016b) The promotion and integration of human rights in EU external trade relations. Utrecht J Int Eur Law 32(83):41–68
Vogt J (2015) A little less conversation: the EU and the (non) application of labour conditionality in the generalised system of preferences (GSP). Int J Comp Labour Law Ind Relat 31:285–304
Vogt J (2015) The evolution of labor rights and trade—a transatlantic comparison and lessons for the transatlantic trade and investment partnership. J Int Econ Law 18(4):827–860
Vogt J (2017) The Bangladesh sustainability compact: an effective tool for promoting workers' rights? Polit Gov 5(4):80–92. http://dx.doi.org/10.17645/pag.v5i4.1093
Yap J (2013) Beyond "don't be evil": the European Union GSP+ trade preference scheme and the incentivisation of the Sri Lankan garment industry to foster human rights. Eur Law J 19(2):283–301

Papers, Studies and Reports

Ark M, Islam M, Kenner J, Lein B, Peake K (2016) The integration of EU development, trade and human rights policies. FRAME Deliverable 9.4. Available at: https://doi.org/20.500.11825/116. Accessed 23 Mar 2020

Bartels L (2012) The role of civil society in monitoring free trade agreements. Report for the EU European Economic and Social Committee, EESC/COMM/16/2012

Bartels L (2014a) The European Parliament's role in relation to human rights in trade and investment agreements. European Parliament, Directorate-General for External Policies of the Union, Policy Department Study, EXPO/B/DROI/2012-09. Available at: http://www.europarl.europa.eu/cmsdata/86031/Study.pdf. Accessed 14 June 2020

Bartels L (2014b) A model human rights clause for the EU's international trade agreements. German Institute for Human Rights, Misereor. Available at: http://www.institut-fuer-menschenrechte.de/uploads/tx_commerce/Studie_A_Model_Human_Rights_Clause.pdf. Accessed 14 June 2020

Bendini R, Delaunay D (2011) The EU trade agreement with Colombia and Peru. Internal Study, Directorate-General for External Policies of the Union, Policy Department, DG EXPO/B/PolDep/Note/2011_145, Brussels, May 2011, p 12

Bilal S et al (2009) Global financial and economic crisis: analysis of and implications for ACP-EU Economic Partnership Agreements (EPAs). ECDPM Discussion Paper No. 92. Available at: ecdpm.org/publications/analysis-of-and-implications-for-acp-eu-economic-partnership-agreements-epas/. Accessed 14 June 2020

Bürgi Bonanomi E (2014) EU trade agreements and their impacts on human rights. Study Commissioned by the German Federal Ministry for Economic Cooperation and Development (BMZ). CDE Working Paper 1, Centre for Development and Environment (CDE), Bern, Switzerland. https://pdfs.semanticscholar.org/5521/e44302044f5c56bb43057d6fda7382b59171.pdf?_ga=2.123865679.418745594.1568745681-49948745.1568745681. Accessed 20 Mar 2020

Bürgi Bonanomi E (2016) Improving the methodology for measuring social and human rights impacts of trade agreements. Paper presented at the Conference 'EU Trade Policy at the Crossroads: between Economic Liberalism and Democratic Challenges', Austrian Foundation for Development Research, Vienna, Austria, 4–6 Feb 2016

CARIS (2010) Mid-term evaluation of the EU's generalised system of preferences. Report commissioned by the EC, Brighton: Centre for the Analysis of Regional Integration, University of Sussex, Sussex. Available at: http://www.sussex.ac.uk/caris/projects; the final report is available at: http://trade.ec.europa.eu/doclib/docs/2010/may/tradoc_146196.pdf, both accessed 20 Mar 2020

CEPII-CIREM (2008) An impact study of the EU-ACP Economic Partnership Agreements (EPAs) in the six ACP regions. Final report. http://www.cepii.fr/PDF_PUB/wp/2008/wp2008-04.pdf. Accessed 14 June 2020

Compa L, Gottwald E, Vogt J (2018) Wrong turn for workers' rights: the US-Guatemala CAFTA labour arbitration ruling- and what to do about it. In: International labour rights forum. Available at: https://laborrights.org/publications/wrong-turn-workers%E2%80%99-rights-us-guatemala-cafta-labor-arbitration-ruling-%E2%80%93-and-what-do. Accessed 23 Mar 2020

Dados N, Cornell R (2012) The global south. Contexts 12–13. Available at: https://journals.sagepub.com/doi/pdf/10.1177/1536504212436479. Accessed 14 June 2020

de Andrade Correa F The integration of sustainable development in trade agreements of the European Union. In: Kleimann D, EU preferential trade agreements: commerce, foreign policy and development aspects. International Trade Observatory and Relex Working Group, European University Institute, Robert Schuman Centre for Advanced Studies. Available at: cadmus.eui.eu/handle/1814/27661. Accessed 20 Mar 2020

De Ville F, Orbie J, Van den Putte L (2016a) TTIP and labour standards. Study for the Employment and Social Affairs Committee of the European Parliament, IP/A/EMPL/2015-07, PE 578.992, Brussels, Belgium

Douma W The promotion of sustainable development through EU trade instruments. In: Pantaleo L, Andenas M (eds), Reul C (ass ed) The European Union as a global model for trade and investment. University of Oslo Faculty of Law, Legal Studies Research Paper Series, No. 2016-02
FES (2016) Evaluation of the Korea-EU FTA's labour standards provisions and their implementation status. Interim Report, Friedrich Ebert Stiftung. Available at: http://fes-korea.org/pages/english/publications/books-and-studies.php. Accessed 20 Mar 2020
Ebert FC (2009) Between political goodwill and WTO-law: human rights conditionality in the community's new scheme of generalized tariff preferences (GSP). ZERP-Arbeitspapier 8/2009. Available at: http://ssrn.com/abstract=1721678. Accessed 14 June 2020
Ebert FC, Posthuma A (2011) Labour provisions in trade arrangements: current trends and perspectives. Discussion Paper Series, International Institute for Labour Studies, ILO, Geneva, Switzerland. Available at: https://www.ilo.org/wcmsp5/groups/public/---dgreports/---inst/documents/publication/wcms_192807.pdf. Accessed 14 June 2020
Greven T (2005) Social standards in Bilateral and Regional Trade and investment agreements instruments. Occasional Paper No. 16, Friedrich-Ebert-Stiftung, Geneva. Available at: http://library.fes.de/pdf-files/iez/global/50087.pdf. Accessed 14 June 2020
Hoang TMH et al (2014) Labour provisions in preferential trade agreements: potential opportunities or challenges to Vietnam? SECO Working Paper 2/14, World Trade Institute, University of Bern. Available at: http://www.wti.org/media/filer_public/32/31/3231e444-9a9b-4fe2-a24f-38acc5aefa98/wti_seco_wp_02_2014.pdf. Accessed 20 Mar 2020
Hossain J, Mostafiz A, Hasan Sharif J (2018) Linking trade and decent work in global supply chains in Bangladesh. Friedrich-Ebert-Stiftung. Available at: http://library.fes.de/pdf-files/bueros/bangladesch/14406-20180614.pdf. Accessed 23 Mar 2020
Jones VC (2015) Generalized system of preferences: background and renewal debate. Congressional Research Service, CRS Report. Available at: https://www.fas.org/sgp/crs/misc/RL33663.pdf. Accessed 20 Mar 2020
Kenner J (2013) Shaping the social dimension of globalization? An analysis of the strategic partnership between the EU and the ILO. Paper presented at the Labour Law Research Network Inaugural Conference, Barcelona, 14–15 June 2013
Kwa A, Lunenborg P, Musonge W (2014) African, Caribbean and Pacific (ACP) countries' position on Economic Partnership Agreements (EPAs). Study for the EU Parliament, Directorate-General for External Policies of the Union, Directorate B, Policy Department, Brussels, April 2014, EXPO/B/DEVE/2013/30
Mbangu L (2005) Recent cases of article 96 consultations. European Centre for Development Policy Management (ECDPM), Discussion Paper No. 64C
Moore M, Scherrer C (2017) Conditional or promotional trade agreements—is enforcement possible? How international labour standards can be enforced through US and EU social chapters. Friedrich Ebert Stiftung, Singapore. Available at: https://www.fes-asia.org/news/conditional-or-promotional-trade-agreements-is-enforcement-possible/. Accessed 14 June 2020
Orbie J, Martens D, Van den Putte L (2016) Civil society meetings in European Union trade agreements: features, purposes and evaluation, vol 3. Centre for the Law of EU External Relations (CLEER) Papers 1
Portela C (2018) Enforcing respect for labour standards with targeted sanctions. CLS + core labour standards plus. Linking trade and decent work in global supply chains. Friedrich-Ebert-Stiftung. Available at: http://library.fes.de/pdf-files/bueros/singapur/14689.pdf. Accessed 23 Mar 2020
PricewaterhouseCoopers (2007) Sustainability impact assessment of the EU-ACP economic partnership agreements. Available at: https://www.wto.org/english/tratop_e/sps_e/private_standards_june07_e/sia_summary_e.pdf. Accessed 14 June 2020
Ramopoulos T, Wouters J (2015) Charting the legal landscape of EU external relations post-Lisbon. Leuven Centre for Global Governance Studies Working Paper No. 156, March 2015. Available at: https://ghum.kuleuven.be/ggs/publications/working_papers/new_series/wp151-160/wp156-ramopoulos-wouters.pdf. Accessed 20 Mar 2020

Raube K, Wouters J (2016) The many facets of parliamentary involvement and interaction in EU external relations. Working Paper No. 174, Leuven Centre for Global Governance Studies
Schmieg E (2015) Trade and investment agreements for sustainable development? Lessons from the EU's economic partnership agreement with the Caribbean. SWP Research Paper 2015/RP 06. Stiftung Wissenschaft und Politik (German Institute for International Affairs), Berlin. Available at: https://www.swp-berlin.org/fileadmin/contents/products/research_papers/2015_RP06_scm.pdf. Accessed 14 June 2020
Siroën J-M (2013) Core labour standards, bilateral relations and international trade. Available at: http://www.etsg.org/ETSG2013/Papers/083.pdf. Accessed 23 Mar 2020
Stevens C, Kennan J (2011) Reform of the generalized system of preferences. Study, Directorate-General for External Policies of the Union, Policy Department, INTA, PE 433. 858, Brussels, April 2011
Van den Abeele E Integrating social and environmental dimensions in public procurement: one small step for the Internal Market, one giant leap for the EU? ETUI Working Paper 2014.08. Available at: http://www.etui.org/Publications2/Working-Papers. Accessed 20 Mar 2020
Van den Putte L et al What social face of the new EU trade agreements? Beyond the 'soft' approach. ETUI Policy Brief, No. 13/2015
Velluti S (2016c) The promotion of social rights and labour standards in the EU external trade relations, vol 5. Centre for the Law of EU External Relations (CLEER), Papers 83-113

Other

Doctorate dissertations

Van den Putte L (2016) The European Union's trade-labour linkage: beyond the soft approach? University of Ghent (unpublished doctoral thesis, on file with author)

Interviews

Interview with Marco Ferri, First Counsellor in Social Affairs of the Permanent Delegation to the United Nations Office and other International Organizations in Geneva, 24 May 2013, Geneva, Switzerland

Policy briefs, position papers and blogposts

Addo A (2015) Core Labour Standards and International Trade. Lessons from the Regional Context. Springer, Heidelberg
Ahmad R (2015) Millennium development goals: Dhaka ready to face new challenges. The Daily Star. Dhaka, 18 Sept 2015. www.thedailystar.net/backpage/dhaka-ready-face-new-challenges-143818. Accessed 20 Mar 2020
Business Europe (2015) TTIP: the sustainability chapter. Position Paper, Brussels, Belgium, May 2015. Available at: https://www.businesseurope.eu/sites/buseur/files/media/imported/2015-00382-E.pdf. Accessed 14 June 2020

Democracy Reporting International (2017) GSP+ and Sri Lanka, Aug 2017. Available at: http://democracy-reporting.org/wp-content/uploads/2018/04/GSP-English_August-2017.pdf. Accessed 20 Mar 2020

ETUC/AFL-CIO, Declaration of Joint Principles 10.07.2014, Brussels, Belgium. Available at: https://www.etuc.org/sites/default/files/document/files/afl-cio_ttip_report_uk_1.pdf. Accessed 14 June 2020

GATT, Relationship of Internationally Recognized Labour Standards to International Trade, Communication from the United States, 28 October 1987, quoted in Kofi Addo, Core Labour Standards and International Trade, Heidelberg: Springer 2015, p. 148.

Global South Studies Centre (2015) Concepts of the global south. Voices issue 1. Available at: https://web.archive.org/web/20160904205139/http://gssc.uni-koeln.de/node/451. Accessed 14 June 2020

Goldhammer S, Gottwald E (2014) Justice delayed…the long road of the Guatemala CAFTA complaint. International Labor Rights Forum, 10 Dec 2014. Available at: https://laborrights.org/blog/201412/justice-delayed%E2%80%A6the-long-road-guatemala-cafta-complaint. Accessed 23 Mar 2020

Granger C, Siroën J-M (2006) Core labour standards in trade agreements. From multilateralism to bilateralism, Oct 2006, pp. 1-25. Available at: https://basepub.dauphine.fr/bitstream/handle/123456789/255/2ECFE995d01.pdf?sequence=2. Accessed 20 Mar 2020

Corporate Europe Observatory, European and Canadian Civil Society Groups Call for Rejection of CETA, 28.11.2016. Available at: https://corporateeurope.org/en/international-trade/2016/11/european-and-canadian-civil-society-groups-call-rejection-ceta. Accessed 14 June 2020

Hornbeck JF (2009) Free trade agreements: US promotion and oversight of Latin American implementation, December 2009. Inter-American Development Bank Policy Brief IDB-PB-102. Available at: https://publications.iadb.org/en/publication/free-trade-agreements-us-promotion-and-oversight-latin-american-implementation. Accessed 14 June 2020

Human Rights Watch (2016) Bangladesh: garment worker's union rights bleak, 21 Apr 2016. Available at: https://www.hrw.org/news/2016/04/21/bangladesh-garment-workers-union-rights-bleak. Accessed 23 March 2020

Jansen M, Lee E (2007) Trade and employment. Challenges for policy research—a joint study of the International Labour Office and the Secretariat of the World Trade Organization. WTO Secretariat, Geneva, Switzerland, 2007. Available at: https://www.wto.org/english/res_e/booksp_e/ilo_e.pdf. Accessed 20 Mar 2020

International Federation for Human Rights (FIDH) (2017) Contribution to the mid-term evaluation of the EU GSP, May 2017. Available at: https://www.fidh.org/en/international-advocacy/european-union/contribution-to-the-mid-term-evaluation-of-the-eu-gsp. Accessed 14 June 2020

ITUC-CCC, Complaint to the European Ombudsman. Alleging maladministration by the European Commission in its failure to investigate the status of Bangladesh under the GSP, Brussels, Belgium, 6 June 2018. Available at: https://www.ituc-csi.org/IMG/pdf/bangladesh_ombudsman_complaint_final_2018_06_06_clean.pdf. Accessed 14 June 2020

International Trade Union Confederation (ITUC): condemnation in 2019 of South Korea's delay in bringing its own labour legislation in line with international labour standards. Available at: https://www.ituc-csi.org/fundamental-labour-rights-under. Accessed 14 June 2020

Lamy P (2006a) Humanising globalization. Speech, Santiago de Chile, Chile, 30 Jan 2006. Available at: http://www.wto.org/english/news_e/sppl_e/sppl16_e.htm. Accessed 14 June 2020

Lamy P (2006b) Making trade work for development: time for a Geneva consensus. Emile Noel Lecture New York University Law School, New York, 30 Oct 2006. Available at: http://www.wto.org/english/news_e/sppl_e/sppl45_e.htm. Accessed 14 June 2020

Lukas K, Steinkellner A (2010) Social standards in sustainability chapters of bilateral free trade agreements. Ludwig Boltzmann Institute of Human Rights, Vienna, Austria, June 2010. Available at: https://www.arbeiterkammer.at/infopool/akportal/Studie_Nachhaltigkeit_englisch.pdf. Accessed 14 June 2020

Malmström C (2015) TTIP—what's in it for labour, environment and sustainable development?, 6 Nov 2015. Available at: http://trade.ec.europa.eu/doclib/press/index.cfm?id=1393. Accessed 14 June 2020

Oxfam (2008) Partnership or Power Play? How Europe should bring development into its trade deals with African, Caribbean, and Pacific countries. Available at: https://policy-practice.oxfam.org.uk/publications/partnership-or-power-play-how-europe-should-bring-development-into-its-trade-de-114561. Accessed 14 June 2020

Sibbel L (2010) The labour provisions in the US-Jordan free trade agreement. Impact and lessons learnt. Available at: https://docplayer.net/59476291-The-labour-provisions-in-the-u-s-jordan-free-trade-agreement.html. Accessed 14 June 2020

Stevens C et al (2011) The poverty impact of the proposed graduation threshold in the generalized system of preferences (GSP) scheme. Overseas Development Institute, London. Available at: https://www.odi.org/sites/odi.org.uk/files/odi-assets/publications-opinion-files/7341.pdf. Accessed 20 Mar 2020

Tasioulas J (2020) On human rights. Available at: http://fivebooks.com/interview/human-rights/. Accessed 20 Mar 2020

ILO (2013), Report on the social dimensions of free trade agreements, 6 November 2013, 6–7, available at http://www.ilo.org/global/research/publications/WCMS_228965/lang--en/index.htm

Chapter 6
The Nature of the European Union's Human Rights Obligations in Its External Trade Relations After Lisbon

Samantha Velluti

6.1 Introduction

Human rights permeate almost every aspect of European Union (EU) action or, put differently, every action of the EU, whether internal or external, has human rights implications. A set of internal rules within the EU—that is the Treaty on EU (TEU)[1] and the Treaty on the Functioning of the EU (TFEU)[2] and the EU Charter of Fundamental Rights (EUCFR)—[3] and various external norms—that is international law sources—[4] impose human rights obligations on the EU. As the EU has become a prominent actor on the global scene it has become increasingly bound by human rights obligations towards "distant strangers"—[5] namely, non-Union persons outside the territory of its member states—who are affected by its trade and investment policies.[6]

This chapter seeks to flesh out the content and scope of human rights obligations of the EU outside its borders. In particular, it seeks to examine how and the extent to which the commitment to uphold and promote human rights abroad may determine the legality of EU external action. In this context, the analysis will touch upon issues

[1]Consolidated Version of the Treaty on European Union [2008] OJ C115/13.

[2]Consolidated Version of the Treaty on the Functioning of the European Union [2008] OJ C 115/01.

[3]Charter of Fundamental Rights of the European Union [2000] OJ C364/01.

[4]E.g. customary international law; bilateral, regional and multilateral agreements concluded by the EU, which impose international obligations on the Union and form an integral part of the EU legal order; and, multilateral human rights conventions; for commentary and analysis, see de Jesús Butler (2008), Ahmed and de Jesús (2006), de Jesús and De Schutter (2008).

[5]Ganesh (2016).

[6]Berkes (2018).

I am indebted to Francesca Martines and Vassilis Tzevelekos for reading an earlier draft of this chapter and for their invaluable comments. Any errors or omissions are my own. Section 2 of this chapter is partly based on an introductory article to a Special Issue co-edited with Velluti and Tzevelekos (2018).

S. Velluti, *The Role of the EU in the Promotion of Human Rights and International Labour Standards in Its External Trade Relations*,
https://doi.org/10.1007/978-3-030-56748-4_6

of "extraterritoriality"[7] and see whether it is an apposite lens to examine the nature of the EU's human rights obligations outside its borders. The aim here is not to provide a comprehensive account of the phenomenon of extraterritorial jurisdiction or the exercise of legal power beyond territorial borders in the field of human rights vis-à-vis EU external action but, more modestly, the aim is to contribute to the debate on the extraterritorial effects produced by the laws and conduct of the EU on the international plane.

The EU uses law as a vehicle for conducting its foreign policy and promoting its interests chiefly through its exclusive competence in the Common Commercial Policy (CCP). As shown throughout the book, since the 2009 Treaty of Lisbon (TL)[8] the CCP has become an important and powerful foreign policy tool, no longer limited in scope to trade. For this reason, the CCP is generally considered as "the mother of all EU external relation policies"[9] because of its strong link with the EU's Internal Market integration process. Over the years the building of the EU integration project has also acquired an external dimension in the context of which the EU acts as a global regulatory actor committed to multilateral solutions to common problems and good governance. Domestic policies and the instruments employed therein extend the impact of EU legislation beyond the borders of the Union so that its power to act internally is projected externally.[10] Moreover, within the framework of its foreign policy, and in accordance with international law, the EU has developed a complex web of relations within 'a multi-layered process of unilateral, bilateral and multilateral normative interactions which cannot be categorized simply as either norm export or import'.[11] However, when the EU acts as an international player it still does so within its overarching mantra of preserving the autonomy of the EU legal order. In this respect, the Court of Justice of the EU (CJEU) in *Opinion 2/13*, citing the *Kadi* and *Internationale Handelsgesellschaft* cases,[12] held that while fundamental rights as recognised by the EUCFR were at the heart of the Union's legal structure, 'the autonomy enjoyed by EU law in relation to the laws of the member states and in relation to international law requires that the interpretation of those fundamental rights be ensured within the framework of the structure and objectives of the EU'.[13] Autonomy was thus the underlying reason for finding the draft agreement on the accession of the EU to the European

[7] The quotation marks intend to highlight the ambiguity and difficulty of pinning down the meaning of extraterritoriality and whether it is possible in fact to define the effects of the EU's laws and conduct beyond its borders as extraterritorial.

[8] Treaty of Lisbon Amending the Treaty on European Union and the Treaty Establishing the European Community, 13 December 2007, 2007/C 306/01.

[9] Van Vooren and Wessel (2014).

[10] Cremona (2019), at p. 64.

[11] Ibid. for a comprehensive account of the contribution of EU law to international law from the perspective of the international legal order, see Wessel (2016).

[12] Case 11/70, *Internationale Handelsgesellschaft* (ECLI:EU:C:1970:114), para. 4, and Case C-402/05 P and C-415/05 P, *Kadi and Al Barakaat International Foundation v. Council and Commission* (ECLI:EU:C:2008:461), paras. 281–285.

[13] *Opinion 2/13* (ECLI:EU: C:2014:2454), para. 170.

Convention on Human Rights (ECHR) to be incompatible with the Treaties.[14] This explains why the principles of EU law not only contribute to the development of international law but also impose constraints on the EU's ability to participate in external regulatory regimes.[15] In this respect Klabbers argues that: 'the EU has always been highly ambivalent towards international law and has carved out an ethos to justify this: what matters—and has always mattered—is the protection of the integrity of the EU legal order and the autonomy of EU law'.[16] 'Yet—as Van Vooren and Wessel aptly note—without international law, the EU would not exist.'[17] In its external legal relations the EU must act under international law and it also has to respect its basic rules.[18] The CJEU has thus had the challenging task of finding an adequate solution between the EU's autonomy towards and dependence on international law.[19]

Since the TL, the EU's external action's instruments are regularly employed as mechanisms for the promotion of its values (including human rights), 'as part of the EU's external mandate under Articles 3(5) and 21 TEU'.[20] As propounded in Chap. 2,[21] a revised notion of the EU's international role as a normative actor requires an approach that goes beyond the "norms versus interests" contrast to understand the complex and inter-twined connections between interests, values, norms and institutions in the EU. Even though interests are largely non-normative in nature and concerned with power politics, as Jaremba, Kanetake and Koning posit: 'long-term commercial gain and competitiveness may well be achieved by upholding human rights and sustainable development, and, in this sense, normative goals that the EU's external action ought to accommodate are not always contradictory.'[22]

In the context of the EU's external trade policy, therefore, questions about its values and interests should not be posed in dichotomic terms, but rather, should be addressed from an interdependence perspective. From this viewpoint, the focus should not be on whether the EU is a large and powerful trade bloc in pursuit of its own interests or rather a facilitator of world-wide free trade; or again—as a rule-based system itself—on whether the EU hinders or contributes to the formation of a rule-based approach in the international trade context. Interests might help the EU to shape its values and vice versa.[23] Any examination of the EU as a global actor should not be limited to the *content* and *substance* of the norms and regulations that the EU

---

[14]This decision was subject to extensive criticism, *e.g.* De Witte and Imamović (2015), at 704. For critical analysis, see Spaventa (2015), Eeckhout (2015).

[15]Cremona, above no. 10, at p. 68.

[16]Klabbers (2015), at p. 55; specifically in relation to the autonomy of EU law vis-à-vis human rights and the proposal of relying on the principle of limited and shared jurisdiction to govern the relationship between the two European Courts in view of the EU's accession to the European Convention on Human Rights (ECHR), see also Eeckhout (2013).

[17]Van Vooren and Wessel, above no. 9, p. 208.

[18]Ibid.

[19]Ibid. pp. 208–209.

[20]Cremona and Scott (2019), at p. 2.

[21]See Section 2 of Chapter 2.

[22]Jaremba et al. (2019), [4].

[23]Tocci (2007), at p. 3.

externalizes but it should also extend to the *way* they are promoted, in addition to the *scale* and *level* of impact that they have.

The 2016 *Global Strategy* itself recognises that the EU's interests and values coincide and that it is in the EU's interests to see its values more widely accepted.[24] To project this new identity the EU has come up with the notion of "principled pragmatism".[25] At the same time, the relationship between the EU's values and interests is mired in tension and, inevitably, this friction also extends to the international role of the EU and the global reach of its laws and values.[26] Hence while, on the one hand, the EU promotes and attempts to apply rules of international law to third countries by which it is itself constrained, on the other hand, it also attempts to promote values and standards which it does not consistently comply with, raising questions about its accountability and credibility.[27]

At the same time, excessive interdependence between values and interests runs the risk of forging the legal values of the EU according to the political interests prevailing across its member states. As Kuner argues, it is important that 'the EU should not cloak the assertion of its political interests in the language of fundamental legal values, in order to keep a degree of integrity in the law that is resistant to changing political pressures'.[28]

This complexity is also exacerbated by the fact that the principle of consistency is not 'well substantiated as a constitutional principle of EU law', and that the 'case law of the Court of Justice of the EU explicitly dealing with the principle is scarce and lacks concretization.'[29] The Court's case-law on consistency is neither 'value-driven, nor does it forge a constitutional interpretative tool in the Dworkinian sense of consistency as integrity'[30] but rather is driven by the objective of ensuring EU competence and the full effectiveness of EU law.[31]

Against this backdrop, the chapter employs Ryngaert's jurisdictional model to determine the geographic locus and scope of application of EU human rights obligations in the context of its external trade policy; namely an "internal-territorial" model,

---

[24]European External Action Service (EEAS), *A Global Strategy for the European Union's Foreign and Security Policy—Shared Vision, Common Action: A Stronger Europe*, June 2016, at 13, available at: https://eeas.europa.eu/sites/eeas/files/eugs_review_web_0.pdf, accessed on 14 June 2020.

[25]The concept of "principled pragmatism" is based on the respect of democratic values by EU institutions and its member states as the primary instrument of their international promotion, more flexible partnerships between the EU and other international actors, and renovated multilateralism to allow the EU to reach its full potential on the international scene; see Tocci (2016).

[26]Cremona and Scott, above no. 20, at p. 2.

[27]Ibid.

[28]Kuner (2019).

[29]Den Hertog and Stroß (2013), at p. 375; see also Hettne et al. (2017).

[30]Herlin-Karnell and Konstantinidis (2013), at p. 152.

[31]Ibid. Pisillo Mazzeschi talks about the shift from a "law of rules" to a "law of values", which implies a paradigmatic and ideological change of the international legal order. In this context, he refers to "coordination" rather than "consistency" to resolve the antinomies between conflicting principles and values. This is not merely a linguistic difference but also one of semantics as the premise is one of a harmonious order, see Pisillo Mazzeschi (2017).

which 'obviates the need for an elaborate conceptualization of "extraterritorial" obligations.'[32] As posited by Ryngaert: 'particularly in the context of international trade agreements, the focus on extraterritoriality may be ineffective, as EU decisions on the conclusion of such agreements cause extraterritorial effects that are not captured by traditional extraterritoriality doctrines,[33] which instead focus on extraterritorial conduct.'[34] If we are to conceive an EU decision on the conclusion of an international agreement of a territorial nature, and thus within the scope of the territoriality principle,[35] the question about the extraterritorial effects of the EUCFR is no longer relevant.[36] Where the EU has the power and competence to act, it has human rights obligations to persons affected by such exercise of power and competence. By extension, constructing the geographical reach of the EUCFR as territorial would reduce the problems of EU accountability that we often encounter in the context of extraterritorial action or effects.

The second lens that the chapter utilizes is that of territorial extension.[37] According to Scott:[38]

> a measure is considered to give rise to territorial extension where its application is triggered by the existence of a territorial connection with the EU (most notably, but not only, market access) but where an assessment of compliance with the law requires an evaluation of foreign conduct and/or third country law. A territorial connection may take the form of conduct within the territory of an EU member state or physical or legal presence within the EU.

The notion of territorial extension of EU law is distinct from that of extraterritoriality or extraterritorial jurisdiction, which is the competence to make, apply and enforce rules of conduct in respect of persons, property or events beyond the EU's territory.[39] This notion is preferred to that of extraterritoriality as the latter applied to the EU is considered to refer broadly to situations of active nationality, i.e. it concerns situations where a measure regulates the foreign conduct of EU citizens. The trigger is thus nationality rather than territory,[40] with the potential of missing a whole range of scenarios.

---

[32]Ryngaert (2018), at 376.

[33]For detailed examination, see among others: Kanalan (2018), at 45–49, Milanovic (2011), Chapter 4; Ryngaert (2008), Chap. 2; Tzevelekos (2014).

[34]Ibid., at 377.

[35]Territory is intrinsically linked with sovereignty as it is one of statehood's constitutive elements. This explains why jurisdiction is to a large extent territorial. Extraterritorial jurisdiction is thus exceptional: the aim is to minimise the interference of the exercise of jurisdiction by one state with the sovereignty of another state—in accordance with sovereign equality; for detailed analysis, see Ryngaert (2008), Ch. 3.

[36]Ibid.

[37]Scott (2014a, b, 2019).

[38]Ibid.

[39]See in this sense, Kamminga (2012). "Prescriptive jurisdiction" refers to a state's authority to lay down legal norms; "enforcement jurisdiction" refers to a state's authority to ensure compliance with its laws.

[40]Scott, above no. 37.

By combining Ryngaert's jurisdictional model with Scott's concept of territorial extension it is possible to take into account the act of prescription that governs a person's legal position and conduct abroad, and the actual enforcement of that act.

The chapter is structured as follows. It starts by unpacking the meaning of extraterritoriality in international human rights law and the problems in attempting to apply this notion to the *sui generis* nature of the EU. It then proceeds to a first examination of the nature of the human rights obligations of the EU, advocating for an obligation to protect human rights beyond its borders. In this context, the analysis focuses on the duty of due diligence, both as a standard of conduct and as a legally binding requirement. The chapter then proceeds to the examination of the afore-mentioned jurisdictional model and its operationalization in the EU context. Here, an argument is presented to explain why a narrow interpretation of the duty of diligence, in the form of strict liability, would befit the EU. The rest of the chapter examines further the nature of the EU's human rights obligations by looking at specific treaty provisions and key decisions of the CJEU. Here, the focus is on how compliance with human rights has become a parameter of legality of EU external action. This analysis provides the basis for the second argument put forward in the chapter, namely, a revisited reading of the principle of implied powers in the form of "functional" human rights competence. The conclusion brings together the chapter's main points with some reflections on the nature of the EU's human rights obligations.

6.2 Understanding Extraterritoriality

6.2.1 Introduction

While the extraterritorial projection of state power is not a phenomenon of recent times in and of itself, its legal regulation and the application of international legal rules by courts is a relatively new development. It is perhaps for this reason that extraterritoriality has many names and different faces[41] encapsulating different scenarios. It is wide-ranging and multidimensional. Terms such as "external governance",[42] "externalisation",[43] "extra-territorialisation",[44] "Brussels effect",[45] "extraterritorial effects",[46] "global reach" of EU law[47] and "territorial extension"[48] all refer to

---

[41] Velluti and Tzevelekos (2018).

[42] Lavenex and Schimmelfennig (2009).

[43] Frelick et al. (2016).

[44] Rijpma and Cremona (2007).

[45] Bradford (2012).

[46] Bartels (2015a).

[47] Fahey (2017).

[48] Scott, above no. 37.

different conceptualizations and frames of analysis of the EU's practice and regulatory impact in various policy areas beyond its territorial borders. These notions also acknowledge the fact that the connection between a given measure and the conduct abroad may be one of influence, incentivization, or manipulation, i.e. a relation of (political) power but, at the same time, the link may be one based on a relation of authority, i.e. a particular measure may also aim at governing conduct overseas.[49]

Ganesh maintains that: 'the correct test for whether a measure engages in extraterritorial jurisdiction is to ask, "where are you when you are being told what to do?" If the answer is "somewhere overseas," then it constitutes extraterritorial jurisdiction. This test takes seriously both the words "extraterritorial" and "jurisdiction"—the latter means "speaking the law".[50] *Prima facie*, this reading of extraterritoriality appears to be somewhat simplistic to the point that any situation where the EU has competence, authority and power to act beyond its borders could be described as extraterritorial. In other words, if the aim of a given measure is to produce some kind of effects in third countries then it is extraterritorial. However, it is well known particularly in the field of international human rights law that extraterritoriality is a complex and multi-faceted legal problem. Complexity in the conceptualization and delimitation of extraterritoriality translates into complexity in the relevant legal framework.[51] By extension, this inherent conceptual complexity explains the diversity of its operation in (and within) different policy areas with the resulting difficulty of drawing clear-cut conclusions.[52]

A first case of extraterritoriality is one based on attribution, which can be either direct or indirect. In the first case, actions that are attributable to a state under international law take place outside its territory. In the second case, particularly in relation to human rights, when the conduct under consideration consists of an omission and a state proves to be negligent in its duty to provide protection to persons that are outside its territory the situation becomes more complex as the criteria as to when states have a duty to protect beyond their borders are not yet fully clear.[53]

---

[49]Ganesh, above no. 5, at 495.

[50]Ganesh, above no. 5, at 503.

[51]Velluti and Tzevelekos, above no. 41.

[52]Cremona and Scott, above no. 20, at p. 3.

[53]The notion of extraterritorial obligations found in the *Maastricht Principles on Extraterritorial Obligations of States in the Area of Economic, Social and Cultural Rights* is helpful in capturing these nuances and related complexities, see Clause 8 which provides a definition of extraterritorial obligations as: (a) 'obligations relating to the acts and omissions of a State, within or beyond its territory, that have effects on the enjoyment of human rights outside of that State's territory; and (b) obligations of a global character that are set out in the Charter of the United Nations and human rights instruments to take action, separately, and jointly through international cooperation, to realize human rights universally.' See ETO Consortium, *Maastricht Principles on Extraterritorial Obligations of States in the Area of Economic, Social and Cultural Rights*, adopted 28 September 2011, available at: https://www.etoconsortium.org/nc/en/main-navigation/library/maastricht-principles/?tx_drblob_pi1%5BdownloadUid%5D = 23, accessed on 20 February 2020; for the official commentary, see De Schutter et al. (2012); for academic commentary, see Wilde (2018), Fons Coomans and Rolf Künnemann (2012), Langford et al. (2012).

However, there are more nuanced situations where, for example, an individual state or the EU may exercise prescriptive jurisdiction by enacting a law that governs an area, which falls outside its borders. This can occur when imposing obligations on its own nationals abroad[54] or on any person, irrespective of nationality, when its conduct can be connected with its legal system such as when the conduct produces effects within the EU.[55] The former scenario concerning nationals is somewhat easier to link to extraterritoriality,[56] and may even correspond to a duty of extraterritorial protection under international human rights law.[57]

The CJEU has increasingly accepted that EU law can also apply to conduct in respect of persons, property or events "outside" the EU's borders.[58] By way of example, the *Air Transportation of America (ATAA)* case,[59] arguably shows the Court's willingness to uphold the validity of EU measures that give rise to territorial extension. The case concerned the EU Emissions Trading System (ETS),[60] which forced airline operators on flights to and from EU destinations to surrender emission allowances for emissions emitted during those flights. A number of American airline companies challenged the directive for being a unilateral and extraterritorial attempt to enforce EU's climate change policies on others and, therefore, in violation of a number of international treaties and principles of customary international law. The CJEU rejected any arguments that the directive putting in place the ETS scheme

[54]Scott, above no. 37, at 94–95, 115 (especially footnote no. 108).

[55]Ibid. pp. 95–96.

[56]Ibid. pp. 94–95.

[57]In this regard, see the notion of "active nationality" as a jurisdictional basis for a home state to regulate and eventually sanction the conduct of investors abroad when their conduct raises human rights concerns. Tzevelekos (2010), at 216–218; see also McCorquodale (2006), Deva (2004).

[58]For the many examples to be found in the Court's case law in different fields of law, see the collection of essays by Cremona and Scott (2019).

[59]Case C-366/10, *Air Transportation of America ex parte Secretary of State for Energy and Climate Change* (*ATAA*) (ECLI:EU:C:2011:864), para. 124; see also Case C-592/14 *European Federation for Cosmetic Ingredients v Secretary of State for Business, Innovation and Skills* ECLI:EU:C:2016:703. The case concerned Article 18(1)(b) of Regulation (EC) No. 1223/2009 of the European Parliament and of the Council of 30 November 2009 on cosmetic products (Text with EEA relevance) OJ L342/59 (the "Cosmetics Regulation"). The provision prohibits the placing on the EU market of cosmetics containing ingredients which, in order to meet the requirements of the Cosmetic Regulation, have been tested on animals. The claimant sought a declaration from the Court that certain type of conduct does not fall within the prohibition and so would not involve the commission of a criminal offence. In particular, the claimant contended that where ingredients are tested in third countries for the purpose of satisfying the legislative or regulatory requirements of that third country, then the use of ingredients in cosmetics placed on the market in the EU does not involve a contravention of the prohibition. The EU's animal welfare laws extend their reach outside its borders—according to the CJEU—'actively promoting use of non-animal alternative methods to ensure the safety of products in the cosmetics sector' (para 34), no matter where in the world that testing happens. For the Court, the focus of the analysis is the use of animal testing data in EU safety assessments, which is an activity that falls within EU jurisdiction, regardless of where any such testing may have taken place.

[60]Directive 2008/101/EC of the European Parliament and of the Council of 19 November 2008 amending Directive 2003/87/EC so as to include aviation activities in the scheme for greenhouse gas emission allowance trading within the Community (Text with EEA relevance) OJ [2009] L8/3.

was in violation of international law. It held that because the directive only applies to aircraft landing and departing from EU territory, i.e. physically present within the EU and thus subject to the unlimited jurisdiction of the EU and its member states, it was in line with the principle of territoriality dismissing any extraterritorial effects as being irrelevant.[61] *ATAA* is a good example of how territorial extension can be unpleasantly overpowering for non-EU states and actors.[62] Scott maintains that the overbearing quality of EU laws' territorial extension is somewhat attenuated where the EU is either seeking to promote international law or it leads to negotiations between the EU and a non-Union state leading to some form of mutual accommodation.[63]

The *Zuchtvieh* case instead shows a Court that construes the remit of EU law in such a broad manner so as to permit its application to foreign conduct and is thus accepting seemingly the extraterritoriality of EU law.[64] In particular, the CJEU held that, in the case of the transportation of goods commencing in the territory of the EU but ending outside of its territory, an EU regulation on the protection of animals during transport and related operations is also applicable to stages of that journey taking place in the territory of one or more third countries outside the EU, the main reason being that, in relation to the authorization of the competent authority, the regulation does not provide for any distinction between transport within the EU and transport with a destination in a third country.[65]

The next section provides an overview of the international human rights legal framework and it examines the extent to which it can be applied to the EU legal order in light of its *sui generis* nature.

6.2.2 The Extraterritoriality of Human Rights Obligations in International Law and the EU Legal Context: Opening Pandora's Box?

The extraterritorial application of human rights obligations is a vexed question. As Yuval Shany cogently puts it: 'the debate over the extraterritorial application of

[61] Case C-366/10, above no. 59, paras. 124–128.

[62] For a discussion of the reaction of the United States (US) to the application of the EU ETS scheme to the US aviation industry, see Fahey (2014), at 371–373.

[63] Scott, above no. 36, at 113–123.

[64] Case C-424/13, *Zuchtvieh-Export GmbH* (ECLI:EU:C:2015:259), paras. 44–46 and 52. The case concerned Council Regulation (EC) No 1/2005 of 22 December 2004 on the protection of animals during transport and related operations and amending Directives 64/432/EEC and 93/119/EC and Regulation (EC) No 1255/97 ("Regulation No 1/2005") OJ L 3/1.

[65] In particular, the legal question related essentially to the granting or refusal of transport approval by the competent authority of the place of departure on the basis of the planning information provided in the journey log submitted to that authority as part of the checks provided for in Article 14 of the contested EU Regulation.

human rights is mired up in a Koskenniemic tension between an ideal (the universality of human rights) and political reality (the principle of effectiveness, which militates against normative overreach).'[66] Linked to this, are also two other tensions at play: one between the need to ensure effective protection of human rights and the continued commitment to territoriality as an organizing principle of the international legal order—as explained further below—even though borders as such are not decisive for ensuring human welfare;[67] and the other one concerning the institutional relationship of courts to governments, or law to politics.[68] As a standard rule jurisdiction is primarily territorial as territory is one of the core elements of statehood and national sovereignty.[69] It follows that the state's competence to exercise legislative, judicial and executive authority applies within its own territory.[70] The common characteristic of the traditional jurisdictional bases is the existence of a link between the state and the person over which it exercises its powers, the only exception being universal jurisdiction.

Extraterritorial jurisdiction is thus exceptional, the reason being a reduction of interference of the exercise of jurisdiction by one state with the sovereignty of another state in line with sovereign equality, which 'is a fundamental axiomatic premise of the international legal order'.[71] In addition, there are certain limits as to how and when a state may exercise extraterritorial jurisdiction: although prescriptive jurisdiction is in principle unlimited, laws cannot be enforced on the territory of another state without its consent.

With regard to international human rights law, jurisdiction has been circumscribed by the criterion of "effective control". According to the European Court of Human Rights (ECtHR), for a state to be responsible for extraterritorial human rights breaches, it must first be established that it exercises jurisdiction.[72] Secondly, that a state is found to exercise effective control[73] over a person or a territory and, in particular, over the situation raising human rights concerns. If these conditions are

---

[66] Shany (2011).

[67] Ibid.

[68] Ibid.

[69] See for instance ICJ, *Legal Consequences of the Construction of a Wall in the Occupied Palestinian Territory*, Advisory Opinion, 09 July 2004, para 109 and ECtHR, *Banković and others v. Belgium, the Czech Republic, Denmark, France, Germany, Greece, Hungary, Iceland, Italy, Luxembourg, the Netherlands, Norway, Poland, Portugal, Spain, Turkey and the United Kingdom*, Application No. 52207/99, 12 December 2001, para. 59. See also the references that the ECtHR makes to scholars supporting this point of view.

[70] However, territory is not the only basis of jurisdiction. On the bases of jurisdiction see, for instance, Higgins (2009); Ryngaert, above no. 35, Chs. 3 and 4.

[71] Kokott (2011).

[72] ECtHR, *Ilaşcu and Others v. Moldova and Russia*, Application No. 48787/99, 8 July 2004, para. 311.

[73] E.g. *Banković*, above no. 23, para. 71; the Bankovic interpretation has been subjected to numerous exceptions, and seems to have been contradicted in a later decision by a single chamber of the ECtHR, see ECtHR *Issa and Others v Turkey*, Application No. 31821/96, 16 November 2004. Cf. with the Human Rights Committee (HRC) notion of effective control and approach to extraterritorial obligations seem to be broader than those of the ECtHR, e.g. HRC, 'General Comment 31: Nature of the General Obligation Imposed on States Parties to the Covenant', UN doc. CCPR/C/21/Rev.1/Add.13

met it follows that a state has an obligation under the ECHR to respect or protect human rights outside its borders. While *respect* for human rights is a negative obligation, namely, the state must abstain from causing a wrongful result through conduct directly attributable to it,[74] *protection* corresponds to positive obligations associated with the principle of due diligence,[75] which imposes obligations of *means* i.e. require or prohibit certain conduct or behavior by states rather than *result*, i.e. require states to bring about a certain situation or result.[76] States are expected to take all actions necessary to protect human rights that are endangered or breached because of the conduct of actors/persons whose conduct is not attributable to the states themselves.[77] The criterion of effective control has been criticised in academia but scholars remain divided.[78] Significantly, in 2017 the Inter-American Court of Human Rights (I-ACtHR) delivered an advisory opinion, which relied on causality rather than the effective control criterion.[79]

When this rather complicated and, to some degree, incomplete legal framework is applied to the EU, which is a unique international legal person, further questions of attribution and allocation of responsibility between the EU and its member states come to the fore.[80] Even though the EU is not a state it is increasingly involved in territorial questions, either of its own or of other states not only in relation to the changing role of borders in its internal market, but also in the context of its role as a global actor.[81] Moreover, with the international role of the EU becoming increasingly important, there has been a growing realization that EU external action can have a significant impact on much more than economic activity and that it can raise profound

(26 May 2004), para. 10; HRC, *Munaf v Romania*, UN doc. CCPR/C?96/D/1539/2006 (21 August 2009).

[74]Indirect attribution instead refers to indirect responsibility for lack of due diligence, see Salmon (2001). In the case of respect for human rights, the ECtHR is stricter when assessing whether effective control can act as a precondition for the exercise of extraterritorial jurisdiction, e.g. ECtHR, *Rantsev v. Cyprus and Russia*, Application No. 25965/04, 07 January 2010, paras. 207–208; *Ilaşcu*, above no. 61, para. 331.

[75]For instance, see HRC, General Comment No. 31: The Nature of the General Legal Obligation Imposed on States Parties to the Covenant, CCPR/C/21/Rev.1/Add. 13, 29 March 2004, para. 8.

[76]Proulx (2012).

[77]For detailed analysis on the meaning of due diligence, see Samuel (2018/2019).

[78]For a critique of the effective control criterion as a precondition for extraterritoriality in human rights law, see Tzevelekos (2015).

[79]I-ACHR, Advisory Opinion *OC-23/17*, The Environment and Human Rights (State obligations in relation to the environment in the context of the protection and guarantee of the rights to life and to personal integrity—interpretation and scope of Articles 4(1) and 5(1) of the American Convention on Human Rights), 15 November 2017. In particular the Court held that: 'the persons whose rights have been breached are under the jurisdiction of the State of origin if there is a causal link between the fact that originates in its territory and the impairment of human rights of persons outside its territory' (para. 101; translation of the authors); for commentary, see A. Berkes, 'A New Extraterritorial Jurisdictional Link Recognised by the IACtHR', EJIL:*Talk!*, available at: https://www.ejiltalk.org/a-new-extraterritorial-jurisdictional-link-recognised-by-the-iacthr/#more-16059, accessed on 29 March 2018.

[80]E.g. see the collection of essays edited by Evans and Koutrakos (2013), d'Aspremont (2014).

[81]Cardwell and Wessel (2020).

questions of social and environmental concern as well as having significant effects in respect of human rights beyond the borders of EU member states.

However, with the exception of the 2008 UN Convention on the Rights of Persons with Disabilities,[82] the EU is not formally bound by any multilateral or regional human rights treaty. Nevertheless, fundamental human rights are part of general international law, which binds international organisations,[83] including supranational entities such as the EU.[84] In the Treaty on European Union, compliance with international law together with, among others, democracy, the rule of law, human rights and fundamental freedoms is presented as one of the principles which have inspired the Union's own creation.[85] Respect for international law effectively is one of the Union's fundamental constitutional principles. In *ATAA* (Air Transport Association of America),[86] the CJEU linked the compliance with international law to the obligation set out in Article 3(5) TEU to reaffirm that the EU is bound, not only by the international agreements it is a party to but also by international customary law. There are then a set of key human rights provisions, which are essentially "EU"-based. Article 2 TEU states that the EU is founded *inter alia* on the value of respect for human rights and Article 3(1) TEU provides that the Union's aims include the promotion of its values. Article 6 TEU is a key human rights provision, which grants legally binding status to the EU Charter of Fundamental Rights (EUCFR), envisages EU accession to the ECHR as an obligation and makes explicit reference to fundamental rights as general principles of EU law.[87] The combined reading of these provisions illustrates the foundational and pervasive character of human rights in EU law.[88]

When we associate these human rights provisions with the extraterritoriality of EU law many questions about its human rights impact as well as the nature of the EU's human rights obligations come to the fore, both from the perspective of international law and EU law. The changes introduced by the TL confirm that the EU intends to have

---

[82]The EU ratified this Convention in 2010, see United Nations Convention on the Rights of Persons with Disabilities, New York, 13 December 2006, available at: https://treaties.un.org/pages/ViewDetails.aspx?src = IND&mtdsg_no = IV-15&chapter = 4&clang = _en, accessed on 29 January 2020.

[83]ICJ, *Interpretation of the Agreement of 25 March 1951 between the WHO and Egypt*, Advisory Opinion, 20 December 1980, para. 37. Among other scholars, see Daugirdas (2016).

[84]See also United Nations Human Rights Office of the High Commissioner (OHCHR), 'The European Union and International Human Rights Law', available at: https://europe.ohchr.org/Documents/Publications/EU_and_International_Law.pdf, accessed on 20 February 2020, p. 23.

[85]Article 21(1) TEU.

[86]Case C-366/10 *Air Transport Association of America v Secretary of State for Energy and Climate Change* [2011] ECLI:EU:C:2011:864, para. 101; see also paras. 102–130.

[87]Long before the constitutionalization in the Treaties of fundamental rights as general principles of EU law, the CJEU played a crucial role in conceiving fundamental rights as general principles of EU law; for an overview and discussion, see de Búrca (2011), Craig and de Búrca (2015); Chapter 11; on the tension between universalism and particularism in the EU context and the CJEU's "judicial colonialism", see Cantabria (2009).

[88]Costello and Moreno Lax (2014), at p. 1660.

a significant role outside its territory,[89] not only in relation to the external dimension of the internal market, but also in relation to normative objectives of global justice such as human rights. The EU has been considering territorial questions from the outset with many references to territory in the EU Treaties and in the CJEU case law,[90] even though they concern mostly member states' territories. In this regard, scholars maintain that: 'it is clearly possible to speak of the emergence of the concept of Union territory, given the autonomous demarcation of the territorial application of EU law defined in the Treaties'.[91] Certainly, we can see the CJEU 'making an intervention into the international legal conversation about jurisdiction and the meaning of territorial borders in a world of globalized production and consumption'.[92]

Questions about the EU's territory, its global reach and that of its laws are particularly important for the pursuit of its normative goals. According to Article 2 TEU, the respect for human dignity and human rights features among the values of the EU. Article 21(2)(b) and (d) TEU includes among the objectives of EU external action human rights and sustainable economic, social and environmental development of developing countries. Furthermore, according to Article 21(2)(b) TEU, one of the goals of the EU in its external action is to 'consolidate and support democracy, the rule of law, human rights and the principles of international law.' These goals apply both to the Union's external action and the external aspects of its other policies.[93] Article 21(3) TEU refers to the external aspects of the Union's other policies and arguably extends the scope of application of the EU's external human rights obligations.[94] Article 3(5) TEU refers, *inter alia*, to the Union upholding and promoting its values in its relations with the wider world. Moreover, from a combined reading of Articles 3(5) and 21 TEU, the EU emerges not only as a passive norm recipient but also as a shaper and generator of international rules. Thus, 'in contrast to the pre-Lisbon era, the Treaties present the EU as an international actor that is committed to protect and promote collective interests and values in accordance with and by means of international law'.[95]

---

[89]As per Articles 52 TEU and 355 TFEU. Article 52(2) TEU points to the territorial scope of the Treaties as specified in Article 355 TFEU, which in turn lists the overseas territories belonging to some of the Member States and the extent to which EU law does or does not apply.

[90]The Court increasingly refers to "territory of the EU", *e.g.* C-177/95 *Ebony Maritime SA and Loten Navigation Co. Ltd v Prefetto della Provincia di Brindisi and others* ECLI:EU:C:1997:89; Case C-34/09 *Gerardo Ruiz Zambrano v Office national de l'emploi* ECLI:EU:C:2011:124.

[91]Kochenov (2019); see Article 4(2) TEU where it provides, *inter alia*, that: 'It [the Union] shall respect their essential state functions, including ensuring the territorial integrity of the state'.

[92]Lawrence (2016)

[93]Article 21(3) TEU; Bartels, above no. 46, at 1074–1075.

[94]Bartels, above no. 46, at 1074–1075.

[95]Velluti and Tzevelekos, above no. 41.

However, the EU does not have a general competence in the field of human rights, i.e. conferred competence within the meaning of Article 5(1) and (2) TEU.[96] Moreover, the above provisions do not require the EU to pursue these objectives in any specific way. Quite the opposite, the Treaties give little specific guidance on how international law should be applied within the EU legal order.[97] Thus far, the Court has failed to make significant use of existing provisions putting emphasis on the EU's commitment to comply with international law or has applied provisions dealing with international law in a restrictive or narrow manner.[98] As a consequence, there is little guidance in practice as to how the EU is to exercise its powers and implement its policies and laws outside its borders particularly those of a non-economic nature.

The above analysis shows why traditional doctrines of extraterritoriality might not be helpful in understanding the global reach of EU law and the nature of the EU's human rights obligations.

The next section starts by examining due diligence, both as a standard and a legally binding obligation in order to see how this duty can be of aid in developing a duty of protection of human rights for the EU beyond its borders. It then looks at Ryngaert's "internal-territorial" model through the lens of territorial extension as coined by Scott. In addition to setting the framework of analysis, this section advocates for the application of a narrow interpretation of the duty of due diligence to the EU in the form of strict liability.

---

[96] See also Article 7 TFEU; for a discussion of the problems raised by the EU's lack of a general competence in the field of human rights for EU external trade relations, see Velluti (2016).

[97] For further analysis, see the contributions to the Special Issue, Moreno-Lax and Gragl (2016), et seq.

[98] While the CJEU has long held that the EU must respect international law in the exercise of its powers and that international law forms an integral part of EU law (see *e.g.* Case C-162/96 *Racke v Hauptzollamt Mainz* ECLI:EU:C:1998:293, para. 45 Case C-286/90 *Anklagemindigheden v Poulsen* ECLI:EU:C:1992:453; Case 181/73 *Haegeman* ECLI:EU:C:1974:41, para. 5), at the same time, it has also forcefully held that the validity of EU law cannot be challenged on the basis of international law, thereby denying giving direct effect to international law, both in the trade and non-trade sphere (with very limited and narrowly interpreted exceptions), *e.g.* Joined Cases 21/72-24/72 *International Fruit Company NV and others* ECLI:EU:C:1972:115, para. 28; *Case C-280/93 Germany v Council* ECLI:EU:C:1994:367, para. 112; Case C-308/06 *Intertanko and Others*, ECLI:EU:C:2008:312, para. 65. The CJEU's resistance is most vividly exemplified by the *Kadi* decisions, Joined Cases C-402/05 P and C-415/05 P *Kadi and Al Barakaat International Foundation v Council and Commission (Kadi I)* ECLI:EU:C:2008:461; Joined Cases C-584/10 P, C-593/10 P, and C-595/10 P *Commission and Others v Yassin Abdullah Kadi (Kadi II)* ECLI:EU:C:2013:518 as well as by Opinion 2/13 on the compatibility with EU law of the draft agreement for EU accession to the European Convention of Human Rights and Fundamental Freedoms (ECHR), ECLI:EU:C:2014:2454.

6.3 Territoriality, Territorial Extension and Human Rights Due Diligence Obligations

6.3.1 The Concept and Role of Due Diligence as a Positive Human Rights Obligation

Due diligence is not a novel concept in international law.[99] Seen by the International Court of Justice (ICJ) as a customary norm[100] or general principle of law,[101] the notion of due diligence, and its associated legal principles and obligations, has become

---

[99]First references to the term "due diligence" can be traced back to the nineteenth century, e.g. *Alabama Arbitration* case which took place in Geneva in 1871. It concerned claims made by the United States ('US') against Great Britain arising from Britain's conduct in relation to not fulfilling its duties of neutrality during the American Civil War (1861–65), see further Bingham (2010).

[100]International Court of Justice (ICJ), *Pulp Mills on the River Uruguay (Argentina v Uruguay)* [2010] ICJ Rep 55–6, para 101. In this case the ICJ was of the view that both procedural (discussed in detail at paras. 80–122) and substantive obligations (their alleged violation is discussed at paras. 169–266) arose out of the treaty obligation of cooperation (para. 77), possessing their own separate existence with accompanying duties of performance as well as potential for breach (paras. 78–79). For further detailed analysis, see Samuel, above no. 77, Sect. 1.5.1. See also Article 1(3) of the UN Charter which refers achieving international cooperation in solving international problems of an economic, social, cultural or humanitarian character and in promoting and encouraging respect for human rights and for fundamental freedoms, Article 56 of the UN Charter, which obliges states to take "joint and separate action" to achieve the objectives set out in Article 55 of the UN Charter, namely, the promotion of: a. higher standards of living, full employment, and conditions of economic and social progress and development; b. solutions of international economic, social, health, and related problems; and international cultural and educational cooperation; and, c. universal respect for, and observance of, human rights and fundamental freedoms for all without distinction as to race, sex, language, or religion. Furthermore, Articles 22 and 28 of the Universal Declaration of Human Rights (UDHR) seemingly imply extraterritorial obligations. Article 22 UDHR provides that: 'Everyone, as a member of society, has the right to social security and is entitled to realization, through national effort and international co-operation and in accordance with the organization and resources of each State, of the economic, social and cultural rights indispensable for his dignity and the free development of his personality.' Article 28 UDHR states that: 'Everyone is entitled to a social and international order in which the rights and freedoms set forth in this Declaration can be fully realized.' Finally, see Article 3(3) of the Declaration on the Right to Development (DRD), which states that: 'States have the duty to co-operate with each other in ensuring development and eliminating obstacles to development. States should realize their rights and fulfil their duties in such a manner as to promote a new international economic order based on sovereign equality, interdependence, mutual interest and co-operation among all States, as well as to encourage the observance and realization of human rights' and Article 4 DRD, which provides that: 'States have the duty to take steps, individually and collectively, to formulate international development policies with a view to facilitating the full realization of the right to development. Sustained action is required to promote more rapid development of developing countries. As a complement to the efforts of developing countries, effective international co-operation is essential in providing these countries with appropriate means and facilities to foster their comprehensive development.' Even though the DRD's status as customary international law is not undisputed its provisions add to the already existent normative evidence of extraterritorial duties to fulfil human rights discussed above.

[101]ICJ, *Corfu Channel,* above no. 98, at p. 22; see also *Trailer Smelter Case (US v Canada)* (1941) 3 RIAA 1905; for an academic definition of due diligence as a basic principle of international law, see

increasingly important globally as a means to ensure adequate protection of human rights. At its core there is the indivisible element of "due, or merited, care".[102] However, 'its definition, parameters and potential reach are often not clearly identified or understood'.[103] Notably, there can be a tendency by scholars and judges to conflate due diligence standards with the corresponding obligations, which is in part due to unclear and fluid conceptualizations.[104] Because of the different legal consequences that can ensue when there is a breach it is necessary to clearly distinguish between what is merely influential and what is formally binding.[105]

International legal scholars broadly define due diligence as a standard of conduct required to discharge an obligation.[106] It is understood as a norm that prescribes the limits of legal conduct while allowing 'a certain margin of attainment within the bounds of reason', as opposed to a "rule", defined as 'capable of strictly logical application'.[107] Generally, standards are intended to encourage both state and non-state actors to comply with substantive legal norms, aimed at improved practice, which are not formally binding upon them.[108] In this context, standards can act as a source of guidance or even interpretation for treaties and customary international law.[109] Moreover, standards can also contribute to the development or even codification of conventional and customary international law norms. Since standards are

Barnidge (2006), at pp. 82, 86 and 91; *contra* McDonald (2019). For detailed analysis, see Samuel, above no. 77, Section 1.5.1.

[102]Barnidge, above no. 101, at 118, citing Carsten Corino (2000).

[103]Samuel, above no. 77, at 1.

[104]Ibid; see also Duffy (2005), at p. 305; see also McDonald, above no. 101.

[105]Ibid.

[106]Bonnitcha and McCorquodale (2017), at 901; see also John Ruggie, Report of the Special Representative of the Secretary-General on the issue of human rights and transnational corporations and other business enterprises, *Protect, Respect and Remedy: A Framework for Business and Human Rights*, Report to the UN Human Rights Council, (Framework Report), UN Doc. A/HRC/8/5, 7 April 2008, available at: https://www.business-humanrights.org/sites/default/files/reports-and-materials/Ruggie-report-7-Apr-2008.pdf, accessed 20 February 2020, note 22, where there is reference to due diligence as defined in *Black's Law Dictionary* (8th edition, Eagan: Thomson West, 2006) as 'the diligence reasonably expected from, and ordinarily exercised by, a person who seeks to satisfy a legal requirement or discharge an obligation', compare with the Merriam-Webster Dictionary's first definition of due diligence is 'the care that a reasonable person exercises to avoid harm to other persons or their property', *Merriam-Webster Dictionary* 'Due Diligence', available at: https://www.merriam-webster.com/dictionary/due%20diligence, accessed on 20 February 2020; see also International Law Commission (ILC), 'International responsibility. Second report by F. v Garcia Amador' (15 February 1957) UN Doc A/CN.4/106, 122, para 3; ILC 'The law of the non-navigational uses of international watercourses' (15 February 1957) UN Doc A/49/10, 103, para 5.

[107]Pound (1921), at 776; see also the individual opinion of Judge Alvarez in the *Corfu Channel* case, who examined what he termed "the obligation of vigilance", a term which seemed to be used as an alternative to "due diligence", in the sense of a non-binding standard, see ICJ, *Corfu Channel (United Kingdom v Albania)*, Judgment, ICJ Reports 1949 *(Corfu Channel case)*, p. 4, Individual Opinion by Judge Alvarez, (Judge Alvarez Opinion), at p. 44.

[108]Samuel, above no. 77, at 5.

[109]A good illustration of how due diligence standards can inform the interpretation of a treaty text and extend its normative content and reach, is the issue of discriminatory conduct or acts of violence towards women. The UN Committee for the Elimination of Discrimination against Women

implemented on a voluntary basis, they are not legally enforceable.[110] At the same time, there is an expectation that the addressees will nevertheless abide by them.[111] The danger here lies in not confusing standards (of conduct) with the obligation of diligence (i.e. to protect). The latter can help shape standards and their content giving them binding status.

Due diligence as a legal obligation requires that states take all reasonable efforts within their power to prevent and repress the commission of internationally wrongful acts by others, that is non-state private actors or other states.[112] Binding due diligence obligations may be provided for expressly or else implied from a treaty text. As Brownlie maintains: 'reasonableness is a golden thread in determining which measures states should take to act in a duly diligent manner',[113] although its meaning is context specific. In practice, a state is required to take all reasonable steps[114] to inform itself of relevant factual and legal matters in relation to any risk associated with a given measure and to have a plan of action to address these risks in a timely and appropriate fashion.[115] If a state fails to take these reasonable steps, for example if it 'knew or ought to have known' about the risks involved with a given action and failed to 'take appropriate measures' or 'to exercise due diligence to prevent' or 'to do all that could be reasonably expected of it'[116]—the state concerned will be

---

has relied on the concept of due diligence to expand the substantive scope of the UN Convention for the Elimination of Discrimination against Women (CEDAW) so as to include domestic violence, in spite of the fact that it happens in the private sphere and is not envisaged in the text of CEDAW, e.g. UN Committee on the Elimination of Discrimination Against Women (CEDAW) (2010), *General Recommendation No. 28 on the Core Obligations of States Parties under Article 2 of the Convention on the Elimination of All Forms of Discrimination against Women*, UN Doc CEDAW/C/GC/28, at para. 19. In so doing, the Committee referred to its own General Recommendation 19 on violence against women according to which: 'under general international law and specific human rights covenants, states may also be responsible for private acts if they fail to act with due diligence to prevent violations of rights', see CEDAW, '*General Recommendation No. 19: Violence against women*', (Eleventh session 1992), at para. 9; see also CEDAW General Recommendation No. 28, above, para. 13, and CEDAW, General recommendation No. 35 *on gender-based violence against women, updating general recommendation No. 19,* 14 July 2017, CEDAW/C/GC/35.

[110]E.g. *OECD Guidelines for Multinational Enterprises,* 25 May 2011, available at: https://www.oecd.org/daf/inv/mne/oecdguidelinesformultinationalenterprises.htm, accessed on 20 February 2020, p. 17, para. 1.

[111]E.g. OHCHR 'Guiding Principles on business and human rights' (21 March 2011) UN Doc. A/HRC/17/31, p. 13, para. 11; p.14, para. 12; p.19, para. 17.

[112]Koivurova (2010), para 2.

[113]Ian Brownlie (2008).

[114]Depending on the specific situation, these reasonable steps may be either one-off or ongoing See *Pulp Mills*, ICJ 2010, above no. 93, pp. 83–84, para. 205.

[115]ILC, *Draft articles on Prevention of Transboundary Harm from Hazardous Activities, with commentaries, Yearbook of the International Law Commission*, 2001, vol II, Part Two, available at: https://legal.un.org/ilc/texts/instruments/english/commentaries/9_7_2001.pdf, accessed on 20 February 2020, p. 154, para. 10.

[116]E.g. UN Human Rights Committee (CCPR) (2004) *General Comment No. 31: The Nature of the General Legal Obligation Imposed on States Parties to the Covenant*, UN Doc CCPR/C/21/Rev.1/Add. 13, paras. 6, 8. ('*CCPR General Comment No. 31*').

considered to have acted negligently and, therefore, to have breached its due diligence obligations.[117] In these circumstances, their breach may constitute a wrongful act for the purpose of triggering international legal responsibility.[118]

Under international human rights law, therefore, due diligence imposes a positive obligation on states that are required to protect human rights against violations committed by third parties, including non-state actors such as corporations.

Following Shue's idea of human rights and the existence of a set of triple duties correlative to the exercise of all rights,[119] this due diligence human rights' obligation can be said to be made up of other obligations, namely, to *protect* and *fulfil* human rights treaty obligations, and to *ensure* adequate remedies in the event of a breach. The obligation to *protect* requires that states act proactively to safeguard those rights guaranteed under a particular human rights treaty and prevent third parties from interfering with an individual's ability to exercise that right.[120] Where a state fails to take proper steps to protect an individual, including through its failure to prevent a human rights violation from occurring in the first place and then by not *ensuring* adequate remedies in the event of a breach, it will be found to have acted negligently and thus in breach of its due diligence obligations.[121] The negative obligation to *respect* a human right is an obligation to avoid measures that hinder or prevent the enjoyment of an individual's right. Related to the latter, the duty to *fulfil* a human right requires states to take the positive measures[122] necessary to allow individuals to exercise their rights without which they could be rendered meaningless or at least less effective.[123]

The existence of due diligence obligations, as opposed to mere standards, has been confirmed by case law. In particular, various human rights bodies and courts

---

[117]These can be either substantive or procedural obligations, e.g. United Nations, *AH Francis (Great Britain) v United Mexican States*, 5 RIAA 100 (1930), at para. 5; see also Judge Alvarez Opinion, *Corfu case*, above no. 100, p. 44.

[118]Samuel, above no. 77, at p. 25.

[119]According to Shue the idea of human rights entails correlative duties to respect, protect and fulfil these rights, thus rejecting the dichotomy between negative and positive rights, see H. Shue, *Basic Rights* (Princeton: Princeton University Press, 1980, 2nd edition 1996). The origin of the classification is attributed to A. Eide, see Commission on Human Rights, *Report of the UN Special Rapporteur on the Right to Food, A. Eide,* UN Doc. E/CN.4/Sub.2/1987/23 (1987), paras. 66–9.

[120]Joseph (2013), at p. 22.

[121]As established by case law, e.g. *Youmans (U.S. v. Mexico),* 4 RIAA 110 (1926), at para. 114; *Janes (U.S. v. Mexico)*, 4 RIAA 82 (1926).

[122]This obligation goes far beyond merely adopting necessary legislation. It requires a comprehensive set of measures to facilitate the implementation, enforcement and monitoring as well as evaluation of results achieved, in this sense see Ziegler, former Special Rapporteur on the Right to Food, who talks about a duty to "support the fulfilment" of International Covenant on Economic, Social and Cultural Rights (ICESCR) rights, see Commission on Human Rights, 'Report of the Special Rapporteur on the right to food, Jean Ziegler', UN doc. E/CN.4/2005/47 (24 January 2005), para. 57. Ziegler uses this term as opposed to "fulfil" recognising that a duty to completely fulfil the right could not realistically be imposed extraterritorially, as such a duty might imply that the territorial state has no such duties.

[123]The duty to *fulfil* may be further broken down into duties to *facilitate*, *promote* and *provide* for the implementation of a right, see Joseph, above no. 113, at p. 22.

have confirmed that states have due diligence obligations to protect individuals from the infringement of their human rights by corporations.[124]

The United Nations (UN) Committee on Economic, Social and Cultural Rights (CESCR) has been interpreting state parties' extraterritorial obligations for some time, on the basis of the unlimited scope of the ICESCR and, in particular, its Article 2(1) on international cooperation.[125] The CESCR interpreted the Covenant as requiring state parties to comply with its positive obligations in relation to the right to health,[126] right to water,[127] the right to social security[128] and the right to just and favourable conditions of work.[129] In particular, the CESCR held that state parties must give due attention to these rights in international agreements and, to that end, should consider the development of further legal instruments taking steps to ensure that these instruments do not adversely impact these rights.

Particular attention has been given to investment policies where states have been recommended to exercise due diligence over corporate nationals abroad by all means at their disposal in all circumstances where they know or should have known about the risk of a human rights violation.[130] In this regard, the Human Rights Committee (HRC) has recommended to state parties that all businesses domiciled in their territory and/or their jurisdiction respect human rights in accordance with the ICESCR during their operations and that they carry out investigations and set up legal redress mechanisms in relation to the harmful activities of such businesses operating abroad.[131] The CESCR has referred to state parties' capacity to influence the conduct of corporations within their jurisdiction so as to respect rights, through legal or political means, in accordance with applicable international law.[132] More recently, the CESCR has

---

[124]In the European context, e.g. ECtHR, *Bevacqua and S. v Bulgaria* App no 71127/01, 12 June 2008, para 53; ECtHR, *Opuz v Turkey*, Application no. 33401/02, 09 June 2009, paras 83–4; *Guerra and Others v Italy* (1998) 26 EHRR 357, para 58; ECtHR, *Osman v The United Kingdom*, Application No. 23452/94, 28 October 1998, para 115.

[125]Article 2(1) ICESCR provides that: 'Each State Party to the present Covenant undertakes to take steps, individually and through international assistance and co-operation, especially economic and technical, to the maximum of its available resources, with a view to achieving progressively the full realization of the rights recognized in the present Covenant by all appropriate means, including particularly the adoption of legislative measures'.

[126]Committee on Economic, Social and Cultural Rights (CESCR) 'General Comment No. 14 (2000)' (11 August 2000) UN Doc. E/C.12/2000/4, para 39 (CESCR, General Comment No. 14).

[127]CESCR, 'General Comment No. 15 (2002)' (20 January 2003) UN Doc. E/C.12/2002/11, paras 31, 33.

[128]CESCR, 'General Comment No. 19' (4 February 2008) UN Doc. E/C.12/GC/19, para 54.

[129]CESCR, 'General comment No. 23 (2016)' (27 April 2016) UN Doc. E/C.12/GC/23, para 70.

[130]For analysis and discussion, see Berkes (2018a).

[131]E.g. UN Human Rights Committee 'Concluding observations: Germany' (12 November 2012) UN Doc CCPR/C/DEU/CO/6, para 16; UN Human Rights Committee 'Concluding observations: Canada' (13 August 2015) UN Doc CCPR/C/CAN/CO/6, para 6.

[132]Including the UN Charter, e.g. CESCR 'General Comment No. 14', above no. 119, para 39; CESCR, 'General Comment No. 15, above no. 120, para 33; CESCR 'Statement on the obligations of States Parties regarding the corporate sector and economic, social and cultural rights' (20 May 2011) UN Doc. E/C.12/2011/1, para 5.

reiterated that 'states parties are required to take the necessary steps to prevent human rights violations abroad by corporations domiciled in their territory and/or jurisdiction'.[133] On this basis, the Maastricht Principles also recognised a state's duty to regulate the extraterritorial operations of its corporate nationals.[134]

In other UN bodies' recommendations there is reference to human rights impact assessments as a way of preventing the violation of human rights in third countries. States are also encouraged to appropriately regulate the investments and activities of their corporations outside their borders[135] ensuring that their legal framework can guarantee the legal accountability of companies and their subsidiaries operating in or managed from the state party's territory in relation to abuses of human rights.[136] In all of these official documents it is clear that due diligence requires positive obligations to protect.

International organizations have equally been entrusted with taking concrete measures to make sure that small and medium-sized enterprises (SMEs) integrate a human rights due diligence approach in the way they operate,[137] as well as promoting the implementation of the UN Guiding Principles on business and human rights[138] and to ensure that they consider the human rights dimension of economic growth.[139]

The above confirms that international organizations are also expected to use its apparatus for purposes of prevention and thus to evaluate the risks of human rights violations by their trade and investment partners within and outside their borders taking all reasonable efforts to avoid such foreseeable human rights violations. Arguably, these positive obligations also bind the EU, as an international legal actor, on the basis of its own internal and external human rights sources. In particular, what is here proposed is that, specifically for the EU, due diligence should be conceived as a standard of conduct which applies to situations of strict liability that does not entail a fault element, with a correlative responsibility to provide a remedy for all its adverse

---

[133] CESCR, 'General Comment No. 24' (23 June 2017) UN Doc. E/C.12/GC/24, para 26.

[134] Maastricht Principles, above no. 50, Article 24; see also Committee on the Rights of the Child (CtRC), 'General comment No. 16 (2013)' (17 April 2013) UN Doc. CRC/C/GC/16, para 43 (CtRC, General comment No. 16); CEDAW 'General recommendation No. 28' (16 December 2010) UN Doc CEDAW/C/GC/28, para 36 (CEDAW, 'General recommendation No. 28').

[135] CtRC, 'Concluding observations: Sweden' (23 January 2012) UN Doc CRC/C/OPSC/SWE/CO/1, para 21.

[136] CtRC, 'Concluding observations: Bosnia and Herzegovina' (29 November 2012) UN Doc CRC/C/BIH/CO/2–4, para 28(a).

[137] HRC, Report of the Working Group on the issue of human rights and transnational corporations and other business enterprises (24 April 2017) UN Doc. A/HRC/35/32, para 77.

[138] OHCHR, Guiding Principles, above no. 103; HRC, 'Report of the Working Group on the issue of human rights and transnational corporations and other business enterprises' (14 March 2013) UN Doc. A/HRC/23/32, para 74; HRC, 'Report of the Working Group on the issue of human rights and transnational corporations and other business enterprises' (10 August 2012) UN Doc. A/67/285, para 78.

[139] HRC, 'Report of the Working Group on the issue of human rights and transnational corporations and other business enterprises on the Asia Forum on Business and Human Rights' (30 May 2016) UN Doc. A/HRC/32/45/Add.2, para 89; see also HRC, 'Resolution No. 28/10' (2 April 2015) UN Doc. A/HRC/RES/28/10, para 38.

human rights impacts, regardless of whether those impacts were unexpected or costly to prevent and regardless of whether those adverse human rights impacts resulted from a failure to act with sufficient diligence or care.[140] One problem with fault, and thus subjective responsibility, is that understood as a psychological attitude of the human will, it is in itself difficult to transfer to the state—as an abstract juridical entity—and *a fortiori* to the EU. The advantage of embracing strict liability as a basis for due diligence obligations is that the latter would express an "objectivized" concept of fault.

The effective application of this understanding of due diligence at EU level would create a special regime at international level that 'would seek to render "imperfect" obligations—obligations that do not clearly belong to any particular agent (by belonging to many agents)—"perfect"'. Once a right becomes part of a corresponding "perfect" obligation, the grounds are provided for making it legally enforceable.[141]

This interpretation of due diligence would have important practical consequences for individuals and communities of non-EU countries whose human rights are impacted by EU trade policies, including domestic policies with external effects. It is acknowledged that presently this reading of due diligence is yet to be fully embraced and accepted by EU Institutions and bodies. However, this reading would not presuppose or entail that the EU or its institutions and bodies would be considered perpetrators of human rights abuses. Rather, the advantage of such reading of due diligence is that it would require the EU to discharge a remedial obligation in cases of breaches of human rights for acts or omissions that have the *effect* of facilitating the impairment of the enjoyment or exercise of rights. This would be in addition to the preventive dimension of due diligence, which has already been incorporated into the EU legal system with impact assessments, although these should be made mandatory across all policy areas of EU action. If the EU is to be a credible global value-driven actor it should become the EU's own ambition to take up this interpretation of due diligence. It is posited that the latter would also befit the jurisdictional model here proposed, which the discussion now turns to.

---

[140]This interpretation of due diligence as entailing strict liability with no fault element is taken from Bonnitcha and McCorquodale, above no. 106.

[141]see M. Salomon, *Global Responsibility for Human Rights* (Oxford: OUP, 2007), at p. 186, citing Arjun Sengupta, *Second Report of the Independent Expert on the Right to Development* (Working Group on the Right to Development, 1st session, 2000) UN Doc E/CN4/2000/WG18/CRP1, available at: https://ap.ohchr.org/documents/E/CHR/report/ECN42000WG18CRP1.pdf, accessed on 20 February 2020, paras 8–9.

6.3.2 *From Extraterritoriality to Territoriality: "Territorializing Extraterritorial Obligations"*[142]

The Union's duty of due diligence, as outlined in the preceding section, has a territorial character. Connoting such human rights requirement as territorial brings with it the benefit of averting classical doctrinal concerns over the scope of the EU's human rights obligations outside of its borders[143] and, in particular, avoids complex doctrinal constructions of extraterritorial obligations over normative and factual connections between the duty-bearer, namely the EU, and the human rights holder necessary to establish the former's extraterritorial obligations. To trigger the Union's human rights obligations what needs to be established is whether its *conduct* or *effects* can be located on its territory.[144] It is not necessary for both conditions to be met: it suffices that territorial effects can be identified, even absent any territorial conduct or instead that territorial conduct can be established, even absent any territorial effects.[145] Ultimately, what is key for territoriality to apply is that the decision to adopt a given external trade instrument and the preparations for the adoption of such decision—be it bilateral or regional or unilateral-[146] have been made by EU Institutions on Union territory.[147] This is the condition for EU territorial human rights obligations to be triggered, which require that the EU follows on its due diligence obligations when adopting a decision concerning an external trade measure, for example, assessing a trade agreement's compatibility with human rights rules before its conclusion, or the latter's effects on the exercise of human rights in the signatory country. When the

[142]This section draws heavily on Ryngaert "internal-territorial" model which departs from the doctrine's classic semantic focus on extraterritoriality [...], which 'clouds rather than illuminates matters of scope of human rights obligations', Ryngaert, above no. 32, at 376. The underlying idea of this model, namely, the territorial character of the EU's human rights obligations—which in Ryngaert's model is limited to the EU bilateral agreements—is here generalized and extended to the Union's entire external trade policy. It also relies on Scott's concept of "territorial extension", above no. 33, to establish the connection/trigger between the duty bearer, i.e. the EU, and the human rights holder, i.e. the national of a third country.

[143]In particular it obviates the need to examine the extent to which the EUCFR can be said to have extraterritorial character, although it could be argued that references to human rights in Article 3(5) and 21 TEU provide a rather solid basis for the Charter to have extraterritorial effects.

[144]Ryngaert, above no. 32, at 384.

[145]Ibid. The former is sometimes denoted as "objective territoriality", and the latter "subjective territoriality", Ryngaert citing J. Bassett Moore, 'Report on Extraterritorial Crime and the Cutting case' (1887) 23 *US Foreign Relations* 575, at 770.

[146]Author's addition.

[147]Ryngaert, above no. 32, at 385.

EU fails to comply with its due diligence obligations in its own territory it triggers the territorial extension of EU law[148] and EU human rights obligations.[149]

By way of example, when the EU decides to conclude an international trade agreement it might facilitate human rights violations by failing to exercise due diligence assessments with regard to the third country concerned, or non-state actors located or established in that country such as corporations (including their subsidiaries, branches, offices or suppliers), with a consequential negative human rights impact. For instance,[150] there might be cases where agreements encouraging exports of labour intensive goods might indirectly encourage child labour in a situation of low labour standards.[151] The economic advantages of exportation of certain agricultural goods might leave poor communities vulnerable to food insecurity; the increase of exportation of water (and land) intensive industries (such as bovine meat) might affect the access to water or increase the risk of land dispute;[152] the regulation of patents related to traditional knowledge could affect the cultural heritage and traditional knowledge of indigenous peoples.[153] Patent protections provisions might raise prices of medicines. The decrease of tax revenues due to the customs duties reduction as a consequence of trade liberalization might impact on the developing country's redistributive measures.[154] In these circumstances, the institutional failure on the part of the EU will classify as territorial precisely because of Union Institutions clearly being located on EU territory,[155] regardless of the extraterritorial effects of such failure, thus triggering the applicability of territorial human rights obligations.[156]

---

[148]Scott, above no. 37, at pp. 22–23. As Scott warns there is still a certain level of disagreement about how a particular jurisdictional trigger should be characterized in relation to the condition of presence, as the dividing line between nationality (i.e. non-territorial connection) and presence (territorial connection) within a member state territory can be difficult to identify in relation to establishment.

[149]Ryngaert elaborates this approach on the basis the ECtHR's *Soering* decision, see ECtHR, *Soering v United Kingdom*, Application No. 14038/88, 07 July 1989.

[150]I am grateful to Francesca Martines for suggesting these examples to help develop the argument put forward here.

[151]Trade agreements with states that have low labour standards or that overlook the use of child labour can indirectly encourage the multiplication of these practices; see G. Vidigal, 'Trade Agreement, EU Law and Occupied Territories (2): The General Court Judgment in *Frente Polisario v Council* and the Protection of Fundamental Rights Abroad', EJIL:*Talk!*, 11 December 2015, available at: https://www.ejiltalk.org/13901-2/, accessed on 25 February 2020.

[152]European Commission, Sustainability Impact Assessment in Support of the Association Agreement Negotiations between the European Union and Mercosur, Interim Report, LSE Consulting, February 2020, available at: https://trade.ec.europa.eu/doclib/docs/2020/February/tradoc_158632.pdf , p. 102. accessed on 10 March 2020.

[153]European Commission, Guidelines on the analysis of human rights impacts in impact assessments for trade-related policy initiatives, 2015, available at: https://trade.ec.europa.eu/doclib/docs/2015/July/tradoc_153591.pdf, p. 8. accessed on 23 February 2020.

[154]J. Cagé and L. Gadenne, 'The Fiscal Cost of Trade Liberalization', 4 June 2012, available at: https://voxeu.org/article/fiscal-cost-trade-liberalisation, accessed on 25 February 2020.

[155]In this respect it suffices that the conduct facilitating the extraterritorial human rights violation, can be situated on EU territory, Ryngaert, above no. 32, at 388.

[156]Ryngaert, above no. 32, at 387.

However, there are also more nuanced situations to consider when the EU decides to conclude an international trade agreement. The obligation for the EU not to contribute to human rights violation in a situation where such action is only potential or a situation of risk, raises the question of identifying the means to fulfill that obligation in such circumstances. This is not an obligation of *result* (obligation to attain a specific result, as it could be, for example, quashing a piece of legislation that discriminates in relation to wage conditions between foreign and national workers, which is clearly an obligation that involves a guaranteed result) since the EU cannot ensure that the risk does not materializes and that human rights are not going to be violated but it is an obligation of *means* or *of endeavor*, that is the EU shall do what is in its power to prevent the occurrence of a certain situation. Beyond the classical nexuses or other possible legal foundations such as a contractual basis, the question that arises here is whether the EU would have a duty to act in a protective manner 'when no jurisdictional bases and links exist between them and the situation calling for protection.'[157] The theory of *effectiveness*—namely the existence of factual/de facto links between a given situation and a state (in this case the EU), which is aware of that situation (or could reasonably be expected to know) and is in a position to protect—might provide further helpful insights. Effectiveness is among the 'factors/bases that activate the duty to protect.'[158] In this regard, Arbour submits that there is a duty of care that is 'based on proximity, justice and reasonableness carrying with it an obligation to act reasonably on the basis of real or imputed knowledge.'[159]

These territorial human rights obligations are of a procedural nature requiring that the EU carries out human rights impact assessments (HRIAs) when negotiating international trade agreements and that it puts in place human rights-sensitive processes in the case of unilateral trade arrangements.[160] More specifically, territorial obligations and rights under EU law will apply, including the EUCFR, without the need to address questions about the Charter's extraterritoriality. In this respect, the European Ombudsman (EO)[161] has already held that under the Charter the EU must conduct a human rights verification test every time it takes decisions that could have an adverse human rights impact. There is recent precedent in the context of trade policy for the EO finding maladministration for failure to act. The EO found failure to conduct a

[157] Tzevelekos and Proukaki (2017), at 454.

[158] Ibid. at 155.

[159] Arbour (2008), at 452.

[160] See sections 3.3. and 3.4 of Chapter 5 of this book.

[161] The European Ombudsman (EO) is an impartial body elected by the EU Parliament that investigates complaints about poor administration or maladministration by EU Institutions or other EU bodies. Instances of maladministration concern a breach of the right to good administration under Article 41 EUCFR, in the activities of the Union institutions, bodies, offices or agencies. The EO office launches investigations either in response to complaints or on its own initiative. Only EU citizens or any natural or legal person residing or having its registered office in a member state can file complaints with the EO, see Articles 228 TFEU and 20(2)(d) TFEU.

human rights impact assessment to be maladministration even where the Commission had discretion, rather than a legal obligation to conduct it.[162] The case centered on human rights concerns accompanying a trade agreement with Vietnam.[163] The EO decided that it was necessary for the EU to investigate the human rights concerns in order to satisfy Article 21 TEU.[164] The latter requires that EU relations with non-EU countries conform to principles including universal human rights, respect for human dignity, democracy, and the rule of law.[165] A few days after delivering its decision the EO said:[166]

> While trade agreements are designed to be good for the economy, it is not necessarily the case that they always bring benefits in the same way for all the peoples of the countries concerned as we can all acknowledge. Trade agreements may at times have negative consequences for the human rights of the peoples affected by those agreements. Consequently, it is important to know whether the EU's Agreement with Vietnam might have negative consequences for the people of Vietnam—a country about which human rights concerns already exist.

In light of those circumstances, even though the EU enjoyed discretion, failure to investigate violated the spirit of Article 21 TEU.[167] The EO suggested that the standard for good administration can be higher than simply fulfilling express obligations and said that:[168]

> While the Commission may not have been legally obliged to conduct a prior human rights impact assessment, its decision not to do so reflected a failure to act in a manner consistent with the highest values and principles on which the EU is based. This, to me, was maladministration.

The example of the Vietnam case makes it clear that inaction by the Commission can constitute maladministration, even where action was not expressly legally required. Arguably, this approach also extends to unilateral trade arrangements such as the Generalised Scheme of Preferences (GSP). While the GSP is not a trade agreement but a regulation enacted unilaterally by the EU, the Commission's responsibility to act according to the EU's principles applies in equal force here.

---

[162] European Ombudsman, Decision in case 1409/2014/MHZ on the European Commission's failure to carry out a prior human rights impact assessment of the EU-Vietnam free trade agreement, (26 February 2016); see also European Ombudsman's Speech on its Decision on the failure of European Commission to conduct a prior human rights impact assessment of the EU Vietnam free trade agreement, 3 March 2016, available at: https://www.ombudsman.europa.eu/activities/speech.faces/en/64453/html.bookmark, accessed on 20 February 2020.

[163] 2019 EU-Vietnam Free Trade Agreement (EVFTA); the text of the agreement is available at: https://trade.ec.europa.eu/doclib/press/index.cfm?id=1437, accessed on 19 February 2020.

[164] Ibid.

[165] Article 21 TEU.

[166] European Ombudsman's Speech, above no. 162.

[167] As well as Article 207(1) TFEU and the 2012 Action Plan on Human Rights and Democracy (Council of the European Union, *Council Conclusions on the Action Plan on Human Rights and Democracy 2015–2019*, doc. 10897/15, 20 July 2015), European Ombudsman, above no. 162, paras 11, 13.

[168] Ibid.

Significantly, in the much discussed *Polisario* case,[169] the Advocate-General Wathelet, cited this EO's decision to say that EU Institutions prior to the conclusion of an international agreement should examine the human rights situation in the other party to the agreement and the impact which the conclusion of the agreement at issue could have there in this regard.[170] The EO confirmed the obligation of prior human rights impact assessment in another inquiry concerning the controversial EU-Turkey Agreement.[171] In this case, the EO noted that 'her office's longstanding view that good administration means, in the first place, observance of and respect for fundamental rights; where fundamental rights are not respected, there cannot be good administration. Accordingly, for all policies and actions of EU institutions and bodies which impact on human beings, any evaluation should contain an explicit consideration of the human rights impact of those policies and actions.'[172] It carried on saying that this requirement is 'fundamental, since the implementation of the Agreement reasonably and necessarily has an impact (a) on the human rights of migrants (direct or indirect) and (b) on the ability of the EU and the member states involved to fulfil their human rights obligations'.[173] In addition, there is case law and other soft law instruments that support the obligation to carry out such impact assessments.[174]

These cases demonstrate that non-Union citizens whose human rights have been affected by EU policies and measures might be able to get a form of remedy by submitting a claim to the EO. In brief, EU measures can have significant impact within third countries not only when they form part of the EU's external relations law and policy but also when they are internal measures as they can have effects beyond the EU's borders. Hence, for the EU to be diligent it should conduct *ex ante* human rights impact assessments, i.e., when designing and negotiating the international agreement, and additionally *ex post*, once the agreement is concluded. Ryngaert suggests that 'in order to prevent undesirable knock-on effects on the EU's

[169]See infra Sect. 6.4 of this Chapter.

[170]Case C-104/16P, *Council of the European Union v Front Populaire pour la libération de la saguia-el-hamra et du rio de oro (Front Polisario)*, ECLI:EU:C:2016:677, Opinion of AG Wathelet, paras. 262–264.

[171]European Council, Council of the European Union, EU-Turkey statement, 18 March 2016, Press release, 18 March 2016, available at: https://www.consilium.europa.eu/en/press/press-releases/2016/03/18/eu-turkey-statement/, accessed on 20 February 2020; see also the EU-Turkey Join Action Plan of 15 October 2015, available at: https://ec.europa.eu/commission/presscorner/detail/en/MEMO_15_5860, accessed on 20 February 2020.

[172]European Ombudsman, Decision in the joint inquiry into complaints 506-509-674-784-927-1381/2016/MHZ against the European Commission concerning a human rights impact assessment in the context of the EU-Turkey Agreement, (18 January 2017), para. 25.

[173]Ibid., para 26.

[174]E.g. C-12/03 P, *Commission v Tetra Laval*, ECLI:EU:C:2005:87; European Commission, Guidelines on the analysis of human rights impacts in impact assessments for trade-related policy initiatives, 2015, available at: https://trade.ec.europa.eu/doclib/docs/2015/July/tradoc_153591.pdf, accessed on 23 February 2020; for detailed analysis of the complexity associated with human rights impact assessments and, in particular, measuring human rights (which is beyond the scope of this chapter), see Gzauthier de Beco (2007), James Harrison (2011).

capacity to enter into international law agreements,' the review of agreements should be restricted to a limited category of fundamental human rights.[175]

6.4 Human Rights Compliance as a Condition of Legality of EU Action

The TL has changed the human rights protection landscape in EU external relations paving the way for further changes in the future.[176] In particular, as seen earlier, it has injected a values-driven vocation in the Treaties as per Article 2 TEU, which 'locates the EU as a project driven by *values*.'[177] Article 2 TEU states that the EU is founded *inter alia* on the value of respect for human rights and Article 3(1) TEU provides that the Union's aims include the promotion of its values. Most importantly, Article 6 TEU—the EU's key human rights provision—has been amended and extended so as to reinforce the human rights dimension of all EU policies, granting legally binding status to the EUCFR, envisaging EU accession to the ECHR as an obligation and making explicit reference to fundamental rights as general principles of EU law.

Compliance with fundamental rights is undisputedly a condition of legality of all EU acts. The CJEU has taken a clear position holding that human rights compliance 'is required of all actions of the EU', including external action.[178] Hence, EU international agreements must comply with EU primary law, including fundamental human rights as protected by the EUCFR. The latter provides a set of minimum standards which both the Union and a given non-EU country concluding the agreement would

[175]Ryngaert, above no. 32, at 393.

[176]S. Velluti, 'The "Inside Looking Out": Mainstreaming Human Rights in EU External Relations in M. Balboni and C. Danisi (eds), *Human Rights as a Horizontal Issue in EU External Policy. Les droits de l'homme comme domaine horizontal de la politique extérieure de l'Union européenne* (Editoriale Scientifica, forthcoming).

[177]Article 2 TEU provides that: 'The Union is founded on the values of respect for human dignity, freedom, democracy, equality, the rule of law and respect for human rights, including the rights of persons belonging to minorities. These values are common to the Member States in a society in which pluralism, non-discrimination, tolerance, justice, solidarity and equality between women and men prevail'; Weatherill (2016).

[178]Case C-263/14, *European Parliament v. Council* (ECLI:EU:C:2016:435), para. 47.

have to comply with.[179] Since *Kadi I*,[180] this obligation has been reiterated in various external action cases after Lisbon, including the conclusion of international agreements. In this respect, *Opinion 1/15*, concerning a proposed agreement with Canada on the transfer by airlines to national security authorities of passenger name record (PNR) data, is a landmark ruling.[181] The Court made it clear that the assessment of compatibility of an international agreement with the Treaties includes compliance with fundamental rights as part of EU primary law.[182] For the first time the Court found a proposed international agreement to be incompatible with the Treaties on the ground that it failed to comply with the EUCFR.[183] This decision follows the *Schrems* case, where it had already held that such transfers of personal data must ensure protection essentially equivalent to that guaranteed within the EU.[184]

---

[179]Failure to comply might entail the risk of either an *ex ante* or *ex post* finding of illegality. For an example of *ex ante* declaration of incompatibility, see the proposed agreement on PNR data with Canada in *Opinion 1/15, discussed below*; for an example of *ex post* declaration of illegality see the *Schrems* case, discussed below, following which it was necessary to renegotiate the EU-US Safe Harbour (Adequacy) Arrangement, see European Commission, 2000/520/EC: Commission Decision of 26 July 2000 pursuant to Directive 95/46/EC of the European Parliament and of the Council on the adequacy of the protection provided by the safe harbour privacy principles and related frequently asked questions issued by the US Department of Commerce (notified under document number C(2000) 2441) (Text with EEA relevance.), OJ [2000] L215/7. Its replacement was the EU-US Privacy Shield, see European Commission, Commission Implementing Decision (EU) 2016/1250 of 12 July 2016 pursuant to Directive 95/46/EC of the European Parliament and of the Council on the adequacy of the protection provided by the EU-U.S. Privacy Shield (notified under document C(2016) 4176) (Text with EEA relevance), C/2016/4176, OJ [2016] L207/1. For further discussion, see Azoulai and Van der Sluis (2016).

[180]Case C-402/05 P and C-415/05 P, above no. 12.

[181]Opinion1/15 the on draft agreement between Canada and the European Union (EU) dealing with the Transfer of Passenger Name Record (PNR) data from the EU to Canada (ECLI:EU:C:2017:592).

[182]Ibid. para. 70.

[183]In its Opinion, the CJEU declared that the Agreement involved particularly serious interferences with the fundamental rights guaranteed in Articles 7 and 8 EUCFR (right to private and family life and right to personal data protection, respectively) as well as Article 21 EUCFR (right to non-discrimination). Accordingly, the transfer of PNR data to Canada required a solid justification, based on grounds other than the protection of public security against terrorism and serious transnational crime. Notably, the CJEU set out in some detail what the limitations of the agreement were from the perspective of the Charter and also went on to say what would be needed to remedy them; Ibid., para. 232, for a discussion of the interference with Articles 7 and 8 EUCFR, see paras. 121–132.

[184]Case C-362/14, *Maximillian Schrems v Data Protection Commissioner, Digital Rights Ireland Ltd.* (ECLI:EU:C:2015:650), paras 72–74. The *Schrems* case is considered to be one of the most important international privacy cases in recent history. It arose from a complaint against Facebook brought to the Irish Data Protection Commissioner by an Austrian privacy advocate named Maximillian Schrems. In the complaint, Mr. Schrems challenged the transfer of his data (and the data of EU citizens' generally) to the US by Facebook, which is incorporated in Ireland. The CJEU invalidated the Safe Harbor (Adequacy Arrangement (above no. 181), which governed data transfers between the EU and the US. See also Joined Cases C-203/15 and C-698/15, *Tele2 Sverige and Watson and others* (ECLI:EU:C:2016:970). For further discussion on the regulation of the use and transfer of personal data globally, including an analysis of the global reach of EU law, see Fahey (2018).

Front Polisario[185] is another important case that merits attention as it reveals significant aspects about the human rights-trade debate, not only in respect of the place of human rights within EU international trade relations but also with regard to the different perspectives of and interpretations given by each of the EU Courts as well as the Advocate General. The General Court (GC) held that assessing the human rights impact of a trade agreement is a procedural requirement, which is enforceable via judicial review rather than merely a matter of good administration. The GC held that even though the Council enjoys a wide margin of appreciation in deciding to conclude such an agreement, the exercise of that discretion is subject to judicial review on grounds of a manifest error of assessment, particularly in relation to the obligation of carefully and impartially examining all the relevant facts before taking its decision.[186] Hence, the human rights impact of the trade agreement on the population of Western Sahara was a factor which should have been taken into account. In particular, the Council should have examined the effects of production of goods for export to the EU under such agreement in the light of specific rights of the EUCFR.[187] Significantly, in order to buttress further its conclusions, the GC referred to the findings of then UN Legal Counsel Hans Corell in relation to these obligations deriving from international law.[188] For the Court it was immaterial that the EU would not be directly responsible for such violations: indirect encouragement or benefits are also prohibited.[189] The Council's failure to do so led the Court to annul the Council's

[185]Case T-512/12, *Front populaire pour la libération de la saguia-el-hamra et du rio de oro (Front Polisario) v. Council of the European Union,* ECLI:EU:T:2015:953; C-104/16 P, above no. 162; see also Case C-266/16 *Western Sahara Campaign UK v Commissioners for Her Majesty's Revenue and Customs, Secretary of State for Environment, Food and Rural Affairs*, ECLI:EU:C:2018:118. The Grand Chamber in this case closely followed the analysis it had made in C-104/16. The CJEU ruled that neither the Fisheries Partnership Agreement nor its Protocol setting out fishing opportunities and financial contributions between the EU and Morocco were applicable to the waters adjacent to the territory of Western Sahara. For academic discussion, see *e.g.* Balboni and Laschi (2017), Ryngaert and Fransen (2018) [20], Kassoti (2017a, b), Odermatt (2017); Vidigal, above no. 150.

[186]Case T-512/12, above no. 185, para. 225.

[187]Ibid. at para. 228; specifically, the rights to human dignity, to life and to the integrity of the person (Articles 1 to 3 EUCFR), the prohibition of slavery and forced labour (Article 5 EUCFR), the freedom to choose an occupation and right to engage in work (Article 15 EUCFR), the freedom to conduct a business (Article 16 EUCFR), the right to property (Article 17 EUCFR), the right to fair and just working conditions and the prohibition of child labour and protection of young people at work (Articles 31 and 32 EUCFR).

[188]Ibid., at para. 229; UN Security Council, Letter dated 29 January 2002 from the Under-Secretary-General for Legal Affairs, the Legal Counsel, addressed to the President of the Security Council, S/2002/161, available at: http://www.arso.org/Olaeng.pdf, accessed on 21 February 2020.

[189]'If the EU allows exports to its member states of products originating in that country that were manufactured or produced under conditions that violate the fundamental rights of the population of the territory from which they come, it might indirectly encourage such violations or benefits therefrom', ibid., at para. 229; see also, Eyal Benvenisti 'The EU Must Consider Threats to Fundamental Rights of Non-EU Nationals by its Potential Trading Partners', available at: http://globaltrust.tau.ac.il/the-e-u-must-consider-threats-to-fundamental-rights-of-non-eu-nationals-by-its-potential-trading-partners/, accessed on 21 February 2020.

decision to conclude a liberalization agreement with Morocco[190] insofar as it was deemed to approve the application of the agreement to the Western Sahara.[191]

The judgment of the GC was reversed on appeal by the CJEU on the ground that there was no legal basis for interpreting the agreement between the EU and Morocco as applicable to the territory of the Western Sahara.[192] It largely followed the Opinion of Advocate General Wathelet who had concluded that the Court should set aside the GC's decision and dismiss the action by *Front Polisario* as inadmissible.[193] The CJEU focused on issues of compliance with international law and analysed three key aspects, namely, the principle of self-determination,[194] Article 29 Vienna Convention on the Law of Treaties on treaties (VCLT)' territorial scope[195] and the relative effect of treaties. It concluded that the people of Western Sahara, according to the Advisory Opinion of the International Court of Justice (ICJ),[196] constituted a third party in this respect and had not expressed their consent. Moreover, even though the Commission and the Council were aware that Morocco had been applying the Association Agreement[197] to Western Sahara for many years and the EU institutions never opposed such application, and although certain tariff preferences de facto applied to products originating in Western Sahara, for the Court these factors did not amount to subsequent practice as per Article 31(3)(b) VCLT.[198] It followed that neither the Association nor the Liberalisation Agreements applied to Western Sahara

---

[190] Council Decision 2012/497/EU of 8 March 2012 on the conclusion of an Agreement in the form of an Exchange of Letters between the European Union and the Kingdom of Morocco concerning reciprocal liberalisation measures on agricultural products, processed agricultural products, fish and fishery products, the replacement of Protocols 1, 2 and 3 and their Annexes and amendments to the Euro-Mediterranean Agreement establishing an association between the European Communities and their Member States, of the one part, and the Kingdom of Morocco, of the other part, OJ [2012] L241/2.

[191] Case T-512/12, above no. 185, at paras. 247 and 251.

[192] C-104/16 P, above no. 170, at paras. 107–108.

[193] Case C-104/16 P, Opinion of AG Wathelet, above no. 170.

[194] The CJEU concluded that given the *erga omnes* nature of the right to self-determination by the peoples of a non-self-governing territory and its status as an essential principle of international law, the GC erred in law when assuming that the agreement also applied to Western Sahara, see Case C-104/16 P, above no. 170, at paras. 105–108.

[195] Article 29 VCLT entitled 'Territorial scope of treaties', provides that: 'Unless a different intention appears from the treaty or is otherwise established, a treaty is binding upon each party in respect of its entire territory.' With regards to Article 29 VCLT the CJEU clarified that "its entire territory" only referred to the territory internationally recognised, and not the territory under Morocco's jurisdiction which would be the wider expression. As such, the Court agreed with the Commission which argued that any extension of the application must be expressed in the agreement, see Case C-104/16 P, above no. 170, at para. 95.

[196] ICJ, *Advisory Opinion on the Western Sahara* [1975] I.C.J. 12.

[197] Euro-Mediterranean Agreement establishing an association between the European Communities and their member states, of the one part, and the Kingdom of Morocco, of the other part, OJ [2000] L70/2.

[198] Article 31 VCLT (on general rule of interpretation) at paragraph 3 provides that: 'There shall be taken into account, together with the context: (b) any subsequent practice in the application of the treaty which establishes the agreement of the parties regarding its interpretation'.

and thus Front Polisario lacked standing before both EU Court. Consequently, the CJEU did not see the need to consider whether the Council's duty to take account of all relevant facts included the requirement to assess the human rights implications of concluding the agreement. Instead Advocate General Wathelet did take issue with the question of whether the Council had such an obligation and concluded that it did.[199] Even though the Advocate General rejected the applicability of the EUCFR outside the EU on the ground that none of the conditions established by the ECtHR for the extraterritorial application of the ECHR were met, he nevertheless accepted the argument that the EU was bound to consider the impact of its external actions as a matter of *erga omnes* and peremptory international law obligations. Hence, for the Advocate General the EU's obligation to uphold human rights in its external action was linked to the duty to comply with international law and in this respect the relevant standards were international law standards.[200] As noted by Cremona, the reaction to the decision of each EU Court in *Front Polisario* 'demonstrates that values and interests do not always pull in the same direction'.[201]

Opinion 1/15 and the *Front Polisario* decisions can be seen as a complement to *Kadi I*,[202] each illustrating the different ways in which the CJEU preserves the legal autonomy of the EU and, at the same time, engages in a dialogue with international law and human rights protection.

In light of these judicial developments, it is lamentable that individuals affected by the extraterritorial effects of EU policies in third countries are still unable to challenge the measures affecting their human rights and thus enforce the human rights obligations of the EU.[203] The reason remains the narrow interpretation of the standing requirements for individual applicants under Article 263(1) and (4) TFEU,[204] which the Court has not lifted despite severe criticism by scholars and members of civil society. The key case to consider for an extraterritorial scenario is

---

[199] C-104/16 P, Opinion of AG Wathelet, above no. 170, paras 220–237.

[200] Cremona, above no. 10, at p. 77.

[201] Ibid., at p. 86; on the issue of values versus interests and the complex issue of occupied territories, see also Sidati (2016). After the decision of the GC Morocco suspended its diplomatic relations with the EU, which were resumed when the Council appealed against it. The decision of the CJEU while *prima facie* a victory for Morocco was also a victory for Front Polisario as the judgment was seen as a blow to Morocco's claim of sovereignty over Western Sahara. See Euractiv (2016); Euractiv (2016); Lonardo (2019); on the economic implications, see Dizard (2019).

[202] Cremona, above no. 10, at p. 79.

[203] Bartels, above no. 46, at 1088; Ganesh, above no. 5, at 487.

[204] Article 263(1) TFEU provides that: 'The Court of Justice of the European Union shall review the legality of legislative acts, of acts of the Council, of the Commission and of the European Central Bank, other than recommendations and opinions, and of acts of the European Parliament and of the European Council intended to produce legal effects vis-à-vis third parties. It shall also review the legality of acts of bodies, offices or agencies of the Union intended to produce legal effects vis-à-vis third parties', and para. 4 of the same Article provides that: 'Any natural or legal person may, under the conditions laid down in the first and second paragraphs, institute proceedings against an act addressed to that person or which is of direct and individual concern to them, and against a regulatory act which is of direct concern to them and does not entail implementing measures'.

Commune de Champagne,[205] where the GC concluded that an EU legal act could never entail any direct effect outside EU territory.[206] In this case, Swiss producers of wine brought a legal action against the Council and the Commission, requesting the GC to annul an agreement between the EU and the Swiss Confederation on trade in agricultural products, which imposed a ban that would prohibit them from marketing wines originating in the Commune Champagne in the canton of Vaud under the name "Champagne" because of the protected designation that a certain type of French sparkling wine enjoys under EU law. Nonetheless, the GC held that the rule applies only to acts within the territory of the EU for two reasons. First, the Court points out 'that the principle of sovereign equality enshrined in Article 2(1) of the UN Charter means that it is, as a rule, a matter for each state to legislate in its own territory and, accordingly, that generally a state may unilaterally impose binding rules only in its own territory'.[207] Second, it held 'that an act of an institution adopted pursuant to the Treaty, as a unilateral act of the Community, cannot create rights and obligations outside the territory thus defined' and therefore 'the scope of the contested decision is limited to that territory and it has no legal effect in the territory of Switzerland'.[208] This results in the exclusion of individuals in third countries from having the standing to challenge an EU unilateral act on the ground of a violation of their human rights extraterritorially.

The reasoning of this decision has been severely criticized for being inconsistent with previous judgments and also for being flawed from the perspective of international law. As Bartels points out the principle of sovereign equality does not *ipso jure* exclude states from exercising their jurisdiction in third states.[209] Indeed, transnational situations always tend to result in potentially parallel and overlapping jurisdiction by the states involved. You could have a scenario whereby one state could be involved territorially whereas another state could be involved extraterritorially, for example, on the basis of nationality.[210] Ganesh, in agreeing with Bartels, refers to a previous decision in which the CJEU interpreted the same provision as not precluding EU rules from having effects outside the territory of the Union.[211] According to Kube: 'the GC seems to err on what constitutes an interference in breach of public international law. Legal effects can be produced under public international law in accordance with the principles allowing for extraterritorial prescriptive jurisdiction.'[212]

[205] Case T–212/02 *Commune de Champagne v Council and Commission* [2007] ECR 2007 II-02017.

[206] Ibid., para. 90.

[207] Ibid., para 89.

[208] Ibid. para 90.

[209] Bartels, above no. 46, at 1088.

[210] I am grateful to Vassilis Tzevelekos for this point.

[211] Ganesh, above no. 5, at 501; see Case C-214/94, *Boukhalfa v Bundesrepublik Deutschland*, ECLI:EU:C:1996:174.

[212] Kube refers to the principle of nationality, the protective principle and the domestic-effects-doctrine as examples; see Kube (2019).

In a similar vein, human rights clauses of bilateral agreements are not justiciable as confirmed in *Mugraby*.[213] Here the GC held that the suspension of the agreement on the basis of the human rights clause is discretionary, that each party to the agreement is free to decide whether there might be an infringement of the clause relating to the respect for fundamental human rights and, significantly, that the discretionary power left afforded to the parties means that the human rights clause cannot have direct effect and confer rights to individuals.[214] In addition, EU trade agreements concluded after 2008 have explicit provisions excluding that the clauses of the agreements can be interpreted as conferring rights or imposing obligations that can be directly invoked before EU or member state courts, namely that they might have any direct legal effect.[215]

6.5 Revisiting the Doctrine of Implied Powers as a Judicial Tool to Protect Human Rights in EU External Action

Any legal or constitutional discussion of human rights issues concerning the EU is still constrained by the lack of or limited EU competence and powers in the field of human rights.[216] In particular, in the context of the EU's internal sphere of action the scope of human rights policy is limited to those areas of EU power or competence,

[213]Case T-292/09 *Muhamad Mugraby v Council of the European Union* and the European Commission ECLI:EU:T:2011:418; Case C-581/11 P, *Muhamad Mugraby v Council of the European Union and European Commission* ECLI:EU:C:2012:466. The case concerned a Lebanese applicant who claimed that the EU failed to adopt appropriate measures, specifically to suspend aid programs, under the human rights clause in the EU-Lebanon Association Agreement (Euro-Mediterranean Agreement establishing an association between the European Community and its Member States, of the one part, and the Republic of Lebanon, of the other part, OJ [2006] L143/2), following Lebanon's fundamental rights violations. The application was dismissed on many grounds but what is noteworthy is that both EU courts did not discuss the issue of extraterritoriality in relation to the alleged human rights violations. However, the CJEU held that 'it follows from Article 17(1) TEU that the Commission, as guardian of the TEU and TFEU Treaties and of the agreements concluded under them, must ensure the correct implementation by a third state of the obligations which it has assumed under an agreement concluded with the EU, using the means provided for by that agreement or by the decisions taken pursuant thereto.' [Case C-581/11 P, at para. 68]. In addition, the Court did not seem to exclude the possibility for a non-EU national to invoke the principle of effective judicial protection outside the EU, as per Article 47 EUCFR [Case C-581/11 P, at para. 81].

[214]Ibid. paras. 59, 61, 71.

[215]Bartels, above no. 46, at 1089. In particular, this preclusion takes the form of a combined reading of several provisions in the text of the agreements and/or in Council decisions concerning their signature, and on the provisional application of the agreement, e.g. the 2011 EU-Korea FTA, Free Trade Agreement between the European Union and its Member States of the one part, and the Republic of Korea of the other part (EU-Korea FTA) *OJ* [2011] L127/6, 14 May 2011, p. 6.; and the 2012 EU- Colombia/Peru Agreement, Trade Agreement between the European Union and its Member States, of the one part, and Colombia and Peru, of the other part *OJ* [2012] L354/3, 21 December 2012, p. 3; see further Semertzi (2014).

[216]See e.g. the horizontal clauses of the EUCFR, namely, arts 51(2) and 52(2).

which directly promote human rights.[217] In addition, the combined reading of Articles 23[218] and 40 TEU[219] seem to indicate that the pursuit of the political objectives laid down by Article 21(1) and (2) TEU—which include human rights—is the primary competence of the Common Foreign and Security Policy(CFSP) and that the other EU substantive policies are prevented from autonomously pursuing the objectives of the CFSP.[220] Nevertheless, in its external sphere of action the EU is given a strong and interventionist role with regard to the promotion of human rights internationally. This fragmented legal framework for the promotion of human rights is somewhat in contradiction with the fact that the EU is bound by human rights obligations, both of its member states and of its own.[221]

---

[217]Cf. TEU art 3(3) concerning human rights within internal EU policies which is quite specific (it provides that the Union 'shall combat social exclusion and discrimination, and shall promote social justice and protection, equality between women and men, solidarity between generations and protection of the rights of the child') and art 3(5) concerning human rights in external relations, which is broader and more general in scope and conceives the protection of human rights as an overarching goal.

[218]Article 23 TEU provides that: 'The Union's action on the international scene, pursuant to this Chapter, shall be guided by the principles, shall pursue the objectives of, and be conducted in accordance with, the general provisions laid down in Chapter 1'.

[219]Article 40 TEU provides that: 'The implementation of the common foreign and security policy shall not affect the application of the procedures and the extent of the powers of the institutions laid down by the Treaties for the exercise of the Union competences referred to in Articles 3–6 of the Treaty on the Functioning of the European Union.

Similarly, the implementation of the policies listed in those Articles shall not affect the application of the procedures and the extent of the powers of the institutions laid down by the Treaties for the exercise of the Union competences under this Chapter.' This provision is known as the reciprocal non-encroachment or non-affectation clause between the CFSP and other Union policies.

[220]Cannizzaro (2015).

[221]Member states are parties to several international human rights treaties. All member states have ratified the International Covenant on Economic, Social and Cultural Rights (adopted 16 December 1966, entered into force 3 January 1976) 993 UNTS 3 (ICESCR); International Covenant on Civil and Political Rights (adopted 16 December 1966, entered into force 23 March 1976) 999 UNTS 171 (ICCPR); Convention on the Elimination of All Forms of Discrimination Against Women (adopted 18 December 1979, entered into force 3 September 1981) 1249 UNTS 13 (CEDAW); Convention on the Rights of the Child (adopted 20 November 1989, entered into force 2 September 1990) 1577 UNTS 3 (CRC); and various conventions of the International Labour Organization (ILO). Member States also have extraterritorial obligations, which can be found, *inter alia*, in Articles 2 and 11 of the ICESCR. See in this sense Committee on Economic, Social and Cultural Rights (CESCR), 'General Comment No 12: The Right to Adequate Food (Art. 11)' adopted at Twentieth Session of the CESCR (12 May 1999) UN Doc E/C.12/1999/5; CESCR, 'General Comment No 15: The Right to Water (Arts. 11 and 12 of the Covenant)' adopted at the Twenty-Ninth Session of the CESCR (20 January 2003) UN Doc E/C.12/2002/11. See also the Maastricht Principles on Extraterritorial Obligations of States in the area of Economic, Social and Cultural Rights (ETO) (ETO Consortium 2012); ILC, 'Report on the Work of Its Fifty-Third Session' (23 April-1 June and 2 July-10 August 2001) UN Doc A/56/10; ILC, 'Articles on Responsibility of States for Internationally Wrongful Acts' (2001) UN Doc A/56/49(Vol. I)/Corr.4 (ARSIWA); ILC, 'Report of the International Law Commission on the Work of its Sixty-Third Session' (26 April to 3 June and 4 July to 12 August 2011) UN Doc A/66/10; ILC, 'Draft Articles on the Responsibility of International Organizations' (2011) UN Doc A/66/473 (DARIO), all of which attempt to clarify the scope of extraterritorial obligations.

In spite of the broad set of objectives laid down by Articles 3(5) and 21 TEU it is still debated whether these two provisions confer new competences on the EU.[222] As Neframi posits, 'whereas specific substantive objectives correspond to specific external action competences conferred to the Union in Part V TFEU, the objective to promote an international system based on stronger multilateral cooperation and good global governance is not linked to a specific competence of the Union.'[223] For Cannizzaro the normative effect of Articles 3(5) and 21 TEU is limited precisely because the restraints deriving from the EU Treaties hinder the possibility for these provisions to be capable of providing a sufficiently strong legal basis for EU action aimed at promoting and protecting human rights. In addition—he argues-Article 21 TEU is limited to the CFSP, on the basis that 'Article 23 TEU assigns the pursuit of the political objectives laid down by Article 21(1) and (2) TEU to the primary competence of the CFSP.'[224] In his view, to entrust the EU with "full" global human rights powers would require further Treaty amendments.[225]

Moreover, it is not clear whether the EUCFR—as the key EU legally binding human rights instrument- establishes any obligations to respect and/or protect human rights beyond the EU's borders and if so, under what conditions and limitations. In this regard, the so-called "horizontal clauses" found in Chap. 7 of the EU Charter are not helpful.[226] Linked to this, the EUCFR does not contain a jurisdictional clause that is similar to the one contained in Article 1 ECHR delimiting its scope of application.[227] While the scope of the EUCFR also applies to EU external policies,[228] it remains unclear what these rights concretely entail for the EU when pursuing its external trade, investment and development policies.

Additionally, it is still settled case law that 'no Treaty provision confers on the Community institutions any general power to enact rules on human rights or to conclude international conventions in this field.'[229] Chiefly, the combined reading of Articles 6(1) subpara. 2 TEU and 51(2) EUCFR make it clear that the provisions of the

[222]Cannizzaro, above no. 220, 1093.

[223]Neframi (2014), at p. 73.

[224]Cannizzaro, above no. 220, at 1098.

[225]Ibid.

[226]See Chap. 7 'General Provisions', Articles 51–54 EUCFR.

[227]Article 51 only states that it is addressed to EU Institutions, bodies, offices and agencies, and to the Member States only when implementing EU law. On the meaning of 'implementing' EU law, see Case C-617/10, *Åklagaren v Hans Åkerberg Fransson*, EU:C:2013:280, where the Court confirmed the continuity between the scope of the Charter and the general principles of EU law. The case, however, focused on the national context and whether it may concern cross-border issues within the EU. Even in this context, it remains unclear what should be considered to fall within the scope of the Charter (and the jurisdictional dimension is not considered), see e.g. van Bockel and Wattel (2013), Fontanelli (2014), Dougan (2015), at 1246.

[228]Interestingly, in referring to Article 21 TEU, the Commission maintains that 'the Charter also applies to the EU's external action', see European Commission, *Strategy for the Effective Implementation of the Charter of Fundamental Rights by the European Union*, COM(2010) 573 final, 4.

[229]Opinion 2/94 on Accession by the Community to the European Convention for the Protection of Human Rights and Fundamental Freedoms, ECLI:EU:C:1996:140, para. 27.

Charter do not extend in any way the competences of the Union or establish any new power or task for the Union, or modify powers and tasks as defined in the Treaties.

However, in addressing Cannizzaro's claim that Article 21 TEU is limited in scope to the CFSP, it could be maintained that Article 23 TEU should not be interpreted as restricting the pursuit of political objectives contained in Article 21 TEU only through the CFSP,[230] as nothing in this provision as drafted supports such interpretation. Moreover, as posited by Engbrink, 'to insist on a rigid separation and interpret Article 40 TEU as strictly prohibiting "contamination" by any element of the respective other policy area [...] would run counter not only to the purpose of Article 21(3) subparagraph 2 TEU, but also to the spirit of the Treaties, which envisage a comprehensive and coherent approach in foreign policy.'[231] Second, if respect for human rights is a condition for the lawfulness of Union acts—as confirmed by the CJEU in many decisions—*a fortiori* the EU institutions have the duty and, therefore, the power in all the areas in which they might exercise conferred competences, to ensure that their acts do not violate fundamental rights. One could call this a "functional" human rights competence.[232] In Eeckhout's words, '[t]hat there must be some measure of competence to conclude human rights treaties follows, in the current state of EU law, simply from the *AETR* (or *ERTA*) principle'.[233] The *ERTA* principle, corresponding to the doctrine of implied powers developed by the CJEU in a line of cases, establishes that the competence of the EU to conclude international agreements may arise not only from an express conferment by the Treaty but may equally flow implicitly from other provisions of the Treaty and from measures adopted, within the framework of those provisions, by EU institutions whenever the EU intends to implement a common policy envisaged by the Treaty and adopts provisions laying down common rules, (whatever form these may take).[234] In a similar vein, Craig and de Búrca maintain that through conferred exclusive, shared or complementary competence in a given policy domain the EU has been given indirect competence to protect and

---

[230] L. Bartels, *The EU's Human Rights Obligations in Relation to Policies with Extraterritorial Effects: Rejoinder to Enzo Cannizzaro*, EJIL: *Talk, Debate!*, 15 January 2015), available at: http://www.ejiltalk.org/rejoinder-to-enzo-cannizzaro/, accessed on 20 February 2020; for the provision contained in Article 23 TEU, see above no. 205.

[231] Even though it would enable the application of the centre of gravity test; Engbrink (2017), at 13–14 and on the legal obligation of coherence, see 21–36.

[232] Eeckhout (2002), at 984.

[233] Eeckhout (2012).

[234] ERTA (or under its French acronym: AETR) stands for the European Agreement concerning the work of crews of vehicles engaged in international road transport, which was at the heart of the legal dispute between the Council and the Commission. The latter sought the annulment of the 'resolution' adopted by the Council relating to the negotiation and conclusion of the AETR by the member states. In this case the CJEU introduced for the first time its implied powers doctrine. As such this decision is considered both a landmark as well as a controversial ruling, see Case 22/70 *Commission of the European Communities v Council of the European Communities* ECLI:EU:C:1971:32, paras. 16–19. For detailed analysis and critical commentary of the doctrine of implied powers, see M. Hodun, *Doctrine of Implied Powers as a Judicial Tool to Build Federal Polities*, PhD dissertation, School of Law, Reykjavik University, available at: https://skemman.is/bitstream/1946/20824/1/Doctrine%20of%20implied%20powers%20as%20a%20judicial.pdf, accessed on 20 February 2020.

promote respect for human rights within that policy domain due to the general provisions that make the promotion and protection of human rights general principles of the Union.[235]

It should also be recalled that the EU is capable of binding itself, within the limits of the powers conferred upon it, to an international human rights instrument, so as to ensure that its legislation and executive acts comply with internationally agreed human rights standards.[236] Nevertheless, the CJEU has yet to examine any such arguments on implied powers and it has not analysed questions of competence in the sphere of human rights protection when scrutinizing the scope of Article 352 TFEU.[237] The CJEU appears reluctant to consider whether, in the light of the changes introduced by the TL, human rights fall within the scope of this provision. To date the CJEU has concluded that Article 352 TFEU cannot be used for the adoption of provisions whose effect would in substance be to amend the Treaty.[238] However, the following factors need to be taken into consideration when assessing the possibility of applying the doctrine of implied powers to the field of human rights. First, a single notion of implied powers in the EU system of government does not exist and the CJEU has developed and applied implied powers in a plurality of situations and for different purposes.[239] Second, and linked to the former, the attribution of implied powers exemplifies how the EU is conceived as a dynamic organization, evolving to meet changing needs and circumstances and, as time goes by, becoming further removed from its Treaty base.[240] It follows that judicial implied powers are derivative in nature rather than autonomous new powers as they constitute a teleological interpretation of explicit Treaty-based powers.

This brings us to Hartley's distinction between a narrow and a wide formulation of implied powers.[241] The narrow notion of implied powers refers to the existence of a given power that implies also the existence of any other power which is reasonably

---

[235]Craig and de Búrca (2011), for similar arguments pre-Lisbon, see Weiler and Fries (1999).

[236]See the preceding section, for key cases as examples of the EU's compliance with international human rights standards.

[237]In particular, Article 352(1) TFEU provides that: 'If action by the Union should prove necessary, within the framework of the policies defined in the Treaties, to attain one of the objectives set out in the Treaties, and the Treaties have not provided the necessary powers, the Council, acting unanimously on a proposal from the Commission and after obtaining the consent of the European Parliament, shall adopt the appropriate measures. Where the measures in question are adopted by the Council in accordance with a special legislative procedure, it shall also act unanimously on a proposal from the Commission and after obtaining the consent of the European Parliament.' From the perspective of input democracy, it is also significant that the provision in paragraph 2 of the Article also envisages the use of the procedure for monitoring the subsidiarity principle in Article 5(3) TEU with the involvement and scrutiny of national parliaments in relation to proposals based on this Article. This permits national parliaments to contribute to the EU's democratic processes, which in the framework and purpose of this provision is important insofar as it seeks to quell concerns about creeping competence of the EU.

[238]Eeckhout, above no. 233.

[239]Hodun, above no. 234, at p. 143.

[240]Bowett (1980).

[241]Hartley (1988).

necessary for the exercise of the former; according to the wide notion, the existence of a given objective or function implies the existence of any power reasonably necessary to attain it. The narrow formulation relies on the idea of necessity and the implied power must be considered to exist by virtue of the express powers. Conversely, the wide notion is more open-ended as it refers to reasonableness of achievement of objectives/purposes and therefore raises questions on its scope.[242] To put it differently, the narrow formulation points to the rule of law, accountability and loyalty, whereas the broad notion is founded on output legitimacy.[243]

In light of the above considerations, when it comes to human rights we can see that a wide formulation of implied powers would allow the EU to have some kind of functional competence in the field of human rights, as argued by Eeckhout and, in slightly different terms, also by Craig and de Búrca. This argument is corroborated by the fact that compliance with human rights is irrefutably a parameter of legality of EU acts, also in the external sphere. It is also supported by the fact that the EU has become a powerful *sui generis* international actor and with great power there must also come great responsibility. Furthermore, the revisited notion of implied powers put forward would not be creating new powers or extending or modifying existing powers. Within the jurisdictional model of territoriality and territorial extension, proposed in this chapter,[244] inferring the existence of competence in the sphere of human rights beyond the Union's borders would equate de facto to applying existing internal powers to the external sphere. In other words, internal powers would be complemented, as per *Kramer*,[245] by powers in the external sphere thus reinforcing the effectiveness and credibility (or output legitimacy) of EU external action.

6.6 Conclusion

> Nearly all men can stand adversity, but if you want to test a man's character, give him power.
> Attributed to US President Abraham Lincoln

The EU sees the global promotion of human rights as being part of both its interests and its self-identification as an international actor. It is now accepted by EU political institutions, the EO and the CJEU that fundamental rights compliance is a condition of legality of EU external action, but the exact nature of such obligation and how this obligation should be put into practice is still not clear.[246] Does the EU have what Joseph has termed "diagonal obligations"[247] towards "distant strangers"—[248] to wit,

[242] Hodun, above no. 234, at pp. 228–229.

[243] Conway (2010).

[244] See section 3, sub-section 3.2. of this Chapter.

[245] In *Kramer* the CJEU developed the so-called "complementarity principle" according to which the external compentence of the EU complements the internal one, Joined cases 3, 4 and 6–76, *Cornelis Kramer and others* ECLI:EU:C:1976:114.

[246] Cremona, above no. 10, at p. 86.

[247] Joseph distinguishes between so-called "vertical obligations", which 'refer to obligations owed by a state to its population with regard to its own conduct'; "horizontal obligations", which 'refer to a state's duty to apply human rights in the private sphere ("horizontally") so as to protect people from harm to their rights from other people or other non-state actors', and "diagonal obligations", which 'refer to a state's duty to the people of another state', see Joseph, above no. 120, at p. 245.

[248] Ganesh, above no. 5.

non-Union persons outside the territory of its member states—who are affected by its trade and investment policies?

Whilst the EU has made the promotion and protection of human rights one of its central pillars, the relationship between (the) EU (external action) and human rights remains strained. The EU, and most notably the CJEU, finds it difficult to clearly position itself as a distinctive (human rights) legal actor within the international legal framework, straddling between the preservation of the autonomy of its legal order and compliance with international law, as exemplified by recent case law.

In a world of global economic interdependence, where many countries do not have the capacity-building of ensuring steady progress towards the fulfilment of economic and social rights beyond minimalist protections without international assistance and cooperation of some sort, positive human rights obligations and the duty of due diligence, as outlined in the present chapter, are arguably necessary to give such rights meaning.[249] A complete denial of the existence of such obligations would deprive people of meaningful avenues to claim redress: 'the "have-nots" in the developing world would have no claim upon the "have" of the developed world, who are in the best position to provide assistance.'[250] The result would be what Craven terms a 'disjunction between the proclamation of rights…and the contingent conditions for their fulfilment'.[251] In the present postcolonial age, there is thus an ethical dimension to the debate concerning the nature of the EU's human rights obligations outside its borders.[252]

This brings us to Salomon's set of criteria for allocating global responsibilities to states in creating a just institutional economic order, namely:[253]

(a) The contribution a state has made to the emergence of a problem (for example, poverty exacerbated by resource depletion under colonization);
(b) The relative power wielded by a state at the international level that is manifested as influence over the direction of finance, trade, and development (effective control); (for example, its influence within the World Trade Organization (WTO));
(c) Whether it is in a position to assist (for example, its level of wealth);
(d) The extent to which a state benefits from the distribution of global wealth and resources. (for example, the extent to which the state has benefited from WTO rules, and other relevant rules of the global economy).

Two important points ought to be made about the above indicators. Firstly, such criteria are not confined to developed states even though they would have extensive responsibilities within this framework. Second, the existence of these obligations towards nationals of other states must not be seen to diminish the duties and responsibilities of those other states towards their own people.[254]

---

[249] Joseph, above no 120, at p. 255.

[250] Ibid.

[251] Craven (2007), at p. 83.

[252] See further section 2 of Chapter 5.

[253] Salomon, above no. 141, p. 193; the examples are provided by Joseph, above no. 120, at p. 260.

[254] Joseph, above no. 120, at p. 260.

If we apply these criteria to the EU, as a *sui generis* representative of collective state conduct, we can see that the EU holds all of these global responsibilities.

The jurisdictional model presented in this chapter—providing a territorial nexus between EU external action and its human rights obligations outside its borders—not only overcomes the "nettlesome issue" of extraterritoriality[255] but it also attempts to bridge the persistent gap in EU international relations between an ethics of care and humaneness[256] and pragmatism and realism. Additionally, the model proposed also goes beyond the values *versus* interests dichotomy[257] in order to propose a more robust and credible conception of normative power Europe. One caveat in relation to social rights. The model proposed would not "solve" their limited justiciability given the existing distinction in the EU context between rights and principles and the lack of clarity of the CJEU's case law,[258] in addition to the problems of standing that individuals have under Article 263 TFEU.

It is suggested that due diligence has an important role to play in determining parameters for the disaggregated appraisal of EU conduct in order to facilitate the attribution of responsibility to otherwise undifferentiated players within the EU itself and, more broadly, the global institutional order.[259] Again, this would be facilitated by the proposed jurisdictional model, as once the responsibility has been attributed within the EU legal order there are a set of grounds and actions for subsequently challenging the legality of an EU measure, even though human rights are likely to continue to be unenforceable before the CJEU in the foreseeable future.[260]

Be that as it may, given the complex interrelationship between EU values, international law and the global reach of EU law, it is not an easy enterprise to understand whose norms the EU is promoting.[261] The EU is intrinsically embedded in international law in many ways from both a formal and substantive perspective.[262] As a subject of international law, the EU is at the same time a norm-generator and a norm-recipient, acting as a legal (and political) "gap-filler".[263] Arguably, the EU is using its own external relations authority and power to promote at once a set of internal constitutional and substantive norms as well as international law. In this way,

[255] Ryngaert, above no. 32, at 388.

[256] For a humanistic philosophy and for humaneness to be the benchmark against which the adequacy and enforcement of EU law and policy across the board should be analysed, see Ferreira (2016), at pp. 9–10.

[257] See section 1 in this chapter; for further analysis, see section 1 of Chapter 2.

[258] See Velluti, above no. 96, at 75; see also Robin-Olivier (2013).

[259] The terms used are taken loosely from Salomon, above no. 141, at p. 186.

[260] With regard to judicial review actions brought by individuals under Article 263 TFEU, the stringent *locus standi* requirements should be uplifted by the CJEU.

[261] Cremona, above no. 10, at p. 87; for a thorough discussion of the interplay between EU law and International Law and for advocating that this relationship be based on "systemic harmonization" as defined by the ECtHR (*Al-Dulimi and Montana Management Inc. v Switzerland*, Application No. 5809/08 (GC), 21 June 2016, para. 140), see Ziegler (2016), and in particular, 687–706.

[262] Ziegler, above no. 261, at 679.

[263] Simma and Pulkowski (2006).

as Cremona posits: 'internal (EU) regulatory choices may be uploaded to the international level via multilateral conventions, and bilateral relations are then used to promote these multilateral norms. The global impact of EU law may involve not only the promotion of the EU's own "home-grown" norms, but also include international norms to which the EU has contributed, and/or wishes to promote.'[264] Yet again, this cross-fertilization between EU law and international law raises pressing questions about their human rights impact and the cases examined throughout illustrate the difficulty of ensuring adequate human rights protection outside EU borders.

References

International Law

Treaties and Conventions

Council of Europe

European Convention on Human Rights and Fundamental Freedoms as amended by Protocols No. 11 and 14, 4 November 1950, ETS 5. Available at: https://www.refworld.org/docid/3ae6b3b04.html. Accessed on 2 Mar 2020

United Nations Treaties

UN General Assembly, *Convention on the Elimination of All Forms of Discrimination against Women*, 18 December 1979, A/RES/34/180. Available at: https://treaties.un.org/Pages/ViewDetails.aspx?src=TREATY&mtdsg_no=IV-8&chapter=4&clang=_en. Accessed on 20 Feb 2020

UN General Assembly, *International Covenant on Economic, Social and Cultural Rights*, 16 December 1966, United Nations, Treaty Series, vol. 993, p. 3. Available at: https://www.ohchr.org/en/professionalinterest/pages/cescr.aspx. Accessed on 20 Feb 2020

UN General Assembly, *International Covenant on Civil and Political Rights* (adopted 16 December 1966, entered into force 23 March 1976) 999 UNTS 171 (ICCPR)

UN Convention on the Rights of the Child (adopted 20 November 1989, entered into force 2 September 1990) 1577 UNTS 3 (CRC)

United Nations, *Vienna Convention on the Law of Treaties*, 23 May 1969, United Nations, Treaty Series, vol. 1155, p. 331

United Nations Convention on the Rights of Persons with Disabilities, New York, 13 December 2006. Available at: https://treaties.un.org/pages/ViewDetails.aspx?src=IND&mtdsg_no=IV-15&chapter=4&clang=_en. Accessed on 20 Feb 2020

United Nations, *Charter of the United Nations*, 24 October 1945, 1 UNTS XVI. Available at: https://www.un.org/en/sections/un-charter/un-charter-full-text/. Accessed on 20 Feb 2020

UN General Assembly, *Universal Declaration of Human Rights*, 10 December 1948, 217 A (III). Available at: https://www.ohchr.org/EN/UDHR/Documents/UDHR_Translations/eng.pdf. Accessed on 20 Feb 2020

---

[264]Cremona, above no. 10, at p. 108.

UN General Assembly, *Declaration on the Right to Development: resolution/adopted by the General Assembly*, 4 December 1986, A/RES/41/128. available at: https://www.ohchr.org/en/professional interest/pages/righttodevelopment.aspx. Accessed on 20 Feb 2020

Documents from International Organizations

Organisation for Economic Co-operation and Development (OECD)

OECD *Guidelines for Multinational Enterprises,* 25 May 2011. Available at: https://www.oecd.org/daf/inv/mne/oecdguidelinesformultinationalenterprises.htm. Accessed on 20 Feb 2020

Committee on the Rights of the Child (CtRC)

CtRC, 'Concluding observations: Sweden' (23 January 2012) UN Doc CRC/C/OPSC/SWE/CO/1
CtRC, 'Concluding observations: Bosnia and Herzegovina' (29 November 2012) UN Doc CtRC/C/BIH/CO/2-4
CtRC, 'General comment No. 16 (2013)' (17 April 2013) UN Doc. CRC/C/GC/16, para 43 (CRC, General comment No. 16)

Committee on the Elimination of All Forms of Discrimination against Women (CEDAW)

CEDAW, '*General Recommendation No. 19: Violence against women*', (Eleventh session 1992)
CEDAW, 'General recommendation No. 28 *on the Core Obligations of States Parties under Article 2 of the Convention on the Elimination of All Forms of Discrimination against Women* (16 December 2010) UN Doc CEDAW/C/GC/28, para 36 (CEDAW, 'General recommendation No. 28')
CEDAW, General recommendation No. 35 *on gender-based violence against women, updating general recommendation No. 19,* 14 July 2017, CEDAW/C/GC/35

Human Rights Committee (HRC)

HRC, General Comment No. 31: The Nature of the General Legal Obligation Imposed on States Parties to the Covenant, CCPR/C/21/Rev.1/Add. 13, 29 March 2004
HRC, 'Report of the Working Group on the issue of human rights and transnational corporations and other business enterprises' (10 August 2012) UN Doc. A/67/285
HRC, 'Report of the Working Group on the issue of human rights and transnational corporations and other business enterprises' (14 March 2013) UN Doc. A/HRC/23/32
HRC, 'Resolution No. 28/10' (2 April 2015) UN Doc. A/HRC/RES/28/10
HRC, 'Report of the Working Group on the issue of human rights and transnational corporations and other business enterprises on the Asia Forum on Business and Human Rights' (30 May 2016) UN Doc. A/HRC/32/45/Add.2
HRC, Report of the Working Group on the issue of human rights and transnational corporations and other business enterprises (24 April 2017) UN Doc. A/HRC/35/32

Committee on Economic, Social and Cultural Rights (CESCR)

CESCR, 'General Comment No. 14 (2000)' (11 August 2000) UN Doc. E/C.12/2000/4
CESCR, 'General Comment No. 15 (2002)' (20 January 2003) UN Doc. E/C.12/2002/11
CESCR, 'General Comment No 12: The Right to Adequate Food (Art. 11)' adopted at Twentieth Session of the CESCR (12 May 1999) UN Doc E/C.12/1999/5
CESCR, 'General Comment No. 19' (4 February 2008) UN Doc. E/C.12/GC/19
CESCR, 'General Comment No. 23 (2016)' (27 April 2016) UN Doc. E/C.12/GC/23
CESCR 'Statement on the obligations of States Parties regarding the corporate sector and economic, social and cultural rights' (20 May 2011) UN Doc. E/C.12/2011/1

International Law Commission (ILC)

ILC, 'International responsibility. Second report by F. v Garcia Amador' (15 February 1957) UN Doc A/CN.4/106, 122
ILC, 'The law of the non-navigational uses of international watercourses' (15 February 1957) UN Doc A/49/10, 103
ILC, 'Report on the Work of Its Fifty-Third Session' (23 April-1 June and 2 July-10 August 2001) UN Doc A/56/10
ILC, *Draft articles on Prevention of Transboundary Harm from Hazardous Activities, with commentaries, Yearbook of the International Law Commission*, 2001, vol II, Part Two. Available at: https://legal.un.org/ilc/texts/instruments/english/commentaries/9_7_2001.pdf. Accessed on 20 Feb 2020
ILC, 'Articles on Responsibility of States for Internationally Wrongful Acts' (2001) UN Doc A/56/49(Vol. I)/Corr.4 (ARSIWA)
ILC, 'Report of the International Law Commission on the Work of its Sixty-Third Session' (26 April to 3 June and 4 July to 12 August 2011) UN Doc A/66/10
ILC, 'Draft Articles on the Responsibility of International Organizations' (2011) UN Doc A/66/473 (DARIO)

United Nations Human Rights Office of the High Commissioner (OHCHR)

OHCHR, 'The European Union and International Human Rights Law'. Available at: https://europe.ohchr.org/Documents/Publications/EU_and_International_Law.pdf. 20 February 2020
OHCHR, 'Guiding Principles on business and human rights' (21 March 2011) UN Doc. A/HRC/17/31

Commission on Human Rights (since 2006 Human Rights Council)

Commission on Human Rights, *Report of the UN Special Rapporteur on the Right to Food, A. Eide*, UN Doc. E/CN.4/Sub.2/1987/23 (1987)
Commission on Human Rights, 'Report of the Special Rapporteur on the right to food, Jean Ziegler', UN doc. E/CN.4/2005/47 (24 January 2005)

Table of cases

Inter-American Court of Human Rights (IACtHR)

IACtHR, Advisory Opinion *OC-23/17*, The Environment and Human Rights (State obligations in relation to the environment in the context of the protection and guarantee of the rights to life and to personal integrity—interpretation and scope of Articles 4(1) and 5(1) of the American Convention on Human Rights), 15 November 2017

United Nations

UN Security Council, Letter dated 29 January 2002 from the Under-Secretary-General for Legal Affairs, the Legal Counsel, addressed to the President of the Security Council, S/2002/161. Available at: http://www.arso.org/Olaeng.pdf. Accessed on 21 Feb 2020

Human Rights Committee (HRC)

HRC, *Munaf v Romania*, (21 August 2009), UN doc. CCPR/C?96/D/1539/2006
HRC, 'Concluding observations: Germany' (12 November 2012) UN Doc CCPR/C/DEU/CO/6
HRC, 'Concluding observations: Canada' (13 August 2015) UN Doc CCPR/C/CAN/CO/6

International Court of Justice (ICJ)

ICJ, *Interpretation of the Agreement of 25 March 1951 between the WHO and Egypt*, Advisory Opinion, 20 December 1980
ICJ, *Legal Consequences of the Construction of a Wall in the Occupied Palestinian Territory*, Advisory Opinion, 09 July 2004
ICJ, *Corfu Channel (United Kingdom v Albania)*, Judgment, ICJ Reports 1949 *(Corfu Channel case)*, p. 4
ICJ, *Advisory Opinion on the Western Sahara* [1975] I.C.J. 12
ICJ, *Pulp Mills on the River Uruguay (Argentina v Uruguay)* [2010] ICJ Rep 55–6

International Arbitral Awards

AH Francis (Great Britain) v United Mexican States, 5 RIAA 100 (1930)
Youmans (U.S. v. Mexico), 4 RIAA 110 (1926)
Janes (U.S. v. Mexico), 4 RIAA 82 (1926)
Trailer Smelter Case (US v Canada) 3 RIAA 1905 (1941)

Council of Europe

European Court of Human Rights (ECtHR)

ECtHR, *Soering v United Kingdom*, Application No. 14038/88, 07 July 1989
ECtHR, *Guerra and Others v Italy*, Application No. 14967/89, 19 February 1998
ECtHR, *Osman v The United Kingdom*, Application No. 23452/94, 28 October 1998
ECtHR *Issa and Others v Turkey*, Application No. 31821/96, 16 November 2004
ECtHR, *Banković and others v. Belgium, the Czech Republic, Denmark, France, Germany, Greece, Hungary, Iceland, Italy, Luxembourg, the Netherlands, Norway, Poland, Portugal, Spain, Turkey and the United Kingdom*, Application No. 52207/99, 12 December 2001
ECtHR, *Ilaşcu and Others v. Moldova and Russia*, Application No. 48787/99, 8 July 2004
ECtHR, *Bevacqua and S. v Bulgaria*, Application No. 71127/01, 12 June 2008
ECtHR, *Opuz v Turkey*, Application no. 33401/02, 09 June 2009
ECtHR, *Rantsev v. Cyprus and Russia*, Application No. 25965/04, 07 January 2010
ECtHR, *Al-Skeini and Others v. the United Kingdom*, Application No. 55721/07, 07 July 2011
ECtHR, *Al-Dulimi and Montana Management Inc. v Switzerland*, Application No. 5809/08 (GC), 21 June 2016

European Union Official Documents

Treaties

Treaty of Lisbon Amending the Treaty on European Union and the Treaty Establishing the European Community, 13 December 2007, 2007/C 306/01
Consolidated Version of the Treaty on European Union [2008] OJ C115/13
Consolidated Version of the Treaty on the Functioning of the European Union [2008] OJ C115/01
Charter of Fundamental Rights of the European Union [2000] OJ C364/01

International Agreements of the European Union

Free Trade Agreement between the European Union and its Member States of the one part, and the Republic of Korea of the other part (EU-Korea FTA) *OJ* [2011] L127/6, 14 May 2011, p. 6
Euro-Mediterranean Agreement establishing an association between the European Community and its Member States, of the one part, and the Republic of Lebanon, of the other part, OJ [2006] L143/2
Euro-Mediterranean Agreement establishing an association between the European Communities and their Member States, of the one part, and the Kingdom of Morocco, of the other part, OJ [2000] L70/2
EU-Vietnam Free Trade Agreement (EVFTA). Available at: https://trade.ec.europa.eu/doclib/press/index.cfm?id=1437. Accessed on 19 Feb 2020
Trade Agreement between the European Union and its Member States, of the one part, and Colombia and Peru, of the other part *OJ* [2012] L354/3, 21 December 2012, p. 3

Table of cases

Cases of the Court of Justice of the European Union

General Court

Case T-212/02 *Commune de Champagne v Council and Commission* [2007] ECR 2007 II-02017

Case T-292/09 *Muhamad Mugraby v Council of the European Union* and the European Commission ECLI:EU:T:2011:418

Case T-512/12 *Front populaire pour la libération de la saguiaelhamra et du rio de oro (Front Polisario) v Council of the European Union*, ECLI:EU:T:2015:953

European Court of Justice

Case 11/70, *Internationale Handelsgesellschaft* (ECLI:EU:C:1970:114)

Case 22/70 *Commission of the European Communities v Council of the European Communities* ECLI:EU:C:1971:32

Joined Cases 21/72–24/72 *International Fruit Company NV and others*, (ECLI:EU:C:1972:115)

Case 181/73 *Haegeman*, (ECLI:EU:C:1974:41)

Joined cases 3, 4 and 6–76, *Cornelis Kramer and others* ECLI:EU:C:1976:114

Case C-286/90 *Anklagemindigheden v Poulsen*, (ECLI:EU:C:1992:453)

Case C-280/93 *Germany v Council*, (ECLI:EU:C:1994:367)

Case C-214/94, *Boukhalfa v Bundesrepublik Deutschland*, ECLI:EU:C:1996:174

C-177/95 *Ebony Maritime SA and Loten Navigation Co. Ltd v Prefetto della Provincia di Brindisi and others* ECLI:EU:C:1997:89

Case C-162/96 *Racke v Hauptzollamt Mainz*, (ECLI:EU:C:1998:293)

C-12/03 P, *Commission v Tetra Laval*, ECLI:EU:C:2005:87

Joined Cases C-402/05 P and C-415/05 P *Kadi and Al Barakaat International Foundation v Council and Commission (Kadi I)*, (ECLI:EU:C:2008:461)

Case C-308/06 *Intertanko and Others*, (ECLI:EU:C:2008:312)

Case C-34/09 *Gerardo Ruiz Zambrano v Office national de l'emploi* ECLI:EU:C:2011:124

Case C-366/10, *Air Transportation of America ex parte Secretary of State for Energy and Climate Change (ATAA)*, (ECLI:EU:C:2011:864)

Case C-617/10, *Åklagaren v Hans Åkerberg Fransson*, EU:C:2013:280

Joined Cases C-584/10 P, C-593/10 P, and C-595/10 P *Commission and Others v Yassin Abdullah Kadi (Kadi II)*, (ECLI:EU:C:2013:518)

Case C-581/11 P, *Muhamad Mugraby v Council of the European Union and European Commission* ECLI:EU:C:2012:466

Case C-424/13, *Zuchtvieh-Export GmbH*, (ECLI:EU:C:2015:259)

C-362/14, *Maximillian Schrems v Data Protection Commissioner, Digital Rights Ireland Ltd.* (ECLI:EU:C:2015:650)

Case C-263/14, *European Parliament v. Council*, (ECLI:EU:C:2016:435)

Case C-592/14 *European Federation for Cosmetic Ingredients v Secretary of State for Business, Innovation and Skills* ECLI:EU:C:2016:703

Joined Cases C-203/15 and C-698/15, *Tele2 Sverige and Watson and others* (ECLI:EU:C:2016:970)

Case C-104/16 P *Council of the European Union v Front populaire pour la libération de la saguia-el-hamra et du rio de oro (Front Polisario)*, ECLI:EU:C:2016:973

Opinion 2/94 on Accession by the Community to the European Convention for the Protection of Human Rights and Fundamental Freedoms, ECLI:EU:C:1996:140

Opinion 2/13 on the compatibility with EU law of the draft agreement for EU accession to the European Convention of Human Rights and Fundamental Freedoms (ECHR), (ECLI:EU:C:2014:2454)
Opinion1/15 on the draft agreement between Canada and the European Union (EU) dealing with the Transfer of Passenger Name Record (PNR) data from the EU to Canada (ECLI:EU:C:2017:592)

Opinions of the Advocate General

Case C-104/16 P, *Council of the European Union v Front Populaire pour la Libération de la Saguia-El-Hamra et du Rio de Oro (Front Polisario)*, Opinion of Advocate General Wathelet, ECLI:EU:C:2016:677

European Ombudsman

European Ombudsman, Decision in case 1409/2014/MHZ on the European Commission's failure to carry out a prior human rights impact assessment of the EU-Vietnam free trade agreement, (26 February 2016)
European Ombudsman, Decision in the joint inquiry into complaints 506–509-674-784-927-1381/2016/MHZ against the European Commission concerning a human rights impact assessment in the context of the EU-Turkey Agreement, (18 January 2017)
European Ombudsman´s Speech on its Decision on the failure of European Commission to conduct a prior human rights impact assessment of the EU Vietnam free trade agreement, 3 March 2016. Available at: https://www.ombudsman.europa.eu/activities/speech.faces/en/64453/html.bookmark. Accessed on 20 Feb 2020

European Commission

Official Documents of the EU Institutions and Bodies

European Commission, 2000/520/EC: Commission Decision of 26 July 2000 pursuant to Directive 95/46/EC of the European Parliament and of the Council on the adequacy of the protection provided by the safe harbour privacy principles and related frequently asked questions issued by the US Department of Commerce (notified under document number C(2000) 2441) (Text with EEA relevance.), OJ [2000] L215/7
European Commission, *Strategy for the Effective Implementation of the Charter of Fundamental Rights by the European Union*, COM(2010) 573 final
European Commission, Guidelines on the analysis of human rights impacts in impact assessments for trade-related policy initiatives, 2015. Available at: https://trade.ec.europa.eu/doclib/docs/2015/july/tradoc_153591.pdf. Accessed on 23 Feb 2020
European Commission, Commission Implementing Decision (EU) 2016/1250 of 12 July 2016 pursuant to Directive 95/46/EC of the European Parliament and of the Council on the adequacy of the protection provided by the EU-U.S. Privacy Shield (notified under document C(2016) 4176) (Text with EEA relevance), C/2016/4176, OJ [2016] L207/1

European Commission, Sustainability Impact Assessment in Support of the Association Agreement Negotiations between the European Union and Mercosur, Interim Report, LSE Consulting, February 2020. Available at: https://trade.ec.europa.eu/doclib/docs/2020/february/tradoc_158632.pdf. p. 102, Accessed on 10 Mar 2020

Council of the European Union

Council Decision 2012/497/EU of 8 March 2012 on the conclusion of an Agreement in the form of an Exchange of Letters between the European Union and the Kingdom of Morocco concerning reciprocal liberalisation measures on agricultural products, processed agricultural products, fish and fishery products, the replacement of Protocols 1, 2 and 3 and their Annexes and amendments to the Euro-Mediterranean Agreement establishing an association between the European Communities and their Member States, of the one part, and the Kingdom of Morocco, of the other part, OJ [2012] L241/2

Council of the European Union, *Council Conclusions on the Action Plan on Human Rights and Democracy 2015–2019*, doc. 10897/15, 20 July 2015

European Parliament and Council of the European Union

Directive 2008/101/EC of the European Parliament and of the Council of 19 November 2008 amending Directive 2003/87/EC so as to include aviation activities in the scheme for greenhouse gas emission allowance trading within the Community (Text with EEA relevance) OJ [2009] L8/3

Regulation (EC) No 1223/2009 of the European Parliament and of the Council of 30 November 2009 on cosmetic products (Text with EEA relevance) OJ L342/59

European External Action Service

European External Action Service (EEAS), *A Global Strategy for the European Union's Foreign and Security Policy—Shared Vision, Common Action: A Stronger Europe*, June 2016. Available at: https://eeas.europa.eu/sites/eeas/files/eugs_review_web_0.pdf. Accessed on 14 June 2020

Books and chapters in books

Balboni M, Laschi G (eds) (2017) The European union approach towards Western Sahara. P.I.E. Peter Lang, Brussels

Berkes A (2018) Extraterritorial responsibility of the home States for MNCs' violations of human rights. In: Radi Y (ed) Research handbook on human rights and investment. Elgar Publishers, Cheltenham, pp 304–343

Bingham T (2010) Alabama arbitration. In: Wolfrum R (ed) Max planck encyclopedia of public international law. OUP, Oxford. Available at: https://opil.ouplaw.com/view/10.1093/law:epil/9780199231690/law-9780199231690-e89. Accessed on 20 Feb 2020

Bowett DW (1980) The law of international institutions. FA Praeger, New York
Brownlie I (2008) Principles of public international law. OUP, Oxford
Cardwell PJ, Wessel RA (2020) EU external relations and international law: divergence on questions of 'territory'? In: Fahey E (ed) Framing convergence with the global order: the EU and the world. Hart, Oxford, pp. 143-161
Coomans F, Künnemann R (eds) (2012) Cases and concepts on extraterritorial obligations in the area of economic, social and cultural rights. Intersentia, Cambridge
Costello C, Moreno Lax V (2014) The extraterritorial application of the EU charter of fundamental rights: from territoriality to facticity, the effectiveness model. In: Peers S, Hervey T, Kenner J, Ward A (eds) The EU charter of fundamental rights—a commentary. Hart Publishing, Oxford, pp 1657–1683, at p. 1660
Craig P, de Búrca G (2015) EU law, text, cases and materials. OUP, Oxford
Craven M (2007) The violence of dispossession: extraterritoriality and economic, social and cultural rights. In: Baderin MA, McCorquodale R (eds) Economic, social and cultural rights in action. OUP, Oxford, pp 71–88
Cremona M, Scott J (eds) EU law beyond EU borders. The extraterritorial reach of EU law. OUP, Oxford
Cremona M (2019) Extending the reach of EU law. The EU as an international legal actor. In: Cremona M, Scott J (eds) EU law beyond EU borders. The extraterritorial reach of EU law. OUP, Oxford, pp 64–111
Cremona M, Scott J (2019) Introduction. EU law beyond EU borders. In: Cremona M, Scott J (eds) The extraterritorial reach of EU law. OUP, Oxford, pp 1–20
d'Aspremont J (2014) A European law of international responsibility? The articles on the responsibility of international organisations and the EU. In: Kosta V et al (eds) The EU accession to the ECHR. Hart Publishing, Oxford, pp 75–85
De Búrca G (2011) The evolution of EU human rights law. In: Craig P, de Búrca G (eds) Evol EU law. OUP, Oxford, pp 465–477
Duffy H (2005) The 'war on terror' and the framework of international law. CUP, Cambridge
Eeckhout P (2012) EU external relations law. OUP, Oxford, pp 99–100
Evans M, Koutrakos P (eds) (2013) The international responsibility of the European union: European and international perspectives. Hart Publishing, Oxford
Fahey E (2017) The global reach of EU law. Routledge, London
Fahey E (2018) Introduction to law and global governance. Elgar Publishing, Cheltenham
Ferreira N (2016) The human face of the European union. Are EU law and policy humane enough? An introduction. In: Ferreira N, Kostakopoulou D (eds) The human face of the European union. Are EU law and policy humane enough? CUP, Cambridge, pp 1–14
Hartley T (1988) The foundations of European Community Law: an introduction to the constitutional and administrative law of the European Community. OUP, Oxford, p 106
Hettne J, Groussot X, Pétursson GT (2017) General principles and the many faces of coherence: between law and ideology in the European union. In: Vogenauer S, Weatherill S (eds) General principles of law: European and comparative perspectives. Hart Publishing, Oxford, pp 77–103
Higgins R (2009) Themes and theories. OUP, Oxford, pp 801–810
Joseph S (2013) Blame it on the WTO? A human rights critique. OUP, Oxford
Kamminga MT (2012) Extraterritoriality. In: Wolfrum R (ed), Max planck encyclopedia of public international law. OUP, Oxford, pp 1070–1077
Klabbers J (2015) Straddling the fence. The EU and international law. In: Arnull A, Chalmers D (eds) The Oxford Handbook of European Union Law. OUP, Oxford, pp 52–71
Kochenov D (2019) European union territory from a legal perspective: a commentary on articles 52 TEU, 355, 349, and 198–204 TFEU. In: Kellerbauer M, Klamert M, Tomkin J (eds) The EU treaties and the charter of fundamental rights—a commentary. OUP, Oxford, pp 334–336
Kochenov D (2019) European union territory from a legal perspective: a commentary on articles 52 TEU, 355, 349, and 198–204 TFEU. In: Kellerbauer M, Klamert M, Tomkin J (eds) The EU treaties and the charter of fundamental rights—a commentary. OUP, Oxford, pp 2058–2062
Kochenov D (2019) European union territory from a legal perspective: a commentary on Articles 52 TEU, 355, 349, and 198–204 TFEU. In: Kellerbauer M, Klamert M, Tomkin J (eds) The EU treaties and the charter of fundamental rights—a commentary. OUP, Oxford, pp 2081–2082

Kochenov D (2019) European union territory from a legal perspective: a commentary on Articles 52 TEU, 355, 349, and 198–204 TFEU. In: Kellerbauer M, Klamert M, Tomkin J (eds) The EU treaties and the charter of fundamental rights—a commentary. OUP, Oxford, pp 2083–2091.
Kochenov D (2019) 'European Union Territory from a Legal Perspective: A Commentary on Articles 52 TEU, 355, 349, and 198–204 TFEU' in M. Kellerbauer, M. Klamert and J. Tomkin (eds), *The EU Treaties and the Charter of Fundamental Rights—A Commentary* (Oxford: OUP, 2019), pp. 334–336; pp. 2058–2062; pp. 2081–2082; pp. 2083–2091
Kokott J (2011) States, sovereign equality. In: Wolfrum R (ed) The max planck encyclopedia of public international law online edition. OUP, Oxford. Available at: https://opil.ouplaw.com/view/10.1093/law:epil/9780199231690/law-9780199231690-e1113. Accessed on 20 Feb 2020
Koivurova T (2010) Due diligence. In: Wolfrum R (ed) Max planck encyclopedia of public international law. OUP, Oxford. Available at: http://opil.ouplaw.com/abstract/10.1093/law:epil/9780199231690/law-9780199231690-1034?prd=EPIL. Accessed on 20 Feb 2020
Kube V (2019) EU human rights, international investment law and participation.Springer, Heidelberg
Kuner C (2019) The internet and the global reach of EU law. In: Cremona M, Scott J (eds) EU law beyond EU borders. The extraterritorial reach of EU law. OUP, Oxford, pp 112–145
Langford M et al (eds) (2012) Global justice, state duties. The extraterritorial scope of economic, social and cultural rights in international law. CUP, Cambridge
Milanovic M ((2011) Extraterritorial application of human rights treaties. Law, principles, and policy. OUP, Oxford
Neframi E (2014) Vertical division of competences and the objectives of the European union's external action. In: Cremona M (ed) The European court of justice and external relations law. Hart Publishing, Oxford, pp 73–94
Proulx V-J (2012) Transnational terrorism and state accountability: a new theory of prevention. Hart Publishing, Oxford, p 270
Ruggie J (2008) Report of the special representative of the secretary-general on the issue of human rights and transnational corporations and other business enterprises, *Protect, Respect and Remedy: A Framework for Business and Human Rights*, Report to the UN Human Rights Council, (Framework Report), UN Doc. A/HRC/8/5, 7 April 2008. Available at: https://www.business-humanrights.org/sites/default/files/reports-and-materials/Ruggie-report-7-Apr-2008.pdf. Accessed 20 Feb 2020
Ryngaert C (2008) Jurisdiction in international law. OUP, Oxford
Ryngaert C (2013) Jurisdiction: towards a reasonableness test. In: Langford M et al (eds) Global justice, state duties: the extraterritorial scope of economic, social and cultural rights in international law. CUP, New York, pp 192–211
Salmon J (ed) (2001) Dictionnaire de Droit international public. Bruylant, Bruxelles
Salomon M (2007) Global responsibility for human rights. OUP, Oxford
Scott J (2019) The global reach of EU law. In: Cremona M, Scott J (eds) EU law beyond EU borders. The extraterritorial reach of EU law. OUP, Oxford, pp 21-63
Shue H (1996) Basic rights, 2nd edn. Princeton University Press, Princeton
Sidati M (2016) The EU's Morocco problem, *Politico*, 23 December 2016, available at: https://www.politico.eu/article/the-eus-morocco-problem-western-sahara-trade-judgment/. Accessed on 19 February 2020
Staker C (2014) Jurisdiction. In: Evans MD (ed) International law, 4th edn. OUP, Oxford, pp 309–335.
Van Vooren B, Wessel RA (2014) EU external relations law: Text, cases and materials. CUP, Cambridge
Velluti S The "inside looking out": mainstreaming human rights in EU external relations. In: Balboni M, Danisi C (eds) Human Rights as a Horizontal Issue in EU External Policy. Les droits de l'homme comme domaine horizontal de la politique extérieure de l'Union européenne (Editoriale Scientifica, forthcoming)
Weatherill S (2016) Law and values in the European union. OUP, Oxford
Weiler JHH, Fries SC (1999) A human rights policy for the European Community and Union: the question of competences. In: Alston P, Bustelo M, Heenan J (ed) The EU and human rights. OUP, Oxford, pp 147–166

Wilde R (2018) Socioeconomic rights, extraterritorially. In: Benvenisiti E, Nolte G (eds) Community obligations in contemporary international law. OUP, Oxford, pp 381–395

Journal Articles

Ahmed T, de Jesús Butler I (2006) The European Union and Human Rights: an International Law Perspective. Eur J Int Law 17(4):771–801
Arbour L (2008) The responsibility to protect as a duty of care in international law and practice Rev Int Stud 34(3):445–458
Azoulai L, Van der Sluis M (2016) Institutionalising personal data protection in times of global institutional distrust: schrems Common Mark Law Rev 53(5):1343–1371
Barnidge R (2006) The due diligence principle under international law Int Commun Law Rev 8(1):81–121
Bartels L (2015) The EU's human rights obligations in relation to policies with extraterritorial effects. Eur J Int Law 1 25(4):1071–1091
Bassett Moore J (1887) Report on extraterritorial crime and the cutting case. US Foreign Relat 23:575
Berkes A (2018) The extraterritorial human rights obligations of the EU in its external trade and investment policies. Eur World: Law Rev 2(1):1–22. http://doi.org/10.14324/111.444.ewlj.2018.05
Bonnitcha J, McCorquodale R (2017) The concept of "due diligence" in the UN guiding principles on business and human rights Eur J Int Law 28(3):899–919
Bradford A (2012) The brussels effect. Northwest Univ Law Rev 107(1):1–68
Cannizzaro E (2015) The EU's human rights obligations in relation to policies with extraterritorial effects: a reply to lorand bartels Eur J Int Law 25(4):1093–1099
Cantabria M (2009) Europe and rights: taking dialogue seriously Eur Const Law Rev 5(1):5–31
Conway G (2010) Conflict of competence norms in EU law and the legal reasoning of the ECJ. Ger Law J 11(9):966–1005
Corino C (2000) Environmental due diligence. Eur Environ Law Rev 9(4):120–124
Daugirdas K (2016) How and why international law binds international organizations harvard. Int Law J 57(2):325–381
de Beco G (2007) Measuring human rights: underlying approach. Eur Hum Rights Law Rev 3:266–278
de Jesús Butler I (2008) The European Union and International Human Rights Law, United Nations Human Rights Office of the High Commissioner, Regional Office for Europe, Brussels. Available at: https://europe.ohchr.org/Documents/Publications/EU_and_International_Law.pdf. Accessed 19 Feb 2020
de Jesús BI, De Schutter O (2008) Binding the EU to International Human Rights Law. Yearb Eur Law 27(1):277–320
De Schutter O, Eide A, Khalfan A, Orellana M, Salomon ME, Seiderman I (2012) Commentary to the maastricht principles on extraterritorial obligations of states in the area of economic, social and cultural rights. Hum Rights Q 34(4):1084–1169
De Witte B, Imamović Š (2015) Opinion 2/13 on accession to the ECHR: defending the EU legal order against a foreign human rights court. Eur Law Rev 40(5):683–705
den Hertog L, Stroß S (2013) Coherence in EU external relations: concepts and legal rooting of an ambiguous term. Eur Foreign Aff Rev 18(3):373–388
Deva S (2004) Acting extraterritorially to tame multinational corporations for human rights violations: who should 'bell the cat' Melb J Int Law 5:37–65
Dougan M (2015) Judicial review of member state action under the general principles and the charter: defining the "scope of union law". Common Mark Law Rev 52(5):1201–1245
Dover R, Frosini J (2012) The extraterritorial effects of legislation and policies in the EU and US. Study for the European parliament, directorate-general for external policies of the union, directorate b, policy department, Brussels, May 2012. Available at: http://edz.bib.uni-mannheim.de/daten/edz-ma/ep/12/EST73891.pdf. Accessed on 30 Jan 2018

Eeckhout P (2002) The EU Charter of Fundamental Rights and the Federal Question. Common Mark Law Rev 39(5):945–994
Eeckhout P (2015) Opinion 2/13 on EU accession to the ECHR and judicial dialogue—autonomy or autarky? Fordham Int Law J 38(4):955–992
Eeckhout P (2013) Human rights and the autonomy of EU law: pluralism or integration? Curr Leg Probl 66(1):169–202
Engbrink D (2017) The European union's external action: coherence in European union foreign policy despite separate legal orders? Leg Issues Econ Integr 44(1):5–48
ETO Consortium, *Maastricht Principles on Extraterritorial Obligations of States in the Area of Economic, Social and Cultural Rights*, adopted 28 September 2011, available at: https://www.etoconsortium.org/nc/en/main-navigation/library/maastricht-principles/?tx_drblob_pi1%5BdownloadUid%5D=23. accessed on 20 February 2020
Fahey E (2014) On the use of law in transatlantic relations: legal dialogues between the EU and the US. Eur Law J 20(3):368–384
Fontanelli F (2014) Implementation of EU law through domestic measures after fransson: the court of justice buys time and "non-preclusion" troubles loom large. Eur Law Rev 39(5):782–800
Frelick B, Kysel IM, Podkul J (2016) The impact of externalisation of migrant controls on the rights of asylum seekers and other migrants. J Migr Hum Secur 4(4):190–220
Ganesh A (2016) The European Union's Human Rights Obligations Towards Distant Strangers. Mich J Int Law 37(3):475–538
Harrison J (2011) Human rights measurement: reflections on the current practice and future potential of human rights impact assessment J Hum Rights Pract 3(2):162–187
Herlin-Karnell E, Konstantinidis T (2013) The rise and expressions of consistency in EU law: legal and strategic implications for European integration. Camb Yearb Eur Leg Stud 15:139–167
Jaremba U, Kanetake M, Koning I (2019) Economic and non-economic values and objectives in the EU's international trade: normative tensions, actors and processes. Eur World: Law Rev 3(1):6. https://doi.org/10.14324/111.444.ewlj.2019.16
Kanalan I (2018) Extraterritorial state obligations beyond the concept of jurisdiction. Ger Law J 19(1): 43–64
Kassoti E (2017) The council v front polisario case: the court of justice's selective reliance on international rules on treaty interpretation (second part) Eur Pap 2(1):23–42
Kassoti E (2017) The front polisario v council case: the general court, Völkerrechtsfreundlichkeit and the external aspect of European integration (first part) Eur Pap Insights 2(1):339–356
Lavenex S, Schimmelfennig F (2009) EU rules beyond EU borders: theorizing external governance in European politics. J Eur Public Policy 16(6):791–812
McDonald N (2019) The role of due diligence in international law Int Comp Law Q 68(4):1041–1054
McCorquodale R (2006) Spreading weeds beyond their garden: extraterritorial responsibility of states for violations of human rights by corporate nationals. Am Soc Int Law Leg Proc 100:95–102
Moreno-Lax V, Gragl P (eds) (2016) EU law and public international law: co-implication, embeddedness and interdependency Yearb Eur Law 35(1):455
Odermatt J (2017) Council of the European Union v. Front Populaire Pour La Libération De La Saguia-El-Hamra Et Du Rio De Oro (Front Polisario) Am J Int Law 111(3):731–738
Pound R (1921) Standards in international law. Harv Law Rev 34(7):776–779
Rijpma JJ, Cremona M (2007) The extra-territorialisation of EU migration policies and the rule of law. EUI working papers, law 2007/01
Robin-Olivier S (2013) The contribution of the charter of fundamental rights to the protection of social rights in the European union: a first assessment after lisbon. Eur J Hum Rights 1:109–134
Ryngaert C (2018) EU trade agreements and human rights: from extraterritorial to territorial obligations. Int Community Law Rev 20(3/4):374–393
Ryngaert C, Fransen R (2018) EU extraterritorial obligations with respect to trade with occupied territories: reflections after the case of front polisario before EU courts 2(1):7. https://doi.org/10.14324/111.444.ewlj.2018.07
Semertzi A (2014) The preclusion of direct effect in the recently concluded EU free trade agreements Common Mark Law Rev 51(4):1125–1158

Sengupta A (2000) Second Report of the Independent Expert on the Right to Development (Working Group on the Right to Development, 1st session, 2000) UN Doc E/CN4/2000/WG18/CRP1. Available at: https://ap.ohchr.org/documents/E/CHR/report/ECN42000WG18CRP1.pdf. Accessed on 20 Feb 2020

Samuel KLH (2018/2019) The legal character of due diligence: standards, obligations or both? 1 (2018/2019 Forthcoming). Available at: SSRN: https://ssrn.com/abstract=3264764. Accessed on 20 Feb 2020

Scott J (2014) Extraterritoriality and territorial extension in EU law. Am J Comp Law 62(1):87–125

Scott J (2014) The new EU 'extraterritoriality'. Common Mark Law Rev 51:1343–1380

Simma B, Pulkowski D (2006) Of planets and the universe: self-contained regimes in international law. Eur J Int Law 17(3):483–529

Spaventa E (2015) A very fearful court? The protection of fundamental rights in the European union after opinion 2/13. Maastricht J Eur Comp Law 22(1):35–56

Tocci N (2007) Profiling normative foreign policy: the European union and its global partners. CEPS Working Document No. 279, December 2007

Tocci N (2016) The making of the EU global strategy. Contemp Secur Policy 37(3):461–472

Tzevelekos VP (2010) In search of alternative solutions. Can the state of origin be held internationally responsible for investors' human rights abuses which are not attributable to it? Brooklyn J Int Law 35:155–231

Tzevelekos VP (2015) Reconstructing the effective control criterion in extraterritorial human rights breaches: direct attribution of wrongfulness, due diligence, and concurrent responsibility. Mich J Int Law 36(1):129–178

Tzevelekos V, Proukaki EK (2017) Migrants at sea: a duty of plural states to protect (Extraterritorially)? Nord J Int Law 86(4):427–469

van Bockel B, Wattel P (2013) New wine into old wineskins: the scope of the charter of fundamental rights of the EU after Åkerberg Fransson Eur Law Rev 38(6):866–883

Velluti S (2016) The promotion and integration of human rights in EU external trade relations Utrecht J Int Eur Law 32(83):41–68

Velluti S, Tzevelekos VP (2018) Extraterritoriality of EU law and human rights after Lisbon: the case of trade and public procurement Eur World A Law Rev 2(1):3. https://doi.org/10.14324/111.444.ewlj.2018.10

Wessel RA (2016) Flipping the question: the reception of EU law in the international legal order. Yearb Eur Law 35(1):533–561

Ziegler KS (2016) Beyond pluralism and autonomy: systemic harmonisation as a paradigm for the interaction of EU law and international law. Yearb Eur Law 35(1):667–711

Doctorate dissertations

Hodun M Doctrine of implied powers as a judicial tool to build federal polities. PhD dissertation, School of Law, Reykjavik University. Available at: https://skemman.is/bitstream/1946/20824/1/Doctrine%20of%20implied%20powers%20as%20a%20judicial.pdf. Accessed on 20 Feb 2020

Blogposts

Bartels L (2015) The EU's Human Rights Obligations in Relation to Policies with Extraterritorial Effects: Rejoinder to Enzo Cannizzaro, EJIL: Talk, Debate!, 15 January 2015. Available at: http://www.ejiltalk.org/rejoinder-to-enzo-cannizzaro/. Accessed on 20 Feb 2020

Berkes A (2018) A new extraterritorial jurisdictional link recognised by the IACtHR. EJIL: *Talk!*, 28 March 2018. Available at: https://www.ejiltalk.org/a-new-extraterritorial-jurisdictional-link-recognised-by-the-iacthr/#more-16059. Accessed on 20 Feb 2020

Benvenisti E The EU must consider threats to fundamental rights of non-eu nationals by its potential trading partners. Available at: http://globaltrust.tau.ac.il/the-e-u-must-consider-threats-to-fundamental-rights-of-non-eu-nationals-by-its-potential-trading-partners/. Accessed on 21 Feb 2020

Lawrence J (2016) The extraterritorial reach of EU animal welfare rules (again): Case C-592/14 European Federation for Cosmetic Ingredients. European law Blog, 16 November 2016. Available at: https://europeanlawblog.eu/2016/11/16/the-extraterritorial-reach-of-eu-animal-welfare-rules-again-case-c-59214-european-federation-for-cosmetic-ingredients/. Accessed on 20 February 2020

Shany Y (2020) Bad cases make bad law, but good law books! EJIL: talk! 1 Dec 2011. Available at: https://www.ejiltalk.org/bad-cases-make-bad-law-but-good-law-books/. Accessed on 20 Feb 2020

Vidigal G (2015) Trade agreements, EU law, and occupied territories (2): The General Court Judgment in *Frente Polisario v Council* and the Protection of Fundamental Rights Abroad' EJIL: *Talk!*, 11 December 2015. Available at: https://www.ejiltalk.org/13901–2/. Accessed on 20 Feb 2020

Other

Online sources

Cagé J, Gadenne L (2012) The fiscal cost of trade liberalization. 4 June 2012. Available at: https://voxeu.org/article/fiscal-cost-trade-liberalisation. Accessed on 25 Feb 2020

Dizard J (2019) Polisario case reveals high stakes behind investors. ESG enthusiasm—legal action over disputed African territory affects EU links with Morocco. Financial Times, 17 May 2019. Available at: https://www.ft.com/content/f27754de-4288-3cf0-98b1-73bd7440bbf4. Accessed on 19 Feb 2020

Euractiv (2016) Mogherini heads to Morocco after EU ties suspended, 4 March 2016. Available at: https://www.euractiv.com/section/global-europe/news/mogherini-heads-to-morocco-after-eu-ties-suspended/. Accessed on 19 Feb 2020

Euractiv (2016) EU court lawyer says decision to stop EU-Morocco trade deal was wrong, 13 September 2016. Available at: https://www.euractiv.com/section/trade-society/news/eu-court-lawyer-says-decision-to-stop-eu-morocco-trade-deal-was-wrong/. Accessed on 19 Feb 2019

Lonardo L (2019) The EU's "diplomatic accident" with Morocco shows the perils of judge-led foreign policy. LSE Blogs. Available at: http://bit.ly/1M2eEfY. Accessed on 20 Feb 2019

Pisillo Mazzeschi R (2017) Coordination of different principles and values in international law. In: European Society of International Law Conference Paper Series, No. 11/2017, 2017 ESIL Conference, Naples, 7–9 Sept 2017. Available at: https://papers.ssrn.com/sol3/papers.cfm?abstract_id=3163099. Accessed on 23 Mar 2020

Sidati M (2016) The EU's Morocco problem. Politico, 23 December 2016. Available at: https://www.politico.eu/article/the-eus-morocco-problem-western-sahara-trade-judgment/. Accessed on 19 Feb 2020

Dictionaries

Due Diligence (2006) in Black's Law Dictionary, 8th edn. Eagan, Thomson West

Due Diligence in Merriam-Webster Dictionary. Available at: https://www.merriam-webster.com/dictionary/due%20diligence. Accessed on 20 Feb 2020

Chapter 7
Conclusion—The Merits of EU Conditionality in a World of Contrasts

Francesca Martines and Samantha Velluti

7.1 The Common Commercial Policy After Lisbon

The Common Commercial Policy (CCP) is a key strategic field of external relations of the European Union (EU) not only for its scope, in qualitative and quantitative terms, but also for what it reveals about the EU's complexity in relation to its multi-faceted identity, conflicting objectives and clashing values and interests.

All the components of the CCP are well summarized in a statement of the European Parliament (EP), which defines the CCP as comprising 'a body of trade agreements and legislative measures to safeguard the Union's offensive and defensive trade interests, contribute to sustainable growth and decent job creation, ensure that EU rules and standards are observed, safeguard states' right to regulate and citizens' well-being, and promote EU values.'[1]

The changes brought about by the 2009 Treaty of Lisbon (TL),[2] which expanded the substantive scope of the CCP (covering trade in services, commercial aspects of intellectual property and foreign direct investment (FDI)), are meant to support the Union's economic interests, its competitive advantage and its "deep trade agenda". At the same time, the CCP is also a powerful policy instrument for the promotion of EU values, which cannot be defined as being ancillary components of EU external trade relations. Indeed, through Articles 3(5) and 21 TEU, the pre-existent normative dimension of the CCP has been codified and reinforced.

In short, the TL's extension of the CCP's reach and scope beyond the traditional realm of trade policy has increased and strengthened the global trade power of the EU

[1] European Parliament, Annual report on the implementation of the Common Commercial Policy, 7.5.2018, (2017/2070(INI).

[2] Treaty of Lisbon Amending the Treaty on European Union and the Treaty Establishing the European Community, 13 December 2007, 2007/C 306/01.

S. Velluti, *The Role of the EU in the Promotion of Human Rights and International Labour Standards in Its External Trade Relations*,
https://doi.org/10.1007/978-3-030-56748-4_7

in order to pursue economic liberalization goals[3] while enhancing also the competitiveness of its industries, particularly via the EU's panoply of the new generation of trade agreements. The latter exemplify the duality of the CCP's goals: on the one hand, these trade agreements aim at pursuing the EU's economic interests, such as the designation of standards and regulatory convergence and, on the other hand, they aim at pursuing non-trade values, such as sustainable development and social standards.

The challenging coexistence of economic interests (that are to be protected) and non-trade values (that are to be promoted) in the implementation of the CCP gives a conflicting picture of the EU that contrasts with the pursuit of the principle of coherence that permeates the whole of EU external action. The complexity of the EU's reality explains why a *third way* in-between normative power Europe (NPE) and its "nemesis" of market power Europe (MPE), might help go beyond the limitative dichotomy of values *versus* interests. Conceiving the EU as both a value promoter—through non coercive means such as the Trade and Sustainable Development (TSD) Chapters of the EU's free trade agreements (FTAs)—and defender of its economic competitiveness helps to better understand the flexibilities, inconsistencies and flaws in the promotion of non-trade values.

In this context, the changes introduced by the TL reinforce the normative dimension of the CCP, providing the legal basis for making the EU a potentially transformative normative power *through* trade.

If trade agreements have become tools through which the EU can project its values and defend its economic interests abroad, the capacity of the EU to give effect to the overarching objectives set up in the Treaties—what Larik defines as the Union's "milieu goals" of a world-wide scope-[4] is dependent on the actual remit of the CCP and its institutional mechanisms. The capacity of the CCP to expand and develop, beyond the confines of the internal market—through the combination of treaty amendments and the (renewed) expansive interpretation of the Court of Justice of the EU (CJEU) after the set back of the 90s—is crucial as it allows the positioning of the EU in the global trade context, which has undergone (and is undergoing) many changes (inter alia, the rise in importance of trade in services, the fragmentation of value and supply chains and the focus on regulatory cooperation). With the exception of FDI, which still requires mixity for the conclusion of trade and investment agreements, the EU has acquired an almost absolute exclusive competence in external trade extending to all fields of the multilateral trading system. The broader scope of the CCP reflects the "trade for all" approach put forward by the European Commission who has been advocating for a reconceptualization of trade policy for several years. In its 2015 *Trade for All* Communication the European Commission maintained that: 'trade policy can be a powerful tool to further the advancement of human rights in third countries in conjunction with other EU policies, in particular foreign policy and

---

[3]As per Article 206 TFEU and Article 21(2)(e) TEU. A traditional goal dating back to the origins of the CCP. The Custom Union (CU) set up by the European Economic Community (EEC) Treaty was designed to remove tariff and non-tariff obstacles among member states as a trade liberalization tool within the Union and globally.

[4]Larik (2013), pp. 7–22, at p. 9.

development cooperation.'[5] These developments have transformed the CCP into an even more powerful EU foreign policy instrument. The increased involvement of the EP in the decision-making process of the CCP is also significant, as it enhances its politicization and democraticization.

7.2 The EU in the World: In Pursuit of Non-trade Values…the *Will* but not the *Way*?

In turning to the other key change of the TL, that is the inclusion of the CCP within the framework of the EU's external action's normative goals as envisaged by Articles 3(5) and 21 TEU, the first point to be made is that it is in these EU primary law provisions that the legal dimension of the EU's global normative role finds its most vigorous expression. As a consequence, the EU's obligation to work towards a rule-of-law based provision of global public good in its foreign policy *lato sensu* is of a constitutional nature, making the promotion and respect for non-trade values a legal duty in all of the EU's external policies.

However, as shown in the book, the Treaties do not specify how this overarching obligation is to be fulfilled. Particularly in relation to human rights, the analysis also demonstrated the interconnectedness between the negative duty of respect with the positive duty of protection[6] and the argument put forward is that through a combined reading of Articles 3(5), 6 and 21 TEU the EU also has a duty to protect human rights externally. Or better said, these constitutional provisions ought to be interpreted by the CJEU in a manner which also includes a duty of protection. This line of thinking is also based on and reinforced by the fact that compliance with human rights is a parameter of legality for all EU acts as confirmed by the CJEU in many landmark cases examined in this study.[7] It also derives from the fact that the EU Charter of Fundamental Rights (EUCFR) post-Lisbon is not only legally binding but it also has the same legal value as the Treaties.[8]

Two distinct but connected questions arise from this claim. First, how to ensure the EU's compliance with its dual duty to respect and protect human rights, including labour rights, effectively and consistently. The other question is how to reconcile the normative vocation of the EU with its other goals, namely, the competitiveness of its economy and its aspiration to establish itself as a global standard setter and promoter in the broader context of an "inter-polar" world.[9]

---

[5]European Commission, Communication from the Commission to the European Parliament, the Council, the European Economic and Social Committee and the Committee of the Regions 'Trade for all. Towards a more responsible trade and investment policy', COM(2015) 497 final, p. 19.

[6]See Chap. 4 of this book.

[7]See Chap. 6 of this book.

[8]Article 6(1) TEU.

[9]Grevi (2020).

Former Trade Commissioner Karel de Gucht once said: 'First, European trade policy can play a key role in maximising the benefits of globalization. It can boost economic growth both at home in Europe and in the developing world. Conversely, we can use trade policy to actively minimise globalization's disadvantages. Europe's strong position in trade makes trade policy a tool in promoting our values in the realms of human rights and sustainable development'.[10]

Beyond this rhetoric, a closer look reveals that any concrete way forward stumbles into a number of tensions and problems of implementation, due to a lack of clarity in relation to the nature and extent of the EU's competence in enforcing human rights beyond its borders. This remains a moot point as the TL has not resolved the human rights competence question. Hence, the array of instruments available to the EU is the one that was designed and put in place long before the TL came into force. The new typology of instruments that have been put in place after Lisbon largely classify as soft law instruments, such as TSD Chapters in the new EU's FTAs or the GSP+ incentive scheme for unilateral trade arrangements, with all their in-built limitations.[11] Certainly, they retain an important socialization, knowledge exchange and mutual learning function in relation to introducing change. However, they should not be used as a replacement for hard law measures and for avoiding adequate levels of human rights and labour standards protection. Hence, the constitutionalization of the obligation to project non-economic values in the EU's external relations and, specifically, the stronger legal basis and legal commitment to respect and promote human rights abroad requires a more coherent and efficient use of the hybrid toolbox that the EU has acquired since the entry into force of the TL.

However, in taking the analysis further another problem emerges. The book has showed that the two overarching goals which make up the overall mission of the CCP largely coexist in "mutual ignorance" rather than to their "mutual benefit". Quite expectedly, Larik talks about "cosmopolitan romanticism" when looking at the promotion of non-trade values enshrined in Articles 3(5) and 21 TEU,[12] which captures the tension between 'the cosmopolitanist imagination of the world as it ought to be by the EU and the harsh realities and global upheavals confronting the EU's ideals.'[13] The book revealed how this underlying tension in the pursuit of these conflicting goals has not been fully tackled by EU institutions. This can be explained in part by the CJEU's obsessive concern for protecting the autonomy of the EU legal and judicial order but also by the fact that the EU struggles to speak with a single voice.

[10]De Gucht (2014).

[11]See Chap. 5 of this book.

[12]Larik (2011), p. 37.

[13]van Vooren et al. (2013), p. 325.

7.3 Recommendations for Change

Be that as it may, the EU must ensure that the pursuit of non-economic objectives is not sidelined by the imperatives of its trade objectives. The EU should thus use its trade power as a leverage for ensuring policy coherence in its external action. Hence, 'the EU must take care not to axiomatically overstate or assume the significance and "correctness" of its own internal achievements'[14] to date. To put it shortly, the EU cannot remain complacent and must act upon the points raised by its critics.

In this regard, the book put forward some tentative suggestions for reform in order to refine and strengthen the use of the EU's instruments at its disposal. These suggestions can be subdivided into two categories. In the first group the changes proposed concern the nature of the EU's external human rights obligations. In the second group, the recommendations concern specific aspects of these obligations and, in particular, the instruments employed to ensure compliance with these obligations.

With regard to the first group, since the causal link between a given trade agreement and human rights violations is contentious and not easily identifiable, it is submitted that the EU's duty not to contribute to human rights violation in a situation where such action is only potential should be considered as an obligation of endeavor, that is the EU shall do all that is in its power to prevent the occurrence of a breach. A due diligence duty has been called for in this scenario[15] requiring the EU to evaluate all possible risks *ex ante* and taking all reasonable efforts to avoid any foreseeable human rights violations. This obligation is met through impact assessments (IAs). The use of the latter is not new: the European Commission has been carrying out Sustainable Impact Assessments (SIAs) for several years.[16] What is posited is that this procedural obligation to carry out IAs should be standardised and extended to all EU trade agreements, on the basis of improved methodologies, rather than being carried out at the discretion of the European Commission. The findings of IAs should not become a substitute for political judgement (as IAs cannot fully detect the causal links between the agreement and human rights).[17] Rather they should be used as an aid for the decision-maker, in this case the EU, to comply with its human rights obligations. Moreover, IAs provide the basis for enhancing and stimulating discussion and public awareness through the consultation process that is part of the assessment. The reason why IAs are particularly invaluable is because they can provide the EU with a tool that—while not perfect- can give some guarantee that the implementation of a particular trade agreement will not lead to human rights violations by the states concerned. In this case 'the links between the trade agreement and possible future harm will need to be analysed against the relevant legal tests for causation.'[18] Linked to this, IAs also enable the EU to identify possible strategies

[14] Ibid., p. 338.

[15] See Chap. 6 of this book.

[16] This is examined in Chap. 5 of the book.

[17] Zerk (2019), p. 14.

[18] Ibid., p. 15.

for reducing the risks of adverse human rights impact.[19] Here, the aim should focus on understanding the nature and sources of different types of risk, the mitigating options realistically available for the state concerned and their likely effectiveness.[20] The second objective of IAs fits in with the narrow conception of due diligence based on strict liability that is presented in Chap. 6, better responding to the EU obligation to effectively protect human rights. As explained in Chap. 5, *ex ante* IAs, whether HRIAs or SIAs, should provide the basis for effectively negotiating the inclusion of those changes to the clauses of a given agreement that are necessary for minimizing, if not fully removing, the potential negative human rights consequences of the agreement. The model proposed in Chap. 6 combines these *ex ante* IAs with *ex post* evaluations where unforeseen effects of the agreement on human rights and causality could emerge. While ex post IAs have mainly been devoted to assessing trade chapters of the EU's international agreements[21] there are also cases of ex post evaluations that contemplate a human rights analysis.[22] In other IAs, human rights considerations have been made part of the assessment, as in the case of the 2011 EU-Korea FTA.[23] In this context, the analysis also addressed the vexing question of extraterritoriality and showed how it might not be an appropriate lens for fully capturing the nature of the effects of EU law beyond its borders. For this reason, the template proposed combines an internal-territorial model (that is within the scope of the territoriality principle) with territorial extension.

With regard to the second group of recommendations, the book showed how EU social and human rights conditionalities, while being the key tool to promote non-economic values in EU external relations, are in need of reform. EU conditionality raises several problems that have attracted criticism of incoherence, ineffectiveness and disguised protectionist purposes. Indeed, for the EU to be a credible global human rights actor it is not enough to include human rights, social clauses, tariff incentives or sustainable development chapters in its trade instruments to make them more palatable to public opinion and its critics. Conditionality tools can be effective as counterweights to the EU's trade instruments' market liberalizing provisions only if the EU fully engages in the protection of non-trade values. However, this is where the "realpolitik" of foreign policy kicks in: the application of conditionality involves a very highly politicized decision. This is why sanctioning is a tool that the EU clearly does not want to inflate and one that shall be applied "prudently".[24] The suspension of the agreement in the case of human rights violations is used only as a

[19]Ibid.

[20]Ibid.

[21]European Commission (2019).

[22]For example, in the Inception Report of the ex-post evaluation of the 2008 (CARIFORUM-EU EPA), the grid for the evaluation of the agreement includes the 'identification of unintended human rights impacts in EU economic, social, gender, human rights and environmental impacts (in short referred to as sustainability impacts) of the EPA', see Economic Partnership (2008), European Commission (2019).

[23]European Commission (2018); see Free Trade Agreement (2011).

[24]De Gucht (2014), p. 10.

last resort since it would deprive the EU of the possibility of using instruments such as EU-funded co-operation programmes to support the reform process.[25]

Hence, the sanctioning approach of conditionality has a limited scope of application due to political and material constraints.[26] Since it is practically impossible, even if it were its intention, for the EU to trigger conditionality in all cases of serious breaches of non-economic values, the EU restricts negative conditionality or sanctioning to blatant cases of democratic and rule of law violations. Nevertheless, there would still be space for the EU to explore the possibility of resorting to other type of measures that would be legitimate under the non-execution clause (which refers to "appropriate measures"), including reliance on positive measures.

In particular, if one considers that the essential element clause has an autonomous value, then it is possible to argue that it can be used as a legal basis for discussion and dialogue with the EU partner country, that is positive measures. In other words, the EU could use the agreement containing a human rights clause for setting up regular and formal dialogues or for upgrading existing human rights dialogue, from local to high level dialogues. In this regard, the case of Vietnam is illustrative.[27]

As suggested in Chap. 5, inconsistency could also be overcome by creating common structured and permanent monitoring bodies in all trade agreements. Existing enforcement mechanisms could be strengthened. For instance, domestic advisory groups provided for in TSD Chapters of FTAs could include independent representatives of civil society.[28] The request of the panel of experts provided for in some agreements, which are subject to the willingness of the parties to use it, could be made compulsory upon the request of one of the parties, although there is a risk that this could lead to a delay in the conclusion of the agreement. In some cases, the EU might use *ex ante* conditionality, as in the case of the (Generalised System of Trade Preferences) GSP+ incentive scheme, to envisage the possibility of conditioning the conclusion of the agreement to the ratification of some core labour/human rights conventions. Even though mere ratification does not ensure enforcement, this could be a demonstration of good faith by the partner in the commitment to respect those rights.

Another problematic aspect concerning the GSP scheme are the eligibility criteria, which set standards that are too low thus allowing countries that notoriously violate human rights to become beneficiaries to the scheme(s). In addition, more weight should be given to reports of all the International Labour Organization (ILO) supervisory and monitoring bodies, particularly for the GSP+ as well as those set up by the conventions that have been ratified by GSP+ beneficiaries. Even though it is acknowledged that in the context of the GSP scheme geopolitical realities can play a decisive role, nevertheless it is submitted that the EU should refrain from its double standards approach in its application of GSP conditionality.

---

[25]European Ombudsman, Decision of the European Ombudsman on complaint 933/2004/JMA against the European Commission, decision of 25 June 2005.

[26]This is examined in detail in Chaps. 4 and 5 of the book.

[27]See Chap. 5 of this book.

[28]See European Parliament (2018).

Another proposal concerns the involvement of private parties in the mechanisms of human rights conditionality so as to enhance their effectiveness. For example, the EU GSP enforcement mechanism could adopt a model akin to the one applied in the United States (US) African Growth and Opportunity Act (AGOA), which envisages the possibility for the private sector or 'any interested person, at any time' to file a petition with respect to the 'compliance' of a country 'with eligibility requirements'.[29] Another agreement to consider is the North American Agreement on Labour Cooperation (NAALC), which allows any person with a recognized interest under the law to submit complaints or petitions to any of the three parties in relation to occupational safety and health, child labour, minimum wage or technical labour standards.[30]

As Bartels aptly observes, 'the EU's trade agreements lag noticeably behind other countries, such as the United States and Canada by not giving individuals, civil society and even other EU institutions any role in its decision to enforce the human rights obligations of other countries.'[31]

Besides individual direct involvement in specific complaint mechanisms, civil society can play a key role in promoting EU trade policy that is responsive to human rights protection in non-EU countries. Negotiations for the Transatlantic Trade and Investment Partnership Agreement between the EU and the US (TTIP)[32] has stirred up both interest and concern and it has stimulated a public debate on EU trade and investment policy that is no longer confined to an inner circle of experts or politicians.

This interest and concern, that can be translated in specific requests concerning the modification of the content of the agreement, can be channeled through national parliaments (as was the case with the Walloon parliament's scrutiny and then rejection of the 2014 EU-Canada Comprehensive Economic Trade Agreement (CETA))[33] or through the key role of the EP. The latter can use its power of consent under Article 218(6)(a) TFEU to reject an agreement that it considers flawed and subordinate its consent to a set of detailed benchmarks to measure progress made by the state authorities of the country concerned.[34]

Civil society and, in particular NGOs, can bring the issue to the fore and stimulate debates. Moreover, EP committees, such as the Committee on International Trade

---

[29]See Section 107 §3, letter A of The Trade Preferences Extension Act (TPEA) of 2015 (H.R. 1295) of June 29, 2015. Renewal and extension of AGOA is incorporated into the TPEA as "Title I-Extension of African Growth and Opportunity Act."; the original act was signed in 2000, United States (US) Public Law 106-200, May 18, 2000, 114 Stat. 251.

[30]See Articles 3(2) and 4 of the NAALC as well as Article 27 of NAALC; the more controversial areas of freedom of association, right to bargain collectively and forced labour are excluded; see the side agreement North American Agreement on Labour Cooperation (NAALC), 32 I.L.M. 1499 (1993).

[31]Bartels (2014).

[32]For detailed information, European Commission, 'TTIP—News Archive', Department for Trade (DG Trade), https://trade.ec.europa.eu/doclib/press/index.cfm?id=1230, accessed on 14 June 2020.

[33]Comprehensive Economic and Trade Agreement between Canada, of the one part, and the European Union and its Member States of the other part, Consolidate Text published 26 September 2014 available at http://trade.ec.europa.eu/doclib/docs/2014/september/tradoc_152806.pdf, accessed on 22 March 2020.

[34]E.g. European Parliament resolution of 12 March 2019.

(INTA) usually meet in public. Transparency and public discussion are crucial for exercising control and engaging the responsibility of decision-makers. In February 2020, a number of NGOs made a request to the EP to postpone its consent on the conclusion of the EU-Vietnam Free Trade Agreement (EVFTA) and Investment Protection Agreement (IPA).[35] This followed an opinion of the EP Foreign Affairs Committee, which was also not in favour of giving consent to the draft agreement. However, the EP INTA Committee rejected this request motivating its vote in favour of the EP giving its consent to the agreement with certain positive developments that had taken place in Vietnam, such as the adoption of a roadmap to finalise core ILO Conventions.[36] This case demonstrates that the EP is not always a champion of human rights protection[37] and confirms the importance of increasing transparency and public debate with the increased involvement of civil society.[38]

7.4 Some Final Reflections on the Status Quo and the Road Ahead

In 1993 Curtin famously defined the EU as a "Europe of bits and pieces".[39] Almost thirty years later the EU remains largely fragmented and is still in search of its own identity. The main difference is the level of interconnectedness and complexity. The EU, and the way it conducts its external relations, in many respects epitomises this globalizing world. In this context, the crises engulfing the EU are not abating.[40] Brexit is a stark reminder for EU leaders that the Union, however constructed, remains a contested project. In its external action there appears to be a schism between a rule of law–based approach and geopolitical reality, in spite of human rights, labour standards, and global governance becoming a sources of normative negotiations

[35]The NGOs requested to make consent subordinate to a number of conditions to improve the human rights situation in Vietnam. The EP's Committee on Foreign Affairs recommended to subordinate consent to the release of political prisoners. See EP Committee on Foreign Affairs (2018); e.g. Human Rights Watch (2020).

[36]ILO Press Release (2019).

[37]A case where the EP did act as a promoter of human rights concerns is the case of Turkmenistan where the European Parliament suggested subordinating the conclusion of the trade agreement to the actual ratification of core human rights conventions or to various reforms, see European Parliament, above no. 34.

[38]E.g. the STOP TTIP citizens' initiative, for information visit: https://europa.eu/citizens-initiative/initiatives/details/2017/000008_en, accessed on 22 March 2020. The European Commission was asked to recommend to the Council the cancellation of the mandate that the later granted to the Commission to negotiate the TTIP. The European Commission refused register the initiative and its decision to refuse to register the initiative was quashed by the General Court, see General Court, Case T-754/14 *Michael Efler and others v Commission*, ECLI:EU:T:2017:323.

[39]Curtin (1993), pp. 17–69.

[40]Eeckhout and Lopez-Escudero (2016), pp. 3–9, at p. 3.

and legal transplants that aim at changing the normative paradigm in international economic law.[41]

The findings of the book show that there is a need for a more comprehensive and coherent approach to the trade and human rights/international labour standards linkages.[42] Since the TL, the duty of consistency features prominently in the Union's constitutional texts[43] and has acquired the status of a general principle of EU law applicable to all areas of EU external action.[44] However, the challenge of translating the concept of coherence 'into *specific legal obligations* is not straightforward [also because] the case law of the Court of Justice (CJEU) is scarce and lacks concretization.'[45]

The way forward for the EU is not so much the envisionment of a new grand strategy but rather focusing on improving the effectiveness of the various instruments that it already has at its disposal and matching its practice with its purported normative and ethical aspirations, clearly enshrined in the Treaties further to the changes introduced by the TL. Additionally, the EU should also consider solidarity, which Articles 2, 3(5) and 21(1) TEU conceive as an overarching principle that extends to all areas of EU action. The term solidarity is not defined in the Treaties. As a value shared by member states solidarity applies to inter-individual relationships within national societies ("infra-national solidarity")[46] but it equally defines the relationship between member states in the implementation of EU policies.[47] As a constitutional principle solidarity also guides the EU in its external relations. In this context, the application of solidarity, in combination with all the other Union's values and principles, should be interpreted as giving policies a more human-centred dimension. Indeed, more than ever the lodestar of EU action should be the betterment of humanity's wellbeing.

---

[41]Voiculescu (2013), pp. 49–64, at 50–51.

[42]den Hertog and Stroβ (2013), pp. 373–388, 376.

[43]Article 21(3), second subpara. TEU; see also Article 13(1), 16(6), second and third subparas., Article 18(4), 26(2), second subpara. TEU and Article 7 TFEU.

[44]Casolari (2012), pp. 11–34, 13.

[45]den Hertog and Stroβ (2013), 42, 378.

[46]In this sense see also Chap. 4 of the EUCFR.

[47]E.g. Common Foreign Security Policy (CFSP) Articles 24, 31, 32, 42(7) TEU; in the context of the Area of Freedom, Security and Justice (AFSJ), Articles 67 and 80 TFEU; economic policy, Article 122 TFEU; energy, Article 194 TFEU; and a dedicated provision which is Article 222 TFEU (the "solidarity clause").

References

Official Documents of the European Union

EU Treaties

Treaty of Lisbon Amending the Treaty on European Union and the Treaty Establishing the European Community, 13 December 2007, 2007/C 306/01

EU International Agreements

Comprehensive Economic and Trade Agreement between Canada, of the one part, and the European Union and its Member States of the other part, Consolidate Text published 26 September 2014 available at http://trade.ec.europa.eu/doclib/docs/2014/september/tradoc_152806.pdf. Accessed on 13 June 2020
Economic Partnership between the CARIFORUM States, of the one part, and the European Community and its Member States, of the other part, OJ L289/I/3, 30.10.2008
Free Trade Agreement between the European Union and its Member States of the one part, and the Republic of Korea of the other part, OJ [2011] L127/6, 14 May 2011, p. 6

European Parliament

European Parliament, Annual report on the implementation of the Common Commercial Policy, 7.5.2018, (2017/2070(INI)
EP Committee on Foreign Affairs, 'Opinion on the draft Council decision on the conclusion of the Free Trade Agreement' (2018/0356 M(NLE), 5 February 2019 between the European Union and the Socialist Republic of Viet Nam(2018/0356 M(NLE))
European Parliament, Draft Opinion of the Committee of Foreign Affairs for the Committee on International Trade on the draft Council decision on the conclusion of the Free Trade Agreement (2018/0356 M(NLE), 16.10.2019 between the European Union and the Socialist Republic of Viet Nam(2018/0356 M(NLE))
European Parliament resolution of 12 March 2019 on the draft Council and Commission decision on the conclusion by the European Union and the European Atomic Energy Community of the Partnership and Cooperation Agreement establishing a Partnership between the European Communities and their Member States, of the one part, and Turkmenistan, of the other part (12183/1/2011–C8-0059/2015), 12 Mar 2019

European Commission

European Commission, Evaluation of the impact of trade chapters of the Euro-Mediterranean association agreements with six partners: Algeria, Egypt, Jordan, Lebanon, Morocco and Tunisia,

July 2019, available at: https://trade.ec.europa.eu/doclib/docs/2019/september/tradoc_158332.pdf. Accessed on 13 June 2020

European Commission, Inception Report of the ex post evaluation of the EPA between the EU and its member states and the CARIFORUM member states, commissioned by the directorate-general for trade directorate sustainable development; economic partnership agreements—July 2019, available at: https://trade.ec.europa.eu/doclib/docs/2019/july/tradoc_158300.pdf. Accessed on 13 June 2020

European Commission, Evaluation of the Implementation of the Free Trade Agreement between the EU and its Member States and the Republic of Korea, Final Report: Main Report, May 2018, available at: https://trade.ec.europa.eu/doclib/docs/2019/march/tradoc_157716.pdf. Accessed on 13 June 2020

European Ombudsman

European Ombudsman, Decision of the European Ombudsman on complaint 933/2004/JMA against the European Commission, decision of 25 June 2005

Table of Cases

General Court, Case T-754/14 *Michael Efler and others v Commission*, ECLI:EU:T:2017:323

Official Documents of the United States (US)

United States (US) Public Law 106–200, May 18, 2000, 114 Stat. 251

The Trade Preferences Extension Act (TPEA) of 2015 (H.R. 1295) of June 29, 2015. Renewal and extension of AGOA is incorporated into the TPEA as "Title I-Extension of African Growth and Opportunity Act."

North American Agreement on Labour Cooperation (NAALC), 32 I.L.M. 1499 (1993)

Books and chapters in books

Casolari F (2012) The Principle of loyal co-operation: a "Master Key" for EU external representation? In: Blockmans S, Wessel RA (eds) Principles and practices of EU external representation CLEER working papers 5/2012, pp 11–34

Eeckhout P, Lopez-Escudero M (2016) Introduction. In: Eeckhout P, Lopez-Escudero M (eds) The European Union's external action in times of crisis. Hart Publishing, Oxford. pp 3–9

Larik J (2013) Entrenching global governance: the EU's constitutional objectives caught between a sanguine world view and a daunting reality. In: van Vooren B, Blockmans S, Wouters J (eds) The EU's role in global governance. The legal dimension, pp 7–22. OUP, Oxford van Vooren B, Blockmans S, Wouters J (2013) Conclusion: the role of the EU in the legal dimension of global governance. In: van Vooren B, Blockmans S, Wouters J (eds), The EU's role in global governance. The legal dimension. OUP, Oxford, pp 325–350

Journal Articles and reports

Bartels L (2014) The European Parliament's role in relation to human rights in trade and investment agreements. Study for the European Parliament, Directorate-General for External Policies of the Union, Directorate B, Policy Department, 2014 433.751, February 2014, 18

Curtin D (1993) The constitutional structure of the Union: a europe of bits and pieces. Common Market Law Review 30(1):17–69

den Hertog L, Stroβ S (2013) Coherence in EU external relations: concepts and legal rooting of an ambiguous term. Eur Foreign Aff Rev 18(3):373–388

Grevi G (2020) The interpolar world: a new scenario (2009) *Occasional paper* No. 79, EU-ISS, Paris, June 2009, available at: https://www.iss.europa.eu/content/interpolar-world-new-scenario, accessed on 14 June 2020

Larik J (2011) Shaping the international order as a Union objective and the dynamic internationalisation of constitutional law. CLEER Working Papers 2011/5

Voiculescu A (2013) Human rights, corporate social responsibility and the shaping of the European Union's linkage strategy: 'A Peaceful Revolution'?'. In: Tamara T, Andrea O, Angelos D (eds), Linking trade and non-commercial interests: the EU as a global role model? CLEER Working Paper 2013/4, pp 49–64

Other

STOP TTIP citizens' initiative, for information visit: https://europa.eu/citizens-initiative/initiatives/details/2017/000008_en. Accessed on 22 Mar 2020

European Commission, 'TTIP—News Archive', Department for Trade (DG Trade), https://trade.ec.europa.eu/doclib/press/index.cfm?id=1230. Accessed on 14 June 2020

De Gucht (2014) EU Trade Policy as a Means to Influence Globalization, Humboldt-Universität zu Berlin, Berlin, 22 May 2014, available at: https://ec.europa.eu/commission/presscorner/detail/fr/SPEECH_14_405. Accessed on 23 Mar 2020

Human Rights Watch (2020) NGOs Urge European Parliament to Postpone Consent to EU-Vietnam Trade Deals. Letter of 4 Feb 2020, available at: https://www.hrw.org/news/2020/02/04/ngos-urge-european-parliament-postpone-consent-eu-vietnam-trade-deals. Accessed on 22 Mar 2020

International Labour Organisation (ILO) Press Release, 'ILO welcomes Viet Nam's vote to ratify ILO fundamental convention on collective bargaining', 14 June 2019, available at: https://www.ilo.org/hanoi/Informationresources/Publicinformation/newsitems/WCMS_710542/lang–en/index.htm. Accessed on 23 Mar 2020

Zerk JA (2019) Human rights impact assessment of trade agreements. Chatham House Research paper, 18 Feb 2019, available at: https://www.chathamhouse.org/publication/human-rights-impact-assessment-trade-agreements. Accessed on 20 Mar 2020

The manufacturer's authorised representative in the EU is Springer Nature Customer Service Centre GmbH, Europaplatz 3, 69115 Heidelberg, Germany. If you have any concerns regarding our products, please contact ProductSafety@springernature.com

Printed and bound by CPI Group (UK) Ltd, Croydon, CR0 4YY
30/09/2026
02225706-0006